Personality Development

Personality Development

The Chronology of Experience

Leon Rappoport
Kansas State University

Scott, Foresman and Company
Glenview, Illinois   London

For Karen, Paul, Alex, and Minnie
and to the memory of our friend Jack Gore

Cover Photograph by James L. Ballard.

ACKNOWLEDGMENTS

Grateful acknowledgment is made for permission to quote from other sources as follows:

Allport: From *Pattern and Growth in Personality* by G. W. Allport. Copyright © 1961 by Holt, Rinehart and Winston, Inc. and reprinted with their permission.

Baumrind: From "Authoritarian vs. Authoritative Parental Control" by D. Baumrind. *Adolescence* 3 (1968): 267–269. Copyright © 1968 by Libra Publishers, Inc. Reprinted by permission.

Bell: From "The Marital Expectations of Adolescents" by R. R. Bell, from *Understanding Adolescence: Current Developments in Adolescent Psychology*, ed. James F. Adams. Copyright © 1968 by Allyn and Bacon, Inc. Reprinted by permission of the author, editor, and publisher.

Bettelheim: Reprinted with permission of The Macmillan Company from *Love Is Not Enough* by Bruno Bettelheim. Copyright 1950 by The Free Press, a Corporation.

Brown: Reprinted with permission of The Macmillan Company and Jonathan Cape Ltd. from *Manchild in the Promised Land* by Claude Brown. Copyright © Claude Brown 1965.

Burke and Van Heusen: From "Swinging on a Star" by Johnny Burke and Jimmy Van Heusen. Copyright 1944 by Burke & Van Heusen, Inc. and Dorsey Brothers Music, Inc. All Rights Reserved. Used by permission of the publisher.

Butler: From "The Life Review: An Interpretation of Reminiscence in the Aged" by R. N. Butler. Abridged from *Psychiatry* 26:1 (February 1963). Copyright 1963 by The William Alanson White Psychiatric Foundation.

Cicero: From *On Old Age and On Friendship* by Cicero. Trans. Frank O. Copley. Copyright © 1967 by The University of Michigan.

Clausen: From *Socialization and Society*, ed. John A. Clausen. Pages 23, 153, 167, 173, 223. Copyright © by Little, Brown and Company (Inc.). Reprinted by permission.

De Ropp: From *Drugs and the Mind* by Robert de Ropp. Copyright © 1957, 1961 by Robert de Ropp. Originally published by St. Martin's Press. Reprinted by permission of the author.

Dollard and Miller: From *Personality and Psychotherapy* by J. Dollard and N.E. Miller. Copyright 1950 by McGraw-Hill Book Company. Used by permission of McGraw-Hill Book Company.

Douvan and Adelson: From *The Adolescent Experience* by E. Douvan and J. Adelson. Copyright © 1966 by John Wiley & Sons, Inc. Reprinted by permission.

Elkind: From "Cognitive Development in Adolescence" by D. Elkind, from *Understanding Adolescence: Current Developments in Adolescent Psychology*, ed. James F. Adams. Copyright © 1968 by Allyn and Bacon, Inc. Reprinted by permission of the author, editor, and publisher.

Erikson: Reprinted from *Childhood and Society*, Second Edition, Revised, by Erik H. Erikson. By permission of W. W. Norton & Company, Inc. and Chatto and Windus Ltd. Copyright 1950, © 1963 by W. W. Norton & Company, Inc.

Fitzgerald: From *The Crack-Up* by F. Scott Fitzgerald. Copyright 1931 by Charles Scribner's Sons, copyright 1936 by Esquire, Inc. Copyright 1945 by New Directions Publishing Corporation. Reprinted by permission of New Directions Publishing Corporation and The Bodley Head, publisher of *The Bodley Head Scott Fitzgerald*, Volume 6.

Flavell: From *The Developmental Psychology of Jean Piaget* by John H. Flavell. Copyright © 1963 by Litton Educational Publishing Inc. Reprinted by permission of Van Nostrand Reinhold Company.

Gawein: From *Gawein* 249:56 (May 1965), a Dutch journal.

Hackman: From "Vocational Counseling with Adolescents" by R. B. Hackman, from *Understanding Adolescence: Current Developments in Adolescent Psychology*, ed. James F. Adams. Copyright © 1968 by Allyn and Bacon, Inc. Reprinted by permission of the author, editor, and publisher.

Preface

All serious teachers probably nurture an ideal concerning the sort of textbook they would like to have for their classes. My own ideal for a personality development course serving students in such diverse areas as education, counseling, philosophy, sociology, biology, anthropology, the general humanities, and even psychology, is based on two main criteria. *First*, the book should introduce the subject matter in a rich fashion, as befits material standing at the juncture of science, philosophy, and art. *Second*, it should carry the reader through the available knowledge about personality development in an orderly, common sense manner, starting at birth and ending at old age.

Because no such book existed, it was necessary to write one. So much for ideals: they may be difficult to formulate, but they are much more difficult to execute, and mine required about five years. Furthermore, during those years certain additional considerations came to exert an increasing influence upon the form and substance of the book.

In the matter of style, simplicity and narrative continuity emerged as a primary goal. Kurt Vonnegut in his novel *Cat's Cradle* has a famous scientist say: "Any scientist who cannot explain his work to an eight-year-old child is a charlatan." One may question whether this standard should be applied to all college textbooks; one cannot question that such books should be understandable and interesting to *eighteen*-year-olds. Consequently, each chapter of this book was written as an extended essay. And since pictures, cartoons, diagrams, and tables tend to inhibit rather than aid the essay format, they have not been added.

With respect to subject matter, it should be said immediately that while the book begins with three chapters (Part I), offering broad general perspectives on the study of personality, the eight remaining chapters (Part II) treat the developing person in a very personal way. The primary focus here is upon the *patterns of his experience* that determine important trends in his development from infancy through old age. To understand these patterns, it is necessary to consider a diverse body of theory and research without losing sight of the whole developing individual. Very briefly, then, I have tried to keep the person always in view—not as a specimen for psychological dissection, and not as a pliable organism to be molded or shaped by others, but as the protagonist of the entire developmental affair—coping as best he can with changing internal needs, changing environmental demands, and even changing attempts by others to manipulate him.

This last point deserves further amplification. Current psychology shows a strong tendency to emphasize procedures for the deliberate molding or programing of human behavior, while comparatively little attention is given to just what is being molded. Without detracting from the legitimate importance of behavior modification research, it ought to be made clear that men have always known how to mold each other's behavior: at first through the use of brute force and quasi-religious rituals or superstitions, later by means of chemicals and simple conditioning procedures, and most recently via programed sequences of rewards and punishments (reinforcement schedules). Indeed, some of the new methods are so subtle that the target person–child or adult–may remain unaware of what is going on.

Consider the following example. In some of the applied psychology offered to teachers and parents, it is suggested that instead of the traditional instruments of reward and punishment used on children (viz.: candy bars and spankings) one may obtain good results by carefully controlling the smiles and frowns aimed at children. This technique can be quite powerful in certain situations, but if it is followed, what is it liable to mean for those concerned? At the very least, adult practitioners must train themselves to inhibit spontaneous expressions of emotion in favor of expressions arranged to produce some desired behavior in the child. And assuming that the child "learns" to produce that which may never even be openly demanded of him, he may also eventually learn that smiles and frowns are not genuine signs of reflexive emotions, but rather are signals indicating how well he is conforming to authority. In sum, the legitimate emotional meaning of facial expressions may become corrupted for both adults and children. Apart from the fact that the world probably already contains an overabundance of reward-punishment signals, the great danger here for students of personality is that they may accept a knowledge of manipulative techniques (the more subtle the better) as the primary basis for understanding the most complex area of psychology–the development of a personality.

Finally, since the aim of this book is to provide a broad-gauge understanding of personality development, each distinctive age period in development has been examined in an open, diversified fashion, without imposing arbitrary preconceptions. The contents accordingly range over a wide variety of theories, research studies, clinical case material, biographies, and occasional personal experiences of the author. To inject a manageable unity and coherence, I have singled out what seemed to me to be the most critical problems at each developmental period, looking first at how they present themselves to the developing person and then at how the major theories interpret what is happening.

The distinguished psychologist Sigmund Koch said a few years ago that he thought the time had come for psychologists to concentrate on trying to recover their own humanity. On my good days, I think this book may be a fair step in that direction.

Acknowledgments

Since the idea for this book—its structure, content, and style—grew out of experience in undergraduate classes on personality development with students at Kansas State University, it is necessary to acknowledge a debt to all of them. And some of them who over the years shared this experience in a more significant way leading us toward friendship (Racek, Cornella, Foster, Rhodes, Harenchar, Irvine, Cousins, Zielke, Jones, and others) deserve special thanks.

To George Jacobson and Hope Wyngarden, who worked hard and to good effect editing the completed manuscript, I can now pay the ultimate compliment of any author: you were right at least 51 percent of the times we disagreed.

There is no direct way for me adequately to thank or to compliment Mrs. Carolyn R. Tessendorf, however. In addition to typing the entire manuscript, she has worked with me on this book from the rough outlines at the beginning to the final galley proofreading at the end. Her enthusiastic efforts and good critical judgments have been essential throughout, and it is no exaggeration to state that this book is truly her achievement as well as mine.

There is also no adequate way to acknowledge the role of my wife and children except by saying *very heavy*. Indeed, my experience as husband and father has been an invaluable aid in interpreting the "objective" evidence of academic psychology.

Leon Rappoport

Table of Contents

Personality Development

One

An Introduction to Personality

The material in this section is no more—and no less—than an elaborate attempt to answer the question "What is personality?" Like so many other questions that can be stated with deceptive simplicity ("What is love?" "What is the foreign policy of the United States?"), this one contains innumerable hidden dimensions. Of course, for every deceptively simple question there are always several deceptively simple answers available to throw at people who insist upon having them, and every profession has a great supply of such answers. The problem for any honest professional, however, is to go beyond easy answers, and to explain as best he can why it is necessary to do so. This, then, is the goal of the following three chapters.

Chapter One concerns the question of a formal definition for personality. The easy answers can be found in dictionaries and textbooks that may devote only a few words to the subject, but the real substance of this confusing question can only be glimpsed when it is traced to the phenomenological and behavioristic roots of modern psychology. Exposing some of the roots of this problem should not be seen as an exercise in dry formalism: how one will seek to learn about personality, and how he will interpret whatever it is he thinks he has learned, will depend in good part upon whether he defines it according to narrow criteria, or whether he maintains a more flexible, eclectic attitude.

In addition to the theoretical statements that may define it, any important concept must also be understood in a historical context. Personality is therefore treated in Chapter Two as an evolving philosophical idea, starting with the earliest evidence of man as a self-conscious being, and continuing through to the placement of personality in the framework of modern psychology. This historical-philosophical perspective seems especially important when one sees a growing tendency to reduce personality to technical matter, to just another factor that must be programed into the design of man-machine systems.

Chapter Three completes the introduction by examining personality from the viewpoint of modern biochemistry. The new information accumulated in this area during the past several years is nothing short of revolutionary, because it is beginning to reveal a substantial material basis for many psychological processes that have traditionally been treated as virtual mysteries.

1

On Definition and Research Strategy

DEFINING PERSONALITY

The genuine interest that most people bring to the study of personality often turns quickly into confusion, and eventually into indifference. This passage from interest to confusion to indifference can occur in any area, but the study of personality is particularly susceptible because certain contradictions are rooted in the subject matter. Just what is studied in the study of personality? According to Webster's dictionary (1961) there are a number of alternatives:

(1) The quality or state of being a person and not an abstraction, thing, or lower being.

(2) The complex of characteristics that distinguishes a particular individual or individualizes or characterizes him in his relationships with others.

(3) The totality of an individual's emergent tendencies to act or behave especially self-consciously or to act on, interact with, perceive, react to, or otherwise meaningfully influence or experience his environment.

(4) The organization of the individual's distinguishing character traits, attitudes, or habits (p. 1687).

These alternative definitions convey some of the contradictions that plague every student of personality, whether he is a sophomore, professor emeritus, therapist, or director of a research institute. The first alternative represents a rather global, philosophical point of view: what does it mean to be a human being? A nice question, but one that most psychologists reject as being too broad. There are religious leaders, physicists, philosophers, novelists, and many others who have as much to say on this matter as the psychologist.

The second definition apparently provides a firmer foundation for research. Transcendental issues can be set aside and persons can be compared with one another according to their distinguishing characteristics. But exactly what characteristics or complex of characteristics should be examined?

At one time or another almost every human attribute has been studied as a distinguishing characteristic, and the range is extraordinary: bumps on the head, dreams, urine chemistry, food preferences, electrical activity in the brain, inkblot interpretations, muscular tension, handwriting, family history, birth-order, reaction time, body type, vocabulary size, handedness, word-associations, and political-social-economic attitudes; not to mention *everything* that has to do with sex.

All of these things can be seen as "distinguishing characteristics," and all have in some fashion or another been studied as a way of explaining individual differences in behavior. Several of the characteristics given above have in fact been used as a basis for defining personality "types." For example, body-type theory categorizes what we might think of as the typical football player as a *mesomorph*. According to Sheldon (1940), the inhabitant of such a body is typically an aggressive, bold, competitive, courageous person. By contrast, the owner of an *endomorphic* or pear-shaped body is described as one who is tolerant, complacent, and loves physical comfort.

The difficulty with this typology is not that it is all wrong—one does indeed encounter muscular types and flabby, fat types that show the psychological characteristics suggested by Sheldon. It is rather that researchers have found that (a) there are a substantial number of exceptions to the psychological descriptions laid down by Sheldon; (b) there are many persons who simply do not fit the pure body-type categories defined by Sheldon; and (c) contrary to Sheldon's assertions, the body type of an individual may change drastically as a result of diet, exercise, or other special treatments. One also cannot help thinking in this context of a remark, attributed to the British novelist Kingsley Amis, that "Inside every fat man there is a thin one struggling to get out."

Criticisms similar in principle to those leveled against Sheldon can be applied to most other typologies as well, insofar as they are founded on the postulation of pure-type categories. People often do not fit any of the fundamental categories; those that do may not show the inclinations specified for the categories; and most important, people change. But if personality cannot be satisfactorily captured by relatively loose definitions based on "distinguishing characteristics," what alternatives remain? The two definitions discussed below appear to be more specific. However, each of them comes with a certain intellectual price tag.

As some see it, the price for definition (3) is nothing less than humanism. This definition, emphasizing the study of behavior, represents the pervasive view that if psychology is to be scientific, it must only deal with what is observable. Behavior is observable, hence psychology must be the study of behavior. In practice, the doctrine has been applied in such a way that sweaty palms are acceptable as legitimate evidence of tension, but statements like "I am tense today because my conscience is bothering me" are not acceptable, especially in the absence of sweaty palms. Critics of simple behaviorism suggest that in their pursuit of scientific precision, behaviorists ignore what is peculiarly human in their subject matter. Asch (1952) notes: "Because physicists cannot speak with stars or electric currents, psychologists have often been hesitant to speak to their human subjects. . . . There are psychologists who would readily acknowledge the reality of conscience or of a sense of honor if they could certify to their presence in oxen and chicks" (p. ix). A rather extreme polemic view perhaps, but no more extreme than the views of those who disagree with it. The relatively humanistic position implied by definition (4) which suggests consideration of individual character, traits, or habits, is criticized as intensively for its apparent *mentalism* as definition (3) is criticized for its apparent *inhumanity*. As many experts see it, the price paid for the former position is nothing less than science itself.

How, then, is one to study characteristic traits, attitudes, or habits? These terms refer to nothing that is palpable; they are just convenient ways to denote mental states that presumably underlie various behavior patterns. Of course one is free to study mental states, but such work should be titled mentalism, not science. B. F. Skinner, who is as strong a critic of mentalism as Asch is of behaviorism, suggests that mentalistic explanations of human behavior originate in "primitive animism":

An organism as complex as man often seems to behave capriciously. It is tempting to attribute the visible behavior to another organism inside—to a little man or homunculus. . . . Nor can we escape from the primitive features by breaking the little man into pieces and dealing with his wishes, cognitions, motives, and so on, bit by bit. The objection is not that these things are mental but that they offer no real explanation and stand in the way of a more effective analysis (in Wann, 1964, pp. 79–80).

At this point, one may be bewildered or disgusted by the fact that radically different viewpoints appear to be responsible for the range of alternative definitions found in Webster. One may, however, take this state of affairs as a challenge to further inquiry: forget the dictionary; how do scholars of personality handle the definition problem? One influential theorist and scholar, Gordon Allport (1937), surveyed references to personality in various kinds of literature—legal, sociological, philosophical, biological, theological, historical—and enumerated 49 different definitions before adding a 50th of his own, which is given below.

Looking at the situation somewhat differently, Hall and Lindzey (1957) state that there simply is no general definition of personality; that one's definition depends upon one's theoretical preference. In the introduction to their text on theories of personality, these authors suggest that personality is defined by the concepts employed by the theorist, and they provide a table comparing the degree to which seventeen different theorists emphasize eighteen different concepts.[1] For example, in Freud's work there is high emphasis on rewards, early experience, and unconscious determinants, while in Allport's work the emphasis on these three concepts is low.

The definition problem can be pursued in much more detail, but this brief examination should be sufficient to show that no definition exists that will satisfy everyone. Those who would like further evidence need only read the following statements from various contemporary textbooks on personality.

---

[1]According to Shaffer and Sinnett (1964), these 18 concepts represent five general categories or clusters of concepts: structural-constitutional, inner experience, learning, unconscious and early experience, social experience.

. . . by personality is meant those relatively enduring traits and dispositions of the individual that have, over time, jelled into a pattern that distinguishes him from other individuals (Sarnoff, 1962, p. 11).

Thus, we arrive at the conclusion that personality is a complex hypothetical construct. It is a hypothetical construct because we develop it—from behavioral observations, of course. It is complex because we assume that it is composed of lesser units—traits, or needs, or id, ego, and superego, and so on (Baughman and Welsh, 1964, p. 31).

In this text, the personality of an individual will be defined as the combination of all the relatively enduring dimensions of individual differences on which he can be measured (Byrne, 1966, p. 15).

Personality consists of the specific contents and consequences of behavior and the processes responsible for these contents and consequences (Gordon, 1963, p. 17).

Starting with a simple operational definition of a person as something one can point to, we have concluded with a definition of personality as the most adequate conceptualization of a person's behavior in all its detail that the scientist can give at a moment in time. . . . Personality is a theoretical interpretation derived from all a person's behavior (McClelland, 1951, p. 69).

Personality is the dynamic organization within the individual of those psychophysical systems that determine his characteristic behavior and thought (Allport, 1961, p. 28).

It should be clear, finally, that depending upon one's philosophy, he may select a particular definition of personality from among a wide range of theoretically respectable alternatives. Allport (1961) is one of the few writers who make this point very clear:

All books on the psychology of personality are at the same time books on the philosophy of the person. . . . In most psychological texts, however, the philosophy is hidden. Only a sophisticated reader can detect it. . . . My own view is that, taken in the large, the evidence before us does not depict man as a reactive robot (p. xi).

The researcher usually is pleased to view personality as a theoretical construct because this view provides the maximum scope and freedom for his work. The therapist, however, usually prefers something more substantially descriptive because his work is directly concerned with the mental condition of patients. The interested beginning student of personality will not go far wrong if he can maintain an eclectic viewpoint, neither accepting nor rejecting any one definition or interpretation until he has examined things more carefully for himself. The eclectic view further implies that we pay special attention to ideas that are important to virtually all theoretical statements. *Individuality* is one such idea. Behaviorist or mentalist, therapist or physiologist, all are occupied to a large extent with individual differences. It follows that if one learns something about the factors that are generally conceded to cause wide individual differences, then he is learning something about personality, regardless of how it is defined.

In this connection, all of us—layman and professional alike—find it plausible to consider that "as the twig is bent the tree shall grow." Thus, the largest part of the material presented in this book concerns early experience: the immediate and long-term effects of experience in infancy, childhood, and adolescence. It is quite remarkable that most of this material can be appreciated as it stands, without recourse to a particular definition of personality. For example, when discussing intelligence it will be shown that both animals and humans suffer serious losses when they grow up in socially deprived environments. The evidence is quite conclusive, and the research quite fascinating, regardless of one's definition of personality, or even if one does not believe that there is such a thing as personality. But it is a truism in science that facts do not speak for themselves; they must be organized with theoretical statements that are economical and sensible. Any statement linking intelligence to personality would therefore have to be put in the form of a theoretical proposition that might eventually be tested. Now it is just at this point that there is a good deal of agreement among personality theorists, because the standards for testing theoretical propositions are well established. Thus, we are brought at last to a conclusion that sounds facetious and may seem confusing, but nevertheless appears to be appropriate: while theorists tend to *disagree* over definitions of personality, they tend to *agree* on the criteria that should be applied to research on personality.

The definition problem has been raised only to be discussed as a source of difficulty, and to suggest, especially for the new student, a policy of eclecticism. It should be added that enlightened eclecticism is not an easy policy to maintain. It has been suggested that just as it may be said of politicians that "patriotism is the last refuge of the scoundrel," it may be said of scientists that "eclecticism is the last refuge. . . ." One can only reply that as in politics, where occasions can occur such that patriotism is appropriate for nonscoundrels, so it may also occur in science that on occasions we must dare to be eclectic. Perhaps it will be useful to go one step further with this argument by way of an illustration from the clinical literature.

During World War II a young B-25 bombardier named Pearson Brack developed a peculiar symptom. On successive missions he passed out when his plane reached the altitude of 10,000 feet. His flight surgeon discovered that on a prior mission Brack had been injured in very frightening circumstances. While making a bombing run at about 10,000 feet, his aircraft had been under heavy enemy fighter and antiaircraft attack, and it suddenly turned over and began to fall out of control. Brack was thrown against his bombsight so hard that he began to cough blood, but at the last moment the plane was brought under control. Brack went on to complete the mission and returned safely after releasing his bombs on the target. He was hospitalized for two weeks and then sent back to duty. The fainting incidents occurred on his next two missions.

This case was first reported by Grinker and Spiegel (1945), who also described the traditional psychiatric treatment that was subsequently administered. Interviews conducted with the aid of pentothal injections indicated that Brack had a rather weak adult adjustment. He consistently denied ever being afraid in combat, and he insisted on maintaining the role of a carefree, truculent fighter. Brack's childhood had apparently been quite insecure because his father was a heavy drinker; but while he consciously rejected his father and recognized the childhood situation, he refused to see any connection with his current problem.

He was then asked if possibly he did not also feel bad because his behavior had been evasive and he had escaped facing his responsibilities in the same way as his father escaped similar responsibilities. He said, "No, I don't drink." He was told that his way of escaping was not through drinking but through failing to face his real feelings. He was then reminded that overseas he had failed to face up to his own anxiety and fear of flying. He answered that he did not know at that time he was afraid. He was asked if he knew it now, and he said he was not sure (p. 203).

The case report ends with a statement by the psychiatrist to the effect that Brack should not be returned to flying duty because of his history of personal insecurity and the trauma associated with his injury. The dramatic quality of this case has kept it alive in clinical literature. White (1964) described the case to show how a person can suffer from severe anxiety without being aware of its source. More recently, Mischel (1968) employed it as a vehicle for criticizing traditional psychiatric approaches to behavior problems. Examining the case from the standpoint of social learning and behavior modification theories, he disagreed strongly with the traditional depth-psychology view.

In Brack's case, for example, social behavior theory probably would have led to a treatment program of counter-conditioning and gradual extinction not dissimilar to the one he requested spontaneously. Brack's goals — to be helped to fly again and to overcome the aftermath of his injury — would be accepted as reasonable, rather than as the defensive façade of a brittle and immature individual from whom unconscious anxieties had to be extracted, in spite of himself (pp. 271 – 272).

Over the past decade many clinicians have come to share Mischel's orientation to behavior problems. The idea that such problems can be treated directly, through application of learning and conditioning principles, is having a revolutionary effect on clinical practice. From an *eclectic* standpoint, however, both the old psychiatric approach and the new learning theory approach are, in and of themselves, unsatisfactory. The former tends to ignore the immediate behavior problem in its search for predisposing causes; the latter tends to ignore predisposing causes in its concentration on the immediate behavior problem. An eclectic can endorse a symptom-treating procedure which has been shown by recent evidence to be effective. But at the same time we cannot help asking about causes: Why was Brack the only member of his crew to develop a neurotic symptom? Why did he not tremble at the mere sight of an airplane instead of being affected just at 10,000 feet? Did he start out, as did so many aircrewmen in World War ii, in a pilot-training program and then get shifted to a bombardier program? And if so, why? Was he an only child? A first- or secondborn child? (There is evidence suggesting that secondborns are less prone to severe anxiety reactions under stress than firstborns.) What sort of relationship did he have with his mother? Answers to all these questions would help us gain an understanding of the man's personality.

RESEARCH STRATEGIES

In personality as in all areas of empirical inquiry, the research strategy issue boils down to the question of "How are we to gain knowledge about our subject matter?"

The two alternative research strategies that characterize personality work are generally described as *cross-sectional* and *longitudinal*. Allport (1961) discussed these alternatives in detail, in the context of his distinction between *nomothetic* and *idiographic* methods.[2] As he explained it, the nomothetic approach is usually followed by those scientists who explicitly seek to discover universal laws, and who concern themselves with variables rather than individual persons. For example, the generalization that frustration leads to aggression is a nomothetic statement because it only refers to a relationship between two psychological variables. It tells us nothing about the interplay between frustration and aggression in any individual person. Yet we can certainly expect different persons to be more or less susceptible to frustration by different events. Furthermore, we know that aggression can take different forms and directions. It can be physical or symbolic, direct or displaced, aimed outward toward others or inward toward oneself. The nomothetic scientist, however, ". . . is interested only in separate dimensions whereby he can compare many persons. He is interested in hearts (yours and mine) or in lungs (yours and mine) but not in the mutual interaction of my heart with my lungs, or your heart with your lungs" (Allport, 1961, p. 8). Idiographic investigators, by contrast, are primarily concerned with individuals; they seek the sort of knowledge that cannot be obtained through nomothetic methods.

Essentially, the issue before us involves a choice between learning a little about a lot of people, or learning a lot about a few people. And while at this point it may not sound especially dramatic, as the implications of this issue become clear it can properly be seen as a fundamental paradox for much of modern science. We can examine the issue more carefully and see the relation between different methods and research strategies better, with the aid of a simple hypothetical problem: suppose that we want to investigate changes in vocabulary as a function of age.

Assuming that a satisfactory vocabulary test is available, the conventional cross-sectional strategy is to administer the test to samples of different ages. Let us further assume that we collect vocabulary test scores from 70 nine-year-olds, 70 eleven-year-olds and 70 thirteen-year-olds. The three sets of scores can be analyzed in terms of simple descriptive statistics to provide some very useful information. First, if the samples are representative of populations of different ages in the community, we will have a normative description of vocabulary levels. The mean or average score for each sample indicates what vocabulary level is typical for each age group. The variance shows the typical spread of scores—the range or interval within which we can expect most scores to be found. Perhaps most important, however, de-

---

[2]With his usual scholarly flair, Allport (p. 9) indicates that the terms were used originally by Windelbrand in 1904 and that they derive from Greek: *nomothetikos*, the giving of laws; *idios*, one's own.

scriptive cross-sectional data of this type also tell us what can be considered to be a truly unusual score.

The data can be useful even if our samples are not representative. They can show where different children stand in relation to one another. The younger child with a high score might be moved to an older group for his reading lessons while an older child with a low score might be given special instruction. Very few people would deny that such cross-sectional data can be extremely valuable. But a good many theorists do deny that this kind of material can really enhance our understanding, even of such a relatively innocuous phenomenon as vocabulary changes.

The longitudinal or idiographic theorist would point out that no matter how much cross-sectional data was available, it still would not be possible to predict the future score of a given child. That is, knowing what score a child makes at the age of nine would not allow us to predict with full certainty what score he would make at the age of eleven. It would be possible to make a reasonably good prediction if we had longitudinal data which showed, for example, that most children below the mean at age nine are also below the mean at age eleven. But data of this type are more difficult to obtain and do not eliminate the possibility of a mistaken prediction, because there will always be some children who score below the mean at one point but above it at another.

The difficulty of individual prediction, however, is only one superficial criticism that would be made by extreme idiographic theorists. Their real argument is this: cross-sectional data cannot tell us what vocabulary and vocabulary changes *mean* to individuals. If pressed for a concrete suggestion they might further suggest that the conventional cross-sectional strategy should be turned on its ear. Instead of getting a single score from each one of 210 individuals, it would be better to get 210 scores from a single individual. (Although a more moderate theorist might suggest that 70 scores from each of three individuals would be better.) What can be gained if the longitudinal-idiographic approach is taken?

Campbell and Fiske (1959) introduced the principles of convergent and discriminant validity. They suggested that when a psychological attribute is to be tested or measured, it is desirable to use several different tests to make certain that the results obtained are not largely determined by the type of test used. *Convergent validity* is attained when a person makes similar scores on several different tests of a given attribute. *Discriminant validity* requires the use of tests that are thought to measure different, unrelated attributes. The investigator tries to specify not only tests that should yield very similar results because they measure the same thing, but also tests that give different results because they measure different things. In a developmental study of vocabulary, we would therefore probably use tests of single word meanings, of antonyms and synonyms, and of phrase or sentence meanings, expecting all these scores to be highly related to one another. If we added some further tests, say of musical and mechanical ability, we would expect the latter scores to be unrelated to the former.

It is most important to note here that the widely accepted principles of convergent and discriminant validity implicitly push the researcher toward an idiographic position. If he is to fulfill the demands of these principles, he must of necessity expend more time and effort with each of his subjects. Furthermore, because both subjects and researchers are not indefatigable, the effort to get larger quantities of information from each subject will usually be spread over an extended period of time. In this way, research begins to take on a longitudinal character.

Finally, as one considers the ultimate question of validity, "How do you know what you are testing or measuring is what you think it is?" different research approaches to the vocabulary problem begin to suggest themselves. For example, consider the following two sentences: (1) The fat cat saw a rat in his hat. (2) The corpulent feline discovered a rodent in his headgear. Children with very good vocabularies might not only show better comprehension of the second sentence, but they might also select the second sentence as more interesting and amusing. If we explicitly aim at increasing our understanding of the vocabulary phenomenon, the "test" possibilities grow very large indeed. Perhaps we could tape-record conversations that the child has with other children and adults, and analyze them for vocabulary content. Perhaps we could observe how the child responds when someone uses a word with which he is not familiar. Perhaps we could determine how effectively the child can infer the meaning of a new word from the context in which the word appears. In brief, it should be clear that we might obtain a great deal of potentially valuable material if we were able to make 70 different tests or observations of vocabulary-relevant behavior.

So is it to be the cross-sectional – nomothetic or the longitudinal – idiographic strategy? Advocates of the former typically support their position with claims for objectivity and generality. They will argue that the more persons studied, however briefly, the less likely are their results to be limited to a few individual cases. And they promise general theoretical statements about personality. For example, "the highly anxious person generally tends to be pessimistic about his chances of success." There are exceptions, of course. Water doesn't really boil at exactly 100°C most places on earth; even precisely at sea level the boiling point will vary depending upon the purity of the water sample. Exceptions or individual differences characterize every scientific generality, but the generalities nevertheless remain valid and useful.

Advocates of the alternative strategy argue that the real task for science is to understand the *meaning* of things. What does it mean to be anxious, or pessimistic, or both? The goal to work toward is an understanding of how or why feelings of anxiety lead to a pessimistic outlook, just as a physical chemist works toward an understanding of how or why water turns from liquid to vapor under certain conditions.

It should be apparent that the research strategy issue is in principle not very different from the definition problem. The content of the arguments made in support of varying definitions is different from the content of the arguments adduced in support of varying research strategies, but both issues can be argued almost endlessly. Because these issues appear throughout the recorded history of Western philosophy, in one form or another, many scholars in many different disciplines are able to trace their theoretical-philosophical ancestry at least to Plato and Aristotle.

Holt (1962) and Wann (1964) both provide relatively detailed descriptions of how the opposed viewpoints discussed above afflict modern psychology. The former traces many of the current differences between personality theorists to the romantic tradition established in philosophy by the end of the eighteenth century. The latter discusses behavioristic and phenomenological trends in contemporary experimental psychology. But even the boundaries of the controversies can themselves be controversial. Steinar Kvale (Kvale and Greness, 1967), who would describe himself as a phenomenological experimental psychologist, argues that Skinner, who appears in Wann (1964) as a major spokesman for behaviorism, really is closer to some current European phenomenologists than is McCleod, who appears in Wann as a major spokesman for phenomenology!

If this all finally begins to take on an *Alice in Wonderland* quality, so much the better, for therein lies a good part of the unique charm of theoretical speculation. It often takes students years to realize that at the frontiers of all basic research one encounters an adversary system, not unlike that which characterizes the legal profession. Nothing is truly certain here except three things: (1) if they are diligent and persistent, the partisans of different theoretical positions will have their day in court, via the pages of a book or scientific journal; (2) the partisan theorist will either be misunderstood, or will claim to be misunderstood, by many of his colleagues; (3) with the passage of time, one or another partisan position will either come to dominate the field, or else all will be forgotten as the field develops along other lines. Obviously a great capacity to tolerate ambiguity is required if one is to live with this state of affairs. Perhaps that is why so few choose to enter and remain in the basic-research arena.

Among historians it is said that each generation interprets history to suit itself; this also tends to be true of scientific theory. Ultimately, each one of us adopts some kind of posture toward the issues raised above. Deliberately or willy-nilly, we become more or less mentalistic or behavioristic, nomothetic or idiographic, depending upon the kind of interpretation that sits well with us. Organized elaborations of the posture then follow almost automatically. Those selecting a more substantive definition of personality as behavior, frequently adopt a nomothetic—cross-sectional strategy; the idiographic-longitudinal strategy typically appeals most to those who opt for a relatively mentalistic definition of personality.

What, then, is the interested student to make of all of this?

Q: "If there is no real consensus about *what* you are studying, and even less about *how* it should be studied, then what is there?"

A: "A great deal of interesting and rather important material that you should know about."

Q: "How's that?"

A: "Because! Despite controversy, uncertainties, and confusion you can learn a lot that will help your thinking when you have to make crucial decisions of your own concerning personality and personality development. Do you have anything to do with members of the opposite sex? Children? Employers or employees? Parents? There exists a large body of factual and speculative material that should drastically influence your thinking on these subjects, regardless of how you may feel about definition and research-strategy issues. The sheer volume of material available is such that it has something for everyone, partisans and eclectics alike. Moreover, the major saving grace of science is that in the long run the evidence is cumulative. A given generalization that may initially be suggested by results from cross-sectional research will usually be studied further in longitudinal research, and vice versa. However bizarre and inefficient it may seem to the neophyte, the adversary system of science virtually guarantees that alternatives will always be explored, implications will be pursued, and conclusions repeatedly checked. Above all, the material is interesting. Why not give it a try?"

References

Allport, G. W. *Personality: A psychological interpretation.* New York: Holt, Rinehart & Winston, Inc., 1937.

Allport, G. W. *Pattern and growth in personality.* New York: Holt, Rinehart & Winston, Inc., 1961.

Asch, S. E. *Social psychology.* New York: Prentice-Hall, Inc., 1952.

Baughman, E. E., & Welsh, G. S. *Personality: A behavioral science.* Englewood Cliffs: Prentice-Hall, Inc., 1964.

Byrne, D. *An introduction to personality.* Englewood Cliffs: Prentice-Hall, Inc., 1966.

Campbell, D., & Fiske, D. Convergent and discriminant validation by the multitrait-multimethod matrix. *Psychological Bulletin,* 1959, *56,* 81 – 105.

Gordon, J. E. *Personality and behavior.* New York: The Macmillan Company, 1963.

Grinker, R. R., & Spiegel, J. P. *Men under stress.* Philadelphia: Blakiston, 1945.

Hall, C. S., & Lindzey, G. *Theories of personality.* New York: John Wiley & Sons, Inc., 1957.

Holt, R. R. Individuality and generalization in the psychology of personality. *Journal of Personality,* 1962, *30,* 377 – 402.

Kvale, S., & Greness, C. E. Skinner and Sartre: Towards a radical phenomenology of behavior? *Review of Existential Psychology and Psychiatry,* 1967, *7,* 128 – 150.

McClelland, D. *Personality.* New York: Dryden Press, 1951.

Mischel, W. *Personality and assessment.* New York: John Wiley & Sons, Inc., 1968.

Sarnoff, I. *Personality dynamics and development.* New York: John Wiley & Sons, Inc., 1962.

Shaffer, J. P., & Sinnett, E. R. A factor analysis of Hall and Lindzey's ratings of personality theories. *Acta Psychologica,* 1964, *22,* 135 – 144.

Sheldon, W. H., Stevens, S. S., & Tucker, W. B. *The varieties of human physique.* New York: Harper & Row, Publishers, 1940.

Wann, T. W. (Ed.) *Behaviorism and phenomenology.* Chicago: The University of Chicago Press, 1964.

Webster, N. *Webster's 3rd International Dictionary.* Springfield, Mass.: G. & C. Merriam Co., 1961.

White, R. W. *The abnormal personality.* New York: The Ronald Press Company, 1964.

2

Some Historical Perspectives

INTRODUCTION

It is no accident that all responsible scholars share the belief that to achieve fair understanding of almost anything, one needs a reasonably good grasp of its history. How did the thing of interest, whether it be an object, idea, person, or some combination of all three, get to be what it is today? The question is provocative both as an abstraction and as a practical tool for working through specific problems.

For example, consider the relationship of sex and romantic love. Most of us in Western cultures spend a substantial part of our lives struggling to come to terms with the sex-romance paradox. It is perhaps disturbing, but nevertheless true, that while we may be deeply committed to a romantic love relationship, we can at the same time be sexually and emotionally aroused by casual contact with a complete stranger. So it may come as a fascinating bit of knowledge to discover that the concept of romantic love, as apart from lust, is in fact a social-psychological invention of the Middle Ages.

Historical research indicates that the idea originated at the court of Eleanor of Aquitaine, located in the Provence area of southern France, in the eleventh or twelfth century. Some scholars theorize that the pleasant environment influenced troubadors to elaborate an idealization of love spontaneously. Others contend that the idea may have been derived from the poetry of Moslem Spain. Painter (1957) followed the first theory, offering a plausible, fictionalized hypothesis about the invention of romantic love:

One day toward the middle of the eleventh century a very hungry minstrel who was wandering about the duchy of Aquitaine came to a castle where he hoped that his tales of battles . . . would earn him a good dinner. Unfortunately he found the lord absent and the lady heartily tired of hearing about endless battles. Then it occurred to the minstrel that if he composed a song in praise of the lady's beauty and virtue and described their effect on him in glowing terms, he might get the dinner after all. The experiment was successful, and soon the minstrel was recommending the same

13

course to his colleagues. It was not long before the baronial halls of southern France were ringing with songs in praise of ladies who were able to dispense lavish hospitality (p. 111).

While this bit of history will certainly not solve any of our personal sex-romance problems, it may very well influence the way we think about them.

The imperative quality of historical knowledge has been codified in a number of aphorisms. According to Sorensen (1966), President Kennedy thought that a great deal of political-strategic wisdom was summed up in the quotation "He who does not know the mistakes of the past is condemned to repeat them." And in the world of science and technology today this one is virtually a cliché: "If we see so far today it is only because we stand on the shoulders of giants."

There is really no point in trying to discuss in detail what the scholar or scientist derives from his historical knowledge because the answer is too gross: practically everything, including his understanding of the current problems in his area, his ability to evaluate efforts to work on these problems, his attempts to train students – in brief, his total sense of what it means to be a chemist, sociologist, psychologist, or what have you. The question that *does* require discussion is what the reasonable student can expect to gain from historical knowledge. The best answer to this question is *a sense of proportion*. In the abstract, a sense of proportion can be defined as the ability to make a reasonable or desirable estimation or assignment of relative value. Concretely, it is the presence of a sense of proportion that keeps the scholar from turning into a pedant, the gourmet from becoming a gourmand, the lover from becoming a sex fiend.

To achieve a sense of proportion is to achieve a broad balance or economy of thought that is our only defense against the absurd. It often goes under the name *common sense*. But this would be a misnomer, because common sense usually denotes an evaluation according to criteria of superficial plausibility. Common sense can be applied to specifics in such a way that given parts of a whole may be plausible, while the sum of the parts is not. So it is common sense to suggest "look before you leap," and "he who hesitates is lost." Yet taken together, the sum of these two bits of common sense is nonsense; one wants something more.

It seems clear that absurdity can follow from thinking based on the narrow perspective either of common sense *or* of formal logic. And such thinking lends itself to the absurd with remarkable speed when the subject matter is psychology. The college student studying psychology for the first time is a stock figure of fun in our culture. He comes home on vacation and proceeds to explain all the problems of his parents, siblings, and their relations with one another, on the basis of textbook generalizations. Freudian generalizations about defense mechanisms are especially seductive in this connection because they have such a nice fit to everyday experience. Haven't we all seen the frail boy who "compensates" by working for high grades; the poor achiever who "rationalizes" a bad grade by explaining that the teacher dislikes him; the rigid moralist who "projects" his sexual desires by condemning sinful sex practices in loving detail? The extremes to which an improvident sophomore may go, when he is armed with a list of seven or eight such defense mechanisms, can be extraordinary. Nor is enthusiastic overgeneralization the only problem. Specific matters of interpretation can also get out of hand.

For example, a student whose wife was expecting a child sought advice concerning circumcision! A pediatrician had recommended this operation for the child if it were male. In browsing through the *Psychoanalytic Quarterly*, however, the student found an article indicating that circumcision had a traumatic effect from which some males never recovered. He was quite worried about both the future of his hypothetically circumcised son, and the revealed contradiction between psychiatry and pediatrics. His psychology professor reassured him on the first point by saying that there was no really decisive evidence supporting this notion, and that even if there were, most of us feel that other forms of early experience have a much more crucial effect upon personality than does circumcision. It was impossible to reassure him about the second point.

If a sense of proportion is necessary to avoid the absurd, how is one to achieve it? Knowledge of subject matter alone does not seem to be sufficient. Such knowledge must be accompanied by at least some of the broad perspectives that we can attain directly from a wide range of personal experience, or indirectly from the wide range of vicarious experience available to us in the form of literature and history.

It used to be said almost as a cliché that one could never properly understand human personality until he had read Dostoevski. The difficulty with the literary approach is that in suggesting it one is suggesting a lifelong amorphous enterprise. The following historical material has the minimal virtue of hewing closer to the formally recognized line of personality.

To keep the discussion within reasonable boundaries, the remainder of this chapter is organized so as to present three different perspectives relevant to the study of personality. We will examine first what appears to be the most direct, primitive form of gaining relevant knowledge. From the earliest cave dwellers to the present, men have doubtless stared into each other's faces seeking some truth about personality. This phenomenon may be called the *physiognomic tradition*.

Second, we move directly into the domain of philosophy. Scientific attempts to study personality have a relatively meager history; perhaps 150 years. But the essential question provoking these attempts – What is the nature of man? – has been with us for a much longer time. A number of historically salient views are discussed under the heading *conceptions of human nature*.

Finally, we go to a more dynamic perspective based on an historical-psychological explanation for the evolution of empirical and metaphysical views of personality. Should personality be picked apart with the conceptual apparatus of science, as other natural phenomena are examined, or should it be enshrined whole and intact, as befits a supernatural phenomenon? The issues here are discussed as *metaphysical and empirical alternatives*.

THE PHYSIOGNOMIC TRADITION

The word *personality* is derived from the Latin *persona*, meaning mask. Apparently the Greek dramatists, faced with the problem of poor lighting and relatively large audiences, adopted the practice of having actors wear masks designed to convey the essence of their roles. This technique, in which the "inner man" is presumably revealed by surface characteristics, can be seen today in traditional Oriental theaters. The tradition still survives in modern Western theaters as the more subtle art of makeup and costuming.

As always in human affairs, however, ideas of magnitude do not exist in isolation. The idea that personality is reflected by appearance was not limited to Greek theater. Aristotle wrote on the subject of *physiognomy* – the reading of character in habitual facial expressions and body movements. We have artistic and scientific traditions of physiognomic perception[1] that remain with us today.

Throughout several centuries of European painting, for example, the suffering mystic is drawn as a lean, elongated figure. Members of the establishment, by contrast, are typically given a fleshy, opulent look. The same pattern can be found in literature: Hamlet is thin, his stepfather is corpulent. Literature also provides a full range of metaphors based on the physiognomic qualities of animals, such as "cunning as a fox" or "wise as an owl."

Animal metaphors had a frightening literal form as idols in pre-Grecian civilizations: "In Mesopotamia, bas-reliefs of bestial shapes unlike any beast ever known, men with birds' heads and lions with bulls' heads and both with eagles' wings, creations of artists who were intent upon producing something never seen except in their own minds, the very consummation of unreality" (Hamilton, 1959, p. 16). Unreal in terms of physical reality, perhaps, but understandable as the products of primitive imaginations stirred by a physiognomic mode of cognition.

Bruner (1962) suggested that the deep emotional impact of such metaphors lies in the fact that a single image or symbol can suddenly bridge the gap between different experiences. He gives as an example the mythical centaur. "To combine man with horse is to connect the image of man's rational gift with a renewed image of virility: sexuality and strength, the fleetness and mobility of Hermes, instinctual dignity. An image is created connecting things that were previously separate in experience, an image that bridges rationality and impulses" (p. 62).

Modern scientific attempts to infer personality characteristics from physiognomic cues have evolved out of the philosophy and pseudoscience of earlier times. Psychology here has a quackish ancestry much as chemistry has alchemy and astronomy has astrology. Allport (1961) reported that physiog-

---

[1]As it appears in current psychology, the phrase *physiognomic perception* was elaborated by Werner (1961) to mean many forms of judgment based on the feeling, tone, or emotions aroused by sensory experiences. "Things perceived in this way may appear 'animate' and, even though actually lifeless, seem to express some inner form of life. All of us, at some time or another, have had this experience. A landscape, for instance, may be seen suddenly in immediacy as expressing a certain mood – it may be gay or melancholy or pensive. . . . there is one field where objects are commonly perceived as directly expressing an inner life. This is in our perception of the faces and bodily movements of human beings and higher animals. Because the human physiognomy can be adequately perceived only in terms of its immediate expression, I have proposed the term *physiognomic perception* for this mode of cognition in general" (p. 69).

nomic psychology became such a problem in the seventeenth and eighteenth centuries that in England, laws were passed to punish those caught practicing it.

Rigorous modern efforts in this area can be catalogued conveniently according to the types of physiognomic cues emphasized. The previously mentioned work of Sheldon (1940) concerned gross bodily cues to personality. Another physiognomic category is termed *expressive movement*. Allport and Vernon (1933) studied such factors as length and speed of walking stride, strength of handshake grip, speed and area of handwriting, and voice intensity. The logic underlying this approach is quite direct: an individual who is hesitant and slow in his expressive behavior is likely to be a relatively indecisive, passive person. One who is quick, confident, speaks loudly, and writes with bold strokes, should be the opposite.

Yet another more abstract attack on the problem of how movement influences judgments of personality can be found in the work of Heider and Simmel (1944). They produced a film showing a circle and triangle in various attitudes of approach, avoidance, and pursuit of one another. Persons viewing the film tended to see it in human interaction terms, and to describe the scenario in words having a dynamic, intentional quality, such as "running away," "chasing," "protecting," or "forcing." And, what is most impressive, they attributed human motives to the circle and triangle. Rappoport (1968) worked on this phenomenon also, arranging cartoon displays to determine how variations in movement and form influence subjects to judge a circle or triangle as friendly or unfriendly, aggressive or passive, strong or weak.

No discussion of physiognomic perception is complete without mention of the straightforward, ingenious studies described by Brunswik (1956). He presented subjects with carefully constructed "schematic faces," which were drawn so that all features (nose length, forehead height, eye separation) were systematically varied. Results showed interesting relationships between physiognomy and judgments of personality. ". . . variation of 'mouth' elicits the most extreme responses, high mouth (chin) appearing as gay and young, low chin as sad, old, and bad. A note of ambivalence is injected by the fact that high chin, while favorable in some respects, swings down to unfavorableness as we proceed to apparent intelligence and energy. Wide eyes and short nose exert influences somewhat similar to those of high mouth even though to a lesser extent. The longest noses are unfavorable throughout. . . . And for all facial features the medium variant tends to be on the favorable side, reminding us of the 'golden mean' so celebrated in antiquity" (p. 105).

Brunswik's final comment makes his own sense of proportion very clear. His reference to the classical Greek "golden mean" carries our discussion almost full circle to its starting point. Indeed, it is well to end the discussion here, because there is little more of a fundamental nature to be said. Directly or indirectly, men have sought personality in physiognomy for centuries. The burden of evidence accumulated, however, indicates that physiognomic cues are not important signs of core personality attributes. Studies show that most of us—like the Greeks—tend to think of personality at least partially in terms of surface characteristics. And we can even make some reasonably good peripheral judgments of personality on this basis. After all, certain characteristics of an individual *are* suggested by his body type, posture, gestures, and the like. But these features do not tell us whether he is honest, intelligent, creative, independent, liberal, or conservative. When judging serious core personality attributes of this type, surface features are as much a source of confusion as of enlightenment.

CONCEPTIONS OF HUMAN NATURE

Certainly the question of human nature is more fundamental to philosophy than psychology. But the original, literal, meaning of philosophy is "love of wisdom." Hence all of us possessing some degree of honest curiosity have a license to prowl that area.

Primitive concepts

When we try to start on the problem of how men view themselves at the earliest possible point, there is not much evidence to go on. It is known, however, that Neanderthal man, the most widely distributed of our nonlineal ancestors, who walked only partially erect and lived about 100,000 years ago, appears to have had a rudimentary consciousness of self. Excavations of Neanderthal grave sites show that the dead were buried in special postures with weapons and food. Muller (1961) suggests that this evidence of special regard for the dead indicates a significant, distinctly nonanimal self-consciousness, because otherwise, careful burial procedures would not have occurred.

Cro-Magnon man, the first true variety of *Homo sapiens*, stood erect and evolved a more elaborate culture. His dead were not only buried with their personal ornaments, but were dusted with red ocher. (Muller speculated that the coloring might have been an attempt to give the dead a more lifelike appearance.) Realistic, multicolored drawings found in Cro-Magnon cave dwellings provide strong indications of primitive religious forms: female figures drawn with exaggerated breasts and vulva suggest some type of earth-mother Goddess.

Anthropological evidence shows that all sorts of objects were worshipped by our hunting ancestors: animals, trees, the sun, and the stars. Van Der Post (1961) reports that among surviving bands of Bushmen roaming the Kalahari desert, various stars and constellations are seen as mighty hunters pursuing prey through the night sky. In general, as extended families and tribes developed toward the end of the Cro-Magnon period, each distinct group seems to have evolved their own distinct set of gods.

The idea of sacrificing to one's gods apparently originates in the competitive nature of primitive religion. One's own gods can be strengthened by giving them choice morsels of food. And one can strengthen his own sense of identity by identifying with his god via communal ceremonies of eating; either setting aside some of the available food for the god, or actually consuming food that is thought to be physically a part of the god. Thus, if a bull is worshipped for its strength, eating parts of a bull is a way to gain strength and enhance one's common identity with him. (If this sort of analysis seems a bit weird or unbelievable, think of all the products sold today on the strength of endorsements from athletes, which allow children to put into their bodies what all those champions are supposed to be putting into theirs.)

The transition of man from cave dweller and hunter to tribal villager and agriculturist is thought to have occurred about 10,000 years ago, during the Neolithic period. No one is certain just how agriculture was discovered, but most experts agree that it must have been a trial-and-error process, with women occupying a primary role. Muller (1961) noted that during this period of magical religion, the supernatural beings are all female. "The Mother Goddess was emerging – the great mother of all life, who would become known as Inanna, Astarte, Cybele, Isis, Demeter, and Diana of the Ephesians, among many other goddesses, and who as the Virgin Mary would restore the feminine element excluded from the Christian Godhead. In the early Neolithic village she apparently had it all her own way, for there is no sign of a male deity until civilization approaches" (p. 19).

Summary

The material presented above shows that if early man differed at all from other ape-like primates, the difference was mainly in the former's awareness of death, and his inclination to construct superstitious rituals around the fact of death. Then, as the struggle for survival was reduced by the development of hunting weapons, and later agriculture, superstition was elaborated into different varieties of anthropomorphic religion. Yet we can draw at least two important generalizations from this material. Kahler (1943) saw the development of superstitious ritual as leading men toward an expanded time perspective and toward social organization.

If men pass their magical ceremonies down from one generation to another, they must be operating from premises based on an extended time perspective; an awareness of events preceding their own immediate life experience and of events that will follow after they are gone. So to the extent that men feared their gods sufficiently to invent rituals, they were also inventing a device that enforced a sense of continuity through time. Kahler also suggested that an inevitable consequence of complex religious ritual is social organization. Rites and rituals require experts to perform them properly, and as such experts or "high priests" emerge, they assume positions of leadership, for if people are superstitious they will naturally consult an authority on the supernatural whenever a difficult decision must be made. Thus the role of chieftain or king began to evolve by the end of the Neolithic period.

Altogether then, it can be argued that out of the superstitious thinking characteristic of our ancestors, there grew two very important human phenomena: extended time perspective and social organization. Both of these were prerequisite to the development of civilization, and both remain today as important factors in personality.

Early Civilizations

The pre-Grecian conceptions of man

The earliest civilizations known to us are the Sumerian and Egyptian. Experts date their rise at about 4000 B.C., usually giving priority to the Sumerians. All of the early civilizations developed in the great river valleys of the east: the Sumerian in the Tigris-Euphrates area of Mesopotamia; the Egyptian along the Nile; and the slightly later Indian along the Indus. All were based on the development of an irrigation technology that could produce surplus crop yields.

What distinguishes a civilization from a collection of primitive farming villages can be argued at length, but we can list three straightforward criteria. Civilization means *cities*. To exist, cities depend on *commerce*, and commerce requires a *written language*. Why have cities in the first place? If people are going to build anything substantial, such as an irrigation canal, and have no modern transportation, their work force must live near the job, and they must be supplied. This means the beginning of a city, instead of a village where each man is daily occupied getting his living out of the field.

The general conceptions of man that dominated life in these early civilizations are not very attractive. Parkes (1960) was eloquent on this subject: "Man's first answer to the social and political problems involved in the rise of civilization was to strip himself of all responsibility for his own destiny and project all authority upon the gods. The priests who organized the building of irrigation canals and the establishment of central governments attributed their capacity for initiative and creativity to divine inspiration and demanded unquestioning obedience from their dependents on the ground that they were the vehicles of the divine will . . ." (p. 53).

From any modern perspective, then, life in this period must be described as being lived in the grip of a heavy-handed, theocratic tyranny. Muller agreed with Parkes that men generally thought in terms of "miracle, mystery, and authority." However, he also described the essentially new possibilities that were opened up by city life. The early cities created a need to make moral and intellectual decisions of such complexity that they simply could not all be covered by religious dogma. Morality in small villages had been taken for granted as traditional, enforced by sets of taboos that were blindly accepted.

By contrast, in the cities, where men lived cheek by jowl with one another and engaged in business transactions and could almost every day have dealings with people who were otherwise strangers, questions of proper conduct, of moral or immoral behavior, became quite serious.

The Sumerians developed a moral code which included such ideals as truthfulness, justice, and mercy. At various times their kings made efforts to improve life by pressing for religious reforms and social justice. Some of the Sumerian proverbs found inscribed on stone tablets, and translated by Kramer (1956), indicate how close they came to modern ideas – on friends and family. "Friendship lasts a day, kinship endures forever"; on sex, "For his pleasure: marriage, on his thinking it over: divorce"; and on the subject of poverty, "The poor man is better dead than alive; if he has bread, he has no salt, if he has salt he has no bread."

As the early theocratic civilizations grew stronger, they became imperialist. Priest-kings became emperors who measured their achievements in terms of conquest. To have an empire, however, it is necessary to have armies and bureaucracies of administrators. These new elements of government inevitably became secular power factions. Authority was siphoned from religious hierarchies to the extent that a powerful general might assume control by deposing a priest-king, or a coalition of generals and administrators might successfully oppose a king in defense of their interests. Conditions like these, evolving over many hundreds of years, eventually transformed government from a matter of handing down divine orders to a matter of practical politics.

If we now skip lightly over huge chunks of history, the stage is set for the entrance of our two major players: the ancient Hebrews and Greeks. In the accomplishments of these two peoples we can find the direct antecedents of virtually every broad conception of humanity or personality that concerns us today.

The Hebrew and Greek traditions

"The two peoples that succeeded in transcending their own particularity, that initiated the concept of humanity proper and its complement, the concept of human individuality—for one corresponds to the other, one calls for the other—these two peoples, that thereby founded our civilization, were the Jews and the Greeks" (Kahler, 1943, p. 64).

Just where and how the wandering Semitic tribes of the Near East picked up the idea of monotheism remains historically obscure. It has been suggested that during his time in Egypt, Moses may have been influenced by the ideas of the Pharoah Akhenaton, who believed in an all powerful sun-god. But the concept of an all-powerful god existed among the wandering tribes of Hebrews long before the advent of Moses. The most plausible interpretation is that the idea of a personal, invisible, omnipotent god evolved from such very primitive beginnings as visions and dreams in the minds of nomadic tribesmen. With characteristic flair, Muller (1961) suggested that we can think of Jehovah as a specifically tribal, "local god who made good," and he described the original conception: "They worshiped their god Yahweh (Jehovah) at 'high places' marked by immemorial stones. He was a purely tribal god. The 'covenant' that the patriarchs made with him, as described in Genesis, was a kind of contractual agreement profitable to both sides: in return for their exclusive devotion, he agreed to devote himself exclusively to them. He fulfilled his share of the bargain by showing no concern whatever for the rest of mankind except to slaughter them when they got in the way of his own people; so Moses could exult, 'The Lord is a man of war!'" (p. 117).

The extraordinary achievement of the Hebrew tribesmen was to roll up diversity in unity. Prior to their conception of one god, men everywhere had faced a multitude of gods with uncertain characteristics and overlapping powers. The images men had of themselves were therefore as diverse as their gods; each god being a different looking glass that reflected a different picture. All this changed drastically by the time Moses led his people to their promised land. By an ingenious application of the principle of centralism, the Hebrew leadership rationalized the preexisting metaphysical hodgepodge, turning it into a smooth, clean-cut model that could be understood and followed with little difficulty by average men. The reason they would want to follow it is obvious: compared to what had gone before, Jehovah was a god with marvelously functional attributes. He was invisible and abhorred idols; hence one traveled light with him, which was no mean thing for people on the move without modern transport. He was omnipotent and One, and different ceremonials and forms of metaphysical bookkeeping could therefore be eliminated. He didn't care for human sacrifice but would take a goat or sheep or whatever else was handy; it was the spirit of the thing that counted. He could be approached directly and personally by any individual. Most important for our discussion is the fact that any individual could guide his own behavior according to a universalistic moral code, the Ten Commandments. By keeping to these rules, the individual could be sure that he was good, and that he would eventually collect a proper reward.

The Greek innovation was of course very different from that of the Hebrews, even though at a certain level of abstraction we can suggest some interesting similarities between the two. Faced with the same general state of affairs as the Hebrews – a confusing multiplicity of gods – the Greeks found an elegant solution based on metaphysical diversity instead of unity. Man was raised to a new level of importance by the Hebrews because they placed the individual in direct, constant contact with one deadly serious god. The Greeks raised the status of man by placing him in juxtaposition to a wide variety of whimsical gods. When grouped with a handful of idols that stand much higher than himself, man is overshadowed. But placed among a whole platoon of idols, none of whom is much bigger than he is, man is salient. The ultimate achievement of the Greeks was to divide the gods in such a way that man could comprehend them.

Traces of this divide-and-conquer strategy can be seen in the earliest Greek literature of Homer. In the Odyssey a clever, practical man survives a whole series of engagements with super-human phenomena. From the beginning of their recorded history the Greeks stand out as a tough, pragmatic people, who focused their energy on human affairs to such a degree that the statues of their gods were patterned after idealized men rather than fantastic animals. Just why they should have been this way is not clear. Bowra (1959) believed that their character was the result of their hard physical environment: they had to be tough, practical, and independent to survive. Edith Hamilton (1959) took a more romantic view suggesting that the Greek conception of man was something like a miracle – a "revolution in thought" – because for the first time in human history it placed man at the center of the universe.

Greek conceptions of human nature evolved slowly. According to Bowra (1959) the earliest of the ancient Greeks did not address themselves to the question of whether man was inherently good or evil. Instead, like some contemporary existentialist and Zen philosophers, they made their value judgments only on the basis of grace-in-action.

This view is simply that a man is only good insofar as he is good *at* things, and that man is best who is good at the greatest number of things. A remarkably flexible morality follows from this view, for if good is only seen in terms of action, so it also must be with evil. One therefore does not carry the burden of making global judgments about others or about oneself. Good and evil can be treated as technical matters. Such a conception has obvious attractions and uses, especially for those living under unstable conditions that require frequent action: adventurers, gamblers, explorers, or revolutionaries.

Life under more organized, stable conditions, however, carries one away from existential moral criteria. Bowra (1959) suggested that with the growth of Greek city-states, the conception of what a man should be was elaborated into four cardinal virtues (today we call them personality traits!): *courage, temperance, justice,* and *wisdom.*

The establishment of this quartet is thought to have been the work of Pythagoras, and even if he inherited it from traditional wisdom, he may have given it a neater form and a wider currency. . . . It embodied what the Greeks admired in theory and sought in practice, and most of them would have thought that if a man exercises these virtues and applies them to each situation as it arises, he does as much as can be expected of him (p. 98).

As did the Hebrews, the Greeks developed a set of criteria for goodness which define a kind of moral end-zone for man. The outstanding problem then becomes one of process. How is a man to reach this end-zone? The Greek answer, formalized by Socrates, was characteristically direct: know thyself. The Hebrew answer, gradually developed through the teachings of a long line of prophets, was stated briefly by the prophet Micah, "What doth the Lord require of thee, but to do justly, and to love mercy, and to walk humbly with thy God?" Nothing here about self-insight—instead, the keynote is obedience.

The two peoples were thus not very far apart on matters of personal ethics: both emphasized concepts of justice, wisdom, temperance, or mercy. But they diverged sharply in their metaphysics. As Micah indicates, the Hebrews took their one god very seriously; with few exceptions, humility was the dominant theme of their relationship to Him. By contrast, the attitude of the Greeks toward their gods seems almost playful; their mythology is full of practical jokes, political intrigues, and adventures.

Moreover, when ancient Hebrews and Greeks occasionally came into contact with one another through trade or the misadventures of travel, their mutual impressions were predictably negative. The Hebrews considered the Greeks to be heathen; irreverent even to their own false gods. And the Greek concern with physical beauty, their love of wine, their acceptance of homosexuality and slavery, made them appear entirely corrupt to the critical Hebrew eye. To the critical Greek eye, however, the Hebrews appeared puritanical, rigid, and intolerably smug. Far from admiring beauty, they might avert their eyes from it to avoid temptation. They would not acknowledge the possibility that any god other than their own Jehovah could exist, and, worst of all, they would explain that after having chosen them, and made a contract with them, their one god watched every move they made.

How is it that these two very different peoples, neither of them notably large or powerful in comparison with other peoples of their time, were able to produce moral systems, metaphysics, literature, and art—in short, complete philosophies and methodologies of life—that have come to dominate our world and influence all our lives? As was noted earlier, no straightforward historical analysis can provide an adequate explanation, but there is an intriguing psychological thesis that engages this question.

Franz Alexander (1942) suggested that the great philosophical achievements of the Hebrews and Greeks were produced as a response to adversity. Later elaborated by McClelland (1951), Alexander's thesis was that the harsh conditions of nomadic life in the desert forced the Hebrews to turn inward and thus led to the development of an interior, personal god. It is argued that the Greeks' greatest contributions to philosophy only occurred after the Peloponnesian Wars had reduced them to a state of poverty. They also turned inward, developing personal principles that stressed self-knowledge.

A dramatic form of evidence for this type of analysis can be found in two of the most powerful legends or myths[2] produced by the Hebrews and Greeks: the stories of Job and Socrates. (Powerful is used advisedly. An indication of their power is the fact that almost every reader of this book will already know these stories.) Job's story stands as the preeminent Hebrew model for behavior in the face of external disasters. It shows that questioning, rational analysis, and logical argument are all fruitless when one has been put down by the hand of God, or Fate, or what have you. It further shows how it can actually be wrong for one even to *try* to understand these things because in so doing, one is putting himself on the same plane as God. The emerging principle is that proper behavior requires acceptance; faith in the ultimate workings of unknowable forces.

The story of Socrates has two essential elements. First, he is the outstanding proponent of self-knowledge. The defeats and confusion plaguing Athens in his time led him to abandon as hopeless any effort to seriously shape external affairs. Instead, he interprets the oracular statement "Know thyself," to mean that individual men can only hope to shape their own personal conduct. And even this is difficult because most men delude themselves with easy rationalizations or uncritical acceptance of prevailing opinions. The second essential to the Socrates myth is individual courage. He dies by his own hand—in an ultimate demonstration of individual control of fate—rather than recant his ideas or dilute their force by going off into exile. He is thus finally a martyr to the principle that individuals must be free to seek truth; that "the unexamined life is not worth living."

Before leaving Job and Socrates, another interesting fact should be mentioned. No historian has ever found evidence linking these two very different stories, yet they both occur at approximately the same time in history. The Book of Job is dated in the fourth century B.C., and Socrates is supposed to have lived from 469 to 399 B.C. If nothing else, this coincidence of timing can be seen as the first of many ways in which the Hebrew and Greek traditions intertwine in the history of Western Man.

Besides analysis of myth, there is at least one more compelling argument

---

[2]*Myth* is used here in its technical sense—as a cultural model or pattern for proper behavior.

that can be cited in support of Alexander's "philosophy as a reaction to adversity" thesis. The evidence resides one way or another in all of our everyday lives. One good example can best be observed on a sunny afternoon in spring, on or near any university campus. It is a clearly unique American contribution to Western culture: the convertible full of young blondes, apparently male and female, all bathed in the sound of acid-folk-rock. The sight is almost enough to make one think that an unexamined life *is* worth living. It is an epitome of Tom Wolfe's *Kandy-Kolored Tangerine-Flake Streamline Baby*. But now consider: what happens when streamlined babies get a breakdown, or get into an accident? Philosophy then suddenly becomes real. Since breakdowns and accidents are, metaphorically speaking, a part of the furnishings of everyone's life, everyone can to some extent validate Alexander's thesis for himself. As individuals we are forced to think seriously about the human condition when the going gets rough[3] — either that or retreat into psychosis. The only uncertainty here is whether one's philosophical reaction to adversity will go in the direction of the Hebrews or the Greeks. This is a very serious issue for whole societies as well as for individuals, because depending upon how it is resolved, either a metaphysical or empirical approach is likely to become the dominant theme of reactions to disaster.

THE METAPHYSICAL AND EMPIRICAL ALTERNATIVES

A metaphysical response to disaster usually involves externalization or projection of crucial problems: "The thing is beyond comprehension; it must somehow all be for the best." Such a response is obviously consonant with much of the Hebrew tradition. By contrast, an empirical response implies internalization of problems: "What went wrong, how can it be corrected?" And this approach clearly follows the Greek tradition. If disaster is connected with the injunction to know thyself, it will entail review and scrutiny of prior behavior. Such a review will inevitably embrace prior circumstances, including conceptions of physical and social phenomena. The movement toward self-knowledge, therefore, quickly broadens to become a generally active investigative process; an empirical enterprise leading ultimately to change and innovation.

Taken together, the two alternatives form an abstraction, an analytical tool, that can help us understand many different kinds of social phenomena. The social philosopher Arthur Koestler has used just such a tool in writing two books whose titles alone — *The Yogi and the Commissar* and *The Lotus and the Robot* — are enough to indicate his approach to the examination of whole societies. Applied to the study of modern European cultures, the abstraction allows us to see the drama of their development as a long struggle between incompatible alternatives. Until the Renaissance, with its emphasis on reformation of the Church, individuality, and the like, European man lived largely in accord with a metaphysical philosophy that was interpreted

[3]This line of argument can easily be extended to the claim that pain and suffering are *good* for people because they make them think. Obviously, some people do emerge stronger from ordeals, but there are great individual differences. On this subject, Kurt Lewin is supposed to have said "The same heat that melts the butter hardens the egg."

and enforced by the Church of Rome. The phrase *Dark Ages* not only denotes an historical period, but it also conveys the flavor of a major human experience. However, even the Dark Ages had a dynamic which can be understood as a metaphysical-empirical antithesis. Freemantle (1962) suggests that this dynamic involved a contest between two kinds of medieval philosophers: ". . . those who believed that 'since God has spoken to us it is no longer necessary for us to think,' and the others who believed that 'the divine law required man to seek God by the rational methods of philosophy' because it is man's first duty to use his Godgiven reason" (p. 6).

On an individual level, the decisive implications of the metaphysical-empirical abstraction can be seen in what many scholars and philosophers consider to be *the* major event of modern history: the Nazi effort to exterminate European Jews. A number of authorities on this event, some of whom experienced it as victims, point out that on occasions when Jews might have resisted with some possibility of success, they did not. There were, of course, at least two documented instances in which an heroic resistance *was* organized: at the Treblinka camp (Steiner, 1967) and in the Warsaw ghetto (Hersey, 1958). But the available information indicates that these two cases were exceptional. Why was resistance so infrequent? There are several general interpretations available here; for example, Jews had a tradition of survival through passive forms of resistance; their religious values were against violence; they had no effective political leadership. There is even the rationale held by many of the Nazis that Jews were an inferior race or were constitutional cowards.

Evidence discussed by such authorities as Bettelheim (1960) and Arendt (1965), suggested that effective resistance was difficult to organize because many of the victims could not resolve the metaphysical-empirical paradox. Having followed a metaphysical philosophy stressing individualized relationships with God (there is no formal ministry in the Jewish faith) for centuries, the majority of people could not easily accept proposals for action that could only be ultimately justified through an appeal to empirical philosophy.[4] This can be better understood by keeping in mind that effective resistance is entirely incompatible with individualism. Such action requires organization in which the individual subordinates himself to group goals and places himself under group discipline.

Relevant evidence is abundant. Bettelheim reports keeping his personality intact while in Dachau by making efforts to study the psychological effects of the concentration camp environment — an empirical activity. Other sources show that in east European Jewish communities, appeals for resistance were made by young members of Zionist groups. These appeals were

---

[4]Let us try to see the situation here concretely. Suppose these prisoners discover that they can escape if they kill a guard. But they don't know who the guard on duty is; perhaps it will be a fellow who has shown them some kindness or humanity. More important, which of the three will actually do it? Believing in the Old Testament, all three know that they will eventually be judged. Shall one take a life coldly, premeditatedly, in the hope of saving his own? So a discussion ensues. Then a fourth man enters the scene, perhaps a scholar or sage known to them by reputation. He says, in effect. "How is it, brothers, that you plan murder? To escape injustice? Is that what our presence here means? But we know that God works in mysterious ways. Is it not possible that we are here being tested, just as our ancestors were tested to see if they were worthy of the covenant?" And so forth. The metaphysical alternative (or, in the rhetoric of the old radical American labor leaders: "Pie in the sky") works against direct action.

usually rejected because the Zionist organizations were socialistic in their ideology. Many of the younger people then left their communities to join national partisan groups. But since many of the partisans were recruited from an anti-Semitic peasantry, this alternative was not always successful.

So it is possible to understand one important aspect of a terrible modern tragedy by application of the metaphysical-empirical abstraction. And should this material seem remote, an isolated instance, one need only examine some of the problems experienced by black leaders in our country today. Conservative spokesmen, labeled "Toms" by the militant youth, are often sincere persons who argue from a metaphysical position.

The Empirical Tradition in Psychology

The preceding material conveys some sense of the origins and implications of metaphysical and empirical philosophies. The history of modern science represents an accelerating move toward the empirical. It grows as much out of religious ferment, philosophical discourse, and the great voyages of discovery in the fifteenth, sixteenth, and seventeenth centuries, as it does out of primitive test tubes or microscopes.

The details of the emergence of psychology as a specific empirical discipline can be pursued in Boring (1950), Heidbreder (1933), and Allport (1954). In general, it stands on three philosophical foundations which had become clear by the eighteenth century: the British empiricist-associationist school (which would include Locke, Hume, and the two Mills); the French materialist school (beginning with Descartes and including La Mettrie and Cabanis); and the German phenomenology culminating in Kant. Our concern with these different philosophical schools or traditions is not just a matter of dull scholarship, for each in its own way leads eventually to a major branch of modern empirical psychology.

By the end of the nineteenth century, British associationism had become a psychology of learning. The German Hermann Ebbinghaus elaborated the British philosophical view that learning and memory could be understood through principles of association, into an experimental or laboratory discipline. Much of this whole tradition entered America in the person of E. B. Titchener, "who kept on being an Englishman thinking German thoughts while he lived in America . . ." (Boring, 1950, p. 386). Most authorities also agree that the later growth of American behaviorism occurred partially as a negative reaction to the introspective associationism represented by Titchener.

German phenomenology had more than one important offshoot. Philosophers such as Husserl were able to formalize their interest in immediate experience — that which is often described today as *sensation* and *perception* — so convincingly that they influenced both ends of a broad intellectual spectrum. A whole line of phenomenological scholars, including the distinguished modern writers Sartre, Bergson, and Merleau-Ponty, follow more or less directly in this tradition. On the other hand, many workers in a medical tradition were influenced to turn their attention to the physiological basis of experience. Wundt, who is credited with starting the first experimental psychology laboratory in Germany in 1879, but who began with a medical degree, is one example of this trend. Freud, who began as a physician and physiological researcher, can be included as a later illustration. In brief, it can be argued that the formal experimental study of psychology began in Germany as a hybrid offspring of phenomenology and physiology.

Finally, the French school somehow took an odd turn away from the British and Germans to become the substantial basis for modern social and clinical psychology. Perhaps this trend, which moved from Descartes up through Voltaire, Diderot, Rousseau, and Comte, should be attributed to the French Monarchy. Their diligent efforts to exile, proscribe, and otherwise harass philosophers at various times would naturally incline these philosophers to reflect upon questions of sociology and psychopathology. We have from this source both the French revolution, with its emphasis on social justice and the rights of man, and the first important center for the study and treatment of psychopathology, the Salpêtrière in Paris, originally made famous by Charcot and where Freud eventually spent time studying. Other relevant efforts such as Wundt's multivolume study of "folk psychology" notwithstanding, it is clear that the French tradition provided the strongest impetus to the study of man as a social being.

As so many other things have done, the different philosophical ideas underlying contemporary psychology end inextricably tied up with one another in America. (It is like American cuisine: where else in the world can people have a dinner of French onion soup, English roast beef, Italian ices, German coffee cake, and never think twice about it? Or where else can you see an army with assault rations ranging from Vienna sausages to spaghetti and meatballs, that taste equally bad?) One can only despair at the task of unraveling it all. Instead, we will employ as an ordering device the "doctrines of man" concept introduced by Asch (1952).

The Three Paths of Empirical Psychology

Asch[5] (1952) suggested that three overlapping but essentially different concepts of man characterize modern studies of social behavior and personality. As we describe these concepts — the biological, the sociological, and the psychoanalytic — and present some illustrative material for each, readers will note several connections to the definition and methodology issues discussed in the previous chapter. This circularity, such as it is, is unavoidable — it comes with a sense of proportion.

The biological view of man is based mainly on the work of Charles Darwin. By establishing continuity between man and animal through his theory of evolution, Darwin laid the conceptual foundation for continuity between analyses of animal and human behavior. As it exists in modern psychology, the biological concept involves two fundamental premises. One is that animals and men are similar because most of their behavior can be traced to the necessity for satisfying such physiological needs as food, water, and sex. The second premise is that the major difference between even the highest mam-

---

[5]Asch can be identified as being in the German phenomenological tradition insofar as he is known as a Gestalt theorist, and insofar as Gestalt psychology was developed in Germany as a theory of perceptual phenomena.

mals and man—the reason for the apparent complexity of the latter as compared with the former—lies in the fact that so much human behavior is *learned*. The school of psychology known as American Behaviorism is essentially grounded on these two premises. They explain why learning theories and learning experiments have had such a large place in psychology texts for the past forty years; and why so much of that research involves rats, pigeons, and chimps.

With respect to the higher forms of human behavior such as altruism, art, and culture, the behaviorist view holds that these things can be understood as secondary or tertiary drives. In essence, this means that the "higher" behaviors ultimately can be linked in a causal chain to physiological needs, by applying learning theory concepts such as conditioning, trial and error, positive and negative reinforcement, and stimulus generalization. Some learning theorists further suggest that to be raised in a human society is to be raised in a huge conditioning apparatus or Skinner box. The individual learns to behave in ways that lead to rewards and to avoid behaving in ways that lead to punishment. A good part of "personality" thereby is shaped in a manner analogous to the way one can shape the behavior of an animal in the laboratory.

The biological concept of man has as its extreme opposite the sociological concept of man. Most authorities credit the main theoretical work here, as well as the title "father of modern sociology," to Émile Durkheim (1898), whose most fundamental statement expounded the idea that man is a social creature. He asserted that great differences in behavior can everywhere be seen between men living in different societies. Yet, since men are everywhere very similar in their biological structure, any explanation of human behavior must rest upon sociological rather than biological factors. It was further argued that where men live together in groups, standardized forms of behavior (ceremonials, rituals, normative ways of thinking and responding) called *collective representations*, become characteristic of the groups. These collective representations are independent of any individual group member; they persist across generations and despite disasters such as war or famine.

From a sociological standpoint, then, personality is seen as being determined by social institutions and cultural practices. Child-rearing methods, educational institutions, religions, art, and entertainment are some of the crucial forces that shape the individual. Whatever aspects of individual personality are *not* hammered out by such forces—variations in personal styles or personal abilities—must appear relatively trivial to the extreme partisan of the sociological concept of man.

We come finally to the third doctrine of man, the psychoanalytic or Freudian. Asch (1952) was especially eloquent in his summary of this view. "It is the principal thesis of Freud that society suppresses human impulses, that the social order is built on instinctual repression" (p. 17). The reference here is, of course, to the instincts of sex and aggression that Freud saw as fundamental to the psychological makeup of every individual. Society must restrain free expression of these instincts if an orderly civilization is to be maintained. Parents and teachers are the witting or unwitting agents of society in this matter, because they discourage children from acting out their primitive instincts, and encourage them instead to channel their energies into more acceptable activities. According to Asch, "It is in fact the clash between the instincts and the interdictions erected by society which, according to Freud, produces the specifically human psychological constitution; in the struggle to master the conflict between himself and society the child's psychological structure undergoes certain characteristic transformations which form the substance of his character and the marks of which he carries through life" (p. 17).

We therefore find that Freudian efforts to understand human behavior, whether these efforts involve clinical cases, historical phenomena, or laboratory experiments, all have one thing in common: explanations are sought in very deep-lying causes. On an individual clinical level, this means a search backward toward the person's early childhood experiences. On the level of group or social phenomena, Freudians often seek explanations by interpreting the primitive origins of social practices as solutions to problems generated by instinctive needs. And in the laboratory, Freudians tend to design experiments relevant to what they see as typical childhood conflicts and fears.

How should one evaluate or choose between these three concepts of man? While Asch would probably have agreed that they denote the major empirical paths followed by modern psychology, he was nevertheless critical of all three. As indicated in the previous chapter, his criticism was essentially humanistic. He felt that in one way or another, these views were all too grim; they did not provide a sufficient basis for understanding the full potential of man. His posture on this matter might be summarized briefly by saying that the three doctrines all followed more from what is worst, rather than what is best, in man.

By questioning the prevailing doctrines Asch provokes the serious critical thought that can lead to scientific progress. So the biological concept, elaborated into a psychology of learning, tells us, for example, how simple rewards and punishments can "stamp in" or "stamp out" behaviors. But after fifty years of research, learning experts can explain little about how children learn at play. And work based on the sociological doctrine may tell us that juvenile delinquency is primarily a sociocultural phenomenon, but it says nothing about why some persons with delinquent backgrounds can go on to useful careers while many others cannot.

If the psychoanalytic doctrine appears more promising than either of the others because it contains important elements of both, it is also more disappointing. Socially inhibited biological instincts must certainly have a role in personality, but when this conception is used to explain phenomena ranging from war to incest to the political decisions of Woodrow Wilson, the explanations can exceed the reach of the concept. Theoretically speaking, the Freudian doctrine has the quality of a good rubber band. It conveniently holds together a great many things and it can be stretched to include more than at first seems likely; but the more it is stretched, the weaker it gets.

We are at a point now, about 20 years after Asch's original discussion, that allows us to better appreciate the validity of his views, and also to see somewhat beyond them. There is little doubt that his bold portrait of the three doctrines answered very well the question of where psychology had been, up to, say, 1950 or 1955. The question he could not then answer was where it would be in the future. An attempt at answering this question is now possible, because at least two important events have occurred since Asch's 1952 book.

These events may be termed the *computer revolution,* which has had an enormous impact on *all* scientific work, and the *cognitive* revolution, which has had a great impact on our prior conceptions of man. While all the implications and effects of these two events as yet await detailed discussion by the historians of modern science, some of their major consequences for psychology are already clear. During the last 10 years, psychology has shown vastly increased tendencies to (a) study the "higher processes" in man; (b) explain behavior as the outcome of rational, though perhaps sloppy, thought processes; (c) examine behavior developmentally, exploring sequences of age-related abilities; (d) discriminate between maintenance behaviors, those related to physiological needs, and growth behaviors, those related to the forward developmental thrust of human personality; (e) determine how certain aspects of personality, such as intelligence, can be seen as *either* innate or acquired; and (f) emphasize the role of uniquely human abilities such as language, intentionality, and other symbolic processes, in all the above matters. There is, furthermore, a corresponding shift away from monolithic interpretations of behavior as largely a function of learning, social structures, or unconscious mental processes.

In sum, while the three traditional doctrines are by no means gone, they have been substantially compressed or transformed. Learning and motivation theorists these days will talk in terms of language and intrinsic rewards. Freudians will describe themselves frequently as ego-oriented, and sociology is marked by new concern with value structures. The three traditional doctrines surely remain in our background, but they no longer account directly for much of our empirical research. Instead, we have in psychology an emerging new conception of man as preeminently *cognitive.*

CHAPTER SUMMARY

An attempt has been made in this chapter to discuss material that can provide the reader with some sense of proportion regarding the subject matter of personality. There is first a discussion of what is meant by a sense of proportion as the essence of good judgment. No one can hope to come to grips with the core issues of personality without harnessing his judgment to the task. Then, the major approaches that can be taken to personality are given, starting with the *physiognomic.* In this category can be placed most attempts, primitive or sophisticated, to understand personality from the outside in. The early Greek dramatists might have agreed with McLuhan that "the medium is the message."

The second major approach considered is based on *historical conceptions* of human nature. A vast area indeed, but some smattering of relevant ideas is necessary to draw attention to the fact that our views of personality have interesting historical roots. Whether or not, as serious Marxists suggest, *all* attempts to understand personality should be seen as historically determined is another question.

A third major avenue toward understanding personality follows from Western cultural traditions originating with the ancient Hebrews and Greeks. This is perhaps the most interesting material to explore because it contains so much that is directly relevant to us today. Our effort to sketch the *metaphysical* and *empirical* alternatives that must inevitably influence responses to adversity, seems especially important at a time when historians and philosophers argue that value concepts can no longer be tied with iron confidence to either the idea of God *or* Science. Some people maintain that we are entering a new period in which value concepts can be tied to *man*, but the issue must remain in doubt. Certainly it is true that our concepts of man are changing. He once stood as entirely the creature of God, and modification of the human condition was to be largely God's business. More recently, man has been taken as a creature of nature, and changes in the human condition were to be the business of a science that could manipulate nature. But in the face of recent historical events, a fundamentalist faith in science grows more and more difficult to maintain. So philosophical and historical thinkers sense in the confused social friction of our times – drug problems, morality shifts, struggles for social equality, inefficient counter-insurgency warfare – the makings of a new concept of man.

To the extent that psychology may participate in whatever new value system eventually emerges, it already seems clear that it will do so on some basis other than the traditional doctrines discussed by Asch. The biological, sociological, and Freudian views that have dominated the development of psychology in the first half of the twentieth century have lost most of their force. We see instead an increasing emphasis being placed on man as a thinking or cognitive being. Furthermore, the instinct-driven emotions that were once thought to be so disruptive to individuals and societies, are beginning to be understood differently today: less as a threat and more as a promise. Narrowly defined forms of dealing with emotionality, such as individual psychotherapy, are giving way to broad-spectrum approaches designed to be preventative as well as curative. These techniques range from group therapy, to T-groups, to micro-labs, and include the total immersion in emotionality provided by marathon "sensitivity" sessions (with and without clothes on). All of them aim to open the individual so that he can accept and understand a wider span of his own emotional potential. It is not entirely implausible, then, that taken together the strong trends in current psychology to see man as both more cognitive, and more capable of dealing harmoniously with his emotions, will contribute to the foundation of a newer, richer conception of our species.

References

Alexander, F. *Our age of unreason.* Philadelphia: J. B. Lippincott Co., 1942.

Allport, G. W. The historical background of modern social psychology. In G. Lindzey (Ed.), *Handbook of social psychology.* Cambridge: Addison-Wesley Publishing Co., Inc., 1954.

Allport, G. W. *Pattern and growth in personality.* New York: Holt, Rinehart and Winston, Inc., 1961.

Allport, G. W., & Vernon, P. E. *Studies in expressive movement.* New York: The Macmillan Company, 1933.

Arendt, H. *Eichmann in Jerusalem: A report on the banality of evil.* New York: The Viking Press, Inc., 1965.

Asch, S. E. *Social psychology.* New York: Prentice-Hall, Inc., 1952.

Bettelheim, B. *The informed heart: Autonomy in a mass age.* Glencoe, Ill.: The Free Press, 1960.

Boring, E. *A history of experimental psychology.* New York: Appleton-Century-Crofts, 1950.

Bowra, C. M. *The Greek experience.* New York: Mentor Books, 1959.

Bruner, J. *On knowing: Essays for the left hand.* Cambridge: Belknap Press, 1962.

Brunswik, E. *Perception and the representative design of experiments.* Berkeley: University of California Press, 1956.

Durkheim, E. Réprésentations individuelles et Réprésentations collectives. *Revue de Métaphysique,* 1898, *6,* 274–302.

Freemantel, A. The age of belief. In *The great ages of Western philosophy,* Vol. 1. Boston: Houghton Mifflin Company, 1962.

Hamilton, E. *Mythology.* New York: Mentor Books, 1959.

Heidbreder, E. *Seven psychologies.* New York: Appleton-Century-Crofts, 1933.

Heider, F., & Simmel, M. An experimental study of apparent behavior. *American Journal of Psychology,* 1944, *57,* 243–259.

Hersey, J. *The wall.* New York: Alfred A. Knopf, Inc., 1958.

Kahler, E. *Man the measure.* New York: Pantheon Books, Inc., 1943.

Kramer, S. N. *From the tablets of Sumer.* Indian Hills, Colo.: Falcon's Wing Press, 1956.

McClelland, D. C. *Personality.* New York: Dryden Press, 1951.

Muller, H. J. *Freedom in the ancient world.* New York: Harper & Brothers, 1961.

Painter, S. *French chivalry.* Ithaca: Cornell University Press, 1957.

Parkes, H. B. *Gods and men.* London: Routledge and Kegan Paul Ltd., 1960.

Rappoport, L. Impressions of personality as a function of physical and behavioral properties of artificial social objects. *Human Relations,* 1968, *21,* 363–371.

Sorensen, T. *Kennedy.* New York: Bantam Books, Inc., 1966.

Steiner, J. *Treblinka.* New York: Simon & Schuster, Inc., 1967.

Van Der Post, L. *The heart of the hunter.* New York: William Morrow & Co., Inc., 1961.

Werner, H. *Comparative psychology of mental development.* New York: Science Editions, Inc., 1961.

Psychobiology:
Some Neurophysiological and Biochemical
Perspectives on Personality

ON PAIN

Whenever I visit an old friend living near Portland, Maine, we go through a lobster dinner ritual. It begins with loading the children into a car and driving to the local pound to select our lobster. The climax occurs in my friend's kitchen when his wife takes a firm stance and (a) holds the lid of a tub of boiling water in her left hand, (b) clutches the lobster by the body with her right hand, then (c) after standing poised for a moment shrouded in steam, with one swooping motion plunges the waving lobster into the pot and slams the lid in place. She now lets out a great sigh of relief, rolls her eyes, and with a prim sincerity that seems unique to the women of old New England families, poses the fundamental question: "I wonder if they feel pain?" The ritual ends later in discussion of the philosophical implications associated with the question of whether lobsters feel pain when they are boiled alive. The thing is, nobody knows.

Anatol Rapoport (in Scher, 1962) summed up the issue for both psychology and philosophy with the following remarks.

We readily agree that human beings feel pain and that stones feel no pain. We assume that animals resembling us also feel pain. With regard to remote animals like oysters or polyps, we may say we do not know. But how can we find out? If no conceivable procedure of verification can be established, assertions on this subject are technically meaningless. But at what stage do they become meaningless? (p. 272).

The deeper issue here is not simply that we don't know enough to answer the lobster question as a scientist would like to (lobsters do or do not possess certain neurophysiological structures, therefore, they do or do not feel pain); it is rather that we are just now reaching the point at which intensive, serious efforts are being made to understand the total biochemical-neurophysiological basis for experience. In the matter of pain as experienced by humans, medical practitioners have traditionally operated on the understanding that pain is a sensation transmitted to the brain by the nervous system, or some such definition. This definition is undoubtedly correct since, after all, pain associated with damage to a body part can be eliminated by cutting the nerve fibers ascending from that part to the brain. Pain is also recognized medically as having important functional properties: it serves as a signal, warning us to avoid potentially damaging circumstances (such as extreme heat or cold), or to keep damaged parts out of service.

But the neat simplicity of these remarks does not hold up very well under close scrutiny. For one thing, efforts to relieve pain by surgery on neural tracts are not always effective, although no one is sure why. Neurologists disagree about whether pain should be conceptualized in terms of a specificity theory or a pattern theory. Gardner (1968) put the question as follows: "Certainly, the specificity theory neglects the psychological aspects, the fact that surgical operations. . . . may fail to relieve pain, and that the quality and degree of pain are susceptible to a variety of influences. The pattern theory, on the other hand . . . neglects the specificity of receptors and their responses . . ." (p. 180).

Gardner describes other difficulties for neurologists dealing with pain; for example, the problems of *referred pain* and *phantom limb sensations*. The former involves the experience of pain in areas of the body that are not damaged: in some forms of heart disease, pain may be felt along the left arm; a kidney stone may cause pain to be felt in the groin or the back; and lung damage can cause pain near the shoulder blades. Phantom limb experiences occur when an amputee feels as if his missing limb is still present. One who has lost his entire left leg may thus report feeling pain or an itch in his left foot. Presumably, this phenomenon is due to stimulation of nerve fibers in the stump of the missing leg, and these stimuli are interpreted in the brain as coming from the absent foot. Gardner (1968) made a nice historical comment in this connection: "It is interesting that in medical history and in folklore, there are references to the practice of digging up amputated parts which had been buried, in order to straighten out the fingers or toes in the belief that this would relieve painful spasms of the absent limb. These spasms were attributed to the devil" (p. 185).

Anyone who has seen his doctor try to decide whether he is suffering from an inflamed appendix or indigestion, and who has had to cooperate in this venture by trying to describe his pains as the doctor pokes about his abdomen, might agree that knowledge of sensations mediated by the nervous system is still quite primitive. Modern medical technology and charts of the nervous system notwithstanding, diagnosis often depends upon questions about where it hurts, how it hurts, and how much it hurts.

A recent addition to the psychological literature in this area concerns individual differences in the experience of pain. Petrie (1967) demonstrated that people vary greatly in their sensitivity to many sensory experiences, including pain. Three categories or types of persons are identified in her study. *Augmenters* are those who exaggerate or intensify sensory experiences; *reducers* are those who minimize sensory experiences; and *moderates* are those who neither exaggerate nor minimize to any significant extent. Using tasks designed to measure what is called *perceptual reactance,* Petrie reported that augmenters classified mounting pain as "unbearable" much sooner than moderates, and that when they were asked to estimate the size of an unknown object by touch alone, augmenters overestimated size much more that did moderates. Reducers *underestimate* both pain and size more than moderates.

These findings are reminiscent of earlier work by Bruner and Tajfel (1961), who also studied individual differences in perception. They identified persons as being either *broad* or *narrow categorizers.* Gardner (1953) dealt with similar differences by identifying persons as perceptual *levelers* or *sharpeners;* the former (broad categorizers or levelers) tend to minimize the differences between perceived objects, the latter tend to exaggerate such differences. One would expect that future research will examine the possibility of establishing a linkage between perceptual tendencies to level or sharpen, on the one hand, and to augment or reduce on the other. Extended research on issues of this type might illuminate many applied problems. For example, Petrie suggests that serious individual differences in sensitivity to pain may explain susceptibility to certain pathological conditions. Thus, alcoholics may be augmenters who try to deaden their senses by excessive drinking. And many schizophrenics, who seem extremely insensitive to pain, may originally have been augmenters who developed a withdrawal psychosis as a defense against their hypersensitivity.

We have discussed the phenomenon of pain at some length, beginning with uncertainty about its presence in a lower species, and ending with uncertainty about how it is experienced in humans, for two reasons. It is, first of all, an intrinsically interesting topic. We all have considerable personal experience with it, and we are all ultimately alone with it, as with some secret, individualized mystery that can never be shared except occasionally through great art.[1] Second, and perhaps more important for didactic purposes, is the fact that pain stands as the most brutally obvious facet of the mind-body issue. It provides an immediate focal point for discussion because it is an experience clearly at the interface between mental and physical events. In this context, pain is merely a vexing, direct manifestation of a much larger matter. If scientific knowledge about pain is still inadequate—it can be manipulated and controlled by mechanical and chemical techniques, but these techniques are quite imprecise—our knowledge about other everyday mind-body phenomena such as sleeping and dreaming is as yet even less adequate. We will, nevertheless, go on in this chapter to discuss mind-body questions that seem directly related to personality.

The past fifteen years have seen a mushrooming of new efforts to investigate such subjects as sleeping, the genetic basis of individual differences, and the biochemistry and biophysics of brain functioning. No unimpeachable summary of all these recent developments can be given because

---

[1]One can understand Hemingway's novel, *The Old Man and the Sea,* as an effort to externalize the internal experience of pain and dying via the metaphor of an epic, three-sided battle between a courageous old man, a huge powerful fish, and a school of vicious sharks. The novel is very much like a symphonic composition on the theme of pain. It includes all the major and minor variations: pain as dull but cumulative, slowly mounting and receding; pain as sharp but short, cycling through quick explosive bursts; and many combinations of both.

most of the material is too recent. Moreover, as one looks through the original research literature in these fields, the general impression received is that experimentation is proliferating so rapidly that no one active in it wants to take time out to write a global review. If he does, his work is liable to be obsolete by the time it is published. The following material therefore has the character of a fairly arbitrary overview; things that catch the theoretical eye. Starting with a short historical briefing on the mind-body problem, we will discuss (a) brain functioning, (b) the gross biochemistry of individual differences, (c) psychopharmacology, (d) the functional properties of sleeping and dreaming, (e) the fine biochemistry of intelligence, and (f) several aspects of theory and research in genetics.

THE TRADITIONAL MIND-BODY PROBLEM

It is the same with the mind-body problem as it is with so many things in science: the origins go back to the ancient Greeks. Initially, the question raised by the ancient thinkers was simply a matter of gross anatomy — "Where is the mind?" Any sort of investigation of the carcasses of animals and men quickly reveals the general location of most vital functions. But where is all the thinking, decision making, anxiety, and passion going on? Some suggested the brain, but consensus on this point was a long time coming. Boring (1950) traced out the controversy, noting that the ancient Egyptians localized thinking in the heart but judgment in the head or kidneys. Pythagoras and Plato, however, placed thinking in the brain, and Galen later described animal spirits as originating in the brain before moving to the heart and out through the arteries.

Through the middle ages, and up to the eighteenth century, the relationship between events of the body and events of the mind remained almost totally obscure. Certain outstanding anatomists did indeed suggest specific functions for parts of the brain that were at times quite close to modern views, but most of these early speculations had little or no impact because philosophers were distracted by quasi-religious aspects of the mind-body problem. Descartes is an outstanding protagonist of this condition. In the seventeenth century he argued for an almost complete psychophysical dualism: the mind is one thing, the body is another. The only interaction between the two might occur when, by an exertion of mind, the "animal spirits" of the body could be influenced (as in daydreaming about food, sex, or violence). He identified the *pineal gland* at the base of the brain as the point of contact between mind and body, and the idea of localizing the "soul" in this little gland, for which no one at the time could find any other function, became quite popular.

The mind-body problem therefore stayed more or less by default in the domain of metaphysics for hundreds of years. It is noteworthy, in this connection, that even as late as 1890 William James thought it proper to begin his *Principles of Psychology* by addressing the "soul-theory" tradition of explaining mental processes.

Early in the nineteenth century, two respectable Viennese brain anatomists, Gall and Spurzheim, collaborated on a book which gave rise to what we now call the pseudoscience of *phrenology* – the effort to read a person's character and personality according to variance in the shape of his skull. It was based on a perfectly logical but rash three-step interpretation of the localization of function doctrine. There is first the doctrine itself, that all major aspects of behavior are centered in, or controlled by, different specific areas of the brain. The second step is the proposition that any conspicuous aspect of individual personality, such as an exceptional imagination or sense of humor, will be accompanied by a corresponding growth in the brain area controlling that aspect of personality, and the third step is the possibility that the skull enclosing the brain will vary according to variations in the shape of the brain. Phrenologists thus sought bumps on the skulls of individuals that would correspond with their behavioral propensities.

As a means of understanding or predicting behavior, phrenology can be dismissed as claptrap because it just doesn't work. But as a way-station on the road to modern brain research, phrenology is most important. It inspired a great general interest in the problem of brain functioning which culminated in the rigorous localization studies of the late nineteenth and early twentieth centuries. These studies yielded results allowing us to map the brain in such a way that we can now reliably identify areas controlling motor action, vision, audition, and touch. For a time it seemed that localization studies might continue to accumulate findings until the "mind" could in fact be entirely understood as finely subdivided areas of the brain controlling the body. But this optimistic view finally had to be discarded. To understand what went wrong, it is necessary to understand the way much of the research was accomplished.

Most localization-of-function studies were based on a very simple research strategy. Researchers sought to determine the relation between physical attributes of the brain and behavior however they could. For example, after a patient known to have suffered from a substantial speech or motor disorder finally dies, his brain can be excised and examined in detail for any abnormalities. A more sophisticated version of this strategy is possible when one works with nonhuman species, and can therefore carry out operations on the brain. Areas in the brains of rats may be systematically destroyed to record the behavioral consequences of the destruction. Much work has been done in this fashion to study the effects of brain damage on learning. One here either teaches a rat (or dog or monkey) to make a certain response, destroys a part of his brain, and then tests to see if the response is still present; or else one first destroys part of the brain and then tests to see if a given response can be learned. Ingenious variations on the learning-destruction strategy have preoccupied many physiological psychologists for many years. However, the difficulty with research of this type began to be clear by the 1920's.

It was observed more and more frequently that an organism which had lost a particular function because of brain damage, could partially or fully recover that function, even though the damage was permanent. After much work on this problem, Lashley (1929) announced the principles of equipotentiality and mass action. *"Equipotentiality* means that one part of the cortex is as good as another in contributing to a certain function, like learning and 'intelligence.' *Mass action* means that all equipotential parts work together and that the loss of one diminishes efficiency in proportion to the magnitude of the loss, no matter where the loss occurs" (Boring, 1950, p. 76). Of course, these principles cannot be applied in all circumstances: when some parts of the brain are destroyed, certain functions are lost permanently. But the effect of Lashley's pronouncement was to shift research drastically from the idea of perfect correspondence between brain structure and behavior. Sketches that map the functions of different brain areas are still present in current textbooks. Compared with similar sketches of the nineteenth century, however, the new ones are much less specific. And while we recognize that specific brain losses cause specific impairments in behavior, it will become clear in a later discussion of contemporary research that we approach such phenomena very differently today.

Aside from efforts to understand the relationship between brain and behavior, the mind-body problem has been elaborated over the past 100 years in psychological theories and through medical research. In the former category, we have already discussed body-type theories of personality. Another outstanding item here, however, is the James-Lange theory of emotion. Introduced in the late 1880's and revised in the 1890's, the theory goes against the common sense idea that emotional feelings determine behavior. Instead of maintaining that one cries because he is sad, or smiles because he is happy, the theory suggests that in many instances the act of weeping can produce a feeling of sadness; the act of smiling a feeling of happiness. One can easily observe good examples of this proposition in young children. Almost every parent tries emotional manipulation in line with the James-Lange theory when he makes funny faces for a hurt or frightened child.

Modern medical research bears on the mind-body problem in several ways. There is now a good-sized literature on what are called *psychosomatic ailments*. It includes such disorders as migraine headaches, asthma, various allergies, skin diseases, frigidity and impotence, high blood pressure, ulcers, and arthritis. Not that all of these problems are known to proceed entirely from mental causes, but they all seem to have some significant, if mysterious, mental component. Why, for example, should it be that some women who want children, but fail to conceive despite great efforts, are able to do so after they have *adopted* a child? Or consider a textbook description of rheumatoid arthritis, which is much more common among women than men. Strange (1965) explained that the typical case involves very active women inclined to act out masculine roles. When they find themselves in situations making this impossible, they are liable to "escape" through an attack of rheumatoid arthritis.

One can even find psychological approaches to such extreme body disorders as cancer. Simmons (1956) speculated that long-term emotional problems could predispose persons toward cancer, and that a sudden, severe, psychic shock or trauma could trigger it off. Ramifications of the mind-body problem show up so frequently, and in so many different areas of modern clinical medicine, that for illustrative purposes it becomes useless to pursue the matter any further. Suffice it to say that no well-trained medical practitioner today should ignore potentially important psychological aspects of physical ailments.

BRAIN FUNCTIONING

The part of the brain controlling most, if not all, of the uniquely human "higher functions"—thinking, judgment, memory—is the cerebral cortex. This is also where most of our past experience or memories are stored. Penfield (1959) introduced the subject as follows.

The human brain is the master organ of the human race. It differs from the brains of other mammals particularly in the greater extent of its cerebral cortex. The gray matter, or cortex, that covers the two cerebral hemispheres of the brain of man is so vast in nerve cell population that it could never have been contained within the human skull if it were not folded upon itself, and refolded, so as to form a very large number of fissures and convolutions. The fissures are so deep and so devious that by far the greater portion of this ganglionic carpet (about 65 percent) is hidden in them, below the surface (p. 1719).

While it exercises a general control function, this fantastic cortex of ours does not serve as the ultimate *source* of all behavior. Just below the cortex, in the cerebral hemispheres, are located the neural centers for vision, audition, motor activity, and the sensory characteristics that we have in common with so many lower species. The crucial thing to understand here is that fibers connect the cortex to the neural centers in a two-way fashion. This arrangement is what makes it possible for humans to maintain their uniquely high degree of control over behavior. The lower we look on the phylogenetic scale, the smaller is the cortex and the fewer are the fibers connecting it to the hemispheric centers. To a greater extent than any other species, therefore, we humans can inhibit or override responses to stimuli reaching the neural centers, and we can initiate actions in the absence of direct stimulation coming from the centers.

Recent research provides fascinating examples of cortical functioning. It has been shown that when the cortex is removed from the brain of an otherwise unimpaired dog, he will give total rage reactions to even mildly offensive stimuli. This is thought to occur because the rage response is fully organized in a lower center which can be triggered by external events. Without the inhibitory control provided by the cortex, the response is no longer graded to the stimulus; the dog loses his "judgmental" capacity. Presumably, many emotional reactions in men as well as animals are thus cortically controlled.

Penfield (1959) described work demonstrating that electrical stimulation of a region he terms the "interpretive cortex" can produce either *experiential* or *interpretive* responses. He illustrated the former response in the case of a woman who reports hearing an orchestra: "The music stopped when the electrode was removed. It came again when the electrode was reapplied. On request, she hummed the tune, while the electrode was held in place, accompanying the orchestra. . . . Over and over again, restimulation at the same spot produced the same song. . . . She believed that a gramophone was being turned on in the operating room on each occasion, and she asserted her belief stoutly in a conversation some days after the operation" (p. 1720).

Interpretive responses resulting from similar stimulation in the same region of the cortex have a more perceptual character. The person reports anomalies of vision, hearing, or thinking, often with an awareness that these things are absurd. No one as yet has a good answer to the question of why the same type of electrical stimulation applied to the same region of the cortex will produce different types of responses. However, as one goes through this and other material to be mentioned below, one can't help beginning to think of it all in terms of a compelling aphorism: "Experience is electricity." Certainly as one looks to relevant findings concerning another area of the brain called the *ascending reticular arousal* or *activating system (ARAS)*, the aphorism gains strength.

Located at the base of the brain (the *brainstem*), in an area that is a bit above the nape of the neck, the ARAS is stimulated by excitatory currents which can originate almost anywhere in the body prior to ascending the central neural tracts leading to the brain. In turn, when the ARAS is stimulated, it sets off increased electrical activity in the cortex. Gross monitoring studies such as *electroencephalograph* recordings *(EEG)* have shown that such electrical activity of the cortex is generally quite low during sleep, greater in a waking but relaxed state, and still greater in a condition of high tension. The ARAS is therefore especially interesting as the source of this cortical activity.

The most important general statement that studies (see Samuels, 1959) allow us to make about the ARAS is that it serves as a kind of tuning device for the cortex as a whole. The cortex will not function properly unless an optimum level of electrical activity is maintained in it by the ARAS. If this activity is insufficient, the organism goes into a state of apathy; if the activity is too great, overstimulated behavior states similar to what can be observed in some epileptic seizures can occur. Unfortunately, the neat simplicity of the above statements, while quite justified 10 years ago, and certainly not entirely unjustified now, are turning out to be too simple. Thompson (1967) cited experiments indicating that the ARAS does not *fully* control cortex electrical activity. The whole matter is beginning to look more complicated than before. "Finally, it would seem that sleep-wake cycles and 'attentive' behavior can occur in animals with virtually complete destruction of the ARAS and that animals with lesions limited to sensory pathways may be much impaired in alerting and 'attentive' aspects of behavior. To assert that the ARAS has any clear or paramount unitary function would seem at present to be somewhat premature" (p. 457).

Note that the thrust of Thompson's comment is not to categorically deny earlier generalizations, but rather, by raising exceptions, to make us uncomfortable with them. So it is that life on a scientific frontier tends to be dangerous. On reaching such a situation, it seems wisest to emulate the classic frontiersman who was always ready to move on to new territory.

GROSS BIOCHEMICAL CONSIDERATIONS

Probably because brain functioning has a traditionally grand air of mystery about it, people readily accept its importance for personality. By contrast, the gross biochemistry of the body seems a deadly-dull affair with about as much apparent dramatic potential as a sack of potatoes. We grow up to a chorus of our parents' groans and belches, discussion of Aunt Sophie's operations, loose talk about livers, kidneys, hearts, spleens, and cholesterol levels, and direct commands to eat balanced meals. And all of this occurs against a commercial mass-media background urging us to consume products that will either make us strong and sexy ("My wife is as slim as our teen-age daughter even though she's had 12 children.") or cure us from the effects of our consumption errors (Announcer: "Give your stomach a chance." Stomach: "I'll try if he will."). If body chemistry is to be discussed properly as an influence on personality, we must first put aside all that mundane nonsense.

Barker (1958) provided a good statement of basic principle by suggesting that we can consider the body to be a "tool for action." The most obvious aspect of the body conceived as a tool for action is its general shape: big or small, wide or narrow, and so forth. It is this sort of material that led to development of body-type theories of personality. A less obvious, but perhaps more important, factor determining capabilities for action is the manner in which vital body functions are performed. Most persons are not aware of the extraordinary range defining the normal size limits of glands which do the heavy chemical work of the body.

Postmortem data collected by Williams (1956) showed that the weight of normal thyroid glands can vary from 8 to 50 grams; adrenals from 7 to 20 grams; pituitaries from 350 to 1100 milligrams. Normal glandular variability is thus on the order of 300 to 500 percent! A basic constituent of the nervous system is the *myelin sheath* that surrounds or insulates nerve fibers. The thickness of this sheath is thought to influence the speed of action currents passing along the nerve fibers, and analyses show that normal myelination can also vary on the order of normal gland weight. Evidence of this type makes it quite likely that much of what we see as individual differences in personality may have their origin in biochemical functioning. Furthermore, because glandular and neuroanatomical differences are all internal, and because they do not typically have clear-cut effects on physique, they are not open to discovery by the naked eye. We can thus see traditional body-type theory as an effort to relate *overt* body characteristics to personality, while the present discussion is an effort to relate *covert* body characteristics to personality.

For the sake of illustration, consider some research findings concerning sex. Sex activity is influenced by chemical agents *(hormones)* secreted into the bloodstream by sex glands: in males the *testes*, in females the *ovaries*. Williams (1956) said normal human testes vary in weight from 10 to 45 grams, and ovaries from 2 to 10 grams. Evidence based on extensive experimentation with lower mammals indicates that significant mating behavior will not occur unless a sufficient concentration of sex hormones is present in the blood. Furthermore, sex activity can be directly stimulated in lower species by the administration of sex hormones. The problem is complicated by the fact that sex activity may not be entirely or immediately eliminated in animals that have been castrated and therefore lack sex hormones. Following such an operation, the decline in sexual behavior will vary a good deal from one rat to another, and this variability is related to the intensity of the precastrational sex drive of the individual: "Apparently the precastrational differences in sexual drive are due, not to differences in the amount of hormone secreted by the testis, but to individual differences in the sensitivity of the target tissues which react to testicular secretions" (Beach, 1958, p. 275). The point made here is especially interesting because it goes against the idea that sexual behavior can be systematically manipulated by simple hormone treatments. One reads occasionally about rich, elderly "beautiful people" who visit mysterious-sounding private clinics in Switzerland to receive hormone treatments designed to restore lost capabilities. The results must be disappointing to many of them.

Another aspect of covert body chemistry that has direct psychological implications involves oxygen. At sea level, air is about 20 percent oxygen. When that 20 percent is altered to any significant degree, human beings suffer very odd psychological effects. If supplementary oxygen is not available as one goes above 10 to 12 thousand feet, he begins to feel dizzy, weak, and nauseated. These physical symptoms serve as sufficient body warnings to mountain climbers who inch their way upward to high altitudes. But the early test pilots who could reach high altitudes without such slow effort often went quickly into hallucinations or delusions characterized by a terrific sense of well-being or omnipotence. Jacques Cousteau was the first to describe similar effects of anoxia experienced by skin divers at extreme depths. He called the euphoric feeling "rapture of the deep." It results from high pressure which reduces the amount of oxygen reaching the brain. By contrast, however, a reasonable oversupply of oxygen has quite positive effects because it helps to eliminate fatigue. During World War II overtired pilots learned to turn on their oxygen masks before reaching altitude to recover alert combat reactions. And oxygen tanks can be found at the bench of every pro football team today for similar reasons.

Impressive support for the old cliché "You are what you eat" can be found in the amazing range of psychological effects associated with vitamin deficiencies. Consequences of *pellagra* (a disease involving general deficiency of the B vitamin group) include memory losses, mental retardation, anxiety, hysteria, delusions, and depression. Persons with the disease *beriberi* (caused by thiamine deficiency) are described in medical texts as forgetful, irritable, quarrelsome, apathetic, confused, depressed, restless, and anxious. In a class discussion recently, a student explained that while serving in the Peace Corps on a remote island in the Pacific, he developed what was later diagnosed as a serious vitamin-C deficiency. The psychological symptom he was most aware of was a recurring series of severe nightmares.

Some of the behavior observed in connection with the deficiency diseases is so like the behavior of hospitalized psychotics that researchers have attempted to treat psychoses with vitamin therapy. According to Eiduson and his co-workers (1964) the administration of niacin is useful with many psychotic patients who have no history of vitamin deficiency. It is known only that niacin has some sort of positive influence on brain metabolism.

Variations in thyroid-gland functioning also can produce a wide range of psychological symptoms. Insufficient production of *thyroxin*, the hormone secreted by the thyroid gland, leads to *cretinism* when it occurs in newborn children. Such *hypothyroid* children rarely attain normal levels of intelligence. When this condition develops in adults it is called *myxedema*. Adult symptoms include apathy, slowed reaction times, intellectual dullness, irritability, and inability to concentrate. In severe cases, psychotic behavior patterns such as delusions and extreme depressions will occur.

A *hyperthyroid* condition (oversupply of thyroxin) leads to extreme excitability, drastic mood shifts, anxiety, and sleeplessness. In general, variations in the supply of thyroxin seem to have effects analogous to variations in the electricity input to electronic systems: too little and the system slows down or fails; too much and the system sparks over or burns itself out.

Before leaving this section, it is valuable to reconsider the work by Williams showing the very great size ranges of normal body organs. Most of the material we have presented here comes inevitably from descriptions of effects produced by the *abnormal* functioning of such organs. However, if many of these effects are scaled down to some extent, and Williams' evidence suggests that it may not be necessary to scale them down very much, then one can see what a Pandora's box of individual differences in personality must ultimately spring from gross biochemical differences between individuals.

PSYCHOPHARMACOLOGY

As the linguistic structure of the word implies, *psychopharmacology* can be defined as the science of manipulating psychological or mental states through the use of drugs or chemicals. It is presently conventional to think of psychopharmacology solely in terms of how chemicals may influence emotions. And this convention will be followed in this text, even though researchers are beginning to probe the possibilities of influencing cognitive as well as emotional states. For example, a controversial report by Babich, Jacobson, Bubash & Jacobson (1965) showed that a response learned by specially trained rats could be acquired by untrained rats when *ribonucleic acid (RNA)* extracted from the brains of the former was injected into the latter. But as will be seen later in this chapter, learning through chemistry is not yet a feasible proposition.

Immense public interest in the manipulation of emotions through drugs began with the introduction of tranquilizers in the late 1950's, and it has continued to grow, nurtured by publicity given to the *psychic energizers* (*amphetamines* or "speed"), and the *hallucinogens* ("mind-benders") such as *LSD*. Partly because of all the public interest, and partly because these new compounds have escaped, so to speak, from official control, much confusion exists about them. If we are to discuss the topic in an organized way, we must first have some technical terminology.

All of the chemical agents that have a direct, heavy impact on experience are generally referred to as *psychoactive compounds*. They are classified according to their psychological effects as being either *tranquilizers*, *energizers*, or *hallucinogens*. Berger (1960) indicated that no single system of classifying the psychoactive compounds is entirely satisfactory.[2] He shows that tranquilizers may be divided into four different categories of differing chemical structures. These differences, in turn, determine what part of the brain will be the site of action for the drug. In brief, different compounds may all have the same general tranquilizing effect, but they may be working in either the cortex, the hypothalamus, the limbic system, or the reticular formation. It is also pointed out in this connection that sóme tranquilizers serve as *autonomic suppressants*, while others are *central relaxants*. The foregoing material explains why the subject of psychopharmacology cannot be discussed in a unified fashion: it is too complex. Moreover, this material should further explain why any scholar of the subject is doubly outraged to hear of persons who use psychoactive compounds indiscriminately, for kicks. Such mixed usage is not only astonishing for its rashness, it is also scientifically frustrating because it makes the task of understanding effects infinitely more difficult.

Tranquilizers

The clinical effects of compounds in this category are most generally described as "reducing excitement and agitation without clouding consciousness," or "having a sedative effect without enforcing sleep." It has already been mentioned that different tranquilizers act in different regions of the brain to achieve their effects on behavior. But how are we to understand the process by which tranquilizers (and, as we shall presently see, the other psychoactive compounds as well) cause dramatic behavioral changes?

First of all, it is generally understood that all psychoactive compounds owe their effects to the way they influence the *neurohumors*. Neurohumors, sometimes referred to as *chemical transmitters* or *neurotransmitters*, are chemical compounds in the brain that are found in the space between individual brain cells (the synaptic space). Some of these compounds directly facilitate, and others directly inhibit, the transmission of neural impulses from one cell to another. They do this by changing the electrical potential on the membranes of fibers extending into the synaptic space. What makes things wonderfully complicated, however, is that there are still other neurohumors that *indirectly* influence action in the synaptic space by inhibiting or facilitating the concentration of *directly* facilitating or inhibiting neurohumors.

Let us now take a running jump into the problem by examining the functioning of one of the more important tranquilizing compounds, *reserpine*, in some detail. According to Himwich (1960), reserpine is especially useful in

---

[2]DeRopp (1957) indicated that one of the earliest modern efforts to treat psychoactive compounds systematically can be seen in the work of a German toxicologist, Lewin (1924). "Lewin distinguished five classes of drugs that influence mind and emotions. He called them *euphorica, phantastica, inebriantia, hypnotica*, and *excitantia*. Today we use somewhat different terms. Instead of *phantastica* we speak of *hallucinogens*, drugs capable of producing hallucinations, of which LSD-25 and mescaline are examples. His *hypnotica*, sleep-producing drugs such as the barbiturates, are more commonly referred to now as *sedatives*. In addition we have a new group of drugs, the *ataraxics* (a term recently introduced by Dr. Howard Fabing), that tranquilize without producing drowsiness. Finally Lewin's *excitantia*, a class which includes such stimulants of the nervous system as cocaine or 'Benzedrine,' are more generally known today as *analeptics*. They have an action opposite to that of the sedatives, arousing and stimulating instead of soothing and calming" (p. 5).

calming excessively combative or destructive schizoid patients; it is known to have a sharp negative effect on the neurohumor *serotonin*. Knowledge of serotonin is still somewhat vague, but abnormal concentrations of this substance – either too much or too little – are found in persons suffering from a variety of mental aberrations. Himwich describes one study showing that a rabbit injected with a dose of reserpine has its normal level of serotonin reduced by about 90 percent within four hours of receiving the injection. Another study showed that after mental patients received reserpine, their urine contained above-average amounts of an acid that is a primary constituent of serotonin.

Besides its action on serotonin, reserpine also acts to inhibit the concentration of the neurohumors *noradrenaline* and *adrenaline*. After the administration of reserpine, all three of these neurohumors follow the same time pattern as they gradually rebuild to their prereserpine levels. The final important thing to note here is that the three neurohumors in question all have their site of action in the hypothalamus which, it will be recalled, is a subcortical region of the brain controlling emotionality.

In summary, our running jump at the problem of how tranquilizers work has landed us in a pool of biochemical data that suggests one clear generalization: the tranquilizing compounds achieve their effects on behavior by influencing chemical concentrations at neural junction points in the brain. One cannot leave the subject of tranquilizers, however, without saying something about their truly revolutionary impact on the treatment of mental disorders. Havemann (1968) provided an excellent summary. In the middle 1950's there were 560,000 mental patients hospitalized under variable, sometimes awful conditions. But now:

The atmosphere in the mental hospitals has totally changed. They are less crowded now – 425,000 patients instead of 560,000. The patients are far less destructive, far less terrified, far more "normal" in their behavior. The staffs have more time to treat the patients, with individual or group psychotherapy as well as medicine. And patients do recover; more than twice as many as before go back to rejoin their families and to work at jobs, like anybody else. In human terms, the improvement is nothing short of magnificent (p. 111).

Energizers

The psychic energizer compounds, often called *antidepressants* or *stimulants*, function so as to reduce fatigue and stimulate activity. Berger (1960) divided the energizers into three general categories. (1) The *analeptics* (e.g., the *amphetamine, benzedrine*) which have a global stimulating effect on the central nervous system because they curtail the action of compounds that normally act as depressants. (2) Indirect inhibitors such as *imipramine* and *iproniazid*. The latter is a *monoamine oxidase inhibitor* best known by its trade name, Marsalid. These compounds have a more specific stimulating action than the analeptics. They are referred to as *indirect inhibitors* because they seem to produce their stimulating effects by reducing the supply of chemicals (e.g., the enzyme monoamine oxidase) needed by the body to manufacture various neurohumors which *inhibit* neural activity in the brain. (3) Chemical constituents of *acetylcholine*. Because acetylcholine is a direct chemical transmitter of neural impulses in the brain, the administration of compounds (*cholinergic* agents) used in the manufacture of this transmitter increases its concentration and may thus facilitate neural activity.

From the research literature it appears that the indirect inhibitors have become the compounds most frequently used for therapeutic purposes by a process of elimination. The analeptics or amphetamines get a good deal of publicity, but their effects are too strong and too global to be useful medically. These compounds are so broadly stimulating that they may produce active behavior that is more pathological than the original depressed behavior. And the aftereffects of the analeptics are severe.

The cholinergic agents which increase the supply of acetylcholine are not widely used because the functioning of these agents is not sufficiently understood to justify the risk of side effects. Altogether then, as we have seen with the tranquilizers, and as we will see with the hallucinogenic compounds, the psychic energizers in wide medical usage are those that influence the action of certain neurohumors located in the hypothalamic region of the brain. These energizers have relatively narrow-gauge effects; they seem to alleviate depression without causing overexcitement, by indirectly facilitating neural transmissions in brain centers associated with emotionality.

Hallucinogens

The hallucinogenic compounds are often referred to in the technical literature as *psychotomimetics*, because early researchers were impressed by the degree to which behavior caused by these compounds mimics behavior typical of psychotics. It is interesting that under a wide variety of common names, nature provides a lavish supply of hallucinogens: peyote, hashish, mescaline, opium, ayahuasco vine, coca leaf, ololiuqui, soma, Syrian rue, cohoba, teonanacatl, iboga, betel nut, kavakava, and others. Indeed, those who, like Timothy Leary, argue that hallucinogenic drug experiences offer mankind a new form of self-understanding akin to religion, sometimes cite the profusion of hallucinogens in nature as evidence that man was meant to have these experiences; that the exploration of "inner space" is, so to speak, preordained. Be this as it may, the prevailing opinion among psychophysiological workers is that these drugs produce hallucinations, not visionary or mystical experiences, although one must grant that the difference between a hallucination and a vision has always been debatable.

Russell (1960) gave a widely accepted clinical viewpoint in his discussion of mescaline:

Self-experiments with mescaline were first reported about 1896. From this and many more recent reports, certain special characteristics of the behavior changes produced stand out clearly. Perception of the environment is disturbed. Time appears to be changed, to become fragmentary and discontinuous. Consciousness varies from a rather detached self-evaluation to extreme drowsiness. Certain experiences belonging to one sense become attached to another. Sensory illusions, particularly visual and tactile, appear. Frequently, but not always, these experiences are described as having been very pleasant (pp. 22–23).

Of LSD, Russell says:

Like mescaline, it produces serious disorganizations of normal behavior, including disturbances of perception and thinking, changes in mood, and the appearance of hallucinations and delusions. It produces a marked aggravation of the abnormal symptoms of schizophrenic patients, and it produces mild schizophrenic-like symptoms in normal subjects (p. 23).

Because of its popularity and the availability of research findings, our discussion of the hallucinogens will be limited to LSD. Its full chemical name is *d-lysergic acid diethylamide tartrate*, abbreviated by chemists as LSD-25. According to DeRopp (1957), its hallucinogenic properties were first discovered accidentally by a Swiss chemist named Hofman, who was working with lysergic acid and added to it a diethylamine compound. DeRopp gave the following report of the event:

Last Friday, April 16th [wrote Hofman in his laboratory report], in the midst of my afternoon work in the laboratory I had to give up working. I had to go home because I experienced a very peculiar restlessness which was associated with a slight attack of dizziness. At home I went to bed and got into a not unpleasant state of drunkenness which was characterized by an extremely stimulating fantasy. When I closed my eyes (the day light was most unpleasant to me) I experienced fantastic images of an extraordinary plasticity. They were associated with an intense kaleidoscopic play of colors. After about two hours this condition disappeared (p. 187).

In more systematic studies that soon followed Hofman's discovery, the sequence of experiences following the administration of LSD have been reported in more detail. Rinkel, De Shon, Morimoto, York & Salvatore (1955) explained that at first there are physical changes: trembling, sweating, weakness. After about an hour comes irritability, anxiety. By the second hour subjects begin to withdraw from reality; they seem apathetic, lethargic, or confused. And finally the hallucinations set in. These include strange feelings of nonexistence, that parts of the body have disappeared, loss of conventional time sense, separation of self from body, and a host of sensory illusions involving touch, vision, hearing, and taste.

Opinions vary on the question of how to interpret the illusions or hallucinations experienced under LSD. Strictly speaking, a hallucination involves the experience of events that are not real. But it has also been reported by some persons that LSD provides a heightened sensitivity to reality or an awareness of new forms of internal reality. From our understanding of the neurophysiological evidence to be presented below, however, we would argue that neither of the above interpretations is entirely correct. LSD influences neurohumoral activity in the brain, nothing else. Therefore, the only thing that LSD can do is change the way standard sensory inputs to the brain are processed. It cannot change what our peripheral sense receptors pick up, nor can it put into the brain any new material—experiences, or memories,—that were not previously present. So it should be clear that LSD is not a ticket for a trip into a new world.

Himwich (1960) explained that the chemical composition of LSD is very similar to that of serotonin. He described some studies which suggest that LSD replaces serotonin at its synaptic site of action, and that LSD will in some ways act like serotonin. Other studies show that LSD can either enhance or inhibit the action of serotonin, depending upon what concentration of LSD is used. It will be recalled from our earlier discussion of tranquilizers, that certain adrenaline compounds also behave like serotonin. Some investigations of psychotomimetic drugs have accordingly focused on adrenaline and have found that a derivative called *adrenochrome* has the same psychological effects as LSD. Perhaps LSD, which is definitely known to influence serotonin, also has some influence, direct or indirect, on associated adrenaline compounds.

Before leaving the whole subject of psychoactive drugs, it should be mentioned that at least one attempt has been made to explain many of the phenomena we have discussed through a theory of brain chemistry. Marrazzi and Hart (in Himwich, 1960) suggested that normal behavior depends upon the maintenance of a state of neurohumoral equilibrium. Bizarre behavior occurs if the balance between the various neurohumors that facilitate or inhibit neural activity is disturbed. Thus, many psychoses can be understood as resulting from some naturally occurring disturbance to neurohumoral equilibrium, while psychotomimetics can be understood as achieving their effects through an artificial disturbance of this equilibrium. Moreover, the equilibrium theory would also embrace the actions of the tranquilizers and energizers, both of which can be seen as functioning to restore disturbed neurohumoral equilibrium states. Whether or not this theory continues to be supported by research evidence, it has the virtue of clarity, and it provides a conceptual handle for material that is otherwise very slippery.

SLEEPING AND DREAMING

With the exception of Freud's work (1900) on the interpretation of dreams and related works, the student interested in personality had, until quite recently, little reason to concern himself with the phenomenon of sleep. According to a review by Webb (1968), prior to 1960 only two books describing experimental research on sleep had been published; since 1960 there have been at least six. The sudden upsurge began in 1955 with an unexpected observation of eye movements during sleep reported by Kleitman and Aserinsky. Webb (1968) described their discovery as follows:

They soon discovered that several times during the night there were bursts of very rapid, jerky movements of the eyes that would often last as long as an hour. Furthermore, these periods of rapid eye movement (REMs as they have come to be called) were accompanied by physiological changes such as increased heart rate and changes in the pattern of breathing which seemed emotional in character. It occurred to the researchers that these eye movements might be associated with dreaming. On this thought, they awakened subjects during these periods of REM and found that dreams were consistently reported. By contrast, awakenings at other times during sleep resulted in no recall of dreams (p. 25).

By 1957, Dement and Kleitman were able to show in systematic experiments that 80 percent of subjects awakened during their REM periods were having dreams, while only 7 percent awakened during non-REM periods were having dreams. A further important finding was that during REM periods, the brain waves of sleeping subjects (measured through electroencephalograph recording) resembled those of an awake person. A great deal of subsequent research has confirmed and extended these initial findings. It is now generally accepted that when a sleeping person dreams, he is, physiologically speaking, awake. In addition to the wakeful condition of his eyes and brain waves, his breathing, heart rate, brain temperature, and skin resistance are those of an alert, awake person. The dreamer's physiological condition is also related to his dream content: if he is excited or struggling in the dream, his breathing, heart rate, and body movements become concomitantly more intense. All this material has led many experts to refer to the dream state as *paradoxical sleep*, sleep in name only. Hartmann (1967) went even further by proposing that we all live according to a cycle of three psychobiological states: the waking, the sleeping, and the *D state* (*D* for dreaming).

Aside from dreaming, which will be discussed in further detail below, fascinating unsolved questions about sleep concern its function and origin. Why do we sleep as much as we do? Insofar as physiological evidence bears on this question, it suggests that we don't *need* that much sleep. Sleep duration is, furthermore, negatively correlated with age. It has been shown that while newborn infants sleep an average of 16½ hours per day, by the age of 6 months, this average drops to a bit under 14 hours. Mature persons average between 7 and 8 hours, and it is commonly reported by the elderly that they sleep only 5 or 6 hours, or less, per night.

No straightforward physiological reason for such sleep patterns has yet been suggested. But there is evidence indicating that some regular amount of sleep is a physiological necessity. Newborn puppies deprived of sleep will eventually die. And in the human body, after a few days of sleep deprivation the energy-releasing compound *adenosine triphosphate* falls well below its normal production level.

The origin of human sleeping patterns as a species-specific behavior is entirely obscure. One evolutionary thesis, however, deserves mention for its sheer ingenuity. It is based on the premise that, as compared with many predators, man's night vision is quite poor. Therefore, our early ancestors who went hunting or puttering about at night were more likely to be killed than those who stayed safely holed up. One can also appeal to evolution on the basis of hearing. Given equally poor night vision, that species having the best hearing will be most likely to be successful in night operations. In either case, the principles of natural selection and survival of the fittest would function to preserve night-sleeping humans and eliminate nonnight sleepers. Hence most of the time we sleep 7 or 8 hours because this period corresponds to the period of darkness during which our ancestors were at such a disadvantage.

Once the new, REM-based technology for dream research was established, the burst of experimentation that followed soon revealed two important things: people typically dream a great deal more than anyone had thought, and to some unknown degree, dreaming seems necessary for proper personality adjustment. In connection with the former issue, Webb (1968) reported his investigation of 40 males and females of different ages, who were studied for three consecutive nights by means of EEG and eye-movement recordings.

The lowest average amount of dreaming was about one hour during a full night's sleep and the highest was two hours. The overall average was an hour and a half. The average number of dream periods was slightly over three, and about 60 percent of the dreaming occurred in the last third of the night. From the thousands of nights recorded in many laboratories, so far as I know, every subject has shown evidence of dreaming. As Kleitman has put it, Shakespeare's "To sleep, perchance to dream . . ." must be modified to read, less felicitously, "To sleep, perchance to recall a dream . . ." (p. 27).

Dream recall is indeed very poor. It is reported that while 80 to 90 percent of subjects have good recall when awakened during a dream period, within 5 minutes after waking the recall is fragmentary, and that after 10 minutes any recall at all is very unusual. Research has also shown that dream content can be influenced by external manipulations: water dripped on sleeping subjects led to dreams involving water for about 50 percent of these subjects, and names read aloud to sleeping subjects were incorporated into their dreams at about the same 50 percent level. Furthermore, and contrary to popular belief, dream time is not drastically different from "real" time. The evidence showed that a given behavior sequence takes about as much time when it is dreamed, as it does when it is deliberately imagined while awake. The common notion that dream time is shorter than real time seems based on the fact that in dreams we omit much of the detail that ordinarily links salient behavior sequences together. A person might dream of landing at an airport and then being welcomed into his home, having omitted from his dream the wait for luggage and the bus ride that would ordinarily intervene between these two events.

The dream-research findings that are most dramatic of all, however, and that also seem most directly important for the student of personality, involve *dream deprivation*. Here again, Webb (1968) provided a convenient summary:

In 1960 Dement reported an ingenious experiment which firmly established that we have a need for dreams. . . . Eight subjects were prevented from dreaming for six successive nights by being awakened whenever the REM-EEG indications of dreaming occurred. It was necessary to awaken the subjects more and more frequently each night. It seemed as if the longer dreams were kept out of sleep the more they forced their way back in. In addition, during "recovery" nights of uninterrupted sleep the subjects dreamed 30 percent more than they had before dream deprivation. It was as if they were making up for lost dream time. Further, Dement reported the development of so much anxiety and irritability in his subjects that one subject had to withdraw from the experiment. Was this a psychic process being interfered with? Were subjects being deprived of opportunities to clear their psyche? (pp. 28–29).

Unfortunately, as we have seen earlier and as we will certainly see again, on those rare occasions when an experiment provides neat, clean, and exciting results, they invariably tend to grow more complicated with further research. A later study of dream deprivation showed that while dreaming did increase with increasing deprivation, the anxiety and irritability did not occur. The problem here is at least in part a matter of proper experimental control. How is one to separate the anxiety and irritability that develop as a consequence of frequently interrupted sleep, from the anxiety and irritability that may be a specific result of dream deprivation? Another complication comes from the fact that the experiment contradicting Dement's anxiety finding involved only two subjects. And these were subjects who, according to the researchers, seemed to have the ability to "sneak in" dreams after being given the sleep-arousal signal.

One of the subjects consistently reported bizarre, vivid dreams of approximately 1-min. duration when awakened after this signal. The other subject often reported fragmentary mentation and occasionally a brief, vivid dream when awakened. It may be possible that there is a compensatory acceleration of the dreaming process under conditions of deprivation so that within a few seconds there is substantial content. Thus this dreaming, brief as it is, may be sufficient to prevent significant psychic changes (Kales, Hoedemaker, Jacobson & Lichtenstein, 1964, p. 1338).

In closing, one can only surmise that since we spend about a third of our lives asleep, and since approximately 12 to 15 percent of this time is spent dreaming, the new research in this area seems to be pointing the way toward an unexplored universe of psychological functioning.

THE BIOCHEMISTRY OF INTELLIGENCE

Current research on what is loosely termed the *biochemistry of intelligence* involves two different major approaches or strategies which have so far remained quite independent of one another. For the sake of convenience, these approaches can be distinguished according to the chemical compounds primary to each: ribonucleic acid (RNA) vs. cholinesterase (CHE).

The RNA strategy, touched upon briefly at the outset of our discussion of psychopharmacology, involves the chemical transfer of learning, and is based on new knowledge of the microstructure of brain cells. RNA molecules found within these cells are so complex that they can have almost an infinite number of different forms. By comparing the form of RNA molecules in the brain cells of rats that have been trained to perform novel tasks, with those of rats that have not had such training, it has been further discovered that RNA molecules change their form as a result of learning. It is as if learning is stored by being coded in the RNA molecule (see Gaito and Zavala, 1964).

More recently, Hydén and Lange (1965) showed that along with changed RNA molecules, learning also leads to production of new brain proteins. They suggested that the changed RNA functions to "instruct" neural support cells to produce the new protein compounds.

All of this material is still fairly tentative, but it should be sufficient to show that efforts to transfer learning by chemical means relate to intelligence only insofar as memory is essential to intelligence. Certainly another, more directly relevant aspect of intelligence must be the ability to learn quickly and efficiently. And this is the problem under attack by adherents of the "cholinesterase strategy."

We have met the neurohumor acetylcholine (ACh) in an earlier section. It is the direct chemical transmitter of neural impulses across the synaptic space. The CHE strategy described by Rosenzweig, Krech, and Bennett (1958), has to do with the functioning of ACh which must be present in an optimum concentration if neural activity is to go on properly. Either too much or too little will inhibit the passage of neural impulses. Under normal conditions, the chief problem is oversupply of ACh because it is released with every neural transmission. Cholinesterase, however, takes care of this problem by inactivating ACh as soon as it has performed its transmitting function. The more ACh produced, the more CHE is needed. In short, CHE controls the level of ACh.

Starting from such knowledge in 1953, Krech organized a research program to study the chemical basis of intelligence. The work began with an experiment showing that intelligent behavior is related to CHE levels. Rats required to run a certain type of maze typically start by relying on visual cues, and then shift to more efficient spatial cues. In this context, one can identify individual differences in the intelligence of rats according to how quickly they learn to rely on spatial cues. By running a sample of rats on the maze and then sacrificing them to analyze CHE levels in relevant brain regions, Krech and his associates (in Harlow & Woolsey, 1958) established that ". . . animals with lower CHE activity tend to display visual preferences, while animals with higher CHE activity tend to abandon this preference and to develop a spatial preference" (pp. 391–392). A second experiment supported the views of the Krech group by showing that rats given *pentobarbital,* a drug which drastically reduces production of ACh, were unable to learn the spatial preference. *Intelligence = degree of adaptation*

In the second major phase of their work, the Krech group produced strains of maze-bright and maze-dull rats by a selective breeding process. Rats that learned the maze quickly were separated from slow learners. Each group was allowed to inbreed, their progeny were again tested on the maze, and the brightest and dullest were again separated for breeding purposes. After repeating this process for several generations, a set of very bright and a set of very dull rats were obtained. The former had significantly higher levels of CHE than the latter. But the obvious experiment—injecting CHE from the brains of bright rats into the brains of dull rats—failed to produce any improvement in the maze-running of the dull rats. The probable reason for this failure was indicated by later work involving fine microscopic analyses of rat brain structures. Results showed that in addition to the chemical differences

Visual cues = artistic shapes (2D)

between the brains of bright and dull rats, there are also structural differences. As compared with dull rats, bright rats have a better-developed cortex, larger blood vessels, and more *glial cells* which provide nourishment to neural cells.

In a lecture concerning the third and most recent phase of his program, Krech (1965) reported that he was able to produce bright or dull rats by manipulating *either* their heredity or their environment. This extraordinary finding was based on an application of other research studies on the effects of stimulus deprivation, which is described in a later chapter. For the present, it is sufficient to note that both animals and humans reared in enriched environments show higher intelligence later in life than those reared in unstimulating environments. The Head Start program is partially based on this material. Krech arranged a stimulus-rich environment — or Head Start program — for young rats, allowing them to play together, to exercise and run about on interesting wheels and ladders, and the like. Other rats were kept in barren, solitary cages. Subsequent comparison of these stimulated and unstimulated rats with respect to maze-running and brain chemistry and structure yielded results directly parallel to the results of the selective-breeding studies. The stimulated rats had more CHE and structurally better-developed brains than the unstimulated rats.

In summary, it would appear that Krech has been able to vary the chemical and neuroanatomical basis of intelligence by varying either heredity or environment. He agrees, however, with the cautious reactions of many psychologists. That is, what may work for rats may not work in the same fashion for other species, including humans; and while maze-running may or may not be an entirely satisfactory way to define intelligence in rats, it is likely to be unsatisfactory for other species.

Despite qualifications that may limit the generality of Krech's findings, his program seems likely to stand as one of the most important psychobiological explorations of our time. Its implications to such phenomena as "smart pills" are obvious; its implications to what we may have as a future psychology of intelligence or learning are not so obvious, but are no less exciting, particularly when we look forward to an inevitable juncture between the RNA and CHE research discoveries. In this connection, one can't help raising a rhetorical question: is the future royal road to intelligence going to be paved with RNA, CHE, a combination of both, or some as yet unknown substance?

A GENETIC-ANTHROPOLOGICAL PERSPECTIVE

Having moved rather quickly through a jungle of modern psychobiology, with brief stops to explore the major thickets relevant to personality, an intellectual breather seems to be in order. It may be refreshing after so much biochemical detail about brain functioning, therefore, to consider a new general perspective on the *evolution* of the human brain.

Fossil evidence discovered in South Africa and first described by the anthropologists Dart and Leakey about 10 years ago (see Geertz, in Scher,

1962; Ardrey, 1967) indicates that our earliest recognizable ancestor was a species called *Australopithecine*. His physical remains, which date back about a half million years, ". . . show a striking mosaic of primitive and advanced morphological characteristics, in which the most outstanding features are a pelvis and leg formation strikingly similar to that of modern man and a cranial capacity hardly larger than that of living apes" (Geertz, 1962, p. 720). Australopithecine also seems to have walked at least partially erect, and to have developed a simple tool-weapon culture. Mainly using the larger bones of dead animals as weapons, he hunted and killed.

The important feature of this evidence which leads to a new interpretation of brain evolution is the relatively small size of Australopithecine's brain. He was using tools, and was thus the possessor of a rudimentary culture, while his brain was only about one third the size of man's brain today. This means that our brain has largely evolved *after*, rather than prior to, the invention of tools. To put it succinctly, authorities such as Washburn (1959) and Geertz now believe that instead of the evolution of a complex brain leading to the use of tools, the use of tools led to the evolution of a complex brain. And the other unique characteristics of man—his erect stature, reduced jaw and teeth, thumb-dominated hand, relative absence of body hair—are also the consequences of gradual adaptation to a tool culture. Washburn (1959, p. 21) summarized as follows: ". . . it is probably more correct to think of much of our structure as a result of culture rather than to think of men anatomically like ourselves slowly discovering culture." In this connection, it would appear that the two great principles of evolution, natural selection and survival of the fittest, have operated for the past half-million years in favor of species members best able to use tools. Thus man as we know him today is the product of a process of *biocultural* evolution.

The knowledge accumulated about Australopithecines has also been interpreted by some writers as an explanation for man's violent nature. How did we get to be beings who seem innately capable of phylogenetically extraordinary violence, destruction, and cruelty? Ardrey (1967), who set out to investigate the animal origins and nature of man, suggested that the answer is quite obvious: "Man is a predator whose natural instinct is to kill with a weapon" (p. 322). He offered convincing support for this idea by appealing to evidence concerning Australopithecines. Once the proposition is accepted that the primary *functional* difference between our earliest ancestor and other higher apes involved the ability to use tools (weapons), the argument that man has survived and prospered because of his superior capacity as a killer is difficult to refute.

Moreover, the evolution of most of the gross anatomical and physiological characteristics of man fit the killer thesis. Consider erect stature. Wrestling and rough-and-tumble fighting with hands, legs, and teeth can be done well on all fours, but the standing position is virtually prerequisite for a killing blow with a club, or a throw of a rock. The long gut, which allows us to digest animal flesh, would hardly have evolved in a species unable to consistently kill for its living. Nor would a reduced tooth and jaw structure have occurred if these items were needed for fighting.

A criticism that often comes immediately to the minds of those hearing the "killer thesis" for the first time involves altruism. Man is obviously capable of sophisticated cooperative actions and even extreme acts of self-sacrifice; doesn't this sort of material contradict Ardrey? Not really, because he argues that the killer thesis must be understood as a group phenomenon. In other words, man is not only an hereditary killer, as it were, he is also an hereditary social creature. We can comprehend the apparent contradictions in his nature only by reference to both of these assumptions: to be an effective killer, man has to operate in groups, and to maintain the life of his groups, man has to be an effective killer. Thus, all acts of cooperation, self-sacrifice, and the like occur only when such action will enhance the life of an in-group, or is necessary to defend it from some external threat. Serious acts of altruism can hardly ever be observed to cut across in-group boundaries. It can, in fact, be argued that men only delude themselves with thoughts of altruism, because the group-living orientation from which altruism springs is phylogenetically older, and much more widely distributed, than man's unique tool-weapon culture. Free-ranging baboons, and other mammals such as gorillas and whales, all show high degrees of cooperation and occasional dramatic acts of altruism.

Ardrey's writing on altruism and other aspects of human behavior that can be examined from an anthropological-evolutionary viewpoint opens many fascinating new perspectives. In one chapter, for example, he suggests a clever new interpretation for mating activity: the conventional idea is that males select females of their choice by fighting or otherwise achieving dominance over competing males. Ardrey says this notion should be changed — males may fight each other, but they do so primarily to attain *territory*. Females then choose the male who has established his territorial authority. Part of the justification for this argument is that by shifting the final mate decision from male to female, and by changing the criterion according to which the decision is made from fighting to territory, we gain a more obviously valid understanding of both animal and human mating behavior. Would any man who has ever lost a girl friend to an older fellow with a bigger car or better job disagree with this view?

Ardrey's (1967) major theme, however, was the killer thesis. He summarized it in an eloquent but disturbing statement:

Our history reveals the development and contest of superior weapons as *Homo sapiens'* single, universal cultural preoccupation. Peoples may perish, nations dwindle, empires fall; one civilization may surrender its memories to another civilization's sands. But mankind as a whole, with an instinct as true as a meadow-lark's song, has never in a single instance allowed local failure to impede the progress of the weapon, its most significant cultural endowment (p. 324).

Unquestionably, Ardrey's views must be disturbing to anyone with reasonably liberal or progressive attitudes toward humanity. There are always some students who quite properly react to his ideas with remarks to the effect that "Well, if Ardrey is right, then the world really *is* a jungle and men *are* doomed to destroy each other with nuclear weapons." One can, of course, give no final answer to such comments. But there are at least two qualifying conditions that do not conflict with Ardrey's interpretation of the evidence, and yet enable one to take a less pessimistic view. First, there is the fact that the evolution of man is closely tied to culture. As our culture places increasing emphasis on the value of human life, and as it increasingly demands higher levels of cognitive skill, and as the spread or impact of culture is accelerated by the development of mass media communications, it is reasonable to assume that our species must evolve in such a way as to make wholesale violence less probable. It might well be argued that given the violence in our cities and the Vietnam war, this suggestion is ridiculous. But the long-range significance of these events may be the great reaction against them.

Second, and on a more concrete level, one may suggest that technically advanced societies today are basically planned or arranged according to people's understanding of group-living requirements. Insofar as this understanding is inadequate, the planning will be inadequate. Therefore, while it may be true that the "killer thesis" imposes a less rosy view of man than, say, the philosophy of Rousseau, it forces us at the same time to think of redesigning social systems in a more effective fashion. In other words, Ardrey's ideas provide an additional and valuable tool for social planning because they enforce consideration of requirements that might otherwise be ignored.

A case in point is our present social welfare system which was developed in the late 1930's on the premise that people who could not find jobs needed financial help to tide them over until more jobs were available. Because there was no understanding of how technological progress and long periods of idleness accompanied by subsistence payments could yield the problem we now call hard-core unemployment (and several other unforeseen consequences), the system is now seen as inadequate by almost everyone. The point to understand here is that if anyone had rejected the subsistence-payment approach to unemployment as inadequate at the time it was initiated, he would probably have been ignored as a Cassandra. So it is with Ardrey. The pessimism that may follow from a reading of his ideas is a matter of interpretation. One may interpret the ideas in a relatively positive light because by indicating new factors that should be considered when attacking social problems, they can help us do a better job in the future than we have done in the past.

CHAPTER SUMMARY

The wide variety of material in this chapter has one general purpose: to provide a general psychobiological framework for the subject matter of personality. Just as Chapter 2 was planned to convey some of the major philosophical-historical considerations that bear upon personality, the present chapter should convey some of the major neurophysiological and genetic-anthropological considerations.

Beginning with the phenomenon of pain as the most obvious way people experience psychophysical unity, a brief overview of the traditional psychophysical dualism issue was given, followed by discussions of brain functioning, psychopharmacology, sleep and dreams, the biochemistry of intelligence, and some new perspectives in evolutionary theory. Each of these areas has important implications for personality:

(1) The experience of pain can be seen in terms of individual differences demonstrable at either a pure perceptual or pure physiological level.

(2) Many of the important brain functions are becoming better understood as dependent upon specific properties of the central nervous system. Virtually all of the dramatic achievements of psychopharmacology hinge upon the chemical-electrical actions that psychoactive compounds cause to occur at neural junction points in the brain.

(3) Sleep is now seen to involve different states of consciousness apparently associated with a need to dream.

(4) Individual differences in intelligence are seemingly reducible to separate chemical processes underlying knowledge acquisition and storage.

(5) The discovery of evidence concerning Australopithecines has enriched our understanding of man's evolution. On one level, man is now seen to have evolved according to the demands of a tool-weapon culture; on another level, the evidence offers an explanation for the paradoxical spectacle of man as both destroyer and altruist.

In all these areas we can see specific intersections between mind and body. That which has been most obscure throughout most of man's history as an intelligent being is now beginning to be understood. Moreover, as many of the findings discussed in this text begin to be integrated, old ideas about personality will drastically change. One hears already of therapists who hardly talk to patients because they work almost entirely with programed sequences of drugs.

Altogether then, the material discussed in this chapter allows personality to be seen largely through a psychobiological lens, just as a century ago it was largely seen through a religious-philosophical lens. The beginning student of personality must remain open to both of these approaches, as well as to the experiential approach to be considered next, if he is to avoid a premature narrowing of his outlook. Not that specialization is wrong—it is all too easy to join in the currently fashionable intellectual attack on specialists as inferior to generalists—but the specialist will only know the proper meaning of his work when it is based on an adequate general foundation.

References

Ardrey, R. *African genesis.* New York: Dell Publishing Co., Inc., 1967.

Babich, F. R., Jacobson, A. L., Bubash, S., & Jacobson, A. Transfer of a response to naive rats by injection of ribonucleic acid extracted from trained rats. *Science,* 1965, 149(3684), 656–657.

Barker, R. G., et al., quoted in Anastasi, A. Heredity, environment and the question, how? *Psychological Review,* 1958, 65(4), 197–208.

Beach, F. A. Neural and chemical regulation of behavior. In H. Harlow and C. N. Woolsey (Eds.), *Biological and biochemical bases of behavior.* Madison: University of Wisconsin Press, 1958, pp. 263–284.

Berger, F. M. Classification of psychoactive drugs according to their chemical structures and sites of action. In L. Uhr and J. G. Miller (Eds.), *Drugs and behavior.* New York: John Wiley & Sons, Inc., 1960.

Boring, E. G. *A history of experimental psychology*. (2nd Ed.) New York: Appleton-Century-Crofts, 1950.

Bruner, J. S., & Tajfel, H. Cognitive risk and environmental change. *Journal of Abnormal and Social Psychology*, 1961, *62*, 231–241.

De Ropp, R. *Drugs and the mind*. (first published 1957) New York: Grove Press, Inc., 1961.

Eiduson, S., Geller, E., Yuwiler, A., & Eiduson, B. *Biochemistry and behavior*. Princeton: D. Van Nostrand, 1964.

Freud, S. *The interpretation of dreams*. (first published 1900) New York: Basic Books, Inc., Publishers, 1959.

Gaito, J., & Zavala, A. Neurochemistry and learning. *Psychological Bulletin*, 1964, 61(1), 45–62.

Gardner, E. *Fundamentals of neurology*. (5th Ed.) Philadelphia: W. B. Saunders Company, 1968.

Gardner, R. W. Cognitive styles in categorizing behavior. *Journal of Personality*, 1953, *22*, 214–233.

Geertz, C. The growth of culture and the evolution of mind. In J. Scher (Ed.), *Theories of the mind*. New York: The Free Press, 1962.

Hartmann, E. *The biology of dreaming*. Springfield, Ill.: Charles C Thomas, Publisher, 1967.

Havemann, E. Psychochemistry: Personality by prescription. *Playboy*, November 1968, p. 111.

Himwich, H. E. Biochemical and neurophysiological action of psychoactive drugs. In L. Uhr and J. G. Miller (Eds.), *Drugs and behavior*. New York: John Wiley & Sons, Inc., 1960.

Hydén, H., & Lange, P. W. A differentiation in RNA response in neurons early and late during learning. *Proceedings of the United States National Academy of Sciences*, 1965, *53*, 946–952.

James, W. *The Principles of Psychology*, Vol. 1. New York: Dover Publications, Inc., 1950.

Kales, A., Hoedemaker, F. S., Jacobson, A., & Lichtenstein, E. L. Dream deprivation: An experimental reappraisal. *Nature*, 1964, *204*, 1337–1338.

Krech, D. Unpublished lectures on the biochemistry of intelligence. University of Colorado, 1961. Kansas State University, 1965.

Lashley, K. S. *Brain mechanisms and intelligence*. Chicago: The University of Chicago Press, 1929.

Penfield, W. The interpretive cortex. *Science*, 1959, *129*, 1719–1725.

Petrie, A. *Individuality in pain and suffering*. Chicago: The University of Chicago Press, 1967.

Rapoport, A. An essay on mind. In J. Scher (Ed.), *Theories of the mind*. New York: The Free Press, 1962.

Rinkel, M., De Shon, J. H., Morimoto, K., York, R. M., & Salvatore, H. Experimental psychoses. *Scientific American*, 1955, *192*, 34–39.

Rosenzweig, M. R., Krech, D., & Bennett, E. L. Brain chemistry and adaptive behavior. In H. Harlow and C. N. Woolsey (Eds.), *Biological and biochemical bases of behavior*. Madison: University of Wisconsin Press, 1958.

Russell, R. W. Drugs as tools in behavioral research. In L. Uhr and J. G. Miller (Eds.), *Drugs and behavior*. New York: John Wiley & Sons, Inc., 1960.

Samuels, I. Reticular mechanisms and behavior. *Psychological Bulletin*, 1959, *56*, 1–25.

Simmons, H. *The psychosomatic aspects of cancer.* Washington, D.C.: Peabody Press, 1956.

Strange, J. R. *Abnormal psychology.* New York: McGraw-Hill Book Company, 1965.

Thompson, R. F. *Foundations of physiological psychology.* New York: Harper & Row, Publishers, 1967.

Washburn, S. L. Speculations on the interrelations of the history of tools and biological evolution. In J. N. Spuhler (Ed.), *The evolution of man's capacity for culture.* Detroit: Wayne State University Press, 1959.

Webb, W. B. *Sleep: An experimental approach.* New York: The Macmillan Company, 1968.

Williams, R. J. *Biochemical individuality.* New York: John Wiley & Sons, Inc., 1956.

Two

Personality and Experience

Up to this point, personality has been discussed as an abstraction, and while a nicely detached philosopher-scientist orientation is always appropriate for examining abstractions, this orientation is less appropriate when the gross realities of everyday life are engaged at their own level. On the contrary, when it comes to understanding how personality emerges from experience, it is often necessary to get right down there into the muck where the action is, shrinking from neither the diapers of infancy nor the bedpans of old age. And when these realities are presented in a chronological sequence, further changes in general orientation are required.

Research and theory concerning personality are generally not organized in a chronological fashion. Both the technical journals and the majority of books in this area are arranged in categories conforming to specific topics, such as motivation, emotion, intelligence, thinking, achievement, or adjustment, rather than to the growth of personality. And while material in the area of human development, as distinct from personality, *does* present normative growth data in a chronological fashion, these data are typically not discussed in relation to personality development or personality functioning. One encounters charts and descriptions of everything from height and weight to bed-wetting and masturbation, examined as a function of age or developmental stage, but little or no space is given to the question of why such material may be important for personality.

The foregoing remarks purposely exaggerate these tendencies in order to emphasize that there is an important gap in the framework of knowledge available to students of personality. Particularly for students who may not get much more than a survey course in this area, the categorical arrangement of most personality books, and the actuarial character of many developmental books, make it very difficult for personality development to be seen as a forceful, dynamic process. Our solution is to arrange all the relevant material sequentially, following a scheme of development generally acknowledged to be the gross life pattern for every individual.

To accomplish this purpose, it is first of all necessary to consider the basis for assuming that personality development can indeed be described according to a meaningful chronological scheme. Consequently, Chapter Four provides a review of the six different major theories that are relevant to growth sequences in personality. Behaviorism is not included among these theories because it is really a set of assumptions that may be applied to *any* branch of psychology. And insofar as behavioristic assumptions have generated theoretical interpretations of personality, these interpretations are not particularly concerned with development in specific age periods. This is not to say that ideas and research findings emerging from the behaviorist tradition are irrelevant: as will be seen in later chapters, such material receives careful attention. But since the behaviorist principles of conditioning and reinforcement presumably operate at all ages, they do not require discussion in chapters distinguishing between different age periods.

It should be acknowledged that the chronological framework established in Chapter Four involves certain costs as well as benefits. At the very outset, for example, one must make some assumptions about the experiences most of us *do* have from birth to death. Furthermore, research findings organized according to the chronological scheme will necessarily be discussed mainly in terms of their fit to this scheme, rather than their original context. So there will be some loss of "research fidelity" in the sense of comprehensive reporting of every detail. And this condition will extend even to a blurring of traditional boundaries between different theory-research areas, for we will bring together material from such areas as sociology, ethology, and comparative, physiological, and social psychology, without too much regard for origins.

Obviously, it would be absurd to attempt an eclectic, chronological approach if its gains did not appear to outweigh its losses. Some of the potential gains have already been mentioned—the common sense advantages of looking at personality from the beginning as a growth process; the need to bridge the gap between works on personality and works on human development—but there are at least two more.

First, at the level of theory, there is the possibility of developing linkages and relationships between matters that usually have been treated as entirely separate from one another. Thus sexual development and cognitive development, when looked at in a chronological framework, show themselves to stand in an important relationship to one another, especially as both can be seen to bear directly upon the strength of an individual's self-concept, his self-esteem, his sense of competence, and the like. Of equal or greater importance, perhaps, the sexual and cognitive aspects of personality can also be better understood when they are distinguished from one another according to their periods of maximum impact on the individual.

Second, at a purely practical level, the level at which one tries to understand himself, his parents, or his children, the chronological approach can provide illuminating principles that might otherwise remain totally obscure. For example, if the nuclear family is seen as a vehicle defining a good part of the life space of its members and containing most of their essential "life-support" equipment, yet also moving within and through a larger cultural space subject to course variations imposed by chance events as well as by the intentions of its "crew," one can attain valuable perspectives on personality development as a series of systems-management problems. To pursue this NASA-inspired analogy one step further: the internal characteristics of the vehicle (family dynamics) must be coordinated both to changing external factors (sociocultural norms and demands) and to changing crew needs (such as those that come with growth and development), if a successful voyage is to be accomplished.

4

The Chronology of Experience: An Ordered Framework for the Critical Periods and Critical Events in Personality Development

Down through the centuries, many gifted thinkers have tried to summarize the sweep and scope of typical human experience. Their efforts span a wide range including (a) bitter one-liners:

"Life is an incurable disease" (Abraham Cowley).

"Life is one long process of getting tired" (Samuel Butler).

"Life is made up of sobs, sniffles and smiles, with sniffles predominating" (O. Henry).

They extend to (b) cynical epigrams on the human condition:

"Man is the only animal that eats when he is not hungry, drinks when he is not thirsty, and makes love at all seasons" (author unknown).

"All progress is based upon a universal innate desire on the part of every organism to live beyond its income" (Samuel Butler).

And what will concern us most in this chapter, they will also include (c) attempts to capture ordinal sequences of experience. The expressions in this category can also be quite abrupt—"Man is born, he suffers, he dies," but their direction is toward specification of critical life periods:

"At twenty years of age, the will reigns; at thirty, the wit; and at forty, the judgment" (Benjamin Franklin).

Of all the literary statements one can find on this subject, none surpasses the wisdom, wit, and beauty with which Shakespeare gives us the seven ages of man.

All the world's a stage,
And all the men and women merely players:
They have their exits and their entrances;
And one man in his time plays many parts,
His acts being seven ages. At first the infant,
Mewling and puking in the nurse's arms.
And then the whining school-boy, with his satchel,

And shining morning face, creeping like snail
Unwillingly to school. And then the lover,
Sighing like furnace, with a woful ballad
Made to his mistress' eyebrow. Then a soldier,
Full of strange oaths, and bearded like the pard,
Jealous in honour, sudden and quick in quarrel,
Seeking the bubble reputation
Even in the cannon's mouth. And then the justice,
In fair round belly with good capon lin'd,
With eyes severe, and beard of formal cut,
Full of wise saws and modern instances;
And so he plays his part. The sixth age shifts
Into the lean and slipper'd pantaloon,
With spectacles on nose and pouch on side,
His youthful hose well sav'd, a world too wide
For his shrunk shank; and his big manly voice,
Turning again toward childish treble, pipes
And whistles in his sound. Last scene of all,
That ends this strange eventful history,
Is second childishness, and mere oblivion,
Sans teeth, sans eyes, sans taste, sans everything.
(*As You Like It,* Act II, Sc. VII, 139, pp. 260-261, The Oxford Shakespeare)

Age, experience, and literary knowledge notwithstanding, anyone can draw up a history of his life. Consider some material taken from the work of a college student, a counseling-center client who was asked to write his autobiography. He arranged this document in four periods: preschool, grade school, high school, and college. The mere choice of school-oriented period titles is significant, for it suggests the dominant force in his life. In early childhood (preschool) he remembers both parents as hard-working, but as providers of a warm home atmosphere:

Both of my parents worked so my younger sister and I spent most of our daytime hours with a babysitter. Our babysitter was an old lady, quite like a grandmother. She baked cookies and cakes and homemade bread. We, my sister and I, often helped her churn butter by rolling a jar of cream back and forth across the floor.

In grade school he learned easily and had many friends:

Scott and Allen were my two best friends at the time. All of us had chemistry sets. . . . we were fascinated by explosives and tried numerous times unsuccessfully to demolish a chicken house on Allen's property. It was during this period that my parents became more strict. Since both my parents worked, my sister and I had more work around the house than any other kid in the neighborhood. Then it really hacked me off, but it caused no major split in the family relationship.

There was also the usual childhood sex play:

Although it was necessary to play our sex games in the woods, no one seemed to feel any great guilt from them. These were not conducted alone but in groups. At times there were as many as 16 – 18 kids running through the woods in the Emperor's New Clothes. . . .

Then high school:

It was here I first encountered the problem of acceptance by others. . . . My athletic prowess was negligible. I could not receive recognition in that manner. My only apparent salvation was my sense of humor. I could be accepted as a clown. . . . Later, I dated more but my shyness limited this a little. Although I engaged in promiscuous sex play fairly often it only developed into full fledged intercourse twice. For a period of about two weeks after each session of intercourse I felt some anxiety but that was small and rapidly subsided. . . . My home life was quite good I feel. . . .

After attending a junior college where he meets a "way-out" art instructor who inspires him to think seriously about life, he is now finally at a large university, trying to find himself in the midst of much uncertainty:

My grades have hit an alltime low, I do not feel sufficiently motivated. Even a draft deferment does not inspire me to work harder. Now I begin to question whether my choice of curriculum was correct. I'm just not sure any more. I feel there should be more to life than this. I feel isolated and cut off from the real world out there. I feel that I really am missing something. The pioneer-explorer feeling that is being aroused within me is stifled by academics. I get the impression that the individual, the pioneer is dead and I must rechannel my talents to survive. I want freedom and room to breathe, to grow, and I'm not finding it. . . . You ask of my future! I know nothing of the future. My goal is to find my niche in society as a REAL, FUNCTIONING, WORTHWHILE, INDIVIDUAL PERSON.

In his final remarks, this sensitive young student perfectly expresses what is recognized in personality theory as an *identity crisis*. This problem is, by all accounts, the most serious psychological hurdle facing any young person in passage from adolescent to adult. And as we can all testify personally, or see in literary works or such films as "The Graduate," for many it turns out to be a hurdle on the order of Mount Everest.

The preceding literary-philosophical selections and the autobiographical material have been presented to suggest the issues that must be considered as we move toward a chronological framework for experience. The literary remarks convey the detachment and rueful gallows humor that arise from any really broad view of the human condition.

By contrast, the personal fragments taken from a young life-in-progress impose a more actively inquisitive attitude toward experience. Here we have a bright young person raised in relatively innocuous, healthy circumstances, who seems quite suddenly and painfully at odds with himself; alienated, stifled, uncertain about his past and his future. How does such a condition arise? Why is it so general? How is it likely to be resolved? These questions elicit sympathy and curiosity rather than detachment; they lead us toward empirical inquiry instead of fatalistic philosophy. Most of the material we will discuss as relevant to construction of a meaningful framework for experience falls somewhere between the extremes of clinical sympathy and philosophical detachment. To round out these introductory remarks, therefore, let us consider some research concerning the projection of experience through time.

The British psychologist Cohen (in Fraser, 1966) introduced an ingenious technique in which persons were quite literally asked to "lay their lives on the line." However, the line here was just that: a line about ten inches long drawn on a sheet of paper. Future time perspective was studied by labeling the left end of the line "now," and the right end "end of life." Subjects were then asked to mark a point on the line indicating the location ("how far in the future") of their next birthday, when they expected to marry, become a parent, achieve financial security, and other matters of theoretical interest. Past time perspective was studied in the same fashion, by changing labels so that "now" was the right end and "birth" was the left end of the line.

In one variation of this procedure, Cohen found that most subjects represented their short-term *future* time perspective to be about four times as distant from the present as their comparable *past* time perspective. That is, when line markings made for 3 to 6 months in the future were compared with markings for 3 to 6 months in the past, the former were about four times more distant from the present than the latter. Cohen also reported the interesting fact that this exaggeration of future time did not hold for intervals of a year or more. One year in the future was represented by a linear distance only slightly greater than that representing one year in the past. It would appear then, that for many persons the short-term future is more "distant" than the short-term past, but this distortion does not apply to long-term future and past.

This is the kind of *objective* data concerning *subjective* experience that appeals to the empirical intelligence. Perhaps the exaggeration of short-term future accounts in part for the agony of a young man undecided about his life style who says: "I know nothing of the future!" Or perhaps, because it indicates that the immediate past is more real than the immediate future, Cohen's work can help explain why older people have difficulty adapting to new environments or changing societies.

In summarizing his compendium on the problem of time, Fraser (1966) himself suggested specific connections between time-sense and personality:

This new and powerful tool which we recognize as man's knowledge of time, is co-eval and necessary for the establishment of his personal identity. For, only through the combination of expectation and memory can he know in what cumulative way he is different from others. In turn, the discovery of one's personal identity is but a way of recognizing his self-awareness (p. 589).

At another extreme from subjectively oriented studies of time perspective, material relevant to a sequential framework for experience can be found in research projects which follow individuals through many years. Kagan and Moss (1962) summarized an investigation carried out over the past thirty years at the Fels Research Institute. Between 1929 and 1939, 45 girls and 44 boys were enrolled in a longitudinal study of personality development that is still going on. While they were children, the subjects in this study were observed during regular home visits by staff, were given standard tests, and their parents were interviewed at appropriate intervals. Now that they are adults, they are paid to occasionally visit the Institute for interviews. Results so far available indicate that important aspects of adult personality can be recognized during early childhood.

The most dramatic and consistent finding of this study was that many of the behaviors exhibited by the child during the period 6 to 10 years of age, and a few during the age period 3 to 6, were moderately good predictors of theoretically related behaviors during early adulthood. Passive withdrawal from stressful situations, dependency on family, ease-of-anger arousal, involvement in intellectual mastery, social interaction anxiety, sex-role identification, and pattern of sexual behavior in adulthood were each related to reasonably analogous behavioral dispositions during the early school years (Kagan and Moss, 1962, p. 266).

In later chapters, material from this study will be described in more detail. It is valuable to us here because it serves as an illustration of longitudinal research on personality, and because it includes discussion of the key problem in this chapter: the organization of life experience in a chronological framework. Another very interesting example of such research is being carried out by Gardner (1964) at the Menninger Foundation. By regularly testing and interviewing approximately 50 sets of identical twins and one set of triplets through time, he hopes to learn about both hereditary and experiential factors in personality development—any important differences between twins must be due to experience, since heredity is constant. He is also carefully interviewing the twins' parents in this study, which promises to make a very significant contribution to our knowledge.

The most systematic part of the Kagan and Moss study involved the age span from birth to adolescence. This span was divided into four periods: 0 to 3 years, 3 to 6 years, 6 to 10 years, and 10 to 14 years. The authors point out that these periods roughly correspond to important developmental events or epochs. Between 0 to 3 years, the individual experiences infancy and early socialization; from 3 to 6 years he begins relating to other children and breaking away from total dependence on his parents; between 6 to 10 years of age many of his interests, skills and ways of relating to same-sex peers emerge; and from age 10 to 14 opposite-sex peer relationships become important, as well as vocational inclinations and typical defensive reactions. The authors also note that while they would have preferred a finer breakdown of age categories, the data available were not sufficient to permit proper statistical analyses for smaller periods.

Apart from their intrinsic value, the literary remarks in the introduction should have shown how general is the human effort to grasp the sweep and meaning of typical experience. The autobiographical fragments should illustrate how an individual can organize his own experience into meaningful time units and how time perspective may play a significant role in the identity problem. From all this discussion it should be clear that a meaningful chronological framework for experience ought to be of the utmost importance to the student of personality.

Kagan and Moss tried to work out the best possible compromise between their data and the developmental periods generally accepted to be important. But they would have had it otherwise if they could, and the following section goes into this matter in detail, citing the periods or stages of development thought to be of psychological significance,by at least six different theorists. And in the next section of this chapter the chronological scheme followed in succeeding chapters is described. This does not involve age categories that are drastically different from those suggested by major theorists; after all, there are only so many ways to divide the average life. But it emphasizes cer tain ideas that are not explicit in their theories, and it also brings together many of the major ideas contained in these theories.

CHRONOLOGICAL THEORIES OF PERSONALITY DEVELOPMENT

The six major chronological statements about personality that we will discuss here can most readily be distinguished from one another according to their relative emphasis on emotional *vs.* cognitive development.[1] If one thinks of a continuum with six names laid out from left to right as follows:

Freud   Sullivan   Erikson   Harvey, Hunt, & Schroder   Werner   Piaget

and the left end is labeled *emotional* and the right *cognitive*, then our general viewpoint should be clear. The established chronological theories of personality vary between a fairly extreme concentration on emotional development (e.g., Freud) and extreme concentration on cognitive development (e.g., Piaget).

As we move from left to right (political puns are quite plausible here) we find that in Sullivan, and even more so in Erikson, there is an increasing mix between emotional and cognitive aspects of personality. But both theorists give primary attention to emotional development and are considered to be neo-Freudians. The same sort of emotional-cognitive mix is to be found in Werner, and in Harvey, Hunt, and Schroder, but it is in the opposite direction; these authors give cognitive development the higher priority.

If it is important to distinguish between emotional and cognitive developmental theories just for the sake of clarity, it is more important to recognize that this distinction involves a crucial question of causality. Is emotion generally prior to, and causally determinant of, cognition? Or is cognition generally independent of emotion, perhaps even a determinant of emotion? There is research and common sense evidence available to support either position. Most of us know from experience that emotional tension can keep us from thinking clearly at times. We also know that getting a good idea or successfully thinking through a hard problem can make us feel good. Some discussion of why Freud and Piaget stand as theoretical prototypes of these different positions should help convey the core of this issue.

No matter how Freud's ideas are examined, any reasonable evaluation shows that he took emotions to be the bedrock foundation of personality. While it is true that the neo-Freudians, and Freud himself in the latter part of his career, put increasing weight on cognition, it is nonetheless also true that despite this shift of emphasis, emotionality remains for most Freudians as the primary source of mental activity. At least three salient features of Freudian theory can be cited briefly in support of this claim.

---

[1]The phrase *cognitive development* refers to growth in the ability to think; to visualize objects not present, solve problems, make plans, deal with abstractions or symbols. Reading, writing, arithmetic, playing checkers or chess, all require certain cognitive skills. However, the definitions are loose. Terms like *cognitive* and *cognition* are often used to indicate "intelligence" or "conscious awareness."
    The whole affair appears theoretically sloppy, yet in Marcuse's (1964) discussion of operationism and the values of transitivity or surplus meaning in language, one can find good reasons for accepting the sloppiness as a positive virtue.

First, it is a fundamental premise that all psychic energy available to the *ego*, which is the conscious, thinking, cognitive component of personality, must be siphoned off from the available pool of raw emotional energy, which is sexual in nature and referred to as *libido* or *libidinous energy*. Second, the chronological stages of personality development *(oral, anal, phallic, latency, and genital)* are labeled and defined according to emotional-sexual criteria. Third, it is a standard assumption of applied Freudian theory—psychoanalysis as a system of psychotherapy—that almost as blocked-up plumbing can be "freed up" with Drāno, when emotional difficulties are worked out during therapy, cognitive activity is "freed up" so that the patient typically experiences a new capability to deal effectively with the world around him. We might note that this last point is usually explained in terms of the first: it is assumed that as a result of therapy the patient who previously was putting energy into static, ego-defense holding actions, will have more energy available for constructive exploratory activities.

Thus, to the orthodox Freudian, and to a lesser but significant degree to the neo-Freudian, personality development is largely a matter of emotional development.

In what is presently the most authoritative, detailed book on Piaget available in English, Flavell[2] offered an approximate definition of Piaget's aims:

. . . he is primarily interested in the theoretical and experimental investigation of the qualitative development of intellectual structures (1963, p. 15).

This definition is amplified by a discussion showing that emotion and motivation are treated by Piaget as secondary to, or as providing a relatively constant background for, intellectual growth. Aspects of personality such as values and attitudes, which are typically understood to be a product of emotions and basic motives on the one hand, and cultural norms on the other, are seen by Piaget as cognitive systems, or organized structures of thought having the same fundamental characteristics as the more purely intellectual thought structures.

For example, Inhelder and Piaget (1958) indicate that many of the stereotyped features of adolescent personality—the romanticism, the moral and social idealism—can be understood as a consequence of the stage of intellectual development reached by the adolescent. He is for the first time able to think in an abstract, broadly theoretical way. And he can thus imagine a family, a society, or a world as it *might* be; an image which is usually preferable to the world as it is. So it is suggested that much of the adolescent's thought and behavior is, in effect, the result of his being carried away by his

[2]Since Flavell will be relied upon very heavily in many places, it is proper to acknowledge our debt to him immediately. The reader should also know that his rendering of Piaget has the enthusiastic endorsement of Piaget himself. In the foreword to Flavell's book, Piaget wrote: "Naturalist and biologist by training, interested in epistemological problems, without ever having undertaken formal study (nor passed any examinations) in psychology . . . . those who read my work often find themselves confused. Thus a tremendous effort both in focusing and in reinterpreting had to be made to achieve a rendition of my work which is at once clear, well integrated, and fundamentally psychological in nature. Professor Flavell is certainly to be congratulated for having surmounted these difficulties in such an outstanding manner" (p. vii).

It is also necessary to note a great personal debt to Howard Gruber and Jan Smedslund. The former initiated my abiding interest in Piaget long before his work was widely accepted in this country. The latter, through his lectures, discussions, and conversation, opened a path toward the inner workings of Piaget's ideas.

newly acquired intellectual capacity. Inhelder and Piaget therefore call adolescence the *metaphysical age*.

At a more general level, Piaget treats motives mainly as they are related to intellectual growth. Flavell (1963) was quite specific:

Moreover, the motives seen as most important are thought to be intrinsic to intellectual functioning itself and can at least approximately be conveyed by such terms as *exploratory drive, drive to mastery*, etc.; conventional bodily needs as motivators, the perennial favorites of learning theory, are given short shrift in Piaget's system (p. 16).

When it is understood that "conventional bodily needs" include the sex and aggression instincts which generate the energy in Freud's system, the reason for placing Freud and Piaget at opposite poles in the landscape of psychology should be clear.

Of course, the preceding discussion should not be taken as a definitive comparison of Freud and Piaget (interested readers should see Wolff, 1960). The aim here has merely been to show that there is a clear basis for ordering chronological schemes of personality development on an emotional-cognitive continuum. As the different schemes are described below, starting first with the emotional and going toward the emotional-cognitive; then starting with the cognitive and working in toward the cognitive-emotional, the reasons for organizing the material in this fashion should become more apparent.

FREUD AND THE PSYCHOSEXUAL STAGES OF DEVELOPMENT

Freud's basic chronological scheme subdivides the age period from birth to late adolescence (approximately the first 18 years of life) into five stages of development. There is some uncertainty about the age intervals typical for each psychosexual stage. Freud himself was not too specific about this, and most subsequent writers resist being pinned down to precise age statements because they all recognize that growth processes will vary in different persons. However, the generally accepted chronology of psychosexual development is shown below:

The oral stage	. . . 0 to 1 year
The anal stage	. . . 2 to 3 years
The phallic stage	. . . 4 to 5 years
The latency stage	. . . 6 to 12 years
The genital stage	. . . 13 to 18 and beyond

To understand the Freudian interpretation of behavior typical in each stage, as well as the manner in which individuals progress through these stages, it is first necessary to grapple with one of the most difficult concepts in psychoanalytic theory: *libido*. The concept is difficult because it is commonly explained to be a *sexual form of psychic energy*, concentrated in the *erogenous* (sexually excitable) zones of the body. But such explanations can only be meaningful if one knows what Freudians mean by psychic energy and erogenous zones. Before trying to clarify the idea of libido through theoretical discussion, it may be useful to point out how we all presumably experience libido.

According to psychoanalytic theory, during the usual course of lovemaking when an erogenous zone is stimulated, the pleasurable tension felt in that zone is due to the arousal of sexual energy concentrated there. In his introductory lectures on psychoanalysis originally published in 1924, Freud (1960) broached the subject of libido functioning by first discussing sexual perversions.

The kiss to begin with has some claim to be called a perverse act, for it consists of the union of the two erotogenic mouth zones instead of the two genital organs. But no one condemns it as perverse; on the contrary, in the theatre it is permitted as a refined indication of the sexual act. Nevertheless, kissing is a thing that can easily become an absolute perversion — namely, when it occurs in such intensity that orgasm and emission directly accompany it, which happens not at all uncommonly. Further, it will be found that gazing at and handling the object are in one person an indispensable condition of sexual enjoyment, while another at the height of sexual excitement pinches or bites; that in another lover not always the genital region, but some other bodily region in the object, provokes the greatest excitement, and so on in endless variety (p. 331).

In short, libido is the energy associated with sexual excitement. Maximum sexual excitement will involve bodily zones having the highest concentration of libido; sexual perversions can be understood as being determined by the physical locus of libido.

On a more formal theoretical level, Hall and Lindzey (1957) explained that the concept of psychic energy is a fundamental assumption of psychoanalytic theory. Just as physicists take it as fundamental that no physical work can be accomplished without the expenditure of physical energy, Freud assumed that no psychological work (e.g., thinking) can be accomplished without the expenditure of psychic energy. When the idea of psychic energy was first introduced, it was greeted as an entirely arbitrary notion because no one could think of a way to measure it.

Hall and Lindzey (1954) further indicated that as a subvariety of psychic energy, libido has an obscure theoretical status.

Freud's clearest statement of what he meant by libido is found in *Three Contributions to the Theory of Sex* (Freud, 1905). In this monograph he defines libido "as a force of variable quantity by which processes and transformations in the spheres of sexual excitement can be measured" (p. 611) and distinguishes it from general psychic energy by virtue of its origin in the erogenous zones of the body. Since any part or organ of the body can be an erogenous zone, i.e., seat of sexual excitement, the sources of libido are multifarious (p. 146).

Now, granting that some ambiguity must remain in the term *libido*, but having done as much as possible to reduce it to a minimum, we will see the important role it plays in the psychosexual stages of personality development.

The oral stage

The newborn infant's major contact with his environment occurs at the oral area: his lips, tongue, and associated structures provide the means of drawing sustenance from the world. Moreover, as events centered in the oral zone satisfy his basic physiological needs, this zone becomes the infant's locus of pleasure, because all of the good, important, pleasant things happen there: the tensions generated by hunger and thirst are relieved by first crying for food and then sucking it in. In brief, the oral zone is everything to the neonate, a bodily Disneyland as it were. For this reason, libido is initially concentrated at the mouth, and to one degree or another the mouth remains as an important erogenous zone throughout a person's life.

As he grows, the salience of the oral area is further shown by the infant's efforts to experience his environment through his mouth. For example, one of my children spent a good part of his waking time watching the butterfly mobile above his crib. When he began to deliberately reach for it at about 6 or 7 months, we thought it only fair to help him get hold of it. Whereupon he immediately ripped the thing from its mooring and with evident signs of delight began cramming the plastic butterflies into his mouth. (Pity was, we had to stop him. Perhaps in the future someone will manufacture edible mobiles.)

Most of the infant's behavior during this period is described by the phrase *primary narcissism*, meaning that the infant is entirely *egocentric*. He is only concerned with his own gratification, has no conception of the independent existence of objects, and feels himself to be *omnipotent* in the sense that he can call forth from the environment satisfaction of his simple needs for food and physical comfort.

The early phase of infancy is called *oral-dependent* because the infant can play only a relatively passive role with respect to oral events. But once his teeth begin to come in during later infancy (about age 6 months) and he becomes capable of biting as well as exerting stronger, more precise motor control over objects, he is described as being in the *oral-aggressive* phase. Baldwin (1968) suggested an interesting circular process to account for the more aggressive behavior seen in later infancy. When the infant gets teeth, breast nursing becomes more painful for his mother. She therefore starts to wean him, and he experiences frustration which manifests itself in further aggressive behavior. The pain associated with teething is, of course, also relevant here. But many Freudian writers interpret all teething behavior as definitive of *oral-aggressive* needs in the infant.

The anal stage

Elimination activity occurring in the anal region is initially an autonomic or reflexive process for the infant. But as every parent knows, he gradually grows more and more sensitive to, and aware of, events at the anal area. By the age of two, when he is usually getting solid food and therefore producing relatively substantial feces, bowel movements will become a distinct source of pleasure because they remove the discomfort caused by packing of the lower intestine and pressure on the anal sphincter. Libido thus begins to be concentrated in the anal region. This concentration is intensified by the attention parents give to anal events when they begin toilet training. For example, one family kept a potty in their dining room so that the child could be placed upon it right from his high chair. Then, if the child did anything effective, all present were expected to join in a chorus of praise.

More abstractly, with the beginning of toilet training the child must for the first time learn to regulate a reflexive impulse. He must delay anal gratification to receive the approval of parents and avoid the discomfort of dirty diapers. Baldwin (1968) pointed out how feelings of shame or embarrassment can originate during this period:

Another psychological feature of this period is the appearance of shyness, an emotional reaction to being looked at, which is probably based on the closely related feeling of shame. One cause for shame can be a toilet accident; in some homes the child who wets his pants or bed is publicly ridiculed as "being just a baby" (p. 362).

Altogether then, taking into account both the internal physiological character of anal events and the external social factors associated with them, there is a plausible basis for assuming that libido can be concentrated in the anal region. A good Freudian would probably argue for the persistence of anality by pointing to evidence from everyday adult behavior: elaborate toilet rituals, insistence upon absolute privacy, and references to the "throne."

The phallic stage

At about four years of age libido begins to concentrate in the genital region. This new focus for libido is a matter of natural development: at this age the child's genital equipment is developed sufficiently to become, for the first time, an important source of pleasurable stimulation. Most parents will notice the change when children begin to show genital play in the bathtub.

In view of the emphasis on the genital area here, students often question why Freud called this age period *phallic* instead of genital. The answer has to do with the qualitative nature of the sexually stimulating activity that occurs. During the phallic stage the genitals are treated almost entirely as independent objects of pleasure by the child. They are certainly not seen clearly as instrumental to acts of intense intimacy with another person. Use of the term phallic in reference to the child's first serious awareness of the genital region therefore seems appropriate because it concerns the superficial appearance of things.[3]

A good many things Freudians view as important for personality occur during the phallic period, but we will now only note them briefly and save detailed discussion for a later chapter. Female feelings of inferiority vis-à-vis men are said to originate here when the little girl learns that boys have a penis and girls don't. In some instances, Freudians suggest that the girl will think her penis was cut off as punishment for a misdeed. While specific interpretations may vary, general arguments of this type are cited to support the assumption of *penis envy* in women.

A more crucial event assumed to color the whole phallic stage is the Oedipus complex. For young boys this is said to begin with an association between sexual pleasure or sensuality, and the mother. The boy may actually witness

---

[3]One finds in popular literature, for example, frequent use of the phrase *phallic symbol* to describe objects such as the Washington Monument. And the word phallus commonly means an artificial penis.

sex acts between his parents, or he may otherwise, through small cues, become intuitively aware of his mother as a sex object. However it comes about, Freudians make the basic assumption that the little boy wants sex relations with his mother (even though he doesn't really understand what may be involved in this), and further, that he sees his father as a sexual rival who is depriving him of this pleasure. Since the father is, or appears to be, a very powerful, threatening figure, the boy is supposed to be afraid to act out his desire for his mother because if he does, his father may carry out the ultimate punishment of taking away his penis. And it is in this way that *castration anxiety* is said to originate in boys.

As a result of castration anxiety and other more obvious fears centering on his father, the boy begins to resolve his Oedipal conflict by giving up or *repressing* (forcing out of conscious awareness) the desire for his mother, and by imitating or identifying with his father. The latter process is called *identification with the aggressor*. It may seem contrary to common sense for a child to imitate someone he is supposed to fear, but it will be shown in more detail later that identification with the aggressor is a fairly general process. The Freudian argument is that boys acquire a proper masculine identity (sex-role) in this fashion. A strong moral conscience or *superego* is also supposed to be acquired in this fashion because the boy learns (a) to repress a desire strongly disapproved by society as represented by the external authority of the father, and (b) to adopt his father's moral values as part of the general identification with him.

All experts agree, and Freud himself said, that the Oedipal situation for girls is much more obscure than it is for boys. To be sure, the situation for girls is analogous to that of boys because they are supposed to see their mothers as rivals keeping them from having sexual relations with their fathers. This is usually called either the *Electra complex* or the female Oedipus complex. But neither Freud nor any of his theoretical disciples have ever been able to provide as neat an interpretation of the complex for girls as they have for boys. Instead of coming to first fear and then identify with the mother, the girl is thought to retain ambivalent feelings toward her mother. Some fear and threat is certainly posed by the mother as a powerful rival for the father, but supposedly does not reach a very high level. Therefore, while identification with the mother does take place and the girl acquires the correct sex-role in this fashion, the entire process is not so intense as it is for the boy.

One explanation is that since mothers do not have the same apparent power in most families as fathers, they are not as threatening. Another is that not having a penis to start with, the girl cannot develop the same level of fear as the boy regarding mutilation as punishment for an illicit desire. However one chooses to interpret this matter, Freudians argue that because girls do not resolve their conflict as definitively as boys, one can see certain consequences in their sex-role behavior and their sense of morality. The prevalence of masculine behavior in preadolescent girls (tomboyism) is much greater than feminine behavior in boys; and girls are also believed to have a less compulsive moral conscience than boys.

The latency stage

The latency stage in children can be understood most generally as a grand period of rest and recuperation from the elemental desires and fears experienced during the phallic period. Roughly corresponding to the primary-school period (ages 6 to 12), the stage takes its name from the fact that libido is through most of this period *latent* rather than manifest. During this time sex energy is *sublimated*, or channeled into socially acceptable activities.

There are two theoretically plausible reasons for the occurrence of the long latency period. First, the repression associated with resolution of the Oedipus complex is so great, and has such a broad-gauge character, that the child consciously or unconsciously rejects all things involving sex. At this age period most boys and girls have very little to do with one another, and they frequently prefer the company of their like-sexed parent. Second, and no less important, the requirements of starting formal education outside the home absorb virtually all of the child's physical and psychic energy, libido included.

There are always exceptions of course, and in this case they usually take the form of the hetero- and homosexual play that goes on among preadolescents. But the exceptions here tend to occur toward the end of the latency period (ages 10, 11, and 12) when Freudians claim that the great repression and sublimation of libido is beginning to break up anyway.

It is interesting to note that this age period, which for Piagetian theorists is perhaps the greatest age of cognitive development (most of us acquire all the basic symbolic cognitive skills during these years), is for Freudians clearly a period of secondary importance. Hall and Lindzey (1957), for example, did not even discuss the latency period as a distinct developmental epoch.

The genital stage

To put it very grossly, during the genital period libido rises like a phoenix from the ashes of the latency stage. This resurrection of direct sexual energy occurs for reasons of physiological growth: genital organs mature, the endocrine system produces high concentrations of sex hormones; and for purely psychological reasons: the great repression of latency wears off as the child develops a stronger sense of his personal identity and competence, or ego strength.

In the early part of the genital period then, libido is released and begins to be more or less openly expressed toward members of the opposite sex. At first these targets may be similar to the opposite-sexed parents who were earlier renounced as legitimate targets. The "puppy-love" or "crushes" of early adolescence usually involve an opposite-sexed adult—a teacher, neighbor, or favorite brother- or sister-in-law. Some psychoanalytic writers suggest that the adolescent is in this way reliving the Oedipal conflict: working out the remaining Oedipal "bugs" in his heterosexual emotional system, as it were. But as the adolescent finds that, for many reasons, parent substitutes or symbols make unsatisfactory love objects, he finally shifts toward opposite-sexed peers.

From a Freudian perspective, adolescence can perhaps be summarized in one sentence: it is, both theoretically and literally, an awkward period of groping toward satisfactory heterosexual love. Much more can be said about the genital period because Freud left it open ended. Many persons clearly do not achieve a genuinely mature genital sex adjustment until they are far beyond adolescence. Theoretically, in the psychosexual sphere a person can remain functioning at an adolescent or even preadolescent level throughout his life. However, if we push toward the ramifications of genital development, the reasons for things going wrong, or the criteria whereby one can evaluate genital sex adjustment in detail, we will begin to engage psychoanalysis as a system of therapy. For the present, it is enough to say that the distinctly developmental aspect of Freudian theory ends with specification of the genital stage, and the possibility that proper genital adjustment (satisfactory expression of libido through heterosexual love), can be achieved at the end of adolescence.

SULLIVAN AND THE INTERPERSONAL THEORY OF DEVELOPMENT

As suggested by the title of his major theoretical work, *The Interpersonal Theory of Psychiatry*, Sullivan (1953) viewed social relationships as the key to understanding personality. He is often called a neo-Freudian because his work was founded on psychoanalytic theory, and because many of his basic assumptions remained similar to Freud's. But even at the basic level there are very important differences between the two theorists. For example, both accord great significance to the oral and anal areas of the body, particularly at early age periods. Whereas Freud, however, geared discussion of these areas to his theory of libido functioning, Sullivan discussed these areas as *zones of interaction* with the world.

The differences between Freud and Sullivan extend beyond the latter's concern with social processes. Sullivan also placed a heavier theoretical emphasis on cognitive processes. He distinguished three different levels of thought, or modes of experiencing the world, which serve as the basis for his major contribution to psychopathology: a theory of schizophrenic disorders. Briefly, this theory suggests that unfortunate social experiences early in life can lead to the abnormal thought processes characteristically found in schizophrenics. Our immediate concern, however, is his chronological scheme for personality development.

Sullivan specified six stages of personality development. Unlike Freud, he lavished a great deal of theoretical effort on infancy and, in fact, stands as the preeminent psychological theorist on infancy (for this reason we will discuss his work extensively in a later chapter). But like Freud, Sullivan terminated his systematic description of personality development at the end of adolescence. And even more so than with Freud, his stages are difficult to restrict to particular age periods because they are delineated according to the appearance of important events, not chronological age. The few chronological age-statements that Sullivan did make were mainly for illustrative purposes. Efforts to tie the different stages to certain age periods are therefore largely a matter of deduction. Here are the six stages as Sullivan named them. The basis for our age specifications will become clear as we take up each one separately.

Infancy	. . .	0 to 2 years
Childhood	. . .	3 to 5 years
The juvenile era	. . .	6 to 9 years
Preadolescence	. . .	10 to 12 years
Early adolescence	. . .	13 to 17 years
Late adolescence	. . .	18 to 21 years

Infancy

Infancy is defined as spanning the period from birth to the emergence of significant language behavior, which most authorities place at or just before the age of two years. The theoretical importance Sullivan assigned to this period can hardly be overstated. Of the fifteen chapters he devoted to describing "the developmental epochs," five concern infancy (including one happily entitled "the infant as a person") and a sixth concerns the transition from infancy to childhood.

The importance of interpersonal events is stressed from the very outset. As with Freud, the oral zone of interaction has a crucial status because survival depends upon oral events. But while Freud saw the psychological implications of these events mainly in terms of libido, Sullivan saw them as generating a great many of the basic features characterizing all interpersonal situations. To begin with, there is fear. In the degree that an infant's needs for air, food, water, sleep, and warmth are not fully satisfied, he will experience discomfort which can easily escalate into the fearful tension Sullivan called *anxiety*. It is suggested that one can simulate this primitive form of anxiety postulated for the infant by cutting off his air supply. Mild discomfort will be quickly followed by a tense emotional arousal which soon leads to terror. The infant's emotional range of experience is therefore described on a theoretical emotional continuum: when all his needs are satisfied and anxiety is absent, he is presumed to be at the *euphoria* end of the scale. When needs are seriously unfulfilled, as in the case of a lack of air, he will be at the *terror* end of the anxiety scale.

According to Sullivan it is basic that satisfaction of all the infant's needs requires the activity of at least one other person ("the mothering one"). The infant must either passively cooperate with the mother, or actively coordinate his own efforts to hers, if his needs are to be fulfilled. It is further suggested that since no infant can exist without the care of a mother (we will use mother throughout instead of the more abstract "mothering one"), for theoretical purposes the neonate should really be seen not as a single individual, but rather as part of a larger unit that can be called something like "the-mother-and-infant." This type of relationship is what lies beneath Sullivan's emphasis on the interpersonal nature of personality. He saw the patterning of the fundamental social relationship that must exist between the mother and infant as the foundation of personality.

The earliest interpersonal situation is nursing. Sullivan theorized that for the infant, the psychological character of this situation is determined by his experience with his mother's nipple. He can experience "the good nipple" when nursing is satisfactory; "the wrong nipple" when it does not give milk; "the good but unsatisfactory nipple" which can become satisfactory when the infant is hungry enough to suck, but which will remain unsatisfactory if he has received it by mistake, as when his mother erroneously thinks he is crying for food; and finally there is "the evil nipple":

. . . the nipple of an anxious mother which, so far as the infant is concerned, is a nipple preceded by the aura of extremely disagreeable tension—anxiety—which is a signal for avoidance, often even the avoidance of investing the nipple with the lips at all (Sullivan, 1953, p. 80).

Just how the infant senses these different "nipples," particularly the evil one, Sullivan left to a process he called *empathy*, which is discussed in detail later. But the theoretical importance of these nipple discriminations presumably learned in early infancy lies in the assumption that they serve as the basis for the infant's global conceptions of himself and others. Such globally positive or negative conceptions are labeled *personifications*, and they are of practical import because depending upon how he "personifies" himself and others, the infant will expect pleasant or unpleasant experiences (low or high anxiety) to result from his own behavior or the behavior of others.

The infant's personification of himself is elaborated into a rudimentary three-part "self-system" during the latter part of infancy. This system includes three different personifications or self-images: "good-me," "bad-me," and "not-me." According to Sullivan (1953)

Good-me is the beginning personification which organizes experience in which satisfactions have been enhanced by rewarding increments of tenderness, which come to the infant because the mothering one is pleased with the way things are going. . . .

Bad-me, on the other hand, is the beginning personification which organizes experience in which increasing degrees of anxiety are associated with behavior involving the mothering one. . . (pp. 161–162).

The basis for assuming not-me is rather obscure. It can only be understood, paradoxically, as a view of self that rejects some significant part of self. It can perhaps be illustrated in everyday life when people try to evade responsibility for an act by sincerely pleading that "they were not themselves." Functional *amnesia* would be another example. However, suggestions about how the not-me personification may originate in infancy are too elaborate to work out here, and the interested reader is referred to the original work (Sullivan, 1953).

Sullivan assigns considerable importance to crying as the main action available to the infant for the relief of anxiety generated by physical needs.

So far as the infant is concerned, in these very early weeks of life, the cry effects (1) the relief of anoxia by starting the breathing cycle; (2) the relief of thirst and hunger by "producing," in a certain sense, the nipple in the infant's lips, from which the infant sucks relief-giving substance which is swallowed; (3) the relief of subcooling by preventing excessive heat loss; and (4) the removal of noxious physical circumstances, such as a restraint of bodily freedom of movement, painful local pressures, and the like (p. 62).

Obviously, if vocalizing serves the infant effectively as an instrument for obtaining relief, this will influence his personification of himself and others in many ways. Most basically, however, it should promote a positive orientation toward later acquisition of speech.

Cognition is said to go on in a "prototaxic mode" during early infancy, described by Sullivan as:

. . . the simplest, the earliest, and possibly the most abundant mode of experience. Sentience, in the experimental sense, presumably relates to much of what I mean by the prototaxic mode (p. 29).

This form of experience is further discussed as a kind of sensitive awareness of events which we frequently have as adults when we know that something is going on and we can sense, perhaps only vaguely, whether we like it or not.

The "parataxic mode" of cognition appears toward the latter part of infancy. Hall and Lindzey (1957) described it as a form of quasi-logical thought:

The parataxic mode of thinking consists of seeing causal relationship between events that occur at about the same time but which are not logically related. The eminent Czech writer, Franz Kafka, portrays an interesting case of parataxic thinking in one of his short stories. A dog who lived in a kennel surrounded by a high fence was urinating one day when a bone was thrown over the fence. The dog thought, "My urinating made that bone appear." Thereafter whenever he wanted something to eat he lifted his leg. Sullivan believes that much of our thinking does not advance beyond the level of parataxis; that we see causal connections between experiences that have nothing to do with one another. All superstitions, for instance, are examples of parataxic thinking (pp. 140–141).

Finally, the "syntaxic mode" of cognition appears strongly toward the end of infancy and more or less defines the transition to the childhood stage. Syntaxic thought is generally used in language and involves some shared understanding of symbols (words) between persons. The syntaxic mode refers to our symbolic capability. Because it enables us to code and store experience, we are able to represent our past experience to ourselves and others, and to anticipate future events. For the young child this capability, even in a primitive form, means, among other things, that he can be satisfied and reassured with words, and that he can in turn do this for others.

Childhood

Sullivan marked the beginning of childhood by the appearance of significant language ability. Language, and the symbolic capacity that accompanies it, allows the child to accomplish the most important psychological advance of this period: he "fuses" hitherto disparate personifications. This means that instead of thinking in terms of being a good-me or bad-me, or having a good-mother or bad-mother, the self and others are seen to be more unitary, as personifications containing both good and bad elements. The process by which such fusion occurs seems to Sullivan to be inherent in the use of language:

Thanks in no small part to the incredible power which verbal behavior seems to exercise in interpersonal situations, and to the great energy devoted by the more mature people around the very young child to equip him with this most important of all human tools, language, it becomes quite impossible for the child to carry forward any striking surviving evidence of his earliest impression of two mothers — one who gives tenderness and cooperation in the satisfaction of needs, and one who carries anxiety and interferes with the satisfaction of needs. . . . Thus no matter how thoroughly organized the two separate personifications of the good mother and the bad mother were, their individuality is lost or fused into a later personification, in the process of learning language (p. 189).

Sullivan suggests that a number of dynamic personality processes begin to show up in childhood. He refers to one of these as "the theorem of escape," a phenomenon recognized more generally as the *egocentrism* of young children: they will ward off all sorts of unpleasant experiences by seeming to ignore them, by apparently forgetting them with lightning speed. Because it has this interesting feature, the self-system can be extremely resistant to change, even in the face of very intense experiences. The negative aspect of this phenomenon is that in many ways the child seems unable to learn from experience. The positive aspect is that this escape capability can function as a protective shield for his still relatively weak self-system.

For example, when one of my children was three his mother, for the first time in his life, had to be away for several days. The best one can do in these circumstances is bring in a grandmother. However, after an initial tearful parting, the child surprised all of us by showing very few signs of missing his mother. He seemed to forget her. When she returned, we had another surprise: instead of the expected happy greeting, he took one look, burst into tears, and ran off to hide in another room! This episode lasted only a short time, and we understood it as a demonstration of the emotional upheaval that occurs when an escapist defense is shattered. His mother spent a half hour alone with the boy, not forcing herself too much upon him, and things returned to normal.

Another important process is *sublimation*. Sullivan's conception of this process is similar to Freud's, but he elaborates it in a different fashion, without reference to sex energy, as:

the unwitting substitution, for a behavior pattern which encounters anxiety . . . of a socially more acceptable activity pattern which satisfies part of the motivational system that caused trouble (p. 193).

A child may therefore abandon an activity, such as thumb sucking, if he is discouraged by parents who generate anxiety for him whenever he does it. He may then, without consciously choosing to do so, substitute a behavior, such as sucking on a pacifier or toy, which will satisfy at least part of his sucking need.

"As if" performances also emerge during childhood. Such performances may take the form Sullivan called *dramatizations,* in which the child plays at being someone else, acting as if he is his mother, father, or some significant other person. In this connection, dramatizations seem virtually identical to what is known more commonly in social science as *taking the role of the other.*

The final, and most fascinating, of Sullivan's ideas about dynamic processes in childhood is called *the malevolent transformation.* The main thrust of this idea is toward the origin of later behavior pathology, but it is such an ingenious notion that one cannot pass it by lightly. In brief, a child may undergo malevolent transformation if his efforts to get tender reassurance from powerful adult figures are generally repulsed.[4] When such efforts by the child to relieve his anxiety only lead to more anxiety, he may come to anticipate social relationships as being so painful that he will either withdraw from them entirely, or else act out what he anticipates will be the behavior of others: serious rejection that may include attempts to hurt, punish, or otherwise cause pain.

The juvenile era

The beginning of the juvenile era is marked by the appearance of strong social needs that typically extend beyond the boundaries of the immediate family, such that Sullivan explains

I refer to all this as the maturation of the need for compeers, which ushers in what it seems best to call the *juvenile era,* which is particularly the period of formal education. . . (p. 226).

The period corresponds fairly closely to the Freudian latency stage, but Sullivan attaches a greater functional importance to this period than do most Freudians. He sees it as the first developmental era in which idiosyncratic personality features caused by the "limitations and peculiarities" of life in the nuclear family have a chance for being altered. The school society is specifically mentioned as a new source of experience which may correct or modify developmental trends imposed by family experience.

Most of the important achievements of this period are in some way related to the extension of the child's social horizons beyond the family. The child

---

[4]Sullivan explained that "A child may discover that manifesting the need for tenderness toward the potent figures around him leads frequently to his being disadvantaged, being made anxious, being made fun of, and so on, so that, according to the locution used, he is hurt, or in some cases he may be literally hurt. Under those circumstances, the developmental course changes to the point that the perceived need for tenderness brings a foresight of anxiety or pain. The child learns, you see, that it is highly disadvantageous to show any need for tender cooperation from the authoritative figures around him, in which case he shows something else; and that something else is the basic malevolent attitude, the attitude that one really lives among enemies — that is about what it amounts to. And on that basis, there come about the remarkable developments which are seen later in life, when the juvenile makes it practically impossible for anyone to feel tenderly toward him or to treat him kindly; he beats them to it, so to speak, by the display of his attitude. And this is the development of the earlier discovery that the manifestation of any need for tenderness, and so on, would bring anxiety or pain. The other elaborations — the malevolence that shows as a basic attitude toward life, you might say, as a profound problem in one's interpersonal relations — are also just an elaboration of this earlier warp" (pp. 213–215).

learns "social subordination"—how to relate to various new and different authority figures—and "social accommodation"—how to adapt to and accept the different life-styles of his peers. During the course of social subordination he learns to evaluate authority figures, to see them as people. In this way, parents lose their aura of omnipotence because they can be compared with other authorities. The juvenile also learns the meaning of competition and compromise as the basis for social accommodation.

The self-system is said to develop to the point where it attains "control of focal awareness." That is, the juvenile can deliberately control the contents of his mind: he begins to know what he is thinking about; he can selectively attend to or ignore things going on around him. The self-system also comes to include representations of the outside world that help the juvenile fit his behavior to different situations. These representations are called *supervisory patterns*. For example, upon entering a public situation the relevant supervisory pattern is that of the "spectator," and this is the representation the juvenile makes to himself of others' reactions to him.

"Sublimatory reformulation" occurs because the juvenile is said to modify or change many of the defensive behaviors described earlier as "sublimations." He may also acquire "stereotypes," crude general ideas about certain classes or groups of people. These can serve him as an easy technique for coping with novel social situations. The juvenile may have his first experience with "ostracism," rejection by peers, during this period. Such an experience can be important as one of the factors underlying the need for a "chum" that appears in preadolescence.

It is finally suggested that toward the end of the juvenile era there emerges a kind of global adjustment pattern that Sullivan called "the conception of orientation in living." He explained this by saying that an individual is "oriented in living" to the degree that (1) he understands the needs characterizing his interpersonal relations, (2) he sees ways of satisfying these needs and expressing them without undue anxiety, and (3) he acquires goals or values which allow him to forego short-term satisfactions. The importance Sullivan assigns to this phenomenon is clear from his comment on the probable consequences of its absence:

To the extent that a juvenile has been denied an opportunity for a good orientation in living, he will from henceforth show a trait which is a lamentable nuisance: he will be so anxious for the approval and unthinking immediate regard of others that one might well think he lived merely to be liked, or to amuse. And in some cases, that, I fear, is about true (p. 244).

Preadolescence

The preadolescent period is a relatively short one almost entirely defined by the need for a close intimate relationship with a peer of the same sex. Sullivan called this a *chum relationship*. He saw it as the prototype for all serious love relationships that occur later in life. It marks a unique new stage in personality development because, for the first time, the feelings and needs of another person are given equal importance as one's own. In a literal sense, "I" may give way to "we" as the crucial pronoun in a person's life grammar; as Sullivan explained:

. . . if you will look very closely at one of your children when he finally finds a chum—somewhere between eight-and-a-half and ten—you will discover something very different in the relationship—namely, that your child begins to develop a real sensitivity to what matters to another person. And this is not in the sense of "what should I do to get what I want," but instead "what should I do to contribute to the happiness or to support the prestige and feeling of worth-whileness of my chum" (p. 245).

A chum relationship allows the individual to "validate all components of personal worth." Thus he can learn that it is not disastrous to expose serious aspects of his personality to another, and that anxiety about many different behaviors and thoughts can be reduced by sharing them with another person.

Sullivan suggested that important changes can result from the chum relationship. For example, the egocentric individual may be pushed by his strong need for a chum into the realization that his own satisfactions must at times be sacrificed if he is to avoid loneliness. And if a child has gone through something of a malevolent transformation but is still able to acquire a chum, the transformation may be reversed if he learns that tender acceptance by another person is still possible.

Early adolescence

The earlier phase of adolescence as a period of personality development is defined as extending from the eruption of true genital interest, felt as lust, to the patterning of sexual behavior which is the beginning of the last phase of adolescence (Sullivan, p. 263).

Lust is defined as the felt tensions associated with the need to experience sexual orgasm. It is said that this need is not only independent of the need for intimacy underlying chum relationships, but that the two needs may be in opposition to one another, as when the adolescent experiences a conflict between loyalty to same-sex peers, and attraction toward an opposite-sex peer. Or he may encounter the old dichotomy between dating a "good girl" or a "bad girl."

Eventually, however, during adolescence the intimacy need changes its focus from a same-sexed peer to an opposite-sexed peer. Sullivan thought this change occurs partly because of the strong lust need, and partly because the validation of personal worth that accompanies intimacy will be stronger when it originates in a person very different from oneself, such as an opposite-sexed peer.

During early adolescence, the three major needs that characterize most of adult life begin to crystalize. The lust and intimacy needs have already been mentioned; the third is the need for personal security or freedom from anxiety. The great task of early adolescence is to become aware of all three, and to discover how they can be properly integrated. If they are not integrated, any two or all three may collide with one another in ways that can severely handicap subsequent development. For example, Sullivan's discussion of the many pitfalls of adolescent heterosexual experiments implies that a three-way debacle of the following type can occur. If, during the course of lovemaking, a boy has a premature ejaculation, his lust need will be only partially satisfied; he may suffer a loss in personal security because of the anxiety generated by his lack of control, and his need for intimacy can be frustrated if his partner rejects him because of the incident.

Most of Sullivan's material describing this stage of development concerned the pathological consequences of failure to integrate the three major needs, including sexual aberrations such as homosexuality, high levels of autoeroticism (e.g., masturbation), and rejection of the opposite sex (e.g., "They are only good for one thing," or, "They are only after one thing") as persons. Self-rejection can also occur: if the lust need provokes great anxiety, the individual may reject that part of himself related to sex. In extreme cases, this can lead to self-mutilation.

Sullivan closed his discussion of this period by again emphasizing the role of social factors in development. Serious difficulties with sex are not likely to arise if prior psychosocial development has been adequate; if it has been, then the self-system will be strong enough to absorb the anxiety of early-adolescent sex experiences without sustaining any permanent damage.

Late adolescence

This final stage begins when the adolescent makes a satisfactory sexual adjustment:

. . . a person begins late adolescence when he discovers what he likes in the way of genital behavior and how to fit it into the rest of life (Sullivan, p. 297).

Late adolescence goes on until the person establishes a "fully human or mature repertory of interpersonal relations," at which point he may be said to be mature. But some reasonable settlement of genital sex needs must be made before the processes leading to maturity can occur. These processes involve learning in more detail, by personal and vicarious experience, about oneself, others, and the world at large. Most of this experience is in the syntaxic mode, for which the prototype is university education. The person who achieves a satisfactory pattern of sexual behavior, and who then goes to a university, is said to have "a truly extraordinary opportunity" for learning about himself and others. Such learning is prerequisite to mature interpersonal relations because one cannot have them in the absence of the tolerance, perspective, self-respect, and insight into personal needs that come from a broad knowledge of life.

Sullivan ended his discussion of developmental stages by pointing out some of the ways in which adults contrive to function at an immature level. He explained that he did not consider maturity *per se* in any detail because mature people do not frequently come to the attention of a psychiatrist. And his final comment on this matter was that "the greater the degree of maturity, the less will be the interference of anxiety with living. . . ."

ERIKSON AND THE DEVELOPMENT OF PERSONAL IDENTITY

In one of the most interesting books on personality accessible to the general reader, Erikson (1963) offered a developmental framework exclusively concerned with growth of the *conscious self* or *ego*. As a neo-Freudian, his work is generally seen as an extension of Freud's conception of the ego. To understand Erikson, therefore, we must briefly examine Freud's three-part description of personality structure, and the role of the ego in this structure.

Freud believed that personality at first consists of a single component called the *id*, which includes all the basic needs, instincts, and hereditary predispositions of the infant. It operates according to the *pleasure principle* – the id's only concern is to avoid pain and maximize pleasure. It has two means of accomplishing this purpose: *reflex action*, which refers to all automatic, innate capabilities such as crying and sucking; and the *primary process*, which refers to the capacity for wish-fulfilling fantasy or imagination. It is illustrated in adults when, for example, a hungry person daydreams about food.

Ego, the second component of personality, develops because as the infant grows, id alone becomes increasingly incapable of satisfying his needs. Efficient need-satisfaction or maximization of pleasure requires behavior geared to the real world, and the ego is the component of personality that meets this requirement by operating according to the *reality principle*. It is ego's function to match behavior to the objectively real features of the environment. It achieves this purpose by means of the *secondary process*, which is what we ordinarily call *realistic thinking*. This is exemplified in behaviors called *reality testing*, in a child's testing of an action that he thinks will result in some gratification.

The third component of personality to emerge is the *superego* or moral conscience. Superego develops gradually as the child acquires (*internalizes*) the moral values of society transmitted to him by his parents, and later by secular and religious teachings. The primary aim of the superego is to attain approval by distinguishing right from wrong in accord with the standards of society. To do this, it must not only represent these standards, it must also prohibit the expression of socially unacceptable id desires. Superego enforces its prohibitions by imposing guilt feelings if they are violated.

Ego is often described as the harassed mediator of the conflicting demands made by id and superego. It arranges all sorts of compromises that characterize everyday life by specifying the conditions under which id impulses can be gratified without rousing the disapproval of superego. In brief, ego stands as our conscious personality, our self-concept or self-image, our knowledge of who and what we are.

Erikson's major theoretical effort is to show how society influences the growth and development of the ego. The logic whereby psychoanalytic theory indicates that society can shape ego is implied by the manner in which ego develops. If it is to serve as a means of fitting behavior to objective reality, then to the degree that objective reality is determined by social or cultural factors unique to a given society, the ego will in turn be unique to that society. Among persons raised in a highly competitive society, therefore, one will observe highly competitive egos in the sense that such persons will see competitive behaviors as appropriate ways of satisfying their needs.

Erikson's chronological framework for ego development emphasizes how a person's sense of identity evolves during the typical life cycle. His discussion involves the *ego qualities* that emerge at various developmental periods. The life cycle is divided into eight periods. For each period, Erikson gave the particular ego quality that must appear if the person's sense of identity is to develop properly. There is a *crisis* during each age period which takes the form of a conflict between two alternative ego qualities, one being the quality required for healthy normal ego development, the other being the quality associated with abnormal development. The crisis is resolved for most persons when the healthy quality prevails over the unhealthy one. In this connection, Erikson speaks of a *favorable ratio* that should be established for the healthy ego quality.

The following overview lists the eight dichotomous ego qualities, the names of the developmental periods or ages of man when they are supposed to appear, and the chronological age intervals that seem most appropriate.

Ego qualities	Developmental periods	Chronological age
Basic trust vs. basic mistrust	Oral-sensory	0 to 1
Autonomy vs. shame, doubt	Muscular-anal	2 to 3
Initiative vs. guilt	Locomotor-genital	4 to 5
Industry vs. inferiority	Latency	6 to 12
Identity vs. role confusion	Puberty and adolescence	13 to 18
Intimacy vs. isolation	Young adulthood	19 to 25
Generativity vs. stagnation	Adulthood	26 to 40
Ego integrity vs. despair	Maturity	41 - plus

Basic trust vs. basic mistrust

The first indication that an infant is acquiring a basic sense of trust shows up in his physiological need-related behavior. Erikson claimed that such things as ease of feeding and depth of sleep are elementary signs of *social trust*. Then, as the normal mother-child relationship is further developed, a stronger sense of trust is shown when the infant is able to have his mother out of his sight without suffering undue anxiety. Such behavior is thought to demonstrate that the infant's mother has become a stable, reliable feature of his world, an "inner certainty."

The general sense of trust growing out of the consistency and continuity of maternal care does not remain focused entirely on the mother, however. It also includes the infant himself because he becomes able to trust himself. The basis for this self-trust seems to lie in the regularity characterizing mutual activities with the mother. As the infant participates with her in such activities as feeding, he begins to trust his own reactions to be effective and reliable.

Erikson (1963) suggested that the self-trust and trust in mother built up during this period ultimately depend upon the quality of the maternal relationship. His point here is that what the mother does is less important than how she does it.

Mothers create a sense of trust in their children by that kind of administration which in its quality combines sensitive care of the baby's individual needs and a firm sense of personal trustworthiness within the trusted framework of their culture's life style. This forms the basis in the child for a sense of identity which will later combine a sense of being "all right," of being oneself, and of becoming what other people trust one will become (p. 249).

It is also noted that the quality of the maternal relationship serves as a kind of buffer or psychological shock absorber which allows the infant to tolerate the inevitable frustrations he will experience. So long as these frustrations occur in a context of meaningful and continuous care, and an atmosphere of general acceptance, they can be absorbed without ill effects upon personality development.

A sense of basic *mis*trust will develop in infants who experience maternal care which is more or less opposite to what is described above. If the situation is not extreme, then the individual is likely to grow up to be relatively fearful of close, mutual-trust relationships with others. But if the maternal situation is very harsh, then according to Erikson there may be immediate pathological effects such as infantile schizophrenia, or a longer range tendency for the individual to periodically withdraw into solitary states of depression.

Autonomy vs. shame and doubt

During this period the young child first gains muscular control sufficient for purposive actions such as grasping, holding, letting go, crawling, and walking. These abilities allow him to exercise a significant amount of *free choice*, which stands as the primary behavioral basis for a sense of autonomy or independence.

Erikson is careful to warn, however, that the child cannot be left entirely to his own devices; while total permissiveness might provide maximum scope for him to exercise free choice, it will not protect him from seriously harmful consequences. Parents must maintain "firmly reassuring" outer control over the child to protect him against physical harm, and against "the potential anarchy of his as yet untrained sense of discrimination." It seems reasonable to summarize Erikson's view in a colloquial way by saying that the parent's job is not to let the child sink or swim, but to make sure that he learns to swim.

If a simple-minded sink-or-swim policy is adopted, it is likely that instead of being characterized by an increasing sense of autonomy, the child's experience in this period will be dominated by shame and doubt. This can occur when his efforts toward independent action result in frequent failure and/or ridicule. An important aspect of this age period is that along with gross motor skills, the child gains some ability to control his excretory processes. Toilet behavior therefore also provides an opportunity for the exercise of free choice, and the child is very likely to experience shame in this connection if the developmental crisis is not handled appropriately by the parents.

Erikson finally suggests that there can be no autonomy without self-control, but that self-control without self-esteem is not true autonomy. The child who acquires some degree of self-control out of fear may see every new choice situation as dangerously threatening. True autonomy will yield a sense of pride and good will; fearful self-control will yield doubt and shame.

Initiative vs. guilt

Having weathered the stresses of toilet training, and attained a new, vigorous capability for physical action, the four-to-five-year-old displays a zestful, aggressive orientation toward his environment. His behavior is more purposive than ever before and it is organized over longer time intervals. This ability to better organize behavior toward specific goals is what chiefly distinguishes initiative from autonomy. Erikson said that the child delights in his new feeling of power, and experiences great pleasure in the "attack and conquest" of goal objects.

The great danger here, however, is that the child may get carried away with himself. He may throw himself into aggressive or coercive acts that get out of control and thereby generate guilt. For example, one form of pathological behavior in adults occurs when anger leads to the destruction of a love object—human or otherwise—and then is followed almost immediately by extreme guilt and sorrow. But when children show such behavior, say by destroying a favorite toy, it can be understood as a relatively accidental consequence of initiative that has gone out of control.

Erikson also noted that childhood sexuality plays an important role in generating guilt. While he did not go into the details of the Oedipus complex it is clear from his mention of the incest taboo, castration anxiety, and superego, that he saw the child engaging in sex-related rivalries of the traditional Freudian type. It is further argued, however, that out of this situation the child gains sufficient insight to distinguish between socially approved and disapproved domains of behavior. He can exercise initiative and find "pleasurable accomplishment" in the former area.

At any rate, the "oedipal" stage results not only in the oppressive establishment of a moral sense restricting the horizon of the permissible; it also sets the direction toward the possible and the tangible which permits the dreams of early childhood to be attached to the goals of an active adult life (Erikson, p. 258).

Industry vs. inferiority

The next great task for the child is to learn to win approval by becoming productive. This means that he must accommodate himself to a tool world, in which reading, writing, and cooperation with others in constructive activities are the important criteria for acceptance. Therefore, through most of the Freudian latency period, the child should be gaining a sense of industry by acquiring appropriate skills.

The danger of inferiority comes from the possibility that he will not learn the proper skills. When a child fails to master these prerequisites for a sense of industry, he is likely to develop a sense of inadequacy and inferiority, which can leave him in something of an identity limbo: caught between a family context that he has had to renounce, because of the oedipal conflict, and a larger social context (e.g., the school) that he cannot fully enter.

If he despairs of his tools and skills or of his status among his tool partners, he may be discouraged from identification with them and with a section of the tool world. To lose the hope of such "industrial" association may pull him back to the more isolated, less tool-conscious familial rivalry of the oedipal time (Erikson, p. 260).

Erikson refers to this period as being socially decisive because the child should gain a rudimentary sense of the *technological ethos* of his culture. Such a sense seems decisive for the individual because without it, his subsequent development is likely to tend either toward *alienation,* rejection of his culture; or *conformity,* thoughtless submission to the culture.

Identity vs. role confusion

With the onset of puberty and adolescence, the teen-ager goes through a grand reevaluation of his identity. According to Erikson, he questions all the continuities and regularities relied upon earlier in life, and he may "refight many of the battles of earlier years," because he now needs a more sophisticated, better-integrated sense of identity. The most direct cause of this condition is the "physiological revolution" we call puberty.

Genital maturation, with its strong new sex urges, is one major force leading the drive toward a more elaborate ego structure. Another important factor is the speed of bodily growth and change. The youth must incorporate a variety of outward physical changes—body hair, height and weight, sex organs, and usually a good batch of pimples—into his ego. And there is finally the young person's new recognition of the adult tasks that lie ahead of him. How is he to go about functioning in society as an adult? Occupational choice here comes to occupy an important position in his conscious identity. Moreover, since occupational goals and the likelihood of achieving them are intricately involved with status in most societies, and status is in turn related to sexual matters, this particular issue is very salient as an integrating factor in the adolescent's ego structure. Erikson suggested that "the tangible promise of a career" provides a central regularity for the young person, around which he can organize other elements of his ego identity.[5]

Role confusion can occur if the adolescent does not establish a proper sex identity, or more commonly, if he cannot settle on an occupational identity. To cope with this confusion the adolescent may overidentify with certain clique or crowd heroes. Falling in love is said to be another consequence of role confusion. In this instance, however, love will not be primarily a sexual matter. Instead, it is seen as an effort to define personal identity by projecting a poorly integrated ego image upon another person, who may reflect it back in a better-organized fashion. The adolescent might presumably find himself in this way because the other person can provide stability and a standard for sorting out ego elements. Erikson commented that this is why young love may largely be conversation.

[5]This point brings back some relevant examples from my own adolescence. At about the age of 14, I applied for admission to a high prestige high school, took a test, and was given an interview. It was generally known that during the interview one was supposed to emphasize that he wanted to be either a scientist, doctor, or engineer. I was well prepared to do this, but had an attack of precocious integrity at the last moment and said that I didn't really know what I wanted to be. Later, while attending a much less prestigious high school, I was given a routine vocational guidance interview. Since I still didn't know what I wanted to be, the counselor advised me to choose a vocation related to some line of work done by my relatives. But I didn't like any of the things my relatives did, at which point the counselor warned me about the dangers of being a good-for-nothing bum.

He also discussed the adolescent mind as a *moratorium* characterizing the psychosocial stage intermediate to childhood and adulthood. It tends to be an ideological mind, in this connection, because in searching for values that can structure his identity, the adolescent is very sensitive to creeds or programs which define good and evil in ways that he can accept.

Intimacy vs. isolation

The young adult is ready for social as well as sexual intimacy with another person if, by the end of adolescence, he has established a strong personal identity. As Erikson saw it, intimacy is a matter of merging one's own identity with that of another person. Because any such merger involves the risk that one's identity may be obscured or overshadowed, or somehow lost, only persons with a relatively strong identity are able to tolerate the conditions of intimacy. In brief, a person is not likely to expose himself to the hazards of intimacy unless he has a firm sense of who and what he is.

Genuine intimacy is quite different from adolescent love. The former involves commitment to another person, the establishment of "concrete affiliations and partnerships" which require sacrifices of some of one's own desires, and compromises with the desires of the other. Because he saw these conditions as definitive of the fusion of identities necessary for genuine intimacy, Erikson suggested that to maintain such a relationship people must have self-discipline or ethical strength. By contrast, as mentioned earlier, adolescent love may be no more than an effort to explore one's own identity through the use of another person.

Isolation can occur if a person's sense of identity is too weak to sustain the uncertainties of intimacy. In this case one's identity structure is seriously threatened by the demands of intimacy; the commitments and responsibilities will seem harsh, unreasonable, or too restrictive of personal freedom.[6] It also seems clear that a person with a weak ego identity may experience serious ambivalence: on the one hand he will be drawn toward intimate relationships, but on the other he will be repelled or frightened by them when they become intense enough to demand a strong commitment.

Generativity vs. stagnation

In his discussion of this and the following stage of development, Erikson went beyond the periods usually covered by developmental theories. The material here is relatively sparse, because most research does not extend so far into the life cycle. And, as was mentioned regarding Sullivan, the practicing therapist does not often have much experience with older persons who are reasonably well adjusted.

Erikson nevertheless argued for a stage of psychosexual and psychosocial development beyond the genital, which he calls the *generative*. He bases his case on the assumption that the achievement of a relatively happy geni-

---

[6]Erikson's conception of isolation here seems to fit the case of teen-agers who often readily identify themselves with a bachelor uncle or unmarried aunt. The teen-ager responds to an ego structure he sees as similar to his own, while the adult can enjoy the relationship because it does not demand more than he is able to give. This idea is further supported by the fact that such relationships usually die out when the adolescent matures.

tal adjustment will eventually lead toward an "expansion of ego-interests" and to a "libidinal investment" in that which is being generated during sexual intimacy. In other words, the argument seems to be that while at one point in development good heterosexual genital experiences are an end in themselves, if they are achieved on a regular basis they gradually can become a means toward a higher end: producing children. Or, to put it yet another way, part of the felt meaning of good genital sex experiences will come to include the creation of children. Generativity is thus seen to be essentially an interest in one's offspring, a concern with the new generation.

Generativity, then, is primarily the concern in establishing and guiding the next generation, although there are individuals who, through misfortune or because of special and genuine gifts in other directions, do not apply this drive to their own offspring. And indeed, the concept generativity is meant to include such more popular synonyms as *productivity* and *creativity,* which, however, cannot replace it (Erikson, p. 267).

If the enrichment of adult life described as generativity does not develop, stagnation and a sense of personal impoverishment may set in. This is often discussed generally as *middle-aged crisis;* it can manifest itself in complaints about what the person has missed in life, or about the meaninglessness of life. In extreme cases, Erikson suggested that stagnation will lead people to childish forms of self-indulgence: treating themselves as if they were their own children, so to speak. Another related sign of serious stagnation is early invalidism or the excessive self-concern of the hypochondriac. Older men who marry very young women and treat them as pampered children also appear to fit this discussion.

Ego integrity vs. despair

When a person who has lived most of his life stands at the brink of old age, facing the certainty of death, what can sustain him? What can protect him from fear and despair? Erikson said that it must be a quality he called *ego integrity.* Not being able to offer a clear definition of this quality, he spoke instead of the constituents or ingredients of ego integrity: dignity, practical wisdom, belief in the order and meaning of life, acceptance of one's own life pattern, and a sense of continuity with the things that have gone on before one's life and things that will follow after one is gone. Erikson further described ego integrity as the end product of the prior seven stages of development:

Only in him who in some way has taken care of things and people and has adapted himself to the triumphs and disappointments adherent to being, the originator of others or the generator of products and ideas — only in him may gradually ripen the fruit of these seven stages (p. 268).

Theoretically then, ego integrity seems to stand as a final synthesis of all prior ego qualities. Although he did not explain exactly how this final stage comes about, Erikson suggested that it can be achieved in many different ways. The person is described in this connection as a "cultural entity" because the norms of his culture will (a) have determined in large part how his earlier ego conflicts were resolved, and (b) be reflected as important elements in his final state of ego integrity. In a certain sense the integrated mature person can thus be seen as a living microcosm of his culture.

The discussion of ego development ends with a deliberately circular aphorism on the relation between infantile trust and adult integrity. It is a comment which expresses much of Erikson's theoretical understanding of personality development in a form that approximates folk wisdom: ". . . healthy children will not fear life if their elders have integrity enough not to fear death" (p. 269).

THE COGNITIVE DEVELOPMENT THEORIES

At this point the reader must shift the focus of his thinking rather sharply away from the emotional wellsprings of human behavior, and address himself instead to the role of conscious, rational thought. We have heretofore been immersed in processes that are described theoretically with such constructs as libido, anxiety, trust, intimacy, and the like. But in moving to the cognitive end of the theoretical continuum, we enter a different, much calmer conceptual world, one to which such volcanic matters as love, lust, and fear seem quite irrelevant.

If, as we have already indicated, Freud is the chief theoretical proprietor of the netherworld of personality, Piaget has theoretical title to the upper reaches. (The reader who loves metaphorical statements may appreciate a slightly different version of the foregoing: Freud owns personality from the neck down, Piaget from the neck up.) In any case, starting with Piaget, the developmental frameworks discussed below are primarily concerned with the growth of intellect, the manner in which we acquire knowledge of the world, and the way that knowledge influences our behavior.

PIAGET

Piaget's importance can best be conveyed by explaining that in the scientific community, he is increasingly being accorded the same influential place that was once reserved exclusively for Freud. This is because his ideas about intelligence and thinking in children are recognized as having the same sort of revolutionary impact on our conception of man as Freud's work has had. But unlike many of Freud's ideas, Piaget's have not yet been absorbed into the general culture. So it is necessary to begin by explaining a bit about why his work has such importance.

Furth (1969) called Piaget's work revolutionary because it forces revision of most traditional assumptions concerning human intelligence, just as Freud's forced revision of traditional assumptions about human motives. Another parallel between the two theorists is their emphasis on the developmental processes whereby aspects of personality traditionally taken for granted as "givens," actually evolve in a very complex fashion. For example, Freud shows that the moral aspect of personality is not innate, but can be understood to grow out of the prohibitions imposed by parents. Piaget shows that intellectual aspects of personality, (e.g., realistic thinking involving objective time, cause and effect) are also not innate, but grow out of experience with the environment. Finally, just as the ultimate effect of Freud's work has been to revolutionize the emotional side of child care and education, Piaget's seems destined to revolutionize the intellectual side. One hears already of efforts to develop intelligence tests and instructional methods geared to his work.

Piaget described cognitive development as unfolding in four distinct periods, and development within each of these periods follows a sequential pattern in which various cognitive structures are formed through the workings of adaptive thought processes. On the whole, then, his theory can be seen as a hierarchy; a system of four progressive cycles or wheels, each containing its own subordinate cycle or wheel-within-a-wheel. Before going on to discuss the specific periods, however, some of the general theoretical concepts that are important in all of them should be mentioned.

The structural unit of cognitive development is called the *schema* or *cognitive schema*. It is difficult to find a simple definition for this because it refers to virtually all forms of organized knowledge as well as to organized behavioral capabilities which do not seem to involve conscious knowledge. For instance, the sucking and grasping behaviors of the infant are ordinarily described as innate responses. But for Piaget they are schemas, just as reading and writing are schemas, because while the former may appear to be involuntary acts, they are, like the latter, organized forms of behavior that have a definite meaning and purpose. Flavell (1963) noted that a schema can be any set of actions coordinated toward a particular goal; any repeatable, interconnected sequence of acts that have a *core meaning*. Schemas are also *mobile* in the sense that they can function across a variety of situations involving different objects. And schemas are said to be adaptive structures because from primitive, inefficient beginnings they can become highly sophisticated: the year-old child has a much smoother, sophisticated sucking schema than the two-month-old, and the five-year-old who can suck through a straw and blow bubbles has a much more elaborate sucking schema than does the one-year-old. In sum, the schema is an adaptive cognitive structure that allows actions to be coordinated toward specific ends in many different ways in many different situations.

A second important general construct concerns the means by which schemas evolve to fit new situations. This involves two related processes called assimilation and accommodation. Very briefly, *assimilation* is the process whereby new problems are dealt with by employing preexisting schemas. The young infant probably starts sucking his thumb by assimilating this new object into his preexisting nipple-sucking schema. *Accommodation* is the process whereby new schemas develop out of old ones to deal with new problems. For my children, learning to suck through a straw clearly required accommodation of their prior sucking schemas, because both went through quite a bit of frustrating effort before they were able to do it. Another example is learning to ride a tricycle: the prior walking schema must accommodate into a pedaling schema. And when the child changes to a bicycle, it seems as if his prior pedaling schema must be elaborated via accommodation into a pedaling-and-balancing schema.

There is no obvious, definitive criterion that can be used to distinguish between assimilation and accommodation behavior. However, it is plausible to assume that a child is assimilating when he acquires a new ability without much difficulty by making a few minimal changes in a prior schema. Accommodation is indicated by greater difficulty that requires incorporation of a significant new skill or skills into the prior schema. When accommodation takes place, the new schema should appear categorically different from, but inclusive of, the relevant schema that preceded it. In this connection, an example of technology operating to smooth over the difference between assimilation and accommodation can be seen in bicycle riding. Up until a few years ago, the change from tricycle to bicycle was sharp, obvious, and difficult. But now bicycles equipped with training wheels have blurred the distinction to the point where one may not be sure where assimilation ends and accommodation begins.

The final major idea that should be mentioned here is *equilibration*, which denotes a very general process whereby separate schemas become organized into belief systems. An adult who goes to live in a new cultural environment, for example, will acquire a variety of new schemas about that culture. Invariably, he will soon experience some contradictions among these schemas, but they will eventually cease to be disturbing or even noteworthy, as he fits the different schemas together into a harmonious belief system about the new culture. The crucially important aspect of this whole matter is that the frustrations generated by the initial contradictions literally force the person to develop an organized belief system, because without it he will go on having frustrating experiences. Baldwin (1968) suggested that any new, relatively unorganized belief system is likely to contain ideas that will sooner or later collide with one another. These inconsistent or contradictory ideas generate the force toward harmony which leads to equilibration – a process whereby ideas are organized or reorganized into a more coherent system. The essence of this process seems to be its thrust toward resolving discrepancies between the schemas existing at any given stage of cognitive development.[7]

Piaget saw cognitive development proceeding through the four main periods, and following the approximate age sequences that are listed below.

The sensorimotor period . . .	birth to 2 years.
The preoperational period . . .	2 to 7 years.
The concrete operations period . . .	7 to 11 years.
The formal operations period . . .	11 years onward.

The sensorimotor period

This first 2-year interval has been closely studied and resolved into six subperiods of cognitive development which range from abilities given as innate reflexes, to the ability to internally represent (imagine) aspects of the

---

[7]The equilibration process is reminiscent of the dialectic: thesis, antithesis, synthesis. Most psychologists also recognize the same principle of cognitive equilibrium underlying Festinger's idea of *consonance,* Heider's concept of *balance,* and Osgood's notion of *congruity.* (See Flavell, pp. 237–241 for more detail.)

environment. While the six-stage progression cannot be described in full detail here, some of the stages are discussed below to illustrate how carefully Piaget has tried to reconstruct the primary building blocks of human thinking.

During the first month of life the neonate is limited to the exercise of reflexes. Piaget referred to reflexes such as sucking, grasping, and vision as *innate schemas,* because they are organized behaviors which become more sophisticated with the passage of time and the workings of assimilation and accommodation. Briefly, it is argued that the only major difference between certain reflexes and later learned cognitive schemas is that the former are innate. The first clear signs of adaptability or learning appear in the second stage of infancy (1 to 4 months). Thumb sucking is a case in point: during this period the infant seems to know the difference between thumb and nipple sucking, whereas earlier he does not. Another example is the development of vision. During his first month the infant will fix his eyes on a stable object, but during the 1-to-4-month period, he acquires the ability to *look* at an object. That is, instead of fixation, there are small eye movements which seem to circumscribe the object in a way best denoted by the term *looking.* In sum, during this 1-to-4-month period innate schemas such as sucking and vision are said to go through a general process of adaptation. Then, during the next chronological subperiod (4 to 8 months) the general process of adaptation becomes more deliberate or purposive, and Piaget described this third sub-period as being characterized by the *intentional adaptation* of schemas.

Over the whole 2-year span of the sensorimotor period—which takes its name from the fact that most of the schemas here are sensory and/or motor affairs—the infant makes three successive and quite general forms of cog-nitive progress. First he begins to integrate different innate schemas (e.g., he does a more effective job of grasping his bottle as he sucks from it). Along with this sort of integration there is also the ability to coordinate inputs from different sense modalities: auditory and visual stimuli become closely tied cues to familiar events.

The second important form of progress is the infant's ability to perceive his physical environment as stable. Earlier, he behaves as if the environment only exists by virtue of his own direct contact with it. In this connection, Piaget's observations show that the law of early infant perception can be put colloquially as "out of sight out of mind." Later, however, the infant will actively search for lost or hidden objects, and this behavior is inter-preted as evidence for the development of a more stable conception of the en-vironment.

By the end of the sensorimotor period one can observe behaviors being organized in accord with specific intentions or purposes. At the 18-to-24-month age interval the child is quite able to decide that he wants something not physically present (an object that he can internally represent to himself) and then put together a sequence of several actions designed to get it. Behav-ior of this type is ordinarily labeled *goal-oriented* or *goal-directed,* but one of its more important implications tends to be overlooked: in carrying out such activities, the young child is giving evidence of a rudimentary ability to make predictions; to make decisions or judgments in the face of uncertainty and to act upon them.

The preoperational period

During the preoperational subperiod the child is transformed from an organism whose most intelligent functions are sensory-motor, overt acts to one whose upper-limit cognitions are inner, symbolic manipulations of reality (Flavell, 1963, p. 151).

Translating Flavell's statement into phylogenetic terms, it can be argued that development during this period marks a dramatic shift from functioning at the lower-organism level to functioning at the uniquely human level. The most obvious evidence fitting this thesis is the terrific growth of language ability that occurs during this period.

A very general feature of thinking during the preoperational period is its *egocentrism*. Children seem unable to understand or imagine viewpoints other than their own. In many respects, it is as if only his own thought products – predictions, conclusions, perceptions – are real to the preoperational child. At the level of logic, this means that when the child posits some causal sequence and his parents point out that it won't work because of an internal contradiction in the sequence, the child will not understand. At the level of simple morality, egocentrism means that when parents admonish their child not to hurt another because "How would you like it if someone did that to you?" the child will not see the point because he cannot put himself in the position of the other. And at the level of perception, Piaget and others have done experiments which show that the preoperational child cannot shift his perspective. That is, if a child sees a model of a village from the north, he cannot imagine what the display would look like to someone seeing it from the south.

Relevant to egocentrism is what Piaget describes as the preoperational child's apparent inability to *decenter*. Many observations indicate that once he centers his attention on a single striking feature of an object, the child seems unable to take into account other relevant features of the object. This inability to decenter is probably what makes young children so susceptible to visual illusions or garden-variety magic tricks.

Another characteristic of preoperational thought is *irreversibility*, referring to the child's apparent inability to reverse his cognitive operations. Once he accepts a premise, and, in connection with it, pursues a course of reasoning leading to an erroneous conclusion, one cannot tell him that his conclusion is wrong and thus get him to go back over his reasoning to discover the source of error. To an exasperated parent, it may seem as if he simply won't do it, but Piaget's work suggested that he simply can't do it. His cognitive development has not advanced far enough to allow him to reconstruct his own thought patterns. It is noteworthy that many of the characteristics of preoperational thought uncovered by Piaget were traditionally understood as evidence of the willful, selfish nature of preschool children, and such evidence was frequently cited in support of all sorts of atrocious practices designed to correct these evils.

Piaget specified other characteristics of preoperational thought in addition to those mentioned above, but all of them tended to converge on two generalizations. First, preoperational thought has an arbitrary, immediate quality: things are what they seem to be and other things being equal, they are likely to seem to be what the child wants them to be. Second, as Flavell (1963) so aptly noted of the preoperational child, ". . . he thinks but he cannot think about his own thinking."

Why should this be the case? Why shouldn't preoperational thinking develop in a smooth, constructive fashion toward what we recognize as the normal adult capabilities? Piaget offered a complicated explanation (see Flavell's interpretation, 1963, pp. 152–156) based on the assumption of confusion or disturbance in the processes of assimilation and accommodation. Apparently, these processes can be overloaded or swamped by the new verbal and motor skills that develop during the preschool period. Throughout much of this period, the child must be equilibrating schemas from the past, but at the same time he must assimilate new experiences to some of these schemas. As if this were not enough, he must also develop new schemas by accommodating to certain new experiences. Under such conditions, arbitrary and frequently changing modes of behavior and thought seem quite inevitable.

The concrete operations period

It is during this period that the child becomes able to carry out a wide range of relatively concrete mental operations. A heavily researched example of concrete operations involves the *conservation schema:* the principle or rule that a quantity remains the same as long as nothing is added to or subtracted from it. Piaget and others have demonstrated that if a preoperational child is shown a change in the form of a given quantity, as when a ball of clay is kneaded into the form of a long snake, he reports that there is now more clay than before. The same occurs when a given amount of liquid is poured from a wide low beaker into a narrow tube: the younger child reports that there is now more liquid than before because "it looks bigger, taller." But the older, concrete operational child is not led astray. No matter how a quantity is manipulated he will maintain the conservation principle.

Smedslund (1961) described experiments which put children's grasp of the conservation schema to a rigorous test. He arranged a situation in which he could surreptitiously add or subtract a significant amount to a given quantity while changing its form. Children who then responded in accord with conservation by saying there had been no change, were confronted with evidence showing that indeed, the quantity *had* changed. Result: those who did not have a strong conservation schema abandoned it by accepting the fact that a change in form led to a change in quantity. But children with a strong conservation schema did what we would expect most adults to do; they remonstrated with the experimenter, arguing that they must have been tricked, that the experimenter must have cheated. Smedslund's work thus revealed how tenaciously an important cognitive schema will be defended even in the face of contradictory evidence, presumably because it is a keystone in the equilibrated cognitive organization of one who has passed strongly into the stage of concrete operations.

Research by Bruner and his associates (1966) along this line suggested that many of the differences between the preoperational and concrete operational child are due to the former's vulnerability to perceptual evidence.

When the younger child encounters a contradiction between an abstraction and something that appears perceptually compelling, he will abandon the abstraction. Bruner argued that the thinking of younger children is dominated by perception, and most of the relevant research implies that with growth, intelligence becomes more and more liberated from that which is immediate and given by perception.

Along with conservation, the primary-school-age child acquires understanding of a whole spectrum of abstractions involved in adaptation to the everyday environment. In one area, Piaget has done work that is particularly fascinating to social scientists. He showed that younger children ignore intentions when assessing guilt. Thus, in one of the stories created for studying moral thought in children, if a child is described as having spilled ink over his father's papers, younger (preoperational) subjects are not concerned about whether this occurred by accident or not. Instead, they focus upon the amount of damage caused, and set punishments accordingly. Older children try to determine whether or not the act was intentional and tend to ignore the amount of damage caused when setting punishments.

Over and above the changing conceptual principles or cognitive schemas that characterize this period, it is also marked by a new global stability and relative calm in the child's thinking. His schemas are more coherent, better organized, and lie in a substantially equilibrated structure:

Much more than his younger counterpart, he gives the decided impression of possessing a solid cognitive bedrock, something flexible and plastic and yet consistent and enduring, with which he can structure the present in terms of the past without undue strain and dislocation, that is, without the ever-present tendency to tumble into the perplexity and contradiction which mark the preschooler (Flavell, 1963, p. 165).

The formal operations period

Piaget and his associates have studied the course of cognitive development very carefully up through adolescence. This does not necessarily mean that every important feature of thinking is fully established by the end of adolescence; but virtually all of the cognitive development literature stops at this point and, in principle, it seems that the adolescent can have all of the substantive intellectual abilities of the mature adult.

The outstanding aspect of formal operational thinking is its *symbolic* character: the adolescent can deal with his world through symbols. Indeed, the symbolic world may in many instances come to have more meaning to him than the world of physical reality. However, it must be understood that symbolism is being used here in its broadest sense to denote the opposite of physical reality. The adolescent's ability for symbolic thought is nothing less than a broad highroad to intellectual freedom — freedom to conceptualize the world in ways that are not constrained by the imperatives of immediate, physical reality.

The seven-to-eleven-year-old's thinking is freed to some extent from dependence upon perceptual realities, but his symbolic ability is quite limited. He can accomplish relatively simple mental operations that are one step removed from immediate reality, but his general engagement with the world is still very much at the level of immediate experience. By contrast, the adolescent engages the world not only as it appears in his immediate experience, but also as he can imagine it might be under other, hypothetical conditions. He is, in short, able to see that that which is real and immediate is just one special case of that which is possible.

Another approach to cognitive development in adolescence is through Piaget's discussion of formal operational thought as *propositional*. The adolescent goes beyond the younger child's ability to organize his experience according to specific propositional statements (schemas) such as the "if . . . then" rule of conservation. He can also deal with more than one propositional statement at a time by relating them to one another, thereby creating a higher-order logical structure. In this connection, Flavell notes that formal operations ". . . are really operations performed upon the results of prior (concrete) operations," as can be seen in a game of chess.

It is not very hard to learn how all the chess pieces move. But I can remember my own efforts at age eleven or twelve with a friend of the same age: we would usually give up in mutual disgust at our inability to play effectively. By the time we were fourteen we were doing much better. Moreover, we invented a rule for ourselves that clearly reflects one characteristic of formal operational thought. If either one of us made a stupid mistake, we would replay the move. Because of this rule we actually played two games — the real one including our stupid errors, and the one that was possible if we excluded stupid errors.

Other examples of formal operational thinking include algebra, the geometries, and statistics. Historically, all of these can be seen as inventions designed to aid specific kinds of logical thought. They are successful inventions because they organize and serve as external projections or models for certain kinds of formal operational thinking.[8]

The transition from concrete to formal operations seems to be theoretically explainable as a consequence of two cognitive changes. First, as the child moves into adolescence, important cognitive schemas and operations become more and more independent of physical reality. An extreme example from chess is the ability to play without a board when moves are described verbally. Second, it is apparent that as preadolescent cognitive schemas concerning immediate reality become integrated with one another (equilibrated) into harmonious systems, immediate reality can be handled with much greater ease. In theoretical terms, this means that symbolic propositions can be generated more rapidly, and if this is the case then there would seem to be a greater likelihood that thinking *about* propositions will take place.

Because so much can be said about the formal operational period, as indeed, many more things can be said about the other periods as well, it is almost impossible to find a natural stopping place when discussing Piaget. His chronology of cognitive development has been scouted and an attempt to

---

[8]Fascinating questions of epistemology arise here. For example, can a man be a good chess player without being good at math? Since there are such people, the answer must be yes, but one would want to add that such a man would probably be a good *latent* mathematician. In a more formal theoretical connection relevant to studies of human judgment processes, Egon Brunswik commented some years ago that man often behaves as an "intuitive statistician."

convey some of its essential substance and flavor has been made. Subsequent chapters will provide opportunities for further discussion.

WERNER'S ORTHOGENETIC VIEW OF MENTAL DEVELOPMENT

In his *Comparative Psychology of Mental Development* (1961) and in research growing out of his theoretical ideas, Heinz Werner provided a viewpoint for personality development that is unique because, contrary to most other developmental theorists, he did not split apart from one another cognitive and emotional aspects of personality. Instead, a good part of his work proceeded from the assumption that psychological phenomena such as emotions, sensations, perceptions, and thoughts are all bound together in mental life. His frequent use of the phrase *mental life* is also significant: he considered virtually all conscious activity – how people think and behave insofar as these matters can be described by the persons themselves or by an outside observer.

Despite the wide scope of his work, Werner is legitimately called a cognitive theorist because he concentrated upon the development of conscious thinking. The contradiction implied here – how can a cognitive theorist properly emphasize thinking without ignoring or deemphasizing other aspects of personality – is more apparent than real. The genius of Werner's work is precisely that he offered a way through this apparent contradiction by arguing that what we see as everyday adult logical thought develops out of a variegated mass of mental phenomena. For Werner (1961), normal adult thinking is never of a piece; it always partakes in some degree of sensory and emotional forms of experience that frequently cannot be verbalized.

It may be said that mental life has different strata. At one time man behaves "primitively" and at another he becomes relatively "cultured" or "civilized." . . . primitive modes of behavior in the normal adult not only appear under certain extraordinary conditions, but are continually present as the basis of all mental being, and are of vital importance in supporting the highest forms of mentality (Werner, p. 4).

Good examples of what Werner is getting at here can be found in the problem area he called *physiognomic perception*. As adults, we commonly perceive inanimate objects according to their *geometrical-technical* attributes; size, shape, color, and related characteristics. But we form impressions of animate objects such as persons according to dynamic attributes which we take to be expressive of their inner states. For example, when we examine a person's physiognomy – his facial expression – we treat it as indicative of some inner state such as happiness or sadness. Werner therefore uses the phrase physiognomic perception to describe any case in which the physical attributes of an object are used to infer the inner state of that object. Those of us who own German shepherds can always tell their inner state in this fashion by glancing at the carriage of their tail and ears. And a good mechanic can sometimes describe the inner state of a car engine by listening to it. If it is objected that these are simply cases of learning by association rather than physiognomic perception, consider instead the classic physiognomic perception experiment by Krauss (in Werner, 1961). He asked subjects to

match the words *iron, silver,* and *gold* to the three lines below. Eighty percent of subjects invariably chose the first as iron, the second as gold, and the
third as silver. The experiment was first done almost forty years ago in Ham-
burg, but has been repeated in the U.S. with the same basic result. Werner's
contention that normal adult thinking involves much that we ordinarily tend
to ignore or consider childish — the look and feel of a car is supposed to be less
important to an adult than its horsepower — can thus be supported experimentally.

Iron	Silver	Gold

Werner does not provide a general age-related chronology of development. We have here again a kind of paradox: how can a theorist be considered developmental if he does not provide at least a broadly stated chronological scheme for development? But again Werner's ideas pass through and
beyond the apparent paradox. He argues that our understanding of mental
growth (developmental psychology) should not be tied to a literal, age-related
chronology. Instead, specific mental abilities should be seen as following a
sequential pattern that may be quite independent of age *per se.*

At the base of Werner's treatise is the formal principle that every genetic sequence
has an intrinsically required order and direction. This developmental psychology
does not deal with actual historic succession but rather with the functional conditions
for primitive and advanced forms of cognition (Scheerer, 1954, p. 136).

The general principles

Werner's major theoretical ideas about mental development all follow from a
fundamental *orthogenetic principle* or law of development: all living systems grow from an initially simple and relatively undifferentiated state toward a state of complex differentiation and organization. The obvious model
is the human embryo (Werner once taught courses in embryology), in which
various parts slowly emerge, become distinct, and eventually are integrated
into an organized system. Differentiation therefore leads toward integration.
Werner believed that this general law of biological development also held
sway over psychological development.

He saw mental development proceeding in accord with four specific principles, each of which elaborates a different facet of the more general orthogenetic principle.

1. Diffuseness-articulation

This principle concerns the structural aspect of perception and thinking. It
states that all thought structures start by being quite diffuse or broad, and
then become articulated, that is, identifiable as a particular structure with

particular functions. For example, as they acquire language, children begin by using single words or even meaningless syllables to communicate in a very diffuse fashion. The first "word" in the vocabulary of one of my children was "bwah," which meant anything from "I am thirsty (or hungry)" to "I want more dessert" or "How come you don't serve my juice chilled instead of at room temperature?" Linguistic structures of thought become more articulated as the child progresses to the use of real words, phrases, and sentences.

2. Rigidity-flexibility

This principle refers to a developmental trend toward flexibility of response. Such response flexibility can operate in at least two different ways. First, there is flexibility in the degree to which a child learns to grade his response to suit the situation. For example, almost any frustration for a three-year-old may result in a maximum crying response. Older children learn to gear their crying to the level of their frustration. Second, flexibility implies a repertoire of different responses which can be employed in a given situation. The youngster who is hit by another child for the first time may simply stand crying. He will later probably acquire the usual set of options: hitting back, running away, or using the nearest toy as a weapon.

3. Syncretic-discrete

In this distinction between different kinds of experience, Werner suggested that conscious experience is initially a global affair in which everything is rolled together — knowledge, thoughts, and emotions are an undifferentiated mass. Later, experience is sorted into different categories of meaning, thereby becoming more discrete. *Synesthesia*, the crossing over of different sense modalities, is one example of syncretic perception. It involves such phenomena as seeing colors for particular sounds, as when a child may listen to an exciting piece of music and call it "red music." Our language itself reflects a certain degree of syncretism; why else is some music called the blues and not the reds or the greens? Another type of syncretism involves the fusion of structure, function, and emotion. Werner (1961) mentioned an example in which a young child examined a sharp buttonhook and called it "cruel." Its structure is such that it can be used to rip and tear, therefore it is by its nature a cruel instrument.

If several mental functions or phenomena, which would appear as distinct from each other in a mature state of consciousness, are merged without differentiation into one activity or into one phenomenon, we may speak of a *syncretic function* or a *syncretic phenomenon.* . . . Conversely, all those mental contents, acts, and meanings which represent something relatively specific, singular, and unambiguous may be termed *discrete* (1961, p. 53).

4. Concrete-abstract

Werner here was very close to Piaget in stating the principle that conceptual thinking, which is initially concrete in the sense that it is tied to immediate physical reality, gradually becomes more abstract as it becomes independent of immediate reality. In support of this statement Werner cited many of the early studies on causality and time and space carried out by Piaget. It seems clear that the concrete-abstract principle involves virtually the same rationale that was taken up in the prior discussion of the manner in which perception is said to dominate conceptual thinking.

The developmental perspective

It should be reemphasized that Werner saw the four aspects of mental development listed above as very general, applying not so much to individuals of different chronological ages as to mental phenomena *per se*. Even though in a normative sense one tends to see these principles operating at different age levels, and can draw convenient examples that are age specific, it should be clear that for Werner these principles can be operative at any age. When an adult encounters a very novel experience for the first time — say riding in a jet — he is quite liable to go through many if not all of the processes described above. His ideas about jets will at first be concrete, limited to the immediate reality of the first ride; they will certainly be in some degree syncretic — the sound, smell, and feel of the thing will color his rational judgments about jet flight. And his thinking about jets will probably remain somewhat rigid and diffuse until he has gained further experience.

Werner described mental processes characterized by diffusion, rigidity, syncretism, and concreteness as *primitive*. One of his most provocative efforts involved drawing together evidence showing gross similarities between the thinking of children, psychotic mental patients, and primitive or uncivilized people. For persons in all three groups, for example, the gross behavior of another person is often treated as much more important than his intentions. Piaget's work showing this phenomenon in connection with the moral judgments of children was mentioned earlier. Werner quoted anthropological reports showing the same phenomenon in a primitive tribe. A woman who built a fire outside her hut to heat some water was blamed for the death of a child who fell into it. The punishment deemed appropriate in this case was the death of her own child.

The three groups also parallel each other in their belief in magic. Werner's (1961) discussion of "the fundamental ideas of magic as an expression of primitive conceptualization" suggested, among other things, that syncretic modes of thought underlie magical beliefs. Such thinking will lead to the assumption of false causal relationships. Thus, it seems that magical beliefs based on syncretism are what lead some tribesmen to eat the heart of a lion to become braver, and lead a child who wants to be a good swimmer to eat a lot of fish.

Werner did not claim that children, primitives, and psychotics think identically. His comparisons between the three groups were an effort to show universal conformity to the orthogenetic principle. As normal children in civilized societies progress toward the differentiated, organized thought characteristic of adults, they at certain times exhibit primitive thinking characteristic of uncivilized men, for whom thinking probably remains primitive because their environment does not require complexity. Without the infrastructure of civilization, there would seem to be no pressure on thinking to evolve toward such attributes as abstractness and flexibility. Psychotics, finally, are often persons whose experiences in life have been so severe that in one way or another they seek refuge by retreating to a more primitive level of thought. If a person feels extreme guilt at having caused some terrible event, for example, perhaps one way to cope with the feeling is to regress from conventional forms of cause-effect thinking. All of us may approach this condition on occasions when something goes badly for us and we yearn, however momentarily, to be little children again.

Taken together, Werner's ideas contribute an important base for understanding conscious thought processes as these emerge from a mix of cognitive and emotional factors. The orthogenetic principle suggests that a primitive personality is one in which the mix is so fine that cognitive and emotional factors cannot be distinguished from one another. And it seems obvious that the less developed the personality, the more likely it is to be dominated by emotional factors. Of course, this sort of statement might be generated equally well from a Freudian or Piagetian base of ideas. But we are led to it much more easily by virtue of Werner and the invaluable glimpses he provides of how different modes of thought may influence behavior. Anyone interested in Werner's ideas would also do well to read the novel *Steppenwolf* by Herman Hesse, who treats of similar matters in a very dramatic, Freudian manner.

HARVEY, HUNT, AND SCHRODER AND THE CONCEPTUAL-SYSTEMS APPROACH TO PERSONALITY DEVELOPMENT

In *Conceptual Systems and Personality Organization* (Harvey, Hunt, and Schroder 1961), these three theorists made an explicit effort to unite the cognitive and emotional constituents of personality. The key to their effort is the idea of the conceptual system, and they define virtually every ideational element in personality as a concept.

A concept is a system of ordering that serves as the mediating linkage between the input side (stimuli) and the output side (response). In operating as a system of ordering, a concept may be viewed as a categorical schema, an intervening medium, or program through which impinging stimuli are coded, passed, or evaluated on their way to response evocation (p. 1).

This definition is extremely broad; since if a concept is any system for ordering stimuli, it will necessarily be widely inclusive. By extending it to networks or groups of concepts called *conceptual systems*, Harvey et al. were able to use the conceptual system as a unit of analysis that can embrace both cognitive and emotional elements of personality. In other words, the broad-spectrum conceptual-systems notion is adequate for unitary approaches to all elements of personality.

Consider the theoretical status given to the self. Harvey et al. saw all of an individual's ideas about himself as ultimately related to his ideas about everything. That is, in some sense or another our views (concepts) about persons and things in the environment—what we like and dislike in cars, sports, architecture, men, and women—are related to our views of ourselves. Would you prefer a husky or a beagle? Draw poker or stud? All of it ultimately goes to your conception of yourself. By extending this kind of rationale, the self can be treated as an all-inclusive conceptual system. "We define the self as the intertwined totality of one's concepts . . ."(Harvey et al., 1961, p. 6).

Subordinate conceptual systems can be specified within the total self-system. One may abstract a person's ideas about members of the opposite sex, for example, if that person is seeking help for a neurotic sex problem. Harvey et al. see therapy of this sort as an attempt to modify the organization of certain conceptual systems held by the patient.

The joint influence of cognitive and emotional factors on conceptual systems is made clear from the outset. Concepts are considered to develop out of experience with the environment which is partly determined by the nature of the environment, and partly by the internal state of the person. Thus, to use an extreme example, one's concept of snakes is liable to differ greatly if his first experience is catching them in an open field rather than waking up to find a few in his blankets.

The major theme of the work on conceptual systems involves specification of the *concreteness-abstractness* dimension of thought and behavior. Harvey et al. employ this dimension as a hypothetical continuum according to which the functional and structural properties of conceptual systems may be evaluated. In this connection, eight different qualities of thought and behavior are listed as illustrations of relatively concrete or abstract functioning.

1. "Differentiation between the outer and inner worlds in the ego and experience." This concerns the ability to distinguish between wishes, dreams, and other fantasy materials, and reality. In an extremely concrete individual, the distinction is not clear.

2. "Assumption of a mental set wilfully and consciously." Abstract behavior requires this ability. It is akin to shifting one's perspective and being able to try different approaches to a given problem.

3. "Accounting for one's acts to oneself or to others and verbalizing the act." The ability to take the role of the other, or see oneself as others do, is involved here.

4. "Ability to shift reflectively from one aspect of the situation to another." This point refers to flexibility of response; the concrete individual tends to be rigid.

5. "The simultaneous holding in mind of various aspects." Abstract functioning requires that a person be able to attend to more than one thing at a time.

6. "Grasping the essential of a given whole, breaking it up into parts, isolating and synthesizing them." This refers to the ability to organize and interpret experience; to reflect upon it and draw out meaningful generalizations.

7. "The reflective abstraction of common properties and the formation of hierarchic concepts." The ability referred to here involves understanding the

similarities that may exist between superficially different objects. It is essential if one is to group and classify objects into meaningful categories.

8. "Planning ahead ideationally and the assumption of the attitude of 'the mere possible.'" This is the ability to make symbolic manipulations of the future, to see that a given cause may have several different possible effects.

Developmental applications

Harvey and his associates saw the development of conceptual systems as proceeding from concrete to abstract. They postulated four stages for this development and suggested that progress from one stage to the next is contingent upon a process of *differentiation and integration*. That is, the individual at a given stage of conceptual development will, under normal conditions, recognize the limits of that stage because of contradictions or inconsistencies in his conceptual system. This forces him to differentiate elements in the system, to examine them more carefully in an effort to resolve the difficulty. And such differentiation eventually leads to a new integration – a rearrangement of elements in the system such that former confusions are corrected.

For example, consider the case of how children apparently come to understand automobiles. Initially, all cars are alike to them, but they are soon able to distinguish between their family car and all others – not much of a differentiation. With more experience, however, they become aware of different types such as station wagons and sports cars. The confusions or inconsistencies that force the change involve simple things such as the amount of space inside various cars and differences in how they look and feel. So by the age of six or seven, most American children have begun to have a differentiated conceptual system for cars, and some may even be well on the way toward integrating a system involving such elements as models, makes, and styles.

The four stages of development are described below. Chronological age is mentioned occasionally but is not important here for the same reason suggested by Werner: it is argued that conceptual systems develop according to the given four-stage sequence regardless of age.

Stage 1   Unilateral dependence

In this stage, functioning is guided by and depends largely upon outside criteria. Citing evidence collected at the Gesell Institute of Child Development, the authors suggested that typical two-year-old behavior reflects Stage-1 functioning. Thinking is very concrete, behavior is geared to immediate reality, and the child is submissive to external control. Adult examples of this stage include patients in the early phase of psychotherapy who expect the therapist to provide direct, authoritative solutions to their problems.

In children, transition to Stage 2 is promoted by parents who provide a trusting, accepting, and permissive but secure family atmosphere, which is the same sort of situation most therapists try to create when treating patients. The individual consequently develops a sense of self-worth and independence.

Stage 2   Negative independence

This stage involves a strong reaction against outside restraints and is marked by rebellion against authority. H, H, & S describe such behavior as negative independence to make it clear that what is happening is primarily an effort at self-assertion, rather than simple aggression or hostility. In principle, one cannot adequately define himself unless he can establish the borderline between his own power or authority and that of others (in clinical terminology, *testing the limits*), and to do this one must set himself in opposition to others. Gesell Institute data indicate that children will test the limits at about age two-and-a-half, and again at about six. Among adults in therapy, negative independence can be seen in the form of *resistance* by the client once he begins to relax with his therapist.

Transition to Stage 3 is aided by conditions which allow the individual to set himself against external control and, to a certain extent, in this way free himself from dependence on others. Under such conditions there will be a natural swing toward dependency of a new type in which a *sense of autonomy* is mixed with a realistic sense of dependence upon others.

Stage 3   Conditional dependence and mutuality

Third-stage functioning is said to be an empirical affair in which conceptual systems are open to new data in much the same way as a scientist's theory must be open to new data. The individual who has initially depended upon external structure (Stage 1) and then fought successfully against it (Stage 2), is now able to take a more objective or empirical view of himself and his world. Stage-3 functioning is the opposite of Piagetian egocentrism.

Illustrative behavior can be seen in the make-believe and role-playing activities of children. The more sophisticated role-identification behavior of adolescents is also a clear example. In many therapy situations role-playing and/or psychodrama is used to provide patients with greater insight into their own and others' behavior.

Conditions promoting transition to Stage 4 are not clearly described by H, H, & S. However, it seems that the individual must experience situations which allow him to see things as others see them, and yet not feel constrained to limit his judgments entirely to outside standards. If a sufficient latitude to deviate from external standards is maintained, then development should not freeze at the level of conformity to outside norms. The individual will instead be able to progress to the more ego-oriented fourth stage.

Stage 4   Interdependence

The interdependence of the fourth stage refers to integration between external standards and internal or *ego-oriented* standards. The individual functions giving due consideration to both outside norms and autonomous personal values. In the normal course of events, personality at this stage is integrated in such a way that there is no serious conflict between external and internal standards. Both are important, but they do not interfere with each other. It is a condition rather like' the old political gaffe "What's good for General Motors is good for the country"; in this case, however, it might be said that "What is good for the autonomous ego is good for society." Harvey et al. mentioned Erikson's description of ego integrity as approximating what they mean by interdependence.

A major characteristic of Stage-4 functioning is the ability to tolerate anxiety and stress:

> More abstract functioning is based on a conceptual system that has been open to a variety of conflicting forms of subject-object relatedness that have been progressively integrated during development. Consequently there is a greater reservoir of resources to overcome and withstand stress of various forms—failure, control, rejection, or isolation (p. 108).

No age-related examples are given to illustrate full attainment of interdependence. Presumably it will be definitive of the truly mature person. Similarly, psychotherapy situations in which the patient finally terminates treatment because he is "well"—able, say, to mesh his needs with those of others without undue difficulty—might also illustrate attainment of some significant degree of interdependence.

In general it should be obvious that Harvey, Hunt, and Schroder's approach to personality development was more eclectic than any of the other approaches discussed here. Their concrete-abstract framework was the result of a deliberate effort to bring together ideas from Piaget, Werner, and the neo-Freudians. It therefore stands as a very ambitious, systematic attempt to deal with the whole person. Note, for example, their specification of the relationship between an abstract conceptual system and emotional adjustment. The former is said to provide "a greater reservoir of resources" to deal with stress. This kind of generalization epitomizes the theoretical direction of work designed to integrate existing views of cognitive and emotional development.

While the work of the neo-Freudians is also directed toward integration, they generally base their theoretical statements on clinical experience or insights that are difficult to test empirically. The particular value of Harvey, Hunt, and Schroder's work is that it is based more closely upon, and may be more conveniently subjected to, empirical investigation.

Toward an ordered framework

It would be marvelously convenient if at this point a new chronological theory of personality development could be introduced—a synthesis as it were, containing all the best features of the six discussed above. But no such theory exists. Instead, the next several chapters contain a chronological description of personality development that is similar to a catalogue: for each of the salient periods in the typical human life cycle, we will examine whatever seem to be the most important ideas and facts concerning personality. In some instances, this approach may seem to place too much emphasis on either cognitive or emotional factors, but the general aim is to do justice to both. And wherever there seem to be interesting relationships between the two, they are discussed in small theoretical digressions. The overriding concern in the next several chapters is to say to the reader "Look, this is what is generally known about personality in infancy, early childhood . . . , etc." To accomplish this a chronological scheme is employed, based upon the assumption that personality growth can be traced according to a series of *critical events* occurring in *critical periods*.

Why bring up new terminology such as critical events and periods at this juncture, when a heavy burden of terminology already exists in the developmental theories presented earlier? Indeed, why should these theories have been discussed at all if one is going on to an admittedly eclectic chronological scheme? The answer involves at least three separate considerations. First, the prior discussion of developmental theories should provide the reader with a general basis for evaluating subsequent material. If, as most professionals might agree, these theories define the present state of the art with regard to understanding personality development, then they should serve as a general frame of reference, a map showing where the different sources of theoretical action lie.

Second, the chronological nature of these theories should convey a sense of how inescapable is the general principle of sequential development. In one form or another, this principle is embedded as the central theme of every major thought about personality growth.

Third, after reviewing the different theories and reflecting upon them, if any substantial idea at all emerges, it is that when dealing with sequential growth, one must think in terms of critical periods and critical events. This approach seems valid whether the emphasis is upon emotional development, cognitive development, or a combination of both.

The critical-period idea is implicit wherever theoretical analysis suggests that unless an individual is somehow or other structurally ready for an experience, it can have no significant meaning for him. The adolescent's interest in the opposite sex, for example, would not be an outstanding event of the teen-age period were it not for the fact that as an organism, the adolescent is structurally ready for procreation. Piaget's work indicates that cognitive progress is in principle similarly dependent upon structural readiness. There is another side to structural readiness, however, that cannot be seen clearly in our prior discussions. To understand it, we must examine the meaning that the phrase *critical period* has in biology and ethology.

The embryologist can specify critical periods for the development of a fertilized egg. If certain cellular changes do not occur at particular intervals or in proper time sequences, the development of the organism can be irreparably damaged. Ethologists (psychologists who study behavior patterns of animals under natural conditions) point out that there are critical periods for the emergence of certain behaviors. If a given behavior pattern or mechanism does not emerge during the appropriate period, it may never do so at all. The other side of structural readiness can be thought of as structural *un*readiness. That is, a critical period is defined at one end by the fact that the organism has become structurally ready for some change, and at the other by the fact that it is no longer ready: the door has swung shut. With respect to personality, think of Erikson for a moment. The question might arise whether a person can ever achieve a sense of trust in others if, during infancy, he did not achieve it with his mother. The answer is probably "Yes, but it will be difficult and not quite the same as if it had been attained during infancy." In short, so far as one can tell from case histories and research findings, people who do not acquire certain attributes during the period in which they come naturally, usually need either special remedial help (perhaps psychotherapy) or special good luck, if they are to acquire them later.

As personality development is described in succeeding chapters, the critical-period idea will appear as a major organizing principle because specific age intervals are treated as a series of related critical periods. Furthermore, in subsequent chapters discussion will also focus on "critical events."

In ethology, the meaning of the term *instinct* has been clarified with the discovery that many so-called instinctive behaviors emerge instead as reflexes only given in response to specific *triggering* events when the animal is structurally ready to respond to these events. Students of personality are just beginning to learn how general trends in behavior and thinking can be influenced by events or conditions specific to certain age intervals. This is the essential message conveyed by existing theories of development and much new research. Therefore, each critical period will be examined in accord with the critical events or conditions characterizing that period.

This does not mean abandonment of more conventional theoretical ideas and language. In fact, one of the main reasons for reviewing the six theories in this chapter is that their fundamental ideas and language are so important in later chapters. But the critical-period and critical-event concepts are our basic organizational principles. They provide the theoretical perspective and flexibility that are necessary to maintain an eclectic chronological approach, and at the same time avoid being swamped by diversity.

References

Baldwin, A. L. *Theories of child development.* New York: John Wiley & Sons, Inc., 1968.

Bruner, J. S., Olver, R. R., & Greenfield, P. M., et al. *Studies in cognitive growth.* New York: John Wiley & Sons, Inc., 1966.

Cohen, J. Subjective time. In J. T. Fraser (Ed.), *The voices of time.* New York: George Braziller, Inc., 1966, pp. 257–275.

Erikson, E. H. *Childhood and society.* (2nd ed.) New York: W. W. Norton & Company, Inc., 1950, 1963.

Flavell, J. H. *The developmental psychology of Jean Piaget.* New York: D. Van Nostrand Co., Inc., 1963.

Frazer, J. T. The study of time. In J. T. Fraser (Ed.), *The voices of time.* New York: George Braziller, Inc., 1966, pp. 582–592.

Freud, S. *A general introduction to psychoanalysis.* New York: Washington Square Press, 1960.

Furth, H. G. *Piaget and knowledge.* Englewood Cliffs: Prentice-Hall, Inc., 1969.

Gardner, R. W. *The Menninger Foundation study of twins and their parents.* Paper delivered at the APA Convention, 1964.

Hall, C. S., & Lindzey, G. Psychoanalytic theory and its applications in the social sciences. In G. Lindzey (Ed.), *Handbook of social psychology,* Vol. 1. Cambridge: Addison-Wesley Publishing Co., Inc., 1954.

Hall, C. S., & Lindzey, G. *Theories of personality.* New York: John Wiley & Sons, Inc., 1957.

Harvey, O. J., Hunt, D. E., & Schroder, H. M. *Conceptual systems and personality organization.* New York: John Wiley & Sons, Inc., 1961.

Inhelder, B., & Piaget, J. *The growth of logical thinking.* New York: Basic Books, Inc., Publishers, 1958.

Kagan, J., & Moss, H. *Birth to maturity.* New York: John Wiley & Sons, Inc., 1962.

Marcuse, H. *One-dimensional man.* Boston: Beacon Press, 1964.

Scheerer, M. Cognitive theory. In G. Lindzey (Ed.), *Handbook of social psychology,* Vol. 1. Cambridge: Addison–Wesley Publishing Co., Inc., 1954.

Shakespeare, W. *As you like it.* In W. J. Craig (Ed.), *The Oxford Shakespeare.* New York: Oxford University Press, 1959.

Smedslund, J. The acquisition of conservation of substance and weight in children (Parts 1, 2, and 3). *Scandinavian Journal of Psychology,* 1961, *2,* 11–20; 71–84; 85–87.

Sullivan, H. S. *The interpersonal theory of psychiatry.* New York: W. W. Norton & Company, Inc., 1953.

Werner, H. *Comparative psychology of mental development.* New York: Science Editions Inc., 1961.

Wolff, P. The developmental psychologies of Jean Piaget and psychoanalysis. *Psychological Issues, 2*(1), Monograph 5, 1960.

5

Infancy, the Preverbal Period (0 to 18 months)

As a problem area for psychologists, infancy today has about the same character as the interior of Africa had for early nineteenth-century geographers: we know the general shape of the territory, and we are beginning to work our way into it empirically, but it is still basically *terra incognita*. Among laymen this state of affairs has led to the promulgation of myths that have more to do with cultural and ideological values than with fact.

The great problem here, the thing that makes infancy a Dark Continent for psychology, is of course the inscrutable nature of the infant himself — one never knows what he is thinking. During most of his first year and a half of life he only communicates a few very gross states of being: pain or pleasure; apathy or interest. The minimal pain-pleasure/apathy-interest equation for infancy makes this period difficult enough to understand. What makes it even harder, however, is the rapidity with which the infant may move through these different states without giving any word of explanation. This condition led one Freudian writer to describe infancy as fundamentally mysterious:

Since the infant is unable to communicate very much to us, even if he were so inclined, our notions of infantile personality development must necessarily be surrounded by a cloud of dense speculation (Sarnoff, 1962, p. 106).

In short, we have here a communications problem of the first order; one that has gone unsolved throughout man's history. And the result is that man usually does what he has always done in the face of a mystery: he muddles through with the aid of whatever myths seem plausible.

This chapter will first discuss a good deal of material relevant to two salient myths about infancy still prevalent today, which for the sake of discussion may be called the *vegetable hypothesis* and the *TLC hypothesis*. Then the area of infant learning will be examined, giving special attention to feeding and weaning as critical events of this period. Finally, we will look in more detail at the theoretical ideas of Piaget and Sullivan concerning infancy. Their theories are singled out from all others for special attention and review in this chapter, because no other writers have devoted so much systematic effort to the problem of understanding infant personality growth.

THE VEGETABLE HYPOTHESIS

The essence of this view as we construe it for didactic purposes, is that up until the age of 3, 6, 9, or what-have-you months, the human infant is more or less a vegetable. His life is entirely a matter of physical maintenance and growth functions: eating, sleeping, and eliminating. Overly sentimental or anthropomorphic parents will mistakenly interpret his cries, changes of expression or posture, as purposive responses, but this is quite understandable. While it is true that infants vary their expressions, these things are really just unintentional manifestations of autonomic activity. A gas bubble in his stomach causes the infant to reflexively stretch his lips and the simpleminded father announces that his son has smiled at him!

This sort of infant care philosophy is nowhere better expressed than in chapters 10 and 14 of Mary McCarthy's novel *The Group*. She described the way a thoroughly modern (circa 1935) pediatrician and his wife went about raising their newborn son "scientifically." They began by sticking to a rigid nursing schedule despite the fact that the infant cried ten hours a day.

Sloan raised a finger. "In the first place, ten hours is exaggerated. In the second place, what of it? In the third place, the nurses pick him up and fuss over him when he cries." Priss could not answer this. "Of course they do," said Sloan. "So that naturally he cries some more. Already, in the second week of life, he's learned to cry to get attention." He folded his arms and stared, frowning, at Priss (McCarthy, 1963, pp. 257–258).

A few years later, the boy's mother reflected on some of these rules. The boy was by then a very obedient, undemanding child, but his tenacious resistance against toilet training disturbed her.

Could a two-and-a-half-year-old plot and carry out a scheme of revenge? And for what? Alas, in her darkest moments, Priss feared she knew. For the bottle he had got too late, for the schedule he had been held to, on the minute: six, ten, two, six, ten, two. Perhaps even for this "sucking" Norine talked about that he had missed. For never having been picked up when he cried, except to have his diaper changed or be given a drink of water. For the fact, in short, that his father was a pediatrician. . . . The point, Sloan said, was to have the force of character to stick to the system absolutely, except in cases of illness or on trips. Stephen had got a good start in life because Priss had never compromised. This was what Priss endeavored to think herself, encouraged by her friends' admiration. Yet at times she furtively wondered whether when Stephen made messes in his pants he was not getting his own back for being alive at all (pp. 357–358).

The vegetable notion of infancy is one of the more persistent myths that grew out of the now more or less defunct "know nothing behaviorism" psychology of the 1920's and 1930's. Consider the following remarks on child rearing first published in 1928 by the "father" of American behaviorism.

There is a sensible way of treating children. Treat them as though they were young adults. Dress them, bathe them with care and circumspection. Let your behavior always be objective and kindly firm. Never hug and kiss them, never let them sit in your lap. If you must, kiss them once on the forehead when they say good night. Shake hands with them in the morning. Give them a pat on the head if they have made an extraordinarily good job of a difficult task. Try it out. In a week's time you will find how easy it is to be perfectly objective with your child and at the same time kindly. You will be utterly ashamed of the mawkish, sentimental way you have been handling it (Watson, 1928, pp. 81–82).

This appeared in Watson's book titled *Psychological Care of Infant and Child*. It doubtless had a strong influence on McCarthy's pediatrician.

But the underlying question requiring an answer here is serious for both parents and personality theorists: is there something important for personality development going on during the first several months of infancy or not? If not, then as parents we needn't concern ourselves too much with anything beyond maintenance care given according to an optimum set of rules. And as theorists we needn't waste time speculating about this period.

For some of the early behaviorists dedicated to the discovery of regularities coordinating stimuli and responses, the infant could hardly have seemed *in principle* to be very different from a rat, a worm, or even a plant. All show behavior which can be described in stimulus-response terms, and all can be manipulated accordingly. Should it come as any great surprise, therefore, to see that popularized applications of such thinking led to infant care procedures emphasizing maintenance schedules? Moreover, the early Freudians were not able to offer any substantial contradictory evidence: because they could not communicate with infants, they were generally content to take a retrospective view based on untestable assumptions about the later consequences of infant experience. Research on early experience now shows that the postures typical in both schools of thought were wrong.

THE EFFECTS OF STIMULATION

A large volume of research, much of it quite recent and involving both human and animal subjects, is now converging to support the conclusion that a properly stimulating environment is a critical condition for personality development in infancy. In particular, the evidence shows that when neonates from a variety of species including rats, dogs, monkeys, and humans are reared without experiencing the range of stimulation typical of their natural family environments, both their social-emotional and intellectual development is seriously impaired. The standard phrase used to describe work on the negative effects of abnormally low levels of stimulation is "stimulus deprivation." It is worth noting that the initial discoveries of the effects of stimulus deprivation on both children and animals were not dictated or predicted by any theory; researchers in different areas more or less stumbled upon this important phenomenon by accident.

HUMAN RESEARCH

Stimulation and intelligence

The earliest modern studies that now can be related to the stimulus deprivation phenomenon were based on analyses of IQ test scores obtained from poor and culturally backward populations. For example, Sherman and Key (1932) collected data from children in different areas of the Blue Ridge Mountains showing that the more isolated and backward the area, the lower the average IQ. Moreover, in all these areas, the older children had lower scores than the younger children. Gordon (1923), reported similar findings on the reduction of IQ with age among gypsy children and children living on canal boats in England.

These kinds of results were not well understood at the time they were obtained. Some interpretations stated that the cause was genetic, the result of inbreeding in isolated groups of people. Others suggested that perhaps the brighter children moved into the larger society as they got older, leaving only the duller ones to be tested at a later age. And it is always possible to see the tests themselves as the cause: items designed by middle-class professionals and standardized on middle-class children may be too "culture-bound" to serve as effective measures for other populations. All of these interpretations have some degree of plausibility, particularly the last. However, recent findings reported by Coleman (1966) are in certain ways quite similar to those mentioned above and add to the credibility of a stimulus deprivation interpretation.

Having analyzed scholastic achievement test scores collected all over the United States, Coleman showed that in segregated schools the achievement scores of minority group children become steadily lower as they move through successive grades. Furthermore, their scores in first grade are the same as those of minority first-graders in integrated schools, but the latter do not subsequently drop off. If one thinks of school segregation as a form of stimulus deprivation, then all of these findings begin to fit together, indicating that deprivation has cumulatively negative effects on intellectual development. A better feeling for this theory of stimulus deprivation is conveyed by the following studies made in orphanages.

Skeels (1966) described an accidental discovery made in the 1930's that led to a major study of the effects of stimulus deprivation. Two little girls aged 13 and 16 months, both suffering from malnutrition, had to be taken from their mentally defective mothers. They were sent to an institution for the mentally retarded because tests and observation of their behavior showed that they too were retarded. A year later the girls were again tested; Skeels was very surprised to find that they were socially, emotionally, and intellectually normal for their chronological ages. Further investigation revealed that because no other space was available, these children had been living in a ward with retarded adult women having mental ages of 5 to 9. The women had "adopted" the girls, giving them a great deal of affection and attention. Nurses and attendants brought in toys and picture books for them and took them out for rides to the local town. They apparently had received stimulation approximating or perhaps even exceeding that which occurs in a normal family.

This incident was followed up by a study in which 13 children under 3 years of age were taken from an orphanage and placed in an institution for the retarded. They received the same treatment as the two girls. After two years, their average IQ, which had been 64 at the outset, was 92. They were compared with another group of 12 similar-aged children who had an average score of 87 at the outset, but had remained in the orphanage. After two years, the average IQ for the children in the orphanage dropped off to 66.

A number of more recent studies (see Longstreth, 1968, pp. 101–109), in which either retarded, institutionalized, or deprived minority group children had been divided into experimental and control groups, with the former being given various kinds of stimulating preschool experience, all indicate significant IQ gains for the experimental children. One of the more striking projects was carried out by Irwin (1960). Working with deprived families, he paid the mothers of twenty-four 13-month-old children to read to them and tell them stories about pictures for 20 minutes each day. When these children were 30 months old, their verbal ability had risen almost twice as much as the verbal ability of a control group of similar children who did not receive the reading treatment.

Stimulation and general well-being

Early reports concerning the effects of stimulus deprivation on the general well-being of young children – their physical, social, and emotional as well as their intellectual development – were relatively unsystematic and subject to much criticism. But, as we shall presently see, in the light of subsequent work they appear to have been on the right track.

Lowrey (1940), attributed problems of sickliness, speech difficulty, and social negativism in 3 to 5 year old adopted children, to the fact that as institutionalized infants, they had been deprived of intimate maternal care. Ribble (1944), studied 600 infants and their mothers, mainly through personal observation. She reported that a variety of general adjustment and growth problems occurred in cases where infants did not receive adequate physical stimulation from their mothers; that is, close contact in the form of handling, cuddling, and fondling. Her suggestion that infants have an innate biological need for tactile contact with their mothers (n.b. Harlow's work with monkeys 15 years later), was roundly criticized as based on faulty data.

In a methodologically stronger study, Goldfarb (1945) took several measures of personality development in children who had been adopted after being institutionalized up to the age of three, and compared them with similar measures on adopted children who had spent little or no time in an institution. During the age period 7 to 12 years, the former group showed a much lower average IQ than the latter, along with various social-emotional problems: insecurity, apathy, poor emotional control. He concluded that these effects resulted from the substantial custodial period in infancy. Furthermore, in a review of this study and related work published 10 years later, Goldfarb (1955) again specified that the deprivation associated with early experience in an institution reduces subsequent intellectual and social development.

One of the best known and most influential of the earlier projects was carried out by Spitz (1945). He compared 61 infants raised in a foundling home with 69 raised in the nursery section of a women's prison. The foundling home was apparently a model case of stimulus deprivation: babies there spent most of their first year and a half of life in cribs that restricted their visual fields mostly to the ceiling. They were only taken up from their cribs for feeding and changing. The nursery case was quite the opposite: babies there could see around their cribs; they were often cared for by their own mothers (prison inmates), and they were frequently out of their cribs. Using an index that combined tests and observations of physical, social-emotional, and intellectual development, Spitz found that in all these respects, the foundling home sample was drastically inferior to those children raised in the nursery. By the age of two, for example, among the foundling home children there had already been 12 deaths from disease (none died in the nursery); only a few could walk, and most did not have anything resembling the normal verbal ability of two-year-olds.

Following these pioneer efforts, research along this general line began to accumulate rapidly. Bowlby (1952) summarized much of it and then concluded that deprivation in infancy has lasting negative effects on personality development. Casler (1961) criticized Bowlby, arguing that much of the evidence he cited was in one way or another unsound. There now exist two schools of thought on this subject. Both admit that deprivation during infancy has gross, negative, short-range effects. But one claims that these effects are relatively permanent, while the other maintains that normal experience at a later age can wipe them out. Quite probably the truth lies somewhere between these two statements, but research findings do not yet provide a definitive position for moderates.

Findings concerning the effects of stimulus deprivation on children are still ambiguous in another way: are the detrimental effects due to something general, such as the absence of "mothering," or can they be pinned down to specifics such as visual, auditory, and tactile forms of stimulation? The ideal experiment would require systematic manipulation of all these factors for varying lengths of time, using a sample of normal young infants. But knowing what we already know about deprivation, who will be so inhumane as to conduct a systematic program of deprivation with babies?[1] It therefore appears that from here on we must look to animal research.

---

[1]The findings described above have already had a practical impact which makes further research difficult to accomplish. Most, if not all, infant care institutions now try to provide their charges with as much stimulation as they can. One researcher planning to conduct an auditory stimulation experiment with such infants was unable to do so because he discovered that the nurses had beaten him to it—they had heard about stimulus deprivation and consequently kept a radio playing loudly in the ward all day long.

ANIMAL RESEARCH

Rats

The story may be apocryphal, but it is said that at least one line of animal research began by accident in the following way. Newborn rats were each raised in dark barren cages to see whether such treatment would impair their later ability to learn a maze. The experimenters were surprised to find that these rats were able to run a maze just as well as rats raised under normal conditions. Seeking an explanation, they discovered that a student paid to clean cages played with the rats during his chores, fondling and handling them. A study was then arranged to compare the subsequent maze performances of regularly handled and unhandled rats. Results showed the former to be far superior to the latter. Whether or not this story is correct, it is a fact that as early as 1947 Hebb reported that when he raised some laboratory rats in his home as pets, they were later able to learn a standard maze much faster than rats raised under laboratory conditions.

Many studies along this line were done during the 1950's. In a brief summary of the results, King and Eleftheriou (1964) pointed out that systematically handled rats have faster growth rates, and as adults they stand up better to stress, show more activity, and learn faster, then unhandled rats. In short, the handling findings seem parallel to the deprivation findings described earlier for humans. Scott was quite specific on this:

. . . in the usual laboratory situation the environment provides little stimulation other than that which a caretaker provides by adding food and water. The temperature is kept constant, and the room is usually quiet except for noises made by other rats. Consequently, the young rat lives in an unusually calm and constant physical environment. In this way the laboratory environment resembles that of a well-run hospital or orphanage (1968, p. 116).

Later findings showed that handling experience during the rat's first week of life has the maximum positive effect on his subsequent development. More important, however, work done over the past few years has demonstrated that handling *per se* is not the critical factor for rats. Instead, it is *stimulation*. Recent studies (see Scott, pp. 117–118) indicate that all sorts of stimulation including mild electric shocks, mechanical shaking, and even sharply lowered atmospheric temperatures will yield the same positive effects as handling. Moreover, rats will stimulate themselves if they are left alone or with other rats in an "enriched environment"—one that contains various kinds of rat playground equipment.

A general physiological explanation for all these results was offered by Levine and Mullins (1966). It is based on the idea that sensory-motor stimulation, whether it comes in the form of handling or otherwise, places some stress on the young rat which makes for the development of a more robust endocrine gland system. Levine's view is supported by evidence that stimulation increases adrenal gland activity in young rats. It remains to be seen whether this physiological hypothesis can account for all the varied effects of early stimulation on rats, let alone humans. But there is no question that the rat research provides dramatic corroboration of the human studies.

Other species

While the volume of research is greatest for rats—for obvious reasons of convenience—similar findings on the effects of stimulus deprivation have been obtained with other species. For example, songbirds reared in isolation do not later produce songs as sophisticated as those of normally reared birds (Thorpe, 1958). And Melzack (1962) demonstrated that young beagles raised under conditions of subnormal visual stimulation later required much more practice to learn visual discrimination tasks than normally raised beagles.

By far the most compelling animal evidence however, comes out of Harlow's long-term research with monkeys. For a variety of reasons having little to do with any deliberate intention to study stimulus deprivation effects, Harlow raised several monkeys in complete isolation, and discovered that the consequences were very severe. When they were placed in the normal monkey colony at age two, these former isolates were practically psychotic. They withdrew from all contact with others, refusing to engage in typical social grooming and play behavior. When attacked they would not defend themselves, and sexual overtures of any kind put them into a panic. (See Harlow and Harlow, 1962, for more detail.)

Other work by Harlow in which infant monkeys are raised with cloth or wire "surrogate mothers" is by this time so well known that it hardly requires detailed description. These studies clearly demonstrate that monkeys have such a strong need for "contact comfort" that their emotional attachment to a terry-cloth mother who does not give milk far surpasses their attachment to a wire mother who does. In short, the emotional security of young monkeys apparently depends more upon the experience of contact comfort than of nursing.

A final, strikingly suggestive finding reported by Harlow concerns the adult social-emotional adjustment of monkeys raised on surrogate mothers. Among other things, they would not engage in sex:

In a desperate attempt to assist a group of 18 three- to four-year-old cloth-surrogate-raised monkeys, half of them males and half females, we engaged in a group-psychotherapy program, placing these animals for two months on the monkey island in the Madison Zoo. . . . Their summer vacation on the enchanted island was not without avail, and social grooming responses rapidly developed . . . patterns of social ordering developed, and a number of males and females developed friendship patterns. Unfortunately, sexual behavior was infrequent, and the behavior that was observed was completely inadequate—at least from our point of view. In desperation we finally introduced our most experienced, most patient, and most kindly breeding male, Smiley . . . and he rapidly established himself as king of the island and prepared to take full advantage of the wealth of opportunity which surrounded him. Fortunately, the traumatic experiences he encountered with unreceptive females have left no apparent permanent emotional scars, and now that he has been returned to our laboratory breeding colony, he is again making an important contribution to our research program (Harlow, 1962, p. 8).

Eventually, however, some of the females raised on cloth mothers and one raised with a wire mother did manage to become mothers themselves. The result is quite amazing: these females seemed totally inadequate to care for their own offspring.

Month after month female monkeys that never knew a real mother themselves become mothers — helpless, hopeless, heartless mothers devoid, or almost devoid, of any maternal feeling (Harlow, 1962, p. 9).

Summary

The case against the vegetable notion is based on work that at least loosely fits the stimulus deprivation category. But perhaps the argument has gone too far; after all, the vegetable hypothesis is merely a phrase designed to capture all relatively sterile views of infancy, particularly those implying that the infant needn't be thought of as fully human. And perhaps the deprivation research, despite its volume, is not yet coherent enough to warrant theoretical rejection of such views. If a fully definitive answer cannot be given to this question, one pertinent comment can certainly be made. Over the last 10 to 15 years, one finds time and time again research reports indicating that infants have a greater behavioral capability, or are more sensitive to their environment, than was previously thought to be the case. One does not find reports showing lesser capabilities. Therefore, it seems that the most conservative scientific and parental policy is one that will, in the face of some ambiguity, assume more rather than less importance for this period.

Almost as if in response to this proposition, there has arisen over the past twenty years an alternative child-rearing myth which may be called the *TLC hypothesis*. It is more popular today than the vegetable notion, but in a subtle way it can be just as dangerous. It is discussed below in relation to conceptions of mother love.

MOTHER LOVE AND THE TLC HYPOTHESIS

Free associations to the "mother love" concept would probably involve such terms as tenderness, warmth, security, and softness. One might also hear some terms with negative implications such as cloying, sticky, and mushy. But the dominant quality in the pool of meaning associated with mother love would be *sentimentality*. Of course there is nothing intrinsically positive or negative about being sentimental. It is defined as ". . . marked or governed by feeling, sensibility or emotional idealism."

Why then should it be under attack? The rationale underlying criticism of sentimentality in general, and various psychological or pseudo-psychological formulations about the causal properties of love in particular, is quite simple. Sentiment is too frequently put into service as a substitute for thought. However, it should be understood that sentimentality is here being criticized as a *substitute* for thinking, not as an adjunct to thinking. As an adjunctive, mellowing influence, sentiment is what keeps most of us from turning into intellectual monsters.

My own first encounter with sentimentality in the guise of thought occurred during a personality class. It was early in my first semester as an instructor, and it provides a good example of how one becomes sensitized to certain issues through classroom experience.

Instructor to class: "What do you think is most important for personality development in early childhood?"

Young female student: "Tee el see!"

Instructor: "Tee el see?"

Student: "Yes!"

Instructor: "Ah . . ., what do you mean?"

Student: "Tender loving care!"

Instructor: "I see. And what does that involve?"

Student: "Oh, you know, just taking care of the baby and loving it."

Instructor: "Oh."

I have since encountered TLC in many situations, being advised to use it by a greenhouse man selling young trees, an editor explaining how to write a book, a kennel owner selling puppies, a neuroanatomist explaining the use of an electron microscope, a computer programmer, and a Dean of Student Affairs.

The problem with TLC is that like many catch phrases, it expresses something that has no straightforward operational meaning. It is a bit like the prescriptive advice once given during a Sunday morning sermon: "Always strive to walk the straight and narrow path between right and wrong." It sounds fine, but how does one go about it? Having raised trees, dogs, and children, it is clear to me, both professionally and personally, that the important operational factors are knowledge, skill, organization, morale, and a fair share of luck. In the act of changing a noxious diaper for example, one cannot get very far by admonishing himself to think TLC. Diaper changing is a skilled performance of a complex task under conditions of stress. It has always struck me as being more properly analogous to changing a hot machine gun barrel than to a hearts-and-flowers job: under pressure one has to move quickly and get everything in the right place; if not, the whole business won't work.

The TLC hypothesis does have at least one unmistakably *negative* function in our society. As a naively accepted myth, it causes infinite difficulty for young parents who feel inadequate, guilty, or anxious when their emotions do not invariably include tender love. I know one clinician whose practice is largely taken up with group therapy sessions for young mothers in this condition. Much of his work is an effort to counteract their conviction that something must be seriously wrong with them if they occasionally feel downright mad at their babies. (Anyone who has had to duck the geyser that a little boy can produce as he lies stripped on his diaper table will understand these things.)

In all fairness, perhaps it should be said that the TLC cliché at least serves as a useful means of reminding new parents to be careful with their infant. But most parents usually feel sufficient tender love to start with—so much, in fact, that they may have to overcome an excessive fear of hurting the infant; most new fathers are initially afraid to hold the baby.

The ultimate problem here is that vague notions of TLC do not address the hard realities of infant care. Traditional behaviorists see these realities, place the cause in the infant, and thereby provide a barren psychology of mechanical procedures for this period. In reaction, some latter-day humanists see these realities, place the cause in the mother, and thereby give us a psychology of maternal emotions for this period. Enough has already been said to make it clear that as an operational guide to infant care, TLC can be disposed of rather easily. Theoretically, however, TLC presumably springs from mother love. The following discussion shows that there is no strong theoretical or empirical basis for assuming that mother love is an automatic phenomenon which generates TLC.

INTERPRETATIONS OF MOTHER LOVE

Between them, the traditional Freudians and behaviorists, and comparative-experimentalists such as Harlow, offer three different theoretical perspectives on mother love. Contemporary writers in the clinical-personality area such as Rogers and Bettelheim, also provide ideas relevant to this subject.

The Freudian view described by Lomas (1962) stated that maternal love may be based upon either "narcissism" or "masochism." Narcissism refers to extreme self-love; an intense egocentric concern with self. Freud suggested that the exaggerated pride of some parents which is revealed in their inability to recognize faults in their children could be understood by extending the concept of narcissism. The argument is particularly clear in the case of mothers. Since they can see their children as part of themselves, their narcissistic feelings can easily focus on their children. Thus, according to this logic, when a mother lavishes excessive affection upon her child she is really lavishing it upon herself. And this notion of maternal love can be employed to explain all the clichés about parents who try to live their children's lives for them.

Masochism, on the other hand, is commonly understood to mean the enjoyment of pain. In stricter theoretical terms, however, masochism refers only to pleasure experienced from pain that is inflicted by a loved or idealized person. It is suggested, therefore, that mothers accept the self-sacrifice and drudgery of infant care because of a masochistic impulse. They welcome all the difficulties of child rearing as opportunities to show their love for the idealized child. Physical pain thus becomes psychological pleasure. According to this notion one can explain other clichés, such as the mother who scrubs floors to keep her son in an expensive fraternity. In short, for the Freudian, mother love can be explained theoretically either on the basis of narcissism, masochism, or some combination of both.

A behavioristic explanation of mother love would appeal to principles of learning by conditioning and reinforcement. If a mother has no built-in reflex or instinct to show the affectionate behavior we call *mother love,* then it must be learned. And if it is learned, then the conditioning and reinforcement principles governing all significant learning must come into play. Very briefly, the conditioning principle would operate through the medium of culture. As the young female grows up learning the sex-role approved by her culture, she will also acquire the standard behavioral responses expected of mothers in her culture. By the time she is mature, her reaction to babies should be dominated by an almost automatic feeling of affection, if this is expected. The automatic quality of an affectionate response to babies should no more be taken as indicating an "instinct" than the automatic quality of any other conditioned response.

Whatever aspects of mother love cannot be accounted for according to the conditioning principle—for example, mothers reserve their strongest affection for their own children—can be explained according to the reinforcement principle. Mothers behave very affectionately toward their own children because such behavior is reinforced by rewards provided in their environment. The most obvious rewards here are social: the approval and respect of significant persons such as husband, parents, and friends. And one should not forget the negative reinforcement or punishment that will be experienced by mothers who do not show sufficient affection to their infants. Thorndyke's famous "law of effect"—rewards stamp in behavior, punishments stamp out behavior—can be applied as well to maternal love as to any other behavior.

Harlow's experimental approach to mother love, already mentioned, is in the tradition of comparative psychology which often, though not always, seeks explanations for human behavior in the similar behavior of animals. Insofar as Harlow's findings apply to mother love *per se*, they indicate that it is not instinctive. The material suggests that mother love is simply one of many social behaviors that are impaired by early deprivation.

Observations of maternal behavior in other lower species also indicate that such behavior is dependent upon environmental conditions. In severely overcrowded living conditions, for example, female rats neglect their young to the point of death, and in many species the young may perish through cannibalism. Comparative studies of maternal behavior must be interpreted very cautiously when thinking of humans. However, the evidence available does not support any simple instinct theory.

Carl Rogers and Bruno Bettelheim are clinician-theorists originally trained in the Freudian tradition. While much of their writing concerned problems of psychopathology, both produced extensive general discussions of personality (Rogers, 1961; Bettelheim, 1960). Their combined work presents very different perspectives on the subject of mother love.

Rogers' (1959) major thesis was that any person's view of himself, his self-image or ego, develops according to the principle of *self-actualization*. To self-actualize is to make one's potentials as a person real or actual. Because this principle permeates so much of Rogers' work, Maddi (1968) referred to his ideas as a "fulfillment model" of personality. Now in the lives of most women, one major form of self-actualization or fulfillment is having a child. Rogers in fact often uses childbirth as an example of what he means by actualization: normal women have the potential and when they realize it, their self-image is usually much enhanced. The latter point is most important. Self-actualization has its positive effect on personality because, as an act of achievement, it enhances the self-image.

From this standpoint, mother love can be theoretically explained as a self-actualization phenomenon. A mother loves her child because it provides the means for her to achieve an important form of self-actualization. Anyone will presumably have a highly positive emotional feeling for an object that confirms and enhances his own conception of himself as a good, worthwhile person: Freud is said to have once described his books as his children. The logic here can easily be extended to also cover prolonged child care. Mothers carry on because doing a good job of child rearing is in itself self-actualizing. That is, by showing herself adequate to this demanding task the mother further proves her potential as a woman and thus further enhances her image as a good, worthy person.

In this necessarily brief extension of Rogers' ideas to the problem of mother love, it may seem as if mothers simply exploit their children as a means of supporting their own egos. Rogers would probably agree that such things occur in cases of pathology, and in this respect he would come close to the old Freudian idea of narcissism. But he maintains that self-actualization is generally a healthy force in personality growth which does not exploit objects incidental to its functioning because such exploitation would preclude the genuine feelings of self-worth[2] that come from self-actualizing in accord with shared moral standards and values.

In sharp contrast to Rogers and the other theoretical views on mother love thus far described, Bettelheim's argument that "love is not enough" concerns the consequences rather than the causes of mother love. Based on long experience running a therapy center for severely disturbed children, Bettelheim's fundamental position is that a mother's love for her child—whatever its origins—provides no assurance that she will not impose crippling emotional problems upon the child. Mother love is such an amorphous, global idea that it can obscure a wide range of inadequate, irresponsible, or pathological child-rearing practices. Bettelheim's views implied that if gross expressions of affection are accepted as a sufficient criterion of the good mother, then we risk a danger analogous to the one our country has in its relations to foreign governments professing anticommunism: so long as a mother professes herself to be full of love, she can indulge in any excess without criticism.

Bettelheim did not mean that love has no intrinsic merit as a human emotion, especially for mothers. But he showed very convincingly that it can be a sham unless it is translated into effort and knowledge, and kept reasonably free of exploitative elements. In relation to effort and knowledge, he noted how loving parents can unwittingly create conditions that impede their child's development:

. . . it undoubtedly takes more effort and ingenuity, for example, to put breakable things out of the child's reach than to say no! no! to him, or to slap his hands. But the first requires some minimum of planning by the parent, while the second creates in-

---

[2]Self-worth means that one thinks he is a *good* person, not necessarily that he is powerful or successful. The connection between self-actualization and self-worth is a tricky matter. There is probably no really adequate way to distinguish the precise borderline between acts of self-actualization and acts of selfish exploitation. Rogers of course shows how to make gross distinctions between the two, but since one can hear academic people use the self-actualization thesis as a justification for everything from the seduction of young girls to meaningless European junkets, the borderline remains obscure.

conveniences mainly for the child. . . . Again, it seems simple to fence a child in behind gates, with the excuse that he must be protected from hurting himself on the hot kitchen stove. But with only a little imagination it should be possible to fence off the kitchen stove and thus enlarge the realm in which the child may explore safely (1950, pp. 4–5).

And on the exploitative elements that can contaminate mother love, Bettelheim said:

We have known many children who have resented their parents' going through the prescribed motions of "loving" them because they felt it was not genuine. The mother who indulges her child to show the neighbours how good a mother she is will often hurt the child just as much as if she were only indifferent. The child will not understand that his mother may be acting on her fears or anxieties ("The ideal mother never gets irritated as I am so often"). He will sense only that he is being used, in one way or another, and indulgence received to impress others is no indulgence at all; actually, it is painful for him because he is misused for the mother's extraneous purposes (1950, p. 5).

Even if it existed, however, an idealized set of rules for child rearing would not be enough to eliminate the damaging consequences of false or distorted maternal emotions. Bettelheim's ideas here are similar to those expressed in other connections by Sullivan and Erikson — the mother's emotions must be in harmony with her behavior.

Superficially, for example, the mother who does not scold her child for wetting his bed seems more permissive than the one who scolds him severely. Yet if the permissive mother also kicks up a fuss about the labour of washing the sheets, her child may suffer even greater guilt feelings than the one who is scolded for wetting himself. Permissiveness in itself may thus be useless or even harmful if it is more academic than felt (1950, p. 7).

Still another danger inherent in maternal emotions is the manner in which a woman's needs can be transformed into unreasonable demands upon her child. Bettelheim provided a case showing how the need to be a "successful mother" was channeled into an apparently innocuous direction.

One such mother recently told me with pride that she would not dream of beginning to toilet-train her eighteen-month-old son. She said she could wait for that until he could indicate spontaneously that he was ready to make regular use of the toilet. On the other hand, this mother kept a list of the words in his vocabulary and had calculated that he was learning two new words every day — a record she was bent on his keeping up or improving. The new words were discussed early and often in the home, and were the main substance of letters from the mother to her parents and in-laws.

In this case, the pressure for one type of achievement — education to cleanliness — was replaced by the pressure for a much more difficult achievement — verbalization. The mother could allow herself much greater pressure with respect to her son's intellectual progress, since her leniency about toilet training had established her clearly as permissive, not only in her own mind but also before all her enlightened friends. Yet in a way this boy was worse off than if his mother had imposed a too early toilet training. Because the sequence of development was here reversed: the ability to verbalize extensively preceded toilet training instead of coming after it; sphincter control, for which he was by and large ready, was delayed, and verbalization, for which he was by no means yet ready, was pushed (1950, p. 8).

Bettelheim's ideas may seem overly critical to many persons. He did, after all, do a pretty effective hatchet job on naive assumptions about motherhood. But his work raises a major question: if love is indeed not enough, then what is? For one thing, he would like to see knowledge and effort raised to the same high level of public esteem ordinarily reserved for sentimentality. He further implied that instead of basking in the aura of their motherhood or fatherhood, parents should seriously try to gain some insight into their emotional relations with their children. Finally, Bettelheim indicated that a reasonably stable, consistent emotional environment is necessary if a child is to develop any sort of organized personality.

As a critical period for personality development, infancy is often obscured by modern folklore based upon either the vegetable or TLC mythologies. We have discussed both in detail and have tried to show not only that they are misleading, but also that a substantial body of important empirical and theoretical material can be brought to bear upon them. However, while deprivation findings, theories of mother love, and related matters stand as important sources of knowledge about infancy, a third no less important source is the learning that occurs during this period.

LEARNING IN INFANCY

A quantity of research evidence confirms that the infant begins learning through conditioning and/or reinforcement very early in life. Some studies even show that the fetus can be conditioned to respond within the womb. For example, most mothers know that during the last months of pregnancy their unborn child will respond to loud noises with kicking or some other movement, but such stimulation as moderate vibration on the stomach does not produce movement. Spelt (1948) demonstrated intrauterine conditioning by pairing a loud noise (the unconditioned stimulus) with vibration against the mother's abdomen (the conditioned stimulus). After 15 to 20 trials, the fetus would respond to the vibration as he originally did to the noise. Other studies using similar procedures which one psychologist has referred to as "fetus á go-go" experiments, have yielded similar results.

The prenatal learning evidence is also relevant to Otto Rank's theory of the birth trauma. An early follower of Freud, Rank (1929) suggested that birth is a traumatic experience for everyone, and that a person's subsequent personality development depends upon how well he copes with this trauma. But while it is possible to form hypotheses based on this notion (children of mothers having greater difficulty giving birth should have greater personality problems), it is not possible to test such hypotheses because too many other uncontrollable factors enter the picture. There are many different kinds and degrees of difficulty in childbirth, and these may have many different lasting effects on both the child and the mother. Altogether then, apart from its theoretical status as a phenomenon with interesting implications, the fact of prenatal learning does not presently lead to any clear statements about personality development.

The case is very different when *post*natal learning is examined. The following discussion of infant learning is organized around three different critical events or situations that occur during the first 18 months: feeding, weaning, and toilet training. Dollard and Miller (1950) referred to these as "critical training situations." All three require significant learning on the part of the infant, and in all of them the learning may have serious consequences for personality.

Feeding

Feeding in the very young infant is often ignored as a learning phenomenon because the sucking response is instinctive. But recent work demonstrates that from birth the infant can exert significant control over the head movements that play an important role in his nursing. Papousek (1967), and Siqueland and Lipsitt (1966), showed that head movements can be successfully conditioned in infants when the procedure is started as early as three days after birth. And Gunther (1961) indicated the practical side of this and similar infant abilities in a description of the difficulties exhibited by neonates learning to nurse at the breast. Many problems involve the shape of the mother's breast. Some are literally more difficult for the infant to get hold of for proper sucking than others. One particularly nasty little problem can lead an infant of only 4 or 5 days to deliberately avoid the breast. This occurs when his upper lip curls upward during nursing in such a way that the lip blocks his nose, and therefore impedes or totally blocks his breathing. According to Gunther, babies who have had this anoxia experience in their first several tries at nursing will actively fight against being put to the breast by turning their heads away and "boxing" with their fists. The experience is also very upsetting to mothers who have no notion why their babies are rejecting them.

Another relevant report by Newton (1958) concerned the "let-down" reflex in nursing mothers. It is a process whereby once sucking is properly underway, the nipple droops to permit a freer flow of milk. This relaxation response does not occur if the mother is tense or frightened. An anxious mother will make nursing a physically harder job for the infant, who in turn may become more desperate in his efforts, which may then make the mother even more upset and therefore even less able to give milk: a neat vicious cycle allowing both mother and infant to learn that feeding is unpleasant.

Dollard and Miller (1950) noted two general theoretical implications of infant feeding experience for later personality. It can first of all set a pattern leading toward either self-reliant independence or apathy.

If the child is fed when hungry, it can learn that the one simple thing it can do to get results (cry) can make a difference in what happens. Learning to cry as a signal for food is one small unit in its control of the world. Such a trait could be the basis of a later tendency to be "up and doing" when in trouble, of a belief that there is always a way out of a painful situation.

. . . If the child is not fed when it is crying, . . . it can, similarly, learn that there is nothing it can do at that time to change the painful circumstances. Such training may also lay the basis for the habit of apathy and not "trying something else" when in trouble (1950, p. 132).

They went on to suggest that when an infant's hunger is regularly allowed to build up to an intense level, he can learn that a moderate need always tends to become intense, and this could explain how some children learn to give extreme reactions in many situations. If hunger is only satisfied when it is intense enough to provoke extreme activity by the infant, then only his extreme reactions are being reinforced or rewarded. He thus learns to overreact to a moderate need.

The infant's experience with hunger and feeding situations can also lay down the foundation for later social feelings. Dollard and Miller suggested the way a pattern leading toward generally positive or negative social feelings (extroversion vs. introversion) can be set up.

When the hungry infant is fed, some of the wonderful relaxation responses which it experiences can be conditioned to the stimuli of those persons who are caring for the child. Thereafter the mere appearance of the mother can produce a momentary feeling of well-being. . . . Since the mother or caretaker stands at the very head of the parade of persons who become "society" for the child, it is quite important that she evoke such benign and positive responses in the child.[3]

If its food rewards are in various ways cut down and spoiled, it may not care much whether "the others" are there or not. It may tend to be "low in social feeling" (1950, p. 133).

No discussion of infant feeding is complete without some mention of the breast vs. bottle problem. The question is always which is better, and the answer, so far as personality is concerned, is that it all depends. Various studies of the problem done over the past thirty years all converge on the conclusion that breast or bottle feeding *per se* is less important than the manner or style of the feeding process. Peterson and Spano (1941) failed to find any relationship between breast or bottle feeding and later personality at nursery-school age or during adolescence. In 1946 Maslow and his colleagues reported that college students with high scores on a personal security questionnaire were those who had either been entirely bottle- or breast-fed as infants, rather than being shifted from one to the other during early infancy. Sewell and Mussen (1952) collected 26 different adjustment scores from a large sample of five- and six-year-olds. The sample was then divided according to whether their mothers had breast- or bottle-fed them. Comparison showed no significant differences between the two groups on any of the 26 measures.

These and other, similar studies should make it clear that the relative merits of breasts and bottles as apparatus are not psychologically important. The infant is certainly liable to be influenced in many ways by the quality of his feeding experience, but this will depend on more complex things than the mere fact of feeding through breast or bottle.

---

[3]A study by Lu (1967) provided interesting support for this point. Babies approximately 5 months old were fed with a red light on in the background, by mothers wearing red smocks. When later tested, these babies would focus their attention on a red light for a much longer time than others not so conditioned to associate positive experiences with the color red.

Weaning

One of the few great generalizations fitted to the human condition concerns the "adjustment lag" everyone experiences. The lag refers to the fact that by the time most persons become well adjusted to any given period or phase in their lives, they are usually on their way into another, different period. Hence in life as in war, there is a great tendency to fight today's battles with yesterday's weapons.

When breast or bottle is replaced by relatively solid food, the infant has his first serious experience with an adjustment lag and the frustration that inevitably accompanies it. In most instances, this shift to a new form of nourishment occurs just about the time he is nicely habituated to the old form. Weaning is therefore a critical event in infancy because it demands a drastic change in the adjustment pattern relevant to feeding.

The psychological literature on weaning is surprisingly thin – either that or the material one would like to have is hidden away in obscure places. Most of what one finds in book after book are studies of social factors influencing *timing*. In the United States for example, research shows that in the past, weaning varied widely in different social classes, with lower-class mothers postponing it for a much longer time than middle-class mothers (See Davis and Havighurst, 1946). Such studies of weaning practices on different levels of society are difficult to interpret because fads and fashions in this area change fairly rapidly, and any important personality differences related to social class may be the result of many other factors besides weaning.

Equally difficult to interpret are the cross-cultural studies which provide another popular source of weaning data. One finds repeated references to the work of Whiting and Child (1953) which reported that in most primitive societies, children are not weaned until they are 2 or 3 years old. But a conspicuous exception occurs in the Marquesas Islands. Women there are apparently so proud of their breasts that they wean as soon as possible in the first year.

Useful as all such cross-cultural and social-class data on weaning times may be for some purposes, they only allow very speculative statements to be made about the psychological meaning of this event. Are adults raised in cultures or social classes where weaning is *early* generally inclined to drink heavily or chew betel nut? Do pictures of breasts arouse them sexually more than pictures of legs? Perhaps it all has to do with the frustration of oral needs produced by early weaning. Are adults who are weaned *late* more sociable, easygoing, less inclined to be competitive? Perhaps their content in life springs from prolonged early experience with a bountiful breast. Based on combinations of Freudian theory and anthropological data, notions of this sort have a legitimate place in some areas of personality study, but they are not suited to close scrutiny of weaning as a critical factor in personality development. In this connection, Longstreth (1968) mentioned a number of studies of thumb-sucking. One might expect such behavior to be related to certain feeding and weaning practices. But he noted that all the findings relevant to this proposition are quite contradictory or inconsistent.

Dollard and Miller's theoretical examination of weaning as a learning experience, however, allowed them to make substantial statements about its potential impact on personality.

In the case of weaning also, severe traumatic circumstances may arise. If the child is suddenly changed from one type of food or mode of feeding to another, it may go on a hunger strike which the parents obstinately oppose, saying "It will eat when it gets hungry enough." Indeed it will, but in the meantime it may have learned some of the fears or the apathy already listed (1950, p. 134).

Thus, if it is not carried out properly so as to minimize the infant's frustration, weaning can easily lead to the personality problems mentioned earlier in connection with feeding. Furthermore, because the introduction of new food invariably generates some tension—think of your first Chinese or Japanese dinner—there is a good chance that a hungry infant will suffer digestive problems. Dollard and Miller therefore suggested a psychological basis for colic. The infant who refuses new food until he gets very hungry may finally accept it, but he is then liable to eat too quickly, or overeat.

One of the simplest circumstances producing "colic" is that the infant has eaten too much and must regurgitate some of the food or the gases which its digestion produces. Once it has been laboriously walked or patted into parting with food or gas it may be hungry again. Unimaginative parents, not understanding that hunger has innocently recurred, will fail to feed the child. If the mother does feed it, the child may overeat again and the cycle of gastric tension, vomiting, and hunger may recur (1950, pp. 134–135).

Over and above its theoretical status as a source of emotional tension or anxiety which can lead directly to behavior problems, the weaning experience is also the infant's first serious encounter with novelty. Just as application of the stimulus generalization principle enables Dollard and Miller to see the mother as the first representative of society, the same logic allows weaning to be seen as the first representative of novel situations. So the longer range implications of weaning experience concern later reactions to new situations. The child who has not suffered excessive difficulty during weaning is likely to be less fearful of new situations than the child who has. Naturally, many other factors can influence a child's tendency to accept or avoid novelty; but since weaning is the first serious experience most of us have with it, the proposition that learning here may carry over to future novel situations does not seem unreasonable.

Toilet training

Probably the most complex demand that can be made of any child during his first year and a half is the one which requires him to emulate the toilet behavior of adults. Here again, while there is a good supply of descriptive data showing that toilet-training times vary across cultures and social classes,[4] one must look to Dollard and Miller for plausible theoretical discussion. Consider their description of what toilet training can mean psychologically:

[4]Sears, Maccoby, and Levin (1957) found that 77 percent of American mothers begin toilet training when their children are under 15 months old. Almost 50 percent began it prior to 9 months. Other studies (Davis and Havighurst, 1946; Whiting and Child, 1953) showed that this training generally begins later in lower social classes and in most primitive societies.

On pain of losing the parents' love and so exposing itself to the high drives and tensions which occur when they do not support it, and on further pain of immediate punishment, the child must learn to attach anxiety to all the cues produced by excretory materials—to their sight, smell, and touch. It must learn to deposit the feces and urine only in a prescribed and secret place and to clean its body. It must later learn to suppress unnecessary verbal reference to these matters, so that, except for joking references this subject matter is closed out and excluded from social reference for life (1950, p. 137).[5]

Any objective view of what is actually involved in the stringent cleanliness procedures imposed on very young children in most advanced societies makes insistence upon these procedures appear virtually irrational:

Many social scientists have charged that Western Man has made a fetish of cleanliness. . . . For example, toilet training is initiated during very early infancy, and the young child is frequently admonished to wash his hands, brush his teeth, or wipe his nose. We are prone to rationalize that these instructions are important in promoting the child's health, even though we recognize that other civilized countries manage to have equally healthy children without such vigorous scrubbing of toilets and washbasins and without the wrapping of all consumables in cellophane (Brackbill and Thompson, 1967, p. 147).

The English, with their unfailing ability to invent casually appropriate phrases for arduous human problems, refer to toilet training as "potting." Douglas and Blomfield (1958) reported that 60 percent of English mothers begin to pot their children before they are 1 month old, at an age when no voluntary control over elimination is physiologically possible. Only 15 percent of English mothers are apparently patient enough to hold off potting maneuvers until their children are 6 months.[6] Another fact from this study deserves mention: by the time they were 6 years old, 18 percent of the children studied were receiving laxatives at least once a week.

Dollard and Miller pointed out that the child must learn an elaborate sequence of operations during the course of toilet training. The elimination response which is originally tied directly to stimulation from the bladder or large intestine, must be broken down in such a way as to leave room for a number of new stimulus-response elements to be introduced.

The child must learn to suppress the evulsion response to the bowel drive-stimulus alone. It must then insert other responses in the sequence. At first it must learn to call to the parents. It must later learn to insert walking, unbuttoning, and sitting on the toilet chair while it is still suppressing the urgent evulsion response. Only to a new pattern of cues—the bowel stimulus, the cues of the proper room, the sense of freedom of clothes, the pressure of the toilet seat on the child's thighs—may the evulsion response occur without anxiety (1950, p. 137).

[5]The social exclusion can be painfully real for parents as well as children. On certain social occasions, the most embarrassing of which occurred in the formal dining room of a ship crossing from Germany to Denmark, my own offspring have broken things up by referring to their excretory needs with GI expletives.

[6]This material can be tricky, however. It has been suggested that British (and also Chinese) mothers start potting early not really in order to toilet train, but rather to "catch" the infant's droppings and thus save diapers.

They went on to say that all this learning, difficult enough under the best of circumstances, usually goes on under two of the worst conditions for any human learning. First, there is the communication problem. The young child is required to learn a very complex task without the aid of verbal instructions. Second, there is the emotional problem. Parents frequently create a tense emotional atmosphere by watching the child very carefully, forcing him into behaviors that are awkward or impossible, and then showing strong emotional disapproval if he is not cooperative. The result is that the child may learn at least three related things which can seriously influence his personality:

(1) excessive shame and fear of his body functions. If training efforts are such that high anxiety is attached to elimination, the child may become literally afraid of this function, try to hide it, and repress it. In extreme cases, the fear may carry over to associated body parts, so that the penis or vagina and the anal area all become things to be kept hidden or ignored.

(2) generalized insecurity; a weak ego. If parents convey the impression that they are revolted or disgusted by the child's body products, he may come to understand this as a rejection of himself. That is, his feces and urine originate in the child himself and are therefore very intimately a part of him. Being unable to make fine discriminations in these matters, he may associate intense rejection of what he produces with what he is.

(3) inability to express strong emotion. All of the frustrations related to severe toilet training will inevitably make the child angry at his parents. If he expresses this strong emotion openly, they are liable to respond with even greater severity, so it is possible for the child to learn to fear his own anger, because to express it is to bring down even greater frustration, further rejection. And since anger is a very strong impulsive emotion, the child may generalize his inhibition of anger to include other, similarly strong emotions.

Summary

Research findings and theoretical analysis both support the proposition that significant learning goes on throughout the first 18 months of life. Much of this learning has remained obscure because it goes on in the deep recesses of family life; in nooks and crannies of the mother-child relationship that are not open to public investigation.

We have discussed three universal features of infancy—feeding, weaning, and toilet training—as critical events because each one appears to be an important scene for learning. But these three events or situations also deserve the "critical" label because *they only occur once in our lifetimes, during particular intervals, and in fairly definite sequence*. There is no going back, no erasing of mistakes and starting over again. Compensations can of course take place later, either through the natural progression of growth or through the special arrangements of therapy. It should be clear, however, that insofar as experience determines personality, the unique structure of individual personality starts getting erected right from birth, according to the infant's experience in critical situations, and his experience must certainly be cumulative to some degree.

The child satisfied and secure in his early feeding habits will probably accept weaning with less tension than the unsatisfied and insecure child. It stands to reason that one who is generally confident about getting enough of the right stuff to eat will not be terribly threatened by the gradual introduction of some new stuff. And a relatively benign weaning experience should allow this child to stand up better to the later task of dealing with two giants compulsively blundering about with their infernal toilet apparatus.

SOME LONGITUDINAL ASPECTS OF INFANT EXPERIENCE

Since we have already made so much of this period, the question arises "What solid evidence is there that experience in infancy has any long-range influence on personality?" Substantial data on the short-range cognitive and social-emotional effects of deprivation were discussed earlier. But long-range evidence, whether it concerns the effects of deprivation or such things as the secret learning of infancy, is difficult to find. Longitudinal studies are very costly, difficult to run, and those few that are now available were begun 20 to 30 years ago before researchers were aware of many of the things that interest us today. Nevertheless, several different projects deserve mention.

Prediction studies

Shirley (1933) studied 25 infants in detail for 2 years. Personality sketches based on observations, interviews with mothers, pediatrician reports, and psychological tests, were obtained for each baby. Fifteen years later Neilon (1948) tracked down 15 of these subjects who had grown to adolescence, and worked up new personality sketches for them. Ten judges were then asked to match the infant and adolescent sketches. They were able to do so correctly at a much better than chance level. However, an interesting result was that some of the sketches were much easier to match correctly than others. All the judges were right about one subject, but all were wrong about another; the point being that some people are recognizably the same at 2 and 17, but others are not.

More detailed longitudinal studies of personality development indicate that emotional or temperamental characteristics of the infant provide the best basis for long-term predictions (see Freedman, Loring, and Martin, 1967, for a review of this topic). Observations from one study begun over 30 years ago show that the greatest stability is in "active extroverted vs. inactive introverted" behaviors. Another study, which followed persons over a similarly long period, shows that passivity and dependence behaviors remain quite consistent. Behavior patterns of this type can ultimately be traced to the activity levels of infants, and they tend to be stable because they have a physiological base. Depending upon one's metabolism, for example, he may consistently be very active or inactive right from birth. Does the infant squirm about in his crib or is he still most of the time? Does he take the breast or bottle with signs of fierce gusto or quiet contentment? Is his crying *andante* or *allegro*? Such behaviors form gross patterns that are quite meaningful to the trained eye. They don't often discuss it publicly, but maternity ward nurses typically give infants nicknames such as Foxy, Pokey, Bugsy, or Porky (remember Snow White's seven dwarfs?) which are clearly based on activity levels and associated behaviors. The nurses use the nicknames as an effective means of distinguishing the babies, and it saves them considerable time that would otherwise go into reading wristbands.

Apart from physiologically based behavior patterns, long-term consistencies in personality can also be predicted if one sees clear trends in the mother's behavior toward the child. In their report of findings from the Fels Institute study which followed 71 children very closely from birth until they were 14, Kagan and Moss (1962) presented excerpts from home visitor records that illustrate this very well.

Age 20 months: . . . . S wanted to take a doll downstairs with her; she gathered it up in her arms. In so doing, she caught up her dress in front. The mother said, "Put your dress down." S showed no response other than looking at her mother. "I see your stomach. Shame, shame," said the mother. This had no effect, and the mother pulled the dress down herself (p. 215).

Age 3 years, 1 month: The mother told S not to pick the ears off a toy rabbit. S said, "I did pick it off," with some evidence of impudence. Mother said, "What are you doing, defying me or something?" and she struck S two or three light blows with a knitting needle, which brought on a few tears (p. 216).

Age 5 years, 1 month: The mother does not think the nursery school is good for S. After she has been attending, it takes several weeks to cure her of being "fresh." This is definite evidence of a parental attitude that is different from that of the average mother in the sample, she expects her children to obey implicitly; there is no treating them as equals (p. 216).

Age 7 years, 9 months: The mother said that she would not "think of" letting the children go to the store alone or even on the street after twilight. She herself is very timid and insists that the girls take no chances. She has a particular horror of Negro men. She admitted that she was overcautious but said, "It is better to be safe than sorry. My husband tells me that I am babying the girls" (p. 217).

Age 11 years, 10 months: S had a friend visiting, and they sat coyly across the room from me and giggled at whatever was said. S was uncomfortably shy, very uncommunicative and took a long time to warm up.

The mother is a tough customer. She continually insulted the girls, managed to toss off a continual string of withering remarks. Her commands to them are of the "get here" and "get there" variety. Their every move is noted and criticized. For example, S and her friend started upstairs, and the mother demanded, "Now what are you going to do?" S mumbled, "going to the bathroom." The mother replied ominously, "Well, mind what you do up there" (p. 219).

Age 13 years, 1 month: S seems to grow increasingly dull and solemn; she has lost most of her former winsome attractiveness with developing obesity. The mother now calls her fatty when addressing her. She is more slow moving and heavy-footed than ever, galloping and making funny noises whenever she moves around the house. She rarely does anything at home, seems very lethargic, giving the impression that, in face of the mother's restricting and interfering policies, it is easier to simply sit than to initiate any activity and have it squelched (p. 220).

And so it goes. Little imagination is needed to see that passivity, fear of authority, and introversion were probably characteristic of poor S until she became an adult; and probably for the rest of her life as well.

In sum, it appears that long-term predictions can be made with fair accuracy in those cases giving conspicuous evidence of emotional predispositions based on either physiological or home environment factors. But in cases where no particularly strong evidence of this sort is available, long-term predictions of personality remain a hit-or-miss affair.

Birth-order effects

There is no questioning the common-sense idea that first- and laterborn children have grossly different childhood experiences. The mere presence of another older or younger child will influence the whole family climate. Hall and Lindzey (1957, p. 125) summarized a traditional interpretation of birth-order dynamics given by Alfred Adler in the 1930's:

The firstborn or oldest child is given a good deal of attention until the second child is born; then he is suddenly dethroned from his favored position and must share his parents' affections with the new baby. This experience may condition the oldest child in various ways, such as hating people, protecting himself against sudden reversals of fortune, and feeling insecure. Oldest children are also apt to take an interest in the past when they were the center of attention.

Adler and others developed clinical evidence for this position but much of it does not stand up to critical scrutiny. At about the same time Jones (1931) concluded that over two hundred studies had failed to demonstrate any important birth-order effect on personality. However, in 1959 Schacter stimulated new interest in this topic. Earlier studies had largely been surveys, investigating intelligence and general adjustment and not finding anything consistently related to birth order. Schacter developed a new experimental approach to the problem while researching the proposition that "misery loves company." In more technical language, misery is defined as a state of anxiety, and loving company as behavior indicating a need to affiliate with other persons. In a series of experiments designed to create anxiety among college-student subjects, Schacter (1959) found that those who were firstborn or only children consistently preferred to be with others, while laterborns did not.

As a consequence of Schacter's pioneering efforts, many studies of birth-order effects have appeared since 1959. Their findings generally conform to the pattern enumerated below by Sampson.

As compared with the laterborn individual, it appears that the firstborn or the only child (1) is more likely to attain a position of intellectual eminence, particularly in the more scientific fields, (2) is less likely to express overtly aggressive feelings, (3) is more likely to seek the company of others when he is anxious, and to benefit from such affiliative activity, yet (4) is less likely to be a sociable, outgoing, highly rated individual, one who is empathic and sympathetic. In addition, it is probable that, as compared with the laterborn child, the firstborn is (1) more likely to experience a sudden shift in the centrality of his family role, particularly with respect to attention and affection, and (2) more likely to experience a conflict over the issue of dependence *versus* independence (1965, p. 220).

Some of the more interesting, almost bizarre studies of birth-order effects published recently include one showing that firstborns are less inclined than laterborns to participate in such dangerous sports as football, rugby, and soccer (Nisbett, 1968); and another demonstrating that during the New York City black-out in November, 1965, stranded firstborn males were more anxious than stranded laterborns (Zucker, Menosevitz, and Lanyon, 1968).

Still another project (Amir, Sharan, and Kovarsky, 1968) studied factors that can account for individual differences exhibited by firstborns. Amir and his colleagues studied men who applied for officer training in the Israeli army. Officers clearly have fewer opportunities to affiliate with others than enlisted men, particularly in dangerous situations—the "loneliness of command" and all that. The obvious prediction would be that firstborns make fewer applications for officer training than laterborns, but the study showed that family structure could override birth order as a prediction variable. Firstborns from traditional Middle Eastern Israeli families receive preferential treatment as they grow up. These men *exceed* the army average in their applications for officer training. Firstborns from Western European Israeli families are below the army average. While other factors can obviously account for the finding—perhaps Western families do not value warlike behavior as much as Middle Eastern families—it nevertheless indicates that birth-order effects on personality may be contingent upon family structure.

Finally, in a prize-winning doctoral thesis Hilton (1967), showed that birth-order effects could be traced to the mother-child relationship. She arranged an experiment involving both 4-year-old children and their mothers in a problem-solving task. Results indicated that firstborn 4-year-olds were more dependent upon their mothers than laterborns, and the mothers of these firstborns were significantly more "interfering, extreme, and inconsistent" than the mothers of the laterborns.

At present, birth-order research appears to be going in the direction of uncovering just what it is in the early experiences of first- and laterborns that can account for their later tendencies to react differently in the face of anxiety. It also seems obvious that future research in this area will profit from an examination of the relationship between birth order and experience in critical training situations. One would almost have to find gross differences in the feeding, weaning, and toilet-training experiences of first- and laterborns, if only because most parents improve with practice.

Longitudinal variations in infant care

Many of the difficulties which impede efforts to understand the connection between infant experience and adult personality have already been mentioned. But a further difficulty that should be discussed because it is equally important to the theorist and the interested parent, concerns changing fads and fashions in infant care. Wolfenstein (1953) presented a dramatic summary highlighting the quality and magnitude of the changes. Her summary was based on content analysis of the infant-care bulletin issued by the United States Children's Bureau since 1914.

In the first period, 1914–21, the danger of the child's autoerotic impulses was acutely felt. Thumb-sucking and masturbation, if not promptly and rigorously interfered with, would grow beyond control and permanently damage the child. While he was in bed, he was to be bound down hand and foot so that he could not suck his thumb, touch his genitals, or rub his thighs together.

In the next period, 1929–38, the focus of severity shifts. Autoerotism seems less dangerous. Now it is bowel training which must be carried out with great determination as early as possible. Severity in this area increases as compared with the previous period. This is accompanied by a pervasive emphasis on regularity, doing everything by the clock. Weaning and the introduction of solid foods are also to be accomplished with great firmness, never yielding for a moment to the baby's resistance. The main danger which the baby presented at this time was that of dominating the parents. Successful child training meant winning out against the child in the struggle for domination.

In 1942–45, all this was changed. The child became remarkably harmless, in effect, devoid of sexual or dominating impulses. His main active aim was to explore his world; autoerotism was an incidental by-product of such exploration. When not engaged in his exploratory undertakings, the baby needs attention and care; and giving these when he demands them, far from making him a tyrant, will make him less demanding later on. At this time mildness is advocated in all areas; thumb-sucking and masturbation are not to be interfered with; weaning and toilet training are to be accomplished later and more gently.

In 1951 there is an attempt to continue this mildness, but not without some conflicts and misgivings. Autoerotic activities become even more harmless and negligible. Sucking is a permissible though low-grade pleasure (a poor substitute for being held or fed or talked to) and the pacifier (explicitly taboo, 1914–38; not mentioned, 1942–45) is now restored. Rocking and head-banging (not masturbation) are the puzzling things which babies may do in bed and from which they seem to get some satisfaction; perhaps they do it out of boredom. Masturbation is mentioned only in connection with toilet training. While on the toilet, the baby may touch his genitals. This does not amount to anything (not even pleasure), but if it bothers the mother she may give the child a toy. Here the tolerance for autoerotism seems to require increasing denial of its nature. Requirements in toilet training become even more easygoing than in the preceding period. But the anxiety of 1929 that the child may dominate the parents reappears. If one picks up the child whenever he cries, he may become a tyrant. And in the area of toilet training, gentleness is urged out of the consideration that if the mother tries to be tough she cannot win. If she seems to be fighting the child, he can really hold out against her. Thus we get, if we compare 1929 with 1951, the same anxiety about the child's possible domination combined with extremely polarized approaches toward toilet training, on the one hand very strict, on the other, very mild. Neither the problems of the child's autoerotism nor of his possible domination seem to have been quite solved (1953, pp. 121–122).

For the theorist, changes of this sort mean that one of the most valuable features of all scientific enterprises—the cumulative nature of research findings—cannot easily be relied upon to clarify the relationship between infant experience and later personality. By the time the results of a longitudinal study begun in the 1930's are available, the routines and even the apparatus[7] employed in caring for infants have all changed. This state of affairs is not without its uses, however. When called upon to explain puzzling aspects of the current "generation gap," for example, social scientists can fall back on such remarks as "This post-World War II generation was raised more permissively . . . television . . . etc." And they are probably somewhat correct. But no one can be entirely sure, because there is not much data yet on the later personality trends of infants raised according to the 1949 fashion. Except that we all know it was very different from the 1939 fashion.

Vexing as it may be for the theorist, the fashion problem can be more difficult for parents. Theorists are at least trained to look at general principles and make interpretations fitted to concrete situations. Parents usually want to know only what concrete procedures will be "best" for their child, a reasonable question, but one that cannot be answered easily. Wolfenstein offered a pertinent comment:

The mother of 1914 or 1921 was supposed to know that children masturbate in bed, and was told to eradicate this wickedness. The mother of 1951, who is told that masturbation does not amount to anything, is not supposed to know that children masturbate in bed, but may only notice that they sometimes touch their genitals while on the toilet. She is permitted to feel uncomfortable when she observes this and may give the child a toy to relieve her own feelings. But the mother who feels uncomfortable and so must distract her baby may convey, albeit covertly and indecisively, considerable disapproval. And so with other things; changes in behavior too quickly superposed on less quickly alterable feelings may fail to obtain the hoped-for results. The problem remains of how to help people to face the realities of human nature and yet to treat it gently (1953, p. 130).

So far, social scientists have not done very much to help parents in this respect. One current text advises them that no easy rules exist and that they should therefore "be guided by their own creative intelligence. . . ." And a psychiatrist writing in a popular magazine recently closed his advice to an expectant mother saying "Generally, most mothers are best able to do what is right when left to their own devices." In this condition, parents *do* inevitably come up with their own unique answers to specific questions. But the quality of their answers can vary immensely; partly because leftover debris from 50 years of changing child-rearing recommendations still litters the cultural landscape, and partly because modern social science has not done enough to inform people that neither vegetable nor TLC mythology provides a sufficient base for raising children.

DEVELOPMENTAL PERSPECTIVES

How well does the material discussed in this chapter fit the developmental theories sketched in Chapter 4? Piaget and Sullivan are particularly important here because both have written more extensively than any other devel-

---

[7]Surely the advent of disposable diapers, canned formulas, airtight bottles with new rubber nipple designs, not to mention progress in medicine and nutrition, also add up to a significant influence on child care.

opmental theorists on different aspects of infant personality. For Piaget, it will be recalled that infancy is the period of sensorimotor intelligence. He described six substages in this period and suggested how progress through each can be understood as an adaptive process. Sullivan saw infancy as a period of social-emotional development culminating in a three-part self-system: good-me, bad-me, and not-me. On the face of it, the evidence and theory discussed in this chapter—stimulus deprivation, mother love, infant learning, birth order—may seem irrelevant to such notions as sensorimotor intelligence and personifications of self. However, when these matters are examined in more detail, many apparent discrepancies begin to fade.

Piaget

The six substages of sensorimotor intelligence begin with innate reflex activities during the first month of infancy. Piaget's minute descriptions of activity here and in succeeding substages are unique psychological documents. On reading them for the first time one has the feeling of peering into a new, unsuspected world of phenomena—much as one feels on first looking through a microscope. For example, the sucking reflex or schema is initially described as a "blind" activity because it can be triggered by many different environmental conditions. But even in the first month it begins to accommodate to external conditions, since the infant seems able to discriminate between such suckable objects as breast, bottle, and blanket.

In the second substage (1 to 4 months) of "acquired adaptations and primary circular reactions," reflexive schemas show definite change as a result of experience. The infant is said to be adapting to the environment because his reflexive activity "retains something external to itself":

For instance, when the child systematically sucks his thumb, no longer due to chance contacts but through coordination between hand and mouth, this may be called acquired accommodation. Neither the reflexes of the mouth nor of the hand can be provided such coordination by heredity (there is no instinct to suck the thumb!) and experience alone explains its formation (Piaget, 1952, p. 48).

Much of what the infant does during the first 4 months has the character of trial and error groping: trying out reflexive behaviors in new conditions, perhaps encountering a new experience in this fashion, and then repeating the reflexive behavior so as to have it happen again. This kind of activity pattern is called a "primary circular reaction." Piaget observed it in his son Laurent starting at the age of 2 months and 3 days.

—From 0;2 (3) Laurent evidences a circular reaction which will become more definite and will constitute the beginning of systematic grasping; he scratches and tries to grasp, lets go, scratches and grasps again, etc. On 0;2 (3) and 0;2 (6) this can only be observed during the feeding. Laurent gently scratches his mother's bare shoulder. But beginning 0;2 (7) the behavior becomes marked in the cradle itself. Laurent scratches the sheet which is folded over the blankets, then grasps it and holds it a moment, then lets it go, scratches it again and recommences without interruption. At 0;2 (11) this play lasts a quarter of an hour at a time, several times during the day. . . . At 0;2 (14) and 0;2 (16) I note how definitely the spontaneous grasping of the sheet reveals the characteristics of circular reaction — groping at first, then regular rhythmical activity (scratching, grasping, holding and letting go), and finally progressive loss of interest (1952, pp. 91 – 92).

The third substage (4 to 8 months) is characterized by three new adaptation processes: *secondary circular reactions, motor recognition* and *generalization*. The main difference between primary and secondary circular reactions is that in the former, the infant's actions are carried out for their own sake, so to speak. Laurent's scratching and grasping did not have any particular aim, his efforts were not directed at bringing about any change in the environment. However, secondary circular reactions do have an intentional focus, as illustrated in this later observation of Laurent:

At 0;3 (29) Laurent grasps a paper knife which he sees for the first time; he looks at it a moment and then swings it while holding it in his right hand. During these movements the object happens to rub against the wicker of the bassinet: Laurent then waves his arm vigorously and obviously tries to reproduce the sound he has heard, but without understanding the necessity of contact between the paper knife and the wicker and, consequently, without achieving this contact otherwise than by chance.

At 0;4 (3) same reactions, but Laurent looks at the object at the time when it happens to rub against the wicker of the bassinet. The same still occurs at 0;4 (5) but there is slight progress toward systematization.

Finally, at 0;4 (6) the movement becomes intentional: as soon as the child has the object in his hand he rubs it with regularity against the wicker of the bassinet. He does the same, subsequently, with his dolls and rattles (1952, pp. 168 – 169).

Motor recognition occurs a bit later when the infant shows by his motor activity that he recognizes an object, or literally knows what it means. But how are we to know that infant behavior provoked by the sight of an object is appropriate to that object? Because the behavior in question is similar to the secondary circular reactions which usually follow direct contact with the object.

What happens, in effect, is that the child, confronted by objects or sights which habitually set in motion his secondary circular reactions, limits himself to outlining the customary movements instead of actually performing them (Piaget, 1952, p. 185).

Lucienne, who habitually kicked at dolls placed in her bassinet, provided the following illustrations.

At 0;6 (12) Lucienne perceives from a distance two celluloid parrots attached to a chandelier and which she had sometimes had in her bassinet. As soon as she sees them, she definitely but briefly shakes her legs without trying to act upon them from a distance. This can only be a matter of motor recognition. . . .

From 0;7 (27) certain too familiar situations no longer set in motion secondary circular reactions, but simply outlines of schernata. Thus when seeing a doll which she actually swung many times, Lucienne limits herself to opening and closing her hands or shaking her legs, but very briefly and without real effort (Piaget, 1952, pp. 186 – 187).

Generalization is a process whereby the infant abstracts a secondary circular reaction from its original context and uses it as a procedure to control events in the environment. Thus, if something interesting occurs and then stops, the infant may display secondary circular activity to indicate that he wants it to continue.

—Let us finally mention the manner in which Laurent has come to utilize his head movements as "procedures" charged with efficacity. From 0;3 Laurent is able to imitate a lateral displacement of the head. Now, as early as 0;3 (23) I find him moving his head in this way when confronted by a hanging rattle, as though to give it a real movement. . . .

At 0;3 (29) he shakes his head when I stop swinging a paper knife. The following weeks he reacts in the same way as soon as I interrupt a movement he has observed.

At 0;7 (1) he does it to incite me to continue to snap my middle finger against my thumb. At 0;7 (5) same reaction in the presence of a newspaper which I unfolded and which remains motionless (Piaget, 1952, p. 205).

The fourth substage (8 to 12 months) is the first one in which the infant shows unequivocal *intentionality:* the deliberate pursuit of a goal. Here for the first time schemas are coordinated and applied to new situations. The child will remove obstacles blocking the way to desired objects and show understanding of signs signaling the occurrence of important events. At 6 months, for example, Laurent could not deal effectively with an obstacle:

. . .I present Laurent with a matchbox, extending my hand laterally to make an obstacle to his prehension. Laurent tries to pass over my hand, or to the side, but he does not attempt to displace it. As each time I prevent his passage, he ends by storming at the box while waving his hand, shaking himself, wagging his head from side to side, in short, by substituting magic-phenomenalistic "procedures" for prehension rendered impossible. . . . (Piaget, 1952, p. 217).

Later Laurent began to hit at obstacles blocking his way. And later still, the 8-month-old Jacqueline could not only remove obstacles, she could also employ objects as instruments to implement her intentions.

If Jacqueline, at 0;8 (8) has shown herself capable of removing a hand which forms an obstacle to her desires, she has not delayed in making herself capable of the inverse behavior pattern: using the other person's hand as an intermediate in order to produce a coveted result. Thus at 0;8 (13) Jacqueline looks at her mother who is swinging a flounce of material with her hand. When this spectacle is over, Jacqueline, instead of imitating this movement, which she will do shortly thereafter, begins by searching for her mother's hand, places it in front of the flounce and pushes it to make it resume its activity . . . (Piaget, 1952, p. 223).

It is also noted that during this substage children begin to anticipate events:

An adult starts to get up from his chair and the child anticipates the impending departure by crying. Again, the infant sees the mother put her hat on, and since this has been followed by the mother leaving in the past, the child also cries (Flavell, p. 112).

In the fifth substage (12 to 18 months) the child acquires the "tertiary circular reaction." Flavell indicated how it is an advancement over the secondary reaction:

In the secondary reaction, the infant seems at most to sense a dim connection between his behavior and its result and strives simply to reproduce the latter by activating the behavior schema again and again in a mechanical and stereotyped—one is tempted to say "mindless"—way. In the tertiary reaction, on the other hand, there is again repetition, but it is repetition with variation. The infant gives the impression—and here is the real significance of the tertiary reaction for intellectual development—of really exploring the object's potentialities, of really varying the act in order to see how this variation affects the object, of really subordinating his actions to an object seen as a thing apart, something "out there" (p. 114).

The difference between secondary and tertiary reactions is illustrated by observations of Laurent, which also show how more and less advanced processes can occur in close proximity when a child is in transition from one to the other.

—This first example will make us understand the transition between secondary and "tertiary" reactions: that of the well-known behavior pattern by means of which the child explores distant space and constructs his representation of movement, the behavior pattern of letting go or throwing objects in order subsequently to pick them up.

One recalls . . . how, at 0;10 (2) Laurent discovered in "exploring" a case of soap, the possibility of throwing this object and letting it fall. Now, what interested him at first was not the objective phenomenon of the fall—that is to say, the object's trajectory—but the very act of letting go. He therefore limited himself, at the beginning, merely to reproducing the result observed fortuitously, which still constitutes a "secondary" reaction, "derived," it is true, but of typical structure.

On the other hand, at 0;10 (10) the reaction changes and becomes "tertiary." That day Laurent manipulates a small piece of bread (without any alimentary interest: he has never eaten any and has no thought of tasting it) and lets it go continually. He even breaks off fragments which he lets drop. Now, in contradistinction to what has happened on the preceding days, he pays no attention to the act of letting go whereas he watches with great interest the body in motion; in particular, he looks at it for a long time when it has fallen, and picks it up when he can (Piaget, 1952, pp. 268–269).

The child also discovers new means of achieving specific ends during this period. His tertiary reactions are employed in trial and error activities that yield new solutions to many little problems.

An object out of reach rests upon a support of some sort (e.g., a blanket) and the infant draws the object to him by pulling the support. Analogously, he learns that an object with an attached string can be secured by pulling the string alone. Again, he invents the means by which an object can be brought towards him through judicious manipulations of a stick. There are also schemas of a quite different sort. The infant discovers that it is necessary to tilt long objects in order to draw them through the bars of his playpen. He learns to put objects only into containers large enough to receive them, how to make a watch chain or other slender and flexible objects pass through a narrow opening, and so on (Flavell, p. 117).

Finally, in the sixth substage (18 to 24 months and beyond), the child is able to find ways of coping with new situations by an *internal* trial and error process. That is, instead of employing circular reactions in an openly exploratory fashion, he seems able to do this internally, by representing reality to himself or "imagining" the results of exploratory activities.

The child wishes to achieve some end and finds no habitual schema which can serve as means. Thus the beginning of the sequence is identical to that of the stage-5 pattern: no available means exists, one must be discovered. However, instead of fumbling for a solution by an extended series of overt and visible sensory-motor explorations, as in stage 5, the child "invents" one through a covert process which amounts to *internal* experimentation, an *inner* exploration of ways and means. Unlike any previous stage, the acquisition of something genuinely new can now take place covertly—prior to action, instead of through, and only through, a series of actually performed assimilations and accommodations (Flavell, pp. 118–119).

If it is granted that Piaget has accurately described the increasingly intelligent behaviors that emerge during infancy—that his terminology and postulation of cognitive processes are appropriate—then the outstanding question remaining is how his work fits the more conventional material taken up earlier in this chapter. While any detailed answer to such a question is beyond the scope of this text, some brief comments are in order.

First, it seems entirely clear that none of the prior material poses any fundamental contradiction to Piaget's description of sensorimotor intelligence. When Piaget first published (between 1935 and 1945) much of this work, many psychologists were quite skeptical. They felt that he attributed too much to the young infant; that so much significant activity could not be going on so early. But recent deprivation and learning studies seem to confirm the importance Piaget attached to early experience.

Second, we can follow the "reversibility" principle of cognition that Piaget has elsewhere introduced, and consider how his work may help us understand questions raised by stimulus deprivation studies. Conventional research has established that children raised in monotonous, unstimulating environments show impaired cognitive or intellectual capacities, but it has not yet revealed why this occurs. It seems obvious, however, that under conditions of serious deprivation the young infant will not have many opportunities to carry out the activities Piaget sees as definitive of sensorimotor intelligence. For example, how would a classically deprived orphanage infant have an opportunity to show "generalization" if nothing in his environment responded to his circular reactions aimed at controlling external events? Would there even be any interesting events for him to try to prolong? For such a child, most of the activities associated with "intentionality" will also be impossible. How is he to coordinate schemas and apply them to new situations, to removing obstacles, if suitable occasions for such activity are not provided? In fact, to the extent that a traditional orphanage infant *did* show intentional activity, it would probably be seen as annoying or disruptive and therefore be discouraged.

At a more abstract level, the issues here boil down to the argument that a deprivation environment will not provide sufficient opportunity for an infant to develop cognitive schemas through assimilation and accommodation. Sensorimotor intelligence is largely a matter of sensory and motor adaptations to a variable environment. If the environment is monotonous, it will not demand or call out these adaptations, and cognitive development will thus be slowed. In this connection, it could well be argued more specifically that normal progression through primary, secondary, and tertiary circular reactions requires normally variable environmental conditions. Therefore, the apathy or indifference so typical of institutionalized children may reduce to the fact that these children maintain lower order circular reactions for a longer time. But in pointing to the possibilities of gaining a better picture of infant intelligence and learning, we have come well beyond the frontiers of established knowledge. Research on the further dynamics of cognition in infancy must await the attention of a new generation of social scientists.

Sullivan

The most extraordinary thing about many of Sullivan's theoretical ideas about infant social-emotional development is the degree to which they are supported by recent research findings. With the possible exception of birth order, virtually all of the evidence mentioned in this chapter is given plausible status in his interpersonal theory; the pity is that Sullivan did not live long enough[8] to see it, and that many professionals do not yet seem to be aware of it.

Consider his views on nursing as the first important interpersonal situation of infancy (Chapter 4). He suggested, without the benefit of any research evidence so far as one can tell, that the infant is sensitive to the "good" and "evil" nipple. Moreover, in nursing as in other situations with the mother, the good or evil quality of the infant's experience depends upon his sensitivity to her anxiety. Because Sullivan saw this sensitivity as so prevalent in infancy, he elevated it to a general process which he termed *empathy*. Empathy has come into wide usage as a term for sympathy and friendly understanding. This is particularly conspicuous in the vocabulary of those who expound the virtues of *TLC*. When you ask them to explain what *TLC* really means, they frequently fall back on "empathy." So it is all the more enlightening to see what Sullivan himself had to say on the subject:

The tension of anxiety, when present in the mothering one, induces anxiety in the infant. The rationale of this induction—that is, *how* anxiety in the mother induces anxiety in the infant—is thoroughly obscure. This gap, this failure of our grasp on reality, has given rise to some beautifully plausible and perhaps correct explanations of how the anxiety of the mother causes anxiety in the infant; I bridge the gap simply by referring to it as a manifestation of an indefinite—that is, not yet defined—interpersonal process to which I apply the term *empathy*. I have had a good deal of trouble at times with people of a certain type of educational history; since they cannot refer empathy to vision, hearing, or some other special sense receptor, and since they do not know whether it is transmitted by the ether waves or air waves or what not, they find it hard to accept the idea of empathy. But whether the doctrine of empathy is accepted or not, the fact remains that the tension of anxiety when present in the mothering one

---

[8]Sullivan died in 1949. Most of his ideas were first presented in lectures given between 1943 and 1948, long before relevant research was available.

induces anxiety in the infant; that theorem can be proved, I believe, and those who have had pediatric experience or mothering experience actually have data which can be interpreted on no other equally simple hypothetical basis. So although empathy may sound mysterious, remember that there is much that sounds mysterious in the universe, only you have got used to it; and perhaps you will get used to empathy (1953, pp. 41–42).

People have indeed become accustomed to empathy, but not in the way that Sullivan intended. More important is the fact that his conception of empathy can now be supported by substantial evidence. Harlow's specification of "contact comfort" provides one reasonable approach. If infant monkeys are sensitive to, and literally need to have body contact with soft real or artificial mothers, it is not unreasonable to think that human infants may sense the muscular tension that would accompany anxiety in their mothers. Farfetched as it may sound, the idea that via empathy human infants may have a kind of wire or cloth mother experience depending upon whether or not their mothers are anxious, makes some sense.

Another, even clearer collection of evidence for the empathy concept can be found in the section on infant learning. Relatively new discoveries showing (1) that infants can learn by conditioning when they are a few days old, (2) that they will actively avoid nursing from a difficult breast, and especially (3) that anxiety in mothers inhibits the nipple "letdown" reflex, thus making nursing more difficult for the infant—all of these findings suggest that instead of being an obscure mystery, Sullivan's empathy concept can be firmly grounded on empirical evidence.

Besides suggesting the principle of empathy as a basis for understanding the dynamics of infant personality, Sullivan also posits a three-part structure for personality. The infant's emerging self-system is supposed to involve the "personifications" of "good-me," "bad-me," and "not-me." What can we make of this? There is certainly no way to obtain empirical data showing that the infant really thinks of himself in these terms. But on close examination of what Sullivan meant by these terms, as ways in which the infant *organizes* his experience, they appear quite relevant to Dollard and Miller's theoretical analysis of infant learning. For example, the latter writers discussed how feeding and weaning experiences can lead to such habitual behavior patterns as apathy or active interest, independence or conformity, sociability or withdrawal. Their suggestions seem plausible because they follow from applications of traditional learning theory principles. Sullivan said very much the same thing, except that instead of discussing habitual behavior patterns, he spoke on a more abstract level of personifications which include larger categories of infant experience. Thus "bad-me" is said to organize all experiences with the mother that provoke anxiety in the infant, while "good-me" organizes all of the satisfying experiences.

In short, the emotional quality of infant-mother relationships is important to both theoretical positions, but learning theorists see its structural implications in terms of habitual behavior patterns, and Sullivan saw its structural implications in terms of a differentiated self-system. There is no way to decide which position is "correct" or "better"; each leads to very dif-

ferent long-range interpretations of personality development. Sullivan illustrated both the similarity and divergence of these positions in remarks introducing the self-system to a discussion of psychopathology:

> The self-system is struck off in the personality because of the necessity for picking
> one's way through irrational and un-understandable prescriptions of behavior laid
> down by the parents; in other words, the child has to be educated to a very complex
> social order, long before the reason and the good sense of the whole thing can be
> digested, long before it becomes understandable – if it ever does. And the self-sys-
> tem comes to be the organization that controls awareness; all the operations that are
> not primarily of the self go on outside awareness. That can be observed very clearly,
> however difficult it may be to reason it out with pellucid simplicity (1956, p. 4).

Note that the first part of the paragraph could have been written by Dollard
and Miller. The point to emphasize, however, is that different as the learning
and depth-psychiatric positions may be in the long run, they both converge
on the same base of data where infancy is concerned. Whether one scrutinizes
this period through the eyes of a learning theorist or of a practicing psychiatrist, the material one sees as psychologically important is substantially the
same.

CHAPTER SUMMARY

All unknown territories tend to generate some mythology. As a relatively unexplored psychological territory, infancy has generated the vegetable and *TLC*
myths discussed at the outset of this chapter. We have used these myths –
which some people may actually believe – as a means to explore a wide range
of relevant research. Very prominent in connection with the vegetable notion
are studies showing the negative cognitive and social-emotional effects of
stimulus deprivation. *TLC* is evaluated and found wanting on two counts. As
an operational philosophy for child rearing it seems inadequate because it
ignores the knowledge and skills essential to the enterprise. As a construal of
maternal love, it seems inadequate because it is contrary to relevant evidence. Neither animal research nor clinically based personality theories can
support any simple instinct interpretation. Instead, the mother-love mystique
reduces to such understandable matters as contact comfort, social norms,
and ego enhancement.

Analysis of infant learning further clears some of the conceptual smog
surrounding this period. Recent findings indicate that important learning
can occur in the first few months and even in the first few days of life. Dollard and Miller's discussions of feeding, weaning, and toilet training are especially significant here because they point up the critical character of in-
fant-learning situations.

Long-range predictions of later personality as a function of infant experience are difficult to carry out for a variety of practical and theoretical reasons. Nevertheless, the present state of the evidence suggests that one can
make reasonably good judgments about emotional predispositions (passivity,
dependence, introversion vs. extroversion), if clear-cut knowledge about the

physiological characteristics of the infant or his home environment is available. Studies of birth-order effects further support the idea that emotional aspects of personality tend to be relatively stable from early life onward. An outstanding problem for both researchers and parents, however, is posed by the variability of infant-care methods. It is difficult to detect and specify concrete principles when drastic changes come with every generation.

Piaget's, and then Sullivan's, fundamental ideas concerning infancy are discussed in some detail. As the outstanding theoretical writers on this period, their work demands attention out of sheer respect. But very practical matters are also at stake here. Piaget's analysis of sensorimotor intelligence throws considerable light on the probable causes of deprivation effects. And Sullivan's views on empathy and infant personifications are in line with much empirical material concerning the social-emotional impact of early experience.

References

Amir, Y., Sharan, S., & Kovarsky, Y. Birth order, family structure, and avoidance behavior. *Journal of Personality and Social Psychology,* 1968, *10,* 271–278.

Bettelheim. B. *The informed heart.* Glencoe: The Free Press, 1960.

Bettelheim, B. *Love is not enough.* Glencoe: The Free Press, 1950.

Bowlby, J. *Maternal care and mental health.* Geneva: World Health Organization, Monograph Series, 1952.

Brackbill, Y., & Thompson, G. C. (Eds.) *Behavior in infancy and early childhood.* New York: The Free Press, 1967.

Brown, R. *Social psychology.* New York: The Free Press, 1965.

Casler, L. Maternal deprivation: A critical review of the literature. *Monographs of the Society for Research on Child Development,* 1961, *26,* 1–64.

Coleman, J. S., et al. *Equality of educational opportunity.* Washington: U.S. Government Printing Office, 1966.

Davis, A., & Havighurst, R. J. Social class and color differences in child rearing. *American Sociological Review,* 1946, *11,* 698–710.

Dollard, J., & Miller, N. E. *Personality and psychotherapy.* New York: McGraw-Hill Book Company, 1950.

Douglas, J. W. B., & Blomfield, J. M. *Children under five.* London: George Allen & Unwin, Ltd., 1958, pp. 127–132.

Flavell, J. H. *The developmental psychology of Jean Piaget.* New York: D. Van Nostrand Co., Inc., 1963.

Freedman, D. G., Loring, C. B., & Martin, R. M. Emotional behavior and personality development. In Y. Brackbill (Ed.), *Infancy and early childhood.* New York: The Free Press, 1967, pp. 429–502.

Goldfarb, W. Psychological privation in infancy and subsequent adjustment. *American Journal of Orthopsychiatry,* 1945, *15,* 247–255.

Goldfarb, W. Emotional and intellectual consequences of psychological deprivation in infancy: A reevaluation. In P. Hoch, and J. Zubin (Eds.), *Psychopathology of childhood.* New York: Grune & Stratton, Inc., 1955, pp. 105–119.

Gordon, H. Mental and scholastic tests among retarded children. Educational pamphlet #44. London: Board of Education, 1923.

Gunther, M. Infant behavior at the breast. In B. Foss (Ed.), *Determinants of infant behavior.* New York: John Wiley & Sons, Inc., 1961, pp. 37–38.

Hall, C. S., & Lindzey, G. *Theories of personality.* New York: John Wiley & Sons, Inc., 1957.

Harlow, H. The heterosexual affectional system in monkeys. *American Psychologist,* 1962, *17,* 1–9.

Harlow, H., & Harlow, M. Social deprivation in monkeys. *Scientific American,* 1962, *207*(5), 136–146.

Hebb, D. O. The effects of early experience on problem solving at maturity. *American Psychologist,* 1947, *2,* 306–307.

Hilton, I. Differences in the behavior of mothers toward first- and laterborn children. *Journal of Personality and Social Psychology,* 1967, *7,* 282–290.

Irwin, O. C. Infant speech: Effect of systematic reading of stories. *The Journal of Speech and Hearing Research,* 1960, *3,* 187–190.

Jones, H. E. Order of birth. In C. Murchison (Ed.), *A handbook of child psychology.* Worcester, Massachusetts: Clark University Press, 1931, pp. 204–241.

Kagan, J., & Moss, H. A. *Birth to maturity.* New York: John Wiley & Sons, Inc., 1962.

King, J. A., & Eleftheriou, B. E. Effects of early handling upon adult behavior in two subspecies of deermice, *Peromyscus maniculatus.* In S. Ratner and M. R. Denny (Eds.), *Comparative psychology.* Homewood: Dorsey Press, 1964, pp. 410–421.

Levine, S., & Mullins, R. F. Hormonal influences on brain organization in infant rats. *Science,* 1966, *152,* 1585–1592.

Lomas, P. The concept of maternal love. *Psychiatry,* 1962, *25,* 256–262.

Longstreth, L. E. *Psychological development of the child.* New York: The Ronald Press Company, 1968.

Lowrey, L. G. Personality distortion and early institutional care. *American Journal of Orthopsychiatry,* 1940, *10,* 576–585.

Lu, E. G. Early conditioning of perceptual preference. *Child Development,* 1967, *38,* 415–424.

Maddi, S. R. *Personality theories: A comparative analysis.* Homewood: Dorsey Press, 1968.

Maslow, A. H., & Szilagyi-Kessler, I. Security and breast feeding. *Journal of Abnormal and Social Psychology,* 1946, *41,* 83–85.

McCarthy, M. *The group.* New York: Signet Books, New American Library, Inc., 1963.

Melzack, R. Effects of early perceptual restriction on simple visual discrimination. *Science,* 1962, *137,* 978–979.

Neilon, P. Shirley's babies after 15 years: A personality study. *Journal of Genetic Psychology,* 1948, *73,* 175–186.

Newton, N. The influence of the let-down reflex in breast feeding on the mother-child relationship. *Marriage and Family Living,* 1958, *20,* 18–20.

Nisbett, R. E. Birth order and participation in dangerous sports. *Journal of Personality and Social Psychology,* 1968, *8,* 351–353.

Papousek, H. Conditioning during early postnatal development. In Y. Brackbill and G. Thompson (Eds.), *Behavior in infancy and early childhood.* New York: The Free Press, 1967, pp. 259–274.

Peterson, C. H., & Spano, F. L. Breast feeding, maternal rejection and child personality. *Character and Personality,* 1941, *10,* 62–66.

Piaget, J. *The origins of intelligence in children.* New York: International Universities Press, 1952.

Rank, O. *The trauma of birth.* New York: Harcourt Brace Jovanovich, Inc., 1929.

Ribble, M. Infantile experience in relation to personality development. In J. McV. Hunt (Ed.), *Personality and behavior disorders.* New York: The Ronald Press Company, 1944, pp. 621–651.

Rogers, C. R. *On becoming a person.* Boston: Houghton Mifflin Company, 1961.

Rogers, C. R. A theory of therapy, personality and interpersonal relationships, as developed in the client centered framework. In S. Koch (Ed.), *Psychology: A study of a science.* New York: McGraw-Hill Book Company, 1959, Vol. 3.

Sampson, E. E. The study of ordinal position: Antecedents and outcomes. In B. Maher (Ed.), *Progress in experimental personality research,* Vol. 2. New York: Academic Press. Inc., 1965.

Sarnoff, I. *Personality dynamics and development.* New York: John Wiley & Sons, Inc., 1962.

Schacter, S. *The psychology of affiliation.* Stanford: Stanford University Press, 1959.

Scott, J. P. *Early experience and the organization of behavior.* Belmont, Calif.: Wadsworth Publishing Co. Inc., 1968.

Sears, R. R., Maccoby, E. E., & Levin, H. *Patterns of child rearing.* Evanston, Ill.: Row-Peterson, 1957.

Sewell, W. H., & Mussen, P. H. The effects of feeding, weaning and scheduling procedures on childhood adjustment and the formation of oral symptoms. *Child Development,* 1952, *23,* 185–191.

Sherman, M., & Key, C. B. The intelligence of isolated mountain children. *Child Development,* 1932, *3,* 279–290.

Shirley, M. *The first two years, Vol. III: Personality manifestations.* Minneapolis: University of Minnesota Press, 1933.

Siqueland, E. R., & Lipsitt, L. P. Conditioned head turning in human newborns. *Journal of Experimental Child Psychology,* 1966, *3,* 356–376.

Skeels, H. M. Adult status of children with contrasting early life experience. *Monographs of the Society for Research in Child Development,* 1966, *31,* 3.

Spelt, D. K. The conditioning of the human fetus *in utero. Journal of Experimental Psychology,* 1948, *38,* 338–346.

Spitz, R. A. Hospitalism: An inquiry into the genesis of psychiatric conditions in early childhood. In O. Fenichel, et al., (Eds.), *The psychoanalytic study of the child.* Vol. I. New York: International Universities Press, 1945, 53–74.

Sullivan, H. S. *The interpersonal theory of psychiatry.* New York: W. W. Norton & Company, Inc., 1953.

Sullivan, H. S. *Clinical studies in psychiatry.* New York: W. W. Norton & Company, Inc., 1956.

Thorpe, W. H. The learning of song patterns by birds, with a special reference to the song of the chaffinch. *Fringilla coelebs, Ibis,* 1958, *100,* 535–570.

Watson, J. B. *Psychological care of infant and child.* New York: W. W. Norton & Company, Inc., 1928.

Whiting, J. W., & Child, I. L. *Child training and personality: A cross cultural study.* New Haven: Yale University Press, 1953.

Wolfenstein, M. Trends in infant care. *American Journal of Orthopsychiatry,* 1953, *23,* 120–130.

Zucker, R. A., Manosevitz, M., & Lanyon, R. I. Birth order, anxiety, and affiliation during a crisis. *Journal of Personality and Social Psychology,* 1968, *8,* 354–359.

6

The Preschool or Early Childhood Period (2 to 6 years)

The traditional view of many parents, teachers, and social scientists is that the major difficulties with children in this period all have to do with discipline—if discipline is broadly defined as being relevant to all the skills that the young child is presumed to acquire. Entering this period, he has little or no ability to carry out the essentials for life. He cannot communicate well, feed himself efficiently, cooperate with others, defend himself against, or recognize threats to his being, nor maintain minimum standards of personal hygiene.

Lacking all these essentials, the child survives during infancy and early childhood because he is supported by an organized social group. However, the unique feature of early childhood is that the social infrastructure now becomes an aggressively demanding force; the free ride ends here as the child is required to conform to minimal standards of social life. And what is his response? How does he present himself to the eyes of society? As Allport indicates below, the child greets society as a guerrilla fighter greets alien invaders: with guile, stubborn resistance, and nonnegotiable demands for total withdrawal.

Consider first the two-year-old. However much we may love him we are forced to admit that he is an unsocialized horror. Excessively demanding, he can brook no delay in gratifying his impulses. He is pleasure-seeking, impatient, vastly destructive, devoid of conscience, and wholly dependent. His own hunger, his own fatigue, his own bodily urges, his need for activity, play, and comfort—these are his sole concerns. Never does he consider the convenience or welfare of others. He can tolerate no frustration, no rivalry. From his point of view his mother, his family, his world must devote themselves to the instant gratification of his whims. If an adult were half as self-centered as a two-year-old he would be considered a psychopathic criminal. The philosopher Hobbes once said, "The wicked man is but a child grown strong" (Allport, 1961, pp. 196–197).

One social theorist has offered a tongue in cheek suggestion that with every new generation we face the invasion of a barbarian horde. But are all such notions entirely without significance?

Lois Murphy summarized the behavior of a boy aged 2 years and 9 months on first entering nursery school.

In his relations with children, Colin progressed quickly from a quiet, friendly, watching relationship on the first few days to actively hugging the other children. The hugging seemed to be in an excess of friendliness and was only mildly aggressive. Having started hugging he didn't know how to stop, and usually just held on until he pulled the child down to the floor. This was followed very closely by hair pulling. He didn't pull viciously, but still held on long enough to get a good resistance from the child. He grabbed toys from others. When stopped by an adult from any of these acts, he was very responsive to reason, would say, smiling, "I won't do it any more," would tear around the room in disorganized activity, and then return to hugging or pulling hair (1956, p. 12).

So there are some obvious reasons that allow early childhood to be seen as a matter of discipline. It should therefore come as no surprise that the vegetable and *TLC* mythologies surrounding infancy are succeeded by a *barbarian myth* for early childhood. The ideas involved in the latter are even simpler than those in the former. It is also a great conceptual bargain because in addition to being simple, it explains more (a longer time interval), and the evidence for it seems so clear.

The barbarian notion can be described briefly as follows: once a newborn has gotten over being a vegetable, and/or, a roly-poly sponge soaking up *TLC*, he can properly begin to become a human being. To be a human being in our society one must be *socialized*,[1] that is, one must acquire the capabilities necessary for orderly life in an organized society. This is accomplished through the efforts of parents, because if they are remiss in fulfilling their responsibility, the barbarian will survive in the child.

The barbarian idea is, furthermore, deeply embedded in our culture. Language is replete with expressions for conveying appropriate thoughts to children: "Don't act like an animal. . . . Don't eat like a pig." In America today there is a whole generation of parents who as youngsters heard Bing Crosby sing out these warnings:

> . . . if you don't care a feather or a fig
> you might grow up to be a pig.
> And all the monkeys aren't in the Zoo,
> Every day you see quite a few. . . .[2]

Traditional sources for such thinking can be found in the folk literature of Western Europe that is still passed on to children. In Norway, the stories in-

[1]See Clausen (1968) for a complete historical discussion of this term. He traced its earliest use in English to 1828, when *socialize* was defined as "to render social, to make fit for living in society."

He also noted that in the twentieth century, sociological writers had to struggle with their politically oriented colleagues who wanted to restrict meaning of the term to collective ownership of capital goods: ". . . when the original *Encyclopaedia of the Social Sciences* was published in the early 1930's, the article on socialization dealt with the political-economic concept, not the social-psychological one. The forthcoming *International Encyclopaedia of the Social Sciences*, on the other hand, will deal with the socialization of the person, not the means of production" (Clausen, pp. 23–24).

[2]Copyright 1944 by Burke & Van Heusen, Inc., and Dorsey Brothers Music. All Rights Reserved. Used by permission of the publishers.

dicate that trolls and other little people of the forest have an insatiable desire to steal children; any little child that goes off by himself (against orders) is liable to be caught. The trolls themselves are quite childlike in size and personality, and many of their misdeeds are comparable to those of capricious, vindictive children. Thus, these stories both warn of the consequences of disobedience and provide examples of children at their worst.

In Germany there is still published a classic horror of a children's picture book called *Der Struwwelpeter*.[3] It shows the results of disobedience with full-color illustrations of punishments that fit the crime: a little boy who persists in sucking his thumb has both thumbs cut off by *"der schneider"* ("the tailor"), who does the bloody job with a large scissors. Another boy refuses to eat his soup; he grows thin as a rail and ends in the graveyard. A girl who plays with matches is burned into a pile of ashes.

Then there are the Mother Goose rhymes in English. As a creature of folklore, Mother Goose is said to have originated in seventeenth-century France. By 1791 the first clear ancestor of the rhymes that exist today appeared in England under the title *Mother Goose's Melody*. Whippings were a prominent theme, as in this instance of a response to beggars:

> . . . Some gave them white bread,
> And some gave them brown,
> And some gave them a good horsewhip,
> And sent them out of the town.

The old woman who lives in a shoe has too many little mouths to feed, so:

> . . . She gave them some broth without
> any bread.
> She whipped them all soundly and
> put them to bed.

Little Polly Flinders sits in some cinders:

> . . . Her mother came and caught her,
> Whipped her little daughter
> For spoiling her nice new clothes.

Mutilation occurs in the famous case of the three blind mice, and also in some less well-known instances.

> . . . The maid was in the garden,
> Hanging out the clothes;
> When down came a blackbird
> And snapped off her nose.

> . . . There was a man in our town,
> And he was wondrous wise,
> He jumped into a bramble bush,
> And scratched out both his
> eyes, . . .

[3]*The Raggedy (or Sloppy) Peter; Enjoyable Stories and Funny Pictures for Children from 3 to 6 Years Old* by Dr. Heinrich Hoffmann. Frankfurter Originalausgabe, Loewes Verlag Ferdinand Carl.

Jerry Hall, he was so small,
A rat could eat him, hat and all.

Mayhem:

. . . I went to Taffy's house, Taffy was
  in bed,
I took up the marrow bone and
  flung it at his head.

. . . I met a man with bandy legs,
Bandy legs and crooked toes;
I tripped up his heels, and he
  fell on his nose.

. . . There I met an old man
Who wouldn't say his prayers,
I took him by the left leg
And threw him down the stairs.

And even a note on marriage:

Needles and pins, needles and pins,
When a man marries his trouble
  begins.[4]

But times change. In the original story of Little Red Riding Hood, the grandmother is eaten by the wolf who in turn is chopped up by the woodcutter. In a current edition, however, Grandmother merely hides in the forest and the wolf runs away when confronted by the woodcutter.

The barbarian myth is also supported by conditions present in the everyday life of most parents. Consider the situation of the parents of a young child. First, their experience must include a great deal of anxiety about his sheer survival. The motor skills of a young child develop rapidly, and as they develop, his parents must be on guard lest he be seriously injured using them.

What child does not have many close calls during this period? In our family there was a tangle with a cactus plant (at 18 months of age), a mouthful of shattered glass (2 years), a tumble with friends requiring five stitches in the scalp (2½ years), rescue from a construction scaffolding 30 feet above the ground (3 years), and much more. Generally, the parent's situation is made more difficult by the fact that the child seems bent on his own destruction. Out of what White (1959) called an innate motive to develop competence, and what other theorists have labeled *curiosity drive* or *stimulus seeking*, the child frequently appears to be engaged in a contest to elude the protective devices of his parents.

The second major aspect of the situation of parents is ultimately sociological, because they are responsible both by custom and law for the behavior of their children. This means that while the child is preoccupied with his expanding capabilities, his parents are expected to superimpose upon him a

---

[4]These rhymes appear in *The Real Mother Goose,* Chicago: Rand McNally & Co., 1966 (first published, 1916).

vast structure of routine behavior patterns. And they are constantly remind-ed of this by messages from society in the form of remarks from friends, rela-tives, and the mass media. These messages usually have two components: one simply admonishes them to do their civilizing job properly, the other usually implies that they are falling short of the mark.

The third and perhaps most insidious condition of parenthood derives from popularized psychological theories. Widely disseminated versions of behaviorism and psychoanalysis make early childhood the great psychologi-cal killing ground, because according to both, virtually anything that goes wrong with personality development can be traced to events of this early pe-riod. Thus, whenever the perpetrator of an awful crime is apprehended, one of the first things for which feature-story editors look is material on his early childhood. Parents can become excessively concerned about blighting their child's later personality by doing something wrong during his early child-hood, and many adults will trace the cause of their present problems to early childhood experiences.

Altogether then, the claim that the preschool period is largely a matter of housebreaking, or taming, a child to the standards of his culture, is based on an interesting combination of everyday experience, sociological considera-tions, and popularized psychological theory. These lines of thought converge upon one another to provide some people with apparently logical reasons for treating young children atrociously. Nor is it necessary to wait until the child is grown to see consequences. Erikson described the condition of two four-year-olds, each of whom had been driven to employ extreme defensive tac-tics against the efforts of his parents. Note that both used what is probably the young child's ultimate weapon—his bowel movements—in their strug-gles.

Ann, a girl of four, enters the office, half gently pulled, half firmly pushed by her wor-ried mother. While she does not resist or object, her face is pale and sullen, her eyes have a blank and inward look, and she sucks vigorously on her thumb. . . . But her most annoying habit is that of holding on to her bowel movements when requested to relinquish them, and then of stubbornly depositing them in her bed during the night, or rather in the early morning just before her sleepy mother can catch her. Reprimands are borne silently and in reverie behind which lurks obvious despair (1963, p. 49).

I had been told that Peter was retaining his bowel movements, first for a few days at a time, but more recently up to a week. I was urged to hurry when, in addition to a week's supply of fecal matter, Peter had incorporated and retained a large enema in his small, four-year-old body. He looked miserable, and when he thought nobody watched him he leaned his bloated abdomen against a wall for support (1963, p. 53).

In the first case, Erikson found that the little girl was in conflict between al-ternating feelings for her mother and father. Her sequential bowel retention and release behavior presumably expressed the alternating emotional states provoked by her parents. In the second case, it was discovered that the boy had lost a nursemaid who served as a mother substitute, and the emotional impact of this loss had been intensified by later events. Erikson therefore interpreted his bowel retention as part of a general effort to hold onto things, to maintain possession of important objects which, if once relinquished, might never be replaced.

What, then, is to be made of early childhood? We have noted material which supports a barbarian myth, and which certainly can explain the popularity of this myth among many people. (If it looks like a barbarian, and acts like a barbarian, maybe it *is* a barbarian.) On the other hand, we have mentioned some clinical material indicating that the young child can be so sensitive that he may be forced into a serious neurotic condition by the age of four. The only way to avoid this paradox is to recognize that the young child is not all of a piece. While he may indeed act as a barbarian on many occasions, he is also something more. Just what that something is will be discussed in the balance of this chapter, but it should be understood immediately that for at least two obvious reasons no simple barbarian notion is tenable. First, the everyday phenomena already mentioned suggest that one would have to qualify the barbarian theory by saying that, at worst, the young child is a *delicate* barbarian. Yet this statement is such a contradiction in terms that it is about as useless as simple vegetable and *TLC* notions.

Second, there is the basic fact that whatever one may call him, the young child has a past and future. Emphasize future. The great danger of the barbarian theory, and the reason it is discussed in this text is that in their efforts to combat today's barbarian, parents and others may be carried away to the point of damaging tomorrow's person. One can see "overkill" tendencies in socialization practices as well as in warfare. This does not mean that one need go to the opposite extreme. It is not necessary to walk on eggshells with a young child, nor to develop neurotic fears about contaminating his future personality. It *is* necessary to try to penetrate the mythology and to see what really seems to be at stake here.

CRITICAL FACTORS IN EARLY CHILDHOOD

The broad character of this period is established by two major accomplishments: acquisition of language and acquisition of sophisticated perceptual-motor skills. These accomplishments in turn determine the main terrain features that distinguish the psychological topography of early childhood from all other periods. The most prominent of these features is punishment. Call it by whatever name you will, punishment, or frustration imposed upon the child by his parents, stands as the psychological touchstone of this period. During infancy, punishment is not a substantial matter because the child is apparently too young to benefit from it. His behavior runs in brief, primitive sequences that do not seem susceptible to deliberate shaping by his parents. In later periods, punishment is not such a key issue because the older child will have already internalized many of the basic values defining acceptable behavior, and will be able to police himself. But during the 2 to 6 year period, punishment is very salient.

While explicit verbal or physical forms of punishment are often all too easily seen in this period, much of this punishment is also implicit. The 2 to 6 year period has a unique atmosphere of tension because direct or indirect confrontation is so prevalent. As the child moves through the various situations discussed below, parents inevitably greet much of his progress with anxiety—anxiety that the progress be at least minimally safe, minimally fitted to the general standards of society and to their own ambitions. The child invariably senses this anxiety and strains against it. Hence every new addition to the child's behavior repertoire will be accompanied by fluctuations of tension in the parent-child system. Since the new additions come quite rapidly in early childhood, something—either parents' reactions to the child's actions, or the child's changing reactions to his parents' actions—constantly will be making psychological waves. Furthermore, this condition of friction or tension will prevail in some degree in all families, regardless of whatever constant base of love and affection also prevails. Love does not preclude tension, nor is it a guarantee of mutual understanding, particularly when one is speaking of early childhood. Parents hold the upper hand, and through one punitive means or another they usually exercise it in their own interest.

The balance of this chapter discusses first the general sweep of linguistic, physical, and perceptual-motor development in early childhood; then, more specifically, several different aspects of social-emotional development and learning; and finally, important developmental theories.

LANGUAGE

The exact process whereby children learn language is still something of a mystery. Osgood (1953) reported that vocalizations produced by an infant during his first two months of life contain all the speech sounds found in common languages. Most research stresses the idea that conventional speech must develop out of some combination of biological structure and environment. That is, humans are "built to speak" and their social environment teaches them to do so by providing models for them to imitate and rewards for successful imitations. The language mystery persists for several reasons, however, one of which is that there is no agreement about the origins of speech in humans. Osgood noted that there were three "time-honored theories":

(1) The "ding-dong" (mystical) theory assumes that certain objects have the power to evoke certain sounds from man. Once these sounds have been made in association with experiencing the object, the sounds come to mean the objects. . . .

(2) The "bow-wow" (imitative) theory assumes that the beginnings of communication lay in imitating the sounds made by animals and things. Drawing heavily upon onomatopoeic words, such as "buzz," "rumble," and "bark," the theory states that given the idea of thunder, say, and the wish to communicate this idea, the primitive man-ape points skyward and mouths "rumble-rumble." With this as a starter, man goes on elaborating, and his products are standardized by cultural mechanisms. . . .

(3) The "pooh-pooh" (interjectional) theory assumes that various unlearned, emotional vocal responses tended to occur in stereotyped situations: when a bad taste or smell was experienced, "ugh"; when a sudden pain, "ow!"; when pleasant tastes were being enjoyed, "mmm!" Again, this just serves to initiate communication (1953, pp. 682–683).

Learning and normative development

Elements of the above classics appear in more contemporary theories of how children learn language. Mowrer (1960) offered a "babble-luck" formulation. The child's developing vocal structures enable him to babble; occasionally, he has the luck to say something like a word, and his parents reward him accordingly. Mowrer also suggested that such verbal accomplishments were intrinsically rewarding to the child: by reproducing some part of the verbal behavior of his parents, he is re-creating a part of his parents for himself. Thus, because of his ability to reproduce his parents' characteristic sounds, he can comfort himself or make himself feel good in their absence.

Operant conditioning principles also offer a plausibly succinct explanation for the acquisition of speech: the child emits many sounds while babbling, but only those which elicit a positive response from his environment are reinforced, and the others gradually drop out.

Lenneberg (1967; 1969) argued for a stricter biological interpretation of language. After first acknowledging that many different viewpoints exist, and that there is no consensus among experts regarding the general problems of language acquisition, he suggested that this acquisition is a biological endowment of our species for the following six reasons.

(i) It is a form of behavior present in all cultures of the world. (ii) In all cultures its onset is age correlated. (iii) There is only one acquisition strategy—it is the same for all babies everywhere in the world. (iv) It is based intrinsically upon the same formal operating characteristics whatever its outward form. . . . (v) Throughout man's recorded history these operating characteristics have been constant. (vi) It is a form of behavior that may be impaired specifically by circumscribed brain lesions which may leave other mental and motor skills relatively unaffected (1969, p. 635).

However, no matter what theory may be used to explain how children learn language, in the everyday experience of parents their child's linguistic progress becomes notable when he begins to produce intentional cries at about 9 months. Initially these vocalizations may be only meaningful as expressive cues embedded in a general matrix of crying and babbling, but by the time he is a year old, the average child is using one word "sentences" to give quite specific indications of his desires. Starting with single words at one year, the child is using two-word sentences by the age of two, three- to four-word sentences at three, and five- to six-word sentences by the age of six. His vocabulary also increases rapidly. The two-year-old will have a total vocabulary of about 300 words, while the five-year-old's vocabulary has over 2000 words (see Templin, 1957). Pronunciation and grammar follow the same trend; according to Werner and Kaplan (1952), children articulate very well by the age of three-and-a-half, and their use of adjectives, subjects, and predicates in sentences is basically correct by the age of four.

In this connection, it is interesting to note that the language skills of young children in the 1950's were considerably advanced over their counterparts in the 1920's. McCarthy (1959) discussed comparison data and suggested that the progress results from the impact of TV, increased use of preschool nurseries, and the greater amount of time parents now have available to spend with their children. One thing that has not changed is the effect of social class: data from the 1920's and the 1950's both indicate that middle-class children from one to five have larger vocabularies and better sentence structure than lower-class children.

Humans and animals

The normative data described above show that early childhood is a unique period for language, because that is when so much of it is acquired. This is particularly important for the consideration of the meaning of language in the life of the young child. Among other things, it is his fundamental pass-port into human society. Because language, more than any other single at-tribute of man, is what sets him apart from the other mammals, it is no exag-geration to say that as the child masters language, he is mastering that which makes him human in the eyes of society. Brown (1958) provided a good example of this point in his discussion of the famous "wild boy of Avey-ron." In 1797, some hunters in France caught a child of 11 or 12, who appar-ently had lived as an animal on roots and acorns for several years. Given the name of Victor, the boy was placed in the care of Dr. Itard, who ran an insti-tute for deaf-mutes in Paris. Despite Itard's ingenious efforts to teach him language, Victor was never able to progress beyond a rudimentary level. Af-ter 5 years when he could understand a good number of words and phrases, but could only say "God" and "milk," Itard finally concluded that he was of subnormal intelligence and that nothing more could be done. Brown suggest-ed that Victor might have had normal intelligence after all, but that he might have already passed a critical period for learning speech:

Perhaps the impulse to babble which is so evident in infants operates on a matura-tional timetable such that it must receive social support when the readiness is there or the impulse will die (1958, p. 189).

He went on, however, to cite several other cases of wild or severely neglected children. Most were not able to progress much further than Victor, although one girl found at the age of six did achieve normal speech and intelligence by the time she was twelve. Lenneberg (1969) presented the general case for a critical period explanation more forcefully, starting with evidence indicating that the structure and biochemistry of the human brain is fully developed by about age sixteen. This coincides with the approximate age at which most persons cannot learn a new language "naturally," as children do, but must instead learn it as a more formal exercise. Evidence from cases of brain-damaged and deaf children corroborates this view. The latter learn language quite easily at an early primary school age. But if they have not mastered language by the age of 14 or 15, they find it extremely difficult.

Another perspective on this problem involves the question "Do animals have language?" Brown reviewed data running the gamut from bees to chimpanzees and offered the following conditional statement:

If the essence of language is taken to be selective response to categories of stimuli then scarcely any animal lacks a language. If we add that the responses must be treated by other animals in the species as signs of the referent categories there will still be some animal languages. However, if we ask whether there is any set of responses used by animals among themselves that manifests all the properties invariably found in human languages, the answer must be no (1958, p. 172).

Nor can animals be taught to use human language very effectively. The Kelloggs (1933) raised a chimpanzee named Gua with their son Donald. Both had equal exposure to speech but Gua, although she learned to understand over seventy different words or phrases, was never able to speak. Later, Hayes (1951) raised a chimpanzee (Viki) as a child for three years. Special efforts were made to teach her to talk and she was finally able to say three words, but they were very hard for outsiders to understand. A novel project along this line was reported by Gardner and Gardner (1968). They also raised a chimpanzee (Washoe) at home, but instead of trying to teach it verbal speech, they taught it the sign language used by deaf-mutes.[5] The technique seemed to work. At last report, Washoe had an effective vocabulary of over 35 signs. For example:

"Open" . . . hands together, palms down, spread apart while rotating palms upward . . . used at house, room and car doors, the refrigerator and various containers. *"Drink"*. . . fist with thumb extended and placed in mouth . . . used for water, soda pop, etc. *"Flower"* . . . tip of index finger touching nostrils . . . when sees or wants flower, either real or in pictures.

Interesting as this project is, it remains to be seen whether Washoe will ever approximate the vocabulary of a six-year-old human.

Functional meaning

The functional meaning of language for the young child is extremely important. While theorists still are by no means agreed on the details, all see language and thinking as inextricably tied together. Thus many follow Watson's original statement (1914), for which there is plausible evidence, that thinking is implicit speech. There has been research showing that thinking is highly correlated with electrical activity in various muscles. It has also been shown that when persons are instructed to imagine that they are saying something, the activity in their vocal cords is similar to that which can be monitored when they actually speak. Watson's proposition is still debatable, however, because it has not been shown, nor is it generally accepted, that *all* thinking reduces to implicit speech.

An important tradition of empirical research on language and thought in children exists in the Soviet Union. The Russians see speech, language, and thought as related *functional systems* developing from the child's contacts with his environment. For example, Luria (1961) argued very convincingly

[5]The Gardners are apparently the first researchers to test a relatively old idea. Writing in 1934, Vygotsky discussed the notion of teaching chimps sign language, while commenting upon research by Yerkes who even earlier (1925) had suggested that chimps could not approximate human language.

"In principle, language does not depend on the nature of its material. If it is true that the chimpanzee has the intellect for acquiring something analogous to human language, and the whole trouble lies in his lacking vocal imitativeness, then he should be able, in experiments, to master some conventional gestures whose psychological function would be exactly the same as that of conventional sounds" (Vygotsky, 1962, p. 38).

that when a child learns to verbally name an object, this act influences his perception of that object. Naming makes the object salient: it stands out from other stimuli that may be present, and in this sense the act of naming alters the child's environment.

Thus he becomes capable of *actively modifying the environment that influences him;* by using speech for himself, he alters the relative strength of the stimuli acting upon him, and *adapts his behaviour to the influences thus modified* (1961, p. 4).

To illustrate the concrete value of this interpretation, Luria described discrimination learning research carried out by Martsinovskaya and Abramyan. Children ranging in age from three to seven were shown different colored circles superimposed on gray and yellow backgrounds. All the children readily learned to respond to the colors of the circles (the "figures") without being distracted by the background ("ground") colors. Later, however, when the children were instructed to respond to the background colors, only the five- to seven-year-olds were consistently able to do so. The younger children were distracted or confused by the figure colors. This sort of phenomenon has been demonstrated many times by many researchers: young children are not able to shift their attention from perceptually salient stimuli. But Abramyan used an ingenious technique to show that young children can accomplish this shift when they are given suitable verbal help. He first changed the figure stimuli from circles to airplane silhouettes, keeping the same figure and ground colors. Younger children still could not make the shift. Then he added verbal instructions making the yellow and gray backgrounds salient: "the plane can fly when the sun is shining and the sky is yellow," and, "when it's rainy the plane can't fly and has to be stopped." This simple yet compelling verbal aid overrode the perceptual dominance of the silhouettes; a majority of three- and four-year-olds was now able to respond according to the background colors.

These experiments show that speaking to a child can in fact reshape its significant perception of a compound stimulus and thus modify the "rule of force" and make the physically weaker component predominate. In optimum conditions this can be achieved in quite young children (Luria, 1961, p. 6).

At another extreme from this remarkable Russian work, but nevertheless quite relevant to its central proposition that speech modifies the young child's environment, is research carried out by Bernstein (1964). He analyzed the linguistic patterns typical of English middle- and working-class families. In the former, speech served as an "elaborate code" whereby the individual related to his environment. In the latter, it was a "restricted code" because meaning is limited to a much smaller range of alternatives. Working-class children learn to communicate at a lower level of abstraction. Their language is concrete, emphasizing aspects of primary group living and not the individual experience of group members. Bernstein suggested that the different middle- and working-class language codes tend to enforce different priorities for what will be learned or seen as important by children in these classes. He further noted that while their restricted language code might promote the warm loyalties characteristic of working-class families, it also might promote individual passivity and overdependence on group approval.

Similar findings were obtained in a study analyzing the way lower-class mothers in Chicago teach their children language. Hess and Shipman (1965) observed that these mothers of four-year-olds used speech in the relatively narrow, restricted style noted by Bernstein. This style does not demand that the child consider or choose from among different alternatives but instead emphasizes immediate action rather than future consequences. Summarizing the larger implications of their findings, Hess and Shipman offered the following noteworthy remarks.

The picture that is beginning to emerge is that the meaning of deprivation is a deprivation of meaning — a cognitive environment in which behavior is controlled by status rules rather than by attention to the individual characteristics of a specific situation and one in which behavior is not mediated by verbal cues or by teaching that relates events to one another and the present to the future (1965, p. 885).

Other research, just now becoming available and following this same thought, shows that one of the key problems blocking the way to more effective primary education for deprived youngsters is their narrow use of language. Reports indicate that this problem can be attacked successfully in one of two ways — either by arranging preschool programs that will counteract language restriction, or by arranging primary school programs that will be meaningful in the language acquired by the deprived child. Evidence for the value of the first technique was provided in research by Cazden (1965). Working with a group of two-and-a-half-year-olds, she "enlarged" their use of language by responding to their spontaneous verbalizations with relevant further comments. After three months of enlargement training, these children showed markedly better general language ability than a group of similar children who did not receive the enlargement training. Ayers (1968) gave a practical illustration of the second technique by describing an incident in the life of a six-year-old boy:

A few weeks ago, he dictated a story to one of the staff: "We went to look for hoboes today. I was the onliest one who knew where they was. They ain't mean and scary, though. . ." (1968, p. 143).

The boy was very proud of his story. He read it to all who would listen, colored pictures to illustrate it, and finally hung it on the wall in the special education school Ayers is discussing.

To tell Tony that "onliest" isn't a word would have been meaningless and absurd at best, since onliest is a word — widely used and acceptable in Tony's world. Tony doesn't care that "only" cannot be compared and therefore cannot have a superlative. Tony isn't asking for help in grammar or word usage. He is merely expressing himself proudly and openly. To impose my form rather than to deal with his content is to imply that what he said makes no difference, as long as he said it correctly. It is to have a narrow, constricted view of the importance of language and communication (Ayers, p. 144).

Taken together, the substance of the Russian, British, and American work mentioned above all converges on the same generalization: the language acquired by the young child profoundly influences his functional relationship to his environment—his capacity to think about himself, and the persons and things in his world.

Egocentric speech

Apart from the origins of language, the manner of its acquisition, and its functional meaning, which we have just said is huge, one further issue that requires discussion is the egocentric character of language in young children. The essence of the problem is that all through the 2 to 6 year period, particularly in the younger range, children may use speech in an arbitrary, self-centered way commonly described as "egocentric."

Piaget is chiefly responsible for the attention given to this phenomenon. In the 1920's he published observations which indicated that young children engaged in two general kinds of speech: the more or less normal adult kind used to communicate with others, and another kind he called egocentric. The latter was described as an outwardly expressed interior monologue not having any clear meaning to anyone but the child himself. And even this last point was dubious; maybe the child spoke meaningless strings of words aloud just to exercise his vocal equipment.

As compared with socialized speech, the relative degree to which egocentric speech occurs in children is still a debatable issue. Any parent knows that it is often hard to decide whether or not the verbal statements of a young child mean anything. Piaget said that egocentric speech becomes less frequent as the child matures, although he and others report it in children up to and beyond the age of seven. After reviewing a number of descriptive studies, McCarthy (1959) concluded that even in younger children, egocentric speech hardly ever goes beyond 50 percent of total speech output. If it is granted that egocentric speech diminishes and tends to disappear altogether after early childhood, the question of its psychological meaning still remains.

Vygotsky felt that egocentric speech marked an important bend in the child's developmental road toward adult thinking. He began systematic research on this phenomenon by searching for environmental conditions that triggered egocentric speech. The key condition turned out to be frustration:

For instance, when a child was getting ready to draw, he would suddenly find that there was no paper, or no pencil of the color he needed. In other words, by obstructing his free activity we made him face problems. . . .

We found that in these difficult situations the coefficient of egocentric speech almost doubled, in comparison with Piaget's normal figure for the same age and also in comparison with our figure for children not facing these problems. The child would try to grasp and to remedy the situation in talking to himself: "Where's the pencil? I need a blue pencil. Never mind, I'll draw with the red one and wet it with water; it will become dark and look like blue."

In the same activities without impediments, our coefficient of egocentric talk was even slightly lower than Piaget's. It is legitimate to assume, then, that a disruption in the smooth flow of activity is an important stimulus for egocentric speech (Vygotsky, 1962, p. 16).

Going further in a series of related experiments with children of varying ages, Vygotsky discovered that while egocentric speech might start simply as a verbal accompaniment to behavior, it later began to serve as "an instrument of thought" which could *direct* behavior. This transition can be seen in the following example of how a child is accidentally influenced by his own egocentric utterance.

A child of five and a half was drawing a streetcar when the point of his pencil broke. He tried, nevertheless, to finish the circle of a wheel, pressing down on the pencil very hard, but nothing showed on the paper except a deep colorless line. The child muttered to himself, "It's broken," put aside the pencil, took watercolors instead, and began drawing a *broken* streetcar after an accident, continuing to talk to himself from time to time about the change in his picture. The child's accidentally provoked egocentric utterance so manifestly affected his activity that it is impossible to mistake it for a mere by-product, an accompaniment not interfering with the melody. . . . We observed how egocentric speech at first marked the end result or a turning point in an activity, then was gradually shifted toward the middle and finally to the beginning of the activity, taking on a directing, planning function and raising the child's acts to the level of purposeful behavior. What happens here is similar to the well-known developmental sequence in the naming of drawings. A small child draws first, then decides what it is that he has drawn; at a slightly older age, he names his drawing when it is half done; and finally he decides beforehand what he will draw (Vygotsky, p. 17).

Vygotsky was thus led to conclude that egocentric speech is the foundation of thinking. His comments on this matter suggest that the difference between egocentric and socialized speech in children is parallel to the difference between thinking and conventional speech in adults, except that the child's thinking is initially exteriorized as egocentric speech. As he gets older it doesn't drop out, it just becomes interior. This claim is supported with evidence comparing the behavior of younger and older children facing similar problem situations. The younger children would engage in their typical monologues, while the older ones would often study the situation in silence; but when the older children were asked what they were thinking, their answers were substantially equivalent to the egocentric talk of the younger children.

Summary

The material discussed in the preceding sections demonstrates that language is (1) probably a unique biological endowment of our species, the fundamentals of which are (2) largely learned during early childhood, after (3) being "released" or "unlocked" by social stimulation. Research and theory further indicate that language becomes the crucial mediating link between the child and his environment. Because it can determine how he will perceive and react toward physical and social objects, language serves quite literally as a cord plugging the child into his world. Findings demonstrating that the qualitative nature of this "cord" can vary according to how it is used in different social classes suggest the relevance of language to very practical social problems. Finally, Piaget's discovery that the speech of early childhood is both egocentric and socialized, and Vygotsky's brilliant illumination of the functional meaning of egocentric speech, round out a portrait of language as the grand achievement of this period.

PHYSICAL AND PERCEPTUAL-MOTOR DEVELOPMENT

Perhaps because they are so obvious and universal the physical changes that occur during early childhood are often ignored in personality development. However, if one examines the young child as a complex system, the alterations that occur are quite dramatic. The average two-year-old weighs about 30 pounds and stands about 3 feet tall; by age six, his weight is up 50 percent and his height increases about 30 percent. These general changes in the whole system become more interesting when they are seen as a result of differing growth rates in component subsystems. For example, at age two the torso is already almost 45 percent of what its final length will be at age 21; at six it is over 60 percent of its final length. The vital command subsystem is even further advanced. By age six, the average child's brain is at 90 percent of its final adult weight, but the motor subsystem lags behind. Legs are only about 50 percent of their final length by age six.

Variability in growth rates of specific tissues and organs is still larger. The human system has extraordinary biophysical growth properties, which are matched by an equally extraordinary growth in the system's external capabilities (perceptual-motor skills).

Because the 2 to 6 year period is a time of profound change in system properties, unparalleled conditions of uncertainty are created for both the child and his parents. For the child, the uncertainties associated with these changes lead to frequent testing of his new abilities. He is almost constantly engaged in exploratory activities of one kind or another, either perceptual, motor, verbal, or all of these together. For the parents, the uncertainties are in many ways much more severe. They are, first of all, in a fundamentally reactionary position, because they cannot program or predict with any confidence exactly how the child's steadily emerging capacities will reveal themselves. As each new one arrives, they can only react to it. For example, the three-year-old may be hurt by the family cat, and the four- or five-year-old may have to be stopped from giving the cat a bath in the clothes washer. And while the 2-year-old may endanger grandmother's sofa with a urinary accident, at five he may be sawing off the sofa's legs to make a spacecraft. In these and many similar instances, the child is typically testing or exercising new capabilities; but his parents are in a defensive position from which they must cope with rapid changes that can take various forms.

Aside from being in this way forced by circumstances into a reactionary (technically speaking) position, parents also face a more general adaptation problem. By the time they have adjusted or adapted to one phase of the child's development, the child is usually into another one, and their adaptation must change accordingly. It is a bit like "planned obsolescence," only here Nature is the manufacturer, children are the product, and parents are the harassed consumers who can never entirely catch up.

In sum, the rapid growth of early childhood has fundamental psychological implications created by the difficulties of adapting to any complex, changing system. The "adaptation lag" phenomenon virtually always tends to be present in parent-child relationships, and is particularly marked during early childhood. One can observe many parents who continue speaking to their 6-year-old in the same singsong syrupy tones they used when he was two. And there are many who continue to maintain narrow behavior boundaries long after the child can function beyond them. Finally, because the child's behavior can be so variable—advanced at one moment, retrograde at another—many parents despair of matching their behavior to his. They instead begin to "maximize"[6] by following rigid rules regardless of circumstances.

COMPILATION OF THE DISTINCTIVE FEATURES OF EARLY CHILDHOOD

In the preceding sections, punishment, language, and physical and perceptual-motor development are each discussed as a definitive, critical feature of early childhood. It requires no great expertise to see each of them operating in the life of any young child. Nor should it be difficult to understand that all three are uniquely important during this period: punishment is never again so clear or frequent as it is here; language and speech are nowhere else acquired on such a huge scale; physical growth and associated perceptual-motor skills never again proceed so rapidly or change so drastically.

As gross facts of life, all of these points are obvious, but the aim of this discussion has been to emphasize their less obvious functional meaning for personality development. Punishment involves a state of tension between the child and his parents that will color his efforts to master his environment. Language provides the chief means for the child to adapt to his environment but is also an end in itself, since it can determine his perception of the environment. The child's growing perceptual-motor abilities impose severe adaptation problems on his parents, which doubtless contribute to the frequency and quality of punishment he experiences.

SOCIAL-EMOTIONAL DEVELOPMENT

If an adult is asked about his earliest childhood memories, he invariably comes up with material from the 2 to 6 year period. Many psychiatric writers, most notably Alfred Adler, have suggested that such memories are relevant to the adult's current self-concept. Typically, early memories cluster together in a way relevant to the general tone of an adult's life. The case histories presented by Evans (1966) demonstrate this point. "Johnny Rocco," a young man who has lived mainly as a slum street hustler and who has frequently been in trouble with police, remembers brutality and death:

He remembers that when he was a little boy, the family had a dog, Teddy. Teddy got sick and lay beside the kerosene stove, quiet and shivering. Johnny recalls that Teddy was still alive when one of his older brothers put Teddy into a sack half-full of trash, carried him to the garbage dump, and left him there to die (1966, p. 5).

[6]Research on gambling and risk-taking indicates that most persons follow one of two "strategies." "Matching" involves a constant effort to win on every play by adjusting bets to changing circumstances. "Maximizing" is an effort to win over the long run by always betting according to the general odds of the game. A "matcher" might draw to an inside straight; a "maximizer" wouldn't.

Johnny also remembers visiting an older brother in reform school (where he later spent time himself), and, very vividly, the death of his father. One night when he was five, he was awakened by noises, peeked into the kitchen and there saw his father bleeding to death on the kitchen floor.

More formal, literary autobiographies yield similarly characteristic recollections. Vladimir Nabokov *(Speak, Memory)* describes an early childhood filled with sensitive, aesthetic experiences. He remembers sensations of shimmering beauty while playing with the contents of his mother's jewel case, and remembers the delicate perfection of his first butterfly specimens. In contrast, the autobiography of Frank Harris *(My Life and Loves)* contains a detailed description of how at the age of four or five, he developed a technique for peering up the dresses of older girls. There is, however, the problem of false memories: both Adler and Nabokov give examples of childhood experiences they thought were real, but discovered to be false after checking with other persons present at the time.

These accounts should convey the shift in emphasis necessary for the turn from the definitive structure of early childhood – the changing capabilities and general atmosphere of this period – to the specifics of social-emotional development. This shift involves a movement into a more commonly understood and more frequently discussed arena of personality development. The questions here involve the child's emerging conception of himself as an individual, his awareness of sex differences, the development of rudimentary conscience or morality, dispositions toward aggressive or passive behavior, and early orientations toward achievement. Although these everyday elements of personality obviously overlap and intermingle with one another, for the sake of clarity they are discussed separately below.

The emerging self-concept

Development of a conscious awareness of self is surely one of the central events of early childhood. Allport (1961, pp. 113–122) summarizes much theory and research by organizing the child's evolving self-concept into five successive stages. Up to the age of three, he suggests that the child acquires first a sense of *bodily self;* second, a sense of *continuing self-identity;* and third, a sense of *pride or self-esteem.*

Throughout infancy, the child gradually differentiates his body from the rest of the immediate environment. Parents frequently observe how the five- or six-month old "discovers" his toes. By two, the child knows his body directly and his identity includes his own name. Allport notes that the sense of bodily self is so fundamental that most adults are normally unaware of it – it only becomes salient when we are ill or in pain. He gives a striking example of how the natural intimacy of body functions can be exposed as really quite artificial: most persons do not think twice about swallowing their own saliva, but they are liable to be disgusted if asked to salivate into a cup and then drink it. Apparently, most of us retain a very childlike or superficial conception of our bodies, or exercises of this sort would not disgust us.

Enlargement of the self-concept to its second stage, continuing *self-identity,* is promoted by language. The two-year-old knows his name, even though it may take considerably more time until he can use his name and various personal pronouns correctly. He will often speak of himself in the third person, and also will show signs of behaving according to the "good-me bad-me" self-conceptions noted by Sullivan. However, by three it is clear that the child is gaining a unitary knowledge that he is himself, one and indivisible, so to speak, regardless of changing situations.

The importance of the child's name for his new sense of identity can be seen very easily if it is threatened. One of the simplest ways to tease a young child into tearful frustration is by persistently calling him by another name, or mispronouncing his proper name. This is presumably very upsetting to children because it undermines their fragile orientation as distinct individuals.

At three the child gives evidence of burgeoning *pride* by insistent demands to do things for himself, and his subsequent pleasure when successful. Erikson interprets such behavior as expressive of a need for autonomy or independence, but it can also be seen as marking an important evaluative expansion of the self-concept. Another way to approach this matter is in terms of power: the child begins to see himself as having power to alter his environment. In this sense, the realities of pride or self-esteem seem the same for the young child as they are for the adult, because in both, the basis for these feelings reduce to power. In one of his essays on big-game hunting, Ernest Hemingway suggested that its fundamental attraction was that man attains the ultimate power of a god by his ability to deliberately give death. For the young child, however, common attainments of eating by himself, dressing and undressing, building up or smashing down his toy block creations are the proofs of power. The drive for mastery or power is also indicated by the images and phrases used by young children. Lois Murphy's discussion of nursery school behavior contains many examples:

During the succeeding years, we find phrases like the following expressing attitudes, energies, and orientations relevant to Colin's sense of himself: "I'll push," "I'm a big boy"; "I way, way up high," "I got to fix that chimney,". . . Here power, height, or conquest, and repair of damage along with a strong emphasis on visual and motor orientations in connection with each other are implied. . . . Throughout, we find Colin's image of himself dominated by the urge to master, to come to terms with a challenge, to prove his power, and above all to get big (1956, p. 221).

Relevant to Colin's strivings also is the *negativism* so distressing to many parents. Sometime during the 2 to 4 year age interval most children will go through one or more periods of saying no to everything. This clearly seems to be another form of self-assertion. Child-rearing authorities generally agree that the negativism wanes quickly if parents treat it in a matter-of-fact fashion. Some reasonable degree of acquiescence will probably bolster the child's self-esteem; excessive acquiescence or denial are liable to create further difficulties.

During the latter part of early childhood (4 to 6 years), Allport sees the self-concept being elaborated through two further stages: *extension of self* and *self-image*. The former is reflected by jealously possessive behavior: toys, clothing, pets, and parents become things to be guarded against loss, and particularly against appropriation by another child. This behavior can be especially troublesome in play situations. In the eyes of many parents, the child's intense concern for his own "rights" is upsetting; what is even more upsetting is that it is not accompanied by respect for the rights of others. The first time a parent sees his child strike another and take something from him it can be quite disturbing. How is such behavior to be understood? Some people still regard it as evidence that men are actually just greedy little beasts. Allport and others suggest that such behavior is understandable as the first signs of a healthy extension of self. The child is quite literally extending himself beyond former boundaries when he uses the belongings of others; and when he goes to extremes of possessiveness, he is extending himself both into his objects and into a situation in which he can imagine their loss.

Allport described the barely perceptible global self-image of the five-year-old as being little more than a rudimentary model for the conscious self-knowledge, morality, and intentions that will later characterize personality. At five or six, the child begins to see himself somewhat according to these adult criteria, but the view is very dim and narrow.

Detailed processes whereby the self emerges in early childhood have never been worked out empirically. Most of the research on this period concerns relevant, but more specific, issues of the sort to be discussed in the following sections. However, because the idea fits equally well into learning theories, cognitive and psychoanalytic theory, as well as commonsense observation, it is generally accepted that the young child's social environment determines his conception of himself. Mead (1934) expanded this view into the doctrine of the "looking-glass self." That is, the relevant persons in the child's life each serve him as a kind of mirror, because the child will come to think of himself as these others act toward him. If he is treated with consideration, as a valuable person, he will think of himself that way. And if he is treated as a worthless nuisance, he will think of himself *that* way. Burlingham and Anna Freud (1942) mentioned convincing examples of the latter self-view in young British children who were removed from their families during World War II. Many of these children were shifted through various foster homes and nurseries. One five-year-old epitomized the effect of this treatment when he said of himself: "I am nobody's nothing." In general, Burlingham and Freud concluded that because of the psychological damage sustained by so many of these young children, it would have been better to let them stay with their families and risk the hazards of bombing.

Sexual identity and the learning process

According to Gesell's normative data published in 1940,[7] by the age of 30 months most children can say whether they are girls or boys, and other evidence indicates that this discrimination is made even earlier. One can easily see three-year-olds becoming very upset if anyone seems to mistake their gender, and studies show that three- and four-year-olds understand many of the behavioral implications of sex differences. Hartup and Zook (1960) found that when 3- and 4-year-old children are shown pictures of various toys, most

[7]See *Child Development* by Gesell and Ilg, 1949.

boys prefer guns and cowboy dolls while most girls choose cooking utensils and mama dolls.

Another study (Vener and Snyder, 1966), involved children ranging in age from two-and-a-half to five. They were shown a suitcase full of common items of clothing and household goods, and asked to identify each item as being either "Mommy's or Daddy's." The youngest children were almost 75 percent correct in identifying such items as a necktie and screwdriver as Daddy's; hosiery and a dustpan as Mommy's. It was also noted that these children made more errors on the male than on the female items—probably because they are at home with their mothers most of the time and therefore more familiar with the female items. Finally, in still another project, Fauls and Smith (1956) interviewed a number of five-year-olds and discovered that most of them were aware of parental pressures to adopt proper sex-role behaviors.

The interesting question relating to sexual identity in early childhood does not concern its function, because that is obvious: a good part of the child's self-concept and his gross social-emotional development are determined by sex. Instead, it concerns the manner in which sexual identity is acquired. While it may seem a little absurd at first glance, one way to formulate the problem is by raising the question "Are men and women born or made?" Physiologically, of course, they are born. But the general run of research evidence indicates that psychologically they are to a large extent made.

Margaret Mead (1935) argued for an extreme view of sex differences as culturally determined, or as learned rather than hereditary, on the basis of anthropological evidence showing that in some primitive societies women had most of the social-emotional attributes we ordinarily associate with men. In the Tchambuli tribe of New Guinea, for example, women are supposed to be socially domineering and aggressive, while men are dependent and sensitive. Together with other evidence, this led Mead to suggest that most so-called masculine and feminine personality traits are no more tied to physical gender than are clothing or hair styles. Her position can be partially refuted by data showing that among two-year-olds in our society, males are considerably more aggressive than females. And among the higher mammals besides man, males are usually stronger, larger, and more pugnacious than females. Finally, even among the Tchambuli, it is the dependent, sensitive men who go out to fight when tribal warfare erupts. Considerations of this sort force some moderation of Mead's strong stand on cultural determinism. Her position cannot be entirely rejected, however, because too much psychological material supports it.

One of the most striking things observable in any family is the degree to which young children reflect or mimic characteristic behaviors of their parents. This phenomenon is so general that it has been exploited as a means of entertainment. Art Linkletter was a master at eliciting humorous (i.e., revealing) comments from children on a TV quiz program, and Allen Funt's *Candid Camera* also provided many examples of such material.

There are five different general psychological explanations for the fact that by the end of early childhood, most children strongly identify with their same-sexed parent: reinforcement and conditioning; similarity and imitation; internalization of rewarding behaviors; power capturing; and identification with the aggressor.

(1) The reinforcement and conditioning interpretation rests on the same principles we have already encountered in other areas. Parents and other representatives of society reward children for showing appropriate sex-role behavior. A little boy will be encouraged to play at being a cowboy or Indian, and discouraged from playing a housewife. Because they are treated in appropriately sex-relevant ways practically from birth—in names, clothing, toys—children are conditioned to associate themselves with their proper sex. As they grow older, both the reinforcement and conditioning factors shape behavior toward the model provided by the child's same-sexed parent.

(2) The similarity and imitation idea has the virtue of even greater simplicity. Presumably because the young child becomes aware of being generally similar to a same-sexed parent, that parent becomes a model for imitation. It is rather like "monkey see monkey do," when the choice of objects to be imitated is between something similar or dissimilar to oneself.

(3) Internalization of rewarding behaviors is another general principle that can be extended to explain proper sex-role learning. Here the child is thought to imitate those behaviors of his parents that he finds rewarding. He does this to reward himself by making these external behaviors his own. Since the proper sex-role is embedded in the general matrix of parental behavior, the child eventually incorporates this with everything else.

(4) Compared to his parents, the child is relatively powerless, but he envies their power, and tries to capture it in the only way that seems feasible to him: by imitation. The basic idea is similar to the superstition or magical beliefs that have been observed among primitives. By making himself as similar as possible to a powerful figure, the primitive (or child) hopes to capture some of his power for himself. Hence the savage will adopt some of the behavior or wear some of the clothing of one he respects, and the child will do the same with his parents. In most families, power of one kind or another is displayed by both parents sufficiently for girls to imitate their mothers, and boys their fathers. Moreover, the similarity to a same-sexed parent will make magical capture of that parent's power appear much easier for the child.

(5) Identification with the aggressor is a Freudian defense mechanism that supposedly comes into play when an individual cannot defend himself against or escape from a frightening authority figure. Since there is no rational way of coping with the authority, the individual resorts to the semi-rational or magical procedure of making himself similar to the authority figure. The logic involved is that failing all else, if one can make himself similar to the feared authority, perhaps that authority will be less inclined to inflict punishment upon him. This is related to, but somewhat different from, the logic of power-capturing mentioned above.

Bettelheim (1960) saw this identification mechanism operate in a Nazi concentration camp. He observed that many prisoners who did not entirely succumb to the atrocious conditions began to imitate the guards by speaking and dressing like them whenever possible. Anna Freud (1946) provided a more direct illustration by describing the case of a little boy who upset his teacher by making faces in class. It turned out that the boy was frightened of the teacher and whenever he received a scolding, would imitate as best he could the facial expressions of the teacher. In sum, it seems plausible to consider that such a defense mechanism might operate in some families and thus result in imitation of a very domineering parent.

Of the five interpretations of the identification process in young children, which one is most acceptable? Longstreth (1968) reviewed evidence to the first four interpretations and concluded that all are to some extent correct. He further noted that the most convincing material is contained in a study by Hetherington and Frankie (1967). These investigators first used parents' responses to hypothetical situations involving children to determine whether the husband or wife (a) was more dominant in the family, and (b) showed more affection for the child. Then the children of parents categorized in this way were tested on tasks arranged so that they could imitate either their mother's or their father's style of performance. Among other things, the results showed that boys generally imitated their fathers more than their mothers, and vice versa for girls. However, if their mother was dominant, boys and girls both imitated her more than the father; if their father was dominant, boys imitated him more, but girls still imitated their mothers. It was also generally the case that the more affectionate parent, regardless of sex, was imitated more frequently by all children. But if both parents were equally affectionate, the mother was imitated more than the father. This study is particularly valuable because it reveals the complexity of the sexual identification problem. It seems clear that one or more different processes may occur depending upon the characteristics of both parents.

Direct evidence for the identification with the aggressor process is scarce. Like so many Freudian ideas, this one can be supported by certain case history material, but experimental work is lacking because social scientists are not eager to create traumatic conditions for their subjects. An ingenious study by Sarnoff (1951), however, got partially around this problem by analyzing data collected from one hundred Jewish college students. The students were divided into groups showing strong and weak anti-Semitic tendencies as demonstrated by their scores on a "Jewish anti-Semitism" questionnaire. (Note that Sarnoff was dealing with the well-known phenomenon of self-hate in minority groups. He interpreted this to be a form of identification with the aggressor.) Students in both groups were then given extensive personality tests. It was found that those in the highly anti-Semitic group were more insecure and as children seemed to have suffered serious rejection by their parents. Sarnoff therefore argued that identification with the aggressor as manifest in self-hatred is most likely to occur in minority-group adults who have had unfortunate childhoods. If neither parent provides warm acceptance, the child is likely to grow up identifying with outside aggressive forces.

This leads us to an involved hypothesis that seems impossible to test, and may quite probably be wrong, but is intriguing nevertheless. Say a boy has a cold, rejecting mother and a harsh, threatening father; he should by all accounts identify with his father. However, if this condition occurs in a minority-group family, the boy's identification will shift away from the father and focus on more strongly threatening external forces. One finding from the Hetherington and Frankie study tends to corroborate at least the first part of our hypothesis. They found that in families characterized by conflict between parents and by lack of parental affection, children imitated the more aggressive, dominant parent as per the classical Freudian interpretation.

Before closing our discussion of sexual identification in early childhood, it should be emphasized that regardless of dynamics within the family, the cultural environment exerts terrific force toward appropriate sex identification. Beginning in early childhood and increasing with age, social pressures tend to push children irresistibly into their proper sex roles. Proofs for such a strong generalization are very conspicuous in the case histories of homosexuals. For example, boys who grow up to be overt homosexuals tend to have (a) excessively dominant mothers, who (b) reject their husbands, (c) encourage femininity in their sons, and (d) discourage masculine activities by their sons. Furthermore, even in the face of such preconditions, it also takes some sort of relatively pleasant initiation into homosexual practices to finally transform an adolescent male into an active homosexual. Certainly the mere presence or absence of a father figure in the home is not a decisive factor. There are some studies indicating that boys raised in fatherless homes may be somewhat less masculine,[8] but there is no evidence showing this to be a sufficient condition or very strong influence toward later homosexuality. In certain Norwegian fishing villages, virtually all of the active males from 16 to 65 may spend years away from home; yet each generation of boys grows up without becoming effeminate.

Conscience and morality

Any discussion of morality is contingent upon how it is defined. If it is defined as the ability to say that certain things are right and others are wrong, then it is very strong in the average six-year-old. Children at this age commonly know that it is correct to obey authorities, eat with utensils, and be considerate of younger children. They also know that it is wrong to take things that belong to other people, urinate on the floor, and throw stones at passing automobiles. In fact, the six-year-old can list a whole catalogue of things that he is quite certain are right and wrong. But is this what is meant by moral conscience? Most people would agree that while it may be a part of morality, it is the least important part.

What really counts as the definitive element in morality is not the degree to which someone can parrot or act out rules, it is the degree to which he feels guilt if he violates the rules. Note that the emotion specified is guilt, not fear. The four- or five-year-old may be quite frightened of breaking certain rules, but he rarely gives evidence of having guilt feelings. That is, he has no internal standard for proper conduct which, if violated, can cause him to feel sorrow, regret, or chagrin — any of the emotions we loosely associate with the

[8]Results indicate that such boys have more difficulty relating to peers, are generally less mature, less aggressive, less certain about sex-role behaviors, tend to have feminine fantasies about their fathers, and to make lower scores on mathematical aptitude tests. But while they are entirely legitimate, these and other findings on the behavioral correlates of fatherlessness are tricky to interpret.

word *guilt*. In other words, the dichotomy that exists in moral development involves the difference between knowledge and emotion: it is one thing to store knowledge of what is generally considered to be right and wrong behavior; it is quite another to feel an *intrinsic* emotion of rightness or wrongness with respect to such behaviors.

Internalizing rules

It is clear that the young child has no sense of right and wrong as he emerges from infancy. The average toddler gets his first initiation into this matter when he discovers that certain behaviors provoke punishment. Suppose he is crawling around and gets hold of something dangerous – an electric cord attached to a lamp that can fall on him, a plug in a light socket, or whatever. His mother probably separates him from the dangerous object, saying "No, no, mustn't touch," etc. But sooner or later, because of the persistence of most children and the ubiquity of dangerous objects, most mothers will go to the slap on the wrist technique. It is here that one can see the internalization process begin to operate. For instead of abandoning the forbidden activity, many children will return to it mumbling "No, no" and often slapping their own wrists. Parents may see this sort of thing as amusing, and from the standpoint of our earlier discussion of egocentric speech, it would be an illustration of narrative accompaniment. On close examination, however, it appears to be the fundamental basis for moral rule learning. Young children begin by openly imitating punitive actions against themselves, but they soon "interiorize" or internalize these punitive actions.

Simple observation indicates that a young child passes through three general steps in the process of internalizing moral rules. First he will engage in forbidden behavior, imitating punishment when he sees a parent approach. That is, he seems to imitate punishment when cued by the sight of a parent getting ready to inflict it. Later, one can see children start behavior sequences leading toward forbidden action, but stop themselves and imitate punishment either before or while engaging in the action. Finally, children indicate that they have learned the moral rule by avoiding forbidden activities, or by showing fear when caught in them. In brief, whether or not the child obeys the rule, it is clear from his behavior that he knows it. Punishment is no longer openly imitated; it is covertly imagined. If it is very painful, the child may try to avoid it by running away. If it is moderate or mild, he may try to make a game of it by holding out his hand for the slap.

It should be stressed again that according to the imitative process described above, the child comes to internalize moral rules as systematic knowledge that certain activities lead to certain punishments. He does *not* internalize the emotional component of morality. At six he may be a conformist, but he is not the possessor of what we ordinarily call a moral conscience.

Moral sequences in early childhood

Modern studies of moral development were largely stimulated by Piaget's observations first published in *The Moral Judgment of the Child* (1932). He noted some of the basic phenomena described above and provided many illustrations of how children conceive justice to be a matter of conformity to rules. The child under seven or eight was generally described as having *heteronomous* morality—morality in which one is subject to the laws of another. At about nine, the child is said to develop *autonomous* morality because he becomes subject to his own law. Piaget also showed that the young child sees punishment as *expiatory:* wrongdoers should be made to suffer in proportion to the magnitude of their offense, by any convenient means such as spanking. For example, if the crime is spilling ink on important papers, the younger child will suggest that the offender be spanked according to the amount of ink spilled. But older children aged eight or nine see punishment as *reciprocal:* one who spills ink should be made to clean it up; any further punishment should depend upon whether the spillage was accidental or deliberate.

More recently Kohlberg (1970) carried out an extensive program of research on morality. It was based upon Piaget, but went well beyond him in theoretical and methodological detail. Kohlberg's work indicated that at a younger *pre-moral* age, the child simply learns to avoid being punished by parents. After a while, he is able to program himself accordingly. It is not until later, during the age period from six to nine, that he makes the transition to an emotionally internalized morality.

The facts of moral development in early childhood are therefore relatively simple to summarize: the child enters this period entirely ignorant of morality; he leaves it with an extensive, internalized knowledge of rules. Most if not all of the emotional components of morality develop during middle childhood and will be discussed in the next chapter. However, it would be a mistake to pass over early childhood without examining processes that apparently lay the foundation for subsequent enforcement of morality via guilt feelings.

The same general processes that were discussed in connection with development of the child's sexual identity are also thought to explain the emotional side of his moral development. Just as he can internalize appropriate behaviors and feelings about his sex through any or all of five identification processes, so he can presumably also internalize appropriate moral rules and feelings; except that the latter constitutes a narrower, more specific aspect of general identification with parents.

Critical conditions

Empirical research (most notably the Hetherington and Frankie study) showed that in the case of sexual identification the two key causal elements or conditions were parental warmth and dominance. For moral development, research indicates that the critical condition is the style of punishment administered by parents. Hoffman (1963) reviewed studies concerning children's ability to internalize moral values and feel guilt when they are violated. He concluded that when parents employ a "power assertive" style of discipline—emphasizing physical punishment and material deprivation—children tend to grow up with an external orientation to morality. Their main concern is that misbehavior will result in punishment from others. When parents follow a "non-power-assertive" style, emphasizing psychological punishments such as withdrawal of love, children acquire an internal moral orientation. Guilt feelings become their main concern in connection with wrongdoing.

Explanations for the greater efficiency of non-power-assertive discipline in promoting guilt feelings can be drawn from a mixed bag of theoretical interpretations which have been summarized by Hoffman and Saltzstein.

Several explanations of these findings have been advanced, each focusing on a different aspect of the parent's discipline. Thus, Allinsmith and Greening (1955) suggest that the significant variable may be the difference in the model presented by the parent during the disciplinary encounter (i.e., parent openly expresses anger versus parent controls anger). The importance of this factor may lie in the model it provides for the child for channeling his own aggression. Where the parent himself expresses his anger openly, he thereby encourages the child to express his anger openly; where the parent controls his anger, he discourages the child from openly expressing anger and therefore may promote a turning of the anger inward which according to psychoanalytic theory is the process by which the guilt capacity is developed.

Another explanation of the difference between power assertive and nonpower assertive techniques is in terms of the duration of the punishment; that is, whereas nonpower assertive discipline may last a long time, the application of force usually dissipates the parent's anger and thus may relieve the child of his anxiety or guilt rather quickly. A third possibility, suggested by Sears, Maccoby, and Levin (1957), is that punishing the child by withholding love, which is frequently involved in nonpower assertive discipline, has the effect of intensifying the child's efforts to identify with the parent to assure himself of the parent's love.

A still different formulation has recently been suggested by Hill (1960). According to this view, the crucial underlying factor is the timing of the punishment. Love-withdrawal punishment is believed more often to terminate when the child engages in a corrective act (e.g., confession, reparation, overt admission of guilt, etc.), whereas physical punishment is more likely to occur and terminate at the time of the deviant act and prior to any corrective act.

Finally, the important variable may be the information often communicated by nonpower assertive techniques regarding the implications of the child's deviant behavior. For example, Aronfreed's (1961) view is that such information can provide the cognitive and behavioral resources necessary for the child to examine his actions independently and accept responsibility for them (1967, pp. 45–46).

In their own research, Hoffman and Saltzstein obtained test data and ratings relevant to the moral behavior of over 400 seventh-grade children. Many of the children and their parents were also interviewed to determine what style of discipline was used in their homes. The style most consistently associated with guilt feelings as a consequence of wrongdoing was one in which parents point out to the child how his misbehavior can cause pain to others. It was also found that withdrawal of love *per se* was not strongly related to moral development.

The latter finding suggests that recent specifications of withdrawal of love as the most effective means of promoting a strong conscience in children may have to be reconsidered. Hoffman and Saltzstein's results implied that this technique only works to the extent that it includes explanations of the consequences of misbehavior. Previous studies in which punishment styles were categorized as being either physical or psychological (e.g., spankings vs. scoldings and disapproval) found the latter to be most effective. But these studies did not distinguish between the emotional and cognitive components of psychological punishment.

The phrase "withdrawal of love" denotes an emotional procedure. One gets the picture of a parent rejecting the child, devaluing him, telling him by word or deed that he is unworthy. Furthermore, the phrase creates something of a puzzle: how is a parent to employ withdrawal of love when a child is about to dump his oatmeal on his head or heave a rock at his little brother? To avoid disaster, a good part of child rearing requires direct physical intervention. Evidence indicating the value of the cognitive dimension of discipline therefore seems very important, because it removes some of the ambiguity from withdrawal of love. If information about the consequences of misbehavior is given priority over emotional rejection, discipline or punishment becomes a much more straightforward affair. One can at least see restraint and correction in terms of rational instruction, as well as emotionality.

Parental emotions

A related aspect of the punishment and morality problem involves parents' emotions. It is often said that when parents punish children they do it more to make themselves feel good than to instruct the child. Thus, by punishing the child for some transgression, the parent engages in a socially approved means of expressing whatever general hostility he may feel toward the child. Many child-rearing authorities therefore recommend that one should never punish a child in anger. Nor should one show anger or strong emotional arousal while punishing the child even after one has thought it over. These rules are supposed to be followed to avoid giving excessive punishments, and to avoid showing the child a model of uncontrolled emotionality that he can imitate. Bettelheim and other clinical theorists have attacked such ideas (which sound plausible enough in theory), because they suggest that the essential human element be removed from a most characteristically human situation.

If children experience punishment conducted with robot-like efficiency, cold, calculated, and mechanical, how are they to learn that misbehavior can provoke legitimate emotional reactions? And if parents always strive to conceal and control their emotions when provoked, children will sense them anyway, but feel that they are wrong and should be repressed. In short, the interesting theoretical argument here – which cannot be settled empirically unless one can devise an experiment comparing the effects of punishments given with and without expressions of emotion – is between interpretations of punishment as a kind of *technical procedure* for socializing the child, or as an *intrinsic part of human experience* having emotional depth and texture. Pushed to their logical extremes, both interpretations carry certain risks. The former may produce an overcontrolled child who fears his own emotions. The latter may yield an uncontrolled child, overindulgent of his emotional ups and downs. Neither extreme seems attractive, but, happily enough, since most parents are sufficiently human to respond to their children's misbehavior in a mixed rational-emotional fashion, neither extreme poses a serious practical danger.

Timing

On the purely technical side of punishment, the question of timing has interesting empirical and theoretical implications. Empirically, the question is whether punishment is more effective if it is given before or after wrongdoing. Walters, Parke, and Cane (1965) studied children under conditions in which they were punished as they began to break a rule or after they had broken it. Children from the early- and late-punished groups then were shown one of two films. In the first, a child violated a rule and was punished; in the second, a child was rewarded after violating a rule. In sum, the experiment gave children direct experience with punishment prior or subsequent to breaking a rule, and then gave them indirect experience indicating that such behavior could result in punishment or reward. Results from this ingenious study indicate that punishment before the "crime," coupled with examples of punishment for wrongdoing, is the most effective procedure for enforcing rules.

At the everyday level, however, parents are typically in the same position as police: both find it easier to deal with "crimes" *after* they have occurred, and both must be wary of the consequences of being too zealous in their preventive activities. Every parent has probably at least once suffered the pangs of his own conscience when he has been too quick to punish a child with innocent intentions. For this and other reasons, most punishment is only given after some misbehavior has occurred. Moreover, most moral instruction, preventive or otherwise, stresses the *consequences* of misbehavior. Thus, parents frequently warn children about certain activities, and then if children persist in them, they will punish with righteous "I told you so" comments. There is also what may be called *natural punishment* or retribution. If a child is hurt doing something he has been warned against, parents usually point out that he "deserves" the injury. One of the more choice absurdities of family life occurs when children try to conceal injuries from their parents because, having already been hurt, they want to avoid the additional pain of a spanking or scolding.

Theoretically, the fact that punishment usually follows transgressions offers a reasonable explanation for a moral phenomenon that Piaget called *immanent justice*. Children (and some adults) often believe that for some reason they deserve whatever happens to them. If something good happens, it makes them feel that they are themselves good; and if something bad happens, they think of themselves as bad. The more the happening is a matter of chance or luck, the more likely they are to interpret it as significant of their own character. Children grow up with this concept of immanent justice—that we all ultimately get what we deserve—because parents constantly emphasize it. By frequently explaining that rewards and punishments follow from being "good" or "bad" (the Santa Claus theory), parents create an atmosphere of immanent justice.

Summary

Discussion of the primary dynamic theory of moral conscience development in children, Freud's elaboration of the Oedipus complex, which has been omitted thus far, will be taken up later in this chapter under the heading "theoretical perspectives." The present discussion has been limited to the more empirical approaches, which show that moral development in early childhood is largely a matter of rule-learning. Descriptive work by Piaget and Kohlberg and scrutiny of everyday experience make it clear that children initially see morality as heteronomous; the problem being to avoid punishment for breaking other people's rules. And they see punishment itself as expiatory; something to be meted out according to quantitative criteria. Guilt feelings, the emotional component of moral conscience, do not come in strongly until after the age of six. However, research findings indicate that at younger ages, in the course of internalizing rules, the child may encounter parental punishment styles that can predispose him toward an internal guilt-centered morality, or an external fear-centered morality. The former is associated with non-power-assertive punishment which conveys information to the child about how others can suffer from his misbehavior.

Aggression and its causal factors

Much of the material concerning "socialization of aggression" in children, teaching them to control their aggressive impulses, is closely related to work on morality. The two are in fact indistinguishable in everyday life: when one explains to a child that it is wrong to attack others or to take things from them, and punishes him for such behavior, one is simultaneously trying to program his conscience and control his aggression. But since the latter usually has priority, it is fair to say that conscience or morality stand as a psychological by-product of the effort to control aggression.

It will be recalled that in the discussion of morality, power assertive discipline styles such as physical punishment were mentioned as being associated with an externalized morality of fear. Research also demonstrates that physical punishment is associated with high aggression in children. It is reported, for example, that strong physical punishment in the home is a characteristic part of the background of delinquent boys (Glueck and Glueck, 1950). A study of 3- to 6-year-old children by Hollenberg and Sperry (1951) revealed that those who were highly punished for aggression at home were more aggressive in their doll-play than those receiving mild punishment at home. Sears, Whiting, Nowlis, and Sears (1953) rated the aggressiveness of children's nursery school behavior and also evaluated their projective doll-play. The children with nonpunitive mothers showed little aggression in either case. Those with highly punitive mothers showed little aggression in their social behavior, but much came out in their doll-play. A few years later, Sears, Maccoby, and Levin (1957) summarized their own and other work in this area as follows:

Punishment seems to have complex effects. While undoubtedly it often stops a particular form of aggression, it at least momentarily appears to generate more hostility in the child and to lead to further aggressive outbursts at some other time or place. Furthermore, when the parents punish—particularly when they employ physical punishment—they are providing a living example of the use of aggression at the very moment they are trying to teach the child not to be aggressive. The child who copies his parents in many ways, is likely to learn as much from this experience of successful aggression on his parents' part as he is from the pain of punishment (1957, p. 266).

If it is clear that physical punishment is associated with more aggressive behavior in children, the explanation for this association is still obscure. The above quotation suggests that the answer is imitation, which will be discussed in detail later. However, some authorities (e.g., Roger Brown, Ross Parke) note that intrinsic physiological differences between children may explain the relationship of physical punishment to aggression. If some children are stronger and more active by nature, and thus predisposed to aggressive activities, perhaps they provoke their parents into the use of severe punishment. (In their studies of delinquents, the Gluecks observed that action-oriented lawbreakers tend to have the more robust mesomorphic body type.) Furthermore, if such children are severely punished, it follows from the assumption of their basic toughness that they would not be seriously influenced by this experience. (Recall the mention of individual differences in sensitivity to pain, Chapter 3, and Lewin's remark: "The same heat that melts the butter hardens the egg.")

It is all too easy to appeal to individual differences in the face of difficult findings. But in this case, the differences are eminently plausible: who cannot reflect on his own childhood, or scan the behavior of children today, and not come up with good examples of youngsters who seem able to defy all the punishments that society can throw at them? Birth order also seems relevant here. Koch (1960) indicated that boys with older brothers are generally more aggressive than those without siblings.

Apart from the problem of individual differences, another more distinctly conceptual problem makes it difficult to study aggression in children. For example, suppose you observe two four-year-olds playing near each other with some toy cars and blocks. One turns away from his cars for a minute. The other, who perhaps has just finished building a road out of blocks, meanwhile looks around, takes some of the first child's cars, and arranges them on his road. The first child discovers that his cars are missing and takes them back. The two children then begin to struggle for the cars, shouting, crying, perhaps hitting each other. Which child should be scored as aggressive? One might go strictly according to a rule and say that the child who first took something from the other, or who first shouted, or struck the other, was the guilty party. But if his intentions were not clearly aggressive, if he took something without being aware that it was being used by another, or if he hit out in self-defense in the course of a tugging match, most of us might agree that it would be wrong to designate him as the aggressor. In short, particularly for young children, gross behavior is one thing; intentions underlying their behavior are another, and proper categorizing of their activity as aggressive requires that both criteria be considered.

As a practical matter, since it is relatively easy to code gross behavior but difficult to judge intentions, most investigators tend to do only the former. While studying the nursery school behavior of four-year-olds, for instance, Patterson, Littmon, and Bricker (1967) recorded as aggressive any behavior that provoked a strong response from another, or resulted in another suffering loss, pain, or property damage.

Despite the problems posed by individual differences and the coding of intentions, however, much of the empirical research on aggression in children must be granted its proper significance. For one thing, the findings are cumulative and convergent. Different investigators would not have been reaching similar general conclusions over the years if the phenomenon under study were not quite regular, or if their results were merely due to poor control over individual differences or coding procedures. It should be understood that here, as in many other areas of research, it is important to note the problems that can mitigate or water down empirical findings, but it is equally important not to ignore the pattern of findings that have been obtained; not to throw the baby out with the bath water. In this spirit, let us turn to the salient results of studies concerning processes of aggression in children.

We have thus far emphasized material showing that severe punishment is related to aggression. Research findings also support the common sense idea that aggression will increase if it goes *entirely* unpunished. In part of their 1951 study of doll-play among nursery school children, Hollenberg and Sperry rebuked one group of children for aggressive doll-play. Another group of children was allowed to do whatever it liked. The latter group showed a steady, strong increase in both the frequency and intensity of aggression in their doll-playing. Aggression by children in the verbally punished group remained relatively low and stable. Patterson et al. (1967) kept track of the aggressive behavior shown by four-year-olds. Trends in data collected over a considerable period of time revealed that aggression was much lower in structured nursery school settings — where the children's play is organized and they are supervised more carefully — than in permissive settings. It was also observed that when a child's aggression was successful he subsequently increased such behavior. If it was unsuccessful, or provoked retaliatory aggression, then the behavior was subsequently reduced. Sears et al. (1957) also reported that mothers who were inconsistent about aggression, sometimes punishing the child for it and sometimes ignoring it, had highly aggressive children.

In general then, some consistent punishment seems necessary to inhibit aggression in children. It would obviously be interesting to see comparison data on children raised according to a totally permissive regime, but no one has any. Common experience suggests that if such children exist at all, they are very rare. Punishment may vary in form or intensity, and be consistent or inconsistent, but it is never entirely absent. Finally, the fact that inconsistent punishment results in high aggressiveness corresponds with the partial reinforcement principle of traditional learning theory. One of the best established findings in the learning literature is that partially reinforced responses are the most difficult to extinguish. Since it is quite reasonable to think of inconsistent punishment for aggression as partial reinforcement for aggression, learning theory here offers an undeniably good explanation for the aggressiveness of the inconsistently punished.

Another line of research on aggression also in line with the reinforcement-learning principle indicates that adult attention can be an important causal factor. Brown and Elliot (1965) noted that in nursery school situations aggressive children received more attention from teachers. On the assumption that attention from adults was reinforcing or rewarding to a child, these investigators instructed nursery teachers to change their normal pattern of paying most attention to troublesome children. The procedure worked: after 2 weeks of receiving minimal attention for aggressive activity and maximal attention for cooperative activity, three- to four-year-olds showed a significant drop in their physical and verbal expressions of aggression.

The question of why physical punishment should be associated with high levels of aggression has attracted a considerable amount of attention because it seems contrary to common sense and the reinforcement-learning principle. Most authorities are in general agreement with the reasoning that appears in the earlier quotation from Sears et al. (1957). When a parent uses physical punishment, he is providing a model for overt aggression for the child to imitate. The child learns that violence is an appropriate way to express anger. Levin and Sears (1956), for example, found that 5-year-old boys who identified strongly with punitive fathers showed more aggression than any of the other children in their sample. It therefore appears that in the matter of physical punishment for aggression, imitation, or some idea such as identification with the aggressor, is a more important learning principle than negative reinforcement.

The imitation interpretation is further strengthened by studies showing that almost any model of aggressive behavior will be imitated by children. Thus, in experiments where children are shown films containing violence, they are later observed to be more aggressive in their doll-play. But much depends on the qualitative nature of the film. If the film model of aggression also shows that the consequence is punishment, the aggression is not imitated (Bandura, Ross, and Ross, 1963). Bandura (1965) later demonstrated, however, that even though 3- to 6-year-olds do not *imitate* punished aggression, they *learn* it. That is, they are able to describe or reenact the aggressive behavior if the experimenter offers them a reward to do so.

Work on imitation of aggression leads quite naturally to questions concerning the effect of TV violence on children. Because this is a large, popular subject for debate these days, it should be said immediately that no conclusive evidence exists. Virtually all of the survey and experimental research on the association between TV viewing habits and aggressive behavior demonstrates only that there is no simple cause-effect relationship between exposure to TV violence and subsequent aggression. This does not mean that the two are entirely unrelated. One recent study indicated that when the qualitative violence in programs commonly thought to be equally violent is carefully evaluated, the children who prefer the more "truly" violent programs are more aggressive with their peers. But since most of the available research here focuses on middle childhood (6 to 12 years), further discussion will be held for Chapter 7.

In addition to consistency of punishment, type of punishment, adult attention, and imitation, a final causal factor in aggression has been thought to be frustration. The classical frustration-aggression hypothesis formulated by Dollard, Miller, and others in the late 1930's and early 1940's, suggested that frustration always leads to some form of aggression. There is a very large literature on this issue, including work with various animal species, adult humans, and children. It will be sufficient for our present purposes, however, to declare that the results of many studies all indicate that frustration is merely one potential cause of aggression.

Research has established that when children are frustrated they can show a variety of responses including regression to relatively infantile behavior, withdrawal, and sheer passivity. Berkowitz (1969) provided a comprehensive review of research on the frustration-aggression hypothesis which goes into these matters in great detail. It seems generally to be true that aggression is a learned response to frustration, one which is by no means universal, and which probably is more closely associated with the factors mentioned earlier than with frustration *per se*.

The last point that should be made about aggression in early childhood is that it need not remain as a constant feature of personality. The evidence here is ambiguous, however, and takes us back to the definition and coding problems. Byram (1966), reported that 22 boys studied from the age of 3 to 5 years did not show a continuing pattern of aggression. Those who were rated aggressive at three were not rated as similarly aggressive at five. Instead, aggression at age three was a good predictor of masculine and extroverted behavior at five. But in an earlier longitudinal study, Jersild and Markey (1935) found that aggression in nursery school *was* a good predictor of aggression in kindergarten. The difficulties of definition and coding suggest that what appeared as masculine and extroverted in one study was treated as aggressive in the other. In the Kagan and Moss report of the Fels longitudinal project certain extreme behaviors in early childhood—temper tantrums and rage reactions—were good predictors of aggression at later ages. It is probably true that such extreme behaviors are conspicuous, easy to code, and characteristic of the child showing them. Therefore, the only general conclusion warranted at this point is that aggression in early childhood must be very clear before one attaches any long-term significance to it.

Achievement and competence

Depending upon how one looks at the period, early childhood can seem either densely packed with achievement or almost entirely devoid of it. If one's theoretical eyeglasses are designed to admit only conventional formalities, then traditionally recognized achievements—reading, writing, earning money, doing well at sports—are in short supply. But if they admit all concrete accomplishments, then as White (1959) suggested in his discussion of the child's drive to attain competence, the 2 to 6 year period is filled with great achievement. Much of the material discussed in the first part of this chapter concerning language and physical growth conveys the quality and quantity of these achievements. Moreover, if we again consider the child's developing self-concept, it should easily be understood that the stages described by All-port must include the child's emerging sense of competence and orientation toward achievement. No less than the rest of us, the four- or five-year-old will think of himself and generate reactions in others according to his feelings of competence. These in turn will depend upon his track record with such challenges as working zippers and buttons, forks and spoons, getting into and out of coat sleeves and trouser legs, operating pedal-driven wheeled vehicles, and managing drippy ice cream cones.

As usual, it is important to begin with definition. Note that the terms *competence* and *achievement* have been used interchangeably in referring to the child's impetus to master his environment. Both concepts are clearly related to this phenomenon, but they grow out of very different theoretical contexts. In a review of the competence formulation, Smith (in Clausen, 1968) explained that this term was originally introduced by White to counter-act a prevalent tendency to explain all human motives as essentially reactive. In brief, White argued cogently that instead of tracing all motivated behaviors to the physiological survival needs of the organism, some should be recognized as being independent of such needs. He made a strong case for this view by pointing to the apparently innate human drive to attain competence or mastery over the environment, even when no physiological needs are at stake, or even when certain physiological needs must be sacrificed.

Piaget's descriptions of the growth of sensorimotor intelligence (Chapter 5) illustrate how young children begin to be influenced by seeing the consequences of their actions. The idea that such feedback from the environment is intrinsically motivating, that persons and animals will work simply to generate responses from the environment, is well supported by research. Later in this chapter we will discuss an ingenious practical elaboration of this idea by O. K. Moore. For the present, however, it is sufficient to note that while the concept of competence as an innate motive is reasonably well established, it stands otherwise as an unexplained biological phenomenon.

The idea of competence as a biological determinant of behavior has most often been used in research on human infants and lower animal species. The idea of *achievement,* on the other hand, which was introduced by Mc-Clelland and his associates in the early 1950's quite independently of the competence notion, has led to much research directly relevant to early childhood. Probably the main reason for this is that White described competence as innate, while McClelland saw the need for achievement as learned. Parke gave the following general description of achievement:

By achievement, one generally means that the subject is not merely executing a task without assistance, but is trying to perform well with the aim of eliciting positive reinforcement for his demonstrated competence in the task. An emphasis on evaluation of performance against some standard of excellence is the distinguishing characteristic of achievement behavior (1969, p. 303).

Observe how learning is brought into the matter: to achievement theorists the child is not just acting because of an innate desire to see things happen in the environment or to get feedback from it; he is trying to be rewarded, and he is evaluating what he does against a "standard of excellence." A more detailed statement specifying achievement as one of several learned motives, and mentioning conditions which promote its development in children, appears in McClelland, Atkinson, Clark, and Lowell (1953):

In the case of achievement motivation, the situations should involve "standards of excellence," presumably imposed on the child by the culture, or more particularly by the parents as representatives of the culture, and the behavior should involve either "competition" with those standards of excellence or attempts to meet them which, if successful, produce positive affect or, if unsuccessful, negative affect (p. 275).

Measuring achievement motives

Now, if one can see an innate competence drive being expressed in the behavior of infants and young children, how is one to see their learned achievement motives? One way is through their competitive behavior. Greenberg (1932) arranged block-playing sessions with pairs of children ranging in age from 2 to 7 years. At some point in their play, she would ask to see which child could build a bigger, nicer creation. The result was a mixture of achievement and competition. The children tried to outdo each other in their creations, and frequently took each other's blocks. After recording all their behavior, Greenberg found that competitive responses averaged about 50 percent at age three, and rose to almost 90 percent at age five.

Rosen and D'Andrade (1959) scored behavior of nine- to eleven-year-olds on a task requiring them to build a tower of blocks while they were blindfolded and limited to the use of only one hand (try it and you will see that it takes very much achievement motivation). Another popular achievement task has been constructed from the game of ringtoss. This is particularly clever because one can not only infer achievement from the child's persistence, but, depending on how far away he chooses to stand from the peg, one can get a rough idea of his internal standard. The child who wants to stand right over the peg so he can't miss, and the one who wants to stand so far away that he always has an excuse for missing, both presumably have lower achievement standards than children who choose to stand at an intermediate distance.

Aside from such techniques for eliciting achievement behaviors, McClelland and his colleagues have perfected projective tests that yield measures of a generalized "need for achievement" in children and adults. In this procedure, the person is shown ambiguous pictures such as a young man holding a violin and gazing toward a window. Then he is asked to make up a story to fit the picture. High achievement is scored if his story contains themes indicating ambition or accomplishment: "The young man practices for hours every day, staring into space and imagining himself to be the most famous musician in the world." Low achievement is scored if the story reflects other concerns: "The young man is forced to practice although he hates it. Right now he is thinking of slipping out the window."

There are many variations on this projective procedure. McClelland (1961) adapted it to analyze children's stories in different cultures and thereby obtained measures of the relative degree to which achievement is valued in those cultures. Other investigators have noted that various kinds of expressive behaviors are related to achievement motivation. For example, in "doodle" drawings high achievers tend to make lines that are sharper, more discrete, and more frequently diagonal, than low achievers. Those who prefer the color blue tend to have higher achievement motives than those preferring red.

A good body of accumulated evidence snows that the projective test measures of achievement are valid: they can be used to predict achievement behavior in experiments and in natural situations. Without going into detail, many studies demonstrate that persons with higher achievement motive scores generally get better grades in school, will work harder and longer to complete experimental tasks, will only reward themselves for meeting a high standard of performance, and, among adult men, are more successful in business careers. Now then, with all the prior material as background, we can proceed to our main concern: what experiences in early childhood make for high or low achievement motives?

Critical conditions

Winterbottom (1958) carried out the earliest major study of child-rearing practices in relation to achievement. After using a projective storytelling technique to measure motivation in 29 nine-year-old boys, she interviewed their mothers in detail about the demands they made of their sons (e.g., at what age should a boy be able to do regular tasks around the house, have interests or hobbies of his own, eat alone without any help, hang up his own clothes, undress and go to bed by himself). She also learned from the mothers how they rewarded or punished their children for good or bad behavior. In general, her results showed that the high achievement-oriented boys had mothers who made more demands at earlier ages, and placed greater emphasis on training and rewarding independence. Surprisingly, however, in view of other work on morality and aggression, the mothers of high and low achievement scorers showed no significant differences in the frequency and intensity of their punishment practices.

A further noteworthy result involves the number of demands made from children. For five-year-olds, the high achievement mothers made an average of eight different demands, while low achievement mothers average two. By age six, the "low" mothers are up to four demands, but the "highs" are making eleven different demands. This gap does not begin to narrow until age nine, and at age ten, both high and low mothers made approximately the same 18 different demands. The sudden, striking rise in the number of demands made by mothers of low achievement-oriented boys suggests that they are trying to catch up in a hurry, but without success.

Although the Winterbottom study clearly indicated that maternal demands for independence or achievement, coupled with appropriate training, can explain differences in the achievement orientations of youngsters, these findings are largely based on retrospective interview material. One would like to see more direct evidence. Luckily, there is some. Fales (1944) studied two- and three-year-olds in nursery school. He first recorded how many of these children insisted on struggling into their coats every day without any help. Then, one group of children was given special training in this activity. As they became more skillful, they also began to reject help with their coats.

The study was interpreted as showing that with increased skill, children correspondingly increase their level of aspiration: they become more ambitious to do things for themselves according to a higher standard. The study is also in line with the Winterbottom findings, because it illustrates the probable way in which demands and appropriate training in early childhood can operate together to produce a higher achievement orientation.

Case history reports provide direct illustrative evidence. The following selection from Kagan and Moss casts the Winterbottom and Fales results into more personal terms.

At one year of age the home visitor noted:

S is pushed rather vigorously toward developing useful skills and independence by both parents. For example, when the father was given the responsibility of feeding S in the morning, he promptly trained her to feed herself to save him the trouble. The mother is nonchalant and lets S toddle about with minimal protectiveness. The mother fails to bat an eye when S tumbles and cries. S straightens herself out after a perfunctory whimper. S can say half a dozen words and is friendly with all strangers. She is unusually independent and active.

At 4 ½ years of age, S was described as follows:

She had an exceptionally clear voice, and every word of her amazingly large vocabulary was sharply and distinctly enunciated. Her habitual tone was a bellowing shout, but she could modulate it to fit the particular role she was playing. S was one of the group leaders. Her energy, fund of ideas, and verbal manipulation of the world gave her great skills and dominance of peers. S would occasionally attack others if they stood in the way of an object she wanted. She would vary between a diplomatic explanation of, "Well I need it" to simply snatching the toy.

At 6 years of age the Fels' observer wrote:

S has learned to read and vitally enjoys it. She has long, silent periods of concentration and was often enraptured by the story she was reading. She loved trips to the Glen and reveled in the space; sure-footed as a mountain goat and fearless to all danger.

The intellectual challenges provided by the school situation were met and conquered with zeal. She was admired by her peers, for she had a vivid and lively imagination. She enjoyed a battle and adopted a competitive and rivalrous attitude with boys as well as girls.

At 15 years of age her story to Card 17BM of the TAT (picture of a man on a rope) captures her preoccupation with status and mastery goals.

"This is one of the greatest sportsmen of all times, who has broken the record, the speed record for rope climbing. It's the world's record. He is shown going up the rope on one of his latest records that he made."

To Card 14 (silhouette of a person in a window), S verbalized a concern with the acquisition of knowledge.

"This is a high school boy who is interested in studying the stars, but his high school didn't offer the proper education for astronomy, so at night he just stands by the window and wishes with all his might that he could have had the proper education so that he could go on and study things he wanted to study."

S graduated second in her high school class. She was involved in almost all the school activities and devoted special energy to music and athletics (1962, pp. 143–145).

Additional research on achievement provides material which falls into one of three general categories. First, there are studies of the processes underlying acquisition of achievement motives, and the Winterbottom study is one of these. Second, there is work on behaviors highly correlated with achievement, and third, there is some material on the degree to which early childhood achievement orientations remain characteristic of behavior at later ages. The substance typical of each of these categories is sketched briefly below.

(1) Process studies

Findings suggest that three different underlying processes can help explain the origins of achievement motivation: reward, imitation and identification, and processes relevant to mother-father behavior patterns. Reward is indicated in a study by Crandall, Preston, and Robson (1960). They identified nursery school children showing high achievement-oriented behaviors, and discovered that these children had mothers who made a point of rewarding them for achievement at home.

Imitation has been demonstrated by Bandura and Kupers (1964), in a study arranged so that preschool children played a bowling game with adult partners. A dish of candy was present throughout the game. In different conditions of the experiment, the adult partners rewarded themselves by taking candy when they made either high or low scores. And they would say things like: "I did very well this time so I deserve some more candy." Later, each child played the bowling game by himself. Those who had previously played with a partner rewarding himself for low scores also took candy rewards when their scores were low. Those who had a partner with high standards for reward took the most candy when they made their highest scores. The results of this study, and others similar in principle, show that young children will imitate or internalize achievement standards conveyed by adult models.

Styles of mother-father interaction with the child are revealed as a potent force relevant to achievement in the Rosen and D'Andrade (1959) study. Their results were based on work with the families of 9- to 11-year-old boys, but the data are so distinctive that any parent will recognize that the results must also be applicable to early childhood situations. The boys were first ordered into groups having high and low achievement orientations according to their projective stories. In addition to the blind block-building task mentioned earlier, the experiment included ringtoss, anagrams, pattern-matching, and problem-solving tasks. By having parents work with their sons on all five of these tasks, the investigators were able to observe typical family behaviors in achievement situations. They report two important findings: the mothers and fathers of high achievement-oriented boys are alike in setting high performance standards, but they behave quite differently from one another during the performance itself. The mothers take a more domineering role, pushing, encouraging, rewarding, and punishing; while the fathers seem content to let the boys work on their own. The fathers are described as apparently being ". . . competent men who are willing to take a back seat while their sons are performing. They tend to beckon from ahead rather than push from behind" (p. 216).

Among low achievers, the general pattern of parent behavior is reversed: fathers tend to dominate and push, mothers remain relatively uninvolved. Rosen and D'Andrade suggested how given behaviors can have different impacts on a boy, depending upon whether the behavior is typical of his mother or father.

The father who gives the boy a relatively high degree of autonomy provides him with an opportunity to compete on his own ground, to test his skill, and to gain a sense of confidence in his own competence. The dominating father may crush his son (and in so doing destroys the boy's achievement motive), perhaps because he views the boy as a competitor and is viewed as such by his son. On the other hand, the mother who dominates the decision-making process does not seem to have the same effect on the boy, possibly because she is perceived as *imposing her standards* on the boy, while a dominating father is perceived as *imposing himself* on the son. It may be that the mother-son relations are typically more secure than those between father and son, so that the boy is better able to accept higher levels of dominance and rejection from his mother than his father without adverse effect on his need to achieve. Relatively rejecting, dominating fathers, particularly those with less than average warmth — as tended to be the case with the fathers of low *n* Achievement boys — seem to be a threat to the boy[s] and a deterrent to the development of *n* Achievement. On the other hand, above-average dominance and rejection, coupled with above-average warmth, as tends to be the case with mothers of high *n* Achievement boys, appear to be a spur to achievement motivation. It will be remembered that the fathers of high *n* Achievement boys are on the average less Rejecting, less Pushing, and less Dominant — all of which points to their general hands-off policy (1959, pp. 216–217).

(2) Correlates of achievement motivation

Both the ability to delay rewards and to take reasonable risks to attain rewards are reported to be associated with high achievement orientations. Mischel (1961) tested over 100 boys in Trinidad. Those making higher achievement scores on their projective stories showed greater ability to tolerate a delay in gratification. Thus, when asked to choose between receiving a small candy bar "today," or waiting to get a much larger one "next week," most of these youngsters were willing to wait, while most of the low achievement scorers were not. McClelland (1958) categorized 26 five-year-olds as being high or low achievement oriented, and then tested their risk preferences by seeing how far away they stood from a ringtoss peg; noting how many words they were willing to try to memorize in a recall task; and inferring risk from behavior in two other situations as well. In general, the high achievement children took moderate risks while the lows took either very low or very high risks.

It therefore appears that high achievement-oriented children do what one would logically expect them to do when it comes to delay of reward and risk-taking: they will put off collecting rewards when it is worth their while to wait, and they will undertake reasonable risks. As McClelland has pointed out in several publications, both these tendencies characterize the successful adult entrepreneur. Achievement motivation can accordingly be seen as part of a general personality pattern making for economic gain.

(3) Persistence of achievement orientations

How well do signs of achievement in early childhood predict later achievement? Seeking an answer, Longstreth (1968) picked his way through much of the longitudinal data presented by Kagan and Moss. He concluded that activities up to the age of three—such as demonstrations of patience and determination building things out of blocks, stringing beads—are *not* related to later achievement. On the other hand, achievement, competitiveness, and striving for recognition *are* quite consistent from age four to fourteen. He also noted that while boys and girls show equally consistent achievement patterns regarding intellectual matters, boys who are highly motivated toward athletics tend not to care about intellectual achievement. (Recall, however, that the Kagan and Moss data go back to the later 1930's and early 1940's. Several considerations suggest that the athletic-intellectual discrepancy may not be as great for boys growing up today.)

Achievement and competence

According to current formulations, the drive to establish competence is presumed to be innate, while the motive to achieve is learned. But the fundamental issue shaping itself out of the material discussed in this section involves the *relationship* between competence and achievement. How is it that intrinsic competence gives way to an extrinsically programed achievement motive?

Perhaps it is reasonable to think that what is originally innate as competence gets so swamped or contaminated by experience in the first 2 or 3 years that it is lost in a dilute solution of achievement. Or is it more plausible to suggest that a natural growth process is at work; that the seed is competence, the soil is early experience, and the flower (if the soil has enough manure in it) is a high achievement motive? Neither the swamping nor the manure pile interpretation sounds especially attractive, but life is full of unattractive realities. Furthermore, since there can be some truth in both notions, the practical problem for parents is whether to ignore competence—if it is truly innate it should not need much attention—and concentrate on achievement by manipulating rewards and punishments, presenting appropriate models for imitation, and plotting together how to be a demanding mother and undemanding father. The latter course has an unnatural feel to it, rather like the idea of punishing children without showing any emotion. But it might be worth trying if the following question can be answered: does one *want* high achievement motivation in a child and if so, how much? No one has researched varying *degrees* of achievement motivation, nor whether high achievement-oriented children are happy children, or nice to have around the house.

Summary of social-emotional development in early childhood

Five areas or dimensions of development are sketched in the preceding pages. Starting with Allport's review of successive stages in the emerging self-concept of the young child, we have seen how sexual identity, morality, aggression, and achievement all become notable during the 2 to 6 year period. Major lines of research relevant to each of these areas were described. Wherever possible, an attempt has been made to clarify the difference between work demonstrating that certain phenomena exist and can be brought under study, and work designed to explain the phenomena—reveal underlying causal factors or conditions. A broad review and reconsideration of all this material suggests the following generalizations.

First, the definitive features of early childhood described in prior sections of this chapter—punishment, language acquisition, physical growth—determine boundaries for the forms of social-emotional development discussed in this section. For example, in the areas of morality and aggression, one can only do just so much with any child. Overly severe punishment may yield worse behavior than that which it is supposed to eliminate. Verbal explanations are limited by the child's ability to understand them or to grasp such concepts as intentionality. And the child's physical capabilities determine much of what he actually does. Another way to put it is by analogy to a computer system. Punishment, language, and physical growth are like calibration devices: they determine the limits of the system's functioning, and, depending upon how they are set, also determine the quality of its outputs.

Second, in considering specific "outputs" such as sexual identity, morality, aggression, and achievement, the abstractions calibrating early childhood translate into relatively concrete parent activities: styles of punishment, models for imitation, and other, more complex patterns of interaction with the child. These things can be seen as raw material or "inputs" to the child's developing personality system.

Third, the fundamental processes responsible for the impact of parents' behavior on the child's personality involve either (a) extrinsic learning, learning imposed on the child according to principles of reinforcement or conditioning; (b) intrinsic learning originating in the child based on the principle that imitation is intrinsically rewarding; or (c) dynamic, more complicated adjustment processes whereby the child adapts to larger patterns of parental behavior. In this general connection it seems clear that *multiple processes* are at work during early childhood.

The most distinct signal that can be detected above all the theoretical and empirical noise in this period is that no single dynamic, whether it be learning by reinforcement, identification with the aggressor, imitation, innate competence motivation, or whatever, can adequately explain all the phenomena. Theoretically speaking, the motto for the young child might well be that "in my house are many mansions." What he does not acquire in one way he is liable to acquire in another. And what parents set out to give him in one way he may receive in another as something entirely different.

It should be noted, finally, that so far in this chapter any discussion of intelligence has been deliberately avoided because most non-Piagetian developmental studies are tied to IQ test scores. When one sees very little value in such tests because, among other things, there is no way to define what they mean except through the relatively meaningless phrase "intelligence is what intelligence tests measure," and when there is no way to explain the great individual differences in such measures except by appeal to other, more fundamental matters such as social-emotional experience or heredity and brain chemistry, then there is no point trying to foist an arbitrary discussion upon the reader. Traditional views of intelligence as IQ scores are now dying or are already dead. One therefore cannot construe it as anything but an immensely important *theoretical* topic. It is discussed from this standpoint in the next section.

THEORETICAL PERSPECTIVES

It is no exaggeration to say that for most philosophers and scientists who have ever interested themselves in the formation of human personality, the 2 to 6 year period is a great "golden age"; it is here that the organism becomes structurally capable of sustaining sophisticated psychological processes. And yet these structure and process characteristics are not so sophisticated as to be obscure. Theoretical effort is lavished on this period because things are simple enough to look understandable, but complicated enough to make the effort seem worthwhile.

Another way to convey theoretical passion for this period is by analogy to embryology. If you have ever seen a speeded-up film of the development of a fertilized egg cell through successive stages which culminate in a recognizable fetus, you will understand why early childhood is of such interest. Just as cells converge and coalesce to provide rudimentary forms for specific anatomical structures, most of us think that the experiences of the young child converge and coalesce to provide the rudimentary forms for specific aspects of personality.

From almost any angle, therefore, early childhood draws out theoretical interest. In this section, we will first examine the Freudian perspective on social-emotional aspects of development. Such matters as the self-concept, morality, and sexual identity are treated in terms of the ego and superego components of personality; and these, in turn, are related to the dynamics of the Oedipus complex. Relevant ideas in the work of Sullivan and Erikson are also reviewed. Then we will go to Piaget, who described early childhood as the preoperational period of cognitive development, and close finally with some discussion of further work on cognition by Bruner and Moore.

Freud

It will be recalled from Chapter 4 that Freud called the first part of early childhood (2 to 3 years) the anal stage of psycho-sexual development because, at this age, libido presumably concentrates in the anal region. Having already discussed cleanliness training as a critical factor in Chapter 5, no further empirical material is needed here. Theoretically, however, the classic Freudian view is that an individual may become partially "fixated" at the anal stage if he has experienced very harsh cleanliness training. Thus, Freudians describe some adults as having "anal-retentive" personalities. These are people who are typically very stingy, obsessed with detail, easily upset by dirt or disorder, often inclined to become functionaries in bureaucratic organizations. In the latter part of early childhood, one might see direct signs of anal fixation in a child who shows abnormally high tension over bowel movements or dirt.

At about age four, the child enters the "phallic" stage. Libido is now supposed to concentrate in the genital region. In general, 4- to 5-year-old children become interested in their opposite-sex parents as sources of sexual gratification; by the age of six or seven, however, they repress this interest out of fear of punishment from their same-sex parent. The bare bones of the Oedipus complex can thus be described in a single sentence, but it involves two important problems that require much more detail: the origins of Freud's ideas on childhood sexuality, and the dynamics whereby Freud saw resolution of the complex as imposing major changes on the child's personality.

Childhood sexuality first began to seem important to Freud when he was treating neurotic patients at the turn of the century. In one of the famous early cases, for example, a young woman was unable to walk for no apparent medical reason. This condition of hysterical paralysis had set in following the death of her father; her mother had already been dead for some time. Briefly, Freud cured her after therapy sessions had revealed that guilt feelings about her father's death, rooted in her repressed sexual feelings about him, were the cause of the paralysis. Lacking any insight into these things, she had punished herself by becoming a cripple.

For Freud, the important thing about this case, and others like it, was that he kept encountering bits and pieces of material on early sexuality— material suggesting sex as a cause of rivalry between parents and children, and the rivalry seemed to have certain general consequences. The child would repress it, force it out of his consciousness; he would identify strongly with his same-sex parent to cope with fears of punishment; and, finally, he would acquire a fundamental sense of guilt concerning the rivalry. Drawing upon case history data, Freud formalized these ideas in essays first published in 1905. The reaction was generally negative, much of it being of the "dirty old man" variety. But one of the more serious criticisms was that his ideas about childhood sexuality were all deductions based on retrospective evidence: recollections of patients, analysis of their thought associations, and the like. (Freud was by this time interpreting recurrent dreams, slips of the tongue, and other seemingly commonplace things as signs of repressed or unconscious thoughts.)

A few years later, it was a great stroke of luck to have dropped in his lap the case of a phobia in a 5-year-old boy. Even more fortunate, the boy's father was a physician who had heard Freud lecture and who had decided to keep notes on his son's development. Freud specifically acknowledged the value of this case as corroboratory evidence for his fundamental ideas.

I cannot take leave of our small patient's phobia without giving expression to a notion which made its analysis, leading as it did to a recovery, seem of especial value to me. Strictly speaking, I learnt nothing new from this analysis, nothing that I had not already been able to discover (though often less distinctly and more indirectly) from other patients analysed at a more advanced age. But the neuroses of these other patients could in every instance be traced back to the same infantile complexes that were revealed behind Hans's phobia (Freud, 1925, p. 287).

On the face of it, the case was very simple: Hans was afraid to go outside his house because a horse would bite him. Freud unraveled the phobia as follows. In his fear of horses, Hans was really expressing fear of his father. Why? Because he was particularly frightened of white horses wearing dark blinders and bridles. Hans' father often played "horsie" with him, letting the boy ride on his back. Hans once remarked how white his father looked when he saw him without clothing. The father also wore dark glasses and had a black moustache. It was a pretty close match. Why then should Hans be afraid of his father? There was some clear rivalry between them. His father would not let him come into bed to snuggle up to his mother. During a summer vacation, when his father often had to leave the family to go into the city and his mother indulged his snuggling, Hans once said that he wished his father would stay away permanently. Furthermore, in one very gross incident Hans was warned by his mother that if he persisted in playing with his genitals at night, she would have a doctor come to cut off his "widdler." (Remember, his father was a doctor, and we are dealing here with a cultural milieu where "Der Struwwelpeter" stories were quite popular.)

Altogether then, the case of young Hans provided fairly direct evidence for the idea of childhood sexuality as a cause of rivalry with the same-sex parent. Freud viewed the phobia itself as a disguised form of castration anxiety: Hans was afraid to express this fear directly, so he cast his father in the role of a horse that would bite. Once Freud was able to reassure the boy that all children feel some fear and anger toward their fathers, the phobia receded. Freud also noted that in common with most adult neuroses, Hans' phobia had a practical utility. Besides providing a vehicle for the expression of certain emotions, it made his parents give him more attention, much of which had lately been going to his baby sister. Furthermore, the phobia gave him an excuse to stay home with his mother:

After all, Hans's phobia of horses was an obstacle to his going into the street, and could serve as a means of allowing him to stay at home with his beloved mother. In this way, therefore, his affection for his mother triumphantly achieved its aim. In consequence of his phobia, the lover clung to the object of his love—though, to be sure, steps had been taken to make him innocuous (Freud, 1925, p. 248).

There are other ways to interpret the case of little Hans. Roger Brown discussed relevant material in more detail in his *Social Psychology* text, pointing out that a learning and conditioning explanation is also possible. Recent reports of successful treatment of phobias via "desensitization" conditioning techniques support this alternative line of explanation. However, Freud has never lacked critics willing to offer alternative explanations. When he first described Hans' case in 1909, it was said that maybe the boy was just a rare young degenerate, that perhaps the boy's father had been influenced by Freud to read things into his behavior, and that any biased person, such as Freud himself, might easily distort the unreliable behavior of a young child to fit a preconceived pattern. Consequently the case did not dissuade critics when it was first published any more than it does today. It remains, however, as one of the fundamental documents of psychoanalytic theory. Freud made important use of it in elaborating a general explanation for personality development in childhood. Let us now examine how he understood the dynamics of sexual identity and morality in context of the Oedipus complex.

Id is the primary component of personality, the original source of all psychic energy. As the child matures, some id energy is drawn off into the *ego*. This happens because the pleasure principle, according to which the child seeks direct gratification of his id desires, becomes increasingly unsatisfactory as a means of satisfying those desires. It gives way to the reality principle, an ego process. All this occurs by age three or four. By virtue of negative experience with behavior couched on the pleasure principle, and positive experience associated with the reality principle, ego gets stronger as id weakens. But the young child does not yet have a very strong sexual identity or moral conscience. The former is still quite superficial, the latter hardly exists at all except as rule-following.

Freud saw the Oedipus complex as a sexually caused emotional earthquake. The confusion and fear associated with this event forces a restructuring of id and ego, and gives rise to a new moral component of personality, the superego. When the dust settles at about age six, the child's fear of his same-sex parent has turned into identification with that parent. Id-inspired designs on his opposite-sex parent are renounced; energy now goes to superego which enforces obedience to rules against sexual transgressions, as well as transgressions against other common values. These two consequences of the Oedipus complex – identification, and moral conscience or superego formation – go hand in hand. They are the two key pieces the child needs to solve the dangerous family-relations puzzle. A boy, for example, can cope with his anxiety by identifying with his father, but he cannot accomplish this effectively if he does not renounce his mother as a sex object. We will not go into any further detail on the internal logic of the Oedipus complex. Those who reject the idea have never been convinced by detailed discussion; those who find it interesting or plausible will want more detail than can be supplied here.

However, in addition to their internal logic, Freud's ideas on the Oedipus complex also have an external logic; they have a certain good fit to a great variety of human affairs. Once one begins to look for it, sexually based family rivalries seem fairly prevalent in everyday life. Art and literature provide many examples. Shakespeare's *Hamlet* is probably the most famous case in point. The book *Oedipus and Hamlet* by Ernest Jones suggested that Hamlet's unwillingness to act directly against his stepfather, and all his roundabout, indecisive maneuvers, can be understood as resulting from his unresolved Oedipal feelings. Why was he *really* so frightened by his father's ghost? Why did he procrastinate avenging his father's death? Jones suggests it was because he must have been guilty of wishing for that death himself; because to some extent his hatred of his stepfather was based on envy, not simple moral indignation. It was further suggested that the play owes its continuing popularity to the universal appeal of its underlying theme. Watching it, audiences can deal indirectly, and thus safely, with some of their own hidden emotions.

Freud was also very interested in anthropology, and the fact that taboos against incest were reported to be universal seemed to him to be further good evidence for the Oedipus complex. Why should all men view incest, and/or patricide, with such horror? Freud thought that it was because all have had to struggle so hard to repress those inclinations in themselves when they were children. These are the most immoral of crimes because all moral feelings originate in the guilt first experienced in connection with the Oedipus complex.

Sullivan and Erikson

In the neo-Freudian work of H. S. Sullivan and E. H. Erikson, there is a steady retreat from the dramatics of the Oedipus complex. Sullivan backed off a moderate distance; Erikson moved even further away. Recall from Chapter 4 that Sullivan made no important use of the libido concept, and tended to fill the gap created in Freudian theory with more cognitive or ego-relevant material. For example, he defined early childhood according to acquisition and effective use of language.

In such matters as sexual identity and control of aggression, Sullivan discussed "as-if" performances by the child in a way that closely resembles the empirical work on imitation. When the child engages in what Sullivan called "dramatizations"—playing the role of his parents—he is surely imitating them. Much of the research on identification and aggression is therefore quite in agreement with Sullivan's ideas. His thinking is also relevant to studies of morality and achievement. He suggested that children engage in certain "as-if" behaviors to avoid punishment and anxiety. Furthermore, in both Freud and Sullivan's view of "sublimation" (the process of substituting a socially acceptable behavior for one which produces anxiety) morality and achievement are specifically implied. Rewards and punishments tend to shape the direction of the child's sublimation activities.

The most interesting of Sullivan's ideas on early childhood, however, and the one that involves more than translations of terminology, is his statement of the "malevolent transformation." This notion that the child who has had relatively consistent negative social experiences can, as a result, come to see himself as living in a world full of enemies, fits research showing that severe punishment is associated with increased aggression and poor conscience development. But it goes beyond those findings by suggesting that a young child can only sustain a certain degree of harsh punitive experience. If such experiences reach a critical mass, pathology of one sort or another is inevitable. This is not to say that the child should be written off, but it seems likely that the best he can hope for is special treatment or special luck. Learning theorists might speak of the malevolent transformation as a stimulus generalization process wherein the child learns to expect negative consequences from social situations. Sullivan would agree, but he went further by arguing that such expectancies influence the whole personality structure of the child.

Erikson's interest in the development of the ego component of personality took him very far from id and superego processes. He said that in the normal course of events, two general ego qualities emerge during early childhood: autonomy and initiative. Both of these qualities relate very closely to research on competence and achievement. As Erikson described it, the child's sense of autonomy apparently depends upon the outcome of his competence strivings. By age three, if he has made proper gains in mastering his environment, he should think of himself as reasonably capable of dealing with his immediate needs, and he should thus have the sense of pride in himself that Allport mentioned in his review of the emerging self-concept. Initiative comes in by age five as a general sense of pleasure in attaining specific goals. The child here enjoys doing things for himself at his own inspiration. In his discussion of initiative, Erikson to some extent anticipated McClelland's later formulation of the achievement motive. But McClelland's theoretical statements were more specific and tied more closely to learning than Erikson's. The latter only touched upon learning when he suggested that initiative is channeled into socially approved activities as a consequence of the Oedipal situation. The achievement idea also appeared later in Erikson as the sense of industry that should characterize middle childhood.

Piaget

Piaget described the age range 2 to 7 years as the "preoperational" period of cognitive development. The young child's thinking is generally tied to immediate meanings; he does not carry out mental operations. For example, an adult might respond to a novel object by mentally comparing it with other, more familiar objects. But a child will respond to it immediately in terms of its salient perceptual[9] qualities.

The preoperational period is divided into two stages. From 2 to 4 years children are mainly "egocentric" thinkers. And from 4 to 7 years they are described as "intuitive." We have already discussed egocentrism in relation to language. Piaget saw it as broadly characteristic of all the young child's activities. At 2 to 4 years the child not only "thinks" according to his immediate perceptions, but his perceptions are geared to his own self-centered view of the world. This egocentrism is reflected in many common situations. If you bump and hurt a 3-year-old by accident, he generally reacts as he would to deliberate physical punishment. If you make faces and ugly noises playing "monster" with him, he is liable quickly to become frightened, as if you were a legitimate monster. There is also the young child's notorious animism, his tendency to see inanimate things as having an inner life, and anthropomorphism, his tendency to see animate things as having a purposive inner life just like his own.

The 4-to-7-year age range is mentioned as being intuitive mainly because the child is in transition to a higher level of cognitive development; he is moving toward the use of concrete mental operations. When he does this, the child does not suddenly show full-blown, higher-order cognitive abilities. Instead the transition is slow: he seems able to respond more appropriately to more situations as he gets to be 5, 6, and 7. And this increasing frequency of

---

[9]Theoretical distinctions between perception and thinking are difficult to make. Most psychologists agree that perception is prior to thinking in the sense that it usually functions to provide immediate chunks of organized information about the environment. It is the perceptual ability, for example, that allows us to drive in complex traffic patterns without often having to think too much about it. Thinking is secondary in the sense that it enables us to deal with chunks of information more abstractly: we can relate, combine, ignore, store up, or otherwise mess about with perceptual material. Chronologically and phylogenetically, perception also appears to be primary. The child can manipulate objects properly long before he can deal with them symbolically; perception is very good in birds and cats. Present knowledge about the processes of perception and thinking strongly indicates that they are coterminous with one another.

more sophisticated behavior appears to be the result of intuition: like adults known for their good intuitions or hunches, the child can come up with good responses, but he can't explain why or how he does it.

At the end of the previous chapter, we left the child of two at the sixth substage of sensorimotor intelligence. He had a simple representational ability which allowed him to carry out internal trial and error "experiments"; he could maintain a mental image of something not immediately present, and visualize simple changes in it. From two to four, he expands his internal representational ability to cover a much wider range of different and more complex phenomena. For example, the child can probably go from visualizing use of a chair to reach something on top of a drainboard, to visualizing himself climbing on the chair to stand on the drainboard and reach something on the back shelf of a closed cupboard. His representational ability thus becomes a more robust cognitive instrument, able to handle more complicated material. At the same time, however, the child is constantly adapting to new environmental events. Some are assimilated into prior cognitive schemas, and some force him to accommodate by forming new cognitive schemas. So there is a lot of confusion for him because it is difficult for the child to sort things out or "equilibrate" his schemas while new material keeps rolling in.

By the age of four or five, he apparently starts getting caught up with himself, cognitively speaking, because he begins to show better control over his thinking during this intuitive stage:

First, the child becomes noticeably more *testable* in formal experiments from age four or five on. . . . He is much more able to address himself to a specified task and to apply adapted intelligence to it rather than simply assimilate it to some egocentric play schema. It is no accident that the lower age limit in most Piaget experiments is about four years. And not only does the child become testable *per se* in the late preoperational years, he also becomes capable of reasoning about progressively more complex and extended experimental problems or displays in the testing situation (Flavell, 1963, pp. 162–163).

The cognitive progress now underway is a result of the process Piaget called *decentering*. Apparently, as the child gains a greater representational ability, and as he develops more sophisticated, equilibrated schemas, his perception of objects and persons begins to be more complex. Instead of centering his attention on single, salient attributes of objects, he is able to vary the focus of his attention, to consider more than one attribute at a time. The analogy suggesting itself here is to a flashlight beam. The child begins to perceive in sweeping back and forth motions, rather than in a fixed pinpoint fashion. In his summary of this matter, Flavell noted that the progress being made toward concrete operations is at first very tentative:

The rigid, static, and irreversible structures typical of preoperational thought organization begin, in Piaget's phrasing . . . to "thaw out" and become more flexible, mobile, and above all decentered and reversible in their operation. The child of this transitional phase, having first centered on a single, distorting facet of a display, gradually becomes able to decenter and take account of other, correcting aspects. But the decentering process is only fragmentary and semireversible at first . . . (1963, p. 163).

Piaget's work on cognition in early childhood has many implications for personality development, but the most important generalization would seem to be this: he reveals otherwise unsuspected limits or boundaries for what we can demand from young children. Prior material in this chapter shows that substantial social-emotional aspects of personality in the young child are highly related to parental instruction practices. Efforts to socialize the child through rewards, punishments, the presentation of models for imitation, and other devices have a great deal to do with the recognizable substance of his personality by age six. Piaget's work indicated that young children can only absorb finite amounts of such external socializing pressure. It suggests that one might design socializing procedures to fit the contours of the child's growing cognitive abilities, instead of trying to force him – the earlier the better – to fit the contours of parental demands. None of this means that traditional approaches to socialization are invalid. Research makes it abundantly clear that reinforcement, conditioning, and imitation principles *do* provide means to shape the child's personality. What research has *not* made clear is that all such efforts have limits; that they can only be properly effective within certain boundaries. The "arrogance of power" can exist in persons as well as nations. Having so much power relative to the child, parents and others can easily ignore the natural limitations of their power to produce specific results.

Piaget's work allows us to elaborate this idea in a more concrete fashion. His view of decentering as a thawing-out process seems to depend upon a freeing-up or liberalization of the child's perception. Now if a child consistently experiences demands that he cannot understand and is forced into excessively rule-bound behaviors by a heavy-handed positive and negative reinforcement regime, it seems quite likely that decentering will be impeded. For if one lives in a system that ties major pain and pleasure to strict observation of rules, one is not likely to try anything new, perceptually or otherwise. The argument here goes to a central premise of Piaget's work: that thinking develops as a means of adaptation to the environment. The decentering process which carries a child to the higher level adaptation of concrete mental operations seems likely to be impeded if his social environment is hostile to that process. The argument can be pushed a step further by citing clinical evidence. Autism, the most serious form of pathology in young children, has extreme egocentric or non-decentered behavior as its main symptom. Quasi-clinical evidence, such as the rigid child-rearing practices associated with the adult authoritarian personality pattern, also fits here.

Bruner

J. S. Bruner (1966) followed Piaget's general view of cognitive development very closely, but with sufficient differences to perhaps warrant description as a "neo-Piagetian." In any case, he refers to all thinking as a means for the individual to represent his world to himself. Initially the infant is limited to an "enactive" mode of representation; he understands things only through their action properties. In early childhood the mode of representation becomes "ikonic" (visual-perceptual).

Bruner's research program has revealed many of the important details involved in the child's transition to higher-order thinking. One of his major findings concerns the process of decentering. As the intuitive child begins attending to more than one feature of an object or perceptual display at a time, he frequently makes more errors and appears to be more confused than the younger child who remains focused on one thing at a time. Bruner's interpretation of this phenomenon is that the child who is in transition makes more mistakes because he is not yet able to relate different things to one another according to higher-order cognitive schemas. He has, so to speak, begun to abandon a primitive cognitive vehicle before he has mastered the more sophisticated one. In terms of his general performance, therefore, the child who is decentering apparently has to take one step backward before he can go another step forward.

Moore

Completely apart from the context of conventional psychology, sociologist Omar Moore developed a theoretical learning scheme and harnessed it to a new technology for teaching children to read and write at very young ages. The dramatic technical end of his work has been widely publicized in mass media as the "talking typewriter." Used with children as young as four and five, or with older children who seem retarded, Moore's system involves a computer-mated electric typewriter. After a child enters a booth containing the equipment, it works in the following way:

The booth assistant helps him get into the elevated chair (because some children do not like to sit in a *high chair*, in the laboratory we call it an "elevated chair"), turns one switch, tells the child to enjoy himself and to raise his hand if he wants anything. Without further comment the assistant leaves the booth, closes the booth door, and then goes to a control panel mounted on the exterior wall of the booth, presses appropriate buttons, and begins to watch the child through a one-way window located just below the control panel.

The child is alone in the booth confronted with what may appear to him to be a typewriter with colored keys. (Prior to entering the booth his fingernails have been painted with nontoxic water colors. There is a match between the nail colors and the colored typewriter keys so that striking keys with matching fingers constitutes correct fingering. Also, there is a noticeable difference in pressure between the left-hand and the right-hand keys to help the child orient his hands. Behind the keyboard is a lucite housing which permits him to see everything in front of him, but which keeps his fingers out of the moving parts of the typewriter.) Whether or not he believes that the object in front of him is some kind of typewriter—as a matter of fact he is in charge of much more than an electric typewriter—he is at the controls of a computer in-put and read-out device, three distinct memory systems, an audio-recording system, and two visual exhibition systems, all of which are integrated by a central electronic logic and control system. Nevertheless, the operation of this complex instrument is under his management.

Of course, not all of the abilities of the instrument are needed for the child's first session. The booth assistant has set the instrument, which is called the Edison Responsive Environment (E.R.E.), in what is called Phase 1, Free Exploration, i.e., the instrument is set so that the child can explore the keyboard freely. Whenever a key is struck, E.R.E. types the letter (in large type) and pronounces the name of the character that has been typed. (The "reaction time" of E.R.E. to a key operation averages one-tenth of a second.) When a key has been depressed and released no key can be operated for about one second—this gives E.R.E. time to pronounce the name of the character. No two keys can be depressed simultaneously—this makes it impossible to jam or to garble pronunciations. The moment any given pronunciation is completed, the keyboard is automatically unlocked so that the child can go on exploring (Moore, in Gross and Murphy, 1964, pp. 196–197).

In later sessions, the child moves up to a "search and match phase." The machine here flashes a letter on its display window, and the child must find the key that matches it while all other keys are locked. Later still, he goes to "word construction": the machine displays several letters forming a word; after the child matches all of them, a programed voice spells and pronounces the word. As children make progress, they are given handwriting and reading training in addition to their typewriter sessions. There are further variations, but the main thing is that the system works remarkably well. It is impossible not to be impressed when one sees Moore's extraordinary films of 4- and 5-year-olds typing out their own stories. But from a theoretical standpoint, the logic behind this practical accomplishment is more exciting than the accomplishment itself.

Moore and A. R. Anderson first elaborated their conception of "autotelic" (self-directed) activities while analyzing children's games. They were interested in games as a form of training whereby a society or culture encourages its youth to practice the performance of skills essential to that society. For example, in our society there are many cooperative and/or competitive games involving models of important cultural tools, such as weapons, words, and money. These games are autotelic because the players can adapt them to their own particular purposes and styles, and because they are intrinsically enjoyable. Moore gives the following formal statement.

My colleague, Alan Ross Anderson, and I have defined an activity as *autotelic* if engaging in it is done for its own sake rather than for obtaining rewards or avoiding punishments that have no inherent connection with the activity itself (Moore, 1964, p. 184).

It has long seemed obvious that great benefits would result if the energy and effort children put into their games could be channeled toward the purposes of formal education (think of how they enjoy *Sesame Street*). Moore has apparently been able to do this through application of a second major concept, the "responsive environment."

I have defined a *responsive environment* as one which satisfies the following conditions:
  1. It permits the learner to explore freely.
  2. It informs the learner immediately about the consequences of his actions.
  3. It is self-pacing, i.e., events happen within the environment at a rate determined by the learner.

4. It permits the learner to make full use of his capacity for discovering relations of various kinds.

5. Its structure is such that the learner is likely to make a series of interconnected discoveries about the physical, cultural, or social world (Moore, p. 184).

One of the fascinating things about Moore's work is that he has been able to transform his theoretical ideas into a practical system by overseeing a linkage between the technologies of the computer and the electric typewriter.[10] Moreover, while his system has undeniably great practical value, its practical and theoretical implications are still obscure. If, as the evidence so far available suggests, children of four or five can be taught to read and write at a level corresponding to the normal second or third grade, elementary school curricula will have to be drastically changed. At a theoretical level, one wonders how a child given these skills so early would measure up to the progression in cognitive development described by Piaget. Would such a child decenter and move into concrete operations sooner? It seems a reasonable possibility. And how would such skill influence social-emotional aspects of personality? Moore himself says that he thinks it *does* produce deep personality changes, but he limits his discussion to two illustrative cases.

One boy of six was referred for training because he was a discipline problem and had a below-normal IQ (it was 72; the normal average is 100). He made relatively satisfactory progress in Moore's system until reaching the word construction writing (WC-W) phase. He seemed to dislike words. He would mumble to himself "It's not broken" and tell the machine to "Shut up." Yet he had all the skill necessary to do well at this phase. So an interviewer was sent to his home.

His mother said that she had caught Billy "playing with himself," and that she had whipped him and told him he would hurt himself. This made it much clearer what Billy was mumbling about. In WC-W the assistant pointed to his penis when he said, "It's not broken." She said the word "penis" and spelled it. It was put on the dictation equipment for him in a nonautomated booth. He typed the word "penis" twelve times with manifest enjoyment. In his next WC-W storytelling session he said, among other things, "When my dad took the prayers away, my mother got sick and died." The constituent words of this story were made into a word list for the next WC-W typing session. Billy liked these words and now was willing to accept word lists in WC-R (Moore, 1964, p. 211).

After this he made good progress. At the end of 6 months he went into a regular first-grade class and did fairly well. His IQ tested to 79, not a significant change, but he was no longer a discipline problem. Instead of disrupting the class as he used to do when he didn't understand something, he would now ask questions of the teacher. Moore comments:

---

[10]Judging from one of his early unpublished lectures, Moore stumbled on this discovery while trying to entertain his 3-year-old daughter. She enjoyed playing with the family typewriter, and he (or his wife) began verbalizing the letters she struck on it. She liked the "game" so well that he tried it on other children who had the same positive reaction. He then formalized it into a system involving the typewriter and a human monitor, which was tried out in a private elementary school (Hamden Hall, Connecticut). The computer technology was added later. In this connection, Moore feels that a fully automated system is preferable because the child can be distracted by the emotional reactions that even a well-trained monitor will occasionally display.

One year of first grade did not improve Billy's reading significantly—for all practical purposes, he was held back, though his skill at picture interpretation undoubtedly improved. It is my overall impression that Billy is still a vulnerable dependent child who will rebel if he is not skillfully handled. A second year in the laboratory would have afforded him a good deal of protection—it would have been especially helpful if his introduction to arithmetic could have been carried out within the context of a responsive environment.

Billy's family is proud of him, and now they let him work more things out for himself. His mother feels completely vindicated—all the psychologists, social workers, and teachers were wrong—Billy is not dumb, he is simply a "stubborn and lazy" child who needs a good whack (1964, pp. 212–213).

The second case involved a high IQ (139) 4-year-old who was already receiving psychiatric help for neurotic behavior problems. After his entering the program and beginning to make good progress, his mother complained about his changed behavior at home. Prior to this time he had been his mother's close, overprotected companion—she was a well-off divorcée. Now she said he was starting to be rude to her, and would not put away his things. He also refused to show her his skill on the electric typewriter in their home. Several weeks later she removed him from the program. It seems clear that the boy's greater independence vis-à-vis his mother was related to the growth of his reading and writing skills.

To sum it up, Moore's work demands attention on several different counts: it involved an ingenious new practical scheme of instruction; it has important implications for theories of cognitive development; and it suggests interesting connections between cognitive skills and social-emotional personality attributes.

CHAPTER SUMMARY

Early childhood can be described in many different ways. One of the more popular common ideas is that young children are unsocialized barbarians. According to how one reads evidence from everyday life, traditional children's stories and some case histories, this barbarian notion has a certain surface plausibility. It breaks down, however, when one looks beneath the surface. Here it can first of all be seen that punishment, language acquisition, and physical growth stand as the definitive "facts of life" for the young child; they stipulate his existential condition. It does not seem possible to gain an adequate practical or theoretical understanding of personality development without considering them as extended critical events, unique to this period.

We have also been concerned with the social-emotional aspects of the young child's development. That is, while the period as a whole can be encompassed in a triangular frame set by the three critical events mentioned above, the area within it contains specific regions such as the child's self-concept, sexual identity, moral conscience, aggressive tendencies, and achievement orientation. It may be more appropriate to think of these as layers in a mass that has been penetrated by research, each layer having its own width, depth, and dynamic. But no matter what metaphorical structure is preferred, studies have made it clear that all these aspects of personality relate to parental behavior patterns. The tone and texture of the young child's experience is largely determined by his parents. And the underlying psychological processes which render the child sensitive and receptive to this experience can be traced to fundamental learning principles.

Such principles as reinforcement, conditioning, and imitation do not account for everything, however. Neither their respective limits of effectiveness, nor the manner in which they relate to one another, nor the way in which they may gear into hereditary predispositions, are clear. Furthermore, complex mother-father-child relationships, such as those encountered in studies specifying different degrees of affection and dominance for each parent, suggest that multiple processes are operative: the child is not a one- or two-track system.

Finally, in examining major theoretical perspectives on early childhood, one gets a better grasp of longitudinal dynamics. The traditional Freudian view ties the end results of this period to the dramatic workings of the Oedipus complex. Social-emotional components of personality are firmed up as a means of coping with the stress and anxiety created by this complex. Neo-Freudians look to less dramatic social experiences for explanations.

Piaget's work exposes the dynamics of cognitive development: the young child gains an increasing ability for internal representation, his egocentrism diminishes, and as he decenters, his thinking advances from reliance on immediate perception toward simple ("concrete") mental operations. Bruner's work showed that such mental operations involve cognitive schemas which essentially serve to reduce the confusion caused by multiple percepts.

In both Piaget and Bruner, there are indications of important relationships between cognitive and social-emotional aspects of personality development. These seem even clearer in the context of Moore's ingenious system for early reading and writing instruction. Besides demonstrating that a properly designed "autotelic responsive environment" can unlock unsuspected capabilities in young children, he also provided examples of how cognitive and social-emotional aspects of personality mesh. Furthermore, his work poses something of a challenge to conventional learning theory and to Piaget's sequential description of cognitive development. If Moore is correct, then we can probably manage with much less in the way of conditioning and reward-punishment ideas as guides to education. And if children can acquire significant reading and writing skills in the preoperational period of cognitive development, it may be that they can decenter sooner, and thus become concretely operational in their thinking earlier than Piaget's work indicates.[11]

---

[11]Generally accepted research findings show that training based on extrinsic rewards cannot accelerate cognitive development beyond the age limits set by Piaget. But it remains to be seen whether training according to an intrinsic reward system can accomplish this. The reader who observes some apparent contradiction between our discussions of Piaget and Moore is therefore correct. From the former, one derives the idea that child-rearing practices should be limited to fit the cognitive capabilities of the child. From the latter, one gets the idea that if child-rearing practices can be modified to fit autotelic responsive environment principles, cognitive capabilities will take care of themselves. However, perhaps in the long run these ideas amount to the same thing.

References

Allport, G. W. *Pattern and growth in personality.* New York: Holt, Rinehart & Winston, Inc., 1961.

Ayers, W. Discussion: Implementing equal educational opportunity. *Harvard Educational Review,* 1968, *31*(1), 142–148.

Bandura, A. Influence of model's reinforcement contingencies on the acquisition of imitative responses. *Journal of Personality and Social Psychology,* 1965, *1*, 589–595.

Bandura, A., & Kupers, C. Transmission of patterns of self-reinforcement through modeling. *Journal of Abnormal and Social Psychology,* 1964, *69*, 1–9.

Bandura, A., Ross, D., & Ross, S. Vicarious reinforcement and imitative learning. *Journal of Abnormal and Social Psychology,* 1963, *67*, 601–607.

Berkowitz, L. (Ed.) *Roots of aggression: A re-examination of the frustration-aggression hypothesis.* New York: Atherton Press, Inc., 1969.

Bernstein, B. Aspects of language and learning in the genesis of the social process. In D. Hymes (Ed.), *Language in culture and society: A reader in linguistics and anthropology.* New York: Harper & Row, Publishers, 1964, pp. 251–263.

Bettelheim, B. *The informed heart.* Glencoe: The Free Press, 1960.

Brown, P., & Elliot, R. Control of aggression in a nursery school class. *Journal of Experimental Child Psychology,* 1965, *2*, 103–107.

Brown, R. *Words and things.* Glencoe: The Free Press, 1958.

Bruner, J. S., Olver, R. R., & Greenfield, P. M. *Studies in cognitive growth.* New York: John Wiley & Sons, Inc., 1966.

Burlingham, D., & Freud, A. *Young children in wartime: A year's work in a residential war nursery.* London: Allen & Unwin, 1942.

Byram, C. A longitudinal study of aggression and self-assertive behavior in social interaction. Unpublished thesis, Radcliffe College, 1966.

Cazden, Courtney B. Environmental assistance to the child's acquisition of grammar. Unpublished dissertation, Harvard University, 1965.

Clausen, J. A. A historical and comparative view of socialization theory and research. In J. A. Clausen (Ed.), *Socialization and society.* Boston: Little, Brown and Company, 1968, pp. 18–72.

Crandall, V. J., Preston, A., & Rabson, A. Maternal reactions and the development of independence and achievement behavior in young children. *Child Development,* 1960, *31*, 243–251.

Erikson, E. H. *Childhood and society.* New York: W. W. Norton & Company, Inc., 1963.

Evans, J. *Three men.* New York: Vintage Books (Random House, Inc.), 1966.

Fales, E. Genesis of level of aspiration in children from one and one-half to three years of age. Reported in K. Lewin, et al., Level of aspiration. In J. McV. Hunt (Ed.), *Personality and the behavior disorders,* Vol. 1. New York: The Ronald Press Company, 1944, pp. 333–378.

Fauls, L., & Smith, W. D. Sex-role learning of five-year-olds. *Journal of Genetic Psychology,* 1956, *89*, 105–117.

Flavell, J. H. *The developmental psychology of Jean Piaget.* Princeton: D. Van Nostrand & Co., Inc., 1963.

Freud, A. *The ego and the mechanisms of defense.* New York: International Universities Press, 1946.

Freud, S. Analysis of a phobia in a five-year-old boy. In *Collected papers, volume III.* London: Hogarth Press and the Institute of Psychoanalysis, 1925, pp. 149–289.

Gardner, R. A., & Gardner, B. T. Teaching sign language to a chimpanzee: III. Vocabulary demonstrations. Report delivered to the Psychonomic Society, November 1968.

Glueck, S., & Glueck, E. *Unravelling juvenile delinquency.* New York: Commonwealth Fund, 1950.

Greenberg, P. J. Competition in children: An experimental study. *American Journal of Psychology,* 1932, *44,* 221–249.

Hartup, W. W., & Zook, E. A. Sex role preferences in 3 and 4 year old children. *Journal of Consulting Psychology,* 1960, *24,* 420–426.

Hayes, C. *The ape in our house.* New York: Harper & Row, Publishers, 1951.

Hess, R. D., & Shipman, V. C. Early experience and the socialization of cognitive modes in children. *Child Development,* 1965, *36,* 869–886.

Hetherington, E. M., & Frankie, G. Effects of parental dominance, warmth, and conflict on imitation in children. *Journal of Personality and Social Psychology,* 1967, *6,* 119–125.

Hoffman, M. L. Child-rearing practices and moral development: Generalizations from empirical research. *Child Development,* 1963, *34,* 295–318.

Hoffman, M. L., & Saltzstein, H. D. Parent discipline and the child's moral development. *Journal of Personality and Social Psychology,* 1967, *5,* 45–57.

Hollenberg, E., & Sperry, M. Some antecedents of aggression and effects of frustration in doll play. *Journal of Personality,* 1951, *1,* 32–43.

Jersild, A. T., & Markey, F. V. Conflicts between preschool children. *Child Development Monographs,* 1935, #21.

Kagan, J., & Moss, H. A. *Birth to maturity.* New York: John Wiley & Sons, Inc., 1962.

Kellogg, W. N., & Kellogg, L. A. *The ape and the child.* New York: McGraw-Hill Book Company, 1933.

Koch, H. L. The relation of certain formal attributes of siblings to attitudes held toward each other and toward their parents. *Monographs of the Society for Research on Child Development,* 1960, *25*(4), #78.

Kohlberg, L. *Stages in the development of moral thought and action.* New York: Holt, Rinehart & Winston, Inc. In press, 1970.

Lenneberg, E. H. *Biological foundations of language.* New York: John Wiley & Sons, Inc., 1967.

Lenneberg, E. H. On explaining language. *Science,* 1969, *164*(3880), 635–643.

Levin, H., & Sears, R. R. Identification with parents as a determinant of doll-play aggression. *Child Development,* 1956, *27,* 135–153.

Longstreth, L. E. *Psychological development of the child.* New York: The Ronald Press Company, 1968.

Luria, A. R. *The role of speech in the regulation of normal and abnormal behaviour.* London: Pergamon Press, 1961.

McCarthy, D. Research in language development: Retrospect and prospect. *Monographs of the Society for Research on Child Development,* 1959, *24*(5), 3–24.

McClelland, D. C. *The achieving society.* Princeton: D. Van Nostrand & Co., Inc., 1961.

McClelland, D. C. Risk taking in children with high and low need for achievement. In

J. W. Atkinson (Ed.), *Motives in fantasy, action, and society.* Princeton, N.J.: D. Van Nostrand & Co., 1958, pp. 306–321.

McClelland, D. C., Atkinson, J. W., Clark, R., & Lowell, E. *The achievement motive.* New York: Appleton-Century-Crofts, 1953.

Mead, G. H. *Mind, self and society.* Chicago: The University of Chicago Press, 1934.

Mead, M. *Sex and temperament.* New York: William Morrow & Co., Inc., 1935.

Mischel, W. Delay of gratification, need for achievement and acquiescence in another culture. *Journal of Abnormal and Social Psychology,* 1961, *62,* 543–552.

Moore, O. K. Autotelic responsive environments for learning. In R. Gross and J. Murphy (Eds.), *The revolution in the schools.* New York: Harbinger Books, Harcourt Brace Jovanovich, Inc., 1964.

Mowrer, O. H. *Learning theory and the symbolic processes.* New York: John Wiley & Sons, Inc., 1960.

Murphy, Lois. *Personality in young children, Vol. 2.* New York: Basic Books, Inc., Publishers, 1956.

Osgood, C. E. *Method and theory in experimental psychology.* New York: Oxford University Press, 1953.

Parke, R. D. *Readings in social development.* New York: Holt, Rinehart & Winston, Inc., 1969.

Patterson, G. R., Littmon, R. A., & Bricker, W. Assertive behavior in children: A step toward a theory of aggression. *Monographs of the Society for Research in Child Development,* 1967, *32,* No. 5 (Serial No. 113).

Piaget, J. *The moral judgment of the child.* London: Kegan Paul, 1932.

Rosen, B. C., & D'Andrade, R. The psychosocial origins of achievement motivation. *Sociometry,* 1959, *22,* 185–218.

Sarnoff, I. Identification with the aggressor: Some personality correlates of anti-Semitism among Jews. *Journal of Personality,* 1951, *20,* 199–218.

Sears, R. R., Maccoby, E. E., & Levin, H. *Patterns of child rearing.* Evanston: Row, Peterson, 1957.

Sears, R. R., Whiting, J. W., Nowlis, V., & Sears, P. Some childrearing antecedents of aggression and dependency in young children. *Genetic Psychological Monographs,* 1953, *47,* 135–234.

Smith, M. B. Competence and socialization. In J. A. Clausen (Ed.), *Socialization and society.* Boston: Little, Brown and Company, 1968, pp. 270–320.

Templin, M. Certain language skills in children, their development and inter-relationship. *Institute of Child Welfare Monographs,* Minneapolis: University of Minnesota Press, 1957, #26.

Vener, A. M., & Snyder, C. A. The preschool child's awareness and anticipation of adult sex roles. *Sociometry,* 1966, *29,* 159–168.

Vygotsky, L. S. *Thought and language.* Cambridge: The MIT Press, 1962. (First published in the Soviet Union after Vygotsky's death in 1934.)

Walters, R. H., Parke, R. D., & Cane, V. Timing of punishment and the observation of consequences to others as determinants of response inhibition. *Journal of Experimental Child Psychology,* 1965, *2,* 10–30.

Watson. J. B. *Behavior: An introduction to comparative psychology.* New York: Holt, Rinehart & Winston, Inc., 1914.

Werner, H., & Kaplan, E. The acquisition of word meanings: A developmental study. *Society for Research on Child Development Monograph,* 1952, *15,* #1, 506.

White, R. W. Motivation reconsidered: The concept of competence. *Psychological Review*, 1959, *66*, 297–333.

Winterbottom, M. The relation of need for achievement to learning experiences in independence and mastery. In R. D. Parke (Ed.), *Readings in social development.* New York: Holt, Rinehart & Winston, Inc., 1969, pp. 309–321 (first published 1958).

Yerkes, R. M., & Learned, B. W. *Chimpanzee intelligence and its vocal expression.* Baltimore: The Williams & Wilkins Co., 1925.

7

Middle Childhood (6 to 12 years)

Most people look back to middle childhood the way older men look back to the time they were soldiers: the very funny and frightening incidents remain vivid, although some of the frightening things may seem funny in retrospect. Something of this sort can be seen in a childhood memory presented by Dollard and Miller:

One of the authors as a six-year-old boy was permitted to participate in an after-dark session of older boys. They were telling the tale of how Bill Smith, a prominent citizen of the town, had come home and surprised his wife in bed with her lover. Smith thereupon pulled out a spring-loaded jackknife (demonstration of length and viciousness of same by boy telling the story) and proceeded to unman the lover. Such a story does not remain, however, as a mere "fable." It is taken to heart and has the effect of teaching straight-out castration fear to sex motives (1950, p. 146).

Regardless of the interpretations that can be invoked for specific experiences, however, one who seeks to sift out the psychological essence of the 6 to 12 year period soon finds that it has no single, clear dramatic focus. If the period hangs together at all for most of us, it is probably as a chain of exploits combining the exercise of newly acquired skills, evasions of authority, and dangers averted—all of which get incorporated into childhood adventures that stand as exploratory missions into the environment. For those raised in the bygone innocence of the Midwest, this material may approximate the Tom Sawyer model. For those growing up in contemporary big-city slums, the material is liable to be more deadly:

By the time I was nine years old, I had been hit by a bus, thrown into the Harlem River (intentionally), hit by a car, severely beaten with a chain. And I had set the house afire (Claude Brown, *Manchild in the Promised Land*, p. 21).

The picture changes when we back off from specific experiences to generalize. Psychologically, middle childhood seems to be distinguished mainly by its blandness when compared with other periods in the life cycle. It is a relatively open, flat, occasionally bumpy stretch in most of our lives. We get stronger and can handle our bodies much better, but physical growth is slower here than in early childhood. We learn the formalities of reading and writing language, but have already passed through the most significant period of language acquisition. We change in several other ways, but all of them generally involve either extensions and consolidations of prior developments, or conformity to new standards of behavior set by parents, peers, and the school. "Whining schoolboy" was the best Shakespeare could do to epitomize this period. Freud called it the "latency" period because he saw libido being weakened and bottled up during much of this time. Philosophy provides Descartes' observation to the effect, "Give me the child to the age of six and I will answer for the man." So in the search for key factors in personality, middle childhood has never seemed to be very promising territory.

Consider literary works. Virtually no major writer of the type usually cited for psychological insight has been concerned with this period. One finds instead that the "literary psychologists" – Dostoevsky, Proust, Joyce, Wolfe, O'Neill, and others – are concerned mainly with adolescence or post-adolescent periods. There are a few important exceptions, such as Richard Hughes (*High Wind in Jamaica*), Harper Lee (*To Kill a Mockingbird*), and William Golding (*Lord of the Flies*), who perhaps serve to prove the rule. But it is significant that these works centering on middle-childhood experiences are typically not seen as vehicles for understanding children. Serious critics tend to treat the age of the characters here as being of more symbolic than practical importance. When Golding, for example, describes 10- and 12-year-olds as capable of extreme brutality, he is understood to be saying something about the nature of man in general, not children in particular. Furthermore, except for the ambiguous status of certain works by Mark Twain and Robert Louis Stevenson, most writing about middle childhood can be labeled as descriptive adventure, social protest, or, as in the case of Dickens' *Oliver Twist*, both.

Among literary people, the reason for neglect of middle childhood and emphasis on adolescence is obvious: the latter is the age at which sex, and sensitive, self-conscious awareness of self and others first becomes real for most people. Dramatic possibilities are therefore never exhausted. The *Devil in the Flesh* of the 1940's may give way to the *Tea and Sympathy* of the 1950's, and the *Lolita* of the 1960's – one could argue for Lolita as a teeny-bopper-groupie prototype – but the inherent dramatic focus remains fairly constant.

Among psychologists, reasons for the lack of emphasis on middle childhood include historical trends set by major theoretical formulations, basic elements in the scientific ethos, and the evidence of everyday life. Let us take them briefly in order. *First*, we have seen in prior chapters that both Freudians and behaviorists concentrate on experience prior to middle childhood in seeking explanations for personality. For Freudians, the rationale of the Oedipus complex draws attention back to the earlier years. And behaviorists are drawn in the same direction by their learning principles, particularly the stimulus generalization which may follow learning by reinforcement or conditioning. *Second*, psychologists share in the general scientific ethic stressing explanation in terms of first causes. This often means that it is not nearly as satisfactory to explain a personality problem by reference to events at age eight or nine, as it is to explain it according to events at age three or four. *Third*, the evidence of everyday life has as strong an influence on psychologists as it does on others. To most observers who reflect on middle childhood, the period seems hazy and fairly innocuous, a pause before the storms of adolescence.

Middle childhood also comes as something of a relief to most parents. The six- to twelve-year-old is, after all, much less of a physical problem than the infant or preschool child. This is the time when mothers feel they can take a job. The *TLC* and barbarian clichés lose their imperative force. If they are replaced with anything, it is with a kind of general maintenance policy: provide the wherewithal for existence—food, clothing, shelter—and some direction, and the child will take care of himself. After 40 years of work with children from 5 to 16, A. S. Neill gave a succinct statement of this philosophy.

My view is that a child is innately wise and realistic. If left to himself without adult suggestion of any kind, he will develop as far as he is capable of developing (1960, p. 4).

So the question arises, why bother with this period? Why not hasten forward to the *sturm* and *drang* of adolescence? We might easily sketch the normative developments of middle childhood, add a discussion of acculturation processes, and end with Freudian and Piagetian theoretical perspectives. All this will be done, but certain kinds of research evidence suggest that we must try to do more. It is not that any particular study reveals unsuspected depths to middle childhood, or that our common sense views of this period are all wrong. Nor is it that psychologists are generally mistaken in seeking first causes elsewhere. It is rather that laymen and professionals alike tend to miss the *functional meaning* of events in middle childhood. Several sources provide material which suggests that while patterns of personality development originate earlier, they can be modified or crucially altered by middle-childhood experiences.

Neill and Bettelheim, for example, reported that in the permissive atmosphere of their institutions, it generally takes only a few months for children who have previously hated schoolwork to start attending classes of their own free will.

The recovery time is proportionate to the hatred their last school gave them. Our record case was a girl from a convent. She loafed for three years. The average period of recovery from lesson aversion is three months (Neill, 1960, p. 5).

Bettelheim, who works with severely disturbed children, described a similar initial aversion to school: "Most children enter the School with an active aversion to learning, to going to school or to any pressure to do so." He illustrated one way in which an appropriately permissive policy can erode this aversion:

When Leo finally came in, all he did was run around provocatively, and when this produced no reaction he went to the rear door, then back to the side door, pretending at each one to be leaving the room. Finally he did leave, but only to poke his head in every few minutes, shouting, "I'm going out. I'm not coming in." While behaving in this way he also smiled and seemed happy.

The teacher after having said once or twice at the beginning that that was up to him paid no more attention and went on with her work. At last Leo left the room saying, "You have to catch me," and stayed out for several minutes. When nothing happened he finally came in, took his seat, and with no further acting out took up his assignment (a bit of simple work) which was all prepared for him. Nothing further was said, nor was it needed (1950, pp. 135–136).

Kadushin (1967) provided another relevant line of evidence in a study of 91 adopted children. All of them were at least 5 years old when they were put up for adoption after being taken from their parents by court order. The legal separation proceedings rather well guaranteed that all the children had been badly treated. But the surprising finding of the study was that over 75 percent of these children responded quite positively to their new homes. Kadushin also cited prior work that runs in the same direction: of 36 children whose parents were chronic alcoholics and therefore unable to properly care for them, most grew up to be normally well-adjusted adults.

A further indication of the functional importance of middle childhood appears in the longitudinal work of Kagan and Moss. They found that behaviors typical of the child during this period were good predictors of analogous behaviors in the early adult period. And they suggested that important discontinuities between early and middle childhood behavior are due to social pressures encountered in the latter period.

Thus, fragmentary and diverse though it may be, when we draw certain material together, we can begin to glimpse the major functional meaning of middle childhood: it serves both to strengthen and to modify aspects of personality rooted in earlier experience. One must, therefore, see this period as being on the one hand a great time for acquiring new experience in wider environments, and on the other, as a great time for recovery or recuperation from earlier experience. The new cannot eliminate or erase the old, but it can change much of it. Moreover, the forces that can bring about these changes are, in their own ways, no less powerful than the forces operating upon development in infancy and early childhood.

In the following sections of this chapter, we will first examine the global critical event of middle childhood: movement into a world beyond the immediate family. Different dimensions of this event, such as peer-group and school activities, will be analyzed to specify decisive new factors that influence personality.

Substantial social-emotional developments are taken up in the next section. The issues of concern here include elaborations of the self-concept; new elements that appear in the morality, sexual identity, aggression, and achievement areas; and how these begin to close in upon one another to form a more unitary, distinct personality structure.

The final section of this chapter takes up the status of middle childhood as it appears in the major developmental theories. Our chief concern throughout this chapter is to draw together research and theory so as to clarify the functional role of middle childhood, to get a better view of the part it plays in the overall economy of personality growth.

BEYOND THE FAMILY

The essential point to understand at the outset is that almost any serious movement from the familiar to the new is threatening. Whether you think of it in terms of your first days at college, or on a new job, or in marriage, the phenomenon of basic fear or anxiety in the face of major novelty is always there. In many instances we deal with it through formal or informal techniques involving gradualism: orientation sessions, advice and warnings from those who have preceded us, and so forth. But if as adults we recognize that such techniques are never entirely satisfactory ways of softening the impact of drastically new situations, think how much greater must be the impact of new situations on the child.

As he crosses into middle childhood, the child encounters a whole range of new situations that all have at least one fundamental thing in common with one another. He finds himself out of immediate contact with his family. There is usually some preparation for these situations in early childhood via nursery school and baby-sitter experiences, but such things are very pale in comparison with the actual events coming later. Nursery schools, for example, typically involve smaller numbers, shorter time periods, and fewer demands than a regular kindergarten. Besides, any parent will confirm that regardless of his child's nursery school preparation, kindergarten or first grade is a great leap forward. The crux of the matter is that for the five- to six-year-old, activities beyond the family are like sex—some preparation is better than none, but no amount of gradual preparation gives any guarantee of performance with the real thing.

It should be emphasized that adult experience hardly provides any appropriate analogue to the child's movement out of the all-enveloping family cocoon. Some men may approximate this phenomenon when they are discharged after years of military service. Even this model does not hold up too well because the child goes into independent peer activities, and into the schoolroom, without the familiarity and support that sustains returning veterans. The thrust outward from the family seems unique to middle childhood and, therefore, is properly entitled to be treated as a broad critical event defining this period. Before going on to further specification of this event, however, it is important to consider its intrinsic duality.

One way to see this duality is through the reactions of parents. Let us take first attendance at school as a case in point. (You can, by the way, learn a great deal about children just by watching them go inside on opening day.) Most parents treat their child's initial school behavior partly as a matter of acquiring new skills and partly as a test of their child rearing. Any time the child has a serious problem in kindergarten, or in later grades for that matter, they are likely to take it as an occasion to reexamine the way they raised him, looking for mistakes.

Thus, beginning particularly in middle childhood, every substantial new twist in behavior is seen as having dual forward and backward implications. And although there are great differences between them, this is just as true for the child himself as it is for his parents. Parents may worry about what a new behavior portends for the future while they wring their hands over past "errors"; but as the child enters new situations, he inevitably tends to understand the present in terms of the past. That is, when he faces novel situations, the child can only fall back upon his past experience. Since his past experience is relatively small, the limits of his understanding are accordingly narrow, and the threatening quality of new situations is accordingly large; this is why it takes some children considerable time before they can accept the permissiveness of a Neill or Bettelheim. It may also happen that children will meet crucial elements of the past in new situations. Evans (1966) provided an example from the life of Johnny Rocco. His first experience beyond the family was in the streets.

Johnny hadn't been running the streets long when the knowledge was borne in on him that being a Rocco made him "something special"; the reputation of the notorious Roccos, known to neighbors, schools, police, and welfare agencies as "chiselers, thieves, and trouble-makers," preceded him. The cop on the beat, Johnny says, always had some cynical smartcrack to make. Certain homes were barred to him. Certain children were not permitted to play with him. Wherever he went—on the streets, in the neighborhood settlement house, at the welfare agency's penny milk station, at school, where other Roccos had been before him—he recognized himself by a gesture, an oblique remark, a wrong laugh.

"Everybody always knew all about me," he recalls. "I always had a bad name. I felt cheap. Everybody gave me hell" (Evans, p. 11).

In this case, the boy found the abuse he was used to receiving in his family to be continued outside the family. And note the social sensitivity—people knew about him, he felt cheap. The example above illustrates the backward thrust of new experience. For Johnny, the middle-childhood period functioned to strengthen personality patterns carried over from early childhood.

Claude Brown's autobiography allows us to see more clearly from the child's standpoint how he can be set in a *new* direction by novel experience. At age eleven, after growing up in the toughest kind of urban jungle, he was sent to a correctional home. There he met an adult director who did not fit any of his past experience.

I had never met anybody before who never got mad, and I had never met anybody who was always telling the truth like Papanek. But that's the way he was. . . . He would tell you something that left you knowing no more than before you asked him the question, but you would feel kind of satisfied about it. Sometimes he would have you talking about something else altogether different from what you asked him, and most of the time you would never know it. He was smarter than social workers, that was for sure, because he knew how to answer the hard questions without lying. So nobody could ever be mad at him for lying to them. And even though cats up at Wiltwyck lied a whole lot, like me, we didn't like grown-ups to lie to us about important things like the hard questions. Sometimes I used to get real tired of all that damn truth Papanek was telling, but I couldn't get mad at him for it.

For the next year or more, I tried to make life real sad for Papanek. This became harder and harder as time went by, because I grew to like him more and more, just like everybody else (*Manchild in the Promised Land*, pp. 87–88).

Over the years, Claude Brown's encounters with people like Papanek, and his own unusual qualities, combined to change the whole course of his life.

Briefly then, as we discuss specific matters concerning the child's move outward from his family, it should be kept in mind that many middle-childhood events can have dual psychological meanings. New experiences can draw the child ahead toward more sophisticated, positive adjustment patterns — as when Claude Brown discovered that he could trust some adults — or, they can force him backward toward simpler, increasingly negative patterns — as when Rocco found himself generally rejected as a troublemaker. But these are extreme examples. Most children will have a mixed run of experiences.

Peers

Any parent or child can provide personal evidence of the importance of peer-group experiences in middle childhood. Preschool children also have extensive contact with peers; indeed, some of the evidence mentioned below suggests that substantial peer experiences start between the ages of four and five. However, these early contacts do not seem to be of the same quality as those of the school-age child. Piaget and many other observers reported that younger children tend to treat their age-mates more as interesting objects than as significant social beings. All this changes drastically by age six or seven. The four-year-old may complain of another child being nasty if he loses a toy to him, or gets hurt in a scuffle; the six-year-old is quite able to suffer the pangs of chagrin or embarrassment if he is rejected by peers. Clausen summarized the age distinction in his review of socialization processes.

Although preschoolers clearly learn from one another, peer pressures have little meaning at this age level. A few years later, the emergence of structures of prestige and power within the classroom and in informal groups gives to the population of peers a special significance in socialization.

He also noted progressive changes in the child's relationship to his parents:

In the early years we have noted that parental power is very high and that it may be exercised either through the use of superior strength or through direct control of the child's environment. As the child matures, less and less of this physical and social environment is under the direct surveillance or control of the parents. Power can still be used punitively by the parents, but such use is likely to alienate the child and to increase the amount of time spent away from home engaged in activities disapproved by the parents (1968, p. 173).

What is generally happening here is that parental influence on the child decreases as peer influence increases. And while one can accept the validity of this statement on the basis of everyday experience and theoretical logic, it is also supported by empirical findings. In connection with a long-term study of behavior in natural settings conducted by Roger Barker, detailed records have been kept on children's activities in a rural Midwestern community. Wright (1967, p. 207) presented a portion of these data for eight children whose records span the age range two to eleven. The percent of behavior episodes involving adults (including parents) is compared with those involving other children. At age two, over 90 percent of all behavior is with adults. This drops steadily to 55 percent at age six, and 50 percent at age seven. It remains stable at the 50 percent level from age seven to eleven. The percent of behavior with other children shows an opposite trend: it rises sharply from about 5 percent at age four, to 25 percent at five, 38 percent at six and 45 percent at seven. By age eleven, behaviors involving adults and children are approximately equal at 50 percent each.

The decrease in parental influence is indicated further by a study relating discipline to age. Clifford (1959) had parents record all disciplinary incidents with their children for a period of 3 weeks. The average number of such incidents for three-year-olds was about 60; for six-year-olds it approximated 30, and for nine-year-olds it was down to about 15.

Apart from such normative data indicating the rise of peer influence in middle childhood, other research tends to corroborate what many parents first begin to suspect in this period: that after all their efforts and sacrifices through infancy and early childhood, their six- to twelve-year-old frequently seems more concerned to please relative strangers than his own mother and father. It is significant, and wonderfully ironic, for instance, to see the 8-year-old child of a professor of child psychology correct his father on some point of behavior by citing the authority of a teacher who barely passed the father's course.

But teachers can take little comfort in this, because research findings indicate that their influence is in turn weaker than the influence of peers. Berenda (1950) showed that when school children in a conformity experiment are required to make perceptual judgments according to the suggestions of either teachers or peers, they are much more susceptible to the influence of peers. Furthermore, while teen-agers are supposedly notorious for their conformity to peer pressures, findings indicate that in perceptual judgment tasks, such conformity is greater at 6, 7, and 8 than it is at 14, 15, and 16 (see McConnell, 1963).

Normative data thus support a generalization for middle childhood that can easily be validated in everyday life: the parents' salient role in the child's personality development starts to decline as the child spends more time with peers and is more susceptible to their influence. Now let us see what peers do and how they do it.

The functional role of peers

Most authorities agree that the child gets at least four different psychologically important things from his relationships with other children: social support, models for imitation, opportunities for learning social roles, and standards for self-evaluation.

Social support is easy to see. An eight- or nine-year-old, for example, may be able to get a good reasoned discussion from his father on why his allowance is not higher than a fixed amount. But he can get direct sympathy and close support on this problem from one of his age-mates. They can exchange hurt feelings, share fantasies of revenge, and construct alternative schemes for getting money by stealing, working, or selling lemonade. The theoretical dynamics of social support are more obscure.

Children live in an adult world that makes continual demands upon them and gives them little status. Therefore, some theoretical writers argue that children are attracted to one another because "Misery loves company." It is also mentioned that the fundamental dynamic here is similar to what can be observed in psychotherapy; children can unburden themselves of secret, hostile feelings to sympathetic age-mates, just as adults do with sympathetic therapists. And the shared misery idea is supported by the fact that those adults who become good companions to children are often people who in one way or another share in the inferior status of the child. Quite frequently, one sees and hears of children forming close ties with servants, old-maid aunts, alcoholics, or members of minority groups.[1]

Models for imitation are available to the child in all of his activities with peers, but this function is particularly clear when he associates with other children of varying ages. In a technical sense, younger children may serve as "regressive" models. It is not at all unusual, for instance, for a six- or seven-year-old to come home after playing with four-year-olds and lapse into speech or other behavior patterns representative of the younger age group. Or he may, by the same token, try to imitate the behavior of older children he has been playing with, using words he doesn't understand or trying performances that are beyond his ability.

From the standpoint of many parents, however, imitation of peers will be seen at its worst when their child picks up the very things they have been trying to keep him from learning at home. Sometimes the material is trivial—a dirty word he doesn't understand; sometimes it is more serious—a prejudiced racial or religious stereotype; and sometimes it may cut right to the bone, as in teasing or bullying of younger children. Reaction against the potentially corrupting influence of peers may become so strong in parents that they lose sight of the positive benefits of peer-imitation. A great many useful physical and social skills can be learned this way.

Peer activities also provide opportunities for the learning of new *social roles*. As a technical term in the language of social science, a role may be defined as "a structured mode of participation in social life . . . what society expects of an individual occupying a given position in a group" (Allport, 1961, p. 181). Social roles emerging from the peer relations of middle childhood have two important implications. First, by interacting with other children, visiting in their homes, playing at games involving rules and reactions to authority figures, children learn to elaborate their roles as children. This may sound absurd but it is easy to understand. Peer activities encourage the child to expand and extend the way he participates in family life. Thus, children of 6, 7, and 8 show an increasing awareness of fulfilling a standard family role by doing such things as arguing for their rights as children ("All children are allowed to have pets so why can't I keep my snake?"); maintaining the honor of the family against outsiders ("My Daddy can't swim but he has a big office."); or accepting certain responsibilities ("I have to cut the

---

[1]When I was seven or eight, I spent one whole summer as confidant and unpaid assistant to a disreputable handyman at a vacation resort. When I was 20 and working as a disreputable handyman at a summer resort, I was in turn followed everywhere by the young son of an industrialist who was supposed to own half the factories in New England. It is an interesting phenomenon that has never been properly researched.

grass for my allowance."). The increasing complexity of the child's family role is promoted by consensus on such matters existing within peer groups.

Second, and more directly, peer activities allow the child to see and try a number of different roles with his contemporaries. That is, in organized peer groups he encounters the leader, follower, and other diverse roles: the scapegoat, the intellectual, the comedian, the leader's friend. (Think of the old *Our Gang* film series, or such stories as *Winnie the Pooh*.) Children entering organized groups have their first serious experience with the variety of roles that can be filled. And they will typically try out more than one before settling in any particular position. Nor should it be assumed that these roles are as simple as they sound. Leaders can be intellectuals or fighters; comedians can be the leader's friend and/or the butt of all jokes; the roles mix and hyphenate, and children can have considerable difficulty with them.

Processes underlying role learning are also variable. Under some conditions, children are pushed into the roles required by a juvenile culture. Under other conditions, their role develops largely by chance—in Golding's *Lord of the Flies* a boy discovered a conch shell and therefore became "keeper of the conch." Furthermore, roles will frequently shift with age; as a child gets older he may move into a new position in a group, and he will know how to act in it from having observed his predecessor.

Finally, *standards for self-evaluation* emerge from peer activities. No matter how he is treated by parents or other relevant adults, every child comes to judge himself according to peer standards. So while a child's initial self-image may be based upon family behavior toward him, it will be enlarged, deepened, and perhaps changed, depending upon peer responses. This is very clear during the primary school years, when one can see that children who are conspicuously good or bad at various things receive either admiring or contemptuous reactions from peers. The child who lacks the skill to join other children swimming, or riding off on two-wheelers, will inevitably suffer in his own eyes by comparison with them. Moreover, at age 7, 8, and 9, standards of self-evaluation begin to show up in compensatory activities. Children begin to emphasize the things they do well, and avoid those they do badly. In hot weather, for instance, the swimmer will want to be in the water while the good reader may prefer the air conditioner and a book.

As a general rule, parents can only interfere indirectly in the comparison processes of middle childhood. Indirect actions can be very important, however, because successful special instruction or tutoring in areas of difficulty can have great effects on the child's behavior.

The underlying psychological processes at work here are too complex to unravel in a brief discussion. One can appeal to identification, imitation, and other learning principles to explain why a child begins to evaluate himself against peers, and to internalize peer standards that may be contrary to those of his parents. But it is difficult to single out any one dynamic process. Apparently, the child becomes aware of the importance of peer comparisons at some very basic level. The typical six- or seven-year-old will not care very much that he cannot drive a car as his father does, but he will care a great deal if he cannot ride a bike as his friends do. Perhaps it is just a matter of learning: parents encouraging him to measure himself against other children; or perhaps it is an innate reaction to the physical similarities he notes between himself and other children. Various matters relevant to this issue will be discussed in later sections.

Entrance and status in peer groups

Entrance into peer groups can occur in many different ways. An example of the brutally sharp pressures that force many children into peer-group activity is given in the autobiographical reflections of Roberto Sanchez. He told of his initiation to group life in a Mexico City slum when he was about eight or nine.

The law in the Casa Grande was . . . new tenant . . . new fight. To get into the gang, I had to pass through a number of tests. They put their best *gallos* or fighters on the new boy, to see if he was acceptable as a friend. Before, families moved in and out wholesale and there were lots of free-for-alls. Anyone who saw me in the courtyard would hit, pinch, or throw stones at me. If I was carrying something from the store, they would knock it down, and then I would get punished again at home. And so, as the amount of pain the human body can stand has its limit, so patience has its limits, and you find yourself obliged to fight.

One day I was walking by and there in the courtyard, waiting for me, were my brother and the four Ramírez boys. They were waiting for that decisive bout. Manuel had felt obligated to propose me as a member of the gang. But I wasn't going to be their butt just because I was new. My brother said, "Come on, fight." Daniel was going to be the one to test me. I called out to Manuel, but it made him mad that I should be such a coward. "Don't be a slacker. Defend yourself. I won't be fighting for you all your life."

I began to like fighting. I didn't go complaining when they hit me, but would tangle with anybody immediately. Thus, I relieved my brother of the responsibility of having to fight for me. Actually, I never wanted to fight with anybody, but they kept looking for it. I had to defend myself and continued to do so all my life (Lewis, 1961, pp. 72–73).

The environment in Bettelheim's orthogenic school is totally removed from that of a slum, but he is, nevertheless, very careful to minimize the strains of entrance into peer groups. Among other things, he is aware that it is a difficult situation for both the newcomer *and* the group itself: the newcomer has the usual problem of gaining acceptance, but those already in the group have the problem of accommodating themselves to a stranger. So an entrance party is arranged. The newcomer is the occasion of the party, so to speak, and is thus somewhat reassured that he will be accepted. At the same time, the old members of the group can look forward to the treats they will receive at the party. From a learning theory standpoint, the party can be construed as a positive conditioning procedure encompassing the newcomer and the group.[2]

[2] "We find it preferable to admit openly that the addition of the newcomer is a painful imposition on the old group members, one that we regret and for which we apologize. We explain why such things are unavoidable because of the mechanics of the institution and we make it clear that the party is given much more for the old members than for the new one. If, besides the other fun of the party, each child (as well as the newcomer) receives a toy, their loss is in part compensated, or at least symbolically so, by the adult and the School" (Bettelheim, 1950, p. 51).

Research on the problem of entrance into peer groups reveals the underlying stress of this situation in several ways. Phillips, Shenker, and Revitz (1951) observed what happened when six- and seven-year-olds were introduced singly into play groups composed of three others who had been together for some time. The general tendency of the established threesome is to ignore the newcomer. He would respond to this by addressing himself to the adult teacher who was present, apparently seeking to enlist her as a go-between. When the adult would not take this role, the child fell back on imitation, attempting to model his behavior on that of the most active, dominant member of the group. Davitz (1955) studied the friendship patterns of older children living in a summer camp. He found that they preferred those who they perceived to be most like themselves in interests and abilities. There was also a general tendency for children to exaggerate the similarity between themselves and their chosen friends. Davitz interpreted this exaggeration phenomenon in terms of an identification process assumed to be operative in the selection of friends. However, one can also see the relevance of an imitation process which may enhance similarity.

A number of additional factors have been shown to influence acceptance into peer groups. Bonney (1943) obtained measures of the popularity of fourth graders, and compared the behavior characteristics of 20 best-liked and 20 least-liked children. The former were described as standing out in one of two ways; they were either strong, aggressive, and enthusiastic, or attractive, happy, and friendly. Other work on first and third graders shows that the most popular children are those who are physically attractive, known as good sports, friendly, and so on. In first grade boys place a greater emphasis on aggressive, daring behavior, while girls value the ability to get along well with teachers and other children (see Tuddenham, 1952). Studies further indicate that a self-confident adjustment pattern underlies the aggressive, friendly, cheerful, exterior behavior of popular children. D. A. Goslin (1962) reported that children readily accepted by others have a more realistic self-image than unpopular children. Chronically anxious, fearful children tend to be rejected by others. However, F. N. Cox (1953) demonstrated that such children are better received by their age-mates after play therapy sessions have reduced their anxiety. And although it may seem trivial compared to the behavior patterns influencing acceptance and popularity, research by McDavid and Harari (1966) demonstrated that first names can be used as effective predictors of popularity. McDavid and Harari had children rate the attractiveness of 75 different first names in the abstract, without knowing particular individuals having those names. The more unusual or bizarre names were rated lowest. Later, when children rated the popularity of their classmates, those with unusual first names were found to be relatively unpopular. So it would seem that in addition to sticks and stones, first names can also harm you.[3] Social class is also related to peer acceptance. As if it were

---

[3] This work can evoke a nice nostalgia in those of us with unusual first names. "Leon," for instance, rhymes with peon. But while such names may be burdensome, this writer would argue that they can enhance character development, particularly in the area of rough and tumble fighting. Note also the Johnny Cash song about a boy named Sue.

not enough to be born poor, research (Bonney, 1943) suggests that in socio-economically mixed groups, children from poor families are not as popular as those from middle-class families.

Once accepted into a peer group, the child's status within it will depend upon many of the factors already mentioned, as well as long-standing personality attributes such as passivity or independence. Results from the Fels Institute study show that if the child is dependent and submissive in the family environment, he will also appear that way later in activities with peers. Material of this sort makes it clear that children's behavior in groups can be seen as representative of patterns traceable to early childhood. For example, Becker, Peterson, Hallmer, Shoemaker, and Quay (1959) interviewed the parents of 25 six- to twelve-year-olds who were especially shy or timid, and found that these children tended to have excessively domineering, restrictive fathers.

Longitudinal changes

It is to be expected that through the 6 to 12 year period, normative developmental changes in individual children will be matched by changes in their peer-group activities. One normative change involves the social perception skills of children; their ability to judge emotions in others. Work by Dimitrovsky (1964) showed that a substantial rise in the accuracy of such judgments occurs during the 6 to 12 year period. He employed stick figures and tape-recorded vocal expressions to determine how well children could use these cues to judge the emotions *happy, sad, angry*, and *loving*. Children of six made less than 30 percent correct identifications of happy and loving. At 12, the average correct for these emotions was approximately 50 percent. Furthermore, six-year-olds average 45 percent correct identifications for angry, and 74 percent correct for sad. For twelve-year-olds, these figures are 73 percent and 85 percent, respectively. The data here show that social perception skills improve considerably during middle childhood, and that the negative emotions – sad and angry – are the first to be correctly identified. This suggests the rather obvious, depressing notion that sadness and anger are the more salient or better-known emotions for children. Dimitrovsky's data summary showed, incidentally, that loving was mistaken for sad 600 times, while sad was taken for loving only 155 times.

Peer groups as agents of change

Most of the research sketched in the preceding sections only concerns the normative side of peer-group activities. From this perspective, children do not seem to be drastically influenced by peers. Findings generally indicate that peer activities consolidate behavior patterns originating in earlier experience. However, peers can become the most powerful force in a child's life when he is cut off from parents or other stable relations with adults. A very impressive example of this is described by Anna Freud. At the close of World War II she was given charge of six orphaned Jewish children who were rescued from a Nazi concentration camp. All of them had lost their parents before they were a year old. They were raised in a camp "ward for motherless children" by a succession of different inmates. The children displayed an extraordinarily intense attachment to each other by the time they were sent to England when all were between 3 and 4 years old.

The children's positive feelings were centered exclusively in their own group. It was evident that they cared greatly for each other and not at all for anybody or anything else. They had no other wish than to be together and became upset when they were separated from each other, even for short moments (A. Freud, 1951, p. 131).

They were also indifferent or hostile to all adults. These little children apparently created their own "peer-world" in reaction to the threatening adult world they had experienced.

Some interesting parallels to Anna Freud's description of the six orphans can be seen in Bettelheim's work with emotionally disturbed children. The treatment program at his orthogenic school is heavily dependent upon peer-group experience. He suggested that the groups function as substitutes for parents, but do not make the same strong emotional demands as parents. Children who have withdrawn into severe neurotic or psychotic adjustment patterns because they could not cope with their problems, thus find in the groups a refuge from adult pressures. In this connection, Bettelheim believed that much of child pathology originates in unsatisfactory emotional ties with adults. A reasonably well-controlled peer group, however, allows the child to try out various degrees of emotional involvement with others:

The child may submerge his individuality in the group at one moment, and experiment with various degrees of ego distance, of independence, at the next. What is even more important for many of our children is the fact that for some time they can live relatively satisfying lives without any emotional relations to adults because the small emotional involvement they are capable of they can get through the group. On the other hand, while the child can experiment with a close relation to an adult, the presence of the group reassures him that it need not engulf him as he may fear (Bettelheim, 1950, p. 242).

Further illustrations of the important group functions described by Bettelheim can be found in the natural behavior of delinquent boys' gangs. Cohen (1955) analyzed such gangs as "delinquent subcultures" which can supply the child with most of the things he may not be able to get at home — social-emotional support, guarantees of a secure status, and direct aid in satisfying material needs. The gangs are therefore difficult to break up because they are so useful as a means of adjustment. It is appropriate to mention here that Bettelheim drew some of the ideas for his treatment of disturbed children from August Aichorn, who worked with delinquent boys in Germany in the 1920's.

One of the few experimental investigations indicating how peer-group organization can influence normal children is provided by a classic study of social behavior (Lewin, Lippitt, and White, 1939). Eleven-year-old boys were organized into five-member recreational clubs. The boys were all about equal in intelligence, physical development, and such additional attributes as obedience, leadership, and friendliness. Each club was run by an adult leader according to one of the following models: "democratic" — equal participation and majority rule; "authoritarian" — dictatorial rule by the leader; and "laissez-faire"—lack of rule by the leader who does nothing except respond to questions in a nondirective fashion. Results showed that the boys in the democratic club were friendlier with each other, more innovative and independent, less irritable and aggressive, than the others. In the authoritarian club, behavior tended to become passive and apathetic, although in one of the four groups run in this atmosphere, there was an attempt to rebel against the leader. Behavior patterns in the laissez-faire group were more or less intermediate to these two extremes. Obviously, their club activities did not have strong effects on the boys' personalities, because the experiment did not occupy a great space in their lives. Yet the strikingly different behavior patterns emerging in the groups imply that if such atmospheres were intensified and maintained for long periods of time, important permanent effects might easily result.

In general, there is a considerable body of clinical and sociological evidence demonstrating the forceful character of peer groups as agents of change. Because most of this material comes out of unusual situations, however, it is not clear to what extent we should see peer group experience as either consolidating or changing trends in normal personality development. We can only be sure that depending upon circumstances, both are possible.

School

Many different things can be said about primary school experience. It is typically cited as an important factor in development because children spend so much of their time in school, because studies show that throughout childhood and adolescence it is the thing most children worry about, and because schools represent the formal arm of society which is supposed to reach out and gear children toward fulfillment of a proper adult role. The first two points are simple enough, and clearly relevant to personality development. The third is more obscure, because we all know that schools cannot program the lives of their students. Nevertheless, that seems to be the essential mission of the school as a social institution. Clausen gave a more formal description of this mission:

The aims and functions of formal education vary from one society to another, and they have been variously defined from one time to another in the United States. The most general societal functions are transmitting knowledge, norms, and values, along with the orientational and motivational underpinnings that this requires, and recruiting or channeling persons into programs of preparation for social positions allocated on the basis of achievement (1968, p. 153).

Traditionally, the school's functions as a social institution are more properly dealt with in sociology and anthropology than psychology. As recent research on personality has begun to include such topics as competence and achievement motivation, however, controversy over the role of the school has developed in this area. Researchers note that contemporary American schools tend to be either "traditional" or "modern"; the former are organized along lines that fit the concept of achievement, while the latter are better suited to the development of intrinsic competence.

According to Biber and Minuchin, the "traditional" orientation emphasizes factual information and specific skills in a context that depends saliently on the comparative appraisal of achievement. No particular effort is made to encourage the child to incorporate what he learns in his developing self-system. The "modern" orientation, on the other hand, tries to build on the child's native and intrinsic curiosity, on his active initiative in the learning process (Smith, 1965, p. 20).

Smith also noted that the psychological aspect of the controversy over school functioning was firmly stated in remarks by Orville Brim:

Brim gave the sharpest formulation to the underlying issue: Is the development of strong need for achievement an asset or a liability? American society has thrived when it was manned by a middle class that was highly oriented toward achievement—perhaps at a toll for the individual. What position should the school take on the development of achievement motivation? If the school trains children so as to maximize their sense of competence and autonomy, they may choose not to do things that society needs to have done, and that later on they may themselves wish they had chosen to do (1965, p. 21).

The questions raised above can no more be settled at the level of the school than they can at the level of the different theories that give rise to them; recall our discussion of competence and achievement in the previous chapter. Having noted a problem that we will see again in several different forms, let us now turn to the meaning of school at the level of individual personality development.

The school as authority

Theory, research, and common sense all indicate that primary school experience makes an important psychological impact because it is the child's first serious contact with adult authority outside the home. In this connection, most writers on development and education emphasize that children initially see their teachers as mother substitutes. For example, in their behavior profile of the average six-year-old, Gesell and Ilg (1946) observed that school was a new world to him; that the teacher was his "mother" in this world, and that he sometimes got his two mothers confused.

His emotional anchorage remains in the home, but he has to acquire a modified set of emotional moorings in the school. The two orientations are not interchangeable and not mixable. Being inexpert in emotional modulations, the school-beginner cannot always shift readily within the two worlds. An ill-timed visit at school from his mother; a mysterious conversation between his mother and his awesome new teacher may produce some jangle of images and attitudes (1946, p. 96).

Learning theory provides a straightforward theoretical rationale for such confusion: the child generalizes from mother to female teacher because the two often look quite similar, and make similar demands. Mussen, Conger, and Kagan (1963, p. 428), discussed this stimulus generalization phenomenon, noting that children will probably have positive or negative orientations toward teachers depending upon whether they have satisfactory or unsatisfactory relations with their mothers. These authors also suggest that girls may get along much better than boys in the early grades, because boys who are strengthening their masculine identification during this period are liable to struggle against female authority figures.

School impact on personality

If the school is an agency of social authority, and if, in the eyes of the child, the teacher personifies this authority because of her status as a mother substitute, what effects will the child's experience with teachers have on his personality? The general answer to this question is simple, and will be made very clear in the material mentioned below – teachers have a heavy influence over the way children think about themselves. And children's self-images, in turn, relate to their scholastic performances, which then further influence the way teachers act towards them, and so on. We encounter another one of those vicious psychological circles here; easy enough to verbalize, but difficult to really understand, because while we can all remember feeling good or bad depending on our report cards or whether the teacher let us clean her erasers, any adequate sketch of the school impact on personality involves diverse material.

So let us begin at the beginning: what do children think of school before they start? Evidence indicates that the vast majority is positive about it. Stendler and Young (1951) interviewed more than 200 mothers of children about to enter school. Over 90 percent said that their children were looking forward to it; that they were interested in learning to read and write. Other work (Kraus, 1956), demonstrated that even though some children may balk at the last moment and kick up a fuss on entering the building, they adjust quickly. Within a short time they are doing just as well as those who enter calmly. Stendler and Young also interviewed mothers 2 months and 8 months after their children had begun school. On both occasions, a 90 percent majority still said their children were generally favorable. Data collected by Jersild (1952), indicated that by fourth grade, one in five children will admit to an open dislike of the school part of their lives. In answer to the question "What do you dislike about yourself?" 22 percent of a large sample of boys and girls mentioned school-related abilities and attitudes. By grade six, the figure was about 30 percent.

At least three different factors seem to be responsible for the negative changes that occur between first and fourth grade. The attitudes and activities of teachers are foremost, but the mesh between the child's home and school environments, and the quality of what he learns, are also relevant. Most writers in this area include social class as a fourth factor, but since this cuts right across the other three – middle-class values have something to do with all aspects of education in this country – we will take it as it comes instead of setting it up as a special category.

Studies of the general attitudes and values held by schoolteachers relate immediately to middle-class orientations. It is not so much that teachers come from middle-class backgrounds, although many do; it is rather that they believe strongly in the enduring validity of middle-class standards. (There is no time here to discourse on the meaning of middle-class or *bourgeois* standards; suffice it to say briefly that property rights are central.) Hunter (1957) reported that in 1955 a sample of 308 teachers rated stealing, destruction of school property, truancy, and heterosexual activity, in that order, as the most serious behavior problems in children. Lack of interest in their schoolwork was thirteenth down the list. These data were compared with the ratings of 511 teachers made in 1926. The main difference involved sex; masturbation and heterosexual activity came right after stealing as the worst problems of the 1920's.

For children, teachers' socioeconomic backgrounds and associated values will be significant because we know that these things exert a strong bias on virtually all social relationships. In a prior section it was mentioned that research shows children tend to like others they perceive as being similar to themselves. Since the same general finding has been made many times in studies of adults, it is not surprising to see evidence that teachers are better disposed toward pupils who are like themselves. Research shows that even sex differences make a difference. Most primary-school teachers are women, and it is reported (Meyer and Thompson, 1956; Carter, 1952), that girls receive more approval from their teachers than boys. And as one would expect, there is also a bias in favor of children from the upper half of the socioeconomic spectrum. Hoehn (1954) observed that third grade teachers had more positive contacts with upper than with lower socioeconomic status children. During the past few years, findings of this sort have been reported so frequently that they are now widely accepted.

It has also been shown in many different ways that the social-emotional quality of the child's relationship with his teacher is associated with his school achievement. For example, the personal values of teachers are more similar to those of their high achieving pupils than they are to the values of low achievers (McDavid, 1959); high achievers receive more approval from teachers than low achievers (Battle, 1957); and patterns of teacher approval-disapproval are directly related to children's self-concepts (Davidson and Lang, 1960). The latter authors also noted that children with negative self-concepts tend to be poor achievers from lower social class backgrounds.

A question may arise at this point: "Perhaps it is only natural for teachers to like bright, high-achieving kids, and those who conform to middle-class standards of conduct—maybe it should just be accepted as a fact of life." It is, of course, undeniably a fact that in education, as in other areas, them that has, gets. But it is not an *immutable* fact. Quite the contrary. Considerable evidence suggests that teacher approval can be manipulated as a causal agent to improve school achievement. Staines (1958) had teachers praise and encourage the daily performances of students with negative self-concepts. After 3 months of this treatment, most of these students became much more positive in their self-ratings, and their scholastic work was somewhat improved. Furthermore, in an experimental setting outside the school, but using school-related tasks involving reading and writing ability, Sears (1940) showed that regardless of their actual performance, children who were given praise and treated as successful set realistically higher achievement goals for themselves and worked to improve their performances accordingly. Children who were made to feel that they were unsuccessful reacted by setting very low or unrealistically high goals for themselves. The implication of such research is clear: when it comes to getting a child to work effectively in school, his *perception* of his performance—as conveyed by his teacher—seems much more important than his actual or *objective* performance.

Finally, in some very provocative work, Rosenthal and Jacobson (1968) literally hoodwinked teachers into improving the achievement of some of their pupils. They accomplished this by telling teachers at the beginning of the school year that according to new test results, it appeared that certain children in their class were due to show a dramatic rise ("unusual intellectual gains") in their schoolwork. It was a pure fabrication, but the teachers believed it. At the end of the year, the designated children (randomly selected) were not only doing much better scholastically, they also showed sharp gains in their IQ test scores! Moreover, teachers had glowing impressions:

The children from whom intellectual growth was expected were described as having a better chance of being successful in later life and as being happier, more curious and more interesting than the other children. There was also a tendency for the designated children to be seen as more appealing, better adjusted and more affectionate, and as less in need of social approval. In short, the children for whom intellectual growth was expected became more alive and autonomous intellectually, or at least were so perceived by their teachers. These findings were particularly striking among the children in the first grade (Rosenthal and Jacobson, 1968, p. 22).

The explanation for this remarkable phenomenon seems to be that the teachers were sensitized to the designated children and gave them subtle forms of encouragement. Rosenthal and Jacobson explicitly rejected the idea that teachers showed deliberate favoritism.

It would seem that the explanation we are seeking lies in a subtler feature of the interaction of the teacher and her pupils. Her tone of voice, facial expression, touch and posture may be the means by which—probably quite unwittingly—she communicates her expectations to the pupils. Such communication might help the child by changing his conception of himself, his anticipation of his own behavior, his motivation or his cognitive skills. This is an area in which further research is clearly needed.

Why was the effect of teacher expectations most pronounced in the lower grades? It is difficult to be sure, but several hypotheses can be advanced. Younger children may be easier to change than older ones are. They are likely to have less well-established reputations in the school. It may be that they are more sensitive to the processes by which teachers communicate their expectations to pupils (1968, p. 23).

Teachers also exert influence through the social atmospheres they create in classrooms. More or less in line with the Lewin, Lippit, and White findings on democratic and authoritarian atmospheres, later research shows that the social climate of the classroom is an important determinant of classroom behavior. Anderson and Brewer (1946) observed that domineering teachers produce something like an authoritarian atmosphere: children do their bidding passively, and they try to evade tasks by looking around and engaging in stealthy conversations. "Integrative" teachers tend to produce a democratic atmosphere in their rooms; children show more spontaneity, initiative, and easier social relationships. Harvey, Prather, White, and Hoffmeister (1968) found that teachers with abstract belief systems (see Chapter 4 for a discussion of Harvey's work on abstract and concrete cognitive systems) approximate the democratic atmosphere in their classrooms—children tend to be cooperative, enthusiastic, and involved in their schoolwork. The opposite is true of children with teachers having concrete cognitive systems. The relatively dictatorial, punitive behavior of concrete teachers gives their rooms the authoritarian quality, with corresponding effects on children's behavior. Moreover, the average level of achievement in the rooms of abstract teachers is higher than it is in the rooms of concrete teachers.

The general findings here need not be taken as evidence that all "objective" standards of school performance should be abandoned—although in the early grades particularly, this idea appears to have considerable merit. Rather, research showing links between teacher behavior, children's self-images, and school achievement, point to the conclusion that for youngsters in primary school as for men in battle, morale can be decisive, which is a fact that ought to be acceptable to even the most conservative among us.

Teacher-pupil dynamics

Before leaving the subject of teacher influence on children, we should try to understand the everyday difficulties that can preclude satisfactory teacher-pupil relationships. Teachers are not really such great villains of education as they might appear to be from the foregoing material. Not that we should waste any sympathy on the domineering types who can poison the learning atmosphere, but most teachers are just humanly fallible. Witness the fact that even distinguished psychologists may find it difficult to understand children's school behavior.

Kelly (1958) gave a fascinating account of how he finally came to understand "laziness" while providing psychological consulting services to a state school system. At first, Kelly and his colleagues applied their conventional clinical skills to such cases. Through tests and interviews they would try to diagnose the underlying cause of a child's laziness. But after following this procedure for a few years, Kelly began to have second thoughts:

Soon we reached the point in our practice where we routinely used the complaint of "laziness" as a point of departure for reorienting the teacher. It usually happened that there was more to be done with her than there was to be done with the child. So it was, also, with other complaints cast in motivational terms. In general, then, we found that the most practical approach to so-called motivational problems was to try to reorient the people who thought in such terms. Complaints about motivation told us much more about the complainants than it did about their pupils (Kelly, 1958, p. 46).

Kelly and his colleagues then developed some techniques that were effective in helping teachers who felt unable to deal with lazy children.

One technique we came to use was to ask the teacher what the child would do if she did not try to motivate him. Often the teacher would insist that the child would do nothing—absolutely nothing—just sit! Then we would suggest that she try a nonmotivational approach and let him "just sit." We would ask her to observe how he went about "just sitting." Invariably the teacher would be able to report some extremely interesting goings on. An analysis of what the "lazy" child did while he was being lazy often furnished her with her first glimpse into the child's world and provided her with her first solid grounds for communication with him. Some teachers found that their laziest pupils were those who could produce the most novel ideas; others, that the term "laziness" had been applied to activities that they had simply been unable to understand or appreciate (1958, pp. 46–47).

Nor is Kelly's belated recognition that "lazy" children are really doing things, unique. Bruner described a somewhat similar experience.

For two years, while starting other things as well, several of us carried out a study at the Judge Baker Guidance Center on the nature of "learning blocks" in children. . . . We discovered one point of especial value for my own future inquiry. There is a sharp distinction that must be made between behavior that *copes* with the requirements of a problem and behavior that is designed to *defend* against entry into the problem. It is the distinction one might make between playing tennis on the one hand and fighting like fury to stay off the tennis court altogether on the other. The latter is not a distorted version of the former; it is different activity, governed by a different objective and different requirements. The "distortion" in the learning activity of the unfortunate children we were studying and trying to help was not so much a distortion as it was the result of their working on a different set of problems from those the school had set for them. One could say the same thing about them that David Page has said about mathematics learning: when children give wrong answers it is not so often that they are wrong as that they are answering another question, and the job is to find out what question they are in fact answering (1966, pp. 3–4).

Recall also Omar Moore's account of the schoolboy whose difficulty in learning to type words was somehow related to the punishments he received for masturbation. The generality emerging from such instances is that the problem of being a good teacher — as we might define that role in light of current research findings — is extremely difficult. Not only because teachers are human, but also because we are just beginning to grasp the complicated nature of classroom experience. Kelly's remarks suggest that value-laden adjectives such as "lazy" should be stricken from teachers' vocabularies because they serve more to confuse than to enlighten. And Bruner's experience indicates that the phrase "learning block" might well be replaced with "task-coping vs. task-defense." The thing to understand is that teachers cannot be expected to work well in areas where fundamental knowledge of classroom learning processes is lacking.

It should finally be noted that one straightforward way of dealing with the whole teacher-pupil interaction problem is to eliminate the teachers — or drastically curtail their role in the education process. Several authorities on automated teaching systems suggest that in view of the relative difficulties involved, in the long run it will be more efficient to increase *machine*-pupil contacts than to try to reform or modify *teacher*-pupil contacts. Judging from research literature, and the fact that many large companies are diversifying into the education "industry," future generations can look forward to a good deal of both.

Values and content in the school environment

Apart from teachers, who are undoubtedly the strongest psychological element in the school environment, but who are also quite variable, children's reactions to school will be influenced by such constant elements as the general standards of behavior required, and the content of what is taught. When these concrete matters are examined in detail, they can be understood as serious barriers to effective school adjustment. The meaning of social class differences which work against the child from a lower socioeconomic background, and the difficulties of many middle-class children too, for that matter, can be interpreted as outcomes of pressure to conform to alien standards and to absorb alien materials.

For example, the disadvantages of the "disadvantaged child" in conventional schools are frequently explained according to the discrepancy between his family and school environments. Studies indicate that in comparison to the middle-class child, he is (a) less able to tolerate delays in gratification, (b) less familiar with relevant materials such as books and numbers, (c) less exposed to models of adult intellectual activity, (d) less advanced in language skills, (e) less likely to be encouraged and rewarded at home for good school performance, and (f) liable to be undernourished. (It has been demonstrated that in severe poverty areas, free breakfasts and lunches improve school performance.)

Granting the validity of all these things, what do they add up to besides a specification that poor children have drastic odds against them in school? All too often, these findings are interpreted as a direct explanation of why the children of the poor can't learn. This may be correct in certain respects, but it can be very misleading in others, because what these findings really offer is an *indirect* explanation. They tell us why poor children have difficulty *conforming* to the school environment, and that such conformity seems prerequisite to learning in conventional schools. In fact, both poor and middle-class children can have difficulty learning in school. But the learning problems of the poor child will be sharply increased because he has the additional task of conforming to a relatively alien system.

In this vein, Gordon and Wilkerson (1966) criticized most compensatory and/or remedial programs for concentrating entirely on trying to change the child to fit the system, while ignoring the possibility of modifying the system to fit the child. Furthermore, a mass of material indicates that children with all of the disadvantages itemized above are perfectly able to learn—at least they have been known to do so in European ghettos, primitive societies, underdeveloped countries, and sometimes in American slums. Webster (1966) provided three volumes of articles which generally stand in support of the conformity argument (see also Roberts, 1967). As several of the writers in Webster suggested, and as Kozol pointed out in *Death at an Early Age*, deprived children may lack the background experiences required for success in middle-class oriented schools, but they have all sorts of other background experiences that are *potentially* relevant to good schoolwork. And they are well able to learn many things that schools don't teach.

It is especially interesting, in this connection, that Neill (1960), took a similar position when describing the learning difficulties of middle- and upper-class English children:

Parents are slow in realizing how unimportant the learning side of school is. Children, like adults, learn what they want to learn (p. 25).

And he went on to say that the average child is not much interested in material taught in traditional curricula. Note that we are not arguing against the terrible reality of material and cultural deprivation. Such things will certainly hamper learning. However, the magnitude of the learning problem is immensely increased by demands that deprived children conform to a middle-class system.

If conformity to the system is not a great problem for *middle*-class children, it can be argued that regardless of class background, all children have the same difficulties when it comes to learning content. Investigators have been criticizing the material in children's textbooks for many years. Child, Potter, and Levine (1946), for instance, found that the stories in third-grade readers had little to do with reality, and did not encourage independent action or intellectual activity. Children in such stories are frequently shown as getting into nasty situations because they have ignored warnings from adults. They escape through the intervention of benevolent adults, not through exercise of their own ingenuity. And they usually end by promising to be obedient in the future. Cronbach (1963) summarized many reports indicating that story themes in most children's readers are so removed from what is meaningful in their lives, that any reading progress at all seems remarkable. In an article aptly titled "Give Him A Book That Hits Him Where He Lives," Spiegler (in Webster, 1966) showed that surprising progress can be made when intrinsically interesting books are employed.

Another aspect of school operations that can have equally negative effects on all children, and that has been criticized for a long time, concerns individual competition in the classroom. One illustrative study (Stendler, Damrin, and Haines, 1951) compared the performances of second-graders who worked on a painting task for individual and for group prizes. There was much more disruptive, aggressive behavior under the individual prize condition. Jersild (1954) suggested more generally that individual competition is only meaningful to many children as a "reminder of inferiority." It virtually guarantees needless losses in self-esteem.

When a child in such a situation notices that teachers seem to be slaves of a competitive system it will be difficult for him to see how a teacher could like him and respect him when the teacher knows he stands well below the middle rank in his spelling, arithmetic, music, or some other occupation. . . . Reminders of inferiority are inevitable in a school which stresses competitive standards . . . (Jersild, p. 227).

And Bronfenbrenner (1962) argued persuasively that education practices in the Soviet Union which stress group rather than individual activities, yield classroom atmospheres more conducive to learning and orderly behavior.

Inconsistency between competition and cooperation is also a problem. In group situations, children may be criticized for being either insufficiently competitive—shy, passive; or uncooperative—aggressive, hogging the limelight. Moreover, they are supposed to do everything they can to be winners; but if they can't be winners, they are supposed to be good losers. The justification for imposing all this illogical philosophy upon children too young to resist it is that it builds character; an absurdity quite popular among little league baseball practitioners. From what one can observe, they are correct if character means desperation to win at almost any price, sullen acceptance of defeat, and fundamental confusion over the meaning of sport.

Altogether then, various lines of evidence suggest that standards of conduct and instructional materials need not be reduced to some low-level common denominator, but should at least be meaningful to children. When they are, even the deprived or disadvantaged can meet high performance criteria; when they are not, even middle-class children can be alienated from education. However, because the middle-class child is better able to conform, his alienation will probably be expressed as plodding acceptance of school – a necessary evil where one does the minimum to get by. Alienation in the poor child, coupled with lesser ability to conform, may be expressed as a more dramatic reaction against formal education. Personality effects in the two groups will vary accordingly. The influence of school experiences on the self-concept has already been mentioned. Negative experiences will reduce feelings of pride, security, and self-worth in all children. But in the lower-class child who cannot maintain a positive self-concept through general conformity to school standards (if anything, he maintains it by evading or attacking these standards) negative experiences may lead to a broad rejection of all formal authority.

Mass Media

In the early 1950's a prominent psychiatric writer published an attack on comic books, suggesting that they were either directly or indirectly a serious source of corruption in the lives of American children. Attacks on comic books became quite popular for a while. They were obviously filled with violence and sadism. And they were also a safe target. Who would rise to the defense of comic books: certainly not those of us who had spent our preadolescence engrossed in the adventures of Superman, Batman, Green Lantern, and the Captains Marvel, Midnight, and America. Besides, very few people had realized how bad these things were until they were brought under proper psychiatric scrutiny. For example, there were all those stories featuring a mature hero and a boy-adolescent sidekick, neither of whom ever had anything to do with girls. Batman and Robin are the outstanding case.

Here is a rich bachelor keeping a young "ward" in a home where the only female presence is a doddering old aunt. They share a secret life together, having adventures in which they constantly deceive, outwit, and overpower the normal adult world. Conventional authority figures such as police and government officials are portrayed as clumsy clods. Furthermore, these two heroes are forever throwing off their clothes to disport in bizarre, tight-fitting costumes which enhance their physical appeal. And can there be any doubt that their names and costumes signify the quality of their relationship? "Batman" has potent masculine connotations, while "Robin" implies a more fragile feminine character. The former appears entirely covered in grey and black; the latter is bare legged in red and yellow. Altogether, the evidence points to an unmistakable homosexual relationship.

Once one sees the logic of such analyses, it is not difficult to go through whole lists of comic-book characters seeking the worst and finding it. Why was the "Wonder Woman," a voluptuous brunette who wore only a kind of one-piece bathing suit and high-heeled boots, always being bound up in ropes, cords, and chains by evil male, and worse yet, female, enemies? Similar logic can be applied to television programs: why are all those virile, well-off Cartwrights living together on a comfortable ranch without any women?

Whether they search for concealed sexual or drug themes—remember that many heroes swallow pills or potions to be transformed into their superior selves—the fact is that many sincere psychiatric authorities see media such as comic books, television, and movies as very harmful to children. But as will be shown later in connection with TV, it is also a fact that this negative view is not directly supported by research findings. There is even some evidence suggesting that comic books[4] and TV have positive functions. So opinion on the effects of the mass media is divided. All authorities agree that properly entertaining and/or educational material can have great benefits in widening the horizons of children. "Sesame Street," "Misterogers," and "Captain Kangaroo" receive general approval. It is the violence that divides opinion according to two different time-honored theoretical positions. And from here on we will concentrate on television because it excites the greatest attention these days.

One traditional view derived from psychoanalytic theory suggests that exposure to violence can serve as a healthy catharsis, a means of releasing aggression. Children can safely discharge their pent-up aggressive emotions by viewing violence on a screen. Thus, both children and adults are attracted to such programs because participation in violence can occur at a safe distance. One participates vicariously by identifying with the actors engaging in the violence. Moreover, such programs allow expressions of aggression that are otherwise socially disapproved and kept repressed, to be brought to the surface and dealt with in a basically harmless fashion. Although empirical evidence in support of this interpretation is lacking, everyday experience and the popularity of such things as the *James Bond* films make it plausible.[5]

The alternative view originating in behavioristic learning theory is that screen violence is harmful because it provides a model for imitation. A number of investigators (see the section on aggression in Chapter 6) report that children become more directly aggressive and violent in their play after seeing such behavior in films. Working with college students, Berkowitz found evidence that films of justified aggression are the most provocative:

[4]In 1941, Thorndyke reported that the comic books being read by many children contained a more extensive word vocabulary than their school readers.

[5]In a book of essays on movies *(Kiss Kiss Bang Bang)*, Pauline Kael equates the violence of Bond-type movies to the one-dimensional action of comic strips, and suggests that they have the same fundamental appeal. The violence of *Bonnie and Clyde* is something else again: "In a sense, it is the absence of sadism—it is the violence without sadism—that throws the audience off balance at *Bonnie and Clyde*. The brutality that comes out of this innocence is far more shocking than the calculated brutalities of mean killers" (Kael, p. 66).

Rather than feeling purged of their hostility, the students seemed to feel freer to express it . . . justified aggression is precisely the kind that seems likeliest to encourage the expression of aggression by members of the audience (1968, pp. 20–22).

And elsewhere, after reviewing the literature on aggression, he states the general view of those who reject the catharsis idea.

The catharsis notion is an outmoded theoretical conception lacking adequate empirical support which also has potentially dangerous social implications. Violence ultimately produces more violence (1969, p. 73).

As Berkowitz's remarks indicate, most of the experimental data presently available support the learning theory interpretation. But this view cannot yet be accepted as gospel because survey studies of large samples of children do *not* support it.

Himmelweite, Oppenheim, and Vance (1958) studied the TV viewing habits of over 5000 children in England. They found no more aggressive or maladjusted behavior among those who watched TV than among those who did not. Nor were there any differences between these groups in their attitudes toward school and teachers. On the positive side, these authors report that TV viewers have higher aspiration levels for future jobs. In the United States, TV is reported to be positive for children because it increases their general information and vocabulary (Schramm, Lyle, and Parker, 1961). The only clearly negative findings in both these large sample studies concerns TV "addiction." A small percentage of children who show strong feelings of insecurity, apparently withdraw into TV viewing as a passive way of coping with their problems.

These studies concentrated upon total TV viewing time, however, not on the quality of the programs watched. Eron (1963) examined the qualitative viewing habits of third-grade children in over 600 families. He had parents estimate both total viewing time, and the amount of violence shown in the programs preferred by their children. Ratings of the aggressive behavior shown by these children were obtained from their school peers. Results showed that girls seem to be completely out of it—there was no significant relation between their viewing times, programs preferred, and aggressive behavior. For boys, it was found that those spending the greatest amounts of time watching TV were *less* aggressive than others. The one negative finding was that boys who prefer to watch the more violent programs are rated as more aggressive by their peers. But who can say if this last result should be interpreted as cause or effect? It is anybody's guess whether more aggressive little boys seek out more violent programs, or whether watching violent programs makes little boys more aggressive.

In sum, direct research on TV does not support a broad indictment of the medium as harmful to children. It only appears to be negative for those few who use it as a means of withdrawing from reality (who would probably find other means if TV were not available), and for those boys who prefer the more qualitatively violent programs. The benefits of TV, on the other hand, seem quite definite in the broader perspectives and larger vocabulary it promotes.

Embedded in the issue of how TV violence may influence personality is the question of just what is genuinely violent and what is not. Eron noted that parents rate the *Lone Ranger* as a nonviolent program; maybe because the Masked Man still restricts himself to shooting the guns out of outlaws' hands, as he used to on radio. Moreover, Himmelweite et al., observed that children could become quite upset by scenes of verbal aggression between adults, probably because they witness the reality of this sort of thing in arguments between their parents. But there is no systematic material available on the qualitative nature of violence *per se*. It would be interesting to know, for instance, what children derive from such morning cartoon programs as *Tom and Jerry*, where every imaginable variation of trickery and mayhem appears in context of an implicitly friendly relationship. Considerably more research will therefore have to be done before we can further sort out the psychological effects of screen violence. As it stands right now, we do not even have a proper technical vocabulary for describing different types or intensities of violence.

Summary of peers, school, and media as culture

This section was begun with the suggestion that movement beyond the immediate family is the global critical factor or event unique to middle childhood. This movement can be broken down into categories of experience with peers, school, and mass media such as television. When all are taken together, however, they stand as the ingredients of culture. By examining some generally accepted ideas on how culture influences personality, we can conveniently summarize and extend the prior discussion.

Social scientists generally describe culture as all the skills, tools, arts, and standard forms of social behavior typical of any distinct society. A society can be anything from a family unit, to a tribe, to a nation. Cultural investigators are mainly concerned with skills and values—the way things get done in a society, and the way people in that society think things *ought* to get done. From this standpoint, parents are seen as important agents of culture; indeed, anthropologists take various events in the family such as feeding, weaning, and toilet training as primary cultural elements. Nevertheless, one can make a fairly clear distinction between cultural values inherent in parental behavior, and cultural values that the child experiences directly in his contacts with peers, schools, and mass media. The distinction can easily be seen in many first-generation American families. Here a child may be raised through infancy and early childhood according to the ancestral values of his parents, but he typically will be assimilated into the larger American culture during middle childhood. This is the age when such children may begin to refuse to speak any language but American English, and may sometimes feel very embarrassed by their parents' public behavior. These extreme but not uncommon examples illustrate how the larger culture may override the effects of family experience, or family culture, as it were, by providing the child with new skills and standards.

For most children, however, experience with the larger culture will reinforce values acquired in the family. Briefly, the child learns that many of the behaviors encouraged or discouraged by his parents are similarly encouraged or discouraged in the larger culture. And this experience with certain values, which is continuous from infancy onward, shapes what is described as the culturally determined *basic personality*.

Basic personality

In formal terms, the values that predominate in any given society are said to influence personality by sanctioning standard forms for, or models of, proper behavior. Thus a child of five may already know whether belching after meals is considered a fitting compliment to the cook or a cause for embarrassment. Kardiner (1945) and Linton (1945) both popularized the phrase "basic personality type" by suggesting that children acquire the distinctive cultural values of their society through uniformities of experience in the family, with peers, and so on. The basic personality type found in any given society is, therefore, definable according to the pattern of values shared by most members of that society.

The concept of basic personality is raised at this point because by the end of middle childhood, when family, peer, school, and mass media influences have all been at work on the child for some time, it seems clear that his basic personality is well established. The six- or seven-year-old can be moved into a new society, for instance, and will adjust to it quickly, picking up both the language and the values that prevail. But a twelve- or thirteen-year-old will have much more difficulty not merely because of language, but because he already believes that many specific things ought to be done in specific ways, and he will resist change as unnatural.

To see this in a more general perspective, consider the cultural variations that exist with respect to such a universal problem as what to do with dead bodies. Across the different societies in our world, virtually every conceivable disposal technique is somewhere in service, and is believed to be the only right and proper procedure. So we have bodies being put into the ground in horizontal and vertical postures; left lying on top of the ground with and without shelter or markings; put up in the air intact in trees or platforms, or oxidized into smoke and ashes; dropped into the water weighted to sink, or placed on rafts and headed downstream. Nor should the embalming, mummification, and new freezing procedures be ignored. We are even storing specific body parts against the possibility of future use.

Regardless of whatever humor can be got out of this peculiar state of affairs (see Evelyn Waugh's novel *The Loved One* for a superb rendering of the American Forest Lawn style) it should be recognized that differences in tradition and custom concerning the dead can have direct implications for the self-images of the living. And it is sometime in the 6 to 12 year period that most of us accept most of the traditions and customs of our society as the natural order of things. Certainly by the time they are twelve, children the world over can provide culturally determined answers to almost every fundamental problem confronting every human community. How one ought to: dispose of the dead; educate the young; acquire food, clothing and shelter; treat certain wounds and diseases; fight; kill; bargain; persuade; build;

destroy; get along with animals; and even occasionally express love and affection.

Many of the beliefs concerning these things are values having such strong moral force that they might better be termed superstitions. Children in our society may thus have the same magical faith in the healing power of Band-Aids, as primitives have in cobwebs. Within any one society, however, the chief psychological function of shared cultural values is that they serve as a kind of stabilizing mechanism: youngsters learn approximately what to expect from others and what others expect from them. And the importance of this stabilizing function can be judged from the tenacity with which most 11-, 12-, and 13-year-olds defend their cultural values. Nowhere does one find more ardent true believers in the flag, motherhood, and apple pie. It is not until the late teens that their belief systems begin to open up again.

Formal religion and children's games should also be noted as two additional cultural agents that inculcate values. Religion may sometimes be very significant for personality development, though if a child only averages an hour or two a week in Sunday school, he will probably not be too much affected by the experience. Studies report no important differences in moral behavior (e.g., cheating) between children who do or do not go to Sunday school. It has also been found that most children tend to have equally primitive ideas about God, Heaven, and Hell.

Children's games function as important transmitters of culture in several ways. Historically, many games have been traced to medieval and ancient Greek customs that were deadly serious. Blindman's bluff and hopscotch for example, may have originally been used to select persons for human sacrifice (see Spence, 1947, and Opie and Opie, 1959, for detailed discussions of the origins of games). More directly, in their game-playing children learn how to act out various roles, how to behave according to standard rules of conduct, how status hierarchies will operate in different circumstances, and a host of other things relevant to their culture. It is interesting in this connection that the game Monopoly was banned in Nazi Germany – supposedly because Hitler thought it imbued children with crass commercial values. This is not an entirely crackpot idea; it certainly seems true that insofar as games are scaled-down versions of adult activities, they will accordingly convey the social values that go with those activities.

In most of the material so far discussed, emphasis has been placed on the environment of middle childhood, with reference to the psychological meaning of new experiences. Grossly, these experiences work upon the self-concept: children will both consolidate and change the way they think about themselves as a consequence of events outside the home. It is time now to change our perspective – to shift our main focus from the environment to the individual.

SOCIAL-EMOTIONAL DEVELOPMENT

During middle childhood it becomes relatively convenient for the first time to begin treating personality development as an elaborate bookkeeping operation. One can do this by construing personality to be the sum total of the consistent behavior tendencies displayed by any individual, and by choosing a unit of analysis (which is to say, a handle, or metaphor for discourse) that will express consistent behavior tendencies. So one finds some writers describing personality in terms of enduring *motives*.

In its simplest form, this approach can start with the assumption of a grand universal: all persons (and animals) are motivated to maximize pleasure and minimize pain. Add the more unique, higher-order motives that become a part of the self-concept—a child who hero-worships an athlete or policeman, and models himself accordingly; a puny boy like Teddy Roosevelt who puts everything he has into compensation—and you have a full package. It only remains to gather in loose ends and to keep the books straight on the twists and turns of development. Do you see altruism? Greed? Heroism? Cowardice? It is all explicable; just check the books and see which motives are ultimately being satisfied.

Another approach is through the *trait* metaphor for consistent behaviors. In this conception virtually all adjectives that everyday language provides for describing behavior, for example, *honest, shy, friendly, trustworthy, warm, cold,* can be treated as traits of personality. These traits can be measured or assessed with rating scales, questionnaires, interviews, observations of behavior, and other techniques that all have valuable uses and honored places in modern psychology. But neither of these approaches will be followed, even though traits and motives begin to show up very nicely in middle childhood—one sees behavior patterns that fit these metaphors very well, and they provide a convenient means for discussing personality.

The main reason for our departure from convenience is that a profile composed of scores on many traits, or fewer motives, which may serve as a plausible working description of personality at a given point in time, conveys nothing of much relevance to the problem of personality *development*. How do certain traits or motives come out or get changed? Answers can be sought by examining related items on the profile. A child who changes from friendly to unfriendly should also become either shy and inhibited, or aggressive and suspicious. The point being, of course, that traits (and motives) go together in clusters or bundles, and something like unfriendliness would have to fit either a generally aggressive or passive bundle. But if one begins with specific traits or motives, and ends anyway by speaking of them in clusters or bundles that approximate broad social-emotional areas of personality development, it is just as well to stay with these general areas from the outset.

In the following discussions, therefore, our approach will remain tied to the five substantial social-emotional areas that were described as emerging in early childhood: the self-concept, sexual identity, conscience or morality, aggression, and achievement. We will see how these are elaborated in middle childhood and begin to coalesce or fold in upon one another by the end of this period.

The self-concept

As object

In his summary of the different elements that form the self-concept, Allport (see discussion in Chapter 6) ordered development from a sense of bodily self, which originates in infancy, through other senses of self which culminate in a primitive self-image by the beginning of middle childhood. This self-image appears first as a vague, general sense of self as object; a unit encompassing the prior senses of self. Throughout the 6 to 12 year period, the sense of self as object grows stronger. Teachers and peers literally force the child toward a more objective image of himself because their responses to him have an objective character. In school the child is one of many similar children; he is therefore compared with them in a fashion that roughly amounts to a ticking off of his distinguishing features. To a lesser extent, the same thing occurs in the family, where parents and siblings become more evaluative. The child, who may only be dimly aware of what is happening, begins to conceive of himself as a good or bad runner, climber, reader, or drawer of pictures. No matter whether these conceptions originate with teachers, parents, or peers, the brute fact is that evaluative comparisons impose a sense of self as an object with definitive characteristics.

One way to see how a child objectifies himself is to ask him about other children. A first or second grader will describe others—"X is always in trouble with the teacher; Y is the best runner; Z always shares his things"—according to the same criteria he uses on himself. Children also become more concerned about extended family relationships (which cousins belong to which aunts and uncles); they become more conscious of clothes, haircuts, mirrors, and bad breath.

To say that the self-image solidifies through a process of objectification is not, however, to say that this process is "objective" in the sense of being fair or accurate. We have already mentioned how social-class differences influence the self-images of poor children in middle-class school systems. It is also probable that in a smaller school or classroom, there is a greater likelihood that a child having any moderately unusual skill or talent will be discovered and encouraged to use it in ways that will enhance growth of a positive self-image (see Barker and Gump, 1964, for relevant material comparing large and small schools).

Another biasing factor is simple prejudice. Schoolchildren readily absorb the stereotypes of those around them. Studies show that through middle childhood there is a steady increase in the proportion of children expressing common stereotypes and using labels such as wop, honky, nigger, polack, and kike. Radke, Trager, and Davis (1949) showed pictures of scenes including children from various minority groups, to a large sample of 5-, 6-, 7- and 8-year-olds, who were asked to invent stories to fit the pictures. Even the 5-year-olds gave some evidence of prejudice, and the number of those showing strong bias against Negroes and Jews rose sharply among the 7- and 8-year-olds. (This work was done in a white lower-middle-class neighborhood in Philadelphia.)

Other findings (e.g., Hartley, Rosenbaum, and Schwartz, 1948) demonstrated that children begin to describe themselves and others with group labels at about age six. Clark and Clark (1947) showed that the majority of a sample of Negro children did not respond to a doll-preference task as if skin color were an important self-identifying characteristic until they were six. The same general finding has been reported for young white children by Greenwald and Oppenheim (1968).

In sum, an image of self as object develops very strongly during middle childhood as a result of evaluative comparisons that are available in the social environment. And depending upon various conditions, the available comparisons for defining self will probably be biased. Children seem especially susceptible to such biases because they lack perspective; for them the local family-school-peer social matrix is everything. Much of the psychological stress of adolescence occurs when this narrow framework for self-definition later expands.

Self as executive

In the preceding paragraphs the self is discussed as a noun; here we come to it in its verb form. Whether one goes back to early childhood events showing the intrinsic push toward competence, or is content merely to observe behavior in middle childhood, there is clear evidence for an accelerating sense of self as executive; wheeler and dealer; mover and shaker of the environment. At 7, 8, and 9, children become interested in manufacturing things for action: rabbit traps, birdhouses, soapbox cars. Conscious efforts at logical thinking are also in evidence:

At the age of seven we see new evidences of reasonableness and of critical capacity. The 7-year-old is more reflective; he takes time to think; he is interested in conclusions and logical ends. You can reason a little with him even in ethical situations which are charged with emotion. He himself uses language more freely and adaptively; not only to establish rapport, but to make running comments on the matter in hand (Gesell and Ilg, 1946, p. 136).

Allport refers to the child's awareness of his executive planning ability with the phrase "self as rational coper," because the six- to twelve-year-old is increasingly able to handle his problems in a logical fashion. Altogether, the child's conscious ideas about himself, particularly the sense of himself as an executive or rational coper, make up the component of personality that Freud and the neo-Freudians call *ego*. Suffice it for the moment to say that all authorities agree on broadening and deepening of the self-concept, and/or ego, as a primary fact of personality development in middle childhood. As we take up more specific aspects of social-emotional development below, it will become clearer that all of them are not only intimately associated with the self-concept, but, with maturation into adolescence and beyond, they *are* the self-concept.

Sex identity

The 6 to 12 year period is traditionally notorious as the time during which children segregate themselves according to sex. Whether or not this reflects a natural order of things is debatable,[6] but it is certain that many people think

---

[6]Material gathered in certain primitive societies where heterosexual activity goes on through middle childhood indicates that the absence of it in Western technical societies is because of cultural norms. After reviewing evidence on the separation or sexual latency characterizing this developmental period, Blum (1953) suggested that it is mainly due to all the other demands being made upon the child. In effect, the Western child doesn't have time for sex.

so: most of the children of my generation went to school in classrooms divided into boys' and girls' sides. Besides the separation that may be imposed by society, however, the inclination of six- to twelve-year-olds to maintain serious sex boundaries has been interpreted to mean that they are not yet sufficiently confident about their sex identity to risk it in mixed groups. In other words, boys and girls stay apart in middle childhood because their masculine and feminine identities may be too fragile to withstand mixing.

Freudian explanations for this phenomenon should be obvious: the Oedipal situation creates tensions which drive children away from cross-sex contacts. But learning theory offers an equally good rationale: children are conditioned to their sex role, generally rewarded for proper enactment of it and punished for deviations. Why then should a child risk the uncertainties of mixed-sex activities when he can make sure of approval by avoiding them?

Innate behavior predispositions are in the same direction as social learning. Even at very young ages, boys tend to be more active and aggressive than girls (the Harlows have reported similar differences between male and female infant monkeys). In school-aged children these predispositions will be enhanced by general expectations. Tuddenham (1952) reported that six-, eight-, and ten-year-olds see the "typical girl" as being, among other things, quiet, tidy, and friendly, whereas the typical boy is seen as quarrelsome, bossy, and daring. Child, Potter, and Levine (1946) found a similar pattern in children's books—females being described as shy and quiet, males as aggressive and brave. Additional studies show that this general pattern of expectations is also expressed by teachers and parents.

The result of all this pressure toward sex-role conformity is that in middle childhood, male or female sex-role behaviors become one of the most salient features of the self-concept. Moreover, the image of self generated in this fashion keeps behavior within a sexually fixed set of boundaries. It is as if all society conspired to dictate to the child: go this far in being the sort of person you are inclined to be, and no further. If you seriously breach a conventional sex boundary, we lower the boom.

Research that might indicate just how much this state of affairs has changed in the past few years is not yet available. It is certainly true that many of the superficial conventions governing masculine and feminine behavior are breaking up. It can be argued that liberation from the traditional sociocultural tyranny regarding sex-role behavior is desirable and healthy. By freeing boys and girls to engage in activities ordinarily reserved for the opposite sex, some natural forms of self-expression that would otherwise be inhibited might be released.

More specifically, the benefits of exposing both boys and girls to woodworking and cooking, or to sewing and model airplanes, for example, could easily include a stronger self-concept or ego in both. Clinical literature suggests that the greater the number of skills one has, the greater is the sense of overall competence or ego strength. Moreover, while many men might rather field-strip a Browning or drive an APC than cook or change diapers, personal experience suggests that all of these activities can be relevant to ego-strength.

On the other hand, it can be argued—and one hears it fairly frequently—that the breakdown of traditional boundaries between masculine and feminine behavior heralds a breakdown of society. Sexual deviancy will rise, and the family as a basic structural unit of society will thereby be endangered. Something could surely be said for this view if relaxation of rules for masculine and feminine conduct were associated with homosexuality. But research suggests that homosexuality has other primary causes. A more plausible argument is that children gain an important sense of security from having a clear-cut sex-role, just as they gain security from firm boundaries defining other approved and disapproved behaviors. The problem, however, is to determine whether there is a healthy *optimum* boundary for sex-role behavior.

Conscience and morality

Middle-childhood inconsistency
The much-discussed "new morality" of the late 1960's is ordinarily described as a matter of situation ethics, which means that instead of always being defined in terms of rigid rules, right and wrong are only definable in terms of immediate situations. What may be right or moral in one situation may be wrong or immoral in another. This is of interest because it gives a contemporary flavor to a classic study of morality in middle childhood that was made over 40 years ago. Hartshorne and May (1928–1930) tested thousands of children in various situations (classroom, home, playground) arranged to provide opportunities for lying and cheating. Results showed very little consistency in such behavior.[7] For example, children who might refrain from cheating on a spelling test would lie or cheat on the playground 15 minutes later, and vice versa. It was concluded that ". . . a child does not have a uniform generalized code of morals but varies his opinions to suit the situation in which he finds himself" (1930, p. 108). So if the new morality is new for adults, it is not new for children.

This material was not dignified with any high-sounding phrases at the time it appeared. Instead, it was generally taken as evidence of how careful one had to be in raising children to have proper moral fiber. Doubtless there were many who also saw it as evidence of a breakdown in morality. But the important question is why there should be inconsistency in behavior across different situations. And why should there also be inconsistency between the stated moral beliefs of children, and their behavior in relevant situations? For, as reported by Hartshorne and May, and later corroborated by other investigators (e.g., Havighurst and Taba, 1949; Kohlberg, 1964; Pittel and Mendelsohn, 1966), children seem perfectly able to indicate that they strongly believe something is wrong, and then go ahead and do it . . . or not do it.

Explanations can as usual be derived from Freudian theory and behavioristic learning theory. Spokesmen for the former might suggest that the superego is still relatively weak in middle childhood. The learning theorist might explain the inconsistent behavior by pointing to inconsistent rewards and punishments: children surely discover that there are occasions when lying or cheating yield good results.

More complex, less doctrinaire interpretations were offered by Reiss

---

[7]Burton (1963) pointed out that some of the morality tests used in this study were technically unreliable. He reanalyzed the data, dropping out the unreliable material, and though he reported greater consistency in certain areas, no dramatic change in the original conclusion seems warranted.

(1965) and Brown (1965). Although Reiss was mainly concerned with changes in cultural values that go on from one generation to the next—by the time a child grows up the morality imposed by his parents may not fit his adult environment very well—his view can be scaled down for application to the problem of middle-childhood inconsistency. It must frequently happen, for instance, that a child whose family experience has emphasized truth and honesty will find that these values do not hold up in the same way beyond his family. Then there are the contradictions which can be seen in the difficulty most parents have explaining to 6-, 7-, and 8-year-olds why they shouldn't "tell tales," or be an informer. If cheating and stealing are wrong, why shouldn't the well brought up child tell on another who does it? And if a child-informer finds that he is not appreciated, is it not likely that he will change the way he thinks about right and wrong? Another experience that is probably universal in middle childhood is being blamed for something you didn't do; a thought-provoking event. Briefly, all such incidents which dramatize the discrepancy between prior moral instruction and the realities of life beyond (and maybe within) the family are likely to promote inconsistent moral behavior. This line of explanation is reducible to simple reward-punishment formulations, but such formulations do not adequately express the dilemmas and ambiguities in the schoolchild's moral life.

Harari and McDavid (1969) ran a very realistic morality experiment involving 48 middle-class eleven- to thirteen-year-olds. Subtitled "A study of finking," it was arranged as follows.

In order to simulate a realistic event of moral transgression, a contrived "theft" was arranged during regular classes. By arrangement, the teacher was called from the room to take an important telephone call. During her absence, a preinstructed confederate student arose from his seat ostensibly to dispose of his chewing gum into a wastebasket; as he did so, the student scooped up $.75 in silver coins which had been left on a small table at the front of the room, saying "Hey, look; how about that!" He pocketed the money and returned to his seat before the teacher reentered the room. Shortly after the teacher had returned and the classroom activities had been resumed, she received a prearranged call on the local intercom telephone and engaged in a cryptic conversation for a few seconds, repeating, "I don't know," several times. Somewhat later during the class, a messenger entered the classroom to request that students be called from the room one by one for interviews concerning casting a school talent show. As subjects left the room, either singly or in pairs, with the messenger, they were intercepted in the corridor by the experimenter and diverted into an empty office for the experimental interrogation (pp. 240–241).

The results, showing that the social status of the guilty party, and the presence or absence of other peers during the "interrogation," both determine whether or not the child will "fink," are interesting enough to bear repetition in the authors' own words:

Under certain circumstances, every subject interviewed was willing to accuse and incriminate a guilty confederate. When questioned alone, a situation in which the manner of the adult interrogator implies an expectation of moral righteousness and truthfulness, almost all the subjects questioned were willing to confess their full knowledge of the transgression or even to identify the transgressor by name. However, the presence of a peer who also witnessed the simulated transgression appears to deter subjects from making such accusations and identification of the transgressor. The status of the guilty peer seems to be a crucial variable in this context: the implicit peer-group norm against "finking" seems to apply selectively to the question of reporting the guilt of a respected and esteemed classmate, with no evidence of restraint against reporting and identifying a low-status guilty peer. There was pronounced reluctance to identify the high-status transgressor directly by name regardless of whether the guilty person was or was not actually present during the interrogation, and regardless of the seriousness of the transgression . . . (p. 243).

Brown (1965) suggested a broad organizational scheme that encompasses much of the existing empirical material on morality and accordingly helps explain the inconsistencies. His major ideas were that morality should be understood as having three dimensions: knowledge, conduct and emotion; and that four different learning processes relate to "the moralization of the individual." These are cognitive learning or concept formation, operant conditioning, classical conditioning, and imitation. It follows, therefore, that inconsistency in the child can be interpreted as resulting from uneven progress in his knowledge, conduct, and emotion, which will be compounded by the fact that progress in each area involves more than one kind of learning process.

Developmental research

Aside from the general inconsistency revealed by empirical findings, and explainable as we have indicated above, developmental studies by Piaget and Kohlberg suggested that in the 6 to 12 year period, children pass through one or more important stages of moral growth. Piaget (1932) saw peer-group activities as the likeliest force promoting the change from *heteronomous* to *autonomous* morality which occurs at about age seven. Recall that this change is marked by the child's new concern with the intentions underlying behavior, and his understanding that punishment for wrongdoing should be suitably corrective rather than just a matter of expiation. The change to autonomous morality presumably occurs when the child is sufficiently decentered (his egocentrism is sufficiently reduced) so that he can appreciate other viewpoints besides his own. Furthermore, his rule-bound sense of "moral realism," according to which rules are perceived at an earlier age as objective realities rather than man-made conveniences, is also reduced. Peer-group activities come into it because they seem to serve as a medium in which the child acquires a sense of fairness or equal justice. Parents or teachers might convey this if they were to make scrupulous efforts not to take advantage of their superior status to the child, but Piaget thought it was more likely to grow out of relations with peers.

. . . far from being the direct result of parental or scholastic pressure, the idea of equality develops essentially through children's reactions to each other and sometimes even at the adult's expense. It is very often the injustice one has had to endure that makes one take cognizance of the laws of equality. In any case it is hard to see how such a notion could take on any reality for a child before he had come in contact with his equals either in the home or at school. The relation between child and adult as such does not allow for equality. And since equalitarianism is born of the contact of children with one another, its development must at least keep pace with the progress of cooperation between them (Piaget, 1962, p. 275).

Following Piaget, but concentrating his work more narrowly on the specific problem of morality, Kohlberg (1963) suggested that there are six successive stages in moral development. Most of his work involved hypothetical moral dilemmas. For example, should a man desert his official post during an emergency to help his family? Should a man who can't afford the exorbitant price, steal medicine for his sick wife? The answers and explanations persons give in response to such material is coded to indicate their moral stage of development. In the 6 to 12 year period, children are generally at the level of "rule conformity." At six and seven they conform in a hedonistic way to get rewards (stage II). As they approach age ten, rules are followed to maintain the approval and goodwill of others (stage III), and by the end of middle childhood they are entering stage IV, where rules are followed to avoid guilt feelings.

Kohlberg further believed that the stages of moral development he uncovered form a stable sequence: progress to each higher stage cannot be accomplished unless the prior stage is integrated or reorganized to prepare the way. In this his view is similar to Piaget's notion of equilibration, but he is only speaking of moral conceptions, not cognitive schemas in general.

Because Kohlberg's theoretical ideas are based mainly on data collected in interviews, or in response to questionnaires, it is noteworthy that at least one experimental study confirms these ideas. Turiel (1966) used Kohlberg's interview procedure, involving nine different dilemma stories, to establish the moral stage of development of twelve- and thirteen-year-old boys. He selected groups of 11 boys each who were in stages II, III, and IV. Then, to test the idea that the stages are sequential, and that each one must be integrated prior to advancement to the next, he worked with each boy individually, using a role-playing technique to convey moral concepts that were either one stage below, or one or two stages above, the boy's own stage. Afterward, the boys were again given a morality assessment interview to determine whether or not they had been influenced by the exposure to higher- or lower-order concepts than their own. The logic here is that if Kohlberg were correct, then regardless of which stage they were in, the boys would not be influenced by lower-stage concepts; because having integrated and passed beyond that lower stage, they would not find such material plausible—which is how the results turned out. Another finding confirming Kohlberg was that the boys were not influenced by conceptual material two stages above their own. Presumably, this material does not seem plausible because it is too far advanced. A final prediction, also confirmed, was that the boys *should* be influenced by material one stage above their own, since they should be making progress toward integrating their present mode of moral thinking with the next higher one.

Guilt

The direct emotional component of morality, namely guilt feelings, emerges in strength during middle childhood. We have already discussed the Oedipus complex explanation for the origins of guilt, and the empirical work showing that certain parental styles of punishment enhance or retard the development of this emotion. Behavioristic learning theory allows guilt to be interpreted as conditioned fear: having learned to anticipate punishment for wrongdoing, the child automatically feels fear after doing something wrong, even though no one else may be present.

In view of the extensive material mentioned at the beginning of this section showing the child to be inconsistent in his moral behavior and thinking, the question arises whether there is any concrete relationship between guilt and behavior. Perhaps children are inconsistent here also, doing things that will make them feel guilty. But this does not seem to be the case. It is reported that children prone to express guilt tend to be better able to resist temptation (Grinder and McMichael, 1963), and show less delinquent behavior (Bandura and Walters, 1959), than others. And an experiment by Rebelsky, Allinsmith, and Grinder (1963) found that those children who completed a projective story task by having the guilty character confess, were the least likely to cheat on a subsequent task where cheating was both convenient and rewarding.[8]

In general then, morality in middle childhood is fraught with uncertainty, but where guilt feelings are well developed, behavior is consistent with beliefs. Taken together with developmental work showing clearly definable stages of moral growth, all the material suggests that the child's conception of himself will include a strong moral component by the end of this period. That is, as he moves through the 6 to 12 year interval, guilt feelings, and the closer attention that adults and peers devote to such matters as cheating and stealing, should make it increasingly difficult for a child to keep morality apart from his self-concept.

Aggression

The origins and theoretical causes of excessive aggression in children were covered in Chapter Six. In middle childhood, there are three general ways in which aggression and the emotions of hostility and anger presumably accompanying it, are likely to be modified.

Parents
First of all, there is the punitive behavior of parents. Much of the discussion in Chapter Six emphasized how such behavior seems to promote aggression in early childhood. It is the same in middle childhood, but the evidence here is even more clear-cut because children can communicate their feelings more easily, and because the older the child, the easier it is to determine whether his behavior is deliberately aggressive. Kagan (1958) tested and interviewed a sample of 6- to 10-year-old boys known to be highly aggressive. Compared with others, these boys more frequently described their parents as hostile and rejecting. In England, the responses of known delinquents to a

---

[8]It appears that much experimental work on morality has an immoral flavor to it. Investigators use an *agent provocateur* technique, arranging situations that tempt children into breaking a rule. For example, Hartshorne and May used a puzzle task that could only be solved by cheating; and, cruelest of all, a "peeping tom" task in which children were supposed to keep their eyes closed while trying to trace a maze. There are occasions when one thinks a "new morality" may be necessary for social scientists.

projective story-telling task indicated that they felt relatively *detached* from their families (Jackson, 1950).

The latter finding may sound obscure, but it really isn't. Seriously reject-ed children of hostile parents may cope with the situation by repressing their emotions. Clinical material demonstrates that in severe cases, such children cope either by becoming passive and withdrawn (e.g., TV addicts), or by act-ing out their emotions in aggressive, delinquent behavior, and in denying any positive feelings (love or warm friendship is for "suckers"). Jackson's finding agreed with the latter reaction. And one can see this happen in the later childhood of Roberto Sanchez, the boy we have already met learning to fight in the Mexico City *favella*.

When I was about eleven years old and still in the first grade, I ran away for the first time. I went to Veracruz with no more than the clothes on my back.

I traveled alone. I never wanted to take along friends because I have always pre-ferred to go on my own. It is easier for me to get around by myself. I would ask people the way. By asking, you can get to Rome.

When I left home, I felt as though a great weight was lifted off me. To live with other people is hard. I never wanted to be tied to the family again. Sometimes I would ask for lodging for a night and I would stay with a family for a few days. But I wasn't comfortable because what I was looking for was to be free. And so I went, like the air, without difficulty, without direction, free . . . (Lewis, 1961, pp. 74–76).

Roberto made the situation seem attractive, but for all the nice imagery—being free as air, going without difficulty—anyone who has ever really been on the road knows it just isn't so. More to the point are his remarks about the great "weight" being lifted, not wanting any tie to the family, or even any companion on the road. Did you ever know any reasonably normal eleven-year-old who wanted no friends? The narrative only makes sense for a child who has had a very rough time of it, and has been driven to extreme defen-sive tactics.

Many studies converge on the conclusion that rejection by parents is associated with neurotic and/or delinquent behavior during middle childhood and adolescence. The same generalization applies to early childhood, but it is during the 6 to 12 year period that the reactions attract attention, because by this time children can act them out in a serious fashion. Furthermore, during this period it is hard to anticipate when or how the tough aggressive child will go into action.[9]

Another consideration relevant to aggression in middle childhood is that punitive parents are liable to escalate their disciplinary activities as the child gets older. Most parents will treat the misbehavior of a seven- or eight-year-old more severely than the same act by a four-year-old because more inten-tionality is attributed to the older child; he is supposed to "know better." Also, being physically larger, the older child just naturally seems to require a stronger dosage of punishment. On the other hand, the situation isn't all one-

[9]I once spent some time working in a New York City detention home for juveniles called Youth House. The six- to twelve-year-olds (and there were some as young as six), were especially difficult because they seemed to be in constant motion; sometimes with aggressive intentions and sometimes not, it was hard to tell. It was much easier to be with the 15's and 16's because one could see when they were starting to lose control and were ready, in the vernacular of the place, "to pick up a chair."

sided: since he is increasingly capable of planning and executing effective action, the six- to twelve-year-old is better able to deal with punitive parents by concealing his misdeeds, lying, running away. And this is the general image we have of life in high delinquency-poverty areas: those parents who haven't given up entirely, trying to wallop their children into conformity; and children reacting by becoming tougher, more aggressive, finding in gangs the social support they cannot get at home or in school. Ellison (1969), who spent several weeks living as a gang member, said simply that the gang is mother, father, teacher, and clergy for its members. Cohen (1955) said much the same thing in his formal analysis of gangs as social units.

In connection with social class differences, research (e.g., Dolger and Grinandes, 1946) indicates that lower-class children anticipate harsher physical punishment for misbehavior than others, and they are in turn more inclined to use it themselves. Moreover, since direct, physical aggression is a common mode of behavior in city slums, such children come to accept it as a normal response to many situations. An experiment by Davitz (1952) demonstrated how this can occur. He divided 40 boys and girls aged seven to nine into groups that were either given constructive play training (painting pictures, working puzzles) or aggressive training (competitive physical contact games). Then all the children were shown a film and given a bar of candy, but were frustrated by not seeing all the film, and by having the candy taken away. Observation of their free play immediately after the frustration treatment showed that constructive and aggressive behavior could be predicted according to prior training. It has further been shown that in young children (Lovaas, 1961), and college students (Loew, 1967), positive reinforcement for aggressive *verbal* behavior leads to an increase in aggressive *physical* behavior.

Peers

Peer-group activities offer the second general arena for changes in aggression during middle childhood. Gnagey (1960) ran an elaborate experiment demonstrating how peer leaders can disseminate a negative attitude toward adult authority. He first enlisted the cooperation of boy-leaders in fifth-grade classrooms. A woman acting the role of a substitute teacher then showed a film to these classes. The leaders created a disturbance during the film by making loud negative comments about it. At this point, the "teacher" stopped the film, and ordered them to report to the principal's office. In one experimental condition, the trouble-making leaders responded meekly and apologetically. In the other, they were defiant. Following all this, the film was run through and a short time later, the children were questioned about their opinions of female teachers. A small number of those witnessing the passive response to the teacher indicated that their attitudes were more negative than before. But over half of those witnessing the defiant response were more negative than before. It was also demonstrated that this negative effect is much greater when the defiant actors are group leaders rather than followers. These results fit other findings (see Bandura, 1962) suggesting that children are most likely to imitate peers who have prestige, and are physically attractive and powerful.

An extensive investigation of how group and intergroup activities can influence aggression was conducted by Sherif, Harvey, White, Hood, and Sherif (1961). Working with 12-year-old boys in a summer camp, the investigators first allowed natural friendships to spring up, and then broke the friendship patterns by grouping the boys into two teams which lived in separate cabins and competed against each other for a variety of prizes. The boys took the competition very seriously; bitter rivalry developed between the groups; there were fights and name-calling. Original friendships were forgotten as rising intergroup hostility was matched by strong positive feelings within each group. The experimenters were of course demonstrating a principle that goes back to Machiavelli: within limits, threats from an outgroup increases the cohesion of an ingroup. By later placing both groups of boys in situations where they could only attain important goals by cooperating, the hostility between them was substantially reduced.

Mass Media

Arguments concerning the impact of television, which is surely the medium having the greatest effect on children, are yet to be settled. Most of the material available on the problem was discussed earlier. We might mention in passing, however, that virtually all of the research in this area has concentrated on the question of whether exposure to TV violence increases personal violence. There has been little or no study of the information conveyed in movies and TV. Ellison (1969) mentioned that when robbing a store, his gang immobilized the burglar alarm by spraying shaving cream into it from an aerosol can—a trick they picked up from a movie. Johnson and Medinnus (1969) said that when Spanish-American youngsters in Denver saw *City Across the River* (a film about gangs based on a semidocumentary novel called *The Amboy Dukes*) they took it as a model for establishing a gang of their own.

Backing away now from the specifics on aggression, it is difficult to assign this behavior tendency a straightforward place in the 6- to 12-year-old personality. Aggression cannot be treated in the same way as sexual identity or morality, for example, because it is usually not recognized as part of the self-image. In clinical terms, the point is that most aggressive children will show little insight regarding their behavior. It may be objected that children don't show much genuine insight about their sexual identity or morality either, which, at an abstract level, would be true enough. The difference is that children *do* have a rudimentary but reasonably accurate image of themselves with respect to their sex gender and moral values, while they do not have an equally objective view about their aggression.

In this connection, Kagan and Moss (1962, p. 359) presented data comparing the way six- to ten-year-olds rated themselves on aggression, with similar ratings made according to observations of their behavior. Out of 13 different behaviors, including direct and indirect aggression, competitiveness and dominance, only one—dominance—was related to the self-ratings on aggression at a better than chance level. And this relationship was relatively small. By contrast, their data show that self-ratings of sex anxiety (p. 362) are significant predictors of two out of five relevant behaviors, namely, interaction with the opposite sex and activity typical of the opposite sex.

Freud's notion that aggressive behavior is a function of the id component of personality, and thus not conscious or fully open to awareness, is relevant to this point because he was attempting to account for problems that clinicians see very frequently. Also relevant here are the projective techniques we have mentioned so often when describing research. Give children dolls to play with, or ambiguous pictures to use in stories, and they may show aggression in ways that are quite transparent to an observer, while remaining unaware of it themselves.

If the foregoing remarks are more or less correct, how then is aggression to be incorporated into personality? Or should it be dismissed as an unimportant aspect of personality? The latter course would seem to be wrong because too much clinical material and everyday experience suggests that aggressive tendencies are a consistent, distinctive, and important dimension of individual behavior. Kagan and Moss noted that aggression in childhood remains fairly consistent in males, since it is culturally accepted as a masculine attribute. They present an illustrative case from the Fels study. The subject was a rather nasty little fellow at seven and a half, and at 27 he still seemed the same.

An impetuous, irresponsible child with lack of judgment and often purposely mean and malicious. He likes to bust up constructive activities of others with destructive and violent acts. He was noisy most of the time and, in any group, would disrupt its organization. He was rather infantile in these destructive activities.

The mother felt that S was much too aggressive, and he was unpopular with his peers because of this behavior.

After a visit to the Institute when S was 10 years old, the observer wrote:

"S came in with his customary whoop. He dashed cars across the bridge, knocking down portions of it, building it up again with much noise and thumping. During the course of the morning, he managed to demolish the bridge with much pleasure. He bombed the Tinkertoy parts, and, in all, his play was quite destructive."

"Later in the afternoon he raced around in the snow with Mary. He evidently teased her, since she came in very indignantly. Left alone, S amused himself by throwing snowballs at passing college students. . . ."

During the adult interview, when S was 27, he indicated a low threshold for anger and frequent retaliations to personal attack.

E: "Can you remember the last time you were mildly irritated at anyone?"

S: "I get irritated at drivers everyday. I'm driving in traffic—there's usually some idiot that wants to pull out in front of you or something like that. I'm inclined to get too upset about things like that and be criticized for blowing-up like that" (Kagan and Moss, pp. 95–98).

Returning to the primary question—how to understand aggression as part of personality—it appears that for developmental purposes, aggression can be tied to sex identity. In other words, insofar as children are aware of their aggressive (or passive) behavior, they probably see it as part of their sex role. This, at any rate, is the rationale that parents and society provide for children. Furthermore, besides assigning it to the self-image via the back door of sex identity, we can also view aggression as a social-emotional aspect of personality that exists as part of the active executive self, without being clearly understood by the child.

Perhaps the best way to close discussion here is by appealing to everyday experience because we all know children and adults who seem to suffer from their aggression without being aware of it.

Achievement in social relationships and in personality

The origins of achievement motivation in early childhood are obscured somewhat by the difficulty of distinguishing it from a more generalized drive toward competence. However, research makes it clear enough that parental behavior is the major factor in this matter. Since it would seem implausible for mother-father-child patterns of interaction to change very much, the question before us is what can possibly happen to achievement motivation during middle childhood which is not already ordained by continuing styles of parent behavior?

We have already mentioned how teachers and peers can influence children's self-concepts in ways that relate to academic achievement. But from another perspective, it is also necessary to understand that school performance is the definitive criterion for achievement in childhood. Until the child is in school trying to master new skills along with many other children of the same age, there is no convenient way to assess achievement, or to make the concept of achievement motivation meaningful. The motive itself is, to be sure, measurable through analysis of projective stories, and it predicts performances on such tasks as block-building and ringtoss, but both the projective assessment procedure and the validating experimental tasks are generally accepted as important because they relate to formal school achievement. In other words, we would not take the achievement motive seriously if it had not been found to predict academic performance. And because such performances can only occur for the first time during middle childhood, this period is very important for the elaboration of achievement motivation in personality.

The elaboration we have in mind is indicated by longitudinal data (Kagan and Moss) showing that in six- to ten-year-olds, "achievement mastery" is moderately or highly related to such relevant behaviors as competitiveness, striving for recognition, compulsiveness, and expectancy for success. These relationships either do not exist, or are generally lower, during the 3 to 6 year period. By thus uniting with supportive behaviors, achievement seems to expand and to root itself more firmly into personality during middle childhood. Moreover, such things as recognition and competitiveness are not likely to be easily picked up from parents; they are manifestly things of the schoolroom and playground.

A clearer indication of the degree to which achievement can move beyond family control for boys, as compared with girls, is given in a study by Crandall, Dewey, Katkovsky, and Preston (1964). They collected academic achievement test scores on a sample of 120 second-, third-, and fourth-grade girls and boys. The parents of these children were all interviewed in detail about their attitudes and behavior concerning intellectual achievement. Results showed that the behavior of mothers was relevant to achievement, but only for girls; that mothers' attitudes and evaluations of children's academic progress agreed with their actual performances, but fathers' evaluations did not; and that the parents' positive or negative reactions to intellectual effort were related to girls' achievement scores (high scoring girls had encouraging parents) but unrelated to the achievement scores of boys. In short, the performances of boys seem independent of parental approval. The authors cited additional evidence suggesting that girls strive to achieve to win approval from parents, but boys operate from a more internalized achievement motive. This suggests that the achievement motives of boys may be better established, and perhaps more open to influence from nonfamily sources.

However, lest anyone think matters are clear in this area, it should also be noted that research findings are often confusing. McGhee and Crandall (1968) described two studies covering children in the first 12 grades. Measures of the degree to which they perceived their successes and failures in academic situations to be their own responsibility, were compared with their achievement motive test scores and school grades. Belief in their own responsibility was a better predictor of grades than of achievement test scores, and the academic performances of boys were more highly related to their feeling of responsibility for failure than for success. Results like these do not fit any simple conception of achievement motivation.

Another way to see factors beyond the family modifying achievement is by considering national survey data on the effects of school integration. Results generally show that minority children achieve at significantly higher levels when they are placed in properly integrated schools. The point being that while family factors are constant, school changes influence achievement. And if there are many possible reasons for this, the one that seems most probable to most authorities is that segregated schools implicitly convey second-rate standards of achievement. Pettigrew (1968) argued that achievement standards are embedded in the school atmosphere; in predominantly white middle-class schools, the achievement standard is higher, and minority children consequently do better.

Negro children from "more than half" white classrooms score higher on both reading and mathematical achievement tests than other Negro children; and this effect is strongest among those who began their interracial schooling in the early grades.

In the schools which can truly be described as "integrated," where most teachers report no racial tension whatsoever, Negro students evince higher verbal achievement, more definite college plans, and more positive racial attitudes than comparable Negro students in tense, merely "desegregated" schools (Pettigrew, pp. 67–72).

There is nothing mysterious in any of this; we have seen studies demonstrating that children internalize achievement standards from those who participate with them in novel tasks (Bandura and Kupers, Chapter 6), and that teachers' expectations for performance influence children's achievement levels (Rosenthal and Jacobson, this chapter).

Finally, it should be mentioned that evidence emphasizing that achievement motivation can become relatively independent of the family in middle childhood (perhaps more so for boys than for girls), is balanced by a report of important progress made by children "when school and home focus on achievement" (Smith and Brahce, 1963). Two elementary schools in Flint,

Michigan, arranged a program which successfully geared school and home activities to the purpose of increasing academic achievement. For their part, teachers made special efforts to improve reading and vocabulary in the classroom, and made appropriate homework assignments in books known to be available. Meanwhile, parents who had been instructed in group meetings and individually supported the effort at home by reading to the children, providing dictionaries, keeping up a special study period, and expressing positive attitudes. Within five months after the program started, the children had made substantial gains, and the parents reported that they themselves had benefited.

As we have with the other aspects of social-emotional development, let us now see how achievement fits into the child's personality. It should be evident that achievement occupies an important place in the self-concept. The child who does well in school, and thereby receives approval from parents and teachers, will obviously have a better self-image, which should show itself in general feelings of self-confidence. And the reverse tends to be true of the poor achiever, notwithstanding traditional myths about wretched bookworms. (In reality, there are very few cases of children who are outstanding school achievers but otherwise totally miserable. If anything, it works the other way: those with serious emotional problems also tend to be poor achievers.)

Innate intelligence does not seem particularly relevant to the role of achievement in personality. Most investigations of achievement motivation have been conducted with children who have similar IQ test scores, and are therefore presumed to have similar innate intelligence. This control technique allows significant differences in the children's academic performances to be related to their achievement motive scores. Children may thus be labelled as under- or overachievers, depending upon whether their academic records are below or above the average levels associated with their IQ scores.

Sex identity appears to be a more important factor than intelligence in determining the role of achievement in personality. McClelland and his associates worked almost entirely with male subjects in their research because culturally determined sex norms prescribe the importance of achievement mainly for men. In their early work, it was found very difficult to validate achievement motive scores for girls. Kagan and Moss also presented data along this line. It showed that during the age interval 6 to 14 years, there is a general drop in the achievement and recognition striving scores for girls as compared with boys. And other findings mentioned earlier in this section suggest that boys internalize achievement motivation to a greater extent than girls.

In general then, achievement first becomes an important part of the self directly, through the approval or disapproval it generates, and indirectly, through its linkage with sex identity.

One last comment on the place of achievement in personality: when looking at behavior in middle childhood, superficial evidence of achievement may mask crucial individual differences. Scrutiny of some case history material will clarify this point. Madison (1969) presented autobiographical accounts written by two college students named Sidney and Phil. Both made equally outstanding records in primary and secondary school without having to work very hard. Both came from equally well-off middle-class families; one's father was a physicist, the other was a lawyer. Both students were asked to describe their intellectual and academic histories. Here is part of Sidney's response.

In kindergarten I enjoyed painting and an introduction to reading. A card with a color and the word for the color being written out on it would be flashed in front of the class; I was particularly good at this, and enjoyed the praise which accompanied each success. First grade was uneventful except that I had been put in the middle rather than the advanced group, but I was promoted to the advanced group in second grade. I enjoyed reading or being read to. My parents were glad to see me promoted to the higher group. I spurted ahead intellectually. My parents, my teacher, and my sister all helped me with my work. . . .

In third grade the outstanding incident was being severely reprimanded for looking up obscene words in the dictionary. There was never much schoolwork that couldn't be done quickly and easily, leaving much time for play. . . . I found that I was more skillful mentally than I was at playing baseball, and used to amaze my friends by telling them obscure facts about the history of the game.

In fourth grade I had a teacher who singled me out for my keen questions. I was very grateful for this, and she has remained in my mind as my favorite teacher. In recent years I was shocked when a former classmate of mine told me that he had thought she was a poor teacher, and had pets.

At this time I was being elected to various class offices but had succeeded in alienating many people, friends, and teachers, by my assertiveness and ostentation. I would look up facts in the encyclopedia at home and then ask questions which the teacher couldn't answer.

In fifth grade I was shocked to encounter two teachers who did not like me. They regarded my questions as showing off and seemed jealous, rather resentful, of my successes; I hated them bitterly and finally asked my parents to complain to them. They did, but the resentment grew. I was relieved to graduate (Madison, pp. 159–160).

Now Phil:

My schooling started with kindergarten. I walked about one mile to school. Then we moved, and I transferred to a new school. Beginning in the first grade I realized my liking for sports. I remember how mad I used to get when our first grade teacher would make us miss play period to write "I will not talk in class" one hundred times. We never missed play period entirely, but it would always cut off some time from our baseball game which we played the year round. I think it was the neighborhood in which I grew up as much as my personal makeup that was responsible for the devotion I have for athletics. There was always some game going on regardless of the time of day. As I grew older, I began to play baseball in school leagues and on summer playgrounds. I would also follow baseball in the papers and on television. The collection of baseball trading cards was a favorite neighborhood pastime.

In the meantime my school work was coming along well. I was making good grades and doing my work, but I did not have the dedication here that I had in my sports. I can hear my father saying to me as he did often, "Do a little more than the teachers ask." It was seldom that I heeded his advice.

My interest in baseball began one day when my father brought me a glove and ball and started tossing a ball with me. I remember picnics—the men would go and play softball. I would go tearing off and chase it, happy as a lark. I guess television helped generate the interest.

There was a group of boys in the area and we always played from sunrise to sunset, taking time out for eating and that's all. Being together, the relationships to those boys, really cemented my interest. My success kept my liking for it going. When I was a boy, I would take that sport page and really study it. I could quote batting averages, pitchers, players for all teams, and who got how many hits each day (p. 166).

Sidney and Phil went to the same university. One of them made a perfect record, winning every award available for academic distinction. The other wound up on probation for poor grades. It was Sidney who won the honors. There are many ramifications to the two cases, and it is unfair to ask for a correct prediction of the honor student, but the outstanding thing about the two excerpts is that for Sidney, academic achievement is central during middle childhood, while it is peripheral for Phil. This difference would be trivial if Phil's boyhood schoolwork were any less distinguished than Sidney's. The fact that they did equally well, however, dramatizes the problem of seeing how achievement fits personality. In short, gross achievement in middle childhood is one thing, but the role it will play in personality is another. Sidney found his personal identity in scholastic achievement; Phil found it in sports, despite his success in the classroom.

Summary of social-emotional development in middle childhood

We have discussed how each of the five main social-emotional aspects of personality evolve during middle childhood as a consequence of experience beyond the family, and, to some lesser extent, as a consequence of changing experience within the family. The three categories of experience described earlier as critical in middle childhood—peers, school, and mass media—should now be understood to have both specific and broadly mixed effects on the self-concept, sexual identity, morality, aggression, and achievement.

For example, it is apparent that rule-following morality based on family experience in early childhood is heavily influenced by peer-group experience in middle childhood. But while sexual identity and aggression will also be modified by experience with peers, these aspects of personality will be susceptible to further influence from mass media and the family. Achievement motivation seems narrowly dependent on some interaction between family and school experience, but the evidence can be interpreted as giving priority to either one. And the self-concept, self as object and executive, appears open to influence from all sources—family, peers, school, and media alike.

This brings us to a second major point: the older the child, the more difficult it becomes to deal with any one aspect of personality without touching on one or more of the others. So while it is surely useful to concentrate on specific areas one at a time, especially when discussing origins or conducting research, it is folly to persist in this too long when speaking of larger trends in personality development. Accordingly, we have tried to organize discussion of the way social-emotional elements coalesce in middle childhood by treating this problem from the perspective of the child himself, in terms of his self-concept. It seems most economical, and most plausible, to see specific areas of development coming more and more under the heading of the self-concept.

To put it less abstractly: the six- to twelve-year-old increasingly sees himself in a unitary fashion; his sex-role, moral values, and achievement standards, which began as separate, somewhat alien impositions, now form an increasingly integral unit. The self-image of an adult typically incorporates all these things in such a tight weave that it may be impossible to make out any distinctions. We only see the components spread apart in abnormal situations, where the smooth organization of personality has for some reason broken down. Middle childhood is clearly the period during which serious organization begins, and this can only be grasped in some such terms as elaboration of the self-concept or ego.

Consider one last chunk of material. In 1946 Jenkins and Glickman first published a description of "common syndromes in child psychiatry." These included three general patterns of symptoms that were abstracted from analysis of 500 clinical cases, and later checked against 5000 more. Note how these syndromes represent, in one unitary form or another, abnormal development of sexual identity, morality, aggression, and/or achievement.

Type I. The overinhibited child, characterized by seclusiveness, shyness, apathy, worrying, sensitiveness, and submissiveness. He is given to daydreaming, feels inferior, lacks close friendships, cries easily, is overdependent, easily depressed, and is discouraged with himself. He has frequent physical complaints and is prone to neurotic illness.

Type II. The unsocialized aggressive child is characterized by assaultive tendencies, initiating fights, cruelty, defiance of authority, malicious mischief, and inadequate guilt feelings. He is selfish, jealous, vengeful, deceitful, and prone to place upon others the responsibility for his own misconduct. He is suspicious of others, profane and obscene in language, and precociously interested in sex.

Type III. The socialized delinquent or pseudosocial child, is characterized by stealing in the company of others, furtive stealing, habitual truancy from school, staying out late at night, desertion of home, bad companions, and gang activities (Jenkins and Glickman, 1946, pp. 244–245).

From our present viewpoint, the syndromes show what abnormally integrated self-systems will look like in children who have had bad luck with one or more of the main social-emotional aspects of personality.

THEORETICAL PERSPECTIVES

Freud

Next to early infancy, middle childhood seems to have been the period of least interest to Freud. In his lexicon of psychosexual development, it is called the "latency" period, because it offers very little open expression of sexual energy (libido). The discussion in Chapter 4 emphasized that libido is diverted into nonsexual activities while the child recovers from the stress of the Oedipus complex. Freud speculated further that libido might be decreased during this period because of physiological changes. And it has also been mentioned (see Blum, 1953) that the six- to twelve-year-old is so busy with other things—formal and informal learning, peer activities,—that he has little energy left for sex.

Traditional Freudian theory could therefore be dismissed as generally irrelevant to middle childhood if it did not contain one important set of ideas: the ego defense mechanisms. The essence of this matter can be summarized briefly as follows. To maintain a positive self-concept, or self-esteem, the child must defend himself against circumstances that threaten it. Any psychological process that has defense of the self-concept as its central purpose, can thus be termed an "ego defense mechanism." And since from early childhood we are all frequently engaged in efforts to maintain self-esteem, Freud saw ego defense mechanisms as a very important feature of everyday life.

Sarnoff (1962) provided a comprehensive discussion of 11 different defense mechanisms. The number is sizable because as persons mature, they obviously will develop more sophisticated defensive techniques. All are briefly described below in a rough chronological order. That is, the first three or four apparently come into operation quite early; several others can be seen by the end of middle childhood, and the last few seem most characteristic of adults.

1. Denial

This is probably the simplest and earliest of all defenses. The young child, and sometimes adults in extreme situations, will ward off threats to the ego by denying that they exist. It is quite common to see denial in four- or five-year-olds who are engaged in an activity that is uncomfortable or dangerous. Consider the child trembling and turning blue with cold while in swimming, who, when asked to come out, denies through chattering teeth that he is cold. Various authorities also point out that some European Jews used denial when confronted with evidence of Hitler's extermination policy.

But Freud saw denial as a function of the id. If it is recalled that arbitrary "wish-fulfillment" is supposed to be the primary process through which id functions, then it should be clear that denial stands as a specific offshoot of that process.

2. Identification with the aggressor

Frequently mentioned by Freudians in connection with the Oedipus complex, this defense, whereby a child or adult identifies with a threatening person to cope with his fear of that person, was discussed in Chapter 6 as one of the origins of sexual identity. In middle childhood one would look for it to show up in peer and school situations, particularly those involving harsh teachers or gang leaders.

Denial and identification with the aggressor are given first place on our list because, as Sarnoff suggested, they are both simple reactions to *external* threats. He further noted that as the child matures, *internal* threats can exist in the form of anxiety-provoking ideas, images, emotions, and these require other defenses such as repression.

3. Repression

Technically, repression is a way of defending the ego against frightening or threatening ideas by forcing them out of awareness. In everyday language, we often see this as "forgetting." Simplified forms of repression seem quite common in children when they honestly forget many things that are painful to remember—either nasty incidents of the past or oppressive chores that have to be done in the present. Forgetting can also be interpreted as a more complex defense when it prevents an act that threatens the self-concept. For example, it is a cliché, but nevertheless often true, that the soldier or hunter about to try to kill for the first time, will finally squeeze only to discover that he has forgotten to release the safety, or that the weapon is empty. Forgetting can be understood here as a last-ditch defense against doing something which is supposed to be morally wrong.

The dynamics of repression as a psychological process are obscure. Suffice it to say that Freudian explanations are complex, involving assumptions about conscious and unconscious mental processes and psychic energy operations[10] that are debatable. So we will forgo extensive discussion, because in this area it can easily turn into a matter of art for art's sake. And for the same reason, we will stay at a descriptive level when discussing the remaining defense mechanisms.

4. Sublimation

Sublimation can be understood briefly this way: id generates many desires that cannot be gratified because they are prohibited by society. (Remember that the superego component of personality contains the internalized set of prohibitions.) Now in some instances, these desires are repressed; in others, they are admitted into consciousness but kept in their place, so to speak, as daydreams or fantasies. In either case, however, the libido associated with these desires must be released. Sublimation is the process in which threatening libido is diverted from its original aim and released in neutral or positively approved ways. For example, a traditional Freudian might suggest that scientists who study sexuality, or poets who write about it, are people who sublimate their personal sexual desires.

5. Displacement

Displacement is the old "kick the dog" mechanism. Aggression which cannot be released on its proper target without threatening the ego is displaced onto a more convenient, less threatening target. Insofar as it is thus a diversionary technique, displacement is similar to sublimation. But sublimation is usually reserved for constructive activities, such as cutting a pile of firewood

---

[10]Psychic energy is supposed to be needed to force material into the unconscious and then keep it there, which is why remote memories may return when one is very tired, or why events that seemed trivial and were forgotten during the day may come disturbingly to mind when one is about to fall asleep at night. With fatigue, the psychic energy "barrier" is weakened.

or writing a novel, while displacement refers to more obviously negative activities such as kicking the dog and performing acts of racial prejudice. A child appears to be displacing aggression when he is bullied by an older child and then turns around to bully one younger than himself. (The learning theorist would of course call this imitation.)

6. Regression

Any substantial retrograde movement in behavior can be termed regression. Confronted with severe threat, and feeling unable to cope with it in a way appropriate to his age, an individual may regress to some developmentally outmoded defense tactic. Regression is said to have occurred frequently among concentration camp prisoners, and it can also be seen occasionally among young men in military service. Briefly, some adults in these extreme situations will regress to denial, identification with the aggressor, or simply lie down and cry for Mama.

7. Rationalization

To "rationalize" is to find a socially acceptable reason for doing something that might otherwise be thought of as wrong. In jargon, one could speak of rationalization as a process of pulling the wool over the eyes of the superego. My seven-year-old knows that it is wrong to eat too many candy bars. But with the aid of TV commercials, he recently came up with a rationalization: candy is good because it has important body-building ingredients. When that same argument is put to him in connection with vegetables, however, the response is denial: "My body is built up enough." On the other hand, parents can always use the "this is for your own good" rationalization to justify harsh treatment of a child.

8. Projection

When thoughts seem unacceptable to the self, and yet are very attractive, one may find a socially acceptable means of entertaining them by projecting them onto others. An adult with many sexual inhibitions, for instance, may delight in giving detailed denunciations of the sex practices of teen-agers, hippies, Negroes, Jews, or whatever group offers itself as a safe target. One of the traditional Freudian explanations of race prejudice in the South is that white males project onto Negroes all the sex desires they cannot accept in themselves. And this projection also provides a rationalization for keeping Negroes in their place. Similar interpretations have also been made of the Nazi prejudice toward Jews.

9. Reaction formation

This one is a bit difficult to convey because it involves acting in a way entirely opposite to the way one really wants to act. Most writers use the example of the overprotective mother to illustrate reaction formation. Suppose she really feels a good deal of hostility toward her child, her id hates it because it frustrates gratification of certain impulses. But she believes or has it as a part of her superego, that every decent mother must only feel total love for her child. So, lacking insight, she tries to smother the hostility by acting directly contrary to that emotion. It can work in other situations as well: a male teacher who is attracted to young girl students but thinks this is immoral may be especially gruff with them.

10. Compartmentalization

According to this technique, one can cope with threatening material by shunting it off into a separate, *nonself* compartment of personality. The ego or *real me* is protected by assigning the unacceptable behavior to a *nonme*, rather like burying a body in your basement and acting as if it's not there. In extreme cases of pathology, this can lead to what is called split personality. *The Three Faces of Eve* is a famous case in point. For most persons, compartmentalization only occurs under very novel, high stress conditions, which give rise to the feeling of depersonalization. In this connection, soldiers may sometimes experience depersonalization in combat, saying that it didn't seem to be happening to them personally; that it was as if they were watching someone else in a film. And after returning to normal situations, they may compartmentalize the experience by not admitting the capacity for extreme brutality as a part of their self-concept. Depersonalization can itself be seen as a defensive reaction to extreme experience—it is often reported by accident victims—but we needn't add anything to an already prolific list.

11. Transference

Transference is supposed to cover special instances when a person, such as a neurotic patient, transfers feelings he has about a significant figure in his life such as his father, to a new authority figure, such as his psychoanalyst. When it happens in therapy that a patient shows very strong emotion toward the therapist (love or hate) for no apparent reason, this transference is interpreted as a defensive tactic being used to forestall the analysis; something that will stop the therapist from probing into painful subject matter.[11] In less specialized circumstances, one can appeal to transference to explain why young children view teachers as surrogate mothers, why adolescents develop crushes on teachers or family friends, and why some young women prefer much older men.

In sum, Freud's idea that persons protect their egos or self-concepts through the use of defense mechanisms is particularly relevant to middle childhood because here, for the first time, the individual has a substantial self-concept to protect. And many of the defense mechanisms seem descriptively appropriate to behaviors that emerge during this period. If some, such as reaction formation and rationalization, demand a fair degree of sophistication to work effectively, others, such as denial, repression, and regression, can easily be applied to typical childhood behavior.

[11]The descriptive dynamics here are also debatable, but they are extremely interesting:

"For all transference reactions, by virtue of unconscious equation between therapist and family figure, represent attempts to alter the actual nature of the psychotherapeutic relationship and to force it to become like other types of relationships that the patient has known. To the extent that this forcing operation is successful, it diverts the enterprise away from its original and enduring goal, the attainment of self-insight on the part of the patient. Thus, if the therapist can, indeed, be enticed into playing the role of an elderly lover, rejecting tyrant, or pampering Nanny, he abdicates, perforce, his psycho-therapeutic function. Obviously, if such an abdication occurs on the psychotherapist's part, the patient's resistance to continued self-probing will have won out, and the original purpose of the relationship will have been defeated" (Sarnoff, 1962, p. 263).

A final word of warning, however. It is at once the genius and the failing of the defense mechanisms that they offer interesting explanations for so many different phenomena. Armed with the preceding list, one can give a plausible account for practically everything—love, war, art, business, revolution, education, so caution is necessary. It takes more than a quick rundown on defense mechanisms to explain most behaviors, even if one wants to do it according to the traditional Freudian model.

Neo-Freudian views

Sullivan

Contrary to Freud, Harry S. Sullivan attached great importance to middle childhood as a period of personality development. He divided it into the "juvenile era" (6 to 9 years) and "preadolescence" (9 to 12 years). And, as we have mentioned on other occasions, his ideas here are again impressive in the degree to which they fit current research trends.

He anticipated the emphasis on peer activities by defining the juvenile era in terms of an emerging need for friends. He discussed the school as an important factor that could modify the child's self-system. Furthermore, current learning theory research concerning the ways children can be influenced by experience with peers and teachers, is relevant to his discussions of "social subordination" and "social accommodation." Since he used these phrases to describe how children learn to get along in groups and with authority figures outside the home, the learning theory explanations in terms of imitation and reinforcement would not be foreign to him.

Sullivan also devoted some thought to the cultural values and stereotypes acquired during the juvenile era. His view of "supervisory patterns" as the child's internalized conception of how he appears to others, is not unlike the anthropologists' view of the cultural values which form basic personality. Stereotypes, moreover, are discussed as an inevitable result of pressures on children to conform to the demands of their immediate environment:

Since there is so much to be done in this era and so much pressure on the juvenile to take over any successful patterns for doing it, in our type of school society at least, one of the conspicuous outcomes is that a great many juveniles arrive at preadolescence with quite rigid stereotypes about all sorts of classes and conditions of mankind. One of these stereotypes is about people of the opposite sex. Unless something fortunate intervenes, juveniles pretty nearly have to adopt gross stereotypes of juveniles of the other sex (Sullivan, 1953, p. 238).

Sullivan offered other ideas that are more ambiguous. One such notion, the "sublimatory reformulation" process, whereby socially approved activities are substituted for ones that are socially disapproved, seems equally relevant to sublimation as an ego defense mechanism, and to more straightforward changes in behavior that occur as a result of learning. And "control of focal awareness," which refers to the child's ability to direct his own thinking in a deliberate fashion, is seemingly related to Piaget's idea of decentering, as well as to certain defense mechanisms; one can at least do a better job of protecting the ego when he can control the focus of his awareness.

Another point worth reproducing here concerns the social learning that enables children to begin perceiving their parents as humans instead of gods:

This discrimination is, to a considerable extent, first gained by discovering merits in particular teachers and then discovering demerits in certain other teachers, with or without communication of these experiences to the authority figures at home.

As a result of all this, if it works right, the juvenile gradually has an opportunity to pare the parents down from godlike figures to people. Another great tributary to this type of learning, which appears in most juveniles probably when they are well on in the second grade, is that they learn from other juveniles about their parents (Sullivan, pp. 230–231).

Finally, one of Sullivan's more important general ideas for this period is "the conception of orientation in living." This awkward sounding phrase refers to the converging nature of personality development in middle childhood; the problem we discussed earlier in connection with the integration of different social-emotional factors in development. Sullivan handles it entirely at a descriptive level:

The degree to which one is *adequately oriented* in living is, I believe, a very much better way of indicating what we often have in mind when we speak about how "well integrated" a person is, or what his "character" is in the sense of good, bad, or indifferent (p. 243).

All in all, his discussions of the first part of middle childhood contain a diverse selection of rich ideas. Some are treated in current research according to learning theory formulations, and some still lie fallow. The latter condition prevails with respect to the "need for interpersonal intimacy" which is supposed to characterize preadolescence.

It is said that development during the nine to twelve year interval is mainly determined by an intimate relationship with a same-sexed peer.

Just as the juvenile era was marked by a significant change—the development of the need for compeers, for playmates rather like oneself—the beginning of preadolescence is equally spectacularly marked, in my scheme of development, by the appearance of a new type of interest in another person.

. . . it is a specific new type of interest in a *particular* member of the same sex who becomes a chum or a close friend. This change represents the beginning of something very like full-blown, psychiatrically defined *love*. In other words, the other fellow takes on a perfectly novel relationship with the person concerned: he becomes of practically equal importance in all fields of value. Nothing remotely like that has ever appeared before (p. 245).

The phenomenon described here seems very important on both practical and theoretical grounds. To begin with, common experience supports it: most of us remember having had chum relationships during this time. Second, certain problems, such as changes to higher-order levels of morality, might be better understood by analyzing the chum relationship. Does a higher sense of justice arise out of the give-and-take of such a relationship? Third, Sullivan suggested that friendly intimacy of this kind can function as a natural form of psychotherapy, allowing children to verbalize and thus deal directly with some of their emotional problems. One encounters many examples of this in case histories and autobiographies. It is also suggested that the chum situation is the forerunner of heterosexual relationships that will develop in adolescence. By having an intimate same-sexed chum, one is in a sense practicing for later intimacy with someone of the opposite sex.

Since it thus offers great possibilities for growth and change, the chum relationship appears to play an important role in personality development. It might be called a critical event. But apart from Bettelheim's calculated use of peer groups for therapy purposes, which is only relevant at a tangent, Sullivan's conception of this whole matter has received little attention.

Erikson

The dominant feature of middle childhood for Erik Erikson was development of a sense of industry. This ego quality seems to come in partly because the child's executive self (ego as actor) is now strong enough to demonstrate its efficiency through significant accomplishments, and partly because the child is not able to remain completely tied into his family. That is, there is an *intrinsic* thrust outward because of the child's increased capabilities – something like a competence drive. And there is an *extrinsic* push outward that Erikson sees as coming from the family itself; resolution of the Oedipus complex makes it clear to the child that he must seek important gratifications elsewhere.

Skill, ability to be productive, a sense of industry, therefore becomes important to the child because it serves as his passport into larger society. If a proper sense of industry is not attained during this period, a child may instead acquire a sense of inferiority. And as was noted briefly in Chapter 4, this can have varied effects. Children may become alienated from society; being unable to hold their own in it according to conventional standards of constructive work, they may turn against it. Or, if they do not become actively alienated, but instead accept the idea that they are truly inferior, children may withdraw into a protective conformity, or even to some pathology such as drug addiction.

Erikson did not deal with defense mechanisms in his chronology of ego development. However, it is clear from his other writings that such processes as sublimation, repression, displacement, and rationalization, will operate here in ways that can either promote or impede acquisition of the sense of industry. So a child may initially be disposed to sublimate energy into school activities, but if this turns out to be ineffective or meaningless to him, he may displace the energy into criminal activities and rationalize this by pointing to injustice in the school.

In general, while Erikson's discussion of industry and inferiority in middle childhood was not lengthy, it fits together with much of the empirical research on this period, particularly with the work on achievement motivation. On the surface, it seems that the child McClelland would label as having a high achievement motive would probably be labeled by Erikson as having a strong sense of industry.

Piaget

Concrete operations. During the age interval 7 to 11 years, cognitive development is said to be at the stage of "concrete operations." It will be recalled from Chapter 6 that in the latter phase of the preoperational stage (4 to 7 years), thinking was described as "intuitive"; the child was becoming decentered, able to consider more than one aspect of a situation at a time. And he was also, presumably as a result of decentering, becoming less generally egocentric; beginning to show awareness of other points of view besides his own.

Now in retrospect, and from a distance, one can observe that the progress being made in the intuitive subperiod has a kind of negative quality—it is as if the four to seven-year-old were gradually having blinders removed. The result of decentering is that he can see many things that either didn't exist for him before, or were very obscure. But here in middle childhood cognitive development has a positive quality; thinking seems to evolve as a constructive response to the child's new, decentered vision of the world. According to Piaget, the essence of this constructive response is the formation of "concrete mental operations."

Flavell (1963) briefly reviewed the progression leading toward such operations:

As the child progresses through the postinfancy years, on the other hand, we know that his cognitive actions become more and more internalized, schematic, and mobile, and of course more and more divested of their concrete, substantial qualities. But most important of all, for present purposes, these now internal, now representational cognitive actions gradually cohere to form increasingly complex and tightly integrated *systems* of actions. These systems are equilibrated, organized affairs in the sense that one action may annul or otherwise compensate for another previously performed; two actions can combine to produce a third, and so on.

When cognitive actions achieve this special status, that is, when they are organized into close-knit totalities with definite, strong structure, they are called by Piaget cognitive *operations* . . . (Flavell, p. 165).

Concrete mental operations therefore emerge as the child's separate cognitive schemas equilibrate or shake down into substantial beliefs about specific aspects of his environment, and as these equilibrated schemas are organized into larger units or systems . . . the "close-knit totalities" mentioned above. These in turn permit the child to carry out the cognitive activities referred to as concrete operations. Such operations involve extended cognitive acts (thinking) which are qualitatively different from anything that has gone on before. The only precedents for these acts occur as occasional intuitive flashes in the prior subperiod. While this does not mean that all things are now perfectly clear to the child, it does make for gross differences to earlier types of thinking:

There are things that he does not understand, true enough, but he no longer gives the impression that he understands something, only to reveal two sentences later that he does not understand it after all (Baldwin, 1968, p. 249).

And apart from the general changes so far mentioned, Flavell added that the child seems to be acting differently because the processes of assimilation and accommodation work much more effectively. He spoke of them as becoming "finely tuned . . . rich and integrated" mechanisms.

Logical and infralogical operations.   Now then, what exactly are concrete mental operations? Flavell (p. 166) indicated that any cognitive representation or thought, which is part of a larger, organized network or system of thoughts, can be called an operation. He listed many of the common intellectual skills acquired during middle childhood as examples. There are "logical operations," such as addition, subtraction, and multiplication; and "infralogical operations," involving ideas about time, space, and interpersonal relations. The difference between logical and infralogical operations is easier to specify by presenting examples than by formal definition. Piaget just did not provide a *directly* understandable one or two sentence definition, and his American interpreters (Flavell, Baldwin) got into elaborate discussions that go beyond our present purposes.[12] So we will merely take up a few generalizations.

During the course of his investigations of thinking in middle childhood, Piaget observed that mental operations of this period have certain common properties. For example, they tend to be *reversible*: older children can review chains of thought and not cling inflexibly to a mistaken conclusion. Thinking is also *associative*: a series of thoughts or cognitive elements are understood to exist independently of their arrangement because they can be associated together in different ways. Piaget saw these and other common properties of mental operations which emerge in middle childhood as similar in principle to the logical properties of mathematical groups. For those of us untutored in this area, Baldwin gave a lucid statement of what mathematical groups are all about.

In mathematics, a *group* is a set of elements whose relations with one another have certain properties. These elements may be thought of as numbers, points, people, classes of objects, operations, or anything. Piaget usually considers the elements as certain logical or numerical operations, such as the operation of combining two classes of objects into a single class or the operation of adding two numbers.

Not every set of elements forms a *group*. For the set to be a *group* there must be some law of combination of elements. Ordinarily this operation is given the general label "multiplication," but it need not be similar to multiplication in arithmetic (pp. 179–180).

To come to the point: Piaget saw logical mental operations as fitting various types of mathematical groups. That is, patterns of logical thought in the older child can be conceptually analyzed according to different types of groupings (laws for combining elements). There are several such groupings, and considerable research has been done to demonstrate how children approximate them when faced with logical problems.

_____

[12]The zealous student will find good sources in English in Flavell, Baldwin, and two works by Inhelder and Piaget (1958, 1964).

One grouping, for instance, is called formally "bi-univocal multiplication of relations." It involves the ability to group elements together in a one-to-one correspondence, even though these elements may only correspond in a relative fashion. Flavell described an illustrative task:

The child is given ten dolls of differing heights and ten little sticks (walking sticks for the dolls) of differing heights. He is then asked to arrange the dolls and sticks "so that each doll can find the stick which belongs to it" . . . ; that is, if the dolls ascend in height from A to J and the sticks from 1 to 10, then the correct one-one correspondence between dolls and sticks would be A-1, B-2, C-3, . . . J-10. The capacity to make such relational correspondences is a concrete operational achievement . . . (p. 194).

Another grouping is called "bi-univocal multiplication of classes." This involves understanding that an element in one class or set can also be in another. Flavell quoted an illustrative problem from a report by Piaget and Inhelder:

There are only three knives in a store. Two of these knives have two blades: they cost 8 francs and 10 francs. Two of these knives have a corkscrew: they cost 10 francs and 12 francs. I choose the one which has two blades and a corkscrew: how much does it cost? (p. 192).

To get the right answer, the child must in principle be performing a logical operation in which the three knives are thought of as elements in sets defined by blades, corkscrews, and prices. The answer (10 francs) can only come by understanding which element is at the appropriate intersect of the sets.

Infralogical groupings are conceptually similar to logical groupings, but they concern mental operations which apply to physical problems, such as when one is dealing with parts of physical wholes. The infralogical operations thus take in situations where the child's perception of compelling physical attributes may seduce him away from a logical principle.

Perhaps it is clear enough by now that Piaget generally views cognitive development in middle childhood as well advanced toward the higher-order abstract level of adult thinking. The mental operations of this period are concrete, however, because they are limited to events in the concretely real, immediate world. Furthermore, while concrete operations can be analyzed as approximating the formal mathematical grouping models, the child cannot yet grasp the idea of thought as a tool for generating new possibilities. He may be able to solve different logical problems, but he cannot construct them; his thinking may be liberated from dependence on perceptual givens, but he is not able fully to utilize this liberty.

Concrete operations and personality. If the general pattern of cognitive development in middle childhood is vastly illuminated by Piaget's work, the manner in which this development can influence personality is not. The child's expanded intellectual capacity is presumed to effect all sorts of social-emotional behavior as well as intellectual activities (see Flavell, p. 200), but most of Piaget's remarks in this connection involved either parallels between morality and other forms of logic, or comments on how social situations may facilitate such processes as decentering and equilibration. The wider social-emotional implications of cognitive development are virtually unexplored.

From the general perspective of other material in this chapter, one interesting speculation is that the self-concept or ego gets established as a multi-faceted unit because the child deploys his intellectual capacity on his own behavior. In other words, he probably organizes, manipulates, and integrates much of his own behavior just as he organizes aspects of the physical world. Technically, the child can see himself as an element belonging to intersecting sets—member of a family, church, peer-group—he can guide his social behavior according to such logical operations of class inclusion as stereotyping; and it might also be agreed that many ego defense mechanisms could not function in the absence of advanced cognitive capacities.

These are not altogether arbitrary notions. Harvey, Hunt, and Schroder (1961) made an elaborate ecumenical effort to bring together cognitive and social-emotional factors in personality.

Harvey, Hunt, and Schroder

The work of O. J. Harvey and his associates D. E. Hunt and H. M. Schroder is especially appropriate to mention here because it is in middle childhood that cognitive and social-emotional lines of development are most likely to converge upon one another. If nothing else, the school experience forces them to converge. In this chapter, and at the end of Chapter 6 when discussing Moore's work on early reading and writing, we have seen many examples of how the child's self-concept can be affected by his cognitive skills. Erikson's discussion of the sense of industry vs. inferiority is also relevant.

The important theoretical contribution of Harvey et al., is that they offer a systematic analysis of how social-emotional aspects of the self-concept may interact with conceptual (cognitive) systems. Briefly, it will be recalled from Chapter 4 that conceptual systems are said to develop through four successive stages, which mark progress from concrete to abstract cognitive functioning. A central feature of this progress is the steady interplay between cognitive and social-emotional factors. Thus, in describing movement from one stage to another, examples are given of how family conditions can influence the transition. It is explicitly assumed that certain social-emotional experiences can facilitate or hold back conceptual system development, and vice versa. For instance, conceptual development will be enhanced in a child raised so that he is socially and emotionally "open" to new experience. On the other hand, failure in conceptual development (say because of sensory impairment or brain damage) can preclude proper social-emotional development, even if the child is raised in a perfectly ideal fashion. It is therefore possible for development of either conceptual systems or social-emotional organization to be arrested or fixated at an early stage, and for any such fixation in one to have negative effects on the other.

The theoretical perspective of Harvey and his associates began as little more than speculation about relationships between trends in cognitive and social-emotional development. But it is now beginning to be tested in research. One preliminary report (Harvey, Prather, et al.) noted earlier in this chapter, demonstrated that the relative concreteness or abstractness of teachers' conceptual systems indicates whether their classrooms will have authoritarian or democratic atmospheres. And a more extensive program of research is in progress. It would appear from other signs as well that the effort to gain an integral understanding of intellectual and emotional factors in personality development is finally beginning to pick up significant momentum.

CHAPTER SUMMARY

At first glance, middle childhood appears to be a dull psychological affair. There are a number of reasons for this, but the chief reason is that it lacks a clear dramatic focus—the eye scanning this period is not caught by any striking metaphor or myth. Artists look further ahead to the dramatics of adolescence; scientists look backward to origins in early childhood and infancy. But it should now be plain that surface banality masks an exciting interior. Studying this period is like getting to know a rumpled little man who turns out to be a secret agent. The life of a six- to twelve-year-old may seem innocuous to casual observers but in psychological reality it involves a series of high adventures.

The global critical event of this period—movement beyond the family—carries the child into novel, challenging, sometimes literally dangerous[13] domains of experience with peers, school and mass media. Each of these can be seen as separate, overlapping forces acting upon personality development. And these forces can act upon personality in harmony with earlier ones: the child with high need for achievement may find this being rewarded by teachers. Or they can be contradictory: the aggressive girl may discover her behavior is contrary to the feminine sex-role. In broad terms, therefore, middle childhood stands as a critical period for personality because the impact of experience beyond the family ("culture," if you will) can either change or intensify preexisting patterns of development.

The 6 to 12 year period is also critical from a more internal standpoint, because social-emotional aspects of personality evolve to the point of intermingling with one another in a unitary fashion. One might look at this matter according to a botanical analogy: morality, sex-identity, achievement grow out of different roots, but by the end of middle childhood their branches are laced together forming a "whole" self or ego. Personality at 6 is still diverse and fragmentary; still spread out over a variety of distinctive, often contradictory characteristics. By 12 it is rather well tied together.

The unifying thrust of middle childhood development is not only important because it is implicit to much of the empirical material, but also because it dominates the theoretical perspectives. Whether you examine Freud and find "ego defense mechanisms"; or the neo-Freudians and find "orienta-

---

[13]According to government statistics, accidental injuries are the major cause of death in five- to fourteen-year-olds.

tion in living" or "a sense of industry"; or Piaget and find "concrete mental operations"; or Harvey et al., and find "conceptual systems"; you can see that they are all somehow focusing their ideas on unifying trends in development.

Let us come full circle and note, finally, that theoretical views of middle childhood have a certain match to the everyday image of this period. If it lacks a dramatic focus for laymen, it also lacks one for the major theorists. Generally speaking, *early* childhood is the original site of such gutsy things as the Oedipus complex, malevolent transformation, decentering, and the sense of initiative. *Middle* childhood is only the site of extension and unification that goes on without the aid of any glamorous new theoretical formulations. And when the whole integrationist movement of middle childhood is over, then the newly smoothed over, neatly packed structure of personality — remember how nice it was to be twelve? — is ready to be submitted to the fires of adolescence.

References

Allport, G. W. *Pattern and growth in personality.* New York: Holt, Rinehart & Winston, 1961.

Anderson, H. H., & Brewer, J. E. Studies of teachers' classroom personalities. II. Effects of teachers' dominative and integrative contacts on children's classroom behavior. *Applied Psychology Monograph,* 1946, #8.

Baldwin, A. L. *Theories of child development.* New York: John Wiley & Sons, Inc., 1968.

Bandura, A. Social learning through imitation. In M. Jones (Ed.), *Nebraska Symposium on Motivation.* Lincoln: University of Nebraska Press, 1962.

Bandura, A., & Walters, R. H. *Adolescent aggression — A study of the influence of child-training practices and family interrelationships.* New York: The Ronald Press Company, 1959.

Barker, R. G., & Gump, P. V. *Big school, small school.* Stanford, Calif.: Stanford University Press, 1964.

Battle, H. Relation between personal values and scholastic achievements. *Journal of Experimental Education,* 1957, *26,* 27–41.

Becker, W. C., Peterson, D. R., Hallmer, L. A., Shoemaker, D. J., & Quay, H. C. Factors in parental behavior and personality as related to problem behavior in children. *Journal of Consulting Psychology,* 1959, *23,* 107–118.

Berenda, R. W. *The influence of the group on the judgments of children.* New York: Kings Crown Press, 1950.

Berkowitz, L. Impulse, aggression and the gun. *Psychology Today,* September 1968, 19–22.

Berkowitz, L. *Control of aggression.* Mimeographed paper discussed in lectures at Kansas State University, Spring, 1969.

Bettelheim, B. *Love is not enough.* Glencoe, Ill.: The Free Press, 1950.

Blum, G. *Psychoanalytic theories of personality.* New York: McGraw-Hill Book Company, 1953.

Bonney, M. E. The constancy of sociometric scores and their relationship to teacher judgments of social success and to personality self-ratings. *Sociometry,* 1943, *6,* 409–424.

Bronfenbrenner, U. Soviet methods of character education: Some implications for research. *American Psychologist*, 1962, *17*, 550–564.

Brown, R. *Social psychology*. New York: The Free Press, 1965.

Bruner, J. *Toward a theory of instruction*. Cambridge: Harvard University Press, 1966.

Burton, R. V. Generality of honesty reconsidered. *Psychological Review*, 1963, *70*, 481–499.

Carter, R. S. How invalid are marks assigned by teachers? *Journal of Educational Psychology*, 1952, *43*, 218–228.

Child, I. L., Potter, E. H., & Levine, E. M. Children's textbooks and personality development: An exploration in the social psychology of education. *Psychological Monographs*, 1946, *60*, #3.

Clark, K. B., & Clark, M. P. Racial identification and preference in Negro children. In H. Proshansky and B. Seidenberg (Eds.), *Basic studies in social psychology*. New York: Holt, Rinehart & Winston, 1965, pp. 308–317.

Clausen, J. A. Perspectives on childhood socialization. In J. Clausen (Ed.), *Socialization and society*. Boston: Little, Brown and Company, 1968, pp. 130–181.

Clifford, E. Discipline in the home: A controlled observational study of parental practices. *Journal of Genetic Psychology*, 1959, *95*, 45–82.

Cohen, A. K. *Delinquent boys*. New York: The Free Press, 1955.

Cox, F. N. Sociometric status and individual adjustment before and after play therapy. *Journal of Abnormal and Social Psychology*, 1953, *48*, 354–356.

Crandall, V., Dewey, R., Katkovsky, W., & Preston, A. Parents' attitudes and behaviors and grade-school children's academic achievements. *Journal of Genetic Psychology*, 1964, *104*, 53–66.

Cronbach, L. J. *Educational psychology*. New York: Harcourt Brace Jovanovich, Inc., 1963.

Davidson, H., & Lang, G. Children's perceptions of their teachers' feelings toward them related to self-perception, school achievement, and behavior. *Journal of Experimental Education,* 1960, *29*, 107–118.

Davitz, J. R. The effects of previous training on post-frustration behavior. *Journal of Abnormal and Social Psychology*, 1952, *47*, 309–315.

Davitz, J. R. Social perception and sociometric choice in children. *Journal of Abnormal and Social Psychology*, 1955, *50*, 173–176.

Dimitrovsky, L. The ability to identify the emotional meaning of vocal expressions at successive age levels. In J. Davitz (Ed.), *The communication of emotional meaning*. New York: McGraw-Hill Book Company, 1964, pp. 69–86.

Dolger, L., & Grinandes, J. Children's attitudes towards discipline as related to socioeconomic status. *Journal of Experimental Education*, 1946, *15*, 161–165.

Dollard, J., & Miller, N. E. *Personality and psychotherapy*. New York: McGraw-Hill Book Company, 1950.

Ellison, H. *Memos from purgatory*. Resada, Calif.: Powell Publications, Inc., 1969.

Erikson, E. H. *Childhood and society*. (2nd ed.) New York: W. W. Norton & Company, Inc., 1950, 1963.

Eron, L. D. Relationship of TV viewing habits and aggressive behavior in children. *Journal of Abnormal and Social Psychology,* 1963, *67,* 193–196.

Evans, J. *Three men*. New York: Vintage Books, Random House, Inc., 1966.

Flavell, J. H. *The developmental psychology of Jean Piaget*. New York: D. Van Nostrand & Co., Inc., 1963.

Freud, A. with Dann, S. An experiment in group upbringing. *Psychoanalytic Study of the Child,* 1951, *6,* 127–168.

Gesell, A., & Ilg, F. *The child from five to ten.* New York: Harper & Bros., 1946.

Gnagey, W. J. Effects on classmates of a deviant student's power and response to a teacher-exerted control technique. *Journal of Educational Psychology,* 1960, *51,* 1–8.

Gordon, E. W., & Wilkerson, D. A. *Compensatory education for the disadvantaged. Programs and practices: Preschool through college.* New York: College Entrance Examination Board, 1966.

Goslin, D. A. Accuracy of self perception and social acceptance. *Sociometry,* 1962, *25,* 283–296.

Greenwald, H. J., & Oppenheim, D. B. Reported magnitude of self-misidentification among Negro children—artifact? *Journal of Personality and Social Psychology,* 1968, *8,* 49–52.

Grinder, R., & McMichael, R. Cultural influence on conscience development: Resistance to temptation and guilt among Samoans and American Caucasians. *Journal of Abnormal and Social Psychology,* 1963, *66,* 503–507.

Harari, H., & McDavid, J. W. Situational influence on moral justice: A study of "finking." *Journal of Personality and Social Psychology,* 1969, *11,* 240–244.

Hartley, E. L., Rosenbaum, M., & Schwartz, S. Children's perception of ethnic group membership. *Journal of Psychology,* 1948, *26,* 387–398.

Hartshorne, H., & May, M. A. *Studies in the nature of character.* Three volumes. New York: Macmillan Publishing Co., 1928, 1929, 1930.

Harvey, O. J., Hunt, D. E., & Schroder, H. M. *Conceptual systems and personality organization.* New York: John Wiley & Sons, Inc., 1961.

Harvey, O. J., Prather, M., White, B. J., & Hoffmeister, J. K. Teachers' beliefs, classroom atmosphere and student behavior. *American Educational Research Journal,* March 1968.

Havighurst, R., & Taba, H. *Adolescent character and personality.* New York: John Wiley & Sons, Inc., 1949.

Himmelweite, H. T., Oppenheim, A. N., & Vance, P. *Television and the child: An empirical study of the effect of television on the young.* New York: Oxford University Press, 1958.

Hoehn, A. J. A study of social class differentiation in the classroom behavior of nineteen third grade teachers. *Journal of Social Psychology,* 1954, *39,* 269–292.

Hunter, E. C. Changes in teachers' attitudes toward children's behavior over the last thirty years. *Mental Hygiene,* 1957, *41,* 3–11.

Inhelder, B., & Piaget, J. *The growth of logical thinking from childhood to adolescence.* New York: Basic Books, Inc., Publishers, 1958.

Inhelder, B., & Piaget, J. *Early growth of logic in the child: Classification and seriation.* New York: Harper & Row, Publishers, 1964.

Jackson, L. A. Emotional attitudes toward the family of normal, neurotic and delinquent children. *British Journal of Psychology,* 1950, *41,* Part I, 35–51; Part II, 173–185.

Jenkins, R. L., & Glickman, Sylvia. Common syndromes in child psychiatry: 1. Deviant behavior traits. *American Journal of Orthopsychiatry,* 1946, *16,* 244–254.

Jersild, A. T. *In search of self.* Bureau of publications, Teachers College, Columbia University, 1952.

Jersild, A. T. *Child psychology*. Englewood Cliffs, N.J.: Prentice-Hall, Inc., 1954.

Johnson, R. C., & Medinnus, G. R. *Child psychology*. New York: John Wiley & Sons, Inc., 1969.

Kadushin, A. Reversibility of trauma: A follow-up study of children adopted when older. *Social Work*, 1967, *12*(4), 22–33.

Kagan, J. Socialization of aggression and the perception of parents in fantasy. *Child Development*, 1958, *29*, 311–320.

Kagan, J., & Moss, H. A. *Birth to maturity*. New York: John Wiley & Sons, Inc., 1962.

Kardiner, A. *The psychological frontiers of society*. New York: Columbia University Press, 1945.

Kelly, G. A. Man's construction of his alternatives. In G. Lindzey (Ed.), *Assessment of human motives*, New York: Rinehart & Company, Inc., 1958, pp. 33–64.

Kohlberg, L. The development of children's orientations toward a moral order: I. Sequence in the development of moral thought. *Vita Humana*, 1963, *6*, 11–33. II. Social experience, social conduct, and the development of moral thought. *Vita Humana*, 1964, Vol. 7.

Kraus, P. E. A longitudinal study of children. Mimeographed paper, New York Board of Education, 1956.

Lewin, K., Lippitt, R., & White, R. K. Patterns of aggressive behavior in experimentally created "social climates." *Journal of Social Psychology*, 1939, *10*, 271–299.

Lewis, O. *The children of Sanchez*. New York: Random House, Inc., 1961.

Linton, R. *The cultural background of personality*. New York: Appleton-Century-Crofts, 1945.

Loew, C. A. Acquisition of a hostile attitude and its relationship to aggressive behavior. *Journal of Personality and Social Psychology*, 1967, *5*, 335–341.

Lovaas, O. I. Interaction between verbal and nonverbal behavior. *Child Development*, 1961, *32*, 329–336.

Madison, P. *Personality development in college*. Reading, Mass.: Addison-Wesley Publishing Co., Inc., 1969.

McConnell, T. R. Suggestibility in children as a function of CA. *Journal of Abnormal and Social Psychology*, 1963, *67*, 286–289.

McDavid, J. Some relationships between social reinforcement and scholastic achievement. *Journal of Consulting Psychology*, 1959, *23*, 151–154.

McDavid, J., & Harari, H. Stereotyping of names and popularity in grade school children. *Child Development*, 1966, *37*, 453–460.

McGhee, P. E., & Crandall, Virginia. Beliefs in internal-external control of reinforcements and academic performance. *Child Development*, 1968, *39*, 91–102.

Meyer, W. J., & Thompson, G. G. Sex differences in the distribution of teacher approval and disapproval among sixth grade children. *Journal of Educational Psychology*, 1956, *47*, 385–396.

Mussen, P. H., Conger, J. J., & Kagan, J. *Child development and personality*. New York: Harper & Row, Publishers, 1963.

Neill, A. S. *Summerhill*. New York: Hart Publishing Co., Inc., 1960.

Opie, I., & Opie, P. *The lore and language of school children*. London: Clarendon Press, Oxford University Press, 1959.

Pettigrew, T. F. Race and equal educational opportunity. *Harvard Educational Review*, 1968, *38*, 66–76.

Phillips, E. L., Shenker, S., & Revitz, P. The assimilation of the new child into the group. *Psychiatry,* 1951, *14,* 319–325.

Piaget, J. *The moral judgment of the child.* New York: Collier Books, The Macmillan Company, 1962.

Pittel, S. M., & Mendelsohn, G. A. Measurement of moral values: A review and critique. *Psychological Bulletin,* 1966, *66,* 22–35.

Radke, M. J., Trager, H. G., & Davis, H. Social perceptions and attitudes of children. *Genetic Psychology Monograph,* 1949, *40,* 327–447.

Rebelsky, F. G., Allinsmith, W., & Grinder, R. E. Resistance to temptation and sex differences in children's use of fantasy confession. *Child Development,* 1963, *34,* 955–962.

Reiss, A. J. Social organization and socialization: Variations on a theme about genera- tions. Mimeographed paper, Center for Research on Social Organization, Uni- versity of Michigan, Ann Arbor, 1965.

Roberts, J. (Ed.) *School children in the urban slum: Readings in social science re- search.* New York: The Free Press, 1967.

Rosenthal, R., & Jacobson, L. Teacher expectations for the disadvantaged. *Scientific American,* 1968, *218*(4), 19–23.

Sarnoff, I. *Personality dynamics and development.* New York: John Wiley & Sons, Inc., 1962.

Schramm, W. A., Lyle, J., & Parker, E. B. *Television in the lives of our children.* Stanford: Stanford University Press, 1961.

Sears, P. Levels of aspiration in academically successful and unsuccessful children. *Journal of Abnormal and Social Psychology,* 1940, *35,* 498–536.

Sherif, M., Harvey, O. J., White, B. J., Hood, D. R., & Sherif, C. W. Inter-group conflict and cooperation: The robbers' cave experiment. Norman, Okla.: University of Okla- homa Press, 1961.

Smith, M. B. Socialization for competence. *Social Science Research Council: Items,* 1965, *19,* 17–25.

Smith, Mildred B., & Brahce, C. I. When school and home focus on achievement. *Edu- cational Leadership,* 1963, *20,* 314–318.

Spence, L. J. *Myth and ritual in dance game and rhyme.* London: Watts Publishing Co., 1947.

Spiegler, C. G. Give him a book that hits him where he lives. In S. Webster (Ed.), *Edu- cating the disadvantaged learner* (Part III of *The disadvantaged learner*), 1966, pp. 524–532.

Staines, J. W. The self picture as a factor in the classroom. *British Journal of Educa- tion,* 1958, *28,* 97–111.

Stendler, C. B., Damrin, D., & Haines, A. C. Studies in cooperation and competition. I. The effects of working for group and individual rewards on the social climate of children's groups. *Journal of Genetic Psychology,* 1951, *79,* 173–197.

Stendler, C. B., & Young, N. Impact of first grade entrance upon the socialization of the child: Changes after eight months of school. *Child Development,* 1951, *22,* 113– 122.

Sullivan, H. S. *The interpersonal theory of psychiatry.* New York: W. W. Norton & Com- pany, Inc., 1953.

Thorndyke, E. L. Words and the comics. *Journal of Experimental Education,* 1941, *17,* 110–113.

Tuddenham, R. D. Studies in reputation: I. Sex and grade differences in school children's evaluation of their peers. II. The diagnoses of social adjustment. *Psychological Monographs*, 1952, *66*, #333.

Turiel, E. An experimental test of the sequentiality of developmental stages in the child's moral judgments. *Journal of Personality and Social Psychology*, 1966, *3*, 611–618.

Webster, S. W. *The disadvantaged learner*, Parts I, II and III. San Francisco: Chandler Publishing Co., 1966.

Wright, H. F. *Recording and analyzing child behavior.* New York: Harper & Row, Publishers, 1967.

8

Adolescence (13 to 17 years)

If you ever need an opening line to introduce the subject of adolescence, try this: "A funny thing happened to me on my way to becoming a person." (It works best with the parents of teen-agers.) The line has some validity because when you look at this developmental period it *is* funny—both peculiar and amusing. What, for instance, could be more peculiar or ghastly-amusing than suddenly to find your body being modified right out from under you? Between thirteen and fifteen a normal boy may grow 6 inches taller and 30 pounds heavier! Girls show a lesser but equally impressive growth spurt between eleven and thirteen (see Tanner, 1955). And that's just for openers. Hair begins arriving all over the place. Boys experience wet dreams ("nocturnal emissions") and girls begin menstruation. The physical changes alone are sufficient to make adolescence a rough period, but when the usual social-emotional stresses are also thrown in, it is a wonder that any of us survives to tell the tale.

Actually, in an emotional sense, most of us don't. Psychotherapists speak of an emotional amnesia in adults who are trying to recall their adolescence. They can remember the events of this period, but not the emotional intensity.

When we work therapeutically with adults we generally have no trouble in obtaining a plausible account of the events of adolescence. After some while, however, it becomes clear that the account is affectively false. The patient may remember easily enough that he had been stirred and disrupted by feeling in adolescence; but usually he will go no further. So he may adopt a lordly, amused, indulgent attitude toward the emotional storms of that time, gently mocking his "puppy love," his outraged sense of injustice, the secrecies and intimacies of close friendship—but unwilling to take them seriously, to re-enter adolescence psychically. It was too passionate a period: hot, angry, sentimental, lustful, guilt-ridden, sullen, anxious, bitter, elated, tormented. The adult, living in a relatively mellifluous, homogenized affect world, seems to tell us, in his emotional quietude, that he has had it, thank you, and will have no more of it (Douvan and Adelson, 1966, p. 3).

Relevant material was also reported by Jersild (1963). He asked a number of adults whether they would act differently if they could relive their adolescence, and all of them said yes. However, when asked whether they would *like* to relive the period knowing what they now know, all of them said no. From such evidence, it might be argued that adults view the teen-age period as something like a disease; you don't really adjust to it, you just try to get over it as soon as possible.

Signs of this condition are quite distinct right at the boundary between childhood and adolescence. Authorities on development describe sharp contrasts in the behavior of typical twelve- and thirteen-year-olds. The former seem full of enthusiasm, vigor, zest for life; the latter appear withdrawn and pensive.

Typical Twelve is blithe. Thirteen is reflective. This climatic difference came into contrast in the developmental interview. Like Twelve, Thirteen was usually co-operative, but not as spontaneously outgoing or as inquisitive. There was less conversation, less humor; his voice was low and sometimes he responded merely by a shrug. . . . Hesitancy seemed to be due to a self-protective guardedness and searching for the right words and phrase; for Thirteen in comparison with Twelve is a precisionist — a critic of his own performance as well as that of others (Gesell, Ilg, and Ames, 1956, p. 141).

The criticism mentioned here is also applied to the family, and commonly leads to some form of the "stolen child" fantasy. For various reasons which will presently be discussed, adolescents are likely to ask themselves "How can a sensitive flower like me have grown on such a dung heap?" And since the event seems impossible, they may conjure up explanatory fantasies: "I was stolen from my true parents by Gypsies" or, "I was given to the wrong family in the maternity hospital." In this connection, many American parents are unwitting accomplices to their own rejection. Having raised their children in the traditional spirit ("You can do better than your daddy"), it is only logical for their adolescents to conclude that Dad must be a clod or he would have done better himself. However, it is fair to add that stolen-child fantasies can also appeal at times to the bewildered parents of adolescents.

The nickname phenomenon is also relevant. Up through adolescence most children take their names for granted. But with the new self-awareness of this period, they may resent the name imposed by their parents and try out a new one.

Yet all these things — the physiological mess, the social-emotional ferment extending into fantasies and name rejections — are part of the conventional image of adolescence. It comes as more of a surprise to discover that this period is unique in having a special history of its own. That is, philosophers and scientists have been specifically concerned with adolescence ever since Aristotle and Plato discussed the physical and social significance of puberty. In a brief review, Horrocks (1962, pp. 20–24) described various approaches to adolescence ranging from the speculation of the ancient Greeks to the work of G. Stanley Hall, one of the founding fathers of American psychology. At the turn of the century, Hall did extensive questionnaire research with teen-agers, and published a two-volume textbook on adolescence. He took a relatively positive view of the period, describing it as a point of rebirth for the individual, because the "higher and more completely human" characteristics are acquired at this time.

Another surprising aspect of adolescence is that its onset seems to be changing over historical time. According to data reviewed by Tanner (1955), physiological puberty[1] occurred as much as 3 years earlier in 1950 as it did in 1850. Moreover, at any given age, children are generally heavier and taller today than they were a century ago. Such historical changes in maturation are all apparently due to better nutrition. It is known, for example, that a high-protein diet leads to earlier maturation than a high-carbohydrate diet. This diet factor also explains some current data: middle- and upper-class American children tend to start puberty about 6 months sooner than lower-class children. (Which is a finding that offers yet another slant on the meaning of poverty and social class differences.)

Quite simply, the earlier onset of puberty means that adolescents are ready for sex sooner than they used to be. Since Tanner indicated an average 3 to 6 month reduction in the age of puberty occurring every 10 years between 1850 and 1950, it is plausible to consider that children today can be sexually mature almost a year sooner than their parents were. And various studies indicate that this physiological shift is reflected in social behavior. Hetzer (1959) found that 10- to 14-year-olds were mentioning opposite-sex peer relationships 3 years sooner than children of the same age in the 1920's. Furthermore, girls have their first dates sooner (Smith, 1952); boys and girls talk of dating earlier (Jones, 1960), and take more of an interest in such topics as love and marriage (Harris, 1959). In short, all of us over 30 have a genuine basis for being surprised at the precocious sex interests of adolescents, because things really *are* changing.

Finally, as one goes through material on this period, and searches his own admittedly faulty memory, it often seems to be a step down instead of a step up. In other words, the twelve-year-old who stands more or less as the monarch of all he surveys in terms of childhood, is, with the coming of puberty, rather suddenly confronted with a new mass of confusion. Any wonder that Peter Pan is a perennial favorite? As one who refuses to move beyond the world of childhood, Peter Pan represents a certain kind of reality for all of us: the wistful remains of a freer life unencumbered by the internal drives, external responsibilities, and mixed insecurities of adolescence and maturity. At twelve one can take life as it comes, living from one excitement to the next, according to something like an idyllic existential model. But as one moves beyond this point things are not at all what they once seemed to be, and one begins again with a meager social status and a grand sense of psychological vulnerability.[2]

CRITICAL FACTORS IN ADOLESCENCE

When the adult world starts closing in during the age period 13 to 17 years, it does so in connection with five related problems: sex, personal identity, family discord, physical growth, and cognitive growth. These problems make a

---

[1]See Hurlock (1967, pp. 33–75) for a good review of material on the "changed body" of the adolescent. Garrison (1968) provided a more physiologically detailed discussion of the changes.

[2]It is noteworthy that writing on a more abstract plane, G. Stanley Hall expressed a somewhat similar viewpoint:

"At dawning adolescence this old unity and harmony with nature is broken up; the child is driven from his paradise and must enter upon a long viaticum of ascent, must conquer a higher kingdom of man for himself, break out a new sphere, and evolve a more modern story to his psychophysical nature" (1904, 2, p. 71).

gauntlet of the path to maturity, and the stress they engender can be sufficient to expose any flaw in prior personality development. It is one of the
higher ironies of development that just when an individual must draw heavily
upon his psychological capital to meet new challenges, he may find that
some of his currency is counterfeit. His parents may not be as wise as he
thought, his religion may not be as perfect as he thought, and he himself
may seem much less attractive.

However, despite the stress endemic to adolescence, there is continued
growth and development. The difficulty for the observer is to do justice to
both the extraordinary strains and accomplishments that characterize this
period. Traditionally, theoretical writers have gone ahead by concentrating
on one or another of the abstract features of adolescence. Beller (1968) surveyed upward of a dozen different theoretical approaches to adolescence,
which fall into five general categories — biological, psychological, sociological, psychoanalytic, and anthropological.

Five keeps turning up as a magic number, as we can see in the more concrete descriptive works on adolescence. Horrocks (p. 25) suggested five "points
of reference" for the period. He describes it as a time (a) "of seeking status as
an individual," (b) "when group relationships become of major importance,"
(c) "of physical development and growth," (d) "of intellectual expansion and
development," and (e) "of development and of evaluation of values."

Jersild (1963, pp. 5–9) listed five basically similar generalizations as the
"goals of adolescent development." He first noted physical, mental, and emotional maturity, and then added "finding the self" and "emancipation from
parents." Mussen, Conger, and Kagan (1963, p. 531) also listed five "problem
areas" which include physical maturation, sex, family relations, vocational
choices involving values and morality, and ego identity.

Altogether, the literature on adolescence indicates that the critical factors defining this period relate to certain problems experienced by most of us
passing through it. These problems are formulated in different ways by different writers, but tend to converge on five general categories: *physiological
change, family relations, relations with the same and opposite sex peers,
cognitive or intellectual growth, and personal identity.*

It should also be clear that the teen-ager's efforts to deal with these problems will be influenced by two critical conditions: his uniquely difficult *social
position,* and the unique *physical changes* known as puberty. In short, when
one looks at this period from the standpoint of the individual, it is definable
according to the five generic problems he faces. And when one looks at it as a
general situation it is definable according to social status and physical
growth factors.

Therefore, to deal effectively with personality development during this
period, the balance of this chapter is organized in three parts. The first concerns critical conditions. Because physical growth and sociocultural status
together set the limits on adolescence — they determine the existential state
of being for the thirteen- to seventeen-year-old — some discussion of the broad
psychological meaning of these conditions is necessary.

Second, the five general problems of adolescence are each discussed.
Here we deviate sharply from the organization of prior chapters by discuss-

ing such influential factors as family, peers, and school in the context of specific problems. Furthermore, the breakdown of personality into social-emotional components is no longer followed, except insofar as certain problems suggest that specific discussions are necessary. In general, a greater fidelity to common experience with no important loss of analytical rigor can be obtained by treating all the social-emotional aspects of personality as integral elements of the adolescent self-concept.

The final section of this chapter presents major theoretical perspectives on adolescence.

CRITICAL CONDITIONS

Physiological changes

Puberty vs. adolescence

One of the basic points stressed by authorities on this period is the distinction that must be made between the physical and social-psychological aspects of adolescence. Puberty is the term reserved for the physical aspect. It is derived from the Latin *pubertas* ("age of manhood") and refers to development of primary and secondary sex characteristics: glandular changes and changes in voice tone, body hair, and body build. We will not go into any detail on the physical changes because other sources for such material are readily available. But the psychological impact of puberty is something else.

Question: "How does the young teen-ager generally respond to changes in his body?" Answer: "Badly." At least that is the traditional answer. Plato mentioned passionate, ardent emotions in connection with puberty, noting that girls should be watched closely and that boys shouldn't be allowed to drink wine until they reach 18 years. G. S. Hall popularized the idea of a storm and stress (*sturm und drang*) behavioral reaction to puberty, because it apparently causes confused, alternating states of extreme emotion.

But these are academic generalities. The everyday truth is that puberty scares many youngsters: they are liable to become very anxious over such things as menstruation and penis erections and emissions. Even in a day of abundant sex education the unexpected qualities of such experiences invariably cause tension.

Horrocks mentioned examples in which girls deliberately slump or wear baggy clothing to conceal developing breasts. Boys may become equally self-conscious:

One boy in particular refused to recite before his class in the tenth grade to the extent of playing truant whenever he thought it likely that he would be called upon to recite. In a discussion with the school psychologist he said that he was easily aroused sexually and often experienced erection. He was in constant terror lest this fact be noted, particularly by members of the opposite sex (Horrocks, 1962, p. 317).

Very few accounts of the direct, social-emotional impact of puberty—the sense of being unusual or set apart from others as the body functions beyond accustomed limits and controls—rank with the following recollection by Mary McCarthy, who spent part of her youth growing up in a convent.

I had waked up one morning, in my convent room, to find a few small spots of blood on my sheet; I had somehow scratched a trifling cut on one of my legs and opened it during the night. I wondered what to do about this, for the nuns were fussy about bed-making, as they were about our white collars and cuffs, and if we had an inspection those spots might count against me. It was best, I decided, to ask the nun on dormitory duty, tall, stout Mother Slattery, for a clean bottom sheet, even though she might scold me for having scratched my leg in my sleep and order me to cut my toenails. You never know what you might be blamed for. But Mother Slattery, when she bustled in to look at the sheet, did not scold me at all; indeed, she hardly seemed to be listening as I explained to her about the cut. She told me to sit down: she would be back in a minute. "You can be excused from athletics today," she added, closing the door. As I waited, I considered this remark, which seemed to me strangely munificent, in view of the unimportance of the cut. In a moment, she returned, but without the sheet. Instead, she produced out of her big pocket a sort of cloth girdle and a peculiar flannel object which I first took to be a bandage, and I began to protest that I did not need or want a bandage; all I needed was a bottom sheet. "The sheet can wait," said Mother Slattery, succinctly, handing me two large safety pins. It was the pins that abruptly enlightened me; I saw Mother Slattery's mistake, even as she was instructing me as to how this flannel article, which I now understood to be a sanitary napkin, was to be put on.

This was only the beginning, however. One gains a sense of the impotence so frustrating to young people as Miss McCarthy described subsequent efforts to explain that her womanhood was all a mistake.

But the more excited I grew, the more soothing, and yet firm, Mother Slattery became. There seemed to be nothing for it but to give up and do as I was bid. I was in the grip of a higher authority, which almost had the power to persuade me that it was right and I was wrong. But of course I was not wrong; that would have been too good to be true. While Mother Slattery waited, just outside my door, I miserably donned the equipment she had given me, for there was no place to hide it, on account of drawer inspection. She led me down the hall to where there was a chute and explained how I was to dispose of the flannel thing, by dropping it down the chute into the laundry.

Then she had an interview with the Mother Superior, who also refused to listen.

Exactly like Mother Slattery, she attributed all my references to the cut to a blind fear of this new, unexpected reality that had supposedly entered my life. Many young girls, she reassured me, were frightened if they had not been prepared. "And you, Mary, have lost your dear mother, who could have made this easier for you." Rocked on Madame MacIllvra's lap, I felt paralysis overtake me and I lay, mutely listening, against her bosom, my face being tickled by her white, starched, fluted wimple, while she explained to me how babies were born, all of which I had heard before.

There was no use fighting the convent. I had to pretend to have become a woman, just as, not long before, I had had to pretend to get my faith back—for the sake of peace. This pretense was decidedly awkward. For fear of being found out by the lay sisters downstairs in the laundry (no doubt an imaginary contingency, but the convent was so very thorough), I reopened the cut on my leg, so as to draw a little blood to stain the napkins, which were issued me regularly, not only on this occasion, but every twenty-eight days thereafter. Eventually, I abandoned this bloodletting, for fear of lockjaw, and trusted to fate. Yet I was in awful dread of detection: my only hope, as

I saw it, was either to be released from the convent or to become a woman in reality, which might take a year at least, since I was only twelve (excerpts from pp. 123–126 in *Memories of a Catholic Girlhood*).

Puberty rites

Most of us do not have the extreme experiences of a Mary McCarthy, or those mentioned earlier, but we all usually manage our share of tension over the mysteries of puberty. In primitive societies, puberty is treated as a literal mystery with ceremonial rites that are explicit and severe. Some writers suggest that primitive ceremonies are really an advantage because they establish a definite change in status for the youngster. A quick, clean ritualistic affair is preferable to the long period of uncertainty imposed on youth in modern societies. Or is it? After examining the general nature of primitive rites of passage from childhood to adulthood, one may not be too keen.

The boy was tested for strength, physical endurance, courage, and ability to endure physical pain. He was tortured in many ways: he was usually isolated from other members of the tribe; he was forced to endure exposure, hunger, thirst, and extreme heat; he was circumcised; he was subjected to physical pain through body laceration, tattooing, knocking out of teeth, and other forms of body maltreatment; he also might be put through humiliating experiences in the presence of his age peers and his elders.

In many of the simple cultures a woman was regarded as "unclean" during her menstrual period. This attitude applied especially to a girl's first menses. At this time she usually was isolated from the other members of the group. It was the custom in some tribes to remove the girl from her family and to place her, for several weeks or a month, in a hut which was completely closed except for a small opening through which water and food were passed to her (Crow and Crow, 1965, pp. 20–21).

Early and late maturation

Studies show that puberty can begin as early as age 10, although the average age of first menses for girls and noticeable pubic hair for boys is between 13 and 14 years. The normal range runs between ages 10 and 15 years. Within this range there are great individual differences traceable to heredity: early maturing parents tend to have early maturing children. Thus, pubertal age differences can be understood as being similar to other constitutional differences involving body type, gland weight, and metabolism.

The psychological importance of individual differences in the onset of puberty comes from the heavy emphasis that adolescents place on physical appearances and capabilities. Douvan and Kaye (1957) found that the majority of a large sample of 11- to 18-year-old girls wanted to change something about their physical appearance. Jersild (1952) mentioned that physical characteristics headed the list of things that junior high school students said they disliked about themselves. And in line with such findings, Dwyer and Mayer (1968) reported that adolescents are quite ignorant of, and therefore more likely to be upset by, standard developmental changes involving obesity and skin eruptions.

Other research studies show that early maturing adolescents have distinct advantages over their later-maturing peers. Interviews, observations, questionnaires, and peer-rating data all indicate that early maturers are generally more stable, tend to fill leadership roles, and are accepted as more reliable by adults. Late maturers are generally described as irresponsible, childish, restless, concerned to get attention. Furthermore, analysis of projective story responses by adolescents (Mussen and Jones, 1957; 1958), showed that as compared with early maturers, late maturing boys are less independent, and feel more inadequate and rejected.

Briefly, all these and many other reports converge on the conclusion that early maturers have an easier time in adolescence. There seem to be two underlying reasons for the advantages enjoyed by this group. First, because they look more like adults, they are respected by their peers, and probably given more freedom by adults. Hence their psychological environment is conducive to self-confidence, pride, and ego strength. Second, because they get over the tensions caused by pubertal changes sooner than others, they are not so distracted by internal events. Altogether, the early maturer is ready to cope with the various problems of adolescence much sooner, and more effectively, than the late maturer. About the only positive thing to be said for late maturers is that they can continue to pay children's prices at the movies for a longer time, which is poor consolation.

George Kennan's *Memoirs* contain an eloquent passage relevant to the difficulties experienced by many late maturers. He apparently arrived to start college work at Princeton at the age of 16 or 17. The following description touches on some of the classical problems suffered by introverted, late maturing adolescents.

I was a year younger than most members of my class, and even more immature in manner than this tender age would suggest.

I could never find the casual tone. My behavior knew only two moods: awkward aloofness and bubbling enthusiasm. I was afflicted from the start, furthermore, by a quality that has pursued me all my life: namely, of being the slowest and last to learn the ropes in any complicated organizational structure. Too shy to ask, I never found out. I went through Princeton as an innocent, always at the end of every line, always uninitiated, knowing few, known by few. Personal failings — pride, oversensitivity, a sullen refusal to be comforted, and insistence on knowing and experiencing the worst in order to be the more deserving of sympathy, at least in my own eyes — added to the discomfort (p. 8).

Kennan's example is emphasized not only because it reflects an extreme late maturer condition, but also because to anyone who knows his distinguished career of public service, it shows that late maturation need not be a lifelong handicap. And though we cannot provide any detail on the subject, it ought to be clear that while early maturation is desirable in adolescence, it can also bring problems. Too much may be demanded of the youngster who looks physically capable. He may move into adult roles that trap him with fixed responsibilities, or he may peak-out too early. One knows enough people who in later life have never been able to equal their high school status as student leaders or athletic heroes.

Social position

The adolescent situation
In modern societies, the adolescent's social position is fairly clear and fairly unique: as compared with older and younger people, he hasn't got one. That is, he moves through the 13 to 17 year period in a kind of formal and informal social limbo, enjoying neither the rights and privileges of the child or of the adult. The child has the social right of having things done for him, and the adult the right of doing things for himself, but what of the adolescent? As Lewin (1939) noted some time ago, the adolescent is no longer a child and not an accepted adult, so he is suspended in a "marginal" situation—a limbo or no-man's-land.

This is not something that needs much documentation, because we can all dredge up some memories of it, and we can see it operating in our educational and legal institutions. The *in loco parentis* doctrine is still very much in force at many universities and in all public high schools. Adolescents can be forbidden to enter school if their hair or clothing style goes against certain adult norms, but if they *choose* not to attend, the law may come after them. And consider how many things are legally wrong for adolescents classified as minors. Apart from trivia—not being able to buy beer, cigarettes or tickets to certain films—since they cannot sign contracts they cannot own property, buy insurance or be married.

Many social commentators note that in view of such facts, to be an adolescent is, by definition, to be a member of an oppressed minority group. Indeed, parallels between the legal status of the nineteenth-century slave and the contemporary adolescent have been mentioned so frequently lately that they are becoming a cliché.

The adolescent's social situation is equally unattractive at the informal level. Behavior that doesn't rate a second glance if it occurs among children or adults is often treated as suspicious if it involves teen-agers. Let five children or adults sit talking in a public park and it is not remarkable; let five teen-agers do it and suspicion (in police or adult observers) may be immediate. And while adults' and children's clubs are generally seen as innocuous, teen-agers' clubs are always suspect. In short, it probably seems to many adolescents, and it is probably true, that in any ambiguous situation, they rarely receive the benefit of the doubt—adults tend automatically to assume the worst.

Psychological consequences of alienation and conformity
It is generally believed that the adolescent's inferior social position leads to a condition of alienation. Gaier summarized the alienation thesis after discussing problems faced by the average middle-class teen-ager.

Through all this, the adolescent sees himself as unloved, rejected, and misunderstood—one whose privacy is invaded at home, whose sense of dignity is violated at school, and whose behavior is assaulted by anyone over 25—at least if one can believe the writings of the academic Holy Trinity speaking for the American adolescent—Edgar Friedenberg, Paul Goodman, and David Riesman. The high school set feels exploited—especially where they may be made pawns in the solution of both political and social problems. The student feels compelled to exhaust himself in the pursuit of status for his parents and his school. If he fails to engage in this type of activity, he may find himself in a setting that makes it untenable for him to remain in school. As a consequence, the *school dropout* becomes the *school pushout* (1969, p. 90).

The alienation idea is easy to understand in principle, particularly if one exaggerates a bit, but it is fairly complex in practice because it can be expressed in different ways. Gould (1969) reviewed theoretical interpretations of alienation[3] which suggested that it involves both marginality (a sense of not belonging) and conformity. In a group-pressure experiment comparing 15 male college students categorized as strongly alienated, with 15 identified as slightly alienated, he found the strongly alienated to be significantly more conforming. He further described six characteristics as typical of the strongly alienated group: they distrust others, reject standard rules of social behavior, tend to be emotionally depressed, socially introverted, given to psychological and physical complaints, and they conform to the majority in ambiguous situations.

In one respect, this description seems inconsistent—why should those who reject conventional standards and distrust others conform to group pressure? The answer is not clear, but it is suggested that the marginal person may feel that there is no point in making an effort to resist the group. Gould also reported that 11 of his 15 strongly alienated students turned out to be firstborn children, while 14 of the 15 slightly alienated were later-borns. This surprising encounter with the birth-order phenomenon (recall the discussion in Chapter 5), led him to suggest a possible predisposition toward alienation depending upon childhood experience.

Conformity shows up in other studies as a general characteristic of adolescents. Friedenberg (1967) tested approximately 250 high-school students on a set of six hypothetical but realistic problems involving relations between students, teachers, and administrators. Their responses indicated a high degree of conformity, acquiescence to the school system, and little sensitivity to the rights of individuals. Costanzo and Shaw (1966) reported similar findings from a developmental group pressure experiment: conformity increases throughout early adolescence, and begins to decline toward the end of this period.

But if conformity is the general outcome of an inferior social position, where is the rebellion one hears so much of these days? Foster (1969) found that a sample of high-school students in Illinois were more radical than college students in Kansas—but such rebellion is not easy to see for at least three reasons. Adolescent rebellion can exist cheek-by-jowl with conformity; it tends to be selective; and it can follow either a traditional or new pattern.

Rebellion

First of all, it should be understood as a general proposition that rebellion can coexist with conformity. One may find a pattern of latent rebellion and overt conformity, as, for example, in the individual who goes along with au-

---

[3]In a widely accepted abstract discussion of alienation, Seeman (1959) suggested that it can be defined according to five criteria: powerlessness, meaninglessness, normlessness, isolation, and self-estrangement.

thority up to a point, and then, seemingly without warning, starts or falls in with extreme acts of rebellion. Coercive pressure typically yields this pattern. When the coercion either grows weak or becomes ineffective because of new developments, the rebellion is forthcoming. Illustrations of this pattern can be seen in racial, religious, and colonial situations where oppressed minorities "suddenly" rebel (see Fanon, 1963).

The two conditions of rebellion and conformity can also coexist in an alternating fashion: a struggle against authority may go on, and then be abandoned for a time, because an objective is attained, a compromise is reached, or exhaustion sets in. If for no other reason than the physical difficulty of maintaining a continuous state of rebellion, one can expect to see it alternating with conformity.

The selective nature of most rebellion is also relevant. Conformity may remain the norm even while rebellion goes on over specific issues. Remember the American colonists who were presumably only concerned with the issue of taxation without representation. In the midst of violent rebellion over this point, they continued to protest their general loyalty to the mother country. And so it is with adolescents. From a survey of 650 adolescents in Sweden, Pîkas (1961) concluded that they accepted "rational" parental authority – authority based on concern for the child's welfare – but they objected to "inhibiting" authority which involves domination or exploitation. A similar indication of selectivity appears in Gold's (1969) review of delinquency and alienation. He described acts of juvenile delinquency as quite specific, and explicitly rejected the idea that lawbreaking signifies a generalized state of rebellion or alienation.

It is also necessary to distinguish between the traditional and the new patterns of adolescent rebellion. Friedenberg provided a succinct statement of the problem:

Neither clashes with authority nor political protest is, as such, novel. But the major reason why there is so much interest in the question today is precisely because we rather generally sense that many young people now reject society in a new and much more fundamental way (1969, p. 21).

He goes on to explain traditional forms of rebellion as efforts to take over: young people who are impatient with the mistakes of their elders are presumably eager to take over and to show that they can do better. Erik Erikson analyzed Hitler's attraction to German youth according to this traditional model of rebellion. In the years after World War I, Germany suffered from social and economic problems which all seemed related to the humiliating Versailles Treaty, so young people had a good basis for feeling that their elders had failed. As a revolutionary, Hitler promised sweeping changes, making direct and indirect appeals to the young. Erikson showed how this was done by scrutinizing a chapter from Hitler's autobiography, *Mein Kampf* (My Struggle):

This chapter, I conclude, is both personal revelation and shrewd propaganda. It convinces German youth that no old man, be he father, emperor, or god need stand in the way of his love for Germany; it impresses on the grownup men that by having betrayed their rebellious adolescence they had become unworthy of leading Germany's youth, which henceforth would "shape its own destiny"; and it asks both fathers and sons to identify with the Führer: *an adolescent who never gave in.*

Psychologists overdo Hitler's father attributes. Hitler is the adolescent who never even aspired to become a father in any connotation, nor, for that matter, a kaiser, or a president. He does not repeat Napoleon's error. He is the Führer: *a glorified older brother*, who replaces the father, taking over all his prerogatives, without over-identifying with him: he calls his father "old while still a child" and reserves for himself the new position of the one who remains young in possession of supreme power. He is the unbroken adolescent who has chosen a career apart from civilian happiness and "peace"; a gang leader who keeps "the boys" together by demanding their admiration, by creating terror, and by shrewdly involving them in crimes from which there is no way back. And he is a ruthless exploiter of parental failures (Erikson, 1942, pp. 480–481).

Erikson's analysis is noteworthy because, even if one is not entirely convinced by his psychoanalytic interpretation, it does seem to get at the essence of traditional adolescent rebellion. Moreover, it is a striking bit of work in its own right: we can only stand in admiration of Erikson's ability to describe Hitler as a super-evil adolescent.

But the new model of adolescent rebellion is very different. Friedenberg noted that it involves wholesale rejection of adult values which have traditionally been definitive of organized society—it is not that today's adolescents want to take over playing the game, it is rather that they reject the game itself. Empirical research on this new rebellion is lacking, mainly because it is still so new. Friedenberg's discussion is speculative, based on general contacts with young people and impressions of current affairs. (He also offers an interesting guide to folk-rock music conveying the spirit of contemporary rebellion.)

A number of other social scientists who study development in childhood and adolescence have also been moved to comment on this phenomenon. Baumrind (1968) discussed the new rebellion in connection with her research on parental discipline. After mentioning some of the conventional difficulties for parents in this area, she suggested that the fundamental credibility of adult values is now being questioned.

The major challenge to authority today is not that the young have no respect for authority, but that they have little reason to have respect for authority. Both youth and their parents are disaffected with their social institutions—with their schools, churches and their government. The mythology of affluence has been exploded. The credibility gap on issues of poverty and war has made extension of trust unfeasible, and open rebellion morally feasible (Baumrind, pp. 267–268).

Another perspective is provided by Gaier (1969), who speculated on the "current imbroglio" concerning adolescence from a Freudian standpoint. He discussed the current generation gap as partly due to a reversal of traditional Freudian priorities: instead of placing id under control of ego, adolescents today are trying to enhance id-impulses—witness the music, dancing, and drugs.

And Carroll (1969) saw the new rebellion as a reaction against the frustration of human needs in modern societies. He identified adolescent rejection of adult values as part of a broad struggle between all those who believe human needs should be our supreme concern, and all those who would subordinate human needs to other considerations.

Social scientists are no more unanimous in prescribing "cures" for adolescent rebellion than is any other group of intellectuals. However, they generally agree that all such rebellion ultimately relates to the social situation of teen-agers; it is a situation of powerlessness, combined with strong needs that cannot be fulfilled legitimately. This fact is used in various ways throughout the literature on adolescence. Marwell (1966) elaborated upon it as an explanation for the behavior of action-oriented juvenile delinquents — they commit crimes to gain either symbolic or real power. For example, car theft is one of the most popular adolescent offenses because in modern societies a car is both a literal and symbolic token of power. It can be argued that high-powered cars (Road Runners, Chargers, Mach-1's) are especially popular among young people (and older people who want to feel young) for the same reason. Powerlessness is also interpreted as a cause for the passive forms of delinquency. Heavy drug use, for instance, is considered a means of withdrawing from reality when one feels powerless to change it.

Furthermore, traditional and new forms of adolescent rebellion are both susceptible to analysis in terms of power. The rationales may be different — in the former case, conventional power is to be seized, while in the latter case it is either to be destroyed or ignored — but the same essential causal element is present in both. Most social commentators, and virtually all social scientists, argue for some redistribution of power. While they may disagree about how much change is necessary, and how it is to be accomplished, they generally agree that certain obvious conditions require attention. Trivial though it may seem in comparison to other problems, consider the case of clothing and hair styles. The high-school youth knows there is no natural law ordaining appropriate school attire. And he knows that hair — in any quantity — has no relationship to learning or social conduct. Authorities must therefore try to enforce behavior norms based on values that cannot stand up to logical scrutiny. When such values are forced on adolescents, conformity may be attained, but only at the price of discrediting other, more defensible social values.

So it is that one writer after another argues for a change in the social position of youth. For the past 50 years, or since the advent of Freud, it has been widely recognized that *traditional* adolescent rebellion can be met on its own ground by parents (and social institutions) who remain receptive and honest in their behavior, and who are willing to consider some sharing of power. Baumrind expressed this view very clearly:

The adolescent needs a parent who has something to say that is worth listening to, and who is fully receptive to what he has to say. The adolescent needs to have someone to argue with in order to develop his own position. His parents can play this role of friendly adversary. The adolescent needs a strongly stated thesis to relate his own thinking to. A convincing antithesis requires a well-formulated thesis. The authoritative parent can state and defend her own thesis vigorously, and yet not limit the freedom of the adolescent to express and argue for his antithesis. The parent must not expect the resultant synthesis to be merely a restatement of her own thesis. By receiving the antithesis presented to her by her adolescent, the parent gains knowledge of that with which she is authorized to deal (Baumrind, 1968, pp. 268–269).

And her further remarks were relevant to newer forms of alienation and rebellion.

Receptivity does not mean listening in order to achieve conformity after talk. It does mean that an antithetical position which may threaten the stability of the system is encouraged to interact with that system. Only in that way can the system continue to perform its function. A system which cannot absorb dissent cannot survive. Revolutionary fervor is nourished by the refusal of constituted authority to receive antithesis, to be renewed by dissent. If constituted authority were as successful in absorbing dissent as Marcuse thinks it is, there would be no basis for the revolutionary fervor he advocates (p. 269).

Summary of puberty and social position

In declaring physical changes and social position to be the two major critical conditions of adolescence, we have shown how each operates to set the psychological tone of this period. The body changes associated with puberty inevitably create some degree of emotional tension or downright fear in young teen-agers. This can have fairly severe effects, particularly when the changes are not understood to be natural events of development.

In addition, the extreme value placed on physical appearances by young people makes them very sensitive to variations caused by individual differences in maturation. Early maturers are generally recognized as having the advantages of looking more grown-up, and getting beyond physically caused emotional turbulence, sooner than late maturers. They consequently tend to move through adolescence with greater self-assurance and a stronger ego.

The teen-ager's social position is basically ambiguous; lacking the security that goes with the status of a child or adult, he is also relatively powerless to influence his situation. The general results of this condition include conformity, alienation, and rebellion, which can apparently occur altogether, singly, or in alternation. Conformity and alienation have been studied sufficiently to say that the former is most prevalent during adolescence. It can be seen in responses to both experimental tasks and field surveys. Alienation is more complex, involving several criteria which form a general pattern of indifference and rejection—rejection of self and peers as well as impersonal society. The whole problem is further complicated by research showing that psychological alienation can lead to apathy or indifference, which may be difficult to distinguish from conformity.

Adolescent rebellion is complicated because it can take the traditional form of a struggle for power, or a new form involving rejection of values underlying adult power. And rebellion in either form can coexist in various ways with conformity. However, despite the absence of "hard" data, it is the opinion of most experts that growing dissatisfaction with adult society can be met by further opening society to the needs and values of youth, and by eliminating the more arbitrary restrictions placed upon them.

One might add that the physical and social facts of adolescence lead to a further argument in favor of reevaluating the situation of young people. If puberty generally arrives earlier as a result of better nutrition, then adolescents' social condition must necessarily grow more intolerable to each succeeding generation of youngsters. Being physically ready for adult status sooner than ever before (and perhaps intellectually too, as a result of better childrearing and primary educational practices), then they are even more likely to be discontented with an inferior social position. At a minimum, changes in the authoritarian structure of schools which impose empty standards, and thereby contaminate youngsters' impressions of society in the very place where they are supposed to be preparing to assume a functional role in it, seem past due.

CRITICAL PROBLEMS

Five areas of adolescent behavior were mentioned earlier as critical for personality development. Described by various writers as the "tasks of adolescence," or the "major problem areas," they include (a) physiological changes, (b) family relations, (c) same- and opposite-sex peer relations, (d) cognitive or intellectual growth, and (e) personal identity. Viewed separately, each of these problems stands as a distinct drama, having its own pace, rhythm, and rhetoric. But if their diversity is self-evident, even celebrated in plays and novels devoted to one or more of them, their unity is obscure. We all know from experience that there *is* unity in the diversity—that after a successful date, for example, a girl may worry less over her complexion, and a boy may be less worried about not being able to do 20 push-ups; but how can one get a theoretical grip on it?

Recall that the major social-emotional aspects of personality were sketched as separate components emerging during infancy and childhood. The *self-concept* seems initially to be just one of these distinct components. As he moves into middle childhood, the child's self-concept steadily expands and extends until, by the end of childhood, all of the social-emotional aspects of personality are more or less unified within a sense of self as object and executive. Thus, up through adolescence, development of the self-concept can be seen as a straightforward affair, involving gradual increases in self-awareness. One can think of the self as a growing structure which encloses and organizes more and more material.

In adolescence this structure becomes almost totally obsolete. In fact, the teen-ager has to renovate, remodel, and reorganize the whole form, because *the structure becomes irrelevant to the building materials, and the edifice itself no longer suits the surrounding terrain.* The self is initially built up in relation to the substance and terrain of childhood; it is just not adequate for adolescence.

Physically, the impact of puberty changes the raw substance of the self-concept. It is as if one had been building in wood and then found the trucks were delivering cement block. The adolescent has to rework prior conceptions of himself to keep pace with unexpected physical changes, so at this level, his prior self-concept is no longer adequate.

Furthermore, the social position of adolescents is such that a child's self-concept will not serve in this new context. Among all the uncertainties facing the adolescent, there is at least one hard fact: prior conceptions of himself no longer apply. He can no longer think of himself in the same moral, sexual, aggressive, and/or achievement terms as he did before. And he can no longer rely on the same kinds of social support that were satisfactory before—parents, peers, and teachers act differently toward fourteen-year-olds than they do toward twelve-year-olds. If an adolescent continues to act like an eleven- or twelve-year-old, that is, behaving in accord with the self-concept of a child, he will probably be rejected by peers, chastised by teachers, and pushed hard by his parents. One can actually see this occur on occasions when an adolescent is placed in a classroom a few years above or below his age level, or when he is moved to a new culture containing very different age behavior norms.

Beyond the physical and social conditions of adolescence, an additional factor likely to provoke changes in the self-concept involves the unfinished developmental business of childhood. Many authorities on personality development, especially Freudians, emphasize that certain fixations can occur during childhood. Apart from the classical oral and anal fixations which are supposed to occur if the young child does not receive adequate gratification of relevant needs, there are the problems which frequently show up in clinical case histories.

For example, the boy who was severely punished for playing with his penis at age five or six, may from that time forward have repressed his sexual feelings. But with the coming of mixed sex activities in adolescence, and puberty changes that include nocturnal emissions, the problem rises again (pun intended), and guilt over sex feelings must be resolved if development is to proceed normally. Similarly, many cases of sexual promiscuity in adolescent girls trace back to earlier childhood rivalries with their mothers, or unsatisfied desires for attention from their fathers. Relations with authority figures in adolescence can also provoke latent problems. If a child was unable to learn constructive means of expressing aggression toward his father, he may, as an adolescent, be burdened with excessive hostility toward all adult authorities. Case histories provide many illustrations along these lines. But the general point is that some of the psychologically bypassed problems of childhood recur as problems in the self-concepts of adolescents. And these problems generate additional force toward restructuring of the self.

In sum, the self-concept emerging in childhood must be radically altered during adolescence in response to new critical conditions and unfinished developmental business carried over from childhood. It will be altered again, for the same general reasons, in maturity and old age, but not in the same sweeping and definitive fashion. Let us now examine the major problems— the psychological battlefields of adolescence where we all become casualties while struggling to attain developmental objectives, and from which lovable children may emerge as scarred, hard-bitten, teen-age veterans.

1. Physical changes

The physical changes that come with puberty can be seen as both a critical condition of adolescence, and a critical problem challenging the adolescent. From the latter viewpoint, a few behavioral facts are clear at the outset: we know that young teen-agers are notoriously preoccupied with appearances. They will spend hours at the mirror seeking pimples, trying hair styles, looking backward through a hand mirror into a wall mirror to catch a glimpse of their backsides. This is all a part of adolescence and most of us can remember twisting our necks out of shape doing it.

We also know that careful reviews of their bodies leave most adolescents quite discouraged; scrutiny of hair, complexion, and anatomy usually only confirm the worst suspicions of inadequacy. And so there may follow bizarre but entirely normal efforts to change appearances. Everything from the latest patent medicines to GI laundry soap may be used on the complexion. Exercises from weight lifting to Yoga may be deployed on the body, not to mention all the miscellaneous technical devices: tooth whiteners, contact lenses, electro-vibrating machines, hair equipments, and the artificials—paddings, wigs, eyelashes—for those who entirely despair of nature.

Finally, we know that most if not all of the above activities are inspired by valued cultural models—movie stars, rock musicians, and those closer to home who seem to approximate such models.

Taken together, the four behaviors mentioned—scrutiny of appearance, dissatisfaction, efforts to change, and culturally determined standards of judgment—make up a sizable, important chunk of adolescent life. Why should this be the case? Perhaps an obvious reason is that the body changes so rapidly during adolescence that it literally needs to be watched if one is to keep up with all new developments. But a more abstract psychological reason seems to involve the body image component of the self-concept.

Since the body image emerges earliest, and is thus chronologically the most basic element in the self-concept, any serious change in the body seems to require change or reorganization in the self-concept as a whole. This proposition stands out very sharply in work with adults who undergo serious body changes. For example, after getting over the initial shock, and making a physical recovery, amputees and persons who have suffered severe burns are customarily given some form of psychotherapy oriented to the changed body image which tends to disrupt their self-concept. Literature on amputees shows that while the new functional limits placed on their behavior require great adjustments, the deeper psychological problem caused by loss of a limb involves personality: reorganization of the self-concept to fit a changed body.

Direct evidence of similar phenomena in adolescents can be found in biographies and case histories, but evidence also shows up indirectly in certain experimental studies. Powell (1955) identified psychological problems by showing persons words related to various areas of adjustment. Employing a standard word association procedure, he required subjects to respond with the first word that came to mind after they were presented with a stimulus word. The psychological meaning of this technique rests on the well-established assumption that the longer it takes for a person to respond, the more tension he feels about the stimulus word. (It is a simple procedure that any-one can demonstrate: give the words *white, day,* and *mother,* and most peo-ple will quickly respond with *black, night,* and *father.* But throw in *penis* or *vagina,* and the response time is usually much longer, presumably because these words arouse sexual tensions.)

In the physical appearance category, Powell included the words *hand-some, shabby, neat, beautiful,* and *ugly.* Results obtained with samples of persons ranging in age from 10 to 30, show that response times to these words are three to seven times longer for 14- to 17-year-old males than they are for 10- to 13-year-old males, or for those over 21. In other words, just at the time when puberty changes become apparent, emotional tension is drasti-cally increased. At 14 years, the average reaction time suddenly triples over what it is at 13 or 12 years. It continues to go up and reaches a high point at age 16, where it is seven times greater than the 13-year-old level. The data are similar for girls, and provide a nice internal validity check. Since their puberty starts a little earlier, one would expect to see girls' reaction times starting to lengthen earlier, and that is what happens. At 13 years, their re-sponses jump to three times what they are at age 12, or over age 21. And they also reach a high point at age 16, with response times being eight times greater than at 12 or over 21.

Another relevant study by Smith and Lebo (1956) involved 42 boys from 12 to 15 years of age who were examined by physicians and rated for physi-cal maturity according to pubic hair growth. The boys were then given a number of tests for social maturity, including the task of drawing male and female human figures. With regard to physical appearance, comparisons between the drawings of boys rated as pre- or postpubescent revealed a number of interesting differences. The postpubescent or more mature boys put much more hair on their male drawings; beards, mustaches, longer head hair. And in comparison to the prepubescent boys, they also made their drawings of males larger than females. This is explained as indicating great-er self-confidence and a sense of masculine superiority. A further result was that the *pre*pubescent boys included many masculine objects – cigars, pipes, cigarettes, scars – in their male drawings. Smith and Lebo interpreted this as a sign of their need to prove masculinity. Lacking it themselves, but wanting it, they emphasize what they see as the more extreme symbols of masculinity.

These studies support the common sense evidence of adolescent preoccu-pations with appearance, but they also suggest that puberty changes cause changes in the body-image which force changes in the self-concept. And while this dynamic process goes on, it is reflected emotionally by feelings of inadequacy. Such feelings of course extend into other areas besides the phys-ical. Many investigations (e.g., Engel, 1959; Berdie, 1968) showed that self-concepts generally become more positive at the end of adolescence. Other factors than the physical relate to this improvement, but it is certainly true that the improvement comes in as the physical impacts of puberty taper off.

There is no great research literature on the exact processes by which adolescents adapt to puberty changes. Some of the Freudian defense mecha-nisms probably operate here, particularly sublimation, repression, and ratio-nalization. And as the adolescent matures, he surely learns to examine cultural models more carefully. Idols that were once accepted as definitive of perfection are reevaluated.

In the final analysis, time is perhaps the most important factor operating in favor of the young adolescent. As he grows past 14 and 15 years of age, things generally get better, if only because they can't get worse. Strictly speaking, the 15- or 16-year-old holds an advanced position over the 13- or 14-year-old: he is in a higher grade, he knows and is known by more peers and adults, and he is liable to have found some ego-supporting social roles (in a club, band, school newspaper). So once the initial impacts of puberty changes are endured, various social psychological processes allow the changes to be incorporated into a reorganized self-concept.

2. Family Relations

Independence

As one traces a path through the foggy, soft terrain of adolescence, the hard, high ground – firm islands of psychological knowledge – stand out and come as a welcome relief. The adolescent's effort to achieve independence from his parents has this quality; it is dead certain that he must emancipate himself. Just how far the independence movement will go is something else, but common experience and everything in the research literature indicates that it must go forward to some important extent if serious neurotic problems are to be avoided.

Douvan and Adelson describe the effort toward independence as the keystone of adolescent family relations, and give this phenomenon the status of a traditional, mythical model for adolescent behavior.

In folklore and in heroic fiction, we find the recurring pattern – the adolescent hero, having received some sign, an inner stirring or an outer call, gets ready to leave the family. The paths to departure vary. Some must struggle to leave, others must flee for their lives; some leave vindictively, full of hate, thrashing the father or mother, while others are themselves beaten or betrayed before they leave; some leave in high expectation, carrying the family's hope for fortune or redemption, and others leave at dead of night, in disgrace, bearing the family's curse. The hero's journey begins with an ending – the breaking of the connection to home (1966, p. 119).

In the same vein, but following a different tack, Jersild (1963) suggested that family relations take the form of a three-act drama. The adolescent is at first dependent on his parents, but is beginning to see them as ordinary human beings. The "Struggle for Emancipation" comes as a second act, when adolescents outgrow dependence on parents and transfer their major loyalties to prospective mates. In the third act, the struggle is supposed to die out as the former adolescent finds an adult role, and parents become peers – respected or not, as the case may be.

Such generalizations about the thrust toward independence are supported by much empirical evidence. Douvan and Adelson, for example, reported specific findings gathered from interviews with a sample of about 2000 adolescent girls. Speaking of their adult ideal, 43 percent of those under 14 years mention their father or mother. Only 31 percent of 17- to 18-year-olds mention one of their parents. Among those under 14, 18 percent say they disagree with some of their parents' ideas, but 41 percent of the 17 to 18's mention some disagreement. And while a majority of those under 14 say they would stay at home to keep a lonely mother company, the majority of 17- to 18-year-olds say they would not.

Similar material is available on boys: 31 percent choose their fathers as ideal models at 14 years of age; only 18 percent do so at 16 years. Other reports show that there is a steady drop in the number of adolescents who prefer discussing their problems with parents rather than friends.

Sources of adolescent-parent conflict

Once the push toward independence is stipulated, two questions immediately arise: why do most teen-agers feel so strongly about gaining independence, and why do most parents resist granting it? In relation to the first, Mussen, Conger, and Kagan (1963) said that the ultimate sources of the adolescent drive for freedom are culture and individual identification processes.

Cultural institutions and traditions in most Western societies place great emphasis on being independent, standing on your own feet, or making your own way. It is the essence of the Protestant Ethic, and the legacy of the French Revolution, and one might note again Douvan and Adelson's remarks on folklore. So the adolescent who absorbs these values is naturally anxious to start operating in accord with them. Moreover, if he does not show such a desire, the adolescent will be pressured by parents and teachers, particularly in the United States. Horatio Alger is a standard name in the American vocabulary. Very few of us raised here have not been told by our parents that when *they* were 13 or 15 years old or whatever, they had already earned or accomplished this, that, or the other. Nor are such lectures prevented by the fact that they may be totally inconsistent with current social conditions.

Identification also functions to enhance the push toward independence. The adolescent who admires and seeks to imitate some valued adult figure will typically see that adult's autonomy, his freedom of choice, as a prerequisite to successful imitation.

In addition to these two explanations a third might be suggested involving the adolescent's inclination to try out his own increasing powers. That is, one of the constant factors appearing through all stages of development seems to involve something like the competence drive—the desire to use or test new capacities as they are acquired. Since teen-agers feel a greater capacity for independent thought and action than they ever had before, it seems natural for them to want to use it.

The second general question—why most parents resist or try to curtail independence in their adolescents, Horatio Alger and the Protestant Ethic notwithstanding—demands a more complex answer. On various earlier occasions the "lag phenomenon" in parental behavior was discussed; the tendency for parents' perceptions generally to lag behind their children's capacities. Parents are thus frequently in the position of reacting to today's problem according to yesterday's diagnosis, and trying to treat it with yesterday's medicine.

The lag seems particularly difficult during adolescence, however, because nature and society both promote it: nature, because growth is so rapid that the teen-ager himself cannot adjust to it smoothly, let alone his parents; and society, because the teen-ager's position in it is so ill-defined, and because prevailing traditions imply that teen-agers cannot be trusted. All too many news stories, for example, emphasize cases in which adolescents have become involved in crime without the knowledge of their upstanding middle-class parents. The implicit moral is, therefore, take nothing for granted and watch your children like a hawk—which usually gets translated into excessive supervision and invasions of privacy. In this connection, it is awe-inspiring to think of all the pornographic books, pictures, and other memorabilia that have probably—to the needless discomfiture of teen-agers—been found hidden among their socks and underwear.

Empirical research offers a fair degree of support for the lag phenomenon as a probable cause of conflict. Schaefer and Bayley (1960) reported that among a sample of mothers, tendencies to be overprotective or restrictive remain fairly constant up through adolescence. Some of the case history material quoted from the Fels Institute research in earlier chapters, also shows this. A study by Bowerman and Kinch (1959) is particularly relevant, however, because after investigating changes in the family orientations of ten- to sixteen-year-olds, they were led to comment directly on the existence of a parental lag. Discussing their finding that parents tend to use external events, such as school graduations, as indicators of when to change their behavior toward children, Bowerman and Kinch noted that a "law of perseveration" seems to hold sway in many human relationships. That is, people react in a constant way to others until they are forced to change by the pressure of external circumstances. But whether one chooses to call this a lag, a law of perseveration, or a principle of social inertia, the phenomenon seems plain enough, and it will obviously cause much difficulty during adolescence.

Another view of parent resistance to demands for autonomy from teen-agers is often suggested by Freudians, who note that growing adolescents may provoke unconscious feelings of threat or jealousy in their parents. Thus, as a child looks more and more as an adult, one or both of his parents may see him (or her) as a potential competitor or opponent, a new force upsetting the old balance of power in the family. Or, merely by their physical presence, youngsters may serve as a reminder of their parents' age, which can be threatening to people living in a youth-oriented culture. The jealousy possibilities hardly need specification: "Here is this kid living off me, only interested in having fun and he's got no respect, while I have to slave away to support him." More specifically, parents may not be fully aware of how much they envy the older teen-ager his vitality and material opportunities.

But if natural lags, and somewhat less natural forms of threat and jealousy exist, they are both probably outweighed by the simple, down-to-earth problems parents have in defining their own degree of responsibility for teen-agers. As Douvan and Adelson suggested, it is hard for parents to strike a perfect balance—loosening their control in proportion to the child's ability to control himself—because equally serious problems can arise from either too little or too much control. Worse, yet, in some instances parents may not be able to judge whether a given problem can be resolved by relaxing or increasing their disciplinary efforts.

Psychological consequences

In bare theoretical terms, the adolescent struggling for independence from the control of his parents is really struggling to establish a clear image of himself. Chaotic as it may seem, the ebb and flow of parent-adolescent conflict only makes sense as an effort by the child to set himself apart from his parents, to distinguish himself as a psychologically separate entity. In this connection, it should be obvious that the average young teen-ager is pretty much the creature of his parents, or the product of situations arranged by his parents. Therefore, much of what he says and does, and much of how he thinks of himself, relates to his parents.

This condition becomes important when the adolescent discovers it for himself, as his knowledge of the world expands because of school, peer, and other forms of experience. Furthermore, as he begins to act according to new views which deviate from those set by his parents, their negative reaction will strengthen his realization of direct or indirect parent control. Briefly, the adolescent becomes seriously aware for the first time that he is on something like a psychological leash. And he also realizes, at least dimly and intuitively, that so long as he remains on it, he cannot establish a relatively uncontaminated or "pure" self-concept.

Increasing conflict with parents through much of adolescence reflects efforts first to stretch the leash, and later on to break it. In principle, the process here seems not unlike the negativism of early childhood. Just as formation of the pride and self-esteem components of the young child's self-concept require him to test the limits of his freedom to say no, proper reorganization of the adolescent's self-concept requires him to test the limits of his ability to go contrary to his parents. But the process now has much more serious implications: having once found limits, and worked out some compromise agreements with his parents, it is only a question of time before the older teen-ager will be trying to break through those limits again.

It would be wrong, however, to assume from this discussion that adolescence is nothing but parent-child friction. Some parents will relinquish their control voluntarily, and in good time to forestall serious struggles. And some adolescents will be less demanding than others. Too much freedom can be as threatening to youngsters who aren't quite ready to handle it, as too much loss of control can be to parents who aren't sure how else to guarantee the well-being of their child. So there is often a ready basis for a series of compromises that can be mutually satisfactory to both parties.

Unfortunately, research does not offer much concrete information along this line. As one finds so often in personality work, there is much greater emphasis on what may go wrong than on what may go approximately right. But there are a few exceptions. Hurlock mentioned studies showing that younger-aged parents frequently enjoy good relations with their adolescents because they tend to share similar values. And survey data collected by Douvan and Adelson suggested to them that in general, middle-class American families provide adolescents with "an easy-going, libertarian milieu," which promotes development of independence or autonomy.

On the negative side, most authorities see parental efforts to retain strong control over teen-agers, to dominate or run their lives for them, as a great source of psychological trouble. The generalization emerging from the literature here is that if parents try to bind their offspring too closely to them, they will only succeed in influencing their teen-agers' push for independence in such a way that it will either detonate with a bang or expire with a whimper. The bang of course refers to a *full-blown* act of rebellion: tear the hell out of things and run away. Not much discussion needed here because the matter is clear; any high-pressure system not given sufficient means to ventilate itself can explode. The whimper reaction is a bit more complex and certainly more prevalent. Here the adolescent tends to give up the struggle for independence, or else never gets it into high gear. Instead of working through friction with parents and finding new sources of self-confidence in his ability to fight his case, he settles out of court, so to speak. Conformity may therefore become his only source of confidence.

Douvan and Adelson mentioned that about one third of their female adolescent sample give very conventional, conforming responses to key questions concerning independence. Thirty-six percent, for instance, say they do not want to participate in family rule-making decisions; 35 percent say they are closer to their families than to any friends of their own age; and 29 percent believe that respect for authority and living up to their parents' expectations are both very important. It is further suggested that such responses indicate curtailed personality development: the full independence from parents needed for genuine autonomy which can later mature into a deep sense of individuality, is not likely to occur. Horrocks, Jersild, Mussen, et al., all offer further data and discussion along the same line. The general point being that if the teen-ager's self-concept remains too closely tied in with his family, if his self-esteem depends too strongly on approval from parents, then he will probably not make an active, flexible effort to develop his own unique potentials.

Thus, some relevant research studies show that teen-agers reporting more friction with their parents aspire to higher occupational careers (Dynes, Clarke, and Dinitz, 1956); that a moderate but not strong attachment to parents is associated with later marital happiness (Hamilton and MacGowan, 1929); and that high-achieving college students remember their parents as encouraging independence (Cross and Allen, 1969). The latter authors also mentioned that higher achievement is associated with feelings of security and self-confidence, that is, a stronger self-concept.

Taking everything together, some degree of parent-adolescent conflict seems inevitable—a fixed fact of life in modern societies. However, the outcomes of such conflicts will vary. If the teen-ager cannot find a satisfactory path toward autonomy, then (with apologies to T. S. Eliot) it is likely that his drive toward independence will either go off with a bang or deteriorate to a whimper. Both of these possibilities can postpone, or prevent entirely, the establishment of a self-concept strong enough to carry the individual toward full realization of his unique potentials.

3. Same- and opposite-sex peer relations

The literature concerning this area of adolescence is large enough to make organization of any discussion a matter of arbitrary selection. Our discussion is divided among three topics: popularity or acceptance in same-sex peer groups; personal relations with individual same-sex friends; and emerging personal relations with opposite-sex peers. In each of these areas, normative studies will be treated very lightly as we pursue the psychological significance of peer relations.

Popularity

All of the factors which influence acceptance and status in peer groups during middle childhood carry over to adolescence. Furthermore, many of the social-psychological meanings of peer relations also remain the same. The individual can try different roles, he can pick up new perspectives, knowledge, skills, and, depending upon how things go generally with peers, his experiences may have a broadly negative or positive impact on his self-concept. So the first serious question arises: is there anything unique about peer relations in adolescence? One might stipulate that the adolescent spends more time with friends, that he is more dependent upon them for various kinds of social support, and that sex poses some novel problems, and then let the topic go as a garden-variety trend in development. This can be done, and it is not wrong; but it is not entirely right, either, because it misses at least two crucial ways in which popularity or acceptance by peers is uniquely important to teen-agers.

Basically, one important consideration is that the adolescent is not a child. The new self-awareness mentioned in our earlier discussion of relations with parents also influences the quality of relations with peers. Popularity has different meanings to the child and the teen-ager:

Before adolescence the child accepts himself as he is; if he is popular or unpopular, if he has many friends or only one or none—this is the way things are; the child may sorrow over it, but he will not generally feel there is much he can do about it. He has not yet made the discovery of the tractable self. Sometime near the start of adolescence, the child develops a consciousness of the self as a social stimulus, modifiable by will and intention. He enters the world of self-help, of books and columns on manners, dating, dress, make-up, chit-chat, the world of rituals and resolutions designed to make or remake the self. He enters friendship with an eagerness to make good, and the conviction that the self can be transformed to that end (Douvan and Adelson, p. 180).

The possibility of doing something to change their status with friends is an important discovery to adolescents. Mary McCarthy mentioned being tagged with the nickname "Cye," which she hated, and remembered that one of her chief pleasures in transferring to a public high school was that the change enabled her to be rid of that name. Malcolm X remembers that at about 14 or 15 years of age, he began to be consciously disturbed by the word *nigger*, and when his white classmates used it, he would silently stare at them until they became uncomfortable.

A second unique feature·of popularity or acceptance during adolescence is the social support it provides. Popularity will of course help support the self-concepts of children and adults as well as adolescents. But it is of special importance to teen-agers who are struggling for independence from parents. Teen-agers would have small chances in the struggle were it not for the support of peers. The situation can be visualized as a psychological seesaw, with parents on one end and the child on the other. If the adolescent sits alone, the weight of his parents can keep him hung up in the air indefinitely; but let a few others join him, and the balance shifts towards equality. Moreover, unless the adolescent can counter the weight of his parents with friends, it is unlikely that he will ever gain sufficient psychological weight to do the trick by himself.

The question of degree or intensity is something else. No one can say what degree of peer-acceptance is necessary to balance various degrees of parental disapproval. Yet, the principle that positive peer relations serve to offset negative parent relations by providing an alternative source of approval comes through in practically all theory and research on this period.

The above proposition is also corroborated by everyday evidence concerning teen-age pathologies. Almost everything teen-agers do which can be defined as wrong according to traditional social values, or as criminal according to law — precocious sex, drugs, petty crime — is generally done in a group, or with the support of a group. And the more serious the transgression, the more dependent the teen-ager is upon the support of peers.

Personal friendships

Intimate, one-to-one friendships also have a special character during adolescence. We have discussed Sullivan's views of such "chum" relationships on several occasions. He placed this phenomenon toward the end of middle childhood, and interpreted its main psychological functions to be either an informal kind of psychotherapy — chums can openly discuss many things that might otherwise be kept hidden — or a rehearsal for the intimacy with opposite-sex peers which occurs later. All of these ideas remain plausible, but the work of several other authorities indicates that chum-like friendships are as important during adolescence as Sullivan says they are during preadolescence.

Douvan and Adelson discussed the hypothetical case of two girls who share all their intimate secrets. Assume that one girl is a bit older or more mature, and therefore has had more experience being on her own and going out with boys. She will be the more active, dominant member of the pair while the other generally will act as an admiring listener or confidante.

Psychologically, the benefit to the listener is that by identifying with her friend, sharing vicariously in the advanced experiences or adventures being described, she can learn how to cope with situations that would otherwise be frightening. And the listener can also project onto her friend impulses or emotions that are still too disturbing for her to admit into her own self-concept. In short, through the mechanisms of identification and projection, the listener can use the relationship as a relatively safe means of tentatively reorganizing her conception of herself.

The active member of the pair benefits equally, but in different ways. First, by telling her adventures, she receives the other's admiration: the "Oh, I wish I could do that" reaction. More importantly, however, while reviewing her behavior she must reconstruct it for herself. This allows her to get a better perspective on her experience—to internalize it, or assimilate it into her own self-concept. Douvan and Adelson added that the telling of exploits may also have the character of a confession. The active partner senses her listener's reactions and these can provide reassurance or relieve guilt feelings. When an individual is not quite sure of his behavior, but describes it to another who says, in effect, "I would have done the same in your shoes," then some of the uncertainties may be removed.

Finally, the active partner, labeled "A" in the quotation below, may use the relationship to test for appropriate limits to her behavior:

But if A's behavior carries her too far from B's willingness to accept or approve, the identification may become too dangerous for B, who will become uneasy in the friendship. B's uneasiness communicates itself to A, who sees herself in danger of being transformed from Glamour Girl to Bad Girl. Through B's response, then, A is able to find limits for her behavior at a time when external norms are uncertain and internal controls weak and confused (Douvan and Adelson, pp. 182–183).

Erikson also emphasized the important role of intimate friendships among adolescents. He saw this matter in much the same way as Douvan and Adelson: the teen-ager uses close relationships with friends as a means of exploring and defining his own self-concept. The latter authors speak of such friendships as a "forum" where youngsters may debate the uncertainties of personality development. Their interviews with fourteen- to sixteen-year-olds show that girls of this age see ideal friends as those who are reliable, loyal, and who will not reveal secrets given in confidence. Briefly then, the burden of evidence suggests that personal friendships are of unique importance during adolescence because they provide the most effective help for teen-agers who are trying to organize a more mature self-concept.

Opposite-sex peer relations

In societies such as ours where girls and boys may remain psychologically and socially apart during middle childhood, opposite-sex peers can become strangely ambiguous figures at the age of puberty. Strange because on the one hand, there may be great familiarity between girls and boys who have been raised in the same community and go to the same school, or are even in the same classroom. On the other hand, the perspective from which one views the opposite sex changes drastically at puberty. "They" take on a new significance and a new character, becoming—rather suddenly—something other than what one thought them to be. Novels and autobiographies are full of relevant examples; the freckled, taken-for-granted twelve-year-old tomboy who one day, a few years later, seems mysteriously beautiful.

But if young adolescents are anxious about associating with opposite-sex peers for many reasons, including rapid caterpillar to butterfly transformations which can turn the familiar into the mysterious, how is it that youngsters ever make the transition to heterosexual activity? It seems ultimately to be a matter of physiology and culture. With maturation of the sex glands a new physiological force operates in favor of cross-sex activity. And culture provides both motivating forces and operational techniques for bridging the early adolescence sex gap.

In our culture, teen-agers who identify with adults will naturally see cross-sex behavior as one of the defining characteristics of their adult models. Bell (1968) suggested that love and marriage are "adult symbols," which teen-agers are eager to acquire as final proofs that they have grown up. The mass media also encourage cross-sex behavior; books, movies, TV, all lay on the glories of young love with a heavy hand, and offer a veritable warehouse of technical information for the teen-ager trying to learn what is expected of him. Clothes, hair styles, music, dialogue: all of it is there to be had for the taking, and much of it may be imposed whether one wants it or not.

Yet by far the most important cultural element encouraging contact between the sexes is the same-sex peer group. The group literally serves as a social-psychological bridge to the opposite sex. Several investigators (e.g., Dunphy, 1963; Havighurst, Bowman, and Liddle, 1962), noted that in their first steps toward heterosexual activity, young adolescents rely on their same-sex peers to provide the structure or framework for cross-sex activity. This reliance can be observed very easily among thirteen- to fifteen-year-olds; the picnics, skating parties, and birthday celebrations serving as occasions for contact. Such activities are a *social* bridge because they bring the sexes together; they are a *psychological* bridge because the nervous adolescent is reassured by the presence of his or her friends.

As association between the sexes progresses, the formalities of dating begin to be learned, and this is no simple matter. Most writers on adolescence emphasize that teen-age dating is a complex ritual involving rules which define the boundaries of permissible behavior. For example, if one wants a date, there is an optimum advance time interval for arranging it, but timing will also depend upon the type or category of date that is involved. A soda or walk in the park is one thing, while a school dance or birthday party is another. Moreover, studies indicate that proper dress and deportment can be problems. One survey reported that 14- and 15-year-old boys were uncertain whether girls wanted them to dress like gentlemen or he-men. And though it may not be true today, Stolz, Jones, and Chaffey (1937) observed that in junior high school, girls begin to "train" their boy classmates to be proper dancers and party escorts.

Regardless of whether or not explicit training for dating still goes on, it is obvious that young teen-agers must learn quite a lot in a relatively short time. In this connection, older siblings and friends are probably the most important sources of information. They can be imitated, observed, or questioned directly. Frank Harris always believed in the direct approach, especially in matters of sex, so it is not surprising to find a good illustration of this point in the direct questions he raised at age 13:

A conversation began one day at dinner between my sister and my eldest brother about making up to girls and winning them. I noticed with astonishment that my brother Vernon was very deferential to my sister's opinion on the matter, so I immediately got hold of Nita after the lunch and asked her to explain to me what she meant by "flattery."

"You said all girls like flattery. What did you mean?"

"I mean," she said, "they all like to be told they are pretty, that they have good eyes or good teeth or good hair, as the case may be, or that they are tall and nicely made. They all like their good points noticed and praised."

"Is that all?" I asked. "Oh no!" she said, "they all like their dress noticed too and especially their hat; if it suits their face, if it's very pretty and so forth. All girls think that if you notice their clothes you really like them, for most men don't."

"Number two," I said to myself. "Is there anything else?"

"Of course," she said, "you must say that the girl you are with is the prettiest girl in the room or in town—in fact, is quite unlike any other girl, superior to all the rest, the only girl in the world for you. All women like to be the only girl in the world for as many men as possible."

"Number three," I said to myself. "Don't they like to be kissed?" I asked.

"That comes afterwards," said my sister. "Lots of men begin with kissing and paw-ing you about before you even like them. That puts you off. Flattery first of looks and dress, then devotion, and afterwards the kissing comes naturally."

"Number four!" I went over these four things again and again to myself and began trying them even on the older girls and women about me and soon found that they all had a better opinion of me almost immediately.

I remember practicing my new knowledge first on the younger Miss Raleigh whom, I thought, Vernon liked. I just praised her as my sister had advised: first her eyes and hair (she had very pretty blue eyes). To my astonishment she smiled on me at once; accordingly I went on to say she was the prettiest girl in town and suddenly she took my head in her hands and kissed me, saying, "You're a dear boy!" (*My Life and Loves*, pp. 41–42).

Harris being Harris, however, he was not content with the formal niceties, but wanted to get to bedrock sex. So he questioned a family friend who had the reputation of being very successful with the ladies. At first, the man brushed off the boy's explicit questions, yet one suspects he must have recognized a kindred spirit in young Harris, because he finally offered the following man-to-man advice.

'You know, your question amused me, and I thought I would try to find an answer to it, and here is one. When you can put a stiff penis in her hand and weep profusely the while, you're getting near any woman's heart. But don't forget the tears.' I found the advice a counsel of perfection; I was unable to weep at such a moment, but I never forgot the words (ibid., p. 43).

Now this is admittedly extreme, and possibly more typical of characters in *Fanny Hill* than American adolescents, but it does highlight an important issue that remains obscure in most academic works on dating—namely, that while teen-agers are learning the social formalities, they are also keen on learning how to satisfy some plain old lust. The elegant comment of Harris' friend may seem far removed from modern American clichés such as "You gotta have a car to make out" and its obverse "If you drink, don't park—accidents make people." Nevertheless, the underlying principle should be clear:

teen-agers are involved in learning both the formalities of dating *and* how to make it with the opposite sex.

There is little doubt, however, about the relative order of these two purposes. Except among young adolescents in low socioeconomic areas where overt sex activity starts early, most fourteen- and fifteen-year-olds are more preoccupied with social formalities than fornication. The common pattern of early adolescent dating is summarized very well in the following quotation:

There develops a kind of characterological fiction—the 'good date.' Its dimensions vary somewhat with age, social status, and other local circumstances, but generally, the good date is someone skilled in keeping impulses and affects under control in a situation that tends to stimulate them. The good date, male or female, can keep the ball rolling, is amiable and verbally facile. The overt expression of impulse is strictly forbidden. One must not be directly sensual or aggressive. Indeed, any extreme of behavior, even a "desirable" extreme, is generally felt to be out of place. One ought to be gay and yet not altogether frivolous; one ought to be bright, and yet not serious or intellectual; one is expected to offer comments on the evening's entertainment, the movie, let us say, and yet without vehemence. The boy can exercise some inventiveness in arranging the evening's activities, but not to the point of deviation. The girl's behavior is probably more strictly regulated than the boy's; she is to be the audience to the boy's offerings of entertainment, yet she must be at the least polite and if possible enthusiastic about it, whatever her secret inclinations may be (Douvan and Adelson, pp. 205–206).

Odd as it may be, this pattern has the useful function of protecting the sensitive adolescent's self-concept while gradually preparing him for more serious activities. In the ritualized but therefore safe structure of dating, adolescent boys and girls needn't expose too much of their still-fragile self-concepts. They can minimize the risk of drastic losses in self-esteem by hiding their "true" selves in the formal structure. At the same time, they can learn how to handle themselves in new situations, explore their conceptions of themselves, experiment with overt sex via necking, and thus make ready for later, riskier exposures of self in more serious heterosexual activities.

Since it is clear that dating does not serve most adolescents as a great outlet for physical sex drives, and since it is also well known that adolescent boys in particular have very high sex drives, it should be obvious why all reports on the subject show that masturbation is almost universal among young American males. Horrocks (pp. 209–213) provided a general review of this material, including the fact that 95 percent of high-school boys admit that they indulge. He also noted that despite clinical and medical studies showing that in and of itself, masturbation is harmless, it can become a source of serious problems for teen-agers who believe otherwise.

The material on masturbation is in principle very similar for females, with one important exception: fewer of them indulge and they do so less frequently. Estimates vary from 50- to 60-odd percent of the general female population, as compared with 95 percent of the male population. Without going into detail, it seems that sex drives in women are tied much more closely to social-emotional considerations than they are in men. Hence physical gratification through self-manipulation is less frequent. But apart from the descriptive data which support this generalization, the further explanations available to explain differences in male and female sex drives are really no more than speculative interpretations. In fact, the whole physiology of female sexual arousal remains as an outstanding scientific mystery. And judging from the mixed public reactions to recent experimentation in this area (Masters and Johnson, 1966) many people will be just as glad to let it stay a mystery.

In general, heterosexual activities will influence adolescent self-concepts in much the same way as all other social activities of this period: positive experiences should increase self-confidence. However, teen-agers' cross-sex experiences have certain unique properties. Dating requires adaptation to a whole new set of social norms. Besides all the superficial role requirements, boys are called upon to act out a masculine performance that is more serious than anything they have encountered before. They have to take initiatives and assume responsibilities that can be quite difficult (any mature man whose wife still complains that he doesn't know how to speak to waiters in restaurants will be able to recall the much greater difficulties of learning to date). For girls, the normative problems are different but equally serious. They must, among other things, learn to follow appropriately safe standards of conduct, being neither too demanding nor too acquiescent, a good sport who can retain her essential femininity.

The deeper, inner meaning of adolescent heterosexual experience is harder to pinpoint. All authorities agree that such experiences serve as an important vehicle for exploring new areas of the self, and reorganizing old ones. But it is not clear exactly how this works. Our earlier discussion of intimate same-sex friendships is surely relevant: opposite-sex teen-agers who go steady and become close friends can help each other work through problems of self-definition in the same general way as same-sex chums. Yet there must be more to it than that—a steady girl friend or boyfriend in whom one confides is going to be different from a close friend of the same sex, because physical sex differences (and possibilities) will color the relationship. We can be sure that in such a relationship, girls and boys discover how to relate themselves to the opposite sex, and how to evaluate themselves from this standpoint. At a very down-to-earth level, for example, Frank Harris seems to have gone through much of his life asking each of his many girl friends what sorts of physical acts gave them the maximum sexual pleasure, and his conception of himself was certainly influenced by their answers. But there is little in the research literature which can be used to explain in more detail how it is that cross-sex relationships work upon the personalities of teen-agers. Erikson speculated that such relationships are of special value because, being so different, girls and boys reflect each other's self-images in unique new ways. However, discussion of this and other theoretical perspectives will be saved for a later section.

It should be noted, finally, that differences between the peer activities of adolescent girls and boys have not been discussed very much because they are not too well understood. There are some well-established *normative* differences. Girls, for example, are reported to see ideal friends as those who can be trusted not to gossip about them, while boys say they look for friends who will be loyal in times of trouble. It is also clear that while male and female sex drives are quite different, no one is confident about what these dif-ferences mean for personality development. Since such differences must ul-timately be related to both culture and physiology in ways that still remain to be investigated in detail, the best one can do is stipulate their potential importance and pass on to other things.

4. Cognitive-intellectual growth

Piaget's work on cognitive growth suggested that it reaches its final, adult level (formal operations) during early adolescence. In prior chapters his basic ideas concerning each developmental period have been described un-der the heading of theoretical perspectives. We will continue that practice here. However, the research literature on adolescent intelligence is large enough and interesting enough to warrant additional discussion as one of the five critical problem areas of adolescent personality development.

Testing
Much of the conventional work in this area involves standard intelligence, achievement, and aptitude tests. Since such tests in earlier discussions have been viewed skeptically for reasons that will be mentioned again in this sec-tion, the reader deserves some explanation for the present concern.

To begin with, the self-concepts of teen-agers are very vulnerable to re-ports of their test performances. Children could hardly care less about such things, although their development may be influenced indirectly if test re-sults are used to categorize them in grade school. But adolescents tend to accept test scores at their face value. Thus, if teen-agers are told that achievement or aptitude tests indicate that they should become mechanics instead of lawyers, or that they are not bright enough to go to college, they are liable to accept the information as scientific fact, and act accordingly. In short, being unaware of the uncertainties involved in this kind of testing, young people can be heavily influenced by it.

Consider one typical problem. Many high school and college students probably take the Strong Vocational Interest Test. The results tell them whether their interests lie in the direction of any of the conventional occupa-tions: from business to engineering to medicine, teaching, and many other fields. They believe that the scores offer an objective prescription for their future occupation. They do not know that items on this test are scored ac-cording to how samples of people in the different occupations once answered them. In other words, the youngster taking the test today gets back results suggesting that he is suited to be an engineer, doctor, or lawyer, based on the way such professionals answered the test 10 or more years ago! The student who takes the test seriously is in effect going to bet on a career choice that can extend 10 or more years into the *future*, according to fallible data col-lected 10, 15, or 20 years in the *past*. Nothing could be more wrong, though in fairness it must be admitted that the test can be useful to those who want to know how their present interests match up to the interests of various pro-fessionals of an earlier generation.

Another important reason for being cautious about tests is that results can change. Many people believe that individual intelligence test scores remain constant. In fact, they can change a great deal. Studies show that such scores can easily vary over an interval of plus or minus ten points, and the interval will occasionally be much larger. It is of course true that given knowledge of a group of children's or adolescents' IQ scores, one can predict adult scores for that group better than one could without such knowledge. But this is a far cry from being able to make precise individual predictions. For instance, Bradway and Thompson (1962) obtained a correlation of .60 between the intelligence scores of individuals tested as children and adolescents. This is a much better than chance relationship, but not high enough to bet any money on making a good individual prediction.

Differentiation and sex differences

In addition to misconceptions about the meaning and reliability of standard tests, there are at least two more reasons for discussing this topic in connection with adolescence. Elkind (1968) reviewed the problems of differentiation in intelligence and sex differences, both of which first become clear during this period, and both of which can have important impacts on the self-concept.

The question of whether intelligence is differentiated or integrated is one of the grand traditional problems in psychology. Debates about whether or not intelligence is a "general factor" in personality still go on. But Elkind's review of the evidence makes one thing very clear: during adolescence, ability scores become progressively differentiated. Measures of such things as verbal, arithmetic, and reasoning skills begin to spread apart after puberty. Scores in these areas tend to be very close together for individual children — the child high or low on one is very likely to be high or low on others. In adolescence, however, an individual may be high in the verbal area and low in arithmetic, or vice versa. No one knows exactly why this spread sets in, but everyone agrees that it probably has to do with experiences which shape the *interests* of adolescents.

Peer groups, and family and school environments, are all frequently mentioned as likely sources of experiences which influence interests. And self-concepts seem to change accordingly. Brookover, Shailor, and Paterson (1964) studied the self-concepts of over 1000 seventh graders in relation to their school achievement. These adolescents all generally showed conceptions of themselves closely related to their demonstrated academic performances. They could be quite positive about themselves in one academic area, and negative in another. So one begins to see how differentiated performances can lead to the development of a more complex, differentiated self-concept.

The second general problem reviewed by Elkind concerned sex differences. He cited a prior detailed summary by Terman and Tyler (1954) showing that while some sex differences in abilities and aptitudes can be seen during childhood, most of the differences first become conspicuous during adolescence. Specific differences include (a) verbal and arithmetic or spatial problems, girls do better on the former, boys on the latter; (b) general school grades, girls are usually higher than boys; (c) science and mathematics, despite their better overall grades, girls are poorer than boys in these subjects;

(d) vocational aptitudes, girls are higher on clerical skills, boys are higher on mechanical skills.

Along with other authorities, Elkind suggested that most of these differences can be understood as originating in cultural pressures to follow stereotyped sex roles. Girls are not "supposed" to be good at science or math; boys are "supposed" to like mechanical things. In this connection, it is obvious that insofar as masculinity and femininity are important aspects of the adolescent's self-concept, they will undoubtedly influence interests and test performances. One sees here that sex-role and intellectual development can be intimately related to one another, with the former exercising major influence over the latter.

Now, the question may arise, "Why bother with sex differences or the differentiation-integration problem if the tests allowing us to see these things are themselves fallible?" And they are indeed fallible; speaking of changes in IQ scores, Elkind noted a number of circumstances that can also influence aptitude and achievement tests:

Since the IQ measures achievement as well as underlying capacity, any factors which affect achievement will also affect the IQ. Environmental experiences which make for self-confidence, which provide or deprive the individual of ample and effective stimulation for learning, may markedly affect the extent of the young person's intellectual achievements. Environmental circumstances, moreover, do not remain constant throughout childhood and adolescence. The family may move, the young person may become a member of a group which is for or against school, or he may encounter a teacher who sets a spark to his intellect or who, contrariwise, kills his interest in learning. All of these factors and more can and do affect performance on intelligence tests and make it difficult to say how stable the IQ will remain from childhood to adolescence (1968, p. 136).

However, the fact that such tests are fallible at the individual level does not mean that they are entirely meaningless. Standardized tests, whether truly representative of individual abilities or not, seem to reveal some important general developmental trends. Thus, one can observe that self-concepts grow more complex as specific abilities become differentiated during adolescence. At the individual level, the teen-ager's scores and school record will surely influence his present self-concept and plans for the future. In short, the prophecy implicit to grades and test scores may be wrong, but if the youngster believes it, he may act in such a way as to fulfill it.

A similar principle operates with respect to sex differences. No one can be certain whether girls and boys really *are* different in their scientific and verbal skills, but so long as such differences are accepted, and are even treated in many situations as being *definitive* of masculinity and femininity, it is to be expected that youngsters anxious about their sexual identities will shape their behavior to fit the safe stereotypes.

Egocentrism

Elkind is one of the few developmental writers who have made serious efforts to work out connections between social-emotional aspects of personality and Piaget's work on cognitive growth. He suggested that as adolescents acquire the capacity for formal mental operations, this ability to think abstractly and hypothetically leads to a new type of self-concern, which can be described as a type of egocentrism:

It is this feeling that others are as concerned with him as he is with himself that is the substance of adolescent *egocentrism*. The child is egocentric in the sense that he is unable to take another person's point of view. The adolescent, on the other hand, takes the other person's point of view to an extreme degree. He is so concerned with the point of view of others and how they regard him that he often loses sight of his own point of view, i.e., his own best interests (Elkind, 1968, p. 153).

Besides offering a cognitive theory base for understanding teen-age behavior, Elkind's concept of adolescent egocentrism is valuable because it zeroes in on the self-concept from a new perspective. We have already seen in the work of Douvan and Adelson how the self-concept is emphasized when Freudian ideas are applied to adolescent social behavior. But now, exaggerated concern with self, and related ego defense mechanisms, can be seen as relevant to adolescent egocentrism. And this congruity ought to be understood as more than just a matter of theoretical language. The fact that different investigators, working independently from different theoretical viewpoints, reach similar conclusions about the central role of the self-concept, offers strong assurance that this is the major underlying factor in personality development during adolescence.

5. Personal identity

This final problem area is the most difficult to deal with because to appreciate it, one must, more or less simultaneously, be able to follow a number of different but converging ideas. The abstract essence of personal identity is *integration*, but to understand this, it is necessary to understand what is integrated, how it is integrated, why integration is crucial to personal identity, and why personal identity, in turn, is crucial to personality development.

Given the difficulties preventing easy understanding, we might begin by emphasizing the importance of this concept: it is the only theoretical vehicle adequate to the task of pulling together the diverse material discussed in preceding sections. And it is also the only theoretical idea that makes sense to most of us: way down deep, most of us know we have a core sense of who we are, an identity. So if one wants to try to grasp the meaning of personality development in adolescence, there is nothing for it but to come to grips with the identity problem.

Identity and the self-concept

More than anyone else, Erikson deserves credit for elaborating the concept of personal identity or "ego identity," and creating a place for it in contemporary studies of personality. But the paradoxical nature of much psychological work should be familiar enough by now, so that it will not be surprising to hear that in all of Erikson's published works on the subject, one cannot find a convenient or easy definition of identity. He discusses it using examples, or general descriptions (e.g., ". . . sense of invigorating sameness and *continu-*

ity") which are only made clear through examples and analogies. We will say more on this matter in the theoretical perspectives section. Identity will generally be treated here as meaning a continuing sense of who and what one is.

Theoretically, the identity concept is essential because it locks together so many diverse elements. All of the things which demonstrably influence the adolescent's self-concept—his ideas about himself as student, date, family member—force reorganization of his self-concept. During the course of this reorganization, however, a sense of identity somehow emerges at the core of the self. Another way to put it is by saying that up to a point, the self-concept of the child and young teen-ager is relatively plastic; it can develop and be organized in different ways depending upon various experiences. For example, a young teen-age boy who is both a bright scholar and fine athlete can go either way. His sense of personal identity can follow either from his conception of himself as scholar or as athlete. But after a certain point, perhaps at age sixteen or seventeen, his sense of being either *primarily* a scholar or athlete crystallizes, and becomes a strong organizing force in its own right.

More abstractly, the argument is that personal identity stands as the central feature of the self-concept. Identity is at first shaped by experiences influencing the self-concept, but later, as the sense of identity gets stronger, a sort of turnabout occurs, and identity begins to shape experiences influencing the self-concept. This progression, which may seem illogical, can be understood by referring to our example of the scholar-athlete. Once his identity centers on one or another of these activities, the other components of his self-concept will be organized accordingly—which means that there will be a strong tendency to shape or program experience so that it will fit the scholarly or athletic orientation. He will probably begin to associate with peers who are known mainly as scholars or athletes; and he will wear clothing, adopt hair styles, and be attracted to adult models who fit one or the other pattern. Furthermore, having once acquired a primary identity as scholar or athlete, his behavior should reflect an appropriate order of priorities. If he has a primary sense of himself as athlete, scholarly pursuits will begin to take second place, and vice versa. Should he stay up late to study and thus break a training rule? Should he spend a day in the library instead of taking off to watch a professional sports competition? All such questions are real and practical, and eventually are decided in terms of identity. Thus, by the end of adolescence, young people can have a sense of identity which begins to act as a strong directive force in their lives.

Origins

We have described identity as "crystallizing"—turning up somehow, by late adolescence, at the core of the self-concept. Where does it come from? It seemingly is formed the way a pearl is formed inside an oyster. More technically, most of the available material suggests that we have to understand identity as the outcome of multiple forces operating on the self-concept. In analogy to physics, personal identity can be thought of as a vector representing the salient psychological forces impinging on the individual's self-concept. How have his family and school experiences influenced him? How does he match up to cultural standards of what a young person should be like? How has he reacted to puberty changes and the peculiar social position of adolescence? If one could sum up all the many important factors in personality development and cast them in the form of a vector diagram, one might be able to specify identity as the resultant.

But of course this cannot be done. The vector scheme can only serve as a hypothetical model which can help us understand why a sense of identity just seems to gradually emerge out of the confused conditions of adolescence.

In searching for a more palpable handle on the identity concept, authorities such as Gold and Douvan (1969) suggested that sex-role factors play the most important part in establishing a sense of identity. That is, studies oriented toward the identity problem converge on youngsters' ideas of masculinity or femininity as being of prime importance. A major common thread to be found in all adolescent problems—puberty, family relations, peer relations, intellectual growth—has to do with sexual identity. Furthermore, Gold and Douvan noted that the Fels longitudinal study also reveals sex-role behaviors to be a consistently good predictor of other activities.

So without going into further detail, it can be argued that one's sense of unique identity grows out of an earlier sense of oneself as masculine or feminine. Various aspects of the self are first linked together by the common denominator of sex role, and this is gradually replaced by a more unique sense of identity: one sees oneself finally as a *particular* kind of young man or woman.

Organizing functions

Turning to the functional side of the identity problem—its practical utility, so to speak—we are on firmer ground, because studies and case histories offer much relevant material. In general, it seems that interests, moral and religious values, vocational choices or predispositions, and related achievement motives, are all sorted out and organized in terms of personal identity. The many different facets of the self are drawn together to form a unitary structure centering on the person's core sense of himself as an individual. In practice, this will of course be a ragged, sloppy operation; only very rarely will a sixteen- or seventeen-year-old have an identity strong enough to unify fully his conceptions of himself. In fact, it will be clear in later chapters that most of us fall short of perfection in this respect as adults. But the unifying trend plainly starts in late adolescence when a substantial sense of identity develops. And this integrating trend has three very important effects.

First, there is a new world view (*"weltanschauung"*): the older adolescent begins to gain a sense of himself which is oriented to a larger, more realistic understanding of his environment. He may have grown up with a great many different notions—about the glories of being a soldier and wearing a uniform, or with ambitions to become a doctor on the Ben Casey model, or just with daydreams about heroic behavior in the face of great danger. But a more realistic world view comes in as he discovers that a soldier's life is not very glamorous, that it is extremely difficult to become a doctor, and that one may experience paralyzing fear in the face of serious danger. In brief, if it is accepted that the older adolescent's identity is a new, continuing sense of who and what he is, then it must also be accepted that this identity is accompanied by a new, more realistic world view. Identity and world view must go hand in glove. A youngster may *prefer* to think of himself as a great fighter and/or thinker, for example, but if he is always getting beaten up in fights, and is always slow to understand things that are clear to others, he will not be able to maintain such unrealistic ideas about himself. His world view will have to include the fact that there are a great many tougher, smarter people than he thought.

The autobiography of Malcolm X provides a straightforward illustration. At about 15, he left his rural hometown in Nebraska for the first time and visited an aunt in Boston. There he discovered a larger, more sophisticated black community than he had ever dreamed existed. He gained a new world view, and his prior conception of himself as one of a handful of odd "colored" persons – a pet, mascot, or village curiosity – was drastically and forever changed.

Another effect associated with a sense of identity concerns the priorities and interpretations given to various experiences. This was mentioned earlier in our example of the athlete-scholar, who eventually must find himself as one or the other, and who will thereafter order his activities accordingly. Common illustrations can be seen on any college campus, where students majoring in engineering, say, may consider the humanities to be dull and ambiguous, and will not be concerned about getting poor grades in that area. Thus, if a student's identity is tied to the field of engineering, any negative experience in other areas can be shrugged off as irrelevant, unimportant, or maybe as being good. (Vocational interest tests suggest that engineers are not *supposed* to enjoy Walt Whitman or Thoreau.)

In this connection, a sharp distinction can be made between the general self-concept and the core sense of identity. The former typically may involve knowledge that one is good at math and poor at English; the latter involves personal values indicating whether or not this state of affairs is satisfactory. Furthermore, although we will not do it here, it should also be obvious that vocational choices, long-range goals or motives, and moral beliefs can all easily be discussed from the standpoint of identity.

The third, and perhaps most directly important functional aspect of identity concerns its effect on general adjustment. That is, if identity actually operates in the ways we have been describing it, as an integrating force, then much research on general adjustment is relevant. Consider, for instance, a recent study by Martin (1969). He asked adolescent boys to describe their self-concepts in three ways: self with family, self with friends, and self in general. Fifteen teen-agers previously classified as neurotic showed much more inconsistency between their three self descriptions than another group of 15 classified as normal. Martin suggested that the neurotics are having a more difficult time establishing their identities, hence the different sides of their self-concepts remain relatively disorganized.

Another study by Akeret (1959) required college freshmen to rate themselves in the areas of academic values, interpersonal relations, sexual adjustment and emotional adjustment. He reported that while the self-concepts of individuals vary considerably across these four areas, ratings in all the areas are significantly related to "total self-acceptance." This material suggests that personal identity must be operating in some such way as indicated in our prior discussion of behavioral priorities and interpretations: by giving different weights to the four self-concept areas, general self-acceptance can be maintained even though ratings in some of the areas may be quite low. (It may also be of interest to know that across all 81 subjects in this study, academic values had the smallest average correlation with self-acceptance.)

Finally, work by Rogers, Kell, and McNeil (1948), involving data on 151 youngsters obtained in two separate studies, showed that self-understanding or insight is the best single predictor of future adjustment. Out of eight different factors relevant to personality, which included such things as family background, general physical condition, education, intelligence, and socio-economic status, self-insight had the highest correlation with measures of later adjustment. The material is all the more impressive because the 151 cases were all drawn from the files of a juvenile delinquency bureau. Rogers et al. noted that since self-understanding stands out as important even when other social-psychological factors in the youngster's life situation are relatively negative, it must be recognized as a crucial element in personality. And these writers make it clear that by self-understanding, they mean several of the things we have discussed under the heading of identity:

The final implication carried by the results of this study is that if the individual's view of himself and reality is so important—the degree of his defensiveness, the degree of acceptance of himself, his realistic appraisal of reality, his degree of independence and planfulness, his ability to be objectively self-critical—then a great deal of research is needed in this area (Rogers et al., 1948, p. 186).

The above quotation, as well as later work by Rogers, shows that for him, self-insight or understanding is apparently the most important functional aspect of personal identity. And most of the other material we have discussed in this section follows a similar line. Now, difficult as it is to describe the personal identity concept with precision, let us try a summary statement.

Our reading of the available evidences suggests that for descriptive and analytical purposes, the adolescent's sense of himself as a unique individual can be seen as an emerging, organizing force, which draws together various facets of the self, and thus enables him to begin resolving the conflicts and confusions characteristic of personality development during this period.

It is a complicated, clumsy statement, but what else will serve to describe a complicated phenomenon occurring in a clumsy period? Besides, if one wants simplicity, perhaps the following statement will be more satisfactory: the storm and stress of adolescence is ultimately resolved by the emergence of a unifying sense of personal identity. Identity seems to be the oil that calms the rolling waters of adolescent personality. We get that soothing oil by slowly and painfully wringing it out of our experience—a drop at a time, like as not, as we face and work through the problems of this period.

Summary of critical problems

Theory, research, and common experience all suggest that the way to understand the psychological meaning of problems concerning puberty, family and peer relations, intellectual growth, and personal identity, is by examining their impacts on the self.

We have noted how events in the first four of these areas are likely to have broadly positive or negative impacts. Youngsters who get quickly through puberty changes, for instance, maintain a positive body image, which makes for greater self-confidence. In family relations, it seems clear that positive effects are produced when the adolescent is sufficiently successful in struggles with his parents to be able to set himself apart from them.

Experience with same- and opposite-sex peers has a number of important effects. Popularity enhances self-esteem; close personal friends help one explore new areas of the self which might be too threatening to tackle alone; and a friendly circle of peers serves as a bridge to activities with the opposite sex. These activities, which generally occur in "safe" ritualized dating situations, provide a means of learning new social roles, and of making progress toward more serious heterosexual relations.

Self-concepts can also be shaped by events in the intellectual sphere. If accepted at their face value, various mental tests may influence self-esteem and career plans. It is not commonly understood that measures of individual intelligence vary with age, and become differentiated according to interests. Elkind's extension of Piaget's ideas on cognitive development suggests that the concept of adolescent egocentrism accounts for the peculiar sensitivities of teen-agers.

Finally, the development of a sense of identity, which constitutes the fifth problem area, seems to alter the adolescent's self-concept at its very heart. Identity is, on the one hand, understandable as the result of experiences influencing different facets of the self, and on the other, as an integrating force drawing those facets together to form a unitary whole. However, the sense of identity remains a difficult idea to explain. It has a status in personality work that the nucleus of the atom once had in physics—necessary to assume as real if one is to make sense of related phenomena, but very hard for anyone to put his finger on. Nevertheless, a continuing sense of identity apparently begins to develop by the end of adolescence, and serves thereafter as the essential, directive core of personality.

THEORETICAL PERSPECTIVES

Most of the major developmental theories come to a slow or abrupt halt at the end of adolescence. Neither Freud, Sullivan, nor Piaget offered any systematic view of personality development beyond this period. The ideas of Werner, and Harvey, Hunt and Schroder, can be applied across the board of development because they are not closely tied to specific age periods; but for this same reason they do not permit clear-cut chronological statements about development. Erikson is the single exception: he provided a cradle-to-the-grave framework. However, he accomplished this by sticking to the conspicuous upper reaches of personality. His discussions of ego development sequences did not bog down in details and qualifications, because Erikson was quite selective in his treatment of subject matter.

A small commentary on the longitudinal character of the developmental theories seems necessary at this point because it may help explain why much of the material gives the impression that personality is basically finished by the end of adolescence. That is, from the general standpoint of Freud or Piaget, one might easily assume that if all has gone well for the growing youngster, he will by this time have attained the criteria of adulthood: genital sexuality and formal mental operations. If this is an oversimplification—Freud and Piaget would undoubtedly place many strong qualifications on the above statement—it is nevertheless true that the main lines of their developmental work terminate at the end of adolescence.

Furthermore, with the exception of Erikson, the relatively short chronological range of the major developmental theories means that beyond adolescence, one is in free theoretical territory. The literature changes drastically: one finds a whole crowd of theoretical writers scattered over the adult personality landscape. It is still possible to categorize most of them as primarily oriented to the social-emotional or cognitive side of personality, but the fairly clear lines of Freudian and Piagetian work we have enjoyed up to this point tend to blur.

Many of the reasons for this diversification of theories will become clearer as we discuss the outstanding approaches to adolescence itself. In general, however, it is assumed that *adult* personality changes mainly involve unresolved problems left over from earlier periods. Since these can take many different forms, the result is that there are many different theoretical formulations.

Freud

Sigmund Freud believed that in adolescence, libido finally concentrates in the genital area of the body. He therefore called this period the genital stage of psychosexual development, and spoke of proper genital sex adjustment as the hallmark of maturity. Yet it cannot be taken for granted that such an adjustment will occur automatically—too many difficulties stand in the way.

To begin with, there is the superego. We are all familiar with the social norms and values which prohibit genital sex relations for teen-agers in most Western societies. Freud saw these prohibitions internalized as the superego component of personality, which emerges strongly in youngsters as a consequence of the Oedipus complex. But as was noted in Chapter 4, with the new upsurge of sex feelings generated by puberty changes, and with the wearing away of repressions toward the end of the latency period, superego prohibitions gradually begin to crumble.

Why should the guilt feelings which have enforced obedience to superego demands up to this point now become weaker or less effective? One reason is that they wear out—more or less like old military fortifications. Guilt feelings relevant to sexual matters take their initial strength from fears associated with the Oedipus complex. By the time of adolescence, these fears are considerably diminished.[4] The guilt feeling "barrier" is thus less able to withstand the onslaughts of newly invigorated sex impulses.

---

[4] The adolescent is bigger, stronger, and understands the world much better than he did at five or six. Therefore, while castration fears traceable to that time may still be strong, they are not nearly as strong as they used to be. For boys, successful identification with adult male figures also helps reduce these fears. For girls, the whole matter is, as usual in Freudian theory, not so clear. However, their growing feminine identification presumably reduces the force of superego prohibitions in some way analogous to the case for boys.

Moreover, the Oedipal fears which form the basis for superego prohibitions against sex can be bypassed, or outflanked, so to speak, because teen-agers find sex objects to serve as replacements for their mothers and fathers. Remember that as a result of the Oedipus complex, the strongest superego prohibitions are supposed to concern sex impulses directed toward parents. The guilt feelings here enforce an incest taboo, and Freud thought that the absence of sex interests during the latency period occurred because the taboo was so strong that it generalized or slopped over to cover all other sex activities. But the new sex drive of the adolescent goes toward opposite-sex peers, not parents, and so the most intense, incest-oriented guilt feelings are not aroused.

This last point leads to another question: why should libido be diverted to opposite-sex peers when it is initially, in early childhood, directed at parents? Very briefly, it is suggested that this diversion occurs when the teen-ager's sex impulse bumps up against the incest taboo. Faced with a still-strong barrier right here, sex impulses get directed toward other, more available objects. (Note, however, that teen-agers are often strongly attracted to older persons of the opposite sex. Freudians see this as evidence of a last-ditch effort by libido to reach its original target: if Momma or Papa aren't available, the next best thing is someone like them.)

And still another question occurs, to which one can only give a makeshift answer. Why does the incest taboo remain strong enough to keep parents out of it, but not strong enough to force repression of all sex impulses? We have already mentioned some relevant ideas: the wearing out of childhood guilt feelings, and the new strength of the sex drive, but another military analogy suggests itself here as a summary statement. Being unable to defend effectively on a broad sexual front, superego pulls back and concentrates its remaining forces in defense of the main citadel: incest.

Stripped to their essentials, Freud's ideas about the outbreak of genital sexuality in adolescence seem to involve three points: (a) Physiological changes give sexual feelings a new strength and urgency. (b) These desires overwhelm superego prohibitions dating back to the Oedipus complex. (c) While adolescent libido may initially focus on opposite-sex parents, it is soon diverted to more acceptable targets outside the family.

However, these ideas about the dynamics whereby sex impulses are finally directed toward opposite-sex peers cover only one side of Freud's analysis of the meaning of genital adjustment. This side concerns the pitfalls. If early fears have been extreme, and/or, been reinforced by harsh experiences involving sex impulses, the young person may not be able to overcome superego prohibitions very well. Or he may be in a situation where acceptable non-family targets for libido are not available. But we must also consider the other side of genital sexuality. Assuming that all goes well, and that neurotic difficulties are avoided, how is a healthy genital sex relationship to be understood as the ultimate criterion of mature personality? The question cannot be answered with a simple statement from Freud or any of his interpreters, because they only provide complex, open-ended discussions. And at another extreme, one finds among many professionals a shorthand description of genital sexuality which adds up to "sex without hang-ups" – which is unsatisfactory because it is *too* simple. The discussion below is an effort to find a middle ground; something that will do justice to Freud's ideas without running off into too much detail.

When a young male and female engage in mutually satisfactory sexual intercourse (and this will apply to older people as well), their bodies are literally joined together, and certain of their bodily substances literally mingle together. Furthermore, in the ideal case, intercourse provides both partners with orgasm—a physical release of tension which gives acute pleasure. This brief, necessarily cold-blooded, description of "good" intercourse is the basis for several important ideas—love, for instance. Freud suggested that genital sex desires produce such high tension, and the need for gratification is so great, that young people in particular see the whole affair through rose-colored glasses. They romanticize sex because it is so pleasurable. In effect, anything that is so wonderful must be very special.

Aside from offering a base for understanding romantic love, however, the problem remains as to why happy sex relations are supposed to have positive effects on personality. It is partly because sexual orgasm serves as an important, perhaps the *most* important, means of releasing id-inspired tensions. In Freudian terms, any important release of id tensions is called a "catharsis," and orgasm is catharsis at its best. It has positive effects on personality because it allows release of tensions that might otherwise have to be kept repressed, displaced, or sublimated. These and other indirect ways of handling id tensions are liable to lead to various behavior problems. In short, orgasm drains away tension that might otherwise cause trouble in the personality system—especially if these tensions build up to the point where they begin to swamp normally innocuous defense mechanisms. It follows logically, in ways that we cannot explain in detail, that orgasm makes for mental health. And some of Freud's followers have even suggested that the quality of one's orgasm is definitive of his total personality adjustment.

Another psychological aspect of orgasm is concerned with the interpersonal or social character of sexual intercourse. After all, most people can create orgasms for themselves. But orgasm with another person whom one likes and respects is supposed to be best, because it involves giving as well as receiving pleasure. And this in turn means that one's ego is being affirmed at the same time as catharsis is attained. In other words, intercourse allows the individual to express the deepest of id-impulses in a way that affirms his sense of being a good and worthwhile person. The more the sex partner is loved, the more pleasure the partner receives, the greater will be the benefit to ego. This is probably the most important idea underlying the meaning of proper genital adjustment, so it deserves further discussion. If a child performs some difficult social act and receives strong approval from a parent or respected peer, his self-concept will be enhanced in ways already discussed. Sexual intercourse is clearly a social act—many clinical authorities believe it is the most fundamental of all social acts—and a successful "performance" will enhance the self-concept of the adolescent or adult here, just as other social achievements will strengthen the self-concept of a child. The effects are similar in principle, but much stronger and more important for the grown-up, because much more is involved; intercourse is usually the culmination of a great deal of social behavior.

It should also be made very clear that in speaking of ego enhancement or affirmation of the self in connection with intercourse, we do not mean simple *egotism*. That is, if an individual uses sex primarily as a vehicle for controlling or manipulating his partner, as a means of demonstrating power to dominate the partner—and there are many case history reports of "sexual athletes" of this type—then they do not meet Freud's criterion of meaningful genital sexuality. Instead, they are using sex in a phallic way; it becomes just another complex mechanism for working out inferiority feelings, and obtaining narrowly selfish pleasure. The real value of genital sex for personality development can only be attained when persons give of themselves as fully and honestly as possible, because only then will they truly affirm themselves in the relationship with their partners. One can't enhance his ego if it is not exposed.

This is why orgasm through masturbation, or with a prostitute, or any easy make, is considered to be a quite inadequate form of genital sex. Freud suggested that these lesser forms of sex may provide a useful release of tension; they are better than nothing, but such stopgap methods should not be confused with the genuine article.

There is, finally, one additional way in which Freud saw proper genital sex adjustment as an important criterion for a fully mature personality. When a person has regular orgasms in intercourse with one for whom he feels significant liking and respect, the catharsis obtained in this way will reduce his need to rely on defense mechanisms: a proper release of libido means that one doesn't have to guard against it so much. Therefore, psychic energy which might otherwise have to be employed for defensive purposes is liberated. And this makes more energy available for creative or constructive purposes. A happy genital sex adjustment is thus supposed to bring with it an invigorated mental life—a life freed from the necessity always to be watching for and keeping down threatening id-impulses. So it is that the person experiencing good catharsis, and related ego enhancement, can, in the mental sphere, find new fields to conquer—he is no longer psychologically chained down by petty (counterproductive) defensive enterprises. From the writings of Freud and other authorities in this area, one gets the image of "Prometheus unbound," man at his best, and so forth. And it is indeed a fact that some persons report having such feelings once they begin to enjoy a satisfactory genital sex life.

For summary purposes then, we can see Freud's conception of genital sex adjustment as involving two general steps. First, the adolescent must break through superego barriers to heterosexual activity, which stand as the psychological legacy of the Oedipus complex. Second, once the breakthrough is accomplished and opposite-sex peers become the objects of sex impulses, the difficult search for a good genital relationship begins. This will be difficult because Freud's criteria are not easy to satisfy. It is an open question whether anyone ever achieves perfect genitality for any length of time. Really, who among us is ready to claim that his sex life contains all of the Freudian elements? Mutually satisfactory tension-releasing orgasms, ego enhancement, and liberation from energy-absorbing defense mechanisms make a sizable package.

We should again emphasize that our discussion only covers the main lines of Freud's ideas about genital sexuality. He believed, at least in theory, that it is possible for persons to achieve a good genital adjustment at the end of adolescence, and that such an adjustment marked the high point of personality development. He also indicated that since in practice most people do not achieve true genitality by this time, the main work of personality development beyond adolescence must involve efforts to remove psychological barriers blocking the way to genitality. In the writings of orthodox Freudians, genital sexuality appears somewhat as the Holy Grail of personality development. One who seeks perfection is more or less condemned to search for it through sex. A difficult program, especially for those over 30 who may get tired. But if this is a criticism of Freud's ideas, most Freudians would probably accept it, and add that that's why so many adults have so many problems.

Sullivan

Speaking very generally, Harry Stack Sullivan saw adolescence in much the same way as Freud. Both defined the period according to genital sexuality, except that Sullivan said it begins when the youngster feels lust. And both divided the period into two phases. Sullivan called the first phase, when the teen-ager is breaking through normative sex prohibitions, *early adolescence*. The next phase, when the young person has a better understanding of sex and seeks relationships Freud would describe as truly genital, is described by Sullivan as *late adolescence*. Thus, so far as development is concerned, it appears that both theorists have similar views about the importance of sex. The following discussion of Sullivan concentrates on early adolescence. His ideas on late adolescence are left for the next chapter, because they are more concerned with material we will present under the heading of adult transition.

Sullivan believed three major personality needs all become clear during early adolescence: the need for security, freedom from anxiety; the need for intimacy, close collaboration with another person; and the need to satisfy lust, achieve orgasms. These needs develop along separate lines, with lust being the last to emerge. However, since all three are operating during early adolescence, the chief general problem of this period is to sort them out and integrate them in a reasonably harmonious fashion. Most of the serious problems causing trouble for adolescents are attributed to underlying confusions or conflicts between the three basic needs.

Consider the potential confusions over lust and personal security. In childhood, the security need is uppermost; children require assurances of acceptance and all the usual things meant by love, if they are to gain a good sense of self-esteem. Even if it is well established earlier, however, this sense of esteem or personal worth can later collide with the lust need, because heterosexual activity may threaten it. Briefly, if a young person's idea of himself as a decent person relates to social values which define adolescent sexuality as bad or evil, he cannot accept his lust need without endangering his personal security. Note that at this level, Sullivan is in principle close to Freud. The security-lust conflict seems very similar to the conflict between superego prohibitions and libido. Yet deeper differences between the theorists involve more than terminology. From Freud one has the impression that once super-ego prohibitions are put in their place, they will no longer be a source of trouble. But from Sullivan one has the impression that conflicts between lust and security needs may always remain a source of trouble. A person may get over adolescent fears concerning sex, but all through life fundamental conflicts between personal security and lust are, in one way or another, liable to come up again.

The need for intimacy emerges during preadolescence; Sullivan accepted the chum relationships typical of ten- to twelve-year-olds as prima facie evidence. And from material presented earlier in this chapter, it should also be plain that intimacy with a same-sex friend carries over to be an important feature of adolescence as well. Now we might mention more or less in passing that teen-agers' needs for security and intimacy can easily collide. In fact, some empirical research indicates that they do, otherwise why would youngsters so often speak of loyalty as one of the important elements in friendship? A friend who betrays secrets or gossips too much clearly violates the need for security. It would seem that intimacy always involves some risk of security. But when intimacy shifts over to focus on opposite-sex peers, the stage is set for collision with lust.

In some instances, the collision is avoided because youngsters keep the two needs separated. They may hang on to same-sex friends while satisfying lust with masturbation, prostitutes, or easy makes. However, this only prevents the intimacy-lust conflict at the expense of personality integration. When the two needs are kept apart behaviorally, they are kept apart psychologically: the person is not accepting both as legitimate elements in himself. Furthermore, like Freud, Sullivan indicated that the two needs will each be better satisfied when they are linked together. Social intimacy will be enhanced by physical intimacy which brings people literally as close together as possible. Lust, for its part, is better satisfied when accompanied by social intimacy because it then takes on much more meaning to the individual.

Sullivan was not too clear on exactly how intimacy-lust collisions occur. Most of his discussion centers on awkwardness or anxiety about physical sex activity as the precipitating cause. For instance, inexperienced young men are liable either to have a premature ejaculation, or to suffer momentary impotence. In either case, the failure to satisfy lust is liable to contaminate the social intimacy built up between him and his partner. They may blame each other for the failure, or, they may feel too much anxiety and embarrassment in each other's presence. Another possibility is that if a young man feels anxiety about sex, he may try to cover it by attacking his objective in a fairly brutal fashion — which can obviously result in destruction of social intimacy.

All in all, it should be plain that Sullivan saw the problems of adolescent personality development being caused by difficulties which prevent integration of the new lust need together with prior needs for personal security and intimacy. These difficulties are in many ways similar to traditional Freudian views of genital sex problems. But for all the superficial similarity between them in this respect, Sullivan was fundamentally different from Freud because he did not assign the same overriding importance to physical sex relationships. Both saw sex creating terriffic *problems* for adolescents, but Sullivan saw these problems as ultimately tied to social factors in personality. The essential difference was that for Sullivan, lust is just a basic physiological need, which has to be integrated with other, social needs, if personality is to develop in a healthy direction. For Freud, lust is a direct manifestation of the all-pervasive libido, which is much more than a simple physiological need.

Erikson

The possibilities of adolescent personality development were understood by Erik Erikson to range between the two poles of "identity" and "role confusion." Healthy development will involve the attainment of a sense of ego identity, which has already been discussed as a general problem for teenagers. But Erikson's particular theoretical contributions included the role confusion interpretation of failure to achieve identity, and emphasis on sexuality and vocational choice as the two main foundations of identity.

It is basic for Erikson that during adolescence, sexual changes and other effects of the "physiological revolution" of puberty force reorganization of the self-concept. Since this general idea has had extensive discussion, it hardly needs further elaboration. However, the role played by vocational choices or career plans in establishing identity is another matter.

Erikson indicated that reorganization of the self, culminating in a strong sense of identity, will depend to an important degree on how the teen-ager sees his future. If youngsters have an idea of what kind of adult role they want to fill, this can serve as a guide or organizing principle for their emerging sense of identity. Or, to put it in still another way, the necessity to reorganize the self is imposed by puberty changes and other related matters, but the forward thrust or direction of the reorganization is determined by career plans (adult role aspirations).

It follows that the teen-ager who is seriously interested in some adult role will begin to shape his identity accordingly. For example, it is trite but nevertheless true that as a teen-ager one of my friends used to devour Perry Mason novels and he is now a successful lawyer. And another who liked historical novels became a history teacher. But such instances in which adolescent interests relate directly to adult careers do not occur very frequently. Perhaps not even in the cases just mentioned; the first friend is in corporation not criminal law, and the second has become a high school principal. Many authorities, and perhaps Erikson himself, would argue that in modern societies, most teen-agers are not able to make a serious vocational choice because they haven't had time to learn about all the different possibilities. In fact, it often seems that the best one can hope for is some conviction among teen-agers concerning what they *don't* want to be.

But while it is possible to debate the relative merits of early vs. late career choices almost endlessly, Erikson's main theoretical point concerning the directive function that can be served by career plans seems quite plausible. He further suggested that the great danger in this period is "role confusion." If a substantial sense of identity does not develop, the young person will probably remain confused about himself; he will not develop a firm idea of who and what he is. And the teen-ager in this condition is likely to seek a stable role by identifying with popular cultural figures, or by falling in love. The underlying principle here seems to be that if the youngster cannot gain a sense of identity through his own internal resources, he will try to gain it by appealing to external resources.

It is easy enough to understand why Erikson suggested that teen-agers might try to strengthen their sense of identity by modelling themselves after popular entertainers, because this is one way for young people to resolve some of their uncertainties and increase their self-esteem. However, the basis for his idea that adolescent love affairs also serve these same purposes is more difficult to grasp. Erikson argued that when an adolescent falls in love, he projects his confused image of himself upon the loved one. Then, depending upon the reactions he receives, the adolescent may be able to clarify some of his confusions and feel increased self-esteem. In principle, the loved one acts as a kind of sounding board for the ideas of the lover, and this is why Erikson said that ". . . so much of young love is conversation."

Finally, Erikson suggested that adolescent preoccupations with ideologies and moral creeds can be understood to be a consequence of role confusion. The teen-ager is groping for new personal values. To the extent that his identity is unstable, he will be attracted to ideologies which offer to provide stability, or at least a solid moral anchorage. In this connection, Erikson referred to the adolescent mind as a "moratorium," because it stands midway between the certainties of childhood and the ethics of adulthood. This middle point in development is marked by a search for social values which can guide identity, and so ideological concerns are said to be characteristic of the "moratorium."

It is intriguing to consider how the moratorium idea might be applied to current problems—the new youth culture and generation gap. If one accepts the notion that many traditional social values are themselves in a rather confused state today, then the "moratorium" resulting from adolescent confusions seems likely to be a very prolonged affair. And at a time when the average American teen-ager can only envision a future containing such things as unpopular wars, the draft system, racial struggles, urban crises, a polluted atmosphere, and so on, the career plans which might otherwise help to reduce role confusion are bound to appear somewhat irrelevant . . . think of *The Graduate*. However, any attempt to second-guess a robust theorist like Erikson seems unwise; we might better hope that he himself will address these new problems.

Piaget

Adolescence sees the last, major step forward in cognitive development. Jean Piaget suggested that the concrete mental operations of the child—his ability to perform symbolic mental operations on objects immediately present—is now succeeded by an ability to perform mental operations on objects *not* immediately present. More generally, Piaget's work indicated that thinking achieves its final liberation during adolescence because it is able to function beyond the constraints of immediate reality.

Flavell noted that the most important functional difference between formal operations and all earlier modes of thought concerns the changed relationship between the *real* and the *possible*. Even when it has progressed to the relatively advanced stage of concrete operations, the child's thinking always proceeds from the real *toward* the possible. In adolescence, thinking may for the first time proceed from the possible to the real. This distinction often seems rather abstract and irrelevant at first glance. But consider a commonplace example.

The other day, in one of those super supermarkets stocking everything from clothing to guns to groceries, my young son discovered a fairly complicated piece of equipment for his bicycle. He saw it in terms of reality: bright colors, shiny chrome, and an illustrative picture showing how wonderfully it would enhance any bicycle. My own immediate reaction, however, was in terms of possibilities. Were all the parts needed for the assembly included in the box? Did the thing really fit all bicycles? Could one manage the operation with an inadequate tool chest and a related tendency to be undone by rusted cotter pins, frozen nuts, and slipping adjustable wrenches? It is in such everyday incidents that one may begin to grasp the difference between thinking geared to reality and possibility. And if any doubt about the distinction still lingers, consider further how difficult it is for possibility-geared thinking to engage reality-geared thinking: my own effort in this direction was pathetically useless. The situation was only saved when we discovered another object with equally appealing concrete characteristics, but much fewer negative possibilities.

But how is the possibility orientation of formal mental operations to be understood? Where does Piaget's idea originate? Here again, as one always finds it in his work, the theoretical statement is grounded in naturalistic experiments and observation. Piaget's studies of how children work problems reveal that adolescents think them through in a developmentally new, hypothetico-deductive fashion. That is, when facing a problem with several possible solutions, the concretely operational child will consider some of the more apparent solutions, and proceed to try them out. The formally operational teen-ager, however, will consider all possible solutions, and then begin trying them out according to some systematic plan.

A standard experimental problem described by Inhelder and Piaget (1958), for instance, involved five bottles containing colorless liquids. Four of them were numbered and the fifth was labeled g. The investigator began by showing his subject two glasses also containing colorless liquids. He added several drops from the g bottle to both glasses, and the liquid in one of them turned yellow. Now the subject was given two new glasses and told that his problem was to discover how to use liquids from the four numbered bottles in such a way as to reproduce the demonstration that a few drops from g will yield yellow. The answer is a mixture of $1 + 3 + g$.

Adolescents usually begin this task with remarks to the effect that they must try g with all combinations from the four bottles. It is as if they were able to visualize a table or matrix containing all the possible mixtures. By contrast, young preoperational children will try a few random mixtures, while older concretely operational children are in between: they try the different single liquids, and several different mixtures with g, but do not systematically try all possible combinations.

This experiment is something of a classic (it is described in detail by most writers who discuss formal operations) because it reveals three distinctive processes which underlie the workings of higher-order logical thought. While demonstrating the teen-ager's new ability to map possibilities, it also shows his ability to think in terms of *hypothesis testing*. Here is a bit of illustrative dialogue from a thirteen-year-old tested by Inhelder and Piaget:

> Perhaps you could add 4 in $1 \times 3 \times g$ to see if it would cancel out the color [he does this]. Liquid 4 cancels it all. You'd have to see if 2 has the same influence [he tries it]. No, so 2 and 4 are not alike, for 4 acts on 1×3 and 2 does not (1958, p. 117).

The hypothesis-testing approach seems to be effective because it is linked with the second process, *"propositional" thinking*. In this connection, Flavell (1963, p. 205) said that adolescents use their prior ability to perform concrete operations as the means of generating propositions which provide the substance of formal operations:

> He takes the *results* of these concrete operations, casts them in the form of propositions, and then proceeds to operate further upon them, i.e., make various kinds of logical connections between them (implication, conjunction, identity, disjunction, etc.). Formal operations, then, are really operations performed upon the results of prior (concrete) operations.

And formal operations further include the third process, the ability to perform *"combinatorial analyses."* The adolescent can think of all specific factors or variables contained in a problem, and he can also think of all the possible combinations which might be produced by these variables.

The discussion to this point has mainly concerned the functional properties of formal operations. But an important part of Piaget's work dealt with its structural properties. His ideas were very complex, involving elaborations of the logical grouping structures sketched in Chapter 7. For this reason, only his general view will be mentioned, and the interested reader will be referred to books by Baldwin, Flavell, and Inhelder and Piaget.

Briefly, the grouping structures underlying concrete mental operations were described in Chapter 7 as logical rules for combining elements in various kinds of sets. In childhood, these groupings are considered to be relatively specific: they characterize mental operations used one at a time, in particular situations. Flavell referred to these groupings as being related to *intra*propositional mental operations. By contrast, the adolescent's thinking involves logical groupings which allow him to perform *inter*propositional mental operations. To accomplish this, the different groupings of childhood must now operate together in a more or less simultaneous fashion. To put it in less abstract terms: when Piaget described formal operations as including all possible solutions to a problem, and being combinatorial in this respect, he suggested that all the possibilities form a "lattice structure" of combinations. And it is the joint functioning of different logical groupings, different rules for combining elements, which produces the lattice containing all possible combinations.

So by way of a very superficial summary, one might say that Piaget understood the structural properties of formal operations to be based upon a higher-order integration of logical groupings. It should be emphasized that Piaget offered much more than this . . . but we are stopping here because any further discussion leads into extensive discourse on mathematical logic.

Formal operations and personality

If adolescent thinking is in fact characterized by a general orientation toward possibility, and supported by new abilities to make combinatorial analyses, formulate propositions, and test hypotheses, what effects should all this have on personality? We can see some of the effects by referring to the egocentrism described by Elkind and the sensitivity to ideology suggested by Erikson.

Remember that Elkind proposed a new kind of egocentrism developing during adolescence. The young child's egocentrism is such that he sees the world mainly from his own perspective, according to his own personal needs. So his thinking appears highly subjective because it has an *internal* focus. Elkind argued that the adolescent's thinking also appears highly subjective, but for a different reason: the teen-ager places too much emphasis on *external* considerations; he is overly concerned and sensitive about what others will think of him. This general notion is obviously in agreement with all sorts of common experience. However, it should now be clear that a fundamental basis for such sensitivity lies in Piaget's specification of the possibility-geared nature of formal mental operations.

As teen-agers begin to think according to possibilities instead of immediate realities, they are, in a manner of speaking, liable to be swept off their feet by this new cognitive capacity. Thus, whereas thinking was once egocentric because it was tied too closely to arbitrary, personal *realities*, in adolescence it may be egocentric because it is tied too closely to arbitrary, personal *possibilities*.

Working from this general angle of cognitive development theory, one might easily go on to formulate explanations for many aspects of adolescent behavior which are ordinarily discussed only in social-emotional terms. It might be suggested, for example, that formal dating rituals reflect formal mental operations, because they are designed to protect against undesirable possibilities. And the close friendships of adolescence can be seen as providing ways of learning about new possibilities. Furthermore, many parent-adolescent conflicts, generation gaps or whatnot, would also appear to be partly caused, and surely aggravated, by the egocentric possibility-orientation of teen-agers.

Another plausible extension of cognitive development theory is to the discovery of social problems by teen-agers. Why should matters that have never before concerned them – war, prejudice, poverty and the like – suddenly become important? And why should adolescents become interested in the ideologies associated with social problems? Erikson discussed this in connection with his moratorium concept: the adolescent is supposed to be searching for values to replace the rules of childhood. But Inhelder and Piaget saw these things in relation to newly liberated thought capacities. They described adolescence as a "metaphysical" age, because so many teen-agers become preoccupied with metaphysical problems. Is man inherently good or evil? If there is a loving God, why does he permit so much injustice in the world? In short, social problems and related philosophical-ideological questions come to the fore because teen-agers are for the first time able to consider them in terms of alternative possibilities.

Being able to think according to rules of objective logic (groupings), the illogic or actual hypocrisy they can see around them becomes very conspicuous. It seems illogical when parents profess belief in democratic ideals but show prejudice in their everyday behavior, or when religious institutions proclaim the importance of charity but spend more money on new buildings than on helping the poor. Moreover, the emotional forces usually associated with moral feelings are liable to make the adolescent's new discoveries here very significant for his emerging sense of identity.

It seems appropriate to end our discussion of Piaget at this point, even though his ideas probably could be used to good effect in relation to many other personality problems in adolescence. However, remember that cognitive development is just beginning to be understood as an important influence on the social-emotional side of personality development. Elkind's work on adolescent egocentrism is only one outstanding example of what may be expected in the future.

CHAPTER SUMMARY

Superficially, adolescence has something of a naive-noble revolutionary atmosphere to it — a romantic aura involving all sorts of storm-stress sensitivity-confusion dramatics. And when one comes to close grips with the period, this general image or free-floating metaphor does not seem too far off the mark. For analytical purposes, we have defined adolescence according to two critical conditions and five critical problems. Most of the material developed around these critical factors stands in support of our initial remarks: it is a wonder that most of us survive it as well as we do, and it is no wonder that most of us would hate to have to do it again.

The puberty condition alone is enough to make strong men shudder. Physiological changes of this order of magnitude must inevitably seem magical to many youngsters. Indeed, among primitives these changes are bound up in ritual and religious mysteries. To make matters worse, however, just when the young teen-ager is well into the ordeal of puberty, and therefore in need of all the social support he can get, the second critical condition of adolescence sets in: inferior social status. The youngster must proceed through most of his teens stripped of the indulgences given to children, yet not allowed to seize the initiatives available to adults. So, having been revolutionized within his skin, the shaken adolescent also finds himself in a social limbo, with difficult social-emotional problems lying ahead of him.

Briefly, these include restructuring of the body image, restructuring relations with parents, elaboration of new, more intense relationships with same- and opposite-sex peers, diversification of intellectual ability according to interests, and acquisition of an integrating sense of identity. In general, the first four problems all relate to specific aspects of the adolescent's self-concept, but these problems have also been discussed as more or less inevitable reactions to the environmental conditions of adolescence. The identity problem is quite different, however. Identity seems to emerge at the core of the self-concept, as a product or vector resulting from multiple forces, and then to serve in turn as an integrating, directive force in personality development.

Among the major theoretical perspectives on adolescence, one can find systematic statements relevant to all the definitive problems we have mentioned. Freud and Sullivan both concerned themselves with the sexual consequences of puberty. Since Freud understood genital sex activity as representing deep-lying forces which energize the whole structure of personality, it is not surprising to see genitality used as the chief criterion of mature development. Sullivan shifted the emphasis on sex toward interpersonal relations. While acknowledging lust as a major new need, he suggested that its functional meaning for personality lies in how it is integrated with prior needs for security and intimacy. Erikson placed even greater emphasis on social experience. The essential basis for adolescent development toward either ego identity or role confusion seems to depend almost entirely on social matters.

Finally, by drawing attention to the development of possibility-geared thinking, Piaget's conception of formal mental operations offered theoretical illumination for the whole terrain of adolescent personality. That is, one can see the major social-emotional problems of this period in a new light, as at least partly a result of the adolescent's new capacity for a complex but very efficient mode of thought. Piaget's ideas suggest that cognitively speaking, the adolescent may be understood as an enthusiastic nouveau riche; he moves awkwardly into previously unknown domains of thinking, without being much aware of their social-emotional implications. Therefore, while the development of formal mental operations is primarily understood as marking the final stage of cognitive growth, one can find in work by Elkind, Harvey et al., Inhelder and Piaget, and others, strong indications that many adolescent problems arise from asynchrony or disharmony between cognitive and social-emotional factors. But at this point we are ready to move on, for, as will be shown in the following chapter, better integration of cognitive and social-emotional factors seems to be one of the main features of the adult transition period.

References

Akeret, R. U. Interrelationships among various dimensions of the self concept. *Journal of Counseling Psychology,* 1959, *6,* 199–201.

Baldwin, A. *Theories of child development.* New York: John Wiley & Sons, Inc., 1968.

Baumrind, D. Authoritarian vs. authoritative parental control. *Adolescence,* 1968, *3,* 255–271.

Bell, R. R. The marital expectations of adolescents. In J. F. Adams (Ed.), *Understanding adolescence.* Boston: Allyn & Bacon, Inc., 1968, pp. 272–286.

Beller, E. K. Theories of adolescent development. In J. F. Adams (Ed.), *Understanding adolescence*. Boston: Allyn & Bacon, Inc., 1968, pp. 70–100.

Berdie, R. F. Personality changes from high school entrance to college matriculation. *Journal of Counseling Psychology*, 1968, *15*, 376–380.

Bowerman, C. E., & Kinch, J. W. Changes in family and peer orientation of children between the fourth and tenth grades. *Social Forces*, 1959, *37*, 206–211.

Bradway, K., & Thompson, C. Intelligence at adulthood: A twenty-five year follow-up. *Journal of Educational Psychology*, 1962, *53*, 1–14.

Brookover, W. B., Shailor, T., & Paterson, A. Self-concept of ability and school achievement. *Sociology of Education*, 1964, *37*, 271–278.

Carroll, J. F. X. Understanding student rebellion. *Adolescence*, 1969, *4*, 163–180.

Costanzo, P. R., & Shaw, M. E. Conformity as a function of age level. *Child Development*, 1966, *37*, 967–975.

Cross, H. J., & Allen, J. G. Relationships between memories of parental behavior and academic achievement in college. *Proceedings* American Psychological Association, 1969, 285–286.

Crow, L. D., & Crow, A. *Adolescent development and adjustment*. (2nd ed.) New York: McGraw-Hill Book Company, 1965.

Douvan, E., & Adelson, J. *The adolescent experience*. New York: John Wiley & Sons, Inc., 1966.

Douvan, E., & Kay, C. *Adolescent girls*. Ann Arbor: Survey Research Center publication, University of Michigan, 1957.

Dunphy, G. P. The social structure of urban adolescent peer groups. *Sociometry*, 1963, *26*, 230–246.

Dwyer, J., & Mayer, J. Psychological effects of variations in physical appearance during adolescence. *Adolescence*, 1968, *3*, 353–380.

Dynes, R. R., Clarke, A. C., & Dinitz, S. Levels of occupational aspiration: Some aspects of family experience as a variable. *American Sociological Review*, April 1956, 212–215.

Elkind, D. Cognitive development in adolescence. In J. F. Adams (Ed.), *Understanding adolescence*. Boston: Allyn & Bacon, Inc., 1968, pp. 128–158.

Engel, Mary. The stability of the self concept in adolescence. *Journal of Abnormal and Social Psychology*, 1959, *58*, 211–215.

Erikson, E. H. *Childhood and society*. (2nd ed.) New York: W. W. Norton & Company, Inc., 1950, 1963.

Erikson, E. H. Hitler's imagery and German youth. *Psychiatry*, 1942, *5*, 475–493.

Fanon, F. *The wretched of the earth*. New York: Grove Press, Inc., 1963.

Flavell, J. H. *The developmental psychology of Jean Piaget*. New York: D. Van Nostrand & Co., Inc., 1963.

Foster, R. Radical opinions in adults, college and high school students: A comparative study. Unpublished undergraduate research, Kansas State University, 1969.

Friedenberg, E. Z. *Coming of age in America: Growth and acquiescence*. New York: Vintage Books, Random House, Inc., 1967.

Friedenberg, E. Z. Current patterns of a generational conflict. *The Journal of Social Issues*, 1969, *25*, 21–38.

Gaier, E. Adolescence: The current imbroglio. *Adolescence*, 1969, *4*, 89–109.

Garrison, K. C. Physiological changes in adolescence. In J. F. Adams (Ed.), *Understanding adolescence*. Boston: Allyn & Bacon, Inc., 1968, pp. 43–69.

Gesell, A., Ilg, F. L., & Ames, L. *Youth, the years from ten to sixteen.* New York: Harper & Row, Publishers, 1956.

Gold, M. Juvenile delinquency as a symptom of alienation. *The Journal of Social Issues*, 1969, *25*, 121–135.

Gold, M., & Douvan, E. *Adolescent development.* Boston: Allyn & Bacon, Inc., 1969.

Gould, L. J. Conformity and marginality: Two faces of alienation. *Journal of Social Issues*, 1969, *25*, 39–63.

Hall, G. S. *Adolescence*, Vol. 2. New York: D. Appleton & Co., 1904.

Hamilton, G. V., & MacGowan, K. *What is wrong with marriage?* New York: Boni, 1929.

Harris, D. B. Sex differences in the life problems and interests of adolescents, 1935 and 1957. *Child Development*, 1959, *30*, 453–459.

Havighurst, R. J., Bowman, P. H., & Liddle, G. P. *Growing up in River City.* New York: John Wiley & Sons, Inc., 1962.

Hetzer, H. Der Körper in der Selbstdarstellung von Kinder im Jahre 1926 und im Jahre 1957 (The body in self-descriptions of children in 1926 and 1957). *Zeitschrift fur Experimentale und Angewandte Psychology*, 1959, *6*, 15–21.

Horrocks, J. E. *The psychology of adolescence.* Boston: Houghton Mifflin Company, 1962.

Hurlock, E. *Adolescent development.* (3rd ed.) New York: McGraw-Hill Book Company, 1967.

Inhelder, B., & Piaget, J. *The growth of logical thinking from childhood to adolescence.* New York: Basic Books, Inc., Publishers, 1958.

Jersild, A. T. *In search of self.* New York: Columbia University Bureau of Publications, 1952.

Jersild, A. T. *The psychology of adolescence.* (2nd ed.) New York: The Macmillan Company, 1963.

Jones, M. C. A comparison of the attitudes and interests of ninth-grade students over two decades. *Journal of Educational Psychology*, 1960, *51*, 175–186.

Lewin, K. Field theory and experiment in social psychology. *The American Journal of Sociology*, 1939, *44*, 868–897.

Martin, D. G. Consistency of self-descriptions under different role sets in neurotic and normal adolescents and adults. *Journal of Abnormal Psychology*, 1969, *74*, 113–116.

Marwell, G. Adolescent powerlessness and delinquent behavior. *Social Problems*, 1966, *14*, 35–47.

Masters, W. H., & Johnson, V. *Human sexual response.* Boston: Little, Brown and Company, 1966.

Mussen, P. H., Conger, J. J., & Kagan, J. *Child development and personality.* (2nd ed.) New York: Harper & Row, Publishers, 1963.

Mussen, P. H., & Jones, M. C. Self conceptions, motivations and interpersonal attitudes of late and early maturing boys. *Child Development,* 1957, *28*, 243–256.

Mussen, P. H., & Jones, M. C. The behavior inferred motivations of late and early maturing boys. *Child Development*, 1958, *29*, 61–67.

Pikas, A. Children's attitudes toward rational versus inhibiting parental authority. *Journal of Abnormal and Social Psychology*, 1961, *62*, 315–321.

Powell, M. Age and sex differences in degree of conflict within certain areas of psychological adjustment. *Psychological Monographs*, 1955, *69*, #387.

Rogers, C. R., Kell, B. L., & McNeil, H. The role of self-understanding in the prediction of behavior. *Journal of Consulting Psychology*, 1948, *12*, 174–186.

Schaefer, E. S., & Bayley, N. Consistency of maternal behavior from infancy to preadolescence. *Journal of Abnormal and Social Psychology*, 1960, *61*, 1–6.

Seeman, M. On the meaning of alienation. *American Sociological Review*, 1959, *24*, 783–791.

Smith, W. M. Rating and dating: A re-study. *Marriage and Family Living*, 1952, *14*, 312–317.

Smith, W. D., & Lebo, D. Some changing aspects of the self-concept of pubescent males. *The Journal of Genetic Psychology*, 1956, *88*, 61–75.

Stolz, H. R., Jones, M. C., & Chaffey, J. The junior high school age. *University High School Journal*, 1937, *15*, 63–72.

Sullivan, H. S. *The interpersonal theory of psychiatry*. New York: W. W. Norton & Company, Inc., 1953.

Tanner, J. M. *Growth at adolescence*. Springfield, Ill.: Charles C Thomas, Publisher, 1955.

Terman, L. M., & Tyler, L. Psychological sex differences. In L. Carmichael (Ed.), *Manual of child psychology*. New York: John Wiley & Sons, Inc., 1954.

9

The Adult Transition (18 to 25 years)

Since it is a rather sizable and interesting piece of psychological real estate, it is surprising to discover that the adult transition period remains an underdeveloped area in personality research. There are some valuable exceptions to this generalization, and good use will be made of them. But despite the fact that much work is done with college students – they are the most convenient subjects for academic psychologists studying everything from rote learning to attitude change – very little work has been done to explain personality development in the interval between adolescence and full maturity.

In one sense, this period can be described as a time in which the individual leaves adolescence behind on his way to becoming a particular kind of adult. It can be argued that the chief developmental mission of the transition period is finally to reduce confusions engendered by adolescence. For example, if one's sense of identity is basically roughed out by the age of 18 or 19, then for the next few years it will inevitably be going through something like a trial and error polishing or refinement process. Is the college sophomore inclined toward the humanities or the sciences? He will probably know the answer to this, but he will probably not know exactly which one of the humanities or the sciences he wants to pursue. Nor will he be able to single out a particular branch of any one discipline.

So where it concerns career plans, the reduction of uncertainty going on during this time is a fine-grain affair; more precise than what has gone on before, and also more urgent, because alternatives rapidly begin to close. In this respect, the 18 to 25 year period in modern societies is like a funnel. As we progress through it, our freedom to maneuver is constantly being reduced. Regardless of whether we twist and turn, or take the line of least resistance, by about 25 years of age most of us are committed to a particular adult role.

Yet the psychological meaning of adult transition can only be partly understood by reference to career choice uncertainties. From a larger, deeper perspective, personality development here has the combined qualities of tragedy and challenge.

The tragedy – if that is the right word for it – is one that seems implicit to every act of passage when the traveler must say good-bye. We are not often fully aware of it, but the forward thrust of development forces us to be always shaking out and shaking off various ideas, persons, and institutions . . . things that may have once been very dear to us but which have become, with the passing of time and our own growth, obsolete or irrelevant. Some knowledge of this condition probably starts late in adolescence. By then a great range of stuff has already been shaken off: security blankets, pets, primary school chums, indulgent grandparents. And parents are not what they used to be either. No longer omnipotent gods, nor even exceptionally great human beings, parents may only be likable people with whom one has something in common, and to whom one looks for certain kinds of support.

It all adds up to a hard price to pay for growth, a "tragedy"; because as the young person moves beyond adolescence, there is no way he can retain the comfortable psychological furnishings of his youth unchanged. To meet the challenges of an independent adult life, he must finally slip out of the social-emotional framework of youth just as a snake sheds its skin. And this means that many warm, cozy, external sources of security have to go by the board. Of course, this is not to say that the young adult becomes a cold-hearted renegade toward his past. It *does* say that whether he likes it or not, whether he retains some strong sentimental attachments or not, his whole order of priorities will be changed. Thus, where it was once enough to do well in school or a job to gain the approval of parents and friends, such a condition will no longer serve as an end in itself. Nor does it work the other way round anymore, for in this period parental *dis*approval also loses much of its force. The positive or negative reactions of relative strangers, a respected employer or teacher, for example, may mean more to the individual than anything coming from parents or friends.

The all-pervasive disengagement from youth going on here is described concretely in many famous biographies, and it can take a variety of forms. For Bertrand Russell, the years as a student at Cambridge changed him from a sensitive, withdrawn student of mathematics, to a broadly knowledgeable philosopher, able to debate ideas with the keenest young men of his time. Frank Harris lived the exciting hard life of a trail driving cowboy, but then gave it up to enroll at the University of Kansas. Malcolm X took a job in Small's Paradise, a Harlem cafe patronized by many successful musicians and hustlers. It was there that he gave up wearing the padded jackets and pegged pants of a zoot-suiter, and changed to more conservative styles favored by the older, high-rolling elite he admired.

For most of us, adult transition may be less dramatic than in some of the examples given above, but it is nonetheless real. A case in point is the psychological shock felt by most persons who return to scenes of their youth after getting well into the transition period. Claude Brown described it very well. By the time he was in his early twenties he had lived away from Harlem for a few years. But he mentioned going back once in a while, walking the streets he once knew so well; wondering at the changes. On the one hand, he still felt that he belonged; on the other, it was clear that he didn't: the streets were changed, the slang language was different. When he bumped into an occasional friend who, like himself, had survived, the talk was mainly of old times, new changes, and how the world had turned. Moreover, there was a certain reserve in those conversations. The former camaraderie was gone because each was on his own adult path.

At an even more concrete level, consider also the sensations most young adults have on returning home after a substantial time away. Everything typically seems shrunk to a smaller size; the neighborhood, the house, the old rooms, and a lot of the people. From this standpoint, the growth tragedy of adult transition can show up as a literal perceptual experience. Altogether then, if not everywhere, then at least in modern America, one constantly finds elaborations of the Thomas Wolfe theme, *You Can't Go Home Again*, being played and replayed in common experience as well as in literature.

But such experience only covers one side of adult transition. There is another, more positive side to be found in the dramatic challenges typical during the period. In fact, as will be apparent to most people, the personal challenges and discoveries made en route from adolescence to adulthood constitute a good part of the force which makes so many of the conditions of youth obsolete. Young adults ordinarily cannot engage themselves in meaningful, intimate relations with someone of the opposite sex and still maintain primary loyalties to parents and peer groups. Nor can they keep these earlier ties intact and still put themselves wholeheartedly into the struggle to find a meaningful career. There is a high probability that either the choice of a mate, or of a career, or both, will run somewhat counter to general expectations held by family and friends.

Problems of this kind force the issues of adult transition by posing a fairly clear question to young people – are they going to live their own lives or be dominated by others? And besides the large, crucial decisions which tend to split off youth from adulthood – those psychological Rubicons which, once crossed, can never be recrossed – there are countless smaller challenges seemingly built into the social institutions most people enter during the 18 to 25 year period. College is a good example. Madison (1969)[1] pointed out that upon entering college, young people are exposed to a wider variety of ideas and life styles than they have ever encountered before. Moreover, this new diversity of behavior is not merely an inert background condition. As he noted in the following statement, young students are actively challenged to respond.

A freshman who had never thought to question his devout views reported being challenged on his conception of God as he was unpacking his trunk; a girl with conservative views in sex found her roommates freely discussing intercourse with their dates, and using sex language more often found in an army barracks; a serious young scholar found himself in a living group devoted to play and easy courses. This great heterogeneity not only exists, but it is inescapable, and it compels response (Madison, p. 2).

But college is only one institution. Suppose the young person enters something very different, such as a factory? The challenges facing him there

---

[1]Madison's work on personality development in college is one of the outstanding exceptions to the earlier comment about adult transition as a relatively unresearched period. Extensive use of his work will be made in this chapter.

are fundamentally similar to what may occur in college. The young new-comer to an industrial setting may be made the butt of jokes and casual horse-play, if nothing worse.

The military provides another, still stronger variant on the same theme. Novels, personal reminiscences, and empirical research all confirm the hard challenges experienced by young people in military institutions. But the generalities became particularly conspicuous while interviewing returned veterans in a study of attitudes to the war in Vietnam (Rappoport and Cvetkovich, 1968).

One of the first things discovered were sharp differences between the opinions of young men (in their early twenties) who had been in intense combat, and those who had not. The former were all dissatisfied with the war and were contemptuous of the South Vietnamese. Many wanted to see the war either scaled up to a full victory-at-any-price struggle, or else closed out via unilateral withdrawal. And these extreme opinions were not difficult to understand: having had a close-up view of the war, some felt that only a clear victory could justify it, while others thought that nothing could justify it.

But the men without combat experience were fairly satisfied with the war policy. They had more favorable opinions of the South Vietnamese, believed that they appreciated Americans, and that the war could be properly resolved if the effort was continued.

Gradually, it became clear that the interview material was also significant in terms of personality development. Although not explicitly concerned to study this, we were impressed by certain differences between those with and without heavy combat experience. The following summary is drawn from unpublished notes made shortly after the interviews were completed.

Taken together, all of these interviews say a great deal that is relevant to the question of mature personality. The men without combat experience seem very clearly to be in a conventional transition period from adolescence to maturity. They rely a good deal upon outside authority, and maintain a comfortable self-image by defining themselves as good citizens serving the cause of their country. All of the standard arguments in favor of the war are frequently mentioned: the need to keep Asia free; the atrocities committed by the enemy, etc.

The young men with heavy combat experience are generally much less sure of themselves. Whatever natural, relatively smooth transition from adolescence to maturity one assumes for theoretical purposes, it is evident in talking with these men that the process has been terribly upsetting. Without exception, they have been unable to maintain a comfortable self-image. They feel somewhat betrayed by their government, and distrustful of it, either because no maximum effort is being made to win the war (in which case they see no point to fighting), or because they see the war as futile, accomplishing nothing but the loss of their friends and destruction of a primitive people. Consequently, they are quite disturbed. Their conception of themselves, which in any case has not yet had much time to solidify, is undermined by the feeling that something is wrong somewhere. It may be in themselves, or it may be in their country's policies which they have up to now taken for granted as correct. Neither hypothesis is easy to live with. Neither inspires the sort of confidence necessary in order to push forward to meet the challenges and uncertainties of adult life: finding a career, a mate, raising a family, etc.

For example, a 23 year old former marine sergeant said that he went to Vietnam viewing the war as a kind of personal adventure in the cause of Freedom. On their first major operation his company received fire while sweeping a village. They were ordered to destroy the village, which they did, burning the huts and grenading all the holes and bunkers. A short time later he learned that noncombatant villagers typically hide in family bunkers when they suspect trouble. This knowledge came as a great shock to him. It transformed the war from adventure to a crucial challenge of his beliefs and values. His next step was admirable. He called his squad together, men he had trained with and who were therefore close friends as well as subordinates, and spoke to them approximately as follows: "We don't really know why we were sent here or what we are really supposed to accomplish. We just have to fight and try to stay alive. But let's try our best not to do anything that we'll regret later."

To this day he wonders how many innocent people were killed in the bunkers blown up on his first operation. But he says with pride that he subsequently never allowed his squad to destroy huts or bunkers before they were checked out. He feels now that the war is all wrong, but at the same time he cannot accept the idea that so many of his friends died in a cause that was "just a mistake." Toward the end of the interview he struggled with his thoughts for a moment and said "The way I feel about the war probably doesn't make any sense to you, does it? Well, it doesn't make any sense to me either." But of course to any competent psychologist his mixed feelings make a great deal of sense.

It should be clear that the notes from our Vietnam study point to difficulties in the combat veterans' sense of identity. Apart from the very severe emotional stresses of fighting, they have been forced to act contrary to many of their basic personal values, and forced to reject many ideas handed down by conventional authority figures. As one man put it, "Let's see how much they still want to save our face in Asia after they go three weeks in the jungle without changing socks." The identities of the combat men are disrupted because they have seen man at his worst—not only in the behavior of the enemy and the local population, but also in themselves. By contrast, the experiences of the noncombat men apparently were not severe enough to expose the roots of their self-identity.

At this point, it may well be asked what all the Vietnam material has to do with the ideas mentioned earlier. The answer is that by discussing the effect of one very extreme type of challenging experience, we can begin to see what the tragedies and challenges of the adult transition period are really all about. The young combat veterans have had a massive, disruptive dose of the disillusioning medicine we all have to take while moving from adolescence to maturity. However, instead of being allowed the usual luxury of gradualism—gradually giving up past ideas and ideals about themselves and others, slowly building up an understanding of the uncertain nature of conventional social values—they have had to take it all at once.

Consider the problem faced by one young man (who had volunteered for service in Vietnam) when he was a 20-year-old corporal. A new officer ordered him to take a small observation party into an area he knew was occupied by the enemy every night. Despite his protests, the officer refused to change the order. So he went out to another, safer area, while reporting that he was in the original one. As this fellow described the incident, he said that it was clear to him that the officer had read the map incorrectly, and that if he followed the order it would mean almost certain death for himself and his men. But in disobeying, and giving a false position report, he was committing a serious offense which he himself found difficult to justify. Now most young adults learn that superiors may occasionally be wrong. They may even quit a job or disobey an order at the risk of being fired. Consequently, they can learn in a relatively mild way that adult role responsibilities may require them to reject constituted authority. The young corporal did not have this luxury; he had to reject authority in a way that still disturbs him, because it forced a drastic change in his view of himself and the army life he had once idealized.

Thus, when we look at it from a larger perspective, the adult transition period appears to have a general quality of disillusionment. Young people are faced with serious challenges which can only be met by accepting rather hard new ideas, and relinquishing old, softer ones. Ordinarily, this process will go on in a more or less orderly fashion: one may steadily reevaluate himself and others while facing problems posed by career plans, choice of a mate, or adjustment to adult roles in large social institutions. But on some occasions, as shown above, the problems may develop so quickly that the young person cannot handle them without undergoing much confusion. Furthermore, it also happens occasionally that several different serious problems may pile up on one another and make confusion or uncertainty the rule rather than the exception.

For example, while one of my former students was serving in Vietnam he sent a single letter mentioning the following topics:

(a) His first close combat action, killing an enemy soldier who had got through perimeter wire: " . . . the individual was caught in the open under a flare burst right in front of me, I fired without thinking . . . ."

(b) His tentative plans to marry a girl from a very different background: "Enough of this place. I would really value your thoughts concerning love and the social aspects of it, as this is my consuming problem."

(c) His uncertainty about a career: "Sometimes I think I should try graduate school, but I'm not sure . . . ."

And he closed the letter with an apology: "Excuse my handwriting, I hope you can read it, at times I am just a little nervous."

Ultimately, after rooting through biographies, textbooks, and various direct accounts of personal experience, the conglomerate of adult transition material begins to fall into a general pattern. Some of the main features of this pattern have been mentioned: challenging decisions to be made in the face of uncertainty; tragic, or at least reluctant, departures from youthful ideas; and changes in direction which may go counter to the expectations of family and friends. It is now time to consider what critical factors influence personality during this period.

CRITICAL FACTORS

Practically all authorities agree with the common sense view that choice of a mate, and choice of a career or educational program, are crucial problems dominating the lives of most young adults. These problems can be seen as the two critical events of adult transition because the final contours of adult personality will depend upon how they are resolved. It might be said that prior development will determine these choices; that a mate and career are *outcomes* rather than *determinants* of personality development. But while such objections have some validity, and must be given due consideration, we would argue that to take them too seriously is to be caught in the logical trap of infinite regress. Thus, a young person's choice among occupations or opposite sex peers may depend upon his sense of identity, which in turn will depend upon how he has come through adolescence, and childhood before that, and so on. This kind of chess-game logic can be useful for some purposes, but life is not a chess game, and even in chess, outcomes are not always determined by the first few moves. It might be added, furthermore, that to understand the forward movement of personality development, it is more important to emphasize how each new event contributes to the total, rather than how it may be determined by all previous events. However, these issues will be discussed later in a less abstract context. For the present, it is necessary to introduce a third factor which seems critical for personality development in this period.

All of the evidence relevant to adult transition indicates that in the technical sense of the term, *disillusionment* is a critical psychological condition. The word *disillusionment* is not being used here with its usual negative connotations. Entry into adulthood is not inevitably accompanied by cynicism, or the loss of all ideals, but typical experience in this period does inevitably force young people to reevaluate and change most of their ideas about themselves and the world. And these changes can best be described in terms of the formal meaning of disillusionment.

The balance of this chapter is taken up first with discussion of the three critical factors: disillusionment, as the general condition of adult transition; and choice of mate and choice of career, as the major developmental events. In the section on theoretical perspectives, the ideas of Sullivan, Erikson, Madison, and others are discussed.

Disillusionment

The idea that adult transition is a time of disillusionment is difficult to convey without getting into polemical arguments. For one thing, some research reports confirm the common observation that many people look back on this period as the happiest time in their lives — gay exploits with the fraternity or sorority, racing about in a convertible, no family responsibilities or financial worries, courtship and the honeymoon — all that sort of thing. Another line of contrary argument can follow from the ego-development theories of personality: such writers as Rogers, Maslow, and Allport stressed an onward, upward thrust to personality development which may seem opposed to disillusionment.

However, as this concept is elaborated, it should become clear that no important contradiction to either everyday experience or theory is necessarily involved. Like every other developmental period, adult transition is a mixed affair. The fact that many people remember it with pleasure and might like to be 21 again does not preclude disillusion as a basic condition. Nor is it precluded by theoretical discussions which concentrate upon growth or self-actualization. In fact, both the commonsense and theoretical material can be interpreted as essential components in the disillusion process, because it is precisely the excitements and growth of this time which force reevaluation and change. But this concept will take some explaining.

In one dictionary an illusion is defined as "a false idea or conception; an unreal or misleading appearance or image." Most of us leave our teens with a number of ideas which change drastically in the next few years. The question of whether or not these ideas or images are false according to some objective standard of truth is hardly relevant; probably they are, but in any case they change, and we become, technically speaking, *dis*illusioned. To follow the dictionary again, there is a "loss of faith in illusions previously held." A synonym for this condition is disenchantment, which is also relevant because, to whatever extent childhood and adolescence may be considered a magical or enchanted time, this quality is lost in the early 20's. Briefly, the point is that on simple, technically descriptive grounds, disillusionment is an appropriate term for changes in the adult transition period.

Beyond its linguistic meaning, however, disillusionment is indicated as a fundamental condition of adult transition by many research findings. For example, when asked to describe important changes in their personalities, college students frequently mention new perceptions of their parents, peers, and their own status as individuals.[2] Parents are typically seen more realistically:

I understand them better. My parents have closed their eyes in several directions and therefore are incapable of understanding how I feel about areas such as sex and religion.

I have started to understand my parents as people having their own emotions and weaknesses.

We get along much better because I am not home long enough to fight.

I used to feel that my parents were giving up a lot to send me to school but now I feel different. They're always telling me what I cost them but don't realize they still get a tax deduction for me.

Relationships with peers are also reevaluated:

Not so many friends I really trust anymore.

Some of the friends which I used to think could do no wrong I now see in a more realistic light . . . I realize they have their faults and are not always right.

[2]The material mentioned here was collected at Kansas State University in the fall of 1969, with the aid of Howard Cohen. Over the years, other surveys of this type have yielded very similar results.

I try to see each person as a unique individual, and not condemn them for being something other than myself.

And comments about the self emphasize a new sense of unique individuality:

I used to think of myself as being like most other people until last year . . . .

I am less insecure about myself because I feel I am finding out what I am really like which actually isn't so bad.

I don't try to conform to any groups anymore. Everyone has to pursue their own beliefs.

Not so dependent on others. Now realize that I am different and cannot be like someone else.

Practically all of this material stands as a clear demonstration of "loss of faith in illusions previously held"; but it should not be confused with loss of faith *per se*. Instead, these comments show that as parents and peers are scrutinized more carefully, there is also an increase in self-confidence – a new recognition of unique personal identity.

Turning to very different material, further evidence for the generality of disillusionment can be found in actuarial studies of college dropouts. Young people who fail to complete college must, almost by definition, experience some serious loss of illusions, and the numbers are surprisingly high. Summerskill (1962) reported that over the years 1913 to 1962, a fairly steady 60 percent of students who started in a given college did not graduate from it. Some of these were transfers, but even so, most estimates indicate that the attrition rate across all colleges is about 50 percent.

The effort to justify disillusionment as a critical condition of adult transition could be continued by piling up all sorts of other evidence suggesting or demonstrating major changes in this period. It is more important, however, to consider the issue from another angle: if disillusionment seems plausible as a critical condition, how does it come about?

The process of disillusionment

Sanford (1966) suggested that a fundamental process of *"challenge and response"* is at work here: young people encounter a progressive series of challenges while passing into maturity, and their efforts to respond involve changes described in this text under the heading of disillusionment. But it is not enough to say that disillusionment is understandable as a response to challenges encountered during adult transition. Nor is it enough to add that in general, society challenges and the individual responds. Considerable research shows that while such ideas can be supported, the process of disillusionment occurs on both a uniquely personal level, and a wider sociocultural level. That is, the causal elements which explain the process lie in the dynamics of individual growth and the workings of social institutions.

We have seen in previous chapters that certain challenges are intrinsic to growth all through development. Many writers follow Havighurst and discuss these challenges as the "developmental tasks" characterizing each period; adult transition is no exception. Yet if the tasks often mentioned here are unique in any particular way, it is because of their disillusioning quality. Farnsworth (1966) provided a typical listing of the tasks facing college-age people. It included (a) establishing independence from parents, (b) learning to deal with authority, (c) learning to accept emotional uncertainties, (d) developing mature sexuality, (e) finding security in a sense of competence and self-esteem, and (f) acquiring standards and values.

These tasks are of course not new to us; Farnsworth drew heavily from Erikson as well as his own psychiatric work at Harvard. But even the briefest examination of what the tasks involve during adult transition reveals a disillusioning trend. Thus, parents are dethroned, authority loses its magic, while sex, personal security, and moral values become more complex matters than ever before. In short, young adults cannot meet the challenges intrinsic to growth during this period and still maintain simple faith in prior notions.

Among college students, personality development often comes to focus on career plans. Madison described the case of a young man who kept a record of his thoughts on this subject. He went to college planning to be a doctor, but as can be seen in the following excerpts from his diary, he was already questioning this plan at the start of his freshman year:

October I see how much money motivated my desire to be a doctor. Although I would enjoy liberal arts more, I will spend my life with science, probably because of money . . . .

I have been questioning my motives for going into medicine: money and freedom of position seem to be the central reasons.

January Fear of becoming a doctor haunts me. I dare not write my thoughts of my motives for medicine for fear they will bring me out of self-rationalization.

Finally, the conflict is resolved in what the student later recalls as something like a moment of divine revelation:

Sometime in my freshman year when I was sitting on a tennis court I had the very sudden and dramatic realization that my life was my own and not my parents', that I could do what I wanted and did not necessarily have to do what they wanted. I think I correlated this with dropping out of the pre-med program. Material values became less and less important from then on (Madison, 1969, pp. 57–58).

It is important to note both the quality and substance of this revelation. The student experienced it as a new insight which involved both his money vs. personal interest dilemma, and his relationship to his parents. Qualitatively, the moment of revelation was one of integration: two previously distinct issues were linked together and resolved by answering the question of whether or not he would live his own life. And more substantially, it is clear that his own personal values had begun to emerge: he would no longer allow himself to be pinned down by simple material considerations.

The sudden loss of adolescent illusions is not unusual in situations of this type, where growth of individual interests and values gradually force a direct reappraisal of prior ideas. Then, once tensions accumulate sufficiently, some psychological last straw may come along—a book, film, conversation, or whatever—which breaks the camel's back and leads to dramatic change. In this particular case, Freudian ideas about defense mechanisms seem relevant; the young student might have been exhausted from playing tennis and therefore have been less able to maintain his repression of unwelcome thoughts.

However, disillusionment probably occurs more frequently as a result of experiences in social institutions which *force* changes. These experiences can also be dramatic: witness the material on the young Vietnam combat veterans. Some biographies provide further examples. After committing a series of burglaries, Malcolm X was sent to prison at the age of 21. There he had time to think through much of his former life, and one result was that he discarded prior illusions about a criminal career. At the same time, he was opened to the teachings of the Muslim religion. Eldridge Cleaver (*Soul on Ice*) mentioned a similar change while in prison, which he attributed to reading Malcolm's book.

Close examination reveals that disillusionment can also exist as a gradual process literally programed into certain institutional experiences. That is, in some cases institutions are deliberately geared to the task of destroying adolescent illusions.

A sociological analysis of junior colleges in California, for example, showed that they are partly designed to separate students from their unrealistic aspirations. Because these schools accept virtually all California high school graduates, they are called "open door colleges." In a report aptly titled *"The 'Cooling-Out' Function in Higher Education,"* Clark (1960) explained that about two-thirds of the students who start programs leading to a bachelor's degree do not complete them. Instead, they terminate after 2 years. The colleges have responded to this condition by working out means of identifying and then "reorienting" these "latent terminal students."

In a typical junior college, reorientation proceeds in five steps. Entering students are first tested for academic achievement and aptitudes. Second, a counseling interview is arranged to help students select courses. The counselor uses test scores and high-school grades as a guide for the advice he offers. Clark quoted one counselor's statement of technique: "I never openly countermand his choice but edge him toward a terminal program by gradually laying out the facts of life." All new students must then enroll in a special course called *Orientation to College*. Here, teacher-counselors carry out a third step by discussing the rules and principles of vocational guidance in an objective fashion. Students learn exactly what is required to pursue various careers. They also write a paper about their own career plans, including in it a "self-appraisal of fitness."

By the time a student has completed one or two semesters of courses, college grades are available and he is ready for the fourth step: "building an educational program." This euphemism means that the counselor's chief task is now to persuade the latent terminal student to change to a terminal program. Since the student has already learned the rules of vocational guidance, since a record of his scores and grades can be set before him, and since counselors can describe alternative nondegree programs in a fairly attractive way, this fourth step is usually enough to bring about the change. But in case he wants to persist despite negative evidence, counselors can go to the fifth step which is their ace in the hole: academic probation. Any student whose grade average falls below *C* can be put on probation and eventually forced to leave college.

Clark's analysis emphasizes the formal characteristics of this cooling-out procedure. It provides for "gradual disengagement" from original intentions, while confronting students with "objective denial" — evidence that they cannot pursue their original aims. It offers "alternative achievement" in the form of substitute programs, and "agents of consolation" in the form of sympathetic counselors. The whole thing seems wonderfully designed to relieve young people of illusions in a relatively efficient, painless fashion. Actually, as Clark indicated, the system can work so well that students may never be quite aware that their illusions are under attack. Perhaps the economics of higher education make such a system necessary. But for those who want to consider its implications, Clark's final summary is worth repeating:

In summary, the cooling-out process in higher education is one whereby systematic discrepancy between aspiration and avenue is covered over and stress for the individual and the system is minimized. The provision of readily available alternative achievements in itself is an important device for alleviating the stress consequent on failure and so preventing anomic and deviant behavior. The general result of cooling-out processes is that society can continue to encourage maximum effort without major disturbance from unfulfilled promises and expectations (1960, p. 576).

Further instruction on the nature of institutionalized sources of disillusionment can be gained from a report by Becker and Geer (1958). Working in the upper reaches of higher education, these authors described "the fate of idealism in medical school." They begin by noting that medical schools (and other professional training institutions) are often accused of producing cynicism in students. However, their study showed that medical students actually go through a more complex process of disillusionment. Contrary to the case of junior-college students, medical students are not so much separated from their ideals as they are induced to put them on the shelf.

In the beginning, enthusiastic new students are disappointed to discover that their first year is going to be just like college: heavy course work with no concrete training in how to help sick people. Furthermore, faculty experts make it clear that no student can really acquire all the knowledge needed to be a perfect doctor, because there is simply too much to be learned in too short a time. After taking a few examinations and seeing the truth of this demonstrated, students begin to concentrate on passing their tests. They try to learn what will satisfy the faculty, they band together in special study groups, and in general they use all the techniques known to bright, "test-wise" college students. So by the end of the first year, ideals typically recede as survival becomes the immediate objective. Yet ideals are not entirely abandoned:

Cynicism, griping, and minor cheating become endemic, but the cynicism is specific to the educational situation, to the first year, and to only parts of it. Thus the students keep their cynicism separate from their idealistic feelings and by postponement protect their belief that medicine is a wonderful thing, that their school is a fine one, and that they will become good doctors (Becker and Geer, 1958, pp. 52–53).

The second year brings more of the same, with even more emphasis placed on passing examinations to stay in school. But in the third and fourth years, formal exams become less important as students begin to work with patients. One might think that then at last, humanitarian ideals may come into their own; not so. The student must now concentrate on understanding the *diseases* present in patients. Moreover, he is not allowed to take much responsibility for patient care in any case. The result is that gradually, and by stages, a student's technical orientation to medicine may increase until he can look like a very tough customer indeed:

Instead of reacting with the layman's horror and sympathy for the patient to the sight of a cancerous organ that has been surgically removed, the student is more likely to regret that he was not allowed to close the incision at the completion of the operation, and to rue the hours that he must spend searching in the fatty flesh for the lymph nodes that will reveal how far the disease has spread. As in other lines of work, he drops lay attitudes for those more relevant to the way the event affects someone in his position (Becker and Geer, p. 54).

Despite all, however, Becker and Geer ended on a positive note: idealism begins to assert itself again as students approach graduation. To be sure, they think about their careers in a different way. Knowing that they have not been able to learn everything, for example, some students decide to specialize, while others say they will at least know enough to refer patients to appropriate specialists. This material indicates that at least some of their primary ideals about medicine are still intact.

A unique study of fraternities and sororities reveals still another way for illusions to be gradually eroded during adult transition. Scott (1965) found that the personal values of fraternity and sorority members change considerably as they progress through college. Contrary to popular notions, it is the younger, newer members who keep these organizations alive, and believe most strongly in the moral and social values they represent. The older members seem to lose interest as they look forward to life beyond college. Scott's suggestion that senior students " . . . no longer derive their principle sources of prestige and security from group membership. . . ." is clearly in agreement with our discussion of disillusionment. The seniors probably lose their once-strong beliefs in the importance of Greek-letter groups because they recognize that membership in such groups will be largely irrelevant to their future concerns.

Summary of disillusionment

It should be clear enough from all the material discussed above, that the disillusionment we see as a definitive condition of adult transition can take many different forms. Sometimes it is felt all at once: individual growth brings cumulative changes which are suddenly recognized as a new insight. It seems more frequent, however, that adolescent illusions are lost or changed gradually in many institutions. The "reorientation" procedures of certain junior colleges are explicitly designed for this purpose, and the rigorous medical school program seems to accomplish this as a matter of tradition, without any formal design.

But in all these instances, the question of how personality development is influenced when young people seriously engage adult realities is not really answered. Disillusionment, which is understandable as a condition arising from the challenges posed by adult realities, is certainly part of the answer; but it is relatively superficial. It only offers a way of beginning to digest the raw behavioral material which characterizes adult transition. If in fact most of us lose our youthful illusions during this period, what does this do to the way we think of ourselves and others? What happens to that unique sense of personal identity which should be unfolding as we move into maturity? Madison spoke of the disillusioning challenges built into college life as an "assault on identity." How do we meet these assaults? These are difficult and provocative questions, which can only be pursued as theoretical issues, because empirical research studies do not provide direct answers. Therefore, further discussion will be postponed until the section on theoretical perspectives.

No one can say for sure which is the more crucial problem for young adults — finding a career or finding a mate. According to common experience and descriptive statistics, both events occur during adult transition: vocational decisions are made at the time most people leave school, and the average age for marriage in America is less than 22 (just under 23 for males; between 20 and 21 for females). Both events also carry obvious implications for personality: adult self-concepts are largely defined in terms of career and marital situations. However, among the parallels between these two events, the most surprising thing is their similar error rate. It would appear that about one out of every four or five Americans makes a mistake in his career or marriage. Twenty-five percent of a sample of 9000 college graduates said they would have preferred to study something else (Havemann and West, 1952); and approximately 21 percent of marriages end in divorce (government statistics, 1960).

On the face of it, therefore, any choice of priorities here must be arbitrary. But first place should probably go to career choice because it seems to have somewhat deeper, more persistent effects on personality. Besides, judging from the way things are going in our general culture — the sexual revolution and everything else — it is probably getting easier to cope with a bad marriage than a bad career choice.

Careers

How do people wind up spending the better part of their lives in particular occupations? Ideally, according to some of the best technical literature on vocational guidance and counseling, young people ready to choose an occupation should have a "vocational identity." Hackman (1968) explained that this begins when older adolescents make preliminary selections of their main field of interest. Within that field, the youngster should then identify particular kinds of jobs that are best suited to his needs, aptitudes, and opportunities for training. The only trouble with this nice model for fitting people to jobs is that it doesn't work.

I doubt if very many people actually choose jobs this way, and if they did, I do not think they would be very successful, even though superficially this approach looks simple and easy and perhaps even scientific (Hackman, 1968, p. 377).

Instead, it is suggested that exposing young people to vocational information is only the first step. They should also be encouraged to evaluate their interests and aptitudes very carefully—psychological tests are mentioned in this connection. Counselors should try to explain how to make "appropriate," "realistic," and "flexible" decisions; young people should be motivated to reach feasible decisions.

Now if this sounds suspiciously similar to the "reorientation" procedure mentioned earlier, it should be emphasized that Hackman made no such specific suggestions: reorientation appears to be the applied creation of others. Actually, the procedure he described grew out of theories of vocational guidance which are closely tied to personality development. Borow (in Adams, 1968) noted that the most prominent work in this area treats occupational decision-making as the outcome of prior developmental experience from early childhood onwards. Thus, according to Super (1957), the growing child's sexual identity, his increasing independence, ability to take responsibility, should all cumulate at the end of adolescence in an occupational choice which reflects and satisfies his conception of himself as an individual. Super therefore spoke of "vocational development" as a particular form of personality development.

Empirical research offered some support for these ideas. Ginzberg, Ginsburg, Axelrad, and Herma (1951) studied the evolution of vocational plans in samples of males spanning the interval from sixth grade to graduate school. They found that occupations are first thought of in terms of *fantasy*. Then there is a period of *tentative* choice which involves the elaboration of interests and personal values, and at about age 17, the *realistic* period begins as young men begin to explore concrete possibilities. The role of early family experience is also emphasized by Roe (1957). She reported that child-rearing conditions influencing sexual identity may relate to career choices. For example, girls who grow up identifying with their fathers are likely to seek masculine careers in science or engineering.

Our brief scan of vocational guidance material indicates that most authorities look back to development in childhood and adolescence for explanations of career choices. They offer very little on how these choices are actually made, nor are they much concerned with how such choices influence later personality development. But this is not the place to debate the wisdom of guidance practices which may close off possibilities for future development, according to interpretations of past development. Biographical material makes the point well enough by showing that vocational decisions are in reality quite dynamic, future-oriented affairs. To the extent that young people have a truly strong "vocational identity," they push on toward their objectives very directly; to the extent that they are uncertain, no formalities can replace the exploratory, trial-and-error experiences typical of adult transition.

Bertrand Russell was a good example of the former: he was fascinated with mathematics from early childhood on, and this, in combination with philosophy, became his life work. A similar illustration of smooth development toward vocation was given by a young biologist:

When I was eight we spent a summer in a town by the ocean. I started developing a very strange feeling, which is very difficult to put into words, about the ocean. The ocean fascinated me, particularly the queer beings that grew in it (in Madison, p. 259).

His subsequent progress through high school, college, and graduate school was marked by an increasingly sophisticated interest in biological problems. We all know and probably envy people such as this: not for them the agonies of indecision, the rigors of vocational guidance, or the pleadings of anxious parents.

At the other extreme, however, are those who for sundry psychological reasons seem unable to fix on any particular career:

Trixie started out with astronomy as her major, and took a program that was heavy in mathematics. In her sophomore year she shifted to psychology, in which she graduated. As a senior, Trixie decided that her real interest and talents were, and had been all along, in English, a fact that she had persistently fought against. English was weak, feminine. She saw science as adventurous, pioneering, and strong (Madison, p. 23).

In this case, the career choice problem is bound up in deeper problems of sexual identity. In many other cases, the reasons for indecision are not as clear, but the names of some former young adult "undecideds" are well known: William James, for instance, who at one point was apparently so confused by the career problem that he postponed it by spending several months in bed with hypochondriacal complaints. And John F. Kennedy planned a career in journalism when he finished college: it took a war, the death of his adored older brother, and several other experiences to make him finally try politics.

George Kennan was another "undecided." His diplomatic career started almost by accident when he heard of a Foreign Service training program:

My decision to try for entry was dictated mainly, if my memory is correct, by the feeling that I did not know what else to do. During my upper-class years at college I had enjoyed the study of international politics and had prospered in it. Milwaukee held no charms for me. I feared falling into some sort of occupational rut and I thought that I would be best protected in the Foreign Service from doing so. The calculation, miraculously, proved to be correct. Some guardian angel must have stood over me at that point. It was the first and last sensible decision I was ever deliberately to make about my occupation (*Memoirs*, p. 16).

A few years later, Kennan was about to resign to attend graduate school when he discovered that the Foreign Service would send him to school if he studied either Chinese, Arabic, or Russian. He chose Russian, and was thus set on the path that would make him a distinguished authority on the Soviet Union.

Frank Harris provided a wonderful illustration of how chance may operate in the determination of careers. While enrolled at Kansas University, he protested a faculty effort to start compulsory religious services. But he had to attend a roll call held in the college chapel. When the hymn-singing began, however, Harris tried to leave. The door was locked – the professors in charge refused to open it – so, having learned to handle himself in such matters during his cowboy days, Harris kicked it open. He was expelled; but promptly started to read law with a local judge, and within a few years found himself with a flourishing law practice and some interesting girl friends. Then he was visited by a former professor:

We passed the whole day together and when he heard how I spent my days in casual reading and occasional speaking and my topsy-turvey nights, he urged me to throw up the law and go to Europe to make myself a real scholar and thinker. But I could not give up Sophy and my ultra-pleasant life. So I resisted, told him he overrated me: I'd easily be the best advocate in the state, I said, and make a lot of money and then I'd go back and do Europe and study as well (*My Life and Loves*, pp. 205–206).

What is really interesting here is that a month later, Harris had one of those personal revelations which seem to be typical of adult transition. He read a speech by Ralph Waldo Emerson (N.B.) who said that many gifted men are corrupted by the pursuit of material gain:

There flashed on me the realization of the truth, that just because wealth was easy to get here, it exercised an incomparable attraction and in its pursuit "perished a thousand thousand" gifted spirits who might have steered humanity to new and nobler accomplishment.

The question imposed itself: "Was I too to sink to fatness, wallow in sensuality, degrade myself for a nerve-thrill?" (ibid., p. 207).

And within a matter of days, he went to study in Europe.

All these stories, and many others like them, suggest that young adults make their occupational decisions according to one of three general patterns. First, there are some whose childhood interests apparently evolve directly toward a career. Athletes, doctors, occasional soldiers and pilots, and many artists and scientists report this. It is as if their adult careers were a natural extension of their youthful interests and aspirations. Second, there are some who seem to be chronically undecided switchers; they may change jobs frequently, or shift through three or four different educational programs for no obvious reasons. People of this sort are often trying to resolve deep-seated personality problems. And then there are a great many undecided young people who grow up without serious problems, but have no special convictions about any particular career. For them, adult transition is often a time of exploration, and their final vocation is liable to be determined by chance happenings and the pressure of circumstances.

It therefore seems clear that standard vocational guidance programs are not likely to have great impacts on the career decisions of young people. Those with deep convictions or serious psychological problems will resist outside influence; and those without either one will have to explore for themselves. Guidance can certainly be helpful as a source of information or for purposes of referral, as when seriously troubled youngsters can benefit from psychiatric attention. But so long as guidance efforts are bounded on the right by vast catalogues of job descriptions, and on the left by questionable psychological tests, they will probably remain largely irrelevant to career choice problems. If this is too harsh a judgment, perhaps it is caused from reading through the remarks by Emerson which so impressed Frank Harris:

You will hear every day the maxims of a low prudence. You will hear that the first duty is to get land and money, place and name. . . .

When you shall say, "As others do, so will I: I renounce, I am sorry for it, my early visions: I must eat the good of the land and let learning and romantic expectations go, until a more convenient season";—then dies the man in you; then once more perish the buds of art, and poetry, and science, as they have died already in a thousand thousand men (Ralph Waldo Emerson, speaking at Dartmouth College, 1838; reprinted in *My Life and Loves*, p. 207).

Career choice and personality

Aside from all the difficulties likely to surround career choices during adult transition, how does commitment to a given occupation influence personality in this period? Some of the preliminary consequences are implicit in the previous examples.

Frank Harris, for example, practically ran away from his lucrative law position when he recognized that it would probably turn him into just another member of the establishment. Kennan entered the Foreign Service because he was afraid that something similar would happen to him if he returned home to Wisconsin. And Erikson (1968, p. 143) cited the same type of event in the life of George Bernard Shaw:

Shaw proceeds to describe a crisis at the age of twenty. This crisis was not caused by lack of success or the absence of a defined role, but by too much of both: "I made good in spite of myself, and found, to my dismay, that Business, instead of expelling me as the worthless imposter I was, was fastening upon me with no intention of letting me go. Behold me, therefore, in my twentieth year, with a business training, in an occupation which I detested as cordially as any sane person lets himself detest anything he cannot escape from. In March 1876 I broke loose." Breaking loose meant to leave family and friends, business and Ireland, and to avoid the danger of success. . . .

These instances, which illustrate certain forms of disillusionment and also show how young people may intuitively recognize the tyranny that an occupation can exert over their lives, should make it clear that commitment to a career is nothing less than commitment to a particular kind of personal identity. What frightens the heroes of our biographies, and many lesser men as well during adult transition, is their awareness of the personal identity abyss looming before them — the very thing expressed by Emerson in 1838.

In the technical language of personality development, career choice can therefore be understood as influencing virtually all important aspects of the self-concept. The daily round of activities imposed by any particular occupation strikes first at peripheral elements: interpersonal relations and social status. But soon personal values also get involved, and before young people may even be well aware of it, all these elements may converge to influence their core sense of identity. (The sales trainee probably becomes a true salesman when the tricks of his trade — a firm handshake, a stock of jokes, a confident tone, a sincere look-them-in-the-eye approach achieved by staring at foreheads — become natural to him.) In brief, the outer structure of behavior imposed by an occupational role can easily influence the inner substance of personality.

Social psychology textbooks provide abundant experimental evidence of this phenomenon. Few persons can hold out for very long against group pressures for conformity; and, under certain conditions, when a person is required to act contrary to his beliefs, he will often change his beliefs to fit his action. So there is good reason to accept the idea that personal identity will be affected by the behavior demanded in an occupation.

It would be wrong, however, to take an entirely negative view of these matters. Young adults may also benefit in very important ways from occupational roles which allow them to find new, constructive meanings in their lives. If the negative instances have been emphasized, it is mainly because they offer a more direct route to understanding. The positive possibilities of the career-personality relationship are shown in another excerpt from Kennan:

Within weeks after entry onto my first tour of duty abroad, I discovered that in this new role as representative (however lowly) of a government rather than of just myself, the more painful personal idiosyncrasies and neuroses tended to leave me, at least in the office. I welcomed with surprised relief the opportunity to assume a new personality behind which the old introverted one could retire, be relieved of some of its helplessness, and even get some measure of perspective on itself. . . .

I had a role to play, a useful, necessary, legitimate role, helpful to others, requiring no justification or apology. If I played it creditably, I acquitted myself; there could be no need for further questions. Under this welcome mask I felt a hitherto unknown strength. . . (*Memoirs*, pp. 19 – 20).

His occupational role was obviously therapeutic; it enabled Kennan to integrate his personality along lines which will be described in a later section.

It might also be noted in closing that psychology does not provide any sure formula for distinguishing between career choices which will have positive or negative consequences for individuals. Many well-intentioned vocational guidance authorities believe that conventional tests, interviews, and the like will help insure a happy outcome. But no amount of testing or counseling can resolve the very serious, classical questions facing young adults: should one follow his interests or go after money? Should one try to satisfy himself even if this means cruel disappointment to parents? Should one ac-

cept the convenient wisdom of vocational advice based on statistical averages, or go forward on his own despite bad odds? Even guidance experts
themselves have to face these questions.

About the only reasonable theoretical statement to be made here is that
when the chips are down, young people with a strong sense of ego identity
should be better able to resist the dictates of "low prudence." And on a more
practical level, it seems that one's best guide often turns out to be his deep,
intuitive, feeling-in-the-tummy.

Marriage or the choice of a mate

Granted that marriage and choice of a mate seem less synonymous these
days than they used to be, they still have the same basic meaning in the
economy of personality development. The crucial fact is that of commitment
to another person. If anything, the main psychological difference between
the decision to cohabit, with or without benefit of a legal ceremony, probably
concerns its credibility—the legal ceremony demonstrates to all that the decision is serious. Therefore, many young people probably gain an important
sense of security from celebrating their decision according to legal and religious traditions. But the present task is to explore how this decision is made,
and what it can mean for the personalities of those making it.

It was suggested earlier that there are at least three interesting parallels
between career choice and choice of a mate: they occur at about the same
time, carry serious implications for the person's self-concept, and have very
similar error rates. However, the technical literature on marriage (for convenience, we will use this term interchangeably with the phrase *choice of a
mate*) reveals one more parallel between these two events of adult transition.
Just as young people can seek career advice from vocational guidance authorities, or have it thrust upon them, they can also be advised by marital
guidance authorities. And the advice given in both areas is couched in the
same rhetoric: young people are urged to be realistic; to make appropriate,
feasible, decisions. On marriage the voice of authority is likely to speak along
the following lines:

A man does not select the type of woman who will make a good wife, all things considered; he almost necessarily selects the sort of woman with whom he can fall in
love, and women likewise select husbands on the same *gloriously irrelevant basis*
(Waller and Hill, 1951, p. 195, italics added).

Now if one wants to be rational and to avoid the gloriously irrelevant
stuff that can lead people astray, this can be accomplished by following the
principles of *similarity* and *complementarity*. According to much research
on friendship patterns (e.g., Newcomb, 1961), and on married couples (e.g.,
Byrne and Blaylock, 1963; Levinger and Breedlove, 1966), the similarity
principle states that likes attract. Persons who share similar attitudes and/or
values, are, other things being equal, more attracted to one another. Furthermore, once people are attracted to one another to the point where they become good friends or get married, research indicates that they will *assume*
similarity between themselves. Among happily married couples, and among

newly engaged couples, it is typically found that in addition to real similarity between their attitudes, they also assume similarity where it may not exist, and exaggerate similarities that do exist.

In view of such findings, marital guidance authorities suggest that similarities in attitudes, values, and interests are a primary criterion for rational mate selection. They further suggest that the best place to look for someone of the opposite sex who will be just like yourself is among those coming from the same general socioeconomic background. Statistical data shows that most people marry within their own religious, ethnic, social and economic categories, and that the divorce rate is higher for those who deviate from this pattern. So the general principle seems obvious: similarity is important, and it can be found most easily among those who have grown up in the same area, with similar backgrounds.

The second main principle for rational choice is *complementarity:* within the boundaries of similarity described above, one should look for complementary social-emotional attributes. For example, the domineering person should find one who is submissive; the independent person one who is dependent, and so on. This principle is usually discussed using the terminology of personality traits or needs; people should seek mates whose traits or needs will have a tongue and groove fit to their own. (See Winch, Ktsanes and Ktsanes, 1955, and Winch, 1958, for research evidence and theoretical elaboration.)

When research on similarity and complementarity first began to appear, it led to some confusion. Exponents of one or the other principle would disagree over which was more important. Practical guidance authorities solve this problem by evaluating couples according to both criteria. It is now even possible to have the problem managed by a computer. Individuals take standard tests of their attitudes, interests, and needs or traits. Their scores go into a computer programed to match up those with similar attitudes and complementary needs, and presto! The thing that has preoccupied poets and philosophers through the ages is done, and the right people can get together. If it is objected that physical attractiveness is neglected here, the answer is that for the time being this can be handled by having people exchange pictures or physical measurements. However, research going on in the area of physical attractiveness may soon lead to more efficient techniques.

Work by Moss (1969) indicated that physical attraction may follow a congruity principle. College students were found to select prospective dates according to certain congruities between the attractiveness ratings they gave themselves, and the ratings given to the prospective dates. It seems that those who are plain-looking know their place and do not aspire to date those who are very attractive. Along a different line, research by Wiggins, Wiggins, and Conger (1968) suggested that male preferences for women with different body builds can be related to certain personality characteristics:

. . . large-breast preference was associated with a *"Playboy"* image; preference for large buttocks was related to an "anal character" syndrome; and preference for large legs and small legs was characterized by social inhibition and participation, respectively (p. 82).

Taking everything together, it might seem that we are approaching a new era of scientific mate selection. Of course, it all reeks of inhumanity – this cold application of similarity, complementarity, and maybe some other principles yet to come, particularly where computers are involved. But aside from the traditional science vs. humanism arguments that can be made here (many of us might agree, better to have loved and lost in a gloriously irrelevant way than to have happy contentment served up untouched by human hands), it is possible to question much of the material on scientific grounds.

Levinger and Breedlove's study of married couples showed that the similarity principle does not work in a blanket fashion. Couples rated as low in marital satisfaction exaggerate the differences between themselves, and couples with high marital satisfaction ratings may only show high similarities in those areas relating to certain important goals. Another odd finding concerns dating couples. Kerckhoff and Davis (1962) reported that similarity is higher among those dating for a relatively short time, than among those who have known each other for a longer time.

Briefly, there are enough contradictory and anomalous research findings available to cast doubt on the similarity principle as a sure, practical guide to marriage. The same is true of the complementarity principle. Murstein (1961) studied newlyweds and middle-aged married couples and found that while some of their needs fit a complementary pattern, others did not. He further mentioned that since needs can change over time, and vary in their intensity in different situations, the complementarity notion cannot be accepted without reservations.

In sum then, while the similarity and complementarity principles appear to provide a straightforward rational scheme for mate selection, these principles should be treated with due caution. "Scientific" dating services and some marriage guidance experts rely heavily on these principles because they have nothing better to go on. But so far as one can tell from empirical research, let alone humanistic values, it may still be possible to get as much valuable knowledge from a caress as from a computer printout. From a strictly neutral statistical perspective, it can certainly be argued that adherence to these principles will provide better results than blind chance. But what kind of results? Would any of us who has ever felt the irrational, quick, exciting sense of intimacy that can happen on a chance meeting be prepared to wipe that off our records? Would we warn others away from it? Of course, painful disappointments may come in their wake, but those romantic, inefficient experiences are not to be traded lightly for a fully rational system.

Perhaps the ultimate criticism here is that guidance authorities too often emphasize the virtues of prudence, while ignoring the possibility of inspiration.

Sex differences

Many writers suggest that careers and marriage have very different meanings for young men and women. Bell (1968) expressed a prevalent opinion:

It is our contention that the most important adult role for the majority of American girls continues to be that of wife-mother. For her to achieve this role, it is customary to first fall in love. The achievement of the boy's most important adult role, that of choosing and entering into an occupation, is not dependent upon his being in love. In fact, the boy may view love as a threat to his occupational achievement (in Adams, pp. 275 – 276).

Where females are concerned, this point seems contrary to our earlier argument that career decisions are generally more important for personality than marital decisions. Yet the difference between the sexes may only look important as long as careers and marriage are discussed on a superficial level. At the individual psychological level, work reviewed by Bell indicated that girls are often raised to anticipate marriage as their career. It is quite possible to argue then, that the functional meaning of these two events is similar for young men and women. Reconsideration of material concerning the development of sexual identity supports this idea.

All through early and later childhood, girls are generally oriented toward wife-mother roles, and boys toward husband-provider roles. During adolescence, these orientations become more concrete. Parents, peers, and cultural institutions clearly promote this. To put it very grossly: boys must find work, and girls must find boys who have found work; the more lucrative the better. Thus, to the degree that marriage is construed as a female career, it remains difficult to pin down the psychological meaning of sex differences in these two areas.

Implications for personality

For males and females alike, however, marriage has a heavy impact on personality, which can be seen immediately in the changed social situation of most newlyweds; parents and peers no longer occupy the same important place in their lives. We are already familiar with the fact that through the end of adolescence, parental influence wanes as the influence of peers increases. With marriage, peers also tend to lose importance. Evidence of the latter change is so common as to seem almost universal. In our questionnaire studies with college students, for instance, the following responses are typical of those who are married:

> I have a lot less to do with my old friends now.
> I wrap all my needs for companionship around my husband.
> Since getting married, I can no longer be completely loyal, even to my best friend.

This point could be elaborated further but it hardly seems necessary: most of us can easily understand that one practical consequence of marriage is to de-emphasize reliance on friends. In this connection, it should be noted that peer groups seemingly cooperate in their own destruction by giving individuals a significant impetus toward marriage. Friends provide social occasions for meeting potential spouses, or may serve literally as matchmakers. Among older teen-agers and young adults, peers promote a general climate of opinion which gives marriage a central, feasible place in the thoughts of individuals. Even among young men who apparently share the conviction that making out without marriage is the highest goal in life, it is remarkable to see how quickly this idea disintegrates during adult transition. Instead of the old gang being broken up by wedding bells, it may be more correct to say that the old gang creates the possibility of wedding bells for its members.

But our main point is that when two young people live together in social and sexual intimacy, they are not likely to maintain intense prior commitments to others. It follows that most of the support one's ego or sense of identity has formerly received from friends or relatives, must now come from his spouse. Furthermore, marriage brings with it a new degree of self-exposure. Clichés about no man being a hero to his own wife are probably true, but the cliché must be pushed one step further to see its significance for personality. If, after exposure of self to another in marriage, one is still reasonably acceptable to the other—not a hero, but at least not a villain either—then self-esteem, confidence, and most of the other attributes associated with a strong sense of ego identity will be increased. The intimacy of marriage can be interpreted as a very severe, interpersonal "test" of the self. To survive it with fair success is to be supported or affirmed as an individual in a newer, more important way than ever before.

A nice practical slant on what we are saying here is given in a story passed on to me about a well-known psychiatrist. When young couples ask him how to tell whether or not they are really in love, he shrugs and says "Who knows? But don't try marriage unless you think you can both use the same toothbrush." The point being, of course, that marital intimacy demands a unique degree of mutual acceptance which must go on in the cold light of day, when passions are low and the gritty stuff of life stands unadorned.

The deeper implications of self-exposure and commitment in marriage are understood theoretically to involve an important extension of self. We will see in the next section how it is that theorists understand the whole structure of the self to be expanded and enhanced as a consequence of intimate living with another. Young people can become more than they were before in the process of accommodating to each other. Or to put it another way: if their relationship is durable, then the self-concept of each is not only affirmed by the other's acceptance, it is also enhanced by accepting the other. On a very simple level, this process is observable as mutual learning in marriage. Husbands may become more sensitive to art, and acquire easier social manners; wives may learn about sports or business. Both may be enhanced as individuals in the sense that their knowledge and abilities are increased.

Sexuality

No discussion of marriage and personality will seem complete without some mention of sex. Traditional Freudian views on the genital stage of psychosexual development suggest to many people that "sexual compatibility" is prerequisite to happy marriage. And a quick review of our summary description in Chapter 8 will demonstrate why. If good orgasms are so important for healthy personality functioning, then it is only logical to give physical sex action a high priority in marriage. Or is it? Much work on marriage and divorce shows that in and of itself, sexual intercourse is not a particularly important factor. This is not to say that Freud's ideas are all wrong, only that sexual matters do not seem to be the central cause of failure or success in marriage.

Over the past 40 years, an accumulation of research and clinical experience on marriage problems indicates that sexual compatibility is more likely to be the *result*, not the *cause*, of happy marriage. For example, after testing and interviewing thousands of married couples, Terman (1938) found that physical sex factors (e.g., frequency and techniques of intercourse; premarital experience) had little to do with general happiness. The only notable exception was a moderate relationship between happiness and "wife's capacity to reach orgasm." Terman concluded – and many later reports agree with his statement – that sex problems are more of a symptom than a cause of unhappy marriages. Couples who are otherwise well suited and content with each other are usually able to tolerate or resolve their sex problems without serious difficulty.

Briefly, most writers on personality development agree that in the absence of any other major social-emotional problems, sexual matters will take care of themselves. Lindgren (1964, p. 418) expressed the general view when he said that we should consider sex to play a "minor but vital" role in marriage. Note that none of the material here demonstrates that Freud's conception of genital sexuality is necessarily wrong; it only demonstrates that so far as one can tell from the available evidence, genital sexuality cannot be interpreted as the crucial factor in marriage. When people use "sexual incompatibility" as a general explanation for marriage problems, they are using a cliché which may cover up more than it reveals.

Summary of Career Choice and Marriage

The two major decisions facing young adults – career choice and choice of a mate – are critical events which commonly define the young person's movement into full adult status. However, psychological discussions of these events can be confusing because they may represent at least three different perspectives. First, most general developmental writers treat careers and marriage as the *tasks* or *goals* of adult transition; things to be achieved which serve as developmental criteria of maturity.

Second, in the applied literature of vocational and marital guidance, these events are treated as the *outcomes* of prior development. Counselors accordingly offer advice based on what they see as the best fit between a young person's past history and present opportunities. In principle, the expertise of the guidance authority is similar to that of the horse-race handicapper, because both are really odds-makers. Third, theoretical writers who see personality development as a dynamic, future-oriented affair, tend to emphasize the future implications of career and marital decisions. They treat these events as important determinants of what a person will become.

Each of these approaches has its own intrinsic logic, and must be granted its own plausibility, although we have been quite critical of certain guidance practices. It can certainly be accepted as a formidable academic generalization, that career choice and marriage are tasks of adult transition which are accomplished according to the individual's prior developmental history, and which in turn shape his future development. Complex compromise statements of this sort can be deceptive, however, if they are allowed to obscure real difficulties.

Therefore, just as an attempt has been made to show why the problems of finding a career and mate should not be reduced to actuarial equations, it has also been emphasized that there is no easy way to describe the effects of these events upon personality. Studies and biographies suggest certain general implications which have been mentioned: the everyday activities imposed by a job will come to influence personal identity; the intimacy of marriage breaks up former ties with peers and can affirm and enhance the self. But to follow up such ideas in proper detail, we must turn to theory.

THEORETICAL PERSPECTIVES

It was remarked in Chapter 8 that beyond adolescence, one enters relatively free theoretical territory. Such writers as Sullivan, Erikson, and Blos extend from classical psychoanalytic theory, reinterpreting and adding new considerations to the idea of psychosexual development. Their territory is free, but familiar, because we enter it on a Freudian approach path. Yet there are other, diverse ideas available to interpret postadolescent development. Such concepts as reintegration (Madison), deficit and growth motives (Maslow), and self-actualization (Rogers), all relate to personality changes during adult transition.

Sullivan

In his discussion of late adolescence, Harry Stack Sullivan was apparently talking about the period we have labeled adult transition. He defines this period according to two events: it begins when young people achieve a satisfactory pattern of genital sexual activity, and it ends when they are capable of genuinely mature interpersonal relationships. Recall that in contrast to Freud, Sullivan saw sex only as a very important need, not as a direct key to understanding personality dynamics. He therefore suggested that after coping with their sex needs, young adults can get on with development of their individual capacities as thoughtful human beings.

The idea that development toward healthy maturity requires a wide range of experience is emphasized in comments about university life. Ideally, this can give young people the opportunity to learn about other people and places; they can evaluate their own past experience according to new criteria, and thus develop themselves in ways that might not otherwise be possible.

Much of the typical experience we have discussed under the heading of disillusionment can be assumed here. And this critical condition also seems relevant to Sullivan's explanation of why some young adults may not benefit from wider experience. He said that if a young person holds an "inadequate or inappropriate" view of himself, then new experience may only provoke anxiety, instead of healthy movement toward maturity. We have had a good example of this in the story of the student who really didn't want to become a doctor, but who became very upset whenever he thought about it. If the young man had not been able to resolve his problem by reorganizing his view of himself and his parents, he might have gone on having to struggle with the anxiety provoked by every new experience which threatened his decision to become a doctor. In other words, he would not have benefited from such experience, because he would have been too busy warding off threats to his self-concept.

Sullivan further suggested that if people with inadequate self-concepts cannot get beyond the barriers created by anxiety, they are liable to suffer "restrictions in freedom of living." These restrictions amount to a defensive, neurotic style of life. To avoid anxiety, the person may avoid new experience, or misinterpret such experiences when they occur. Ritualistic behaviors are also mentioned; these can be observed across the board in science, art, politics, and religion, whenever people seem to be participating in something meaningful but are really just going through the motions.

Another type of restriction in freedom of living may express itself in attitudes toward people. If a person is anxious about himself he may try to cope with this, or cover it, by being very critical of others:

One of the feeblest props for an inadequate self-system is the attitude of disparaging others, which I once boiled down into the doctrine that if you are a molehill then, by God, there shall be no mountains. In a good many ways one can read the whole state of a person's self-respect from his disparagement of others (Sullivan, 1953, p. 309).

(Orthodox Freudians would of course explain restrictions in freedom of living in terms of ego defense mechanisms. Disparagement, for instance, seems to involve the projection mechanism.)

Sullivan's ideas provide a fairly broad base for understanding the potential effects of disillusionment, career choice, and marriage upon personality. The former condition can create anxiety; the latter events may reflect efforts to defend against it, particularly in cases where work and marriage serve primarily as easy havens for those with inadequate self-concepts. In this connection, it seems perfectly reasonable to assume that people who seek extreme security in their work (by following the line of least resistance) and their marriage (by seeking a compliant, conventional mate) may be showing signs of restriction in living.

Erikson

Adult transition is for Erik Erikson a time when young people will develop either a sense of intimacy or isolation. The great difficulty here is that the young person must expose himself to situations which threaten his self-esteem or confidence; having acquired a sense of identity, he must lay it on the line to move ahead to a sense of intimacy. And this means risk. He must:

. . . face the fear of ego loss in situations which call for self-abandon: in the solidarity of close affiliations, in orgasms and sexual unions, in close friendships and in physical combat, in experiences of inspiration by teachers and of intuition from the recesses of the self. The avoidance of such experiences because of a fear of ego loss may lead to a deep sense of isolation and consequent self-absorption (Erikson, 1963, pp. 263–264).

Note the similarity to Sullivan. Erikson was also defining movement toward mature personality according to the young person's engagement with a broad range of social experiences. But he was more specific than Sullivan in his emphasis on the ego quality called intimacy, which involves genital sexuality. Thus, while the two theorists are close together in the importance they assign to social experience during adult transition, they differ sharply when it comes to sex.

Sullivan treated it as something to be placed under reasonable control before further progress can be made; Erikson remains closer to Freud by giving genital sex a more immediate role in the movement toward maturity. His discussion implied that if a young person cannot achieve satisfying intimacy with another through sexual intercourse, this failure will probably make it more difficult for him to relate well to others in less demanding interpersonal situations. The issue seemingly comes down to a matter of personal confidence. Satisfactory sex relations with a loved one provide a base of security which will allow a person to risk more in other situations. Or, to put it another way: the person with a good, meaningful sex relationship is like a businessman with plenty of capital—he can afford to extend his operations and be more generous.

Erikson's comments on genital sex hark back to our earlier summary of Freud's ideas. In some respects he apparently saw genital sexuality in much the same way as Freud. But he did not get into any discussion of libido, nor did he treat genital activity as a key to understanding personality dynamics. Instead, he went contrary to orthodox Freudians by suggesting that people should be able to absorb frustrating sex experiences without suffering any serious consequences. An adult who is committed to an intimate relationship with another person should feel sufficient loyalty to that person, and derive sufficient meaning from the relationship, so that a reasonable degree of frustration can be accepted. Furthermore, Erikson said that sex should eventually become subordinate " . . . to that ethical sense which is the mark of the adult."

Now then, speaking more generally, Erikson's theory indicates that the disillusionment of adult transition can be borne without undue difficulty if the individual's self-concept (ego) is at the same time being affirmed and strengthened by a proper sense of intimacy. This sense of intimacy will depend in good part upon the person's *capacity* to experience satisfying genital sex, but literal, frequent sex gratification is not necessary.

If something approximately like this does not occur—if intimacy does not become a strong ego quality during adult transition—the result can be a sense of isolation. Isolated people are those who fear the commitments of intimacy as being too threatening to their egos. They are liable to suffer "character problems"; and it would seem that the neurotic behaviors mentioned by Sullivan might also occur.

While Erikson did not specifically discuss the career choices we see as critical for adult transition, his comments on earlier periods of development suggest that a satisfactory career will increase the likelihood of attaining a proper sense of intimacy. That is, other things being equal, one who is happy in his work should find it easier to expose himself in intimate situations, because his work will have provided him greater self-confidence. It might also be argued that one whose ego has been affirmed by intimacy should also find it easier to make a meaningful career choice. But the ramifications here are too dependent upon individual circumstances to warrant further discussion.

Integration theories

Most current writers on personality find nothing serious to balk at in the neo-Freudian views of Sullivan and Erikson. Since their general interpretations focus on the changing self-concept in relation to social experience, their ideas tend to be mutually supportive despite differences over the role of genital sexuality. But without contradicting these ideas, other theorists emphasize that the deeper psychological work of adult transition involves *integration:* various strands of personality must be pulled together, particularly those which the individual either would not or could not deal with during adolescence.

Blos
Following Freud, and adding ideas drawn from other neo-Freudians and his own clinical experience, Peter Blos (1962) indicated that postadolescence is most basically a time for the individual to work through his final relationship with his parents. In other words, adult transition involves a final sorting out of personality attributes related to experience with parents. On the surface, young people may seem entirely emancipated from their parents. But underneath, their egos or self-concepts may still be tied to their parents through long-standing repressed (unconscious) identifications.

Not that the typical struggles and rebellions of teen-agers against their parents all go for nothing; quite the reverse. Blos said that adolescents are so concerned to establish their independence that they may go too far: psychologically they may throw the baby out with the bath by rejecting *all* parent values, including those necessary to lead a realistically ordered life in society. Therefore, young people moving into adult roles must, in a manner of speaking, go back over the old battlefields of adolescence to salvage some of the material they once rejected.

From therapeutic work with older adolescents, one learns that the struggle to integrate ego interests and attitudes of the parent of the same sex proves to be a formidable task. In order to reach maturity the young man has to make peace with his father image and the young woman with her mother image. Failure at this juncture of development will result in regressive solutions, ego deformations, or a break with reality (Blos, p. 157).

At a very practical level, the point to stress here is that the young person who begins to act out an adult role will probably be unable to do so in a satisfactory way, unless he understands how this role makes him in certain respects similar to his same-sexed parent. If he doesn't understand this, he may harm himself and others by rejecting the role, or by acting it out at the expense of serious internal conflict. For example, young adults who become mothers and fathers themselves are liable to suffer various pathological problems if they are unable to accept parental attributes from the images of their own mothers and fathers.

Blos' discussion of adult transition may seem very far from common experience at first glance, but it provides an important additional basis for understanding this period. His work suggests that the desirable kind of ego development sketched by Sullivan and Erikson will be prevented if young people cannot integrate images of their parents into their own self-concepts. Failure to achieve such integration would therefore be one ultimate source of the anxiety or fear of self-exposure which impedes progress toward maturity.

At this point, however, we can better pursue implications of the integration theme by turning to the work of Madison.

Madison

Peter Madison's work is based on a unique collection of autobiographical material obtained from several hundred students in four different universities. He suggested (1969) that college students generally go through an "overall pattern of development and change in personality," which includes three distinct phases.

The first phase is called *initial organization*. Most students enter college without much realistic knowledge of what awaits them either socially or academically. Hence their ideas about themselves and others are initially organized in terms of their "precollege personality."

The second phase is *erosion of the initial organization,* which occurs as students become aware of the realities in their situation. Madison's discussion here is very close to what we have described under the heading of disillusionment. That is, as young people settle into college, they inevitably discover contradictions to most of their prior ideas.

Resynthesis is the third phase. It sets in when students begin to understand themselves and others according to the way they have been able to come to terms with the new realities encountered in college. In more familiar terms, we typically see this phase as the more mature organization of personal aims and social behavior which most students show by their junior or senior year.

Madison's most important theoretical contribution did not rest upon this three-phase pattern of change, however. He suggested that a student's initial personality organization, and later erosion of this organization, are ultimately due to the workings of a psychological process involving the *integration* and *reintegration* of prior experiences.

For example, Madison explained that the initial organization of the student ("Sidney") who was planning to become a doctor resulted from adolescent reintegration of certain earlier experiences. While a youngster, he began to place great value on security, money, and high social status. These ideas were conveyed by the general life style and specific concerns of his parents. But while growing up, he also acquired strong humanitarian values about doing good for people (in the social-science jargon, a high "service orientation"). So two different sets of values were integrated into his self-concept, and when it came time to choose a career plan on entering college, he *re*integrated them in the decision to become a doctor. Doctors can help mankind and make money in the bargain, or so it would seem.

Another illustration of how reintegration can provide the initial organization for young people is given in the case of the girl who began college wanting to be an astronomer. As a youngster, she had become interested in ancient history and questions concerning the origins of the earth. Family dynamics also led her to develop a strong masculine identity. So on reaching college, these separately integrated aspects of her self-concept were reintegrated in the decision to study astronomy: it related to some of her intellectual concerns, and it offered a masculine course of study.

But now the question arises why such initial organizations turn out to be inadequate; why they can be eroded in college. (Not all of them are, of course.) The answer seems to be that many initial organizations simply cannot stand up to the tests of close personal scrutiny, introspection, and the realities experienced in college. In this connection, Madison said that the college environment contains various "agents of change," which tend to force students to evaluate their ideas more carefully. The agents of change include course work, faculty, and friends. As the student encounters them, they evoke emotional reactions in him because of their relevance or similarity to important *past* experiences. Even though he may not be directly aware of it, these emotional reactions force him to confront his past anew, to reintegrate significant experiences from the past in relation to the present.

Consider "Sidney's" struggle over the meaning of material success. Every time he read a novel, or heard a philosophy lecture involving conflict between material gain and personal satisfaction, there would be aroused an emotional reaction carrying him either directly or indirectly back to his parents' ideas on success. And how well can those ideas which he once accepted stand up to contradictions offered by Sinclair Lewis, Ayn Rand, or Socrates? The same general thing can occur in social relationships. Madison mentioned a girl whose irrational dislike of her roommate turned out to be caused by certain similarities between her roommate and her younger sister. So it is that the agents of change in college have their effect by arousing important prior experiences which may then be reintegrated in a new way.

Erosion triggered by agents of change is finally said to yield resynthesis: after working over significant material from his past, the student can reorganize his self-concept in a more meaningful fashion. Dilemmas about career plans and social relationships can be resolved as their origins and present meanings are better understood. In short, the reintegration process operates in all phases of development in college, but ideally, it should end by producing a new harmony among the various aspects of personality.

It is difficult properly to air Madison's ideas in a brief discussion. Nevertheless, the summary should make it plain that he, like Blos, saw the main work of personality development during adult transition to be a matter of sorting out the past in relation to one's present situation and hopes for the future.

More specifically, both theorists indicated that prior experiences which have influenced personality in a significant way are aroused during adult transition. Blos was particularly concerned with matters of identification with parents, while Madison went into the whole gamut of issues facing college students. According to both, however, the outcome of adult transition will depend upon how well young adults are able to meld their pasts in with their present activities. If, from this standpoint, we now look back to Sullivan and Erikson for a moment, it would appear that "restrictions in freedom of living," and/or "a sense of isolation," are most likely to occur in young people who cannot deal properly with problems rooted in their past.

Readers with a taste for theoretical speculation will appreciate that another point of interest here is the parallel between integration approaches to adult transition, and Piaget's theory of cognitive development. The reintegration idea is strikingly similar to Piaget's conception of equilibration. It does not take a great stretch of the imagination to see that the reintegrative phenomena described by Madison can be understood as a process of equilibrating cognitive schemas about the self and others. Moreover, the personal revelations or sudden insights reported by young adults seem very similar to what can be observed in children who, as a result of equilibrating diverse cognitive schemas, suddenly are able to understand a new conceptual problem. And in a general way, Piaget's work on the possibility-geared thinking of older adolescents is also relevant, because one can see the broad integration of adult transition as a form of synthesis between thinking geared to reality and possibility. But discussions of this sort only have heuristic value: they indicate theoretical territory still awaiting exploration.

Self-enhancement theories

According to the theories discussed so far, the critical factors of adult transition must be placed within a past-present framework to understand their impact on personality. We come now to other theorists who reject the past-present framework because it neglects the future.

The disagreement here is partly a matter of priorities. Along with several other psychological writers and philosophers, Rogers and Maslow argued that past experience is important only insofar as it directly shapes present experience. Furthermore, they suggest that present personality is determined mainly by how people see their future. For example, if a young person thinks of himself as a poor student and therefore finds it hard to study, his present condition is not so much due to past failures as it is to his anticipation of future failures. And if his view of the future can be altered, this may lead him to change his present behavior. In short, self-enhancement theorists maintain that personality should be studied within a present-future framework. It follows that in their view, the critical factors of adult transition will be better understood as harbingers of the future than as reflections of the past.

Rogers

For several complicated reasons, Carl Rogers has become the best-known spokesman for conceptions of personality variously described as "self-enhancement," "ego-enhancement," "self-actualization," or "existential" theories. The mixture of labels results from the fact that no single, monolithic theory dominates this area. Rogers is prominent because he has drawn together ideas from many sources as well as his own clinical experience, and organized the most persuasive set of theoretical statements describing self-enhancement approaches to personality. At the heart of all self-enhancement formulations is the assumption of a forward thrust to life:

The organism has one basic tendency and striving — to actualize, maintain and enhance the experiencing organism (Rogers, 1951, p. 487).

It should be understood that this actualizing tendency is taken as a biological fact, characteristic of all living things. To "actualize" is to make real that which is potential. Therefore, all behavior which involves the realization of a potential is an expression of the actualizing principle. In humans, this would include such things as infants learning to walk, children learning speech, women having babies. When speaking of personality, however, the actualizing tendency is felt and expressed through one's self-concept. Anything which enhances one's conception of himself is therefore described as self-actualizing.

In Chapter 5 we discussed how the self-actualization concept can be applied to the problem of mother love: by becoming good mothers, women realize one of their main physiological potentials. At the same time, their self-concepts are enhanced because they receive approval from others, and they demonstrate to themselves that they are indeed able to accomplish new, demanding tasks. This latter point usually requires some clarification.

In skiing, for example, you can take a difficult run and feel yourself enhanced or actualized because of admiring glances or direct praise from others. But you can also self-actualize by taking a difficult run all alone, when nobody else is there to see it. It is actualizing because you demonstrate a new level of skill, courage, or whatnot to yourself; and even if there are no witnesses, you may walk away from it feeling great.

Rogers handles this problem theoretically by distinguishing between "the need for positive regard" — respect or admiration from others; and the need for positive "*self*-regard" — self-respect. So self-actualization, which might otherwise be construed as just a type of conformity which brings social rewards, can also be applied to nonconforming behavior, where persons risk social disapproval to maintain or increase self-regard.

There is of course a great deal more to Rogers' position; his 1951 book included 19 different theoretical propositions. But it is not really necessary to go into further detail to see why his work provides an important basis for understanding personality growth during adult transition. From his viewpoint, the critical factors of this period will present opportunities or challenges for self-actualization. Loss of illusions will surely occur as young people encounter adult realities, and career and marriage decisions are liable to be difficult. Yet the forward thrust toward realization of various potentials is the thing to see here.

Rogerian theory suggests that if young adults are sufficiently open to their immediate experiences, and if they strive to maintain a self-concept in harmony with the present, then past experiences will take care of themselves. The problems that arise may indeed relate to past experiences, but these problems can be worked out effectively by appealing to the future. In other words, given a reasonable degree of self-actualization in the present, and reasonable hopes for more of it in the future, the self-concepts of most young people will be so enhanced that they can sustain themselves despite problems rooted in their pasts. Furthermore, as one self-actualizes by engaging the realities of adult life, each forward step makes one better able to rise above his past limitations. Altogether then, no one need be a hostage to his past if he will open himself more fully to his present.

It might be useful to close this discussion with another analogy to skiing.[3] The self-enhancement approach to personality treats critical factors in development as similar to difficult ski runs: they must be taken as they come, following the fall line and keeping the self "open to the slope," as it were. Past spills—the basis for anxiety or fear in the present—may influence the action, but progress comes with practice, and a good success makes past spills seem trivial as one moves on to the next, more challenging run. In this way, self-actualizing experiences in the present remove the sting from the past, while providing new impetus to engage the future.

Maslow

Generally speaking, the fundamental ideas of Carl Rogers and Abraham Maslow are quite similar. Both assumed self-actualization to be an ultimate motivating force in behavior, and both seemingly agree that problems from the past need not contaminate the present and future. However, there is one important difference between them: Maslow emphasized that growth is contingent upon maintenance. Maddi gave a concise statement of this difference:

He (Maslow . . .) recognizes another tendency, common to all men, and therefore part of the core of personality, that does not have the same connotations of fulfillment inherent in the actualizing tendency. Although he never quite puts it this way, this other tendency is *the push to satisfy needs ensuring physical and psychological survival* (1968, p. 81).

In this connection, Maslow (1954) ordered human needs according to a hierarchy, ranging from survival requirements to higher-order psychological growth requirements. We therefore have the basic needs for (a) food and water; (b) safety and security; (c) love and affection; (d) self-esteem; and (e) self-actualization, in that order. These are subdivided into what are called "deficit" and "growth" needs (or motives). It is assumed that self-actualization is not likely to occur if lower-order deficit needs remain unsatisfied.

Applying Maslow's work to the substance of adult transition, it would seem that while he fits our general interpretation of Rogers, his view that self-actualization lies at the top of a motivational staircase imposes certain

---

[3]This sport provides a good model for phenomenological and existential ideas. And there is also a Freudian interpretation of skiing. Being long, narrow, and pointed, skis are phallic symbols; the soft white contours of the slopes symbolize female anatomy; and the exhilarating pleasure of a good fast run is a catharsis equivalent to orgasm. Actually, some male skiers argue that the sport is *better* than sex. What female skiers get out of it is yet another question, but having come this far, readers can easily imagine that a Freudian interpretation would not be flattering to feminine identity.

limitations not found in Rogers. To coin a phrase, the "Maslovian position" suggests that critical factors in adult transition ought to be scrutinized according to their implications for satisfying deficit and growth motives. Perhaps the real dilemma for young adults is finding careers and mates which will satisfy both motives in the right proportions. It certainly appears that the Rogerian goal of living fully and openly in the present, can be qualified by the Maslovian stipulation that this requires a proper infrastructure of need-satisfactions. Maslow is in effect reminding us that an army travels on its stomach.

It is noteworthy, finally, that Maddi found Maslow vulnerable to criticism based on evidence that psychological growth can occur despite severe deprivation conditions. He cited cases of hungry artists, concentration camp prisoners and others who have shown important forms of self-actualization while barely surviving atrocious physical stress. But he also mentioned the counterargument that these instances may be extraordinary exceptions to the rule. As yet, no one has proposed an experiment which would put this issue to an empirical test.

CHAPTER SUMMARY

No matter how one looks at it, loss of youthful illusions and choice of a career and mate provide the general substance of adult transition in most organized societies.

Various ways to understand the psychological meaning of this material have been mentioned. Many sources indicate that adult transition is basically a matter of individual adjustment to social institutions. This view is supported by evidence concerning typical guidance and counseling procedures.

Going a step further, however, it appears that when a young person assumes, or is forced to assume, social roles which define adult status, their impact registers on his self-concept. We have noted how career choices can influence personal identity and how marriage can lead to an extension of self. Both these points will be developed further in the next chapter.

The major personality theories relevant to adult transition all focus on the problem of growth and change in the self-concepts of young people. To present a fair sampling of important ideas, the theories are arranged in three general categories. First, neo-Freudians such as Sullivan and Erikson emphasize developmental movement toward mature social relationships. While they disagree about the role of genital sexuality in adult transition, they point to similar difficulties standing in the way of proper development ("anxiety"; "fear of ego loss"), and similar consequences if these difficulties are not overcome ("restrictions in freedom of living"; "a sense of isolation").

Second, some neo-Freudians such as Blos, and other more eclectic writers such as Madison, see adult transition mainly as a time for the integration of personality. Without contradicting Sullivan or Erikson, these writers argue that if young adults are to achieve the capacity for mature social relationships, they must integrate (or reintegrate) significant past experiences into their present self-concepts.

Finally, the self-enhancement writers break away from explanations which stress the importance of early experience. By appealing to the principle of self-actualization, Rogers and Maslow maintained that the forward thrust of development makes the future more important than the past. A young person's view of himself will be set by his ability to realize his potentials in the present, and his expectations of being able to do so in the future. Given a proper degree of self-actualization, the self-concept will be sufficiently enhanced so that past experiences can be absorbed without serious difficulty. Maslow differed from Rogers because he considered self-actualization to be dependent upon the satisfaction of lower-order needs, but both writers represented the same present-future approach to personality development.

There is no convenient, direct way of reconciling outstanding differences between all the theoretical approaches summarized above. On the other hand, the confusion is not all that bad. When personality in adult transition is examined according to a nonsectarian discussion of critical factors, and according to theories which offer different interpretations of such factors, the emerging picture is not too disorderly.

All the material converges on changing self-concepts. It seems reasonable to think that different theories might be employed to understand different kinds of changes; or perhaps any given change can be profitably examined from more than one perspective. Some of the mildly disturbed young veterans back from Vietnam, for example, obviously need time to integrate their experiences, and will be able to do so better if they go on to realize their individual potentials as civilians. So if we have to contend with diverse theories for academic purposes, then for practical purposes we also have the possibility of finding our own individual unity in that diversity—which is, everything considered, really what adult transition is all about.

References

Becker, H. S., & Geer, B. The fate of idealism in medical school. *American Sociological Review*, 1958, *23*, 50–56.

Bell, R. R. The marital expectations of adolescents. In J. F. Adams (Ed.), *Understanding adolescence*. Boston: Allyn and Bacon, Inc., 1968, pp. 272–286.

Blos, P. *On adolescence*. New York: The Free Press, 1962.

Borow, H. The adolescent in a world of work. In J. Adams (Ed.), *Understanding adolescence*. Boston: Allyn and Bacon, Inc., 1968, pp. 337–360.

Byrne, D., & Blaylock, B. Similarity and assumed similarity of attitudes between husbands and wives. *Journal of Abnormal and Social Psychology*, 1963, 67, 636–640.

Clark, B. R. The "cooling-out" function in higher education. *The American Journal of Sociology*, 1960, *26*, 569–576.

Erikson, E. H. *Childhood and society*. (2nd ed.) New York: W. W. Norton & Company, Inc., 1963.

Erikson, E. H. *Identity: Youth and crisis*. New York: W. W. Norton & Company, Inc., 1968.

Farnsworth, D. L. *Psychiatry, education, and the young adult*. Springfield, Ill.: Charles C Thomas, Publisher, 1966.

Ginzberg, E., Ginsburg, S. W., Axelrad, S., & Herma, J. L. *Occupational choice*. New York: Columbia University Press, 1951.

Hackman, R. B. Vocational counseling with adolescents. In J. Adams (Ed.), *Understanding adolescence*. Boston: Allyn and Bacon, Inc., 1968, pp. 361–386.

Havemann, E., & West, P. *They went to college: The college graduate in America today*. New York: Harcourt Brace Jovanovich, Inc., 1952.

Kerckhoff, A., & Davis, K. E. Value consensus and need complementarity in mate selection. *American Sociological Review*, 1962, *27*, 295–303.

Levinger, G., & Breedlove, J. Interpersonal attraction and agreement: A study of marriage partners. *Journal of Personality and Social Psychology*, 1966, *3*, 367–372.

Lindgren, H. C. *Psychology of personal development*. New York: American Book Company, 1964.

Maddi, S. R. *Personality theories: A comparative analysis*. Homewood, Ill.: The Dorsey Press, 1968.

Madison, P. *Personality development in college*. Reading, Mass.: Addison-Wesley Publishing Company, Inc., 1969.

Maslow, A. H. *Motivation and personality*. New York: Harper & Row, Publishers, 1954.

Moss, M. Social desirability, physical attractiveness and social choice. Unpublished Ph.D. dissertation. Kansas State University, 1969.

Murstein, B. I. The complementarity need hypothesis in newlyweds and middle-aged married couples. *Journal of Abnormal and Social Psychology*, 1961, *63*, 194–197.

Newcomb, T. M. *The acquaintance process*. New York: Holt, Rinehart & Winston, Inc., 1961.

Rappoport, L., & Cvetkovich, G. Opinion on Vietnam: Some findings from three studies. *Proceedings of the American Psychological Association*, 1968, 381–382.

Roe, A. Early determinants of vocational choice. *Journal of Counseling Psychology*, 1957, *4*, 212–217.

Rogers, C. R. *Client-centered therapy; Its current practice, implications and theory*. Boston: Houghton Mifflin Company, 1951.

Sanford, N. *Self and society*. New York: Atherton Press, 1966.

Scott, W. A. *Values and organizations*. Skokie, Ill.: Rand McNally & Company, 1965.

Sullivan, H. S. *The interpersonal theory of psychiatry*. New York: W. W. Norton & Company, Inc., 1953.

Summerskill, J. Dropouts from college. In N. Sanford (Ed.), *The American college*. New York: John Wiley & Sons, Inc., 1962, pp. 627–657.

Super, D. E. *The psychology of careers*. New York: Harper & Brothers, 1957.

Terman, L. M. *Psychological factors in marital happiness*. New York: McGraw-Hill Book Company, Inc., 1938.

Waller, W., & Hill, R. *The family*. New York: The Dryden Press, Inc., 1951.

Wiggins, J. S., Wiggins, N., & Conger, J. C. Correlates of heterosexual somatic preference. *Journal of Personality and Social Psychology*, 1968, *10*, 82–90.

Winch, R. F. *Mate selection: A study of complementary needs*. New York: Harper & Row, Publishers, 1958.

Winch, R. F., Ktsanes, T., & Ktsanes, V. Empirical elaboration of the theory of complementary needs in mate selection. *Journal of Abnormal and Social Psychology*, 1955, *51*, 508–513.

10

Maturity (26 to 50 years)

Ah, the signs of maturity! They come in slowly and by devious routes, each making its own greater or lesser impact: via the waistline – when you can't fit into the jeans you wore in college, or your old soldier suit; in the street – when a policeman stops you and says "Sir"; in the family – when you begin thinking more about what you may do to your kids than what your parents did to you. And perhaps the most significant of all impacts are felt in relation to work: when younger people start getting ahead of you.

For the last nine years, I've been the fastest lineman on the club, and now Gillingham is the fastest lineman on the club. I cursed him for his youth, for his vigor, for his vitality, for all the things I'd lost, and I wondered how much longer I'd be able to play professional football (Jerry Kramer, *Instant Replay*, p. 34).

Kramer was 31 years old at the time. Old enough as athletes go also to begin perceiving his age in comparison with another rookie:

When I joined the Packers in 1958, he was just starting the eighth grade. When I was All-Pro in 1962, he won the Jerry Kramer Award as the best blocker on the Sand Point High School team. Now he's twenty-two, weighs 275 pounds, and he's looking for my job. It doesn't make me feel any younger (ibid., p. 35).

However, the relevant signs and feelings are one thing; their meaning for personality development are another.

There are many different approaches to the psychological subject matter of maturity and confusion starts with the word itself. It is used in the chapter title as a noun describing a period often referred to as "adulthood." Some authorities prefer to use it as a global adjective indicating the general qualities they think an adult ought to have – "so and so has a mature personality." Like a great many of our difficulties in psychology, this one involves a nice linguistic mishmash, because on pushing into the matter it becomes clear that the word *adult* is also ambiguous.

Beyond its legal definition based on chronological age, what does it mean to be an adult? Implicitly, we distinguish between chronological and psychological adults by calling them immature or mature, but then we also speak of a child or adolescent who acts as an adult as being "mature for his age." In view of all the discrepancies between legal, behavioral, and various other technical meanings given to maturity and/or adulthood, this line of discussion could be spun out almost indefinitely—starting with such an intellectual horseshoe nail one can generate half the problems of art and science—so let us drop it, stipulating that we are out to explore sources of behavior characteristic of a particular age range.

This doesn't get us entirely out of the woods, however, because we immediately run up against another ambiguity. What is a proper age-range for the period called maturity, adulthood, or, for that matter, mature adulthood? Granted that age statements for all developmental periods are somewhat arbitrary, in this period the problem is much worse. Chronological ages for earlier periods are at least sanctified by common usage and rough consensus among the developmental theories. For maturity there is little common usage beyond the magical 21 years, or over 30, or Jack Benny's brilliant 39.

Our specification of 26 to 50 is based on certain developmental and didactic considerations. First, it seems apparent that by age 26, give or take a few years, most people will have made some fundamental adjustments to the critical factors of adult transition. And at the other end, by about 50, most people will probably feel themselves to be on the threshold of old age.

This suggestion is not entirely arbitrary. It is supported by one of the very few attempts to study behavioral changes across the normal life span. Using letters, interviews, and other sources, Charlotte Buhler worked up detailed life histories for 140 men and women living in the vicinity of Vienna, Austria. Among her other findings, she described the approximate age range 28 to 50 as the "culmination period." That is, during this time the majority of persons studied had established their careers and families, and gone on to enjoy the most productive portion of their lives. (See report by Else Frenkel, 1936).

The second main reason for the age specification is didactic. At their very worst, ages may be no more than speculative approximations, but they help remind us of important realities by drawing together the world of common experience and the abstractions we use to describe it. For example, to speak of middle age vs. youth is abstract, but to think simultaneously of a friend in his mid-40's who has just had a mild heart attack, and another who has just married for the third time, is reality.

Then too, as one begins to reflect on such age-related experiences—heart attacks, third marriages, and other things more typical of the 40's than the 20's—the over-30 cliché takes on concrete meaning. Most of us *do* show some important changes as we approach and pass through this age. Indeed, it seems that 30 is now more of a magic number than 21 because it has come to symbolize the final closeout on youth. The emphasis has shifted from the legal-traditional *beginning* of adulthood to the practical *ending* of youth. Youngsters can hardly imagine it, and those who have passed through it understand its significance in many different ways.

Up to this point some of the immediate issues associated with the problem of understanding maturity have been sketched. The remainder of the introduction is devoted to a closer examination of typical experiences which set this period apart from others. But the first thing to mention is that the research literature on maturity is very thin. Bernice Neugarten, one of the few investigators who concentrated on adult personality development, was very emphatic about this:

As yet we have no developmental psychology of adulthood; and psychology as a science has just begun to study the five or six decades that constitute the adult portion of the life span with something of the fascination that it has been studying the first two decades that constitute childhood and adolescence (1968, p. 94).

The question arises immediately, "Why should this be the case? Why should the greater part of the life cycle have received so little attention?" One obvious answer is that most psychologists are themselves in this part of the life cycle and, being no different from anyone else, they are probably reluctant to scrutinize problems too close to home. Other plausible explanations have been mentioned earlier: Sullivan said that clinicians don't get to see many healthy adults as clients, and general scientific traditions are such that most investigators tend to seek *fundamental* (early) causes for behavior.

This is not to say that the social science cupboard is entirely bare with respect to maturity; it contains several important items which will presently be considered. But in coming to grips with this period, we will necessarily be relying more upon biographical material, interviews, and theoretical discussions, than upon controlled studies.

ASPECTS OF MATURITY

The Vietnam study

How to begin? In my own work, mature personality was mainly an academic and idiosyncratic personal matter until our interview study with Vietnam combat veterans. Most of the men were young, but several were in their 30's and 40's, and the discovery of consistent differences between the younger and older men came as a real surprise, probably because we had never before really thought about such differences. The following discussion is from unpublished research notes.

All that we have said so far stands in very sharp contrast to impressions gained from talking with older combat veterans, who seem much less disturbed by their experiences. They talk of combat activities — including civilian killings — as regrettable but inevitable given the nature of the war. And they accept the loss of friends in the same vein. Their attitudes reflect a philosophy of *realpolitik;* they keep the war itself apart from their personalities. It appears as if they do not need any particular outcome of the war to help them assimilate their personal experiences. . . .

Most of these men see themselves as professionals and take considerable pride in their ability to adapt to changing environments and changing demands for performance. They are obviously adults committed to a certain style of life who have developed tough-minded, resilient personality structures appropriate for adjustment to the war. In one way or another, many of them are just as critical of the way the war is being conducted as the younger men. But their critical remarks are relatively matter-of-fact; unemotional. Their individual personalities do not seem any more affected by even the gamiest of experiences than is the personality of a surgeon who comes home after a messy operation. A good wash, a couple of stiff drinks, and then dinner with the wife and kids, calm in the knowledge that one has done his best under difficult circumstances.

The general thing one sees here can perhaps best be summarized with an analogy. In their ability to absorb punishing, high-stress experiences, the personalities of the men in our interview sample are like blotters. The older men have a thick defensive nap that can soak up almost anything. The younger men have a much lower saturation point; once it is reached they can only try to catch the spillover with improvised adjustment mechanisms.

A number of atrocity stories have come out of Vietnam since these notes were written in 1968. It is noteworthy that most of the stories were initially "broken" by younger men. And one particular case deserves special mention because it illustrates the age difference discussed above. A 22-year-old infantryman witnessed four men on patrol with him kidnap, rape, and murder a young girl. He was afraid they would kill him too if he interfered. But he reported the incident to his commanding officer, expecting a great reaction. Instead, the older man said that he too had seen some outrageous things, not only in Vietnam, but back in the States as well, and that such things were part of "the system":

What's happened is the way things are, so why try to buck the system? And take it from me, Eriksson, it's even more hopeless to try to buck it in the middle of a war—there's more of a system then than ever. Better relax about that Vietnamese girl, Eriksson. The kind of thing that happened to her—what else can you expect in a combat zone? (in Daniel Lang, *Casualties of War*, pp. 57–58).

In some ways, this sort of material seems to speak for itself. However, it should not be used to support simple notions to the effect that people inevitably grow more insensitive, callous, or amoral with age. Soldiers are a special population; most of the older ones are regulars; and it was *young* men who took part in the rape-murder. The point to be made here is more subtle than a blanket statement concerning apparent insensitivity among those over 30 years of age. It is that age and experience will make people seem tougher because they develop adjustment mechanisms appropriate to their adult situations. Over the years, to protect the self or ego against the onslaughts of severe experience, certain coping techniques become habitual.

These techniques often resemble classic Freudian defense mechanisms: the officer who spoke of "the system" seems to be using it as a basis for rationalization. And the compartmentalization mechanism, whereby one keeps threatening experiences apart from the self, can be fitted across the board to soldiers, surgeons, businessmen, or even men like Adolf Eichmann.[1]

Generally, the tendency to use defensive techniques does indeed seem to

[1]Hannah Arendt's description of Eichmann *(Eichmann in Jerusalem)* showed him to be a very banal, humdrum family man. The story of his participation in genocide seems all the more horrible because he was apparently able to keep his "professional" activities quite separate from the rest of his life.

get stronger in maturity—there is usually more to defend against. But this psychological defense capability we are talking about is not, in and of itself, proof of insensitivity. One may actually turn the whole issue upside down by arguing that really tough people won't need to use defensive techniques as much as the really sensitive; therefore, the more defensive the individual, the more sensitive he must be.

Finally, the psychological defense capability does not seem any more inherently evil or pathological than the capacity of the body to heal itself by forming scar tissue. In this connection, it is appropriate to add a further comment: dispassionate study of atrocious behavior does not preclude a sense of moral outrage. Whether or not we are psychologists, we can and should blame those who *choose* or *accept* an atrocious role; but in view of what we know about defensive capacities it is not clear whether we should blame them for their ability to *adjust* to an atrocious role. Who will cast the first stone when it comes to the adaptability—for good or ill—of human beings? So long as we don't think much about what goes on in slaughter-houses, we go on enjoying our steaks and chops. And as long as we don't know where our mutual funds get invested, we can go on attacking the "military-industrial complex" as evil, while collecting dividends and donating money to peace organizations.

However, let us return to the main issue: the general appearance of toughness or insensitivity which seems to come with maturity. We have seen how striking this can be in different age groups of soldiers. The threatening conditions which produce this phenomenon can also be seen in other walks of life.

Business studies

An interview survey by Johnson (1961) indicated that advancement in business firms is largely a matter of "executive knifing"; one gets ahead by doing in the man holding a higher position and/or beating out others in line for it.

The majority viewpoint is well summed up in this acid statement by a large company department head, "You've got to be a gut fighter somewhere along the line." A vice president added another biting point, "People who don't get dirty don't make it. I'm not defending the practice. I'm simply stating a sad fact that I've learned the hard way. In 30 years, I know of only three men who've reached executive positions cleanly. And I admit I'm not one of the three" (Johnson, p. 15).

Nor should it be assumed that these practices exist because men enjoy them as part of the two-fisted free enterprise system:

Almost without exception, the people we interviewed regretted the prominent part that knifing plays in a company's power pattern. A controller wistfully told us, "I think there are some companies that are pure, where you can move ahead without treachery. There's not much chance to find one, but I certainly wish I worked for one." One top executive, in a moment of revealing candor, said, "I've done my share of dirty work and I don't like it. I think of the men whose careers I've ruined and the shame I've brought to them and their families. The thoughts aren't pleasant to live with. They're a heavy price to pay for success" (Johnson, p. 17).

Furthermore, according to Johnson, business organizations allow all this dirty work to go on because it provides a way of selecting men with the right stuff in them.

Men with the nerve and ability to climb roughshod over others are valuable assets to their companies. If they can survive the rigors of an in-company knifing war, they've got the ruthless drive and aggressiveness that are demanded in the hard-bitten competitive wars of modern business (Johnson, p. 17).

Without questioning Johnson's veracity, one might think at first that perhaps he is too harsh. Surely things can't be that bad, and after all, aren't there supposed to be large companies where "organization men" trade their independence for routine security in a paternalistic system? Not according to the author of *The Organization Man*. Whyte said that while men in the lower echelons of large companies are far removed from competition for top positions, they compete anyway.

They are competing; all but the fools know this—but for what, and against whom? They don't know, and there is the trap. To keep even, they must push ahead, and though they might like to do it only slightly, who is to say what slightly is. Their contemporaries are in precisely the same doubt, and thus they all end up competing against one another as rapaciously as if their hearts were set on the presidency itself (1957, p. 176).

And in case anyone thinks these conditions are unique to American business, he should read what Lewis and Stewart (1961) have to say about European companies:

. . . the young man who thinks that diligence and good results alone will ensure success is going to be disappointed; for, in addition to merit, promotion in business depends on three 'p's'—personality, pull, and push—and on chance (1961, p. 83).

Push, however, is the most essential quality of all. . . . those who are to be powerful in the business world cannot afford to hide their lights under a bushel. In fact, their concern must be to find other people's lights under other people's bushels and appropriate them . . . (1961, p. 85).

We have painted a pretty grim picture of conditions facing adults in the business world because they *are* grim. In seeking to describe this world, which sets the tone of maturity for many people, we have found only two general kinds of source materials: those which ignore the gritty details of personal advancement, and those which lay it out as above. Moreover, strong criticism of business men has existed down through the ages in religion and folklore. Remember Jesus and the money changers, and the line about a camel passing through the eye of a needle easier than a rich man getting into heaven. My mother assures me that my scholarly grandfather was fond of a Yiddish expression which she translates as follows, "The bigger the businessman, the bigger the crook."

Psychologically, however, we can soften this discussion a little by raising an additional consideration: apart from the comfort business people derive from making money, one of their favorite rationalizations—that things are not really much different in other areas of adult life—has considerable truth.

Miscellaneous areas

Consider academics. Mary McCarthy spent some time teaching in an Ivy League college and wrote a scathing novel *(The Groves of Academe)* about the competitive, hypocritical side of faculty life. C. P. Snow provided similar material in *The Masters*, and empirical support for some of what these fiction writers reveal can be found in such studies as *The Academic Marketplace* (Caplow and McGee, 1958).

Consider sports. Jerry Kramer conveyed some of the hard realities that contaminate the life of a successful athlete:

I started training camp without a contract, and Vince made practice almost unbearable. Every block I threw, every move I made, was either slow or wrong or inadequate. "Move, Kramer, move," he'd scream, "you think you're worth so damn much." And the contract negotiations weren't kept at any executive level. They were held at lunch and dinner, at bedtime and during team meetings, and the rest of the coaches joined in, all of them on my back, sniping at me, taking potshots at me. I got bitter, I got jumpy, and then a lot of the other guys, my teammates, began to tease me, to ride me, and the teasing didn't sound like teasing to me because I was getting so much hell from all angles *(Instant Replay, p. 22).*

Consider art. Interview data collected from pop music performers circa 1960, shows the eternal struggle between integrity and commercialism.

If you want to keep on working, you have to put up with some crap once in a while. . . . I don't care. I've got a wife and I want to keep working. If some square comes up and asks me to play the "Beer Barrel Polka" I just smile and play it.

I used to go on a job with the idea to play the best I could, that's all, just play the best I knew how. And now I go on a job and I just automatically think, "What will these people want to hear?" . . . They've really gotten it into me, I guess they've broken my spirit.

It's better to take a job you know you're going to be dragged [depressed] with, where you expect to be dragged, than one in music, where it could be great but isn't. Like you go into business, you don't know anything about it. So you figure it's going to be a drag and you expect it. But music can be so great that it's a big drag when it isn't. (All quotes are from Becker, 1963, pp. 101–119).

It might be argued that all the preceding material is a waste of time, because any garden-variety cynic could have told us that when it comes to making a living, the adult world is a jungle; dog-eat-dog, and all that. The purpose in discussing these things, however, is partly to indicate the kind of psychological stress they entail, and partly to emphasize an important side of adult life which is often ignored in popular psychological works. It is all very well for theoretical writers to describe ideal states of growth, or creative, self-actualizing life styles as criteria for evaluating mature personality (this vein of theory will be covered in a later section), but it ought to be clear that any such development is going to involve a struggle against certain harsh conditions of maturity. As most people come up against these conditions in their adult roles as soldier, businessman, academician, artist, or whatever, they generally begin to cope through heavier use of defense mechanisms, and they inevitably look tougher as the psychological scar tissue accumulates.

None of this should be confused with the disillusionment of adult transition. In the previous chapter, the loss of youthful illusions was tied to initial experiences with adult realities; this chapter is concerned with effects of prolonged exposure to such realities. The essential difference we see between adult transition and maturity is this: in the former period, one loses illusions; in the latter period, one learns to live without them – or put something else in their place. And that "something else" probably involves a narrowing concern with personal survival and protection of the self. Executives compete because there is apparently no other way for them to maintain themselves. Career soldiers will speak of "the system" and seem indifferent to the horrors of war because they have no psychologically practical alternative. And one sees every day academic people who resist any significant changes in curricula or grading systems, for example, because they fear that the standards they understand will be lost.

Briefly, if adult transition is a series of dramatic engagements with disillusioning experiences and uncertain decisions, maturity seems a less dramatic matter of *attrition*. The young adult can command his life like an old-time cavalry officer: maneuvering in a free, fluid fashion, not worrying much about supply lines, always looking for a quick breakthrough. The mature adult is committed to relatively fixed lines; well dug in, maintaining a comfortable flow of supplies, he is preoccupied with static defenses and will only hazard a set-piece advance.

Marriage

Much of what has been said about the meaning of work-roles in maturity also applies to family roles. At any rate, considerable material indicates that the dramatics of marriage in adult transition later on give way to attrition. Consider the research of Pineo (1961).

Analyzing interview data collected from approximately 400 couples, he reported that after the first 5 years of marriage, there is a general decrease in satisfaction and mutual adjustment. Specifically, physical intimacy declines, couples share fewer interests and activities, and more of them mention feeling lonely. Pineo interpreted these findings according to a theory of "marital disenchantment." This idea was based on the proposition that since people marry when they are maximally well suited to one another, as time goes on and individual changes occur, they can only become less suited to each other.

Another study is also relevant. Cutler and Dyer (1965) reported that contrary to popular belief, when young couples experience some serious violation of their expectations in marriage, open discussion of their feelings may not resolve the problem, and may even make it worse.

At a more general level, there are inevitable changes in the marital relationship as husbands and wives get caught up in their private worlds of making a living and raising a family. Whyte (1957, p. 402) described this development in the lives of many young executives:

> . . . you often find wives in deep emotional trouble because they can no longer get understanding or help from their husbands on their social problems. The wife's talk about the court or the block is not just idle gossip; this is the world she and the children must live in, and the personal relationships in it are quite analogous to the ones that are the basis of the husband's worries. But husbands have a double standard on this: office politics they see as part of a vitally important process, but the same kind of relationships in the community they dismiss as trivia, the curse of idle female tongues.

Before leaving the subject of marriage, we ought to present at least one illustration of the way it can fall apart. Bertrand Russell is by no means representative of the average man, but sometimes the best way of understanding average experience is through the testimony of a unique individual. At the time of this quote Russell was about 30 years old, at the height of his creative powers; he had been married for 7 years.

> I went out bicycling one afternoon, and suddenly, as I was riding along a country road, I realized that I no longer loved Alys. I had had no idea until this moment that my love for her was even lessening. The problem presented by this discovery was very grave. We had lived ever since our marriage in the closest possible intimacy.
>
> I knew that she was still devoted to me. I had no wish to be unkind, but I believed in those days (what experience has taught me to think possibly open to doubt) that in intimate relations one should speak the truth.
>
> I did not at once tell her that I no longer loved her, but of course she perceived that something was amiss. She retired to a rest-cure for some months, and when she emerged from it I told her that I no longer wished to share a room, and in the end I confessed that my love was dead. I justified this attitude to her, as well as to myself, by criticisms of her character (*The Autobiography of Bertrand Russell,* Vol. I, pp. 195–196).

The marriage went on, however, as so many do under such circumstances.

> About twice a year I would attempt sex relations with her, in the hope of alleviating her misery, but she no longer attracted me, and the attempt was futile. Looking back over this stretch of years, I feel that I ought to have ceased much sooner to live in the same house with her, but she wished me to stay, and even threatened suicide if I left her. There was no other woman to whom I wished to go, and there seemed therefore no good reason for not doing as she wished (ibid., p. 200).

Taken together, the material on marriage suggests that while it may or may not be a bed of roses at the outset, in maturity couples inevitably begin to feel some thorns. Whether one appeals to such theories as marital disenchantment, or to the everyday sources of domestic stress—child-rearing problems, job-family role conflicts—the attrition experienced in marriage seems quite clear.

Russell's autobiography provides a relatively pure case of marital deterioration. It deserves emphasis precisely because none of the conventional stresses are present: he and his wife had been sexually and intellectually very intimate; they had no children to quarrel over, and no serious money problems. Yet the marriage fell apart when Russell discovered that he no longer felt love.

Friendship

Now, having noted the kinds of attrition facing adults in their work and marriages, the only major area of life remaining is friendship or peer relationships. There is not much empirical literature available to enlighten us in this area, but the general situation can be described as follows. Personal friendships lose much of their importance with movement into maturity because most people satisfy their needs for intimacy through marriage. And if they don't fully succeed in this, they are at least preoccupied with the effort. For men, there will of course be friendly relationships with colleagues at work, and for women there are neighboring housewives and the wives of their husband's colleagues. The difficulty is that for men and women alike, such relationships do not go very deep. Primary loyalties to the family, and ever-present concerns for material advancement or individual achievement tend to prevent the formation of intimate friendships.

In their discussion of differences between friendships formed during adolescence and maturity, Douvan and Adelson provided an excellent summary of the way most psychiatric authorities understand adult friendship patterns. First noting the barriers to intimacy mentioned above, these writers went on to a deeper interpretation of superficial adult socializing.

Adulthood all too often brings with it a retreat into extroversion and, paradoxically, a loss of sensitivity to the other. Aside from those whose work or style of life allows or encourages introspection and insight, the tendency is to abandon the inner resources. To be intimate with another endangers the repressions of drives and affects.

To a disquieting degree, the adult friendship is no more than a mutual flight from boredom — a pact against isolation, with an amendment against intimacy. The interaction focuses on gossip or on leisure interests; in many cases the friendship centers itself on a game — bridge or golf, let us say, the understanding being that anything that does not bear on the game is gauche, embarrassing, or out of bounds. Those things which are crucial to personal integration, such as a person's history, values, or work, are studiously excluded from the interaction (1966, p. 178).

Many illustrations of adult behavior agreeing with Douvan and Adelson's discussion can be found in Goffman (1959). He described such behavior as role-playing, and used the technical language of the theater to analyze adult role "performances."

Summary of the conditions of maturity

From the discussion to this point it would seem that adult life offers nothing but a bleak prospect of attrition. Over the long haul, the forces encountered in work, marriage, and peer relations are generally negative: people appear to become toughened and insensitive as they must cope with threats to their self-concepts coming in from all sides. If the diverse material cited above is accepted at its face value, then personality development in maturity must turn out to be a holding action. That is, the conditions of adulthood must be recognized as forcing people into a psychologically defensive posture which will preclude further growth.

However, important as it is to understand the hard realities encountered in maturity, there is still some reason to think that one should go on living past 30 or 35. To grant that further development may be difficult beyond this point is not to say that it is impossible.

One basis for such an argument can be found in the common experiences of maturity which often go unnoticed. Ask any random sample of 35- to 45-year-old people about adult life and it is a safe bet that practically all of them will confirm our prior discussion of attrition. But ask what keeps them going, or why they put up with the attrition and they may admit to some deep-seated joys in work, or in raising a family; things that don't often come out in response to questionnaires or interviews, and that tend to be covered over by everyday problems. This is speculation of course, although the argument can be maintained by appealing to personal experience or biographical reports. (It is hard to put a metric on the quiet feelings most of us can have while tucking in a child for the night.)

And there are undoubtedly many other sources of satisfaction in maturity. Competitive work situations impose severe tensions, yet simultaneously provide exciting possibilities for achievement. Ulcers and all, a lot of men would never trade their business careers for the proverbial chicken farm; and chicken farmers also have problems. Similarly in marriage, the strains of attrition exist, but if some bedrock mutual affection and respect survives, the relationship can be all the stronger for having been tested across the years.

Another reason for looking past the difficulties of maturity is simply that we don't know enough about this period yet to form any definitive conclusions. The lack of substantial research has already been mentioned and Brim (1968) also pointed this out, commenting on various possibilities for growth and change with the intention of stimulating further investigation.

In the institution of the family, the sizable adult socialization that takes place in new relationships (as between parent and child) and in the changes in continuing human relationships (as between husband and wife) demands study; the impact of the family upon the adult is evident if one takes the time, and perhaps has the courage, to reflect. Notable among the topics here are the influence of children upon adults over the span of child-rearing years and the influence of husband and wife upon each other (1968, p. 223).

It seems appropriate to summarize our introduction to maturity with three generalizations. *First*, conditions encountered in this period are such that in coping, adults appear to grow tougher, less sensitive and less open to change. *Second*, despite the grimmer sides of adult life, maturity is not without its compensations or satisfactions. And *third*, without necessarily contradicting the general picture of attrition in maturity, it should be understood that research has only scratched the surface of this period. No one can write off possibilities for change and growth that have yet to be investigated.

CRITICAL FACTORS

Attrition

It is hardly necessary to further specify why attrition is seen as a definitive, critical factor in maturity. Its dictionary definition: "a wearing away by or as by friction," is clearly in agreement with conspicuous features of adult life. The only additional point worth mentioning is that normative studies of human development also support the idea of attrition as a critical factor.

Scores on intelligence tests, for example, are generally thought to drop off past the age of 30. A classic study by Jones and Conrad (1933) showed moderate to sharp decreases in test scores with each decade of age beyond 20, but as usual in this area, the results are debatable. Some recent studies indicated that the high point in intelligence scores is reached between the age of 25 and 30, while others suggested that scores remain about the same between 25 and 50. Yet the preponderance of data available suggests that whatever it is the tests are measuring, it does not get any better in maturity.

Physiologically, practically everything that can be measured begins to suffer in a significant way by the age of 40. There is an increasing loss of ability to hear high-pitched tones, a sharp drop in visual acuity, and a slow-down of physical metabolism which causes weight problems. In addition, such vital organs as the heart, lungs, kidneys, and liver are more likely to start malfunctioning.

Briefly then, besides all the evidence of attrition visible in the major areas of social behavior during maturity, there is also a "wearing away" of intrinsic capacities. Much of this may not be immediately apparent to the individual, or to those around him, because of certain compensations that come with age. Thus, at 35 or 40 you may not be as good as you once were at taking intelligence tests, or learning new skills, but these things are generally not required. Furthermore, insofar as a work-role *does* demand new learning, the skills, tricks, techniques, or what-have-you acquired from years of relevant experience may easily make up for losses in native ability.

For personality development, however, our crucial problem is to try to understand the psychological impact of attrition. In this connection, it has already been mentioned how defense mechanisms are likely to operate. But on a deeper, more general psychological level, the attrition of maturity seems to produce a demand for personal meaning. That is, under the accumulating pressure of social, psychological, and physical attrition, adults cannot avoid asking themselves "Why?" "What is it all in aid of?" "What does my life add up to?"

Meaning

In work
Perhaps the easiest kind of meaning problem to understand is that which occurs in relation to work. Young adults frequently begin by treating their work as an expediency, a way of making bread; the more the better. Yet after several years, usually when a fair supply of bread is assured, they may start

to question it and to look for something more. Kaplan described this phenomenon in an article on current trends in psychoanalytic theory:

Analysts often see this conflict in patients turning thirty. These patients have settled the question of who they are, and have become interested in leadership, in leaving some mark on the world around them in a palpable way. They talk about parenthood, or career problems, things outside themselves. Stagnation in people nearing thirty is expressed in a prolonged self-absorption of an adolescent kind, a *dread of not finding activities that are worth believing in* (1968, p. 59, italics added).

At a more concrete level, Jersild (in Hamachek, 1965) discussed the problem of meaning in the work of teachers. His definition of meaning emphasized personal involvement; a quality which is obviously important for teachers who influence children as much by their informal style as by their formal actions. Moreover, since Jersild reported survey results indicating that 60 percent of a large sample of teachers are troubled by feelings of meaninglessness, his concern with this problem was quite practical.

When something has meaning, one is committed to it. Where there is meaning, there is conviction. Such commitment and conviction is something different from conformity, or merely playing a part, or living as a cog in a machine, or losing one's individuality in what Kierkegaard has called the "featureless crowd." Where meaning is lacking in one's work as a teacher, the self is uninvolved. The substance is lacking, and teaching is just an empty formality (1965, p. 539).

Jersild went on to mention some of the symptoms of meaninglessness he saw in the work performance of teachers, and these can easily be transposed to fit other professions as well. One symptom is preoccupation with gimmicky techniques promising greater manipulative control over students. Another symptom is excessive worry over formalities of discipline and curriculum. (In universities, this sort of thing is observable all too often among the compulsive attendance-takers, cheater-detectors, and fixed syllabus-makers.) Lack of meaning in work is therefore not only a problem for the individual himself, which he can carry into the analyst's waiting room, it is also a problem for those around him.

However, we should not put all of the putative "blame" for meaninglessness on the individual himself. To the extent that a work-role is defined according to routines emphasizing form and procedure rather than substance, the individual occupying the role will find it difficult to attain meaning. Many school administrators, for instance, give lesson plans, attendance records, and classroom discipline very high priorities. The teacher who is judged deficient in one of these activities is bound to suffer criticism regardless of whatever else he may accomplish with students.

Merton (1940) discussed the way routine job requirements can influence the personalities of those working in bureaucracies. He suggested that people with certain personality attributes – compulsivity, a need for orderliness; what Freudians call the "anal" pattern – are attracted to bureaucratic institutions. And on the other hand, he suggested that such institutions inculcate these attributes in their members. Merton didn't use this example, but anyone who has had dealings with army supply sergeants will recognize the type he has in mind.

Similar ideas on the relationship between work-roles and personality occur in the earlier writings of John Dewey and Thorstein Veblen; while more contemporary, radical extensions of this line of reasoning can be found in the works of Herbert Marcuse and Marshall McLuhan.

Intriguing as it may be, however, the logic whereby failures to find genuine meaning in adult work can be raised to the level of global social criticism is not our primary concern. It is equally important for us to stipulate that difficulties preventing the discovery of meaning relate to basic sources of attrition in the everyday lives of most adults. You can overhear countless renditions of these basics late at night in any hotel bar catering to a convention of business- or professional men.

Those who *do* find meaning in work describe it as a mixture of stimulation, challenge, and achievement. George Kennan, who spent his early 30's working in the American embassy in Moscow, is a good case in point. At the time (1934–1937), the Soviet Union was something of a mystery to the rest of the world. Kennan said that the challenge of living there, and, with a small group of colleagues, trying to understand it, provided the most meaningful period in his life.

Words would fail me if I were to try to convey in this context the excitement, the enjoyment, the fascination, and the frustrations of this initial service in Moscow.

The impressions that crowded in on us from every aspect of our Soviet environment were ones that challenged our own values unceasingly and in the most provocative way. In reacting to them, we felt an unlimited need for discussion among ourselves. These discussions were friendly but serious and sometimes passionate. What the others gained from them, they can say for themselves; but I feel that no experience in life did more to sharpen my mind and to refine my judgments on the whole problem of Russian communism than these daily arguments and explorations (*Memoirs*, pp. 62–63).

Note the phrase "sharpen my mind and refine my judgments"; it touches part of the essence of personal meaning. And the whole exuberant sweep of Kennan's reflections shows that whatever sources of attrition may have been present in his life at that time, they were more than outweighed by an exciting spirit of commitment and discovery.

A similarly exciting but more solitary intellectual form of meaning-in-work was described by Bertrand Russell. He was about 29 when he found a way of unlocking new relationships between mathematics and philosophy:

For years I had been endeavouring to analyse the fundamental notions of mathematics, such as order and cardinal numbers. Suddenly, in the space of a few weeks, I discovered what appeared to be definitive answers to the problems which had baffled me for years. And in the course of discovering these answers, I was introducing a new mathematical technique, by which regions formerly abandoned to the vaguenesses of philosophers were conquered for the precision of exact formulae. Intellectually, the month of September 1900 was the highest point of my life. I went about saying to myself that now at last I had done something worth doing, and I had the feeling that I must be careful not to be run over in the street before I had written it down (*The Autobiography of Bertrand Russell*, Vol. I, p. 192).

It should be plain enough that psychologically speaking, meaning-in-work ultimately comes down to a matter of ego-involvement; a commitment of one's self to an activity which seems to be intrinsically worthwhile, and not just an expediency done for the sake of money, prestige, or any other venial consideration. The same general principle applies in a somewhat different fashion to family situations in maturity, where extrinsic considerations can also operate to the detriment of meaning.

In the family

If work-roles can become meaningless when they are merely instrumentalities—vehicles for achieving some extrinsic end or goal—family roles can suffer the same fate for the same reason. We can begin to unravel part of this problem by starting with the act of marriage itself, which frequently involves such extrinsic considerations as conformity to peer values, material security, and status-seeking. Recall the suggestion in the previous chapter that young women may perceive marriage in much the same way as young men perceive their careers. It therefore seems likely that many of the same considerations which lead men into expedient work situations will lead women into expedient marital situations, and yield the same general kind of meaninglessness in maturity.

On a practical level, the meaning problem facing those who marry for money or prestige is that having once attained this goal, there will be no fundamental reason for them to maintain the relationship over a long period, particularly if the threat of losing material security can be eliminated by alimony payments. Ordinarily, a good part of the mutual meaning couples find in marriage involves a shared effort to achieve material security; the wife who takes a job to help her husband get ahead, for example, can derive an important feeling of participation in his progress, and an equally important sense of being needed. None of this is probable if full material security comes immediately with the marriage ceremony.

Happily enough, since most of us never get a chance to prostitute ourselves in marriage (there are not that many rich folks going around making offers), meaning problems of this sort do not arise very frequently. It does happen fairly often that in maturity, after the ordinary couple is financially secure, the mutual need and shared struggle which gave important meaning to their relationship will be lost. Relevant examples can be seen all the time: the wife who first works hard to help her husband and then gets engrossed in child-rearing may, at 35 or 40, find herself without a meaningful function if her husband and children have become relatively self-sufficient. Furthermore, if things have indeed gone well for him, the husband at this point may not find much meaning in his wife or children. The former may be worn down into a dull *hausfrau*, the latter may see him as a clod, and his dealings with both may center more on a checkbook than anything else. If, in addition, the man is a still-vigorous wheeler-dealer able to turn the heads of young secretaries, then the stage is set for grand melodrama.

It may all sound like a hackneyed plot for a B movie, but some of the realities are like that: actually shocking in their very banality. One of the clichés observable in academic life is the glib, distinguished-looking professor, complete with elegant mustache, sideburns, fancy vests, sports car, and a dowdy wife or ex-wife tucked safely away somewhere in the background.

Another form of meaninglessness can occur in maturity if family life becomes a defensive instrument for maintaining the psychological security of either spouse. This point is difficult to convey without going into clinical detail, but it can be stated generally as follows: faced with all the attrition of adult life, husbands or wives may *use* their family life as a kind of elaborate defense mechanism. A man who feels defeated or bitter about his work, for instance, may release these frustrations on his family in the same way as some men release their sexual frustrations with prostitutes. Or the family may be used for purposes of sublimation and projection: the father who tries to make his son into the doctor or lawyer he himself would have liked to be, the mother who compulsively pushes her daughter toward a glamorous career or marriage, and all parents who rationalize their own disappointments by insisting that they live *for* their children when in fact they are trying to live *through* them.

The varieties of pathology possible when the family is used as a neurotic adjustment mechanism are almost infinite, and almost impossible to sort out from healthy feelings of responsibility and concern unless detailed case histories are available. Yet the problem exists. Moreover, it leads to a logical paradox: how can family life be described as meaningless if it serves a neurotic, but nevertheless important function? The only way to answer this is by appealing briefly to clinical dynamics. Whenever a person or situation takes its meaning from service as a neurotic adjustment mechanism, its genuine, intrinsic meaning will be lost. If family life is exploited in this fashion, it can only provide the individual with artificial or counterfeit meaning. And the trouble with everything counterfeit is that it just doesn't hold up like the real thing. Therefore, it can be argued that given sufficient stress on the family, or significant changes within it, then, like any defense mechanism, its neurotic meaning will give way to a regular deluge of meaninglessness.

What kind of positive meaning can a husband and wife anticipate when the odds are so stacked against them? If sex gets old, and energies are drawn off in different directions, and interests change, what hope is there for continued meaning? We will review some theoretical ideas embracing this issue later, but a few direct comments are in order here.

Bertrand Russell's failed marriage is an instructive example. As he described it, his involvement with his wife was quite total; strong enough to keep him with her long after he would have preferred to live alone. For the first several years this was apparently sufficient to keep the marriage a happy one. Yet throughout his story, even after making due allowance for his inevitable bias, it is abundantly clear that his wife's involvement with him was not nearly so strong as his with her. Now a condition like this can be borne for some time without it becoming a serious source of trouble. But as the years wear on, most people—including one so unique as the brilliant young Russell—will begin to feel it pinch.

The point is that after several years of marriage, its meaning will depend on relatively strong, unconditional *mutual* loyalty and involvement. In fact, this loyalty or trust is about the only truly unique thing that can come out of several years of marriage.[2] All the rest: companionship, sex, shared interests, can be got on the cheap; none of them demands years and years of living together, nor do they necessarily grow out of long-term relationships. But deep-seated trust and loyalty takes time, and can grow stronger over time. This sort of thing does not require that every individual interest or activity be shared on a 50/50 basis; far from it. Instead of the travesty on mutual commitment indicated by atrocious words such as "togetherness," what we are driving at is a relationship strong enough to bear diverging interests, differences of opinion, and/or circumstances imposing "apartness," without deteriorating. In sum, if marriage is to be meaningful over the years, there must be an accumulation of trust, mutual regard, or whatever you want to call it (mature love, maybe) that can not only sustain the partners through the usual domestic stress, but also strengthen them so that each, by virtue of the other's existence, so to speak, is more than he or she would be alone.

Admittedly, this is a tall order, and fortunate indeed is the person who in this respect can look to his own house without fear and trembling, but in Russell's case we have clear evidence that the order was not fulfilled. His wife never relinquished her allegiance to a peculiar philosophy combining fundamentalist religion and women's rights, nor would she set aside family connections with a neurotic mother and brother in favor of her husband. Russell compromised, and indulged her wishes many times, yet hardly ever received similar consideration in return. So in the end they fell apart, with her still trying to hold onto him as an important instrumental object in her life.

Summary and discussion

Formal research provides little in the way of relevant evidence, but our assumption of attrition and meaning as critical factors in maturity is strongly supported by the run of common experience in this period. On the one hand, it seems apparent that most people feel significant forms of attrition by their mid-30's, possibly sooner, and certainly not much later. This generalization applies in both the physiological and social-psychological spheres of life. On the other hand, it is less apparent but probably no less true that at about the same time, people also become aware of meaning problems relating to their work or family situations.

While the two critical factors can each be appreciated separately, it should also be clear that they may stand in a causal relationship to one another. Common sense suggests that if the attrition of maturity does not directly generate meaning problems, it will surely serve to intensify them. Becker (1964) offered a sociological interpretation of stability in adulthood which illuminates this point. He noted that with increasing age, the individual's job, family, and social commitments act as significant constraints on his behavior. The person is virtually held hostage in the social structures of

---

[2]Let it be clear that the question raised here, which is seldom mentioned in all the literature on how to have a happy marriage, is this: "Is there anything of any special value that people can get out of living together for 10 or 15 years, that they can't get from 2 or 3?" In the absence of an affirmative answer to this question, it is hard to find a logical basis for long-term marriage.

which he is a part, because if he initiates any important change, he runs the risk of losing stable adjustment patterns built up over the years. Becker's ideas indicate that were it not for socioeconomic constraints, adults might attempt to cope with their dissatisfactions directly, by seeking new situations. As it is, many are forced to remain in place, skewered on meaning problems and stewing in the juice of attrition. The issue is illustrated dramatically in the following quotation.

Dear Ann Landers: I'm a middle-aged man who has just been offered the promotion he's been dreaming about. It means moving the family several hundred miles from here.

My wife refuses to move. She says the kids are doing well in school and moving would mean leaving friends they have grown up with. She is also close to her family.

What can a man do when he is faced with rebellion like this? My wife says, "Money isn't everything." I agree, but this isn't just money. It's what I've been aiming for. It's satisfaction and progress. I'm 37 years old. If I turn down this promotion, I'll be stuck in this spot the rest of my life. Please help me.—Between the Devil and the Deep Blue Sea.

Dear Between: If the devil wins this battle she is going to have a frustrated, unhappy husband on her hands for many years to come. Maybe forever. In my opinion, your wife is letting you down badly. It is the woman's responsibility to make a home for her man wherever he can best pursue his profession or ply his trade. Remind her of those beautiful words: "Whither thou goest—I goest" (From a syndicated newspaper column, December 23, 1969).

Despite attrition and the defensive reactions it may provoke, however, personality growth can continue as long as people are able to tie their self-concepts to significant meanings. What kind of growth is involved here? It is what Rogers and Maslow would call self-actualizing, and examples of it have already been described in the lives of Kennan and Russell. The former became involved in the task of understanding the Soviet Union: this all-absorbing effort served as an obvious inspiration to personal growth. His study of Russian language, culture, and politics, coupled with relevant professional responsibilities and daily social encounters, eventually changed him into a competent, tough-minded but scholarly man of affairs. His self-concept could hardly fail to be expanded or enhanced with the increasing skills, knowledge, and friendships resulting from his work.

It was the same for Russell. Having given himself over to the study of certain problems in philosophy, we have seen how much their solution meant to him. But the growth preceding and following this great moment should also be apparent because he too developed new capacities and friendships; the grand collaboration with Whitehead is a historically significant case in point.

In a different sphere than work, Russell gave us a further glimpse of quasi-mysterious growth possibilities. The following incident occurred while he and his wife were sharing a house with the Whiteheads:

When we came home, we found Mrs. Whitehead undergoing an unusually severe bout of pain. She seemed cut off from everyone and everything by walls of agony, and the sense of the solitude of each human soul suddenly overwhelmed me.

The Whiteheads' youngest boy, aged three, was in the room. I had previously taken no notice of him, nor he of me. He had to be prevented from troubling his mother in the middle of her paroxysms of pain. I took his hand and led him away. He came willingly, and felt at home with me. From that day to his death in the war in 1918, we were close friends. At the end of those five minutes, I had become a completely different person.

Having been an imperialist, I became during those five minutes a pro-Boer and a pacifist. Having for years cared only for exactness and analysis, I found myself filled with semi-mystical feelings about beauty, with an intense interest in children, and with a desire almost as profound as that of the Buddha to find some philosophy which should make human life endurable. A strange excitement possessed me, containing intense pain but also some element of triumph through the fact that I could dominate pain, and make it, as I thought, a gateway to wisdom. The mystic insight which I then imagined myself to possess has largely faded, and the habit of analysis has reasserted itself. But something of what I thought I saw in that moment has remained always with me, causing my attitude during the first war, my interest in children, my indifference to minor misfortunes, and a certain emotional tone in all my human relations *(The Autobiography of Bertrand Russell,* Vol. I, pp. 193–194).

Russell's remarks carry the flavor of *fin de siècle* melodrama, but that only makes their fit to contemporary life all the more impressive. In addition, by specifying the sweeping changes he felt at this time, his statement paves the way for discussion of growth dynamics according to changes in the core sense of identity maintained by adults. Before going ahead with full-blown theoretical material, however, let us turn over the coin of meaning one more time to examine the real abyss of meaninglessness. It is laid out in excruciating detail – captured, dissected, and fixed forever in the pages of literature, thanks to the courage and brilliance of F. Scott Fitzgerald.

THE FITZGERALD MASTERPIECE

Possibly there are literary people, not to mention psychologists, who would disagree with my judgment of the essays in *The Crack-Up.*[3] Perhaps they do *not* contain the most extraordinary description of the experience of meaninglessness ever put on paper. Be that as it may, here we have the candid reflections of a man who had lived more fully than most, who had created more than most, yet who found himself at the age of 39 without meaning, and could capture this feeling with an unforgettable metaphor:

. . . a feeling that I was standing at twilight on a deserted range, with an empty rifle in

[3]New York: New Directions Paperbook #54, 1956. All page references are to this edition. Quotations are also identified by original essay titles and dates of publication.

In working up this material it has more than once seemed a sacrilege to be picking over the remains of a superb writer thirty years in his grave. Edmund Wilson (editor of *The Crack-Up*) introduced it with a long poem dedicated to Fitzgerald. The last four lines express for us the dilemma and the necessary apology of any scholar who deals with a great artist:
"And I, your scraps and sketches sifting yet,
Can never thus revive one sapphire jet,
However close I look, however late,
But only spell and point and punctuate." (Wilson, p. 9)

my hands and the targets down. No problem set—simply a silence with only the sound of my own breathing ("Handle with Care," 1936, pp. 77–78).

Superficially, his feeling seems easy enough to understand because he was alone. His wife Zelda—as a couple they had epitomized glamour and romance in the 1920's—was living apart from him after suffering a mental collapse. His daughter was in a boarding school. His many friends seemed irrelevant, and probably worst of all, the times were out of joint. Fitzgerald was preeminently a man of the twenties; a celebrity and celebrant of what he called the "Jazz Age." The feeling he had for that time is revealed in the way he wrote about it.

It was an age of miracles, it was an age of art, it was an age of excess, and it was an age of satire.

The ten-year period that, as if reluctant to die outmoded in its bed, leaped to a spectacular death in October, 1929, began about the time of the May Day riots in 1919. . . . The events of 1919 left us cynical rather than revolutionary. . . . It was characteristic of the Jazz Age that it had no interest in politics at all.

But in those days life was like the race in *Alice in Wonderland*, there was a prize for every one.

By 1927 a wide-spread neurosis began to be evident, faintly signalled, like a nervous beating of the feet, by the popularity of cross-word puzzles. I remember a fellow expatriate opening a letter from a mutual friend of ours, urging him to come home and be revitalized by the hardy, bracing qualities of the native soil. It was a strong letter and it affected us both deeply, until we noticed that it was headed from a nerve sanitarium in Pennsylvania.

Now once more the belt is tight and we summon the proper expression of horror as we look back at our wasted youth ("Echoes of the Jazz Age," 1931, pp. 13–22).

Writing five years later, Fitzgerald explained that he was all used up. Psychologically, the belt was drawn much tighter. But the thing that made his confrontation with meaninglessness uniquely different from other works on the subject (e.g., in the novel *The Pawnbroker*) is his way of facing it for what it is, without recourse to any palliative defenses. In the vernacular of our time, Fitzgerald took the experience cold turkey.

He began with a general commentary which ought to be required reading for everyone over 35:

Of course all life is a process of breaking down, but the blows that do the dramatic side of the work—the big sudden blows that come, or seem to come, from outside—the ones you remember and blame things on and, in moments of weakness, tell your friends about, don't show their effect all at once. There is another sort of blow that comes from within—that you don't feel until it's too late to do anything about it, until you realize with finality that in some regard you will never be as good a man again. The first sort of breakage seems to happen quick—the second kind happens almost without your knowing it but is realized suddenly indeed ("The Crack-Up," 1936, p. 69).

Then he continued, casually mentioning a bit of philosophy which prefigures by over a decade certain ideas elaborated by Albert Camus.

One should, for example, be able to see that things are hopeless and yet be determined to make them otherwise. This philosophy fitted on to my early adult life, when I saw the improbable, the implausible, often the "impossible," come true. Life was something you dominated if you were any good. Life yielded easily to intelligence and effort, or to what proportion could be mustered of both.

As the twenties passed, with my own twenties marching a little ahead of them, my two juvenile regrets—at not being big enough (or good enough) to play football in college, and at not getting overseas during the war—resolved themselves into childish waking dreams of imaginary heroism that were good enough to go to sleep on in restless nights. The big problems of life seemed to solve themselves, and if the business of fixing them was difficult, it made one too tired to think of more general problems.

For seventeen years, with a year of deliberate loafing and resting out in the center—things went on like that, with a new chore only a nice prospect for the next day. I was living hard, too, but: "Up to forty-nine it'll be all right," I said. "I can count on that. For a man who's lived as I have, that's all you could ask."

—And then, ten years this side of forty-nine, I suddenly realized that I had prematurely cracked ("The Crack-Up," pp. 69–70).

Fitzgerald did not describe the immediate causes of his crack-up in much detail. He indicated only that after being informed of a serious, possibly fatal health problem, he had a "strong sudden instinct" to be alone. He found himself feeling very tired and thinking mainly of trivial things from the past. Then his health improved, and he suddenly became aware of meaninglessness.

Suffice it to say that after about an hour of solitary pillow-hugging, I began to realize that for two years my life had been a drawing on resources that I did not possess, that I had been mortgaging myself physically and spiritually up to the hilt. What was the small gift of life given back in comparison to that?—when there had once been a pride of direction and a confidence in enduring independence ("The Crack-Up," p. 72).

He had no energy for anything and mentions a conversation with someone who argued with him over this:

I felt a certain reaction to what she said, but I am a slow-thinking man, and it occurred to me simultaneously that of all natural forces, vitality is the incommunicable one. In days when juice came into one as an article without duty, one tried to distribute it—but always without success; to further mix metaphors, vitality never "takes." You have it or you haven't it, like health or brown eyes or honor or a baritone voice. I might have asked some of it from her, neatly wrapped and ready for home cooking and digestion, but I could never have got it—not if I'd waited around for a thousand hours with the tin cup of self-pity. I could walk from her door, holding myself very carefully like cracked crockery, and go away into the world of bitterness, where I was making a home with such materials as are found there—and quote to myself after I left her door:

"Ye are the salt of the earth. But if the salt hath lost its savour, wherewith shall it be salted?" ("The Crack-Up," p. 74).

The man did not give up; instead, he tried to think through his condition. Why, he asked himself, did he feel irrelevant? Why did he even lack faith in his own art as a novelist? We know that part of the answer is that he felt out of place in the relatively humdrum, politicized world of the mid-1930's. Another part of it is that he saw his art becoming obsolete, being devoured or left in the dust by films:

As long past as 1930, I had a hunch that the talkies would make even the best selling novelist as archaic as silent pictures.

. . . there was a rankling indignity, that to me had become almost an obsession, in seeing the power of the written word subordinated to another power, a more glittering, a grosser power. . . .

—this was something I could neither accept nor struggle against, something which tended to make my efforts obsolescent, as the chain stores have crippled the small merchant, an exterior force, unbeatable—("Handle with Care," 1936, p. 78).

Then he went still deeper into himself and concluded that he had not really made enough of an effort to understand his life while he was living it; that for 20 years he had lived on the ideas and according to the examples of others. Consequently, he felt himself to be without a self:

So there was not an "I" any more—not a basis on which I could organize my self-respect—save my limitless capacity for toil that it seemed I possessed no more. It was strange to have no self—to be like a little boy left alone in a big house, who knew that now he could do anything he wanted to do, but found that there was nothing that he wanted to do—("Handle with Care," p. 79).

We reach the last of it when Fitzgerald squared-off on the question of suicide: how is a man without meaning to go on living? Many of his friends had found no answer.

I had stood by while one famous contemporary of mine played with the idea of the Big Out for half a year; I had watched when another, equally eminent, spent months in an asylum unable to endure any contact with his fellow men. And of those who had given up and passed on I could list a score ("Pasting It Together," 1936, p. 81).

However, he decided that survival is possible if one makes a clean break with the past.

A clean break is something you cannot come back from; that is irretrievable because it makes the past cease to exist. So, since I could no longer fulfill the obligations that life had set for me or that I had set for myself, why not slay the empty shell who had been posturing at it for four years? I must continue to be a writer because that was my only way of life, but I would cease any attempts to be a person—to be kind, just or generous. There were plenty of counterfeit coins around that would pass instead of these and I knew where I could get them at a nickel on the dollar. In thirty-nine years an observant eye has learned to detect where the milk is watered and the sugar is sanded, the rhinestone passed for diamond and the stucco for stone. There was to be no more giving of myself—all giving was to be outlawed henceforth under a new name, and that name was Waste.

The heady villainous feeling continued.

I felt like the beady-eyed men I used to see on the commuting train from Great Neck fifteen years back—men who didn't care whether the world tumbled into chaos tomorrow if it spared their houses. I was one with them now, one with the smooth articles who said:

"I'm sorry but business is business." Or:

"You ought to have thought of that before you got into this trouble." Or:

"I'm not the person to see about that."

And a smile—ah, I would get me a smile. I'm still working on that smile. It is to combine the best qualities of a hotel manager, an experienced old social weasel, a headmaster on visitors' day. . . .

The voice too—I am working with a teacher on the voice. When I have perfected it the larynx will show no ring of conviction except the conviction of the person I am talking to. Since it will be largely called upon for the elicitation of the word "Yes," my teacher (a lawyer) and I are concentrating on that, but in extra hours. . . .

And if you were dying of starvation outside my window, I would go out quickly and give you the smile and the voice (if no longer the hand) and stick around till somebody raised a nickel to phone for the ambulance, that is if I thought there would be any copy in it for me ("Pasting It Together," pp. 81–83).

So his answer is to go on, but to do it as a different sort of man. He will live not well, but *wisely*, without the irrelevant white plume.

So what? This is what I think now: that the natural state of the sentient adult is a qualified unhappiness. I think also that in an adult the desire to be finer in grain than you are, "a constant striving" (as those people say who gain their bread by saying it) only adds to this unhappiness in the end—that end that comes to our youth and hope.

I shall manage to live with the new dispensation, though it has taken some months to be certain of the fact. And just as the laughing stoicism which has enabled the American Negro to endure the intolerable conditions of his existence has cost him his sense of the truth—so in my case there is a price to pay. I do not any longer like the postman, nor the grocer, nor the editor, nor the cousin's husband, and he in turn will come to dislike me, so that life will never be very pleasant again, and the sign *Cave Canem* is hung permanently just above my door. I will try to be a correct animal though, and if you throw me a bone with enough meat on it I may even lick your hand ("Pasting It Together," p. 84).

But the dog's life didn't suit him. After working as a Hollywood scriptwriter for a few years and drinking against doctor's orders because he couldn't really stomach it, he was dead of heart failure in 1940.

Now why give all these pages of a textbook to Fitzgerald? His writing skill is fantastic enough to humble any of us who put words on paper, and his subject matter is close enough to that of this text to warrant inclusion, yet these considerations might have been satisfied in much less space, and the attempt here is not to conduct a psychological postmortem. It is just the reverse. Fitzgerald told us so flatly and honestly what it means to encounter true meaninglessness in maturity, that the weight of his experience defies clever analysis.

In the following section a number of theoretical ideas which have some relation to meaning problems in maturity will be discussed. Fitzgerald's work should help keep them in focus *as* theory. He wrote before such terms as self-actualization, ego-integrity, identity crisis had been invented and become clichés. Not that these ideas are irrelevant, but taken out of the context of human realities – as they must be for purposes of theoretical discussion – they can too easily become glib euphemisms allowing us to finesse the terrible fundamentals faced by a man who had been there and knew that ". . . in a real dark night of the soul it is always three o'clock in the morning, day after day."

THEORETICAL PERSPECTIVES

There is a vast supply of speculative theoretical writing on the subject of personality in maturity, ranging from the dynamic to the prescriptive to the moralistic, yet most of the important material falls into two general categories. One of these can be called the broad spectrum approach. It involves efforts to specify all the major personality attributes which people ought to acquire in maturity. Basically, the work here lends itself to organization in the form of checklists, and it will be reviewed accordingly, following summary statements prepared by Allport (1961).

The second category of theory involves the more familiar general factor approach: here we find writers such as Erikson emphasizing a particular dimension of personality as the key to understanding adult development. Besides Erikson, several others also addressed maturity in this fashion, and we will see that despite differences in terminology, all of them were getting at the problem of meaning.

The broad-spectrum approach

At the start of this chapter, it was mentioned that the term *maturity* is confusing because it can be used to denote either a developmental period or a desirable state of personality. The confusion arises partly from traditional research aimed at specifying individual differences in personality. Such studies usually involve the assessment of standard attributes (traits, motives, values) according to standard methods (interviews, tests, ratings), so that people can be compared with respect to their "scores" on the attributes. Confusion begins to develop at this point when investigators interpret particular score patterns or profiles to be definitive of mature personality. Indeed, some tests provide coding schemes allowing scores on certain items such as honesty, sense of responsibility, consideration for others, to be added up into a global score on maturity. It is also possible in this way to convert maturity into a general personality attribute measurable on a par with such things as aggressiveness or emotional stability.

It should be clear that some difficulty will occur at a technical level because different test materials and scoring systems yield somewhat different descriptions of maturity. But at a more abstract theoretical level, the confusion is compounded because maturity is never really defined at all, except by statements treating the mature person as equivalent to the healthy-normal person. Therefore, when a personality test profile is said to indicate maturity, this really means that in the judgment of the speaker, the profile contains a healthy-normal pattern of scores. And since the concept of normalcy remains quite arbitrary in psychology—it can be described according to statistical averages or cultural values—it is this very point which generates most of the uncertainty surrounding the broad spectrum approach.

Maturity as healthy normalcy

Allport suggested that writers working from the standpoint of their clinical experience tend to describe mature, or normal, personality attributes as the opposite of what they see in their patients. So they produce checklists including such things as self-insight, emotional control, ability to love, work, meet responsibilities. For example, Shoben (1957) added to clinical experience a philosophical discussion of what it means to be a human being, and offered a list of five attributes: self-control, personal responsibility, social responsibility, democratic social interests, and ideals.

Another relevant source is Maslow (1954). He approached the problem empirically by examining biographical information from a carefully selected sample of subjects. These were people who by all conventional standards appeared to have lived self-actualized lives, and thus achieved genuine maturity. Careful analysis of their behavior allowed Maslow to produce a list of over a dozen criteria for maturity, including self-acceptance, democratic character, spontaneity, independence, ethical certainty, humor, social feeling, creativity, self-sufficiency and so on.

Allport himself gave a list of six criteria for mature personality which seemed to him to embrace all the basics necessary in a normal-healthy adult (1961, pp. 283–304).

(1) "Extension of the sense of self." This refers to what is often called ego-involvement or commitment. It is achieved when a person gives himself fully to his activities, and is thereby truly participating in life.

(2) "Warm relating of self to others." Allport mentioned here the capacities to give love, and feel intimacy and compassion without jealousy.

(3) "Emotional security (self-acceptance)." A person should feel enough confidence in himself to tolerate frustrating events and his own shortcomings without becoming inwardly bitter or outwardly hostile. Threatening emotional impulses must be accepted, but should be held in check by a sense of moderation lest they produce serious depression or impulsive attacks on others.

(4) "Realistic perception, skills and assignments." This boils down to clear thinking and good judgment: one should be able to function according to reality, finding a place in life suited to his talents. In this connection, Allport commented on the attrition of adult economic life:

To be able to support oneself and one's family (in America with an ever-advancing standard of living) is a frightening demand. To meet it without panic, without self-pity, without giving way to defensive, hostile, self-deceiving behavior is one of the acid tests of maturity (p. 290).

(5) "Self-objectification: insight and humor." The point here is to know

thyself. A mature person should know himself as an object and should understand the difference between what he is, what he would like to be, and what others think of him. Humor is very important because it can prevent pompous self-glorification or affectation. The man who can laugh at himself occasionally will be able to maintain a fair degree of humility.

(6) "The unifying philosophy of life." Allport discussed this idea in several ways, mentioning such things as general value orientations, religious sentiments, and direction in life. Briefly, it is suggested that the mature person will have a strong, unitary sense of purpose underlying his everyday existence. Extreme examples can be seen among dedicated scientists, artists, revolutionaries, or churchmen. Everything in their lives is subordinated to certain aims related to deeply held values. A philosophy of life therefore serves as a kind of master plan or blueprint for meaning.

Even the brief summary given above should indicate that there is much wisdom in Allport's discussion of maturity. Having surveyed the ideas of other theorists and added to them his own knowledge of personality, his six criteria must be acknowledged as representing the broad spectrum approach at its best. At the same time, however, the inherent shortcomings of any such approach to maturity should be apparent: it leads toward elaboration of checklists for an ideal state of development which most writers (including Allport) admit is hardly ever found in reality.

Discussion

Ideals are never to be sneezed at, particularly in theoretical matters where they may provide standards for examining reality. But in this instance, by first treating mature personality as equivalent to healthy-normal personality, and then suggesting multiple criteria according to which adult progress toward this ideal may be evaluated, broad spectrum approaches tend to obscure the things that are most difficult to understand in adult development.

To begin with, there is a logical problem: vague or arbitrary as it may be, if the concept of healthy-normal personality has any importance, then it should be applied across the board of human development, not just as a synonym for mature adulthood. Second, it is not difficult to see that many ideas about normalcy rest on the shifting sand of historical trends and cultural norms. For example, many current events concerned with racism and war reveal that what was thought of as normal at one time may now seem abnormal, and vice versa. Finally, in most broad-spectrum approaches which treat maturity as equivalent to normalcy, it is difficult to find serious discussion of the attrition or meaning problems experienced by adults.

These problems are sometimes mentioned as barriers to the attainment of a healthy maturity, yet their fundamental significance in shaping the psychological contours of adult life are either ignored, or passed over very lightly. According to much of the broad-spectrum literature, one is supposed to overcome barriers blocking the way toward the mature ideal, and to the extent that one fails, it is probably because of defects in earlier personality development, defects in the social order (if society were in better shape we could all be better people), or both. Furthermore, one can always seek psychotherapy. There is surely some important truth in all this, but it takes us too far away from understanding the *personal* side of adult personality development.

The general factor approach

By concentrating on major changes observable in adult behavior, general factor theories avoid the difficulties associated with checklists of criteria for ideal states of development. Furthermore, instead of getting caught up in the logical problem of defining maturity as a healthy-normal ideal, general factor writers tend to treat maturity as an age period during which adult personality will either grow along certain lines, or else remain in a static condition leading toward decay. The following discussion will consider the relevant ideas of Erikson, Buhler, Frankl, and Rogers, showing how each in their own way came to grips with meaning as the general factor underlying adult development.

Erikson

According to Erikson, the basic problem awaiting people who have achieved the proper ego qualities in earlier periods now involves a sense of "generativity" – concern for young people of the next generation. This quality can be understood as a new aspect of personal identity which allows the mature individual to maintain meaning through commitment to those who will come after him.

It should be emphasized immediately that Erikson did not see this quality simply as a matter of altruism or charity: generativity is not a one-way operation whereby those who have everything may divert themselves by practicing good works on younger people. It is rather an expression of expanding personal (self or ego) concerns which literally need a younger generation to be realized. Far from being a matter of altruism, then, generativity apparently refers to a psychologically significant *transaction* between the mature and the young. Erikson even suggested that man's inherent nature has evolved in such a way as to make this transaction an essential feature of mature living.

Evolution has made man a teaching as well as a learning animal, for dependency and maturity are reciprocal: mature man needs to be needed, and maturity is guided by the nature of that which must be cared for (1968, p. 138).

Ordinarily, people will express generativity through concern with their own offspring, although Erikson also included other forms of creative activity under this heading. But he said that no other form of generativity will be as meaningful as the kind which involves one's own children. This stipulation seems arbitrary at first glance: why shouldn't the childless person be able to find perfectly good ways of expressing his generative concerns by working with other people's children, or by doing things for the general benefit of future generations?

It is, of course, acknowledged that considerable satisfaction *can* be found in such ways. However, Erikson indicated that because of the psychosexual dynamics involved in the origins of the generative impulse, no substitute activities can fully replace the meanings to be derived from concern with one's own children. The basis for this argument goes back to genital sexuality:

It has taken psychoanalysis some time to realize that the ability to lose oneself in the meeting of bodies and minds leads to a gradual expansion of ego-interests and to a *libidinal investment in that which is being generated*. Generativity thus is an essential stage on the psychosexual as well as on the psychosocial schedule (1963, p. 267, italics added).

Briefly, Erikson's position appears to be that because psychosexual dynamics play an important role in generativity, this impulse can only find its fullest satisfaction with the children who are a product of genital love. Mature people who fail to achieve generativity may suffer "stagnation." The signs of this condition can be seen in people who are excessively concerned with themselves:

Individuals, then, often begin to indulge themselves as if they were their own—or one another's—one and only child; and where conditions favor it, early invalidism, physical or psychological, becomes the vehicle of self-concern (ibid.).

Yet having children is, in and of itself, no guarantee against stagnation. Erikson gave several possible reasons for personality development going wrong in a way that can prevent people who have children from achieving generativity. He spoke of individual pathology which may yield a lack of "belief in the species."

In general, the view that mature personality development may vary between generativity and stagnation is well suited to our discussion of critical factors for this period. While he did not consider attrition *per se*, this factor seems clearly indicated by Erikson's suggestion that stagnation is marked by a sense of "personal impoverishment"—exactly the sort of thing that was noted in connection with attrition.

On the other hand, however, if mature people can find significant meaning in their lives, the negative consequences of attrition can be avoided. It is noteworthy that for Erikson, all forms of meaning were not equally satisfactory. He specified concern for the next generation and one's own children in particular, as the most important type of meaning which can insure against stagnation. We will see that this idea is quite unique when compared with other theoretical discussions of meaning, yet it is interesting that the two biographies mentioned in this chapter offer supporting evidence. George Kennan recently published a book addressing young people of the "protest" generation; and Bertrand Russell's activities against nuclear armaments and the Vietnam war follow specifically from his concern with young people.

Buhler

Based on her analysis of many normal life histories, Charlotte Buhler described maturity as a "culmination period" because it is a time when most people reach a productive peak in their professional and personal lives. And it is certainly plausible to think that if one is going to have a peak period in his life, it is likely to be somewhere in the interval from 28 years to 50 years. In addition to Buhler's findings, Dennis (1966) also provided relevant evidence. He analyzed material from over 700 life histories of scientists, artists, and scholars who lived to be at least 80 years old. On the average, peak productivity was reached at about 40 years of age, although artists tend to reach the maximum sooner than others.

Underneath the positive tone of Buhler's global view of maturity—that it is the prime of life, so to speak—much of her theoretical discussion relates to problems of attrition and meaning. In a way similar to what we have seen in Erikson, it is suggested that "creative expansion" of the self during the first part of maturity (approximately 25 to 45 years), involves "self-realization in occupation, marriage, and own family" (see Buhler, 1962, pp. 107–111). Self-realization is used here more or less synonymously with the self-actualization concept of Rogers and Maslow. However, Buhler suggested that because of their biological orientation, the former theorists do not pay sufficient attention to the role of personal values. This point will be elaborated later in the discussion of Rogers. It is more important now to emphasize that the attrition experienced by adults is very clear in the life-history evidence cited by Buhler (N.B.).

Self-realization also implies meaning; yet Buhler did not treat the two concepts as equivalent in the overall economy of mature personality. Instead, her work suggested that when people are heavily engaged in efforts toward self-realization, they are not much concerned with meaning. It is only later, during what is called the "climacteric phase" (starting at about age 45), that people seemingly have time to become reflective, or perhaps are driven to a reflective attitude under the accumulating impact of attrition. In any case, Buhler said meaning becomes crucial as people go through a "critical self-assessment":

Even heretofore not very thoughtful persons may unexpectedly be overcome with feelings of guilt regarding the time they wasted or did not use in the most profitable way to obtain what they could have out of life, to accomplish what they should have, to provide security for their old age and a sense of fulfillment for their life as a whole (1962, p. 111).

The critical self-assessment described here is plainly nothing less than a summing up of meaning; practically a balance sheet according to which it is decided whether or not life has been worthwhile. In general, Buhler saw mature personality being shaped first by the effort toward self-realization, and later by the inevitable assessment of how well one has done at it. To the extent that such assessment yields a negative outcome, then, as Erikson did with respect to stagnation, Buhler (1968) suggested that people will show neurotic symptoms, and will even attempt suicide in extreme cases.

This point is strongly supported by a recent analysis of suicide notes. Discussing age differences in the content of suicide notes, Darbonne (1969, p. 49) made the following comments:

Individuals from ages 40 to 49 who committed suicide left a communication of the vanquished. They seemed unequal to the demands of life and were tired or bored

and wanted a way out. . . . It is likely that many of these people have spent their earlier years attempting to achieve above their potential or operating below it. The result
is a defeatist feeling and/or guilty thoughts of a wasted life. In either case the future is
viewed with pessimism.

Frankl

Viktor Frankl's work belongs to a vein of theoretical writing which is hard to
describe. It is quasi-popular, because the style is usually interesting and the
theoretical ideas are usually understandable to general readers. It is quasi-
inspirational, because it usually contains a message: that if one can understand certain things and try to act accordingly (e.g., listen with a third ear,
not escape from freedom), then his life will be better. And it is mostly quasi-
Freudian, because practically all of the writers in this vein—Fromm, Reik,
Ellis, Berne, Frankl, and others—were trained in psychoanalysis but later
struck off for themselves in different directions.

Of those mentioned, Fromm has probably been the most popular, Reik
and Ellis the most sensational, and Berne the most amusing; so why single
out Frankl? The reason is that contrary to the others who all had much to say
about meaning in maturity but who saw it as derivative—a happy consequence resulting from a proper life style—Frankl saw meaning as *the* fundamental of adult personality:

Central to my psychiatric approach known as logotherapy is the principle of the will
to meaning. I counterpose it both to the pleasure principle, which is so pervasive in
psychoanalytic motivational theories, and to the will to power, the concept which
plays such a decisive role in Adlerian psychology (Frankl, 1966, p. 23).

It is difficult to pin down this "will to meaning" idea with a clear-cut
definition. Frankl did not treat it as a biologically given instinct, and he preferred to call it a *will* rather than a need or drive, because needs and drives
can be satisfied in ways that leave men in a state of equilibrium, while the
will to meaning is never really satisfied. Most generally, the will to meaning
is described as a kind of metaphysical human craving to find purpose in
existence. And more substantially, Frankl indicated that the will to meaning
involves something like what the dedicated churchman or communist gets
from his ideology: values and responsibilities which transcend his own life.

Frankl also disagreed with those theorists who see meaning resulting
from self-realization or actualization. He argued instead that self-actualizing
experiences result from the will to meaning. The practical essence of
Frankl's approach can best be appreciated through his psychiatric technique.
Meaning is translated into a concern with values and responsibility: to whom
and to what does the patient feel responsibility, over and above his desire for
personal fulfillment? It is said that therapists following this technique will
often lecture their patients:

. . . an American visitor to Vienna asked me to tell him in one sentence the difference
between logotherapy and psychoanalysis—whereupon I invited him first to tell me
what he regarded as the essence of psychoanalysis. He replied: "In psychoanalysis
the patient must lie down on a couch and tell you things which sometimes are dis-

agreeable to tell." And I quickly responded: "In logotherapy the patient is allowed to sit erect but must hear things which sometimes are disagreeable!" (Frankl, 1966, p. 29).

Rogers

It will be recalled from the previous chapter how self-actualization theory applies to personality during adult transition: briefly, the self is enhanced through positive regard accumulated while one is striving to realize his potentials. Because the Rogerian view also emphasizes forward thrust in development, assigning great importance to present experience and expectations for the future, it is particularly appealing to young people. It is well suited to a developmental period involving disillusionment about the past and uncertainty about the future. For these reasons, self-actualization theory would appear to be an *in*appropriate vehicle for understanding mature personality, yet it is as widely used here as in the earlier period.

Some critics (e.g., Frankl) imply that Rogerian ideas are popular for the wrong reason: by treating fulfillment of the self as a be-all end-all of development, they offer an easy alternative to struggle with the hard problems of meaning.[4] There may be some justification for this criticism, but it cannot help us see how a theory eminently suited to adult transition can also be applied to maturity. To understand this we must consider at least two general points.

First of all, Rogers does not ignore the problem of meaning. As noted earlier, both he and Maslow suggested that meaning will result from self-actualization, and in many writings on this subject meaning is treated as equivalent to actualization. Any experience that helps a person realize his potentials is *ipso facto*, meaningful for him. Furthermore, at the level of concrete experience theoretical differences between Rogerians and others who see personal values as the basis for establishing meaning, tend to disappear.

In most instances, meaningful experiences feel that way because they are immediately relevant to existing personal values. Only on rare occasions do people find it necessary or difficult to distinguish explicitly between stimulating events which relate positively or negatively to their value orientations. To be sure, there are some trends in contemporary art and radical politics that involve use of grossly shocking material; apparently based on the notion that shock equals stimulation equals meaning. And in such cases personal values may be challenged. However, this does not occur frequently enough to invalidate generalizations about the simultaneity of meaning and value in concrete experience.

The second general point to consider is that Rogerian theory "travels" well: it can be applied somewhat differently in different developmental periods. For young adults troubled with disillusionment and uncertainty it provides a philosophy of growth through action, and, where necessary, a form of

---

[4]The difference between Frankl and Rogers is essentially the difference between European and American forms of existential philosophy. The former tend to be more pessimistic than the latter. While commenting on this problem, Gordon Allport summed it up as follows:

"Trends in American existentialism will be (and are) far more optimistic. Sartre says there is 'no exit.' One is reminded of Epictetus the Stoic, who long ago wrote, 'So your nose runs? What then, you fool, be glad you have a sleeve to wipe it on.' Can anyone picture Carl Rogers offering such counsel?" (in May, 1961, p. 97).

psychotherapy allowing expansion of the self. The same things are available to mature people troubled with attrition and meaning problems, but with more direct emphasis upon the self. In Rogerian therapy, for example, the older person who feels trapped by circumstances in a meaningless life situation is encouraged to explore his self-concept so that he may find new perspectives on his situation.

. . . when all of the ways in which the individual perceives himself—all perceptions of the qualities, abilities, impulses, and attitudes of the person, and all perceptions of himself in relation to others—are accepted into the organized conscious concept of the self, then this achievement is accompanied by feelings of comfort and freedom from tension which are experienced as psychological adjustment (Rogers, 1947, p. 363).

While the problem of meaning is not specifically mentioned here, in other statements Rogers makes it very clear that he is talking about the *preconditions* of meaning. If a person can free himself from tensions which may be produced by the attrition of maturity, he ought to be able to find new meanings without necessarily having to change his circumstances. Or, to put it another way, when people can achieve a wider, more accepting view of themselves, they will also view their circumstances differently, and see meaning or opportunities for meaning where they could not see them before.

So it would appear that according to Rogers, the person whose work and/or family life provides him with a reasonable degree of self-actualizing experience should have a self-concept free enough, and sufficiently robust, to weather the strains of attrition. But the person who has not been able to realize his potentials in a significant way will probably be locked into a narrow self-concept, which in turn predisposes him to meaning problems. And if these are serious, the result may be neurotic behavior.

Summary and discussion

In Erikson's generativity, Buhler's critical self-assessment, and Frankl's will to meaning, there are concepts which specifically link mature personality development to meaning, while in Rogers there is the idea that meaning will come if the self is open enough to perceive it.

Both the broad-spectrum theories geared to attributes defining mature (sic: healthy-normal) personality, and general factor theories indicating meaning as decisive during the age of maturity, must be understood as tentative statements demanding further investigation. For several reasons mentioned earlier, the latter approach seems to provide better developmental perspectives. Yet it is an open question as to what kind of meaning can best sustain people through the attrition of maturity.

How, for instance, can one address the "case" of a man like Scott Fitzgerald? The generalizations hardly fit: here is someone who had realized his potentials better than most, and apparently had a strong will to meaning, but could not find it. Of course it is absurd to try to evaluate speculative theories according to the experience of one unique individual; however, such comments are necessary to highlight difficulties that get smoothed over in summary discussions. In this connection, Henry (1968) mentioned a study by Chiraboga which may be a harbinger of future research.

Interested in the problem of "self-actualization in middle-age males," Chiraboga studied a sample of men who were successful, and therefore seemed to have fulfilled themselves in their work. Upon closer examination of their life-styles, he discovered that only about a third of these men satisfied theoretical criteria for mature personality development. The rest included a group which seemed content to live as gross conformists, without any important sense of purpose or meaning, and another group who simply coasted along enjoying opportunities to indulge their impulses, but not committed to anything beyond this.

Such findings suggest different patterns of normal development in maturity. Some are apparently more desirable than others: the idea of reaching a plateau of contented adjustment and just staying there seems pretty dull, but we really need to know more about these things. It is likely that future research will allow us to make clearer distinctions between people who continue to grow, and those who turn their development into a holding operation. With respect to the former, we will probably see high and low risk patterns of growth. And with respect to the latter, it may be that static patterns work well enough until they are put to the test of severe attrition. Then, in the words of Scott Fitzgerald, may come the real dark night of the soul.

CHAPTER SUMMARY

The initial signs of maturity are typically felt as attrition in the physical dimension: a "wearing away as by friction" of good physique, or teeth, or hair. And social-emotional forms of attrition can occur across the board of adult activity in work, marriage, and friendship.

However, while attrition thus stands as a blatant critical factor in maturity, the concept of maturity itself can be confusing because it is treated both as an age period in development, and as a healthy-normal state of adult personality. Following Buhler, the term has been used here to designate an age period running from approximately 26 to 50 years, although in contemporary usage, 30 has come to symbolize the end of youth.

The gap between common adult experience and theories of adult personality makes it difficult to give a firm description of the psychological impact of attrition. But relevant interview and biographical material suggests first a general toughening up process. In this connection, it is possible to amend Kurt Lewin's old remark about heat either melting butter or hardening eggs, by adding that in the moderate heat of everyday attrition, most people seem to react more like eggs than butter. All the familiar defense mechanisms allow us to cope with attrition, and also give us the appearance of toughness or insensitivity.

On the other hand, the question of whether or not adults will melt when the heat of attrition becomes severe seems to depend upon whether they can sustain themselves with important meanings. Our discussion of meaning as a critical factor is based largely on biographical material showing that ego-involvement or commitment of the self in work and marriage determines the meaning to be found in these areas. Marriage is even more difficult than work in this respect, because significant meaning requires the mutual commitment of two people. (Relevant to this point, an older colleague of mine once said that after thinking over his own experiences and those of his contemporaries, it seemed to him that the things they once thought would be hard – advancing their careers, writing books – had turned out to be easy; but the things they thought would be easy – marriage, raising a family – had turned out to be very hard.)

Theoretical perspectives on mature personality can be ordered in two categories according to their basic orientation. Following a broad-spectrum approach, such theorists as Maslow and Allport offered discussions geared to various personality attributes which can be taken as defining a healthy-normal ideal. Aside from the intrinsic psychological-philosophical interest of such work, its chief practical result has been the formulation of checklists which can be useful for assessment purposes, but do not provide much help in understanding development.

By contrast, the general factor approach represented by Erikson, Buhler, Frankl, and Rogers emphasizes the dynamic role of meaning in maturity. All the various concepts we have seen here – generativity, critical self-assessment, will to meaning, self-enhancement through actualization – relate to the central issue of how people respond to the strains of attrition. And the implications of all these ideas are similar: if significant meaning is not forthcoming, then further development ceases, and adults are liable to show neurotic symptoms.

This is obviously an oversimplification, yet logically, the idea holds up fairly well because in the face of attrition, what else is there? One can only turn outward in a self-expanding effort after meaning, or inward, in a self-protective effort leading to behavior commonly recognized as neurotic. Future research will probably allow us to see fine distinctions between the extremes of self-expanding meaning and neurotic self-concern. For the time being, however, that's the way maturity shapes up: you either move up on meaning or get hung up on meaninglessness.

References

Allport, G. W. *Pattern and growth in personality*. New York: Holt, Rinehart & Winston, Inc., 1961.

Becker, H. S. *Outsiders: Studies in the sociology of deviance*. Glencoe, Ill.: The Free Press, 1963.

Becker, H. S. Personal change in adult life. *Sociometry*, 1964, *27*, 40–53.

Brim, O. G. Adult socialization. In J. Clausen (Ed.) *Socialization and society*. Boston: Little, Brown & Company, 1968, pp. 183–226.

Buhler, C. *Psychology for contemporary living*. New York: Hawthorn Books, Inc., 1968.

Buhler, C. *Values in psychotherapy*. Glencoe, Ill.: The Free Press, 1962.

Caplow, T., & McGee, R. J. *The academic marketplace*. New York: Basic Books, Inc., 1958.

Cutler, B., & Dyer, W. G. Initial adjustment processes in young married couples. *Social Forces*, *44*, 1965, 195–201.

Darbonne, A. R. Suicide and age: A suicide note analysis. *Journal of Consulting and Clinical Psychology*, 1969, *33*, 46–50.

Dennis, W. Creative productivity between the ages of 20 and 80 years. *Journal of Gerontology*, 1966, *21*, 1–8.

Douvan E., & Adelson, J. *The adolescent experience.* New York: John Wiley & Sons, Inc., 1966.

Erikson, E. H. *Childhood and society.* (2nd ed.) New York: W. W. Norton & Company, Inc., 1963.

Erikson, E. H. *Identity: Youth and crisis.* New York: W. W. Norton & Company, Inc., 1968.

Frankl, V. E. The will to meaning. In P. Tournier, V. E. Frankl, H. Levinson, H. Thielicke, P. Lehmann, & S. H. Miller, *Are you nobody?* Richmond, Va.: John Knox Press, 1966, 23–31.

Frenkel, E. Studies in biographical psychology. *Character and Personality*, 1936, *5*, 1–34.

Goffman, E. *The presentation of self in everyday life.* New York: Anchor Books, Doubleday & Company, Inc., 1959.

Henry, W. E. Personality change in middle and old age. In E. Norbeck, D. Price-Williams, & W. M. McCord, *The study of personality.* New York: Holt, Rinehart and Winston, Inc., 1968, pp. 209–217.

Jersild, A. T. The search for meaning. In D. Hamachek (Ed.) *The self in growth, teaching and learning.* Englewood Cliffs: Prentice-Hall, Inc., 1965, pp. 539–553.

Johnson, H. R. How to get the boss' job. *Modern Office Procedures*, 1961, *6*, 15–18.

Jones, H. E., & Conrad, H. S. The growth and decline of intelligence: The study of a homogeneous group between the ages of ten and sixty. *Genetic Psychology Monographs*, 1933, *13*, 223–298.

Kaplan, D. M. Since Freud. *Harpers*, August, 1968, 55–60.

Lewis, R., & Stewart, R. *The managers: A new examination of the English, German and American executive.* New York: Mentor Books, 1961.

Maslow, A. H. *Motivation and personality.* New York: Harper & Row, Publishers, 1954.

May, R. (Ed.). *Existential psychology.* New York: Random House, Inc., 1961.

Merton, R. K. Bureaucratic structure and personality. *Social Forces*, 1940, *18*, 560–568.

Neugarten, B. (Ed. and contributor). *Middle age and aging.* Chicago: The University of Chicago Press, 1968.

Pineo, P. C. Disenchantment in the later years of marriage. *Marriage and family living*, 1961, *23*, 3–11.

Rogers, C. R. Some observations on the organization of personality. *American Psychologist*, 1947, *2*, 358–368.

Shoben, E. J. Toward a concept of normal personality. *American Psychologist*, 1957, *12*, 183–189.

Whyte, W. F. *The organization man.* New York: Doubleday Anchor Books, Doubleday & Company, Inc., 1957.

11

Old Age (The 60's and beyond)

Maybe the fundamental thing about old age is this: no one *wants* to get old, but the only alternative is to die young, and most people are not interested in that alternative. One prominent authority on aging introduced this paradox by quoting the Roman philosopher Cicero, who said of old age:

. . . all men long to attain it, only to cry out against it when once secured. Such is the fickleness and perversity of human folly (44 B.C.)! (Kastenbaum, 1965, p. 16).

Cicero should have known what he was talking about; according to Plutarch, he was 62 in 44 B.C., and seems to have accepted a violent death with quiet dignity when it caught up with him in the following year.

Apart from the fact that it brings us closer to death, however, why should old age be so frightening? In the language of Madison Avenue, part of the answer seems to be that old age suffers from a very bad image; one which has not been improved by merchandising campaigns geared to euphemisms such as "senior citizen." More directly, Rosenfelt (1965) suggested that there is a core set of negative ideas and attitudes about old people – what she called an "elderly mystique" – that has come into being in the years following World War II.

The elderly mystique got underway . . . as the psychosocial reflection of rapidly accelerated conditions of technological development, sequelae of the prolonged period of global war. Obsolescent skills of the aging, overcrowding of the ranks of labor, and the growth of social security and retirement plans profoundly changed the anticipations of those entering the aged cohorts. With the changed anticipations, many of a negative sort, there developed new attitudes toward old age itself. (1965, p. 38).

Thus, although we take phrases such as *youth cult* for granted, the current emphasis on youth appears to be a historically recent development tied to cultural patterns which make for rapid human, as well as mechanical, obsolescence. Rosenfelt went on to provide a merciless, bold-stroke portrait of this development:

We know that many a person at some point late in life comes to consider himself old, and this implies he views himself as different in important respects from what he considered himself to have been earlier.

Health and vigor, it is assumed, are gone forever. The senses have lost their acuity. The memory is kaput. Education and new learning are out of the question, as one expects to lose his mental faculties with age. Adventure and creativity are for the young and courageous. They are ruled out for the old, who are, *ipso facto*, timid and lacking in moral stamina. As for the pleasures of sexual relationships—the very thought of the old person in such a context brings smiles.

Nothing is to be expected from the children. They have their own lives to lead. Furthermore, they are leading them, like as not, in distant locations, bridged only by the three-minute phone call on alternate Sundays, if contact is maintained at all.

Let him brace himself for isolation and rejection . . . Worse than isolation is the mental ill health that follows it, this concept being a euphemism for loneliness, which sounds too sentimental for modern usage. The nadir of the process is, of course, institutionalization of the aged—not always a necessary or desirable outcome, to be sure, but a practical method of storage until death.

A vicious circle is set in motion. There is no hope in old age, and those who grow old are quite hopeless. That, in essence, is the elderly mystique. Clearly the world pays dearly for this myopic view of what are sardonically called, "The Golden Years." (Rosenfelt, pp. 38–41).

This is all pretty strong stuff, and like other sweeping statements, it will lead many of us automatically to think of exceptions. Rosenfelt pointed to survey data indicating that many people *think* the elderly mystique is factually correct, but argued that it is "in large measure untrue and misleading." How untrue? How misleading?

Rosenfelt claimed only that we accept negative stereotypes about old age too readily. She acknowledged studies showing major declines in the capabilities of old people, but said that we tend to ignore equally relevant evidence showing that old people *can* benefit from educational programs, hold down useful jobs, and even enjoy some sex. She might also have mentioned some of the outstanding feats regularly accomplished by the elderly: Chichester sailing around the world in his 60's, Bernarr McFadden parachuting into the Hudson River to celebrate his 70th (or 80th) birthday, countless stories about grandmothers taking flying lessons, and many more.

In the long run, however, while it is always a pleasure to attack unfair generalizations, the facts of aging make it difficult to maintain a full-blown posture of righteous indignation. The best one can do is agree with Rosenfelt that in addition to the inevitable pain and indignity *nature* imposes as the price of life for old people, they also suffer needlessly from generalizations imposed by *man*. And it remains a toss-up whether maximum honors in cruelty should go to man or nature. There is no ignoring the fact that biologically, as maturity gives way to old age, gradual attrition accelerates into a pattern of outright deterioration.

THE BIOLOGY OF AGING

Kastenbaum (1965) noted that biological research has revealed one central truth: aging goes on at the cellular level. It is a process whereby formerly healthy body cells begin to degenerate and die. Up to the age of 20 years or so, new cells are continually added as old cells reproduce themselves. Later on there is a reduced capacity for reproduction because the cells do not continue to receive the proper supply of nutrients required for healthy mitosis. Thereafter, in an accelerating cycle, reproduction slows down, the wherewithal for good general cell functioning is further reduced, and cells begin to die. As if this weren't enough, the cells that continue to reproduce start yielding a higher and higher proportion of dysfunctional or unhealthy offspring. Microbiologists such as Curtis (1963) can therefore describe aging in terms of unfavorable mutations occurring among body cells.

While biologists generally agree about the cellular death and disorder associated with aging, they disagree about fundamental causes. Kastenbaum mentioned theories of "somatic mutation," "immunology," and "central control." The latter involves an interesting idea which goes beyond microbiology to general evolutionary theory. According to this conception, in nature's grand scheme of things man—like every other species of animal life—exists to reproduce himself. Once he is past his prime for serving this purpose, he is biologically redundant (excess baggage for the species) and therefore is not endowed with a developmental schedule or program for life beyond the reproductive years.

What happens next, in the postreproductive period? Death terminates the postreproductive period rather abruptly for many animals and for many humans, especially in times gone by. In the wild state not many animals grow old. It is only in our own times that the proportion of aged humans has become truly substantial. Thus, it is difficult to discern a programmed impetus to growing old on the biological level that would parallel the earlier surges to grow up and reproduce.

Comfort, who does not necessarily subscribe to all the speculations involved here, does express a similar thought in his characteristically lucid style: ". . . we probably age because we run out of evolutionary program. In this we resemble a space probe that has been "designed" by selection to pass Mars, but that has no further built-in instructions once it has done so, and no components specifically produced to last longer than that. It will travel on, but the failure rate in its guidance and control mechanisms will steadily increase—and this failure of homeostasis, of self-righting, is exactly what we see in the aging organism" (Kastenbaum, 1965, p. 22).

For abstract discussion purposes, it serves well enough to trace the inroads of aging to cellular processes, and to mention some relevant theoretical ideas, but the really cruel stuff is much more concrete. Normative descriptions of gross bodily changes in this period read like a catalogue for a chamber of horrors. Moreover, there is a kind of weird humor in many textbook discussions because they often criticize the negative stereotypes applied to old people, and then go blithely on to describe awful physical realities which tend to support the stereotypes.

Consider appearance. Changes in the face alone include the following: cheeks become wrinkled and baggy, skin coarsens, moles and warts become more frequent, the chin sags, the nose elongates, eyes grow watery, hair grows out of the ears and nose. Furthermore, while one's face is going to pot, the rest of him is not doing too well either. Shoulders get round; veins stand out in scrawny limbs; there are likely to be general tremors and twitching in hands, arms, and the head – and this is only a partial list. Is it unfair to call old people ugly? Is it hard sometimes to see children recoil from the embrace of an elderly relative? Of course it is, yet it is also clear that none of us is going to get any more attractive as we all get older.

Other normative changes are not as apparent but they are equally severe. Bones get hard, internal organs are subject to atrophy, the central nervous system and brain lose weight and become less efficient, metabolism slows, digestion becomes more difficult, insomnia increases and results in tiredness during the day. If it is wrong to dismiss old people as dull, slow, set in their ways, it is equally wrong not to recognize the general conditions which lend substance to such generalities. It is logic, not prejudice, to understand that the stresses of old age will inevitably force one to put more and more of his waning strength into coping efforts, with the result that there may not be much left over for anything else.

It should be emphasized again that the preceding material concerns *normative* changes that come with age; these things will occur in relatively healthy people, and are ordinarily discussed as the signs or symptoms of *senescence*, growing old. When such declines turn into pathological losses or impairments, the term *senility* or *senile* is applied. Thus, the elderly person who grows forgetful, hard of sight or hearing, and suffers digestive problems would be called *senescent*, while one who often confuses the present with the past, and is blind, deaf, or incontinent would be called *senile*. Technical distinctions here can be quite vague, yet they can be important. Part of the negative stereotype applied to the elderly is probably due to widespread confusion between aging *per se* (senescence) and the pathological disorders associated with old age (senility). Perhaps what is needed to counteract this confusion are a few more TV series with heroes and heroines in their 70's.

Later in this chapter we will see evidence indicating that while senility is associated with old age, it is not really caused by aging alone. Instead, it seems to result from illnesses, injuries, and social-emotional conditions prevalent among the elderly. Biographical statements provide abundant direct testimony on this subject.

BIOGRAPHICAL MATERIAL

At about age 61, after some disastrous political maneuvers that eventually led to his assassination, Cicero went into retirement and composed a dialogue titled *On Old Age*. The text suggested that old age enjoyed no better reputation in ancient Rome than in modern America. But Cicero was able to produce one of the most positive statements ever written on the subject by ignoring the physical ailments associated with advancing age, and by constantly appealing to individual differences. Early in the dialogue, he set his thesis as follows:

People, you see, who have no inner resources for living the good and happy life, find every age a burden. But men who seek all good from within themselves are simply unable to view as evil anything that comes about through nature's law (Cicero, Copley translation, 1967, p. 5).

Most of the dialogue involves a general discussion of the four major complaints against old age, which are first enumerated, and then systematically attacked according to the principles listed below.

Now as a matter of fact, when I review the subject in my mind, I find four reasons why old age is adjudged unhappy, the first, because it takes us away from life's activities, the second, because it diminishes physical vigor, the third, because it deprives us of almost all pleasures, and the fourth, because it is only a short distance from death. Let us see, if you will, how significant each of these charges is, and to what degree each is justified (p. 10).

(1) **Concerning activities:**

Old age need not be a time of lusterless ennui; on the contrary, it may well be very busy indeed, always in the middle of some activity, or projecting some plan—in continuation, of course, of the interests of earlier years. And what of those who take up entirely new interests? Consider Solon, for instance: we know those verses of his in which he proudly tells how as he grew old he "learned something new every day." For that matter, take my own case: after I had passed the age of sixty, I began the study of Greek, and I took to it so eagerly that one might have thought I was trying to slake a long-felt thirst! (p. 15).

(2) **Concerning physical vigor:**

At my age, I don't yearn for the physical vigor of a young man, either (this, you recall, was second in our list of charges against old age) any more than in my youth I yearned for the vigor of a bull or an elephant. Use what you have: that is the right way; do what's to be done in proportion as you have the strength for it. What, now, could be more deserving of contempt than the sentiment expressed by Milo of Croton? One day, after he had become very old, he was watching the athletes working out in the stadium; the story goes that he glanced down at his own body, burst into tears, and cried out, "See! My body is already dead!" Your *body?* No, you idiot! You yourself! You became a famous figure not because of any qualities inherent in you, but only because you had a broad chest and strong muscles (pp. 15–16).

(3) **Concerning pleasures, Cicero is particularly eloquent:**

Archytas declared that nature had afflicted man with no plague more deadly than physical pleasure, since the hope of pleasure roused men's desires to fever-pitch and spurred them on, like wild, unbridled beasts, to attainment. (p. 21).

. . . if we should prove unable to rise above pleasure through the use of philosophic reasoning, we should be very grateful to old age, which causes us no longer to want what we ought never to have wanted (p. 22).

No, it is a wonderful state! We have, so to speak, served out our term to passion, ambition, competition, contention, desire—the whole lot!—and now we are our own masters and, as the saying goes, we can live as our hearts desire. (p. 26).

(4) **Concerning death:**

Oh, you sorry old man, if after all these years you still have not learned that death is nothing to worry about! There are only two possible views: either death is the total extinction of ourselves, in which case it is of no importance whatever, or it conducts us to a place where we shall live forever, in which case it is something to be desired (p. 34).

As for the act of dying, we may have some sensation there, but it will be no more than momentary, especially for the old. After death there will be either a pleasant sensation, or no sensation at all. In any event, from our youngest years we must train ourselves to make light of death, since the man who does not so train himself can never have peace of mind. For die we must, and for all we know, on this very day. Every minute of every hour, death hangs over us; if we live in terror of it, how can we keep our sanity (p. 37)?

Only some of Cicero's more dramatic statements have been quoted, but his general message should be clear enough: old age can be beautiful; if not for everybody, then at least for those who have acquired some wisdom and remain in reasonably good health. Pretty good evidence for this position can be found in other memoirs. For example, writing at the age of 70, Somerset Maugham sounded very much like Cicero.

. . . it occurred to me that the greatest compensation of old age is its freedom of spirit. I suppose that is accompanied by a certain indifference to many of the things that men in their prime think important. Another compensation is that it liberates you from envy, hatred and malice. I do not believe that I envy anyone. I have made the most I could of such gifts as nature provided me with; I do not envy the greater gifts of others; I have had a great deal of success; I do not envy the success of others. I am quite willing to vacate the little niche I have occupied so long and let another step into it. I no longer mind what people think of me. They can take me or leave me. I am mildly pleased when they appear to like me and undisturbed if I know they don't (*A Writer's Notebook*, 1949, pp. 353–354).

Further comments along the same general line can be found in the reflections of Edmund Wilson. At 61, he said that he was quite content to retire from many of his former activities.

I do not want any more to be bothered with the kind of contemporary conflicts that I used to go out to explore. I make no attempt to keep up with the younger American writers; and I only hope to have the time to get through some of the classics I have never read. Old fogeyism is comfortably closing in (*A Piece of My Mind*, 1956, p. 211).

And he offered some interesting remarks on sex:

We may still desire . . . We may even feel occasional symptoms of falling in love again, as we do those of some old ailment—gout or a sneezing from roses—to which we have become accustomed and which by this time we know how to cure. Yet sex has come to seem more irrelevant to the other things that occupy our minds, and we may sometimes push it away with impatience when we are busy with something else (p. 203).

Wilson's urbane attitude can be balanced by a very different, but wonderfully candid perspective on sex among the elderly offered by the hardworking father of the Sanchez family:

Now as for my problem, I couldn't get an erection, see? . . . But, of course, any time you abuse something it's harmful. You drink a lot of alcohol and you go under, you're dead in a few days, eh? Well, it's natural, if you abuse your sex life you can't help getting a bit weak. Now add to this the two hernia operations I've had. The doctor told me some delicate parts were cut, and this weakens a man and his member. . . .

It's hard for a man to satisfy a Mexican woman. I've been told personally, "Oh, *querido*, you've quit on me and I'm not halfway through." Just like that, can you imagine. "Well, look, *mi vida*, I better get you a length of pipe because I'm finished now."

Even when I was younger I didn't overdo it, understand? Once or twice at most, and I mean once or twice a week, and not every day. You see I'm sort of puny, or let's put it, I'm not very strong, and naturally on account of I didn't eat very well when I was a child, I think I'm affected by it today, in my sex life. I've practically stopped my sex life with Lupita a few years ago. But with Delila it's different (in Lewis, 1961, pp. 490 – 492).

A great many people, however, cannot meet old age with the dignity and humor indicated in all the remarks quoted above, because they are suffering too much. Either directly – from the pain of disease, or indirectly – from frustration caused by impaired abilities, or both.

According to the 1966 Hotchner memoir *(Papa Hemingway)* Ernest Hemingway suffered dramatically over the loss of his capacities. So much so that he preferred to die rather than to live without them:

I felt I should get to it quickly now, and I did, but I said it very gently: "Papa, why do you want to kill yourself?"

He hesitated only a moment; then he spoke in his old, deliberate way. "What do you think happens to a man going on sixty-two when he realizes that he can never write the books and stories he promised himself? Or do any of the other things he promised himself in the good days?"

"Hotch, if I can't exist on my own terms, then existence is impossible. Do you understand? That is how I've lived, and that is how I *must* live – or not live" (1966, pp. 327 – 328).

The conversation went on, and eventually Hotchner thought that Hemingway was coming round to a less pessimistic attitude, but he was mistaken.

I felt suddenly elated. "And you should work hard to think about the things you care about and like to do, and not about all those negative things. That's the best thing that can happen."

"Sure. Sure it is. The best things in life and other ballroom bananas. But what the hell? What does a man care about? Staying healthy. Working good. Eating and drinking with his friends. Enjoying himself in bed. I haven't any of them. Do you understand, goddamn it? None of them" (p. 330).

A month later, Hemingway ended his life with a shotgun.[1]

---

[1]Ernest Hemingway's situation deserves further comment, because knowledgeable readers will be aware that by all accounts, he was *not* very ill physically. Instead, he was suffering from hypochondriasis and paranoid delusions of persecution. His death is therefore often attributed to a purely psychological breakdown. After searching through relevant material, my own view is that this interpretation is much too simple for at least two reasons. First, he began to go downhill when he found himself plagued by lapses in memory and a related inability to write. These symptoms must be set apart from other, more typical declines associated with old age. Second, he had a long history of head injuries. It therefore seems probable that his psychological condition was due to the cumulative effect of physical insults to brain cortex, which, in conjunction with the reduced biochemical efficiency of aging, impaired his ability for high-level mental activity, and led to loss of control over his exceptional imagination. In short, the anguish of his last months seems ultimately to be a matter of physical damage of the sort likely to produce symptoms of mental deterioration.

Reflecting upon all these memoirs, we can see that personal experiences of old age range over a wide emotional spectrum: from the enthusiasm of Cicero and the moderate good cheer of Maugham and Wilson; to the passionate disdain of Hemingway. Moreover, it seems fair to suggest that physical well-being determines whether or not reactions to aging will be generally positive or negative. Judging from the tone of their remarks, Hemingway would not hesitate to drink from a fountain of youth, while Cicero, Maugham, and Wilson would certainly want to think it over, and might very well refuse. But perhaps this result could be predicted from the fact that Hemingway lived as a man of action, as well as a man of letters.

There seems to be an atrocious mystique about the elderly which places them in much the same position as any despised minority group. Vast individual differences among them tend to be ignored; they are stereotyped as dull, ugly, incapable; and it is apparent that they suffer from de facto conditions of segregation.

On the other hand, brief examination of the biology of aging shows an atrociously real pattern of deterioration. Normal cell functioning gradually breaks down, producing changes in appearance and reduced efficiency of vital body processes. In this respect, some of the negative stereotypes have a basis in fact.

Finally, material describing personal reactions to old age indicates that the decisive consideration is physical. Those who suffer from serious disorders find it hard to go on when the abilities that have provided the central meanings in their lives have been lost or impaired.

THE CRITICAL FACTORS

Contrary to the state of affairs prevailing in adult transition and maturity, a very substantial research literature is available for old age. It indicates that the three critical factors for personality in this period are deterioration, stimulation, and death or the process of dying. Each of these factors must be understood in the broadest possible way, because each apparently operates across the physical, cognitive, and social-emotional sides of personality.

Deterioration

It was mentioned earlier that in old age the gradual attrition of maturity gives way to a pattern of outright deterioration. The difference between these two terms should be made very clear: *attrition* refers to a gradual wearing away; *deterioration* refers to a process whereby the quality, state, or condition of things become impaired.

It hardly seems necessary to offer any extended justification for considering deterioration to be a major factor in old age. The evidence is so obvious in everyday life that many authorities (e.g., Charlotte Buhler) treat the matter quite casually.

After the age of fifty, most physical, mental, and emotional functions suffer deterioration. This is, of course, only a general rule and may not apply to every case . . . (1968, p. 157).

But the *psychological impact* of physical deterioration in old age requires careful consideration.

The analogy to puberty

Consider some examples of how the psychological impact of deterioration in old age may be equated to the impact of puberty in adolescence.

As in adolescence, the late years of life are characterized by physical, social, and emotional upheavals. But, as in the early years, proper preparation for such changes can prevent them from being too stressful and too disruptive (Pikunas, 1969, p. 366).

Just as newly throbbing drives and new life problems may bring about in puberty a personal crisis, so in the climacteric the loss or diminution of potentialities may create similar problems (Buhler, 1968, p. 157).

This last phase of life has a certain parallelism queerly enough with the age of adolescence; on the one hand, the adolescent leaves the life of childhood; on the other, he must make the transposition to his future life (Frenkel-Brunswik, in Neugarten, 1968, p. 84).

The transition from middle to later adulthood in many ways re-creates some of the stresses of being suddenly propelled from adolescence into early adulthood (McNeil, 1969, p. 239).

If the deterioration of old age does indeed have a broad impact analogous to experience in adolescence, how is this impact felt? Havighurst (in Gorlow and Katkovsky, 1959) summarized traditional understandings of this question by listing five ways in which "old age insults the person." These include (a) "loss of physical attractiveness," (b) "loss of supporting persons," (c) "loss of status," (d) "loss of useful and respected roles," and (e) "lessening of physical health and vigor." He also suggested that such insulting events impose corresponding needs for adjustment. If these are not met successfully, the elderly person is likely to fall back on a variety of defensive techniques, which may involve living in the past, regression to infantile behavior, lapses of memory, sight or hearing, and even hallucinations.

It is interesting that insofar as the defenses of old people include regression and fantasy, they are similar to the defenses of adolescents. Barker and Barker (1961) also reported similarity between adolescents and old people with respect to certain measures of gross behavior. The "territorial range" of people over sixty-five (the number of behavior settings they are typically a part of) is close to the range found for adolescents, and this is much lower than the corresponding range for adults between 18 and 64. The same approximate finding appears when activity *within* behavior settings is analyzed: compared with most adults, the adolescents and elderly were more often on the fringe of social situations as onlookers and guests rather than as active participants.

The dependent socioeconomic condition of old people provides still another parallel to adolescence. McNeil (1969) reported that of those over 65 in America, 27 percent live on pensions, social security and/or relatives; 23 percent live on charity; 31 percent are working; and 19 percent are retired on investments or savings. In short, a good 50 percent are in a more or less dependent condition and this proportion undoubtedly increases with age beyond 65. Any wonder then that like adolescents who find few possibilities for meaningful activity, old people may also resort to withdrawal and fantasy; or that novelists and playwrights occasionally elaborate the theme of mutual sympathy between old people and teen-agers?

Impacts on the self

Kuhlen (in Worchel and Byrne, 1964) reviewed a great many studies of personality changes associated with advancing age. Without going into detail, it appears that except for those who remain in positions of responsibility, such motives as achievement, power seeking, and self-actualization generally decline. Interests and activities tend to shift from emphasis on direct gratification to vicarious or indirect gratification. In this connection, the elderly identify more closely with their children and get more involved in religion.

Results of projective test studies suggest reduced "ego involvement in life." Older people make up less complex, less emotionally intense stories in response to TAT pictures. Other test findings show that personal anxiety and susceptibility to threat increase, but the anxiety issue is complicated by evidence showing differences with respect to specific fears about health, mobility, and mental functioning.

Various studies relevant to changes in the self-concept reveal a broadly negative trend. For example, results from one projective task ("draw a person") show that once past the age of 40, progressively older samples of men and women draw progressively smaller pictures – an indication of decreased self-confidence. Other investigators report that in responding to various questionnaire items involving risk-taking, elderly men (47 to 85) seem more cautious and less self-confident than those of college age. And comparative studies in which older and younger samples are asked to rate themselves and the "ideal person" reveal a greater discrepancy between self and ideal for the older people.

Amid all the projective test material, one brighter spot shows up in several studies of subjective age. When a sample of over 300 people 70 years or older was asked to describe themselves, about half used the term *middle-aged*. Additional work indicates that these "underestimators" are people who have made a better adjustment to the problems of aging. The old adage about only being as old as you feel therefore receives some support. Trivial as it may seem at first glance, this old-as-you-feel catch phrase is shown to be quite important by research focused on individual differences among the elderly.

Individual differences

As sketched above, practically all of the normative data on aging suggests that with advancing age there is a rather straightforward pattern of negative change in personality: physical deterioration and reduced socioeconomic status apparently combine to produce social-emotional deterioration. And as was mentioned earlier, physical deterioration seems to be the critical factor, because otherwise the elderly person might retain his capacities. Work on individual differences among the elderly offers additional support for this interpretation.

The clearest evidence appears in an interdisciplinary study reported by

Butler (1963). The subjects were 47 men from 65 to 91, who were in apparent good health and were living in better than average socioeconomic circumstances. Invited to spend 2 weeks at a special clinic, they were put through an extensive series of medical and psychological tests, including detailed psychiatric interviews. According to medical examination results, 27 of the men were judged to be in optimum health, while 20 showed minimal traces of disease such as minor arthritis, diabetes, or other conditions that were well under control. In general, all the men made a very positive impression on the research team:

Broadly speaking, our men were vigorous, candid, interesting and deeply involved in everyday living. In marked contradiction to the usual stereotype of "rigidity" of the aged, these individuals generally demonstrated mental flexibility and alertness. They continued to be constructive in their living; they were resourceful and optimistic (Butler, p. 724).

The psychological test data obtained from these men were compared with similar data from a young normal-control sample. The only significant differences involved performances on intellectual tests, and these differences were mainly due to the slower working speed of the older men.[2] Recognizing that their sample was composed of select subjects, the researchers nevertheless pointed out that many of the impairments ordinarily thought to be a consequence of old age actually result from disease.

The belief, for example, that cerebral blood flow and oxygen consumption necessarily decrease as the consequence of chronological aging per se was not confirmed: rather it was found that when such changes did occur they were the probable result of arteriosclerosis.

Moreover, psychometric tests appeared unusually sensitive to the presence of minimal disease states including arteriosclerosis.

Our broad conclusion may be stated as follows: As a consequence of a careful multidisciplinary pilot study, we have found evidence to suggest that many manifestations heretofore associated with aging per se reflect instead medical illness, personality variables, and social-cultural effects (Butler, pp. 727–728).

Note the emphasis on arteriosclerosis. It suggests that for otherwise normally functioning old people, the primary *physical* source for *psychological* deterioration lies in reduced arterial blood flow to the brain. This material underscores our assumption of physical deterioration as a critical factor because the other things mentioned – "personality variables, and social-cultural effects" – seem most likely to become serious sources of difficulty when physical well-being is lost. In sum, while showing that elderly persons in relative good health are not much different from younger people, and that they remain able to live in a vigorous, constructive fashion, the Butler report also indicated that for those in good living situations, physical condition can be the most important determinant of individual differences.

[2] It is relevant that after a careful review of research studies concerning the cognitive capacities of old people, Botwinick (1967) found no conclusive evidence of impaired learning or intelligence; but there is good evidence showing losses in speed and performance skills. Apparently, this finding can be added to the list of other things one holds against intelligence testing.

Another study deserves special mention because in both design and results, it is quite complementary to Butler's report. Frances Carp (1969) investigated a representative sample of 295 persons ranging in age from 52 to 92. They were tested on a senility questionnaire which measures personality changes associated with old age (see Cavan, Burgess, Havighurst, and Goldhamer, 1949). They were also given a general diagnostic test of personality (the MMPI). Carp made it clear that items in the senility questionnaire reflect the effects of physical as well as other forms of deterioration.

Some of her main findings are the following: (a) no significant relationship between senility scores and chronological age; (b) a comparison group of college students made a *higher* average score on the senility index than the elderly sample; (c) in a subsample of 100 of the elderly, senility scores were negatively related to ego strength scores obtained from the MMPI. That is, the lower the senility score, the higher the ego strength.

The parallels to Butler should be obvious: Carp's work confirmed and extended his argument against the importance of chronological age *per se*. And if senility index scores *are* partly dependent upon physical well-being, then the negative relationship with ego strength is perfectly in line with Butler's finding that those in good physical condition are also in good psychological condition. The only thing preventing a closer check on Butler's results is the absence of medical data in Carp's study. However, the biographical material presented earlier in this chapter suggests that if such data were available, the elderly with serious physical complaints would show lower ego strength and higher senility scores, regardless of chronological age.

The theory of disengagement

Traditionally, it has been thought that the elderly are forced (by society or physical disabilities) against their wills into a passive social role, the result being such broad personality changes as withdrawal or reduced ego-involvement in life. This view has been summarized as an "activity theory" of aging:

The older person who ages optimally is the person who stays active and who manages to resist the shrinkage of his social world. He maintains the activities of middle age as long as possible and then finds substitutes for those activities he is forced to relinquish: substitutes for work when he is forced to retire; substitutes for friends and loved ones whom he loses by death (Havighurst, Neugarten and Tobin, in Neugarten, 1968, p. 161).

Cumming and Henry (1961) challenged such ideas with their disengagement theory of aging. Based on data collected from approximately 200 elderly men and women ("The Kansas City Study of Adult Life") these authors argued that instead of being forced on the elderly, withdrawal is a natural, intrinsic development of old age. It was suggested that old people *need* to withdraw into themselves, and/or disengage from the bustle of middle age, to maintain their psychological equilibrium. When one is younger, equilibrium or harmony in personality requires a high level of participation in the social environment. But with old age, harmony is best maintained if behavior shifts toward relative passivity. Thus, personality development in this period is primarily a matter of disengagement.

We will examine some cogent objections to this viewpoint soon enough. However, it should first be explained why the theory has received so much attention. Apart from some of the initial Kansas City data, prior studies also showed a comprehensive pattern of withdrawal among the elderly. From a study of over 1200 men and women 60 or more years old, for example, Cavan, Burgess, et al. (1949) concluded that advancing age is associated with reductions in personal companionship, general social participation, feelings of happiness, and interest in life. It seems reasonable to consider that such a broad pattern may not be entirely due to the pressure of circumstances; that it may indeed reflect personal inclinations.

In the Kansas City study, a number of healthy older persons were found who apparently *preferred* a "rocking chair" adjustment. They were described as calm, withdrawn, and contented.

Additional support for the natural disengagement idea can be drawn from a theoretical discussion of reminiscence among the elderly. Butler (in Neugarten, p. 487) argued that the tendency to review past experience – to reminisce, and perhaps to seemingly live in the past – is a normal, functionally important process in old age.

I conceive of the life review as a naturally occurring, universal mental process characterized by the progressive return to consciousness of past experiences, and, particularly, the resurgence of unresolved conflicts; simultaneously, and normally, these revived experiences and conflicts can be surveyed and reintegrated.

If he is correct, then disengagement from everyday life seems understandable as a side effect of reminiscence: one who is busy reviewing his life will presumably have less energy available for contemporary affairs.

Finally, the remarks of people such as Cicero, Wilson, and Maugham also indicate a natural tendency toward disengagement.

But despite the plausibility of disengagement theory, and the enthusiastic attention it received at first, many authorities now reject it as a general interpretation of aging. Interestingly enough, the strongest critique of the theory is based on two additional findings from the Kansas City study.

After keeping track of the subjects for another few years and analyzing further data on their social activity, involvement in the present, and life satisfaction, Havighurst, Neugarten, and Tobin reported that while persons over 70 accepted their reduced activity as inevitable, they also *regretted* it. These authors go on to criticize disengagement theory for ignoring the problem of dual personal values:

There appear to be two sets of values operating simultaneously, if not within the same individual then within the group we have been studying: on the one hand, the desire to stay active in order to maintain a sense of self-worth; on the other hand, the desire to withdraw from social commitments and to pursue a more leisurely and a more contemplative way of life. Neither the activity theory nor the disengagement theory of optimum aging takes sufficient account of this duality in value patterns (Havighurst et al., in Neugarten, pp. 171–172).

This dual values interpretation, which first appeared in 1963 (2 years after the original statement of disengagement theory) was followed in 1965 by another critique based on intensive analysis of personality data from the Kansas City study. The new material came from 59 persons who had been under study for 6 years. With one exception, they were all categorized according to four general personality patterns called the "integrated," "defended," "passive-dependent," and "disintegrated."

The 19 *integrated* personalities were those who seemed competent, satisfied with life and reasonably self-confident. One subgroup was composed of "reorganizers": people who stayed active and reorganized their lives around their activities. Another subgroup included the "focused": those who withdrew from certain activities to concentrate more intensively on specific interests such as hobbies or family matters. And a third subgroup were the "disengaged" mentioned earlier—people who apparently preferred a rocking chair life.

All of the 16 *defended* personalities were people who saw old age as a threat; something to be defended against. They fell into two subgroups. Some tried to ward off the threat by following a "holding on" pattern, struggling to stay as busy and active as possible; the remainder followed a "constricted pattern," which seems to involve a hedgehog defense. They deliberately restricted their activities and minimized chances for new experiences.

The 13 *passive-dependent* personalities included a group called "succorance seeking"—persons who seemed moderately well adjusted as long as they could lean on others—and another group called "apathetic," who were very withdrawn.

The *disintegrated* personalities were 11 people suffering from physical and psychological impairments which led to a disorganized pattern of aging.

It is noteworthy that similar personality data were also reported by Reichard, Livson, and Petersen (1962). In a sample of retired men they found (a) a "mature" group who were making the best of old age; (b) a "rocking chair" group who preferred little activity; (c) a defensive or "armored" group who tried to cope with their fear of aging by keeping active; (d) "angry men" bitter over past failures they blamed on others; and (e) "self-haters" who also thought they were failures but blamed themselves.

The summaries of such personality findings are very brief, yet it should be clear why they lead to criticisms of disengagement theory. Neugarten et al. went beyond criticism and said that responses to aging are an expression of long-standing personality patterns:

There is considerable evidence that, in normal men and women, there is no sharp discontinuity of personality with age, but instead an increasing consistency. Those characteristics that have been central to the personality seem to become even more clearly delineated, and those values the individual has been cherishing become even more salient. In the personality that remains integrated—and in an environment that permits—patterns of overt behavior are likely to become increasingly consonant with the individual's underlying personality needs and his desires (Neugarten, Havighurst, and Tobin, in Neugarten, p. 177).

In general, then, it would seem that while a natural tendency toward disengagement may account for part of the existing evidence on old age, it does not provide a full explanation. Instead, Neugarten and others suggested something like an "age-stress" personality theory: under the physical and social stress of advancing age, people are stripped down to the essence of their personalities. Superficial attributes drop away, and basic reaction tendencies stand out.

This line of thought makes sense if you have ever seen people under prolonged stress; soldiers, for example, who are experiencing extreme weather conditions or live fire for the first time. Some become very active, trying anything and everything to make the situation more bearable; some "disengage," telling dirty stories, playing cards, or eating candy bars; some "defend," arguing that the officers must know what they are doing and that this can't last much longer; while others curl up in a ball, shut their eyes, cover their ears and thus present a perfect picture of withdrawal or apathy.

Altogether the idea that withdrawal from everyday life is a natural, functionally useful, and preferred way of adjusting to old age does not hold up under close scrutiny. While authorities in the field acknowledge its value for some descriptive purposes, they are critical for at least two reasons. First, there seems to be a dual set of value orientations typical among the elderly and the disengagement idea only fits one of them. Second, the various personality patterns found to underlie different adjustments to old age are only partly explainable according to disengagement theory.

Stimulation

The case for deterioration is supported by abundant research evidence, but the assumption that stimulation is a second critical factor in old age depends mainly on deduction and inference. The logic begins with a mass of evidence concerning the importance of keeping active. We have already noted common beliefs in activity as a means of warding off the negative effects of aging. Among social scientists, this idea goes under the name of activity theory; and we have seen that some people use it as a practical strategy for adjustment to old age.

In the physical domain, where activity means exercise, there can be little doubt of its importance: heart specialists and all manner of other medical experts testify to the value of exercise in preventing or slowing down physical deterioration. The popular view is that physiological systems decline from disuse just like automobile engines.

In the social-emotional sphere, where activity means personal contact with other people, the same sort of principle is suggested. Many studies show that retired persons who are engaged in hobbies, clubs, and community affairs of one sort or another seem better off than those who are less active. Pikunas (1969, p. 379) offered a plausible explanation for such findings which is again reminiscent of the auto-engine analogy: he indicated that a person's ideas and emotions will grow stale and flat if they are not exercised or kept in tune via discussion with others.

In addition, although the evidence for this point is not so clear, some authorities think that continued intellectual activity can help prevent the decline of cognitive capacities.

Briefly then, considerable material suggests that the best general medicine for old age is activity; and it hardly matters what kind, so long as it has the effect of keeping physical, social-emotional, and intellectual systems tuned up. In this connection, many writers comment that old people ought to be prepared to substitute new activities for those which are no longer feasible. Hobbies should serve as a substitute for work, and new friends should replace those who are dying off. But can one take these things seriously? It is all very well to have convenient generalizations available as prescriptions for the elderly—join a golden-age club, visit museums, raise roses, baby-sit, go to Berlitz and learn Greek—but does the cry for activity have any meaning beyond the level of actuarial tables, and if it does, what about the *quality* of activity?

Research literature provides no answers to such questions, except by implication. Yet the various relevant implications are important because they indicate a way of getting past normative clichés in our understanding of activity. Right at the outset, a change of terminology seems necessary: instead of talking about the benefits of activity, we might better speak of a *need for stimulation* among the aged. That is, if activity or exercise has positive effects across the whole spectrum of personality, these effects must result from the stimulating properties of activity. Moreover, since a need for stimulation during infancy and early childhood is now well accepted, it is not terribly strange to see such a need at the other end of the life cycle.

In view of other parallels noted between adolescence and old age, one might even argue for a nicely symmetrical "elevator theory" of development, in which the person going down makes the same stops he did on his way up. (The elevator notion is particularly forceful if you start in the basement, with a toothless, hairless, helpless, babbling, incontinent infant, and equate this to the conditions of total senility.)

More substantially, however, the assumption of stimulation as a critical factor in old age rests on our understanding of its functional, biophysical meaning. In infancy stimulation is considered necessary to tune up bodily systems, especially the central nervous system. Among adults, research on stimulus deprivation has shown that when sensory inputs are sharply curtailed, mental processes grow disorderly. So the general run of evidence shows stimulation to be necessary for proper development and maintenance of neural systems.

When this material is ranged next to findings showing positive effects of activity for the elderly, it seems appropriate to recognize stimulation as a critical factor. With it, the old are likely to remain plugged in to life; without it, they are likely to decline much more rapidly. Another point worth considering here is the gross similarity between marasmus in the very young and senility in the very old. Since the apathy and physical decline associated with marasmus is traceable in part to lack of stimulation, why not consider that the same cause is relevant to senility?

Such perspectives also suggest how to organize practical approaches to the question of activity *quality*. One might begin by trying to analyze various activities according to their stimulation potential. Occupations such as TV viewing or other passive activities should be distinguished from those demanding a more active response. The degree to which activities involve social interaction should be considered, as well as their variability or inherent uncertainty. (Gardening may *seem* equivalent to rug weaving, but it involves far more uncertainty.) Ultimately, instead of lumping all activities together, we should be able to weight them according to their stimulation potential and then see whether their psychological benefits are different.

Some hint of how useful such information could be is given in the results of a large-scale investigation by Kutner, Fanshel, Togo, and Langner (1956). Studying 500 persons over 60, these authors reported that those who visited with their children or friends at least once a week had higher morale than those visiting less often. It was also found that among the elderly who worked, morale was directly related to the size of their salary. From our present viewpoint, however, the most interesting finding was that the morale of people who worked but were paid less than twenty-five dollars a week, was equal to that of persons drawing a higher income in total retirement. Thus, a stimulation potential might well be assigned to sources of income.

Another technical approach would be to follow the same research strategy employed to test the effects of stimulation on young children. That is, compare random or matched samples of institutionalized old people who are exposed to particularly stimulating or routine conditions. And if it hasn't already been done, it would be interesting to see some laboratory experiments comparing the effects of stimulating and dull environments on aging animals.

At present, however, it should be clear that our assumptions about stimulation in old age are speculative. Implications drawn from the activity literature, research on stimulus deprivation, and analogies to early childhood, support the idea that stimulation is a critical factor, but we should also consider some counterarguments. Perhaps only those older persons who are in relative good health can benefit from stimulating experiences. Or perhaps activity seems so valuable because those who are incapable of it die off before they can be included in research studies.

Parallels between early childhood and old age can also be questioned: if nothing else, the range of certain individual differences is probably much greater among the elderly. Therefore, the effects of stimulation are liable to be more variable for older people. And it must be admitted that we do not yet know enough about the biophysical workings of stimulation. Electrical activity in the central nervous system depends upon sensory stimulation, and certain levels of electrical activity must be triggered in the brain if it is to function normally, but the relationship between electrical and biochemical processes is not too clear. Nor is it clear how the central nervous system interacts with other bodily systems such as the endocrine glands.

In sum, however, despite all the conceivable objections that can be raised against it, the case for stimulation as a critical factor remains quite persuasive. It is a testable proposition which fits existing research literature, and a great many biographical[3] statements as well. Furthermore, since current census projections indicate that the number of old people is steadily ris-

---

[3]Conspicuous examples of old people reputed never to have suffered serious declines (Freud, Frank Lloyd Wright, Picasso, Bertrand Russell) seem to be those who were able to continue the meaningful activities which characterized their lives.

ing (it is estimated that by the year 2000 at least 25 percent of the U.S. population will be over 65), it seems inevitable that interest in the problems of aging will increase accordingly. And apart from the possibility of breakthroughs in biochemical work—youth pills, maybe—stimulation offers the most promising line for future research.

Death and dying

It is not exactly an upbeat ending, but there's no way around it: death is the Big Finish. However, the interesting thing about death is that it does not require much discussion. Cicero covered it as well as anyone ever has when he noted that one can die at *any* time, and that the only important issue is whether or not one goes on to an afterlife. The fact of death itself—as a discrete event—is dismissed as nothing. Most of the other classical philosophers also took this view, and in one form or another it has remained with us.

In the Troyat biography of Tolstoy, for example, it was reported that while on his deathbed the 82-year-old writer roused himself for a moment, saying "So this is the end!. . . And it's nothing. . . ." According to Hotchner, when Ernest Hemingway was asked about death he replied with characteristic aplomb, calling it "Just another whore." And in a very different vein Shneidman explained that the philosopher-physicist Percy Bridgman disposed of death through a more formal exercise of logic:

Essentially, his concept is that death is not experienceable, that if one could experience it, one would not be dead. One can experience another's dying and another's death and his own dying—although he can never be sure—but no man can experience his own death (1963, p. 207).

Pursuing his discussion of "orientations toward death" a few steps further, Shneidman also provided a relevant quotation from Freud:

Our own death is indeed unimaginable, and whenever we make the attempt to imagine it we can conceive that we really survive as spectators. Hence the psychoanalytic school could venture on the assertion that at bottom no one believes in his own death, or to put the thing in another way, in the unconscious every one of us is convinced of his own immortality (pp. 208–209).

Without getting into any more quotations, it seems that most literary-philosophical approaches to death can be summarized as follows: while practically nobody is interested in death *per se*, everyone is very interested in the *process* of dying.[4]

But this interest in process has only recently become important in the social science literature. In fact, if it did not border on the macabre, dying might accurately be described as a glamorous new research area because it has all the properties which merit such a description. The subject matter carries universal interest, it is inherently dramatic, it has never been studied

---

[4]A conspicuous exception appears in the *Anti-memoirs* of André Malraux. In 1944 he was hit by machine-gun fire in both legs. While lying a captive of the Germans and expecting either to bleed to death or be shot or tortured for his resistance activities, he said that the dying process seemed nothing. What really intrigued him was the idea that he might finally learn some answers about death itself.

thoroughly, it takes considerable fortitude to do the research, and recent reports indicate that many traditional ideas about dying may be all wrong. Thus, physicians commonly do not tell terminal patients the truth about their condition for fear of upsetting them, but new sources (e.g., Kübler-Ross, 1969; Saunders, in Pearson, 1969) suggest that for persons able to cope with it, open discussion of the truth is the best and kindest policy.

Before entering the empirical literature on dying, however, it will be useful to consider a prior issue: why has there been a sudden boom of interest in this research area? On the immediate surface, the answer involves our own rationale for the present discussion—an increasing number of social scientists have come to recognize dying as an important factor in personality. Or, to put it another way, those interested in understanding personality are increasingly aware that the way we end our lives may be just as important a source of knowledge as the way we begin them. A more practical reason is that just as studies of birth and infancy have led to better procedures for handling the very young, work on dying may lead to better procedures for handling the very old. But these answers are superficial because potentially useful applications can always be claimed for basic research, and because it seems obvious that work on infancy has greater potential utility than work on dying. So the question remains: why, starting in the late 1950's, has there been an accelerating interest in the social and psychological processes of dying?

Shneidman (1963) suggested that the world is in such an awful condition that we are now freer to study death.

Pearson (1969) offered an illuminating personal explanation for his interest in the subject:

I first became aware of death as a clinical entity with special psychological impact when consulting at a home for the aged in Chicago some years ago. One day one of the residents failed to appear for our group-therapy session. When I asked about him, the staff member serving as cotherapist with me looked startled. With her face reddening, she said she would tell me about it "later." Then one of the other residents calmly spoke up: "He died last night." This led to a discussion of attitudes toward death as well as toward the dead man. It became apparent that most of the older persons had made some resolution of their feelings toward death. Subsequent talks with staff members, however, revealed much reluctance to discuss the concept (1969, p. vii).

He further noted what many other people working in this area have also observed—that death and dying are relatively taboo matters in our society. His direct experience with this taboo began after he started teaching a course on the subject:

Soon, I became the object of a curious interest on the part of colleagues. At a social gathering of faculty one evening, the host greeted me at the door and led me to the living room, where he introduced me: "And here is our Minister of Death." Students who were studying with me began to acquire a campus reputation as eccentrics, as they often asked questions of friends about death, attitudes toward bereavement, and so on (1969, p. vii).

Among those who have speculated about the peculiar rise of interest in dying, Sarnoff (1962) seemed to have struck on the best single, general explanation. He suggested that the existential philosophers – particularly Sartre and Camus – provided the necessary intellectual springboard.

. . . some members of the existential school of thought are inclined to see in the fact of death the greatest source of human motivation. Thus, they hold that it is the dread of his ultimate end that is the well-spring of man's most significant behavior; that it is the awful awareness of his final fate that drives man to all his excesses of self-deception, of escape, of extravagant works and fantasies whose sole purpose is to blot out or transcend the timelessness of doom.

By calling man's attention so forcefully and relentlessly to his dilemma, they [the existentialists] hope to stir him into constructive action on his own behalf . . . (Sarnoff, pp. 489 – 490).

It remains for scholars in the history of science to judge the influence of existentialism on psychology, although overlaps in timing and among prominent writers indicate a very strong connection between the two. But let us turn back to our immediate problem: how to understand dying as a critical factor in old age.

Fear of death

The best place to begin is with elderly people who are actually on the brink: are they actively frightened of death? This may seem like a trivial question because everyone is supposed to be afraid of it, yet it is not at all clear whether most institutionalized old people really go about with a daily awareness and fear of dying. If they do, then one might see this as an important source of stress on their social-emotional adjustment. If they do not – and it is quite possible for people to defend against such fears through repression or other defense mechanisms – then one might very well ignore the problem.

Unfortunately, no definitive answer is available for this simple question. Some authorities argue that the elderly are not much troubled by fear of death. Weisman and Kastenbaum (1968), for example, said that in a careful study of 80 persons who died in a hospital for the aged, fear of death was only "rarely observed." And they mentioned two other studies which supported their finding.

Strauss (in Pearson, 1969), discussed this problem from a more abstract perspective. He described a general atmosphere of "closed awareness" about death which prevails among staff and patients in institutions for the aged. Death is apparently a taboo subject which people may think of but never discuss openly.

Kübler-Ross (1969) amplified the closed awareness theme in a commentary on possible reasons for depersonalized orientations toward the dying:

Is the reason for this increasingly mechanical, depersonalized approach our own defensiveness? Is this approach our own way to cope with and repress the anxieties that a terminally or critically ill patient evokes in us? Is our concentration on equipment, on blood pressure our desperate attempt to deny the impending death which is so frightening and discomforting to us that we displace all our knowledge onto machines, since they are less close to us than the suffering face of another human being which would remind us once more of our lack of omnipotence, our own limits and failures, and last but not least perhaps our own mortality (1969, p. 8)?

Altogether, it would seem that because of individual inclinations and the typical institutional atmosphere, the odds are entirely against open awareness of death. But another, very contradictory source of information is available. Wolff (1968) maintained that death fears do indeed play a significant role in the lives of most old people.

Appealing to 12 years of psychiatric practice with a total of 240 aged patients, he claimed that while many start by denying fear of death, in later therapy sessions they admit to it. Specifically, he said that concerns centering on impending death were an important factor in the emotional lives of 80 percent of his patients. And Wolff also suggested that restlessness and insomnia in the elderly can frequently be traced to death fears. The discussion of this latter point is illuminating:

. . . they openly admitted that they frequently were afraid to fall asleep or to be alone in their rooms because "something might happen" to them or because they "might not wake up any more." Most of these patients liked to keep the light on as late as possible and frequently called the night nurse to get attention for minor physical ailments. More than half were unable to sleep at all without sedatives or tranquilizing medication at bedtime. Their dreams frequently centered around falling into water or swimming in a lake, symbolizing a return to the uterus. It is interesting that nearly all of the patients who showed very little concern about death were diagnosed as having a schizophrenic reaction. Anxiety of any sort in those patients was much decreased because their emotions were blunted (Wolff, p. 162).

It is even more illuminating to discover evidence that the night fears of elderly, dying patients are not all pure fancy. One investigator kept track of the time nurses took responding to call lights, and found that they were much slower answering the signals from terminal patients than others (in Bowers, Jackson, Knight, and LeShan, 1964).

Wolff's arguments are difficult to deny. Yet in the face of inadequate and contradictory material[5] there is no way to decide how disturbing death fears are to old people except by doing further research. At the very least, however, the present state of the evidence indicates that fear of death ought to be considered an important potential source of stress upon the institutionalized elderly. And on a more practical level, it would certainly be helpful if the following general state of affairs noted by Weisman and Kastenbaum could be changed:

. . . it is an unfortunate fact that patients are not usually allowed, even less encouraged, to express fears and beliefs about death. Even workers experienced in psychological interviewing find themselves avoiding dying patients or inadvertently terminating discussions about death (1968, p. 18).

---

[5]An example of the difficulties one finds here is the disagreement between Weisman and Kastenbaum on the one hand, and Wolff on the other. They are not only split over the general issue of death fears among the elderly, but also about the relevance of psychiatric disorders. The former suggested (1968, p. 35) that "psychiatrically disturbed" patients are more likely to express fear of death, while the latter said that those who express *little* fear are psychiatrically disturbed (show a schizophrenic reaction).

This seems particularly important in the light of reports by Kübler-Ross, Cicely Saunders, Pearson, LeShan, and several others, who all emphasized that dying patients may experience great relief from emotional tension when they are allowed to express some of their fears.

Reminiscence, guilt, and shame

If the impact of death fears upon the personalities of old people is not well understood yet, other social-emotional effects related to dying are very plain. We have already introduced Butler's view that reminiscence and review of the past may be an important, general form of adaptation to dying. One force operating to produce this phenomenon is thought to be an increased sense of self-awareness. Suspecting that the end is in sight, people again turn to the perennial questions of meaning and identity: "Who am I?" "What does my life add up to?" An increased concern with religion may be symptomatic. Reflective attitudes are also triggered by changes in physical appearance. Butler described many instances in line with the following comment of an old man:

I was passing by my mirror. I noticed how old I was. My appearance, well, it prompted me to think of death—and of my past—what I hadn't done, what I had done wrong (in Neugarten, p. 489).

Another condition promoting reminiscence is simple boredom. If one is bedridden or unable to get about easily, if interesting conversation is rare, if one is unable to read for long periods or watch TV, then memories are liable to be the only diversion left—the sole alternative to dreary thoughts of the present or future.

Finally, there may also be a purely organic basis for reminiscence. Many old people report spontaneous "sensory memories" coming back from the remote past: the smell of bread baking in their mother's kitchen, the sound of rain on the roof of their childhood home. Perhaps such things will soon be understood according to the biochemistry of brain functioning in old age.

Apart from causes, however, the effects of reminiscence are our main concern here. Common-sense logic, as well as the observations reported by Butler and others, indicate that the immediate consequence of living on or with memories is likely to be guilt or shame. Note the quotation given above: the old man started by glancing in the mirror, and quickly ended by thinking of what he had done wrong. In a great many cases of depression psychoses among old people, Butler believed that an important precipitating factor was the guilt aroused by reviews of past behavior.

The development of such guilt feelings is easy to understand. Suppose that for some reason or other you are trying to find a bit of pleasure by retreating into your memories. You think of a remote, happy event—maybe a particularly delightful Christmas arranged by your parents when you were a child. Within a few moments, you are *also* likely to be thinking something like: "Ah, after all is said and done, they were really pretty decent people who tried their best; why couldn't I have treated them better later on, when they needed me?" Or possibly you remember a funny incident from high school or college, and then conjure up all those old friends. You might have acted more decently to some of them; maybe it was more cruel than funny always to be having fun at the expense of the awkward types. And does it help to think that by now they may all be dead or decrepit?

It should be emphasized that only a mild exercise in the memory-guilt relationship has been provided. If you want the real strong stuff you have to dig into the unforgettably rotten things all of us manage to accomplish on occasion.[6]

While the guilt and/or shame provoked by reminiscence can be serious enough to cause severe depressions, most elderly people are able to cope if they have opportunities to work through their emotional feelings. Butler, Saunders, LeShan, Kübler-Ross—all the clinically oriented authorities—indicated that psychotherapy, or just sympathetic conversations with decently accepting ward visitors, can be of great help to old people suffering regret or chagrin as they review their past. In this connection, the ultimate effects of reminiscence are not necessarily negative. Butler suggested that a constructive reexamination of his past may eventually lead the elderly person to a more "serene and dignified" attitude toward his impending death.

Here again, the impersonal quality of most institutions for the aged demands comment: they are organized to treat and maintain bodies rather than people. As a result, they provide the exact opposite of the atmosphere needed for working through emotional problems. In the psychological autopsy research to be discussed later, we will see that as matters presently stand in many hospitals, troubled old people often prefer to die and have done with it when they experience severe emotional upsets.

Immediate events

Events in their immediate living situations also contribute to guilt and shame among the infirm elderly. All investigators who have studied this problem invariably report that feelings of guilt for being "a burden on the family" lead the aged to enter institutions. Thus, after reviewing relevant research and conducting his own study, Kalish offered the following conclusions:

The elderly themselves, however, frequently wish to be removed from their home when they become unable to take care of themselves or cannot afford to hire others who can care for them.

Some prefer to be where medical care is more readily available; others prefer the impersonal care; sometimes an aged parent believes that his effect upon the people with whom he lives is destructive. A number of elderly persons also prefer to avoid the role reversal in which the once-dominant parent must regress to the status of helpless infant, nurtured by the children he once nurtured himself; a geriatric facility enables him to maintain the original parent-child relationship intact as long as possible (Kalish, 1965, pp. 91–92).

---

[6]Strikingly powerful illustrations can be found in Alexander Solzhenitsyn's novels, *The Cancer Ward* and *The First Circle*. In the latter, one of the chief characters was an old communist activist named Rubin. While ill, he found himself plagued with memories of the time he was in charge of collectivizing a peasant village, and the men he had to shoot or deport. Logically, he still believed that his actions were necessary, but psychologically he was very disturbed.

Underlying these generalizations one can find case histories illustrating a whole world of embarrassment and shame experienced by old people who must depend on others. Often hard of sight or hearing, they can make awkward errors in conversation. Easily fatigued, they can drop off to sleep in the midst of a family gathering. Prone to becoming disoriented, they may set out on a short walk and become lost on familiar streets. Most pathetic of all embarrassments, however, are those which concern inconveniencing others as a result of illness. In the midst of hemorrhaging, for example, an old person may be more upset by the mess he is making in his daughter-in-law's bathroom than by his physical condition. Weisman and Kastenbaum described the case of a hospitalized, 100-year-old man who one day absent-mindedly emptied his bedpan on the ward floor. After remarking that he would rather die than do such things, he refused to eat or drink and died a few days later.

It should be added that all authorities tend to treat guilt and shame among the elderly as a distinctly culture-bound phenomenon. The "underdeveloped" areas of the world typically contain societies in which the elderly are held in great esteem, and are treated accordingly, despite illness or infirmity. It is also interesting that while going over some of this material a colleague from India remarked that, among his compatriots, America is generally thought to be a good place to study and work, but they all intend to return home before the onset of old age.

Death predictions

Although it does not start out sounding directly relevant to personality, the question of whether a person can predict his own death, and/or whether death can be predicted by an observer, is intrinsically interesting enough to warrant discussion. Both questions can probably be traced to folklore, but both have drawn the attention of recent investigators.

In their study of dying geriatric patients, Weisman and Kastenbaum found several instances which seemingly confirm the validity of death premonitions. Here is one of their more convincing examples.

During most of his three years in the hospital, a 76-year-old widower had been enthusiastic, alert, and convivial. Then, without known precipitant, he declared one day, "My time is almost here!" He began to fear being alone at night, lest he die unattended. Three days before his death, he consulted his lawyer and sold his house. An oversolicitous nurse refused to permit a psychologist to speak with him two days later, because he had been "too worried about death!" Death was attributed to chronic asthma and arteriosclerotic heart disease (1968, pp. 21–22).

However, these authors also reported other cases involving premonitions of death which did not come true. People apparently tend to overemphasize the confirmed cases and forget the others. In general, so far as one can tell from the literature, cases in which people make deliberate, surprisingly accurate predictions of their own deaths are rare. And the element of surprise is very important here: anyone who knows he is in the terminal phase of disease may be able to give an accurate prediction of his death. The "true" premonition is one that occurs in the absence of clear-cut information.

Careful consideration of this issue leads toward a reformulation of the initial question. Instead of speculating about rare and mysterious instances of true premonition, it is much more useful to think in terms of self-fulfilling prophecies. That is, the underlying question is not whether people can *predict* their own demise, but rather, regardless of any public predictions, whether they can *will* their own death. The best available evidence indicates that the answer to this one is a "yes," which must be qualified because it all depends upon how "will" is defined.

When an elderly person announces that he can't bear to go on, and refuses food (as in a case mentioned earlier), or refuses to cooperate with his physicians, then his will to death seems fairly clear—it is almost equivalent to suicide. The will to death is not as clear when an old person appears to lose interest in living. This typically occurs after an emotional shock or disappointment: a last good friend may die; the family may stop visiting. Weisman and Kastenbaum described several cases in which such blows to morale led to sharp declines in physical condition. Ordinarily, in these cases we speak of a loss of the will to live; the person may continue to function and follow doctor's orders, but he becomes apathetic and indifferent:

An 81-year-old childless widower was reported to have lost interest in his customary pastimes. He withdrew from conversations, ate sparingly, retired early, and tended to be confused. After a minor respiratory infection, he was thought to be "going downhill."

A psychiatric consultant learned that a short time before onset of these symptoms, the patient's favorite sister had died.

After discovering that the "downhill" symptoms had probably begun with grief and depression, the staff intervened to improve the situation. . . . Six months later, he was continuing to make an excellent institutional adjustment (Weisman and Kastenbaum, p. 18).

And then there are what seem to be spontaneous cases of lost will to live. For no apparent reason, the individual just gives up:

Five months before his death, a 75-year-old former stone mason first spoke about losing his will to live. Except for diminished vigor, nothing further was noted until he gave up his work in occupational therapy. Then, one morning, he asked for directions to a cemetery near his former home, stating that he was expecting the undertaker! (Weisman and Kastenbaum, p. 16).

The most plausible explanation for such cases may be simply that no one is able to find out what triggers the sudden change. Perhaps this old fellow was disturbed by remote memories or a dream, but kept the thing to himself.

The general point to understand here, however, is that clichés about the will to live appear to have significant meaning, particularly for the very old. Of course, no one has yet developed a scientifically respectable definition or description for the will to live. In philosophy one encounters it under such pseudonyms as "life force" or *"élan vital."* Nevertheless, it is impressive to see this concept emerging as a salient aspect of personality in the elderly.

So much for death premonitions. Some legitimate cases exist, but on close inspection many of these may be explainable as self-fulfilling prophecies—cases in which the person wills his own death. As a distinct issue, the will-to-live problem clearly requires further study. But we now turn to another, equally interesting form of death prediction: can observers tell in advance, without any special information, when a person is likely to die?

To date the most systematic research on this particular problem has been carried out by Lieberman (1965; 1966). His reason for beginning such work shows that the problem is quite real:

The author's interest in examining psychological changes preceding death was stimulated by the observation that the chief nurse in a home for the aged could predict the death of residents with remarkable accuracy several months prior to any marked physical changes. Nevertheless, she could identify no regularities in the pattern of change nor any cues other than that a person nearing death "just seemed to act differently" (1965, p. 181).

Lieberman's first study included 25 residents of an old person's home with no incapacitating physical or psychological ills. They ranged in age from 70 to 89. (Initially, 17 men and 13 women were selected, but five died before the extended study period was over.) They were all given repeated psychological tests. Then, for purposes of analysis, their responses were grouped according to a "death-imminent" vs. "death-delayed" scheme. The death-imminent group included data from eight people who died less than three months after being tested. The death-delayed data were from 17 people still alive a year after testing.

Although the sample size was small, statistically significant differences between the two groups were found with respect to the area and accuracy of their Bender-Gestalt drawings; the complexity of their person drawings; and the amount of activity in their projective stories. That is, in relation to their own initial performances, those in the death-imminent group showed declines in their work, while those in the death-delayed group did not.

These results indicated real cognitive and motor-skill declines which may well serve as subtle cues to impending death. Lieberman's further research (1966) with another sample of elderly subjects suggested that the death-imminent are also distinguished by certain social-emotional changes: they seem to be more sensitive emotionally, and more interested in people. All generalizations here must be carefully qualified because they are based on preliminary findings. But it does appear that there is a substantial basis for observers to make better than chance judgments about approaching death.

Two general schemes

Up to this point, we have concentrated on specific areas of knowledge concerning personality and the dying process. As relevant work accumulates, however, it is necessary to have a more general scheme or framework for organizational purposes. The recent efforts by Kübler-Ross and Weisman and Kastenbaum go exactly in this direction.

Kübler-Ross (1969) provided a descriptive framework based on extensive psychiatric interviews with over 200 dying patients. She described the process of dying as progressing through five distinct psychological stages: "denial," "anger," "bargaining," "depression," and "acceptance."

Denial is the first general reaction to set in after the initial shock of learning that death is imminent.

When his initial feeling of numbness begins to disappear and he can collect himself again, man's usual response is "No, it cannot be me."

Depending very much on how a patient is told, how much time he has to gradually acknowledge the inevitable happening, and how he has been prepared throughout life to cope with stressful situations, he will gradually drop his denial and use less radical defense mechanisms (1969, p. 37).

It is also suggested that patients tend to rely more heavily on denial when hospital staff use it. Thus, despite a clear medical condition indicating death, patients will be encouraged in their denial by staff remarks about sudden cures and surprising recoveries.

The second stage is *anger*. This reaction boils down to an easy-to-understand feeling of outrage and frustration centering on the question, "Why me?" Particularly in younger people, the gross injustice of their situation can produce great bitterness. And it may overflow onto any convenient target. Anger at fate, God, or whatever, is often displaced onto family members, physicians, and nurses. So in this stage patients are liable to be very difficult because they will seize on any real or imaginary slight as an excuse to express their hostility.

The *bargaining* described as the third stage can take several different forms, but essentially it comes down to a kind of foxhole religion, where the person tries negotiation with God: "Oh Lord, if you will only get me out of this one. . . ." Some patients promise to give their bodies to "science" if only the doctors will prolong their lives.

There are two types of *depression* characterizing the fourth stage. When patients are substantially convinced that death is imminent, and when earlier defensive reactions are no longer effective, they first suffer depression over concrete losses. Their illness may be eating up life savings; their business or professional careers may be going down the drain. Such depression is oriented toward the past—it focuses on specific life gains which the person has worked for and is now losing. But the second type of depression is more global and future-oriented. It embraces all the personal or existential losses that will come with death. In this condition, for example, people suffer profound sadness at the thought of soon being parted from their loved ones. Kübler-Ross emphasized that this sorrowful state seems to be a necessary preparation for acceptance.

When it finally comes in as the last stage, *acceptance* may look like a fairly happy state because the prior anger and depression tends to disappear. However, when patients reach this stage (if they do not die in an earlier stage) they are usually running on the last dregs of their energy. They are quite weak and easily tired. At its very best, therefore, acceptance seems to be a stage of serene apathy.

Acceptance should not be mistaken for a happy stage. It is almost void of feelings. It is as if the pain had gone, the struggle is over, and there comes a time for "the final rest before the long journey" as one patient phrased it. This is also the time during which the family needs usually more help, understanding, and support than the patient himself. While the dying patient has found some peace and acceptance, his circle of interest diminishes. He wishes to be left alone or at least not stirred up by news and problems of the outside world. Visitors are often not desired and if they come, the patient is no longer in a talkative mood. He often requests limitation on the number of people and prefers short visits. This is the time when the television is off (p. 100).

Kübler-Ross' descriptive framework is difficult to evaluate. She herself spoke of the work very modestly, as an account of how it was possible to learn from the dying. ("I am simply telling the stories of my patients who shared their agonies, their expectations, and their frustrations with us.") A great part of her book was given to qualitative interview material which cannot be reproduced here. Moreover, it concerns dying at any age, not just among the elderly.

On the other hand, her five-stage framework deserves careful consideration because it offers an important descriptive scheme for organizing research. To be able to specify the phases of dying in a psychologically meaningful way is a great step forward on the road to further knowledge. Furthermore, although it has not been possible to do this aspect of her work justice in a brief discussion, it plainly offers very useful, practical information to anyone who has anything to do with the dying. And in one way or another this will naturally include all of us.

Following a very different research strategy than Kübler-Ross, Weisman and Kastenbaum offered a theoretical approach to dying which is directly concerned with the elderly. Their work has already been referred to for illustrative purposes. But full discussion has been saved for the last because amid all the new psychological literature in this area, they have provided the best single, general source of knowledge. It is no exaggeration to say that if one could only read a single work on dying in the elderly, he should select the Weisman and Kastenbaum monograph. The fact that it is so brief—59 pages—is both a tribute to their skill and an indication of how much still remains to be done on the subject.

Their work began with the assumption that dying in the elderly should be understood as an integral part of the whole developmental cycle:

. . . the authors suggest that there is a preterminal period that may be regarded as a developmental phase. This has been generally ignored by psychiatrists and developmental psychologists. Specific characteristics of the preterminal developmental phase can be described with reasonable accuracy when we begin to observe systematically all aspects of the dying person, not only his medical symptoms and vital signs (Weisman and Kastenbaum, 1968, p. 2).

In addition, they suggested that if we do not recognize dying as part of a natural, "preterminal" period of human development, then it is likely to be treated merely as one more social problem; something to be "solved" with maximum technical efficiency and then put aside. Their position here is worth repeating in detail:

Currently, there is a strong upsurge of interest in the aged, taking form in legislation, research, and action programs. This has created a marked tendency to characterize aging, not as a process, but as a problem. Many essays and proposals on the subject of aging seem to assume that aging, per se, is a mental health problem. The same sequence is now possible with the subject of dying. Proceeding from a viewpoint of neglect, we may now be moving toward a period of "discovery" of dying and then, almost imperceptibly, to the assumption that dying per se is just one more "mental health problem." The authors are not convinced that the translation of every phase of human life into the terms of a "mental health problem" is in the best interests of our society or that it represents the most trenchant scientific approach (pp. 2–3).

It should therefore be clear that while these authors relied more heavily on the standard technical methods of psychological research than Kübler-Ross, their ultimate concerns were no less humanitarian.

Not that their immediate methodology is inhumane; on the contrary, it is based upon use of a very interesting technique called the *psychological autopsy*. This was developed to serve as a relatively objective means for investigating the preterminal phase of life. Used in the context of a hospital for the aged, it is no more than an elaborate staff conference aimed at evaluating the role of social and psychological factors in the hospital careers of recently deceased patients.

Everyone on the staff who has had significant contact with these patients takes part (doctors, nurses, chaplains, psychologists), and all of their impressions are recorded. Efforts are also made to gain summary information about patients' earlier lives. The conference is organized around a list of 15 general questions, of which the following are a small sample:

What were the medical, social, and personal circumstances that led to hospitalization?

How was the patient regarded by those who were in contact with him?

Did the patient ever refer openly to death and dying or give other indications of going downhill?

Was death sudden or gradual?

Data from 80 cases were obtained using the psychological autopsy method, with results being arranged in several categories such as "mental status," "precipitating events," "attitudes toward death." A typical example in the category of "precipitating events" is this case of a social crisis.

An 85-year-old man had suffered with chronic bronchitis and emphysema for many years but was alert and active otherwise. He had eagerly anticipated going to his son's home for Thanksgiving, and when the day arrived he was dressed and ready, but no one came for him. He became more concerned as the hours went by. He asked the nurse about messages, but there were none, and he finally realized that he would spend the holiday at the hospital. After this disappointment, the patient kept more and more to himself, offered little, and accepted minimal care. Within a few weeks he was dead (p. 13).

Occasionally, the findings of an autopsy conference are extraordinary in ways that go far beyond the original intent of the research:

After three years in the hospital, a 74-year-old man died of an acute cerebral hemorrhage. He had been regarded as one of the outstanding members of the hospital population because of his enthusiasm for new ventures, his helpful attitude toward other patients, and his unceasing appetite for learning.

The staff was surprised to discover, at the time of the psychological autopsy, that he had attended school only to the fourth grade and that he had been regarded as a harmless mental defective by his family. Aside from occasional maintenance work, he had had little contact with the world. For over 20 years he had made his home with a female cousin who was an invalid. When she became too feeble to be cared for at home, the family put her in a nursing home and sent the patient to Cushing Hospital, which they thought, erroneously, was an institution for defectives.

It was clear that the patient was at least normally intelligent and had an unusual capacity for inquiry. By seeking out the chaplain and the librarian, he pursued an active, albeit belated, program of self-education. He also learned to play the clarinet, drums, and harmonica and taught himself to paint, play billiards, and to bowl! On the day of his death, he had discussed buying a used clarinet (p. 25).

The wider import of Weisman and Kastenbaum's work can be seen in their concluding discussion. First of all they were led to a better understanding of the preterminal period, defining it as follows:

. . . the transition point beyond which an aged person undergoes, not only the changes of senescence, but the incipient events of the final illness (p. 27).

And their results also support the contention that the preterminal phase is ". . . an observable period of physical and psychological accommodation to the imminence of death . . ." On a more concrete level, it is suggested that the "signs and syndromes" of this period include social apathy, reduced competence, indifference to food, less sensitivity to pain, and a greater incidence of hallucinations and delusions. Impressive similarities between most of the items listed here and some of the Kübler-Ross findings concerning "acceptance" should be obvious.

Another provocative generalization involves discussion of the preterminal phase of life as an adaptation to death. Now the idea that some behavior of the elderly can be understood as a preparation for death is not unusual — we have seen it suggested by several other writers. But it is especially striking here to discover material on hallucinations and delusions which seems directly relevant to our earlier discussion of stimulation in old age. Weisman and Kastenbaum said that hallucinations may well be a way of adapting to "an impoverished world." (In our terms, perhaps a way to satisfy a need for stimulation.) After describing two cases of elderly women who in their last days apparently had pleasant hallucinatory experiences with long-dead friends, relatives, and even a pet dog, the authors offer a more specific version of our deprivation hypothesis:

Both of these aged women suffered from severe organic defects. They were isolated and, for a variety of reasons, were inaccessible to orientation visits by the staff. Consequently, they created their own circumscribed hallucinatory worlds, populated by well-remembered and dearly loved people with whom they had had a significant interchange (p. 20).

If we now back away from the particulars of their separate works, it should be clear why Kübler-Ross and Weisman and Kastenbaum have been given special emphasis. Both sources provide interesting new empirical knowledge, and broad schemes useful for organizing such knowledge. Most important, however, both converge on the systematic personality effects associated with dying. The five-stage description of Kübler-Ross is different from the one big preterminal period suggested by Weisman and Kastenbaum, but the general implications of both are very similar.

At this point in the short history of work on dying as a factor in personality, it is much too early to look for clean theoretical organization. It is *not* too early, however, to judge that if present trends continue, there may soon be a genuine revolution in the way we think about and treat the dying.

It is fitting to end this section with a final observation from an authority who has worked very closely with the dying. He expressed sentiments frequently mentioned by others working in this area.

The therapist who works with patients in a catastrophic situation may find to his surprise that there are real rewards in the work that he did not expect.

One sees clearly the strength and dignity of human beings, the deep altruism, the positive qualities that exist at all levels of personality. Working with people who are under the hammer of fate greatly increases one's respect for them and makes one proud of being a human being (LeShan, in Pearson, p. 46).

Summary

We have spent most of this chapter examining deterioration, stimulation, and death as critical factors acting upon personality in old age. Like most of the factors discussed in previous chapters, each of these must be understood as having more than one side to it, and this is especially the case with deterioration.

There is no denying that an elderly person experiencing the physical, cognitive, social, and emotional blows of deterioration is in a grim situation. He is beset from within—via physiological breakdowns, and from without—via losses of status and negative social stereotypes. The cumulative psychological effects of these gross conditions are so various as to be almost impossible to inventory. We have seen a good number of them sketched briefly in Rosenfelt's "elderly mystique," and have looked more carefully at some of them under the headings of impact on the self, individual differences, and disengagement.

But if the general picture is grim, there are some mitigating circumstances. One is the fact that deterioration occurs gradually and unevenly. As an individual ages, therefore, he ordinarily can adapt himself piecemeal to successive losses. Another important consideration is new research showing that the serious losses are related more to disease than to age itself. In this connection, the evidence indicating that drops in intelligence test scores are caused by reduced working speeds rather than reduced general ability is particularly valuable.

Stimulation arises as a second critical factor because most of the literature on aging emphasizes that activity is the best all-round specific against deterioration. The discussion here is speculative, based on an interpretation of what activity means and how this fits knowledge about the effects of stimulus deprivation on children and adults. It is also impressive to find a similar trend of thought in Weisman and Kastenbaum's remarks concerning hallucinations in the dying.

We come full circle, finally, with material supporting the idea that dying is the last critical factor influencing personality. The clearest effects here are those involving emotional changes associated with fear, guilt, and shame. However, the five-stage framework of Kübler-Ross, and the preterminal period of Weisman and Kastenbaum both provide ample indications of effects on the cognitive and social dimensions of personality. Work in this area is very promising because it already constitutes a theoretical challenge to developmental writers; the practical, humanitarian importance of research on dying can hardly be overstated.

THEORETICAL PERSPECTIVES

From adolescence onward, we have been dropping and adding general theories of personality. That is, the systematic developmental statements of Freud, Sullivan, and Piaget do not extend much beyond adolescence, and so they must be left by the wayside as the life cycle progresses. Yet as we have dropped, we have also added: Madison, Rogers, and Buhler, for example. In old age, one finally runs out of theoretical maneuvering room: there is only Erikson and Buhler, with perhaps Kastenbaum and Birren coming up on the outside.

But the latter two writers cannot be included with the former because they do not provide broad theoretical discussions of personality in old age. While Kastenbaum often seems close to such a contribution, his major efforts have so far been chiefly focused on dying. Birren, whose 1964 book *The Psychology of Aging* is an excellent general resource work, concentrated on the review of empirical findings and avoided developmental theory. In successive chapters, for instance, he was equally concerned with such topics as "psychomotor skills" and "learning" as he was with "personality and aging." It is also relevant that he made only one brief reference to Erikson and none at all to Buhler. Yet in all fairness, it must be admitted that while Erikson and Buhler stand out as the major developmental writers on old age, their work may be *too* general.

Erikson

The final (8th) stage in Erik Erikson's outline of ego development is called *ego integrity vs. despair*. The elderly person must either achieve ego integrity or drift into despair. What is ego integrity? Erikson said that he could not provide a clear-cut definition, but then went on to describe it as a state of mind centering upon a sense of orderliness and meaning. Thus, he offered the following statements. Ego integrity involves:

(1) . . . the ego's accrued assurance of its proclivity for order and meaning.

(2) . . . a post-narcissistic love of the human ego—not of the self—as an experience which conveys some world order and spiritual sense. . . .

(3) . . . the acceptance of one's one and only life cycle as something that had to be and that, by necessity, permitted of no substitutions . . . (Erikson, 1963, p. 268).

Taken together, the various references to order and meaning seem geared to fundamental problems of morality and rationality. If one is to attain ego integrity, he must be able to make sense of his life; and if his life is to make sense, it must be seen as having had both a moral and rational pattern. The possessor of ego integrity will be aware that he might have lived his life differently, and that in other times or places his own pattern might not have been appropriate. But despite such an awareness of relativity, he will maintain confident belief in the value of his own way:

Although aware of the relativity of all the various life styles which have given meaning to human striving, the possessor of integrity is ready to defend the dignity of his own life style against all physical and economic threats. For he knows that an individual life is the accidental coincidence of but one life cycle with but one segment of history; and that for him all human integrity stands or falls with the one style of integrity of which he partakes (Erikson, 1963, p. 268).

Now, if one accepts the concept of ego integrity, two questions remain to be answered: how does it arise, and what are its consequences? Erikson said that integrity will "gradually ripen" as the "fruit" of proper passage through the earlier seven stages of ego development. In other words, it must apparently be taken on faith that if one has been able enough and lucky enough to acquire the healthy ego qualities throughout life, then at the end, integrity will develop by itself, seemingly as a kind of prize or reward for having lived right.

The chief consequence of integrity (aside from the pride and dignity already indicated) is that one will have no great fear of death. It is suggested that ego integrity involves a final consolidation of personality which is so strong that the individual can stare death in the face without flinching. This appears to be an idealized state which few people can achieve. Interestingly enough, however, Erikson's view of this matter seems very similar to Cicero's:

. . . it seems to me that once we have had our fill of all the things that have engaged our interest, we have had our fill of life itself. There are interests that are proper to childhood: does a full-grown man regret their loss? There are interests that belong to early manhood: when we reach full maturity—what is called "middle age"—do we look back to them with longing? Middle age itself has its special concerns; even these have lost their attraction for the old. Finally, there are interests peculiar to old age; these fall away, too, just as did those of the earlier years. When this has happened, a sense of the fullness of life tells us that it is time to die (Copley translation, 1967, pp. 37–38).

And more directly, Buhler (1968, p. 164) quoted a statement by Grandma Moses showing what the sense of ego integrity may feel like to an elderly person:

I look back on my life like a good day's work, it was done and I feel satisfied with it. I was happy and contented, I knew nothing better and made the best out of what life offered. And life is what we make it, always has been, always will be.

Despair is the alternative to ego integrity. Its presence will be signaled by fear of death among old people who cannot accept their own particular life as having been a single, unique, ultimate experience. Briefly, excessive fear of death is interpreted as an expression of despair caused by failure to achieve integrity. The elderly person realizes that he cannot start over or change the path he followed, and so he may despair as the end of his life approaches. Presumably, this phenomenon can be seen in people with great regrets: those who put off marriage or children until it was too late; those who made their big career decisions according to expediency instead of their own deep convictions.

But Erikson further suggested that despair can arise from "a thousand little disgusts" as well as from grand regrets or remorse. His short discussion implied that the highly conventional, conforming life which has neither great mistakes nor great passion or inspiration in it, can also be cause for despair, especially if one has spent himself pursuing a material security which does not enrich life.

Ideas about ego integrity and despair hold up fairly well in the light of empirical research. For one thing, the whole approach fits generalizations concerning the importance of life review and reminiscence in the elderly. Feelings of integrity or despair will necessarily depend upon retrospective reviews of the past. Furthermore, studies showing that the elderly can be classified into personality types (e.g., the integrated or defended categories mentioned by Neugarten et al.; and the mature or angry categories described by Reichard, Livson, and Petersen) suggest the reality of an adjustment continuum ranging from ego integrity to despair.

On the other hand, it is hard to evaluate Erikson's argument that ego integrity more or less precludes fear of death. Since the general empirical issue of death fear cannot be settled yet, it is all the more difficult to judge whether ego integrity is associated with reduction or elimination of such fear. Buhler also touched upon this problem without providing much help. In one place (1968, p. 164) she asserted that while some people may deny it, fear of death is universal. In another, (1962, p. 120) she suggested that people who have fulfilled their life goals may not suffer as much anxiety over death as others. It would be interesting to question Kübler-Ross on this point: perhaps among her patients she has seen some who approximate ego integrity and therefore seem better able to face dying.

Buhler

Doubtless for the sake of theoretical clarity, Charlotte Buhler divided old age into two periods: 65 to 80, and 80 to death. The basic developmental theme of the first period is "self-fulfillment." It involves a general feeling that life as a whole has been worthwhile, and that important aims have been accomplished.

With the term *fulfillment*, we refer to a closure experience that the person who lives with direction seems to be living toward.

To me it seems, from my biographical evidence . . . that we accumulate and assemble fulfillments toward the end where life, for the person who sees his life as a whole, is as a whole experienced as fulfilled (Buhler, 1962, pp. 116–117).

The last quote is a bit tricky (it has probably suffered in translation from German) but the meaning comes across well enough: taking it all together, most elderly people can probably say whether or not their lives have left them with a general feeling of fulfillment.

Buhler added that a feeling of self-fulfillment is particularly important for people who believe that their lives should have involved more than personal gratification. The latent question here seems to be "Did my life add anything to the sum total of human progress or happiness?" But what of all those who *have* lived mainly for personal gratification? They apparently still seek some kind of fulfillment at the end, and Buhler's remarks bordered on sarcasm:

Those on the other hand, whose predominant tendency was toward "happiness," comfort, or security, or also toward inner harmony and peace, or toward a successful adjustment to given circumstances—these people who most likely represent the majority of mankind, are probably not living toward such a pronounced end result as the experience of fulfillment is. Yet they all, it seems, want to feel toward the end that they lived their life "right" or "successfully" or meaningfully and not "in vain" (1962, p. 117).

At the end of this discussion, however, she noted the case of a very old woman who said that her only hope was to be remembered kindly by a few people. For Buhler, this attitude seemed to express all that human beings can honestly aspire to, and she called it a truly human, admirable outlook.

If people live long enough, they enter a final period which resembles the preterminal phase described by Weisman and Kastenbaum. According to Buhler's description, this is not a very attractive period because the main theme is "regression to predominant need satisfaction" and acceptance of death. The regression probably involves a combination of childishness and preoccupation with vegetative functions. However, not enough detail is given to warrant further discussion.

In summary, it should be plain that Erikson and Buhler made grossly similar statements about personality in old age. The concepts of ego-integrity and self-fulfillment both emphasize retrospective meaning as the basis for adjustment. While Erikson was more explicit in his suggestion that despair is the alternative to integrity, Buhler's work also indicated that something like despair may occur in the absence of fulfillment.

The two theorists cannot be judged harshly from the standpoint of available research findings: their ideas stand up quite well as far as they go. But they go only a relatively short distance in relation to the whole problem of personality in old age. Apart from reinforcing the importance of studying reminiscence in relation to different types of adjustment patterns, Erikson and Buhler have only contributed a very general orientation toward personality changes among the elderly. This is not so much a criticism of the theorists as it is a commentary on the state of our knowledge. Much of the material mentioned in this chapter was not available to them when they were writing; the new studies of dying are a conspicuous example. Furthermore, it should be kept in mind that developmental frameworks spanning the life cycle cannot embrace more than the most salient features of any given period. Given these stipulations, and the additional knowledge that no other major scheme of personality development extends into old age, Erikson and Buhler must be recognized as important pioneers.

CHAPTER SUMMARY

For a good many years it has been traditional to summarize personality as developing via interaction between the organism and the environment. Indeed, practically all writers on the subject emphasize this point. And what it finally boils down to is something like this: *adaptation to change*. We have seen that every age period is characterized either by external changes – in the social or physical environment, or internal changes – in physiology, or both. Personality typically develops in response to these changes. It is a convenient term for referring to the general pattern of psychological consequences which follow from our efforts to adapt to change.

But this is all very complicated because so many things go on simultaneously, and because sequences of cause and effect do not remain fixed: yesterday's effect can turn into today's cause; tomorrow's cause may be understood only by virtue of today's effect. The complexity of personality development has been dealt with in this book by employing three scientific tools or abstractions: the concept of developmental periods; the idea that each period contains critical factors for development; and an organizational plan for examining psychological effects according to their cognitive, social and emotional implications.

Old age provides an excellent theoretical vantage point from which to scan adaptation to change in these terms. Here we have a fairly clear-cut period containing drastic changes in physiology and social circumstances that apparently generate drastic changes in the cognitive and social-emotional dimensions of personality. Moreover, sufficient material is available here to see the extraordinary way in which the main trends in an individual's life history come to a general and final focus. This is made very clear in the work of Erikson and Buhler who described personality in old age according to the cumulative meaning the person attaches to his past life. To put it very briefly, one's developmental strengths and weaknesses tend to recapitulate themselves. Ample empirical findings support this proposition and, from Cicero to Maugham, relevant evidence also appears in personal reflections of the elderly.

The pressure or stress of aging is another important consideration. Regardless of whether it is viewed in common sense terms – via discussion of an elderly mystique, or more formally – via discussion of deterioration, the stress of aging tends to simplify personality. Under such pressure many superficial complexities fall away; the individual is revealed as he can never be revealed in less trying circumstances. Fortunate is the person who can accept what he learns about himself in these circumstances.

More generally, the stress of aging reveals indications that the developmental cycle repeats itself. For example, the physical well-being and general stimulation which played an important role early in life show up again as major determinants of individual differences. Add to this the social and physiological analogies to adolescence and a good case for developmental recapitulation can be made. Recall the mention of an "elevator" hypothesis; the idea that one seems to make similar stops on the way down as he did on the way up.

Now then, besides the deterioration making for simplicity, the meanings from the past which can apparently sustain us in the face of deterioration, and the fact that these aspects of old age shed some light on the whole issue of personality as adaptation to change, there remains death.

It is fair to say that as a species, man has even succeeded in adapting his way out of death — at least it seems that as species go on this earth, man is the only one to have found means of living much longer now than he used to. Yet despite all delays, death eventually arrives as a great unknown. The psychological processes associated with *dying,* however, which used to be as much of an unknown as death itself, are beginning to be better understood. And the knowledge accumulated thus far again underscores the importance of adaptation: psychologically, the last great change to which we adapt ourselves is the end of ourselves (or, for those with diverse ideas on this subject, "the end of ourselves as we have thus far known ourselves").

It seems appropriate to admit that one cannot easily judge exactly what important new things about personality development can be learned from studies of dying. Of course, it is valuable to understand the social-emotional specifics in this area: fear, guilt, and the processes by which people are able to accept their death. But on the level of theory, do we learn anything other than how people adapt to very severe stress? Part of the problem is that work on dying has only just accumulated to the point where it seems clear that future studies *may* have a serious impact on the way we understand personality. A further uncertainty concerns the developmental status we assign to dying. It seems likely that dying in the elderly may soon be recognized as a separate developmental period. Instead of treating it as part of old age, therefore, dying should perhaps be interpreted as a new preterminal period in agreement with Weisman and Kastenbaum's suggestion.

So the final theme in this last chapter is similar to the theme of the first chapter: *uncertainty.* The text began with an invitation to enter personality study *despite* its inherent uncertainty, because it can be interesting and useful. The text ends on the same note. But perhaps now some will agree that personality study can be interesting *because* of its inherent uncertainty.

References

Barker, R. G., & Barker, L. S. The psychological ecology of old people in Midwest, Kansas, and Yoredale, Yorkshire. *The Journal of Gerontology,* 1961, *16,* 144–149.

Birren, J. E. *The psychology of aging.* Englewood Cliffs: Prentice-Hall, Inc., 1964.

Botwinick, J. *Cognitive processes in maturity and old age.* New York: Springer, 1967.

Bowers, M. K., Jackson, E. N., Knight, J. A., & LeShan, L. *Counseling the dying.* Camden, N.J.: Thomas Nelson & Sons, 1964.

Buhler, C. *Psychology for contemporary living.* New York: Hawthorn Books, Inc., 1968.

Buhler, C. *Values in psychotherapy.* Glencoe, Ill.: The Free Press, 1962.

Butler, R. N. The life review: An interpretation of reminiscence in the aged. In B. Neugarten (Ed.) *Middle age and aging.* Chicago: The University of Chicago Press, 1968, pp. 486–496.

Butler, R. N. The facade of chronological age: An interpretative summary. *American Journal of Psychiatry,* 1963, *119,* 721–728.

Carp, F. M. Senility or garden-variety maladjustment. *The Journal of Gerontology*, 1969, *24*, 203–208.

Cavan, R. S., Burgess, E. W., Havighurst, R. J., & Goldhamer, H. *Personal adjustment in old age*. Chicago: Science Research Associates, Inc., 1949.

Cicero. *On old age and on friendship* (44 B.C.). F. O. Copley translation. Ann Arbor: University of Michigan Press, 1967.

Cumming, E., & Henry, W. E. *Growing old: The process of disengagement*. New York: Basic Books, Inc., 1961.

Curtis, H. J. Biological mechanisms underlying the aging process. *Science*, 1963, *141*, 686–694.

Erikson, E. H. *Childhood and society*. (2nd ed.) New York: W. W. Norton & Company, Inc., 1963.

Frenkel-Brunswik, E. Adjustments and reorientation in the course of the life span. In B. Neugarten (Ed.) *Middle age and aging*. Chicago: The University of Chicago Press, 1968, pp. 77–84.

Havighurst, R. J. Social and psychological needs of the aging. In L. Gorlow and W. Katkovsky (Eds.) *Readings in the psychology of adjustment*. New York: McGraw-Hill Book Company, Inc., 1959, pp. 439–447.

Havighurst, R. J., Neugarten, B., & Tobin, S. S. Disengagement and patterns of aging. In B. Neugarten (Ed.) *Middle age and aging*. Chicago: The University of Chicago Press, 1968, pp. 161–172.

Kalish, R. A. The aged and the dying process: The inevitable decisions. *The Journal of Social Issues*, 1965, *21*, 87–96.

Kastenbaum, R. Theories of human aging: The search for a conceptual framework. *The Journal of Social Issues*, 1965, *21*, 13–36.

Kübler-Ross, E. *On death and dying*. London: Macmillan & Co., Ltd., 1969.

Kuhlen, R. G. Personality change with age. In P. Worchel and D. Byrne (Eds.) *Personality change*. New York: John Wiley & Sons, Inc., 1964, pp. 524–555.

Kutner, B., Fanshel, D., Togo, A., & Langner, T. S. *Five hundred over sixty: A community survey on aging*. New York: Russell Sage Foundation, 1956.

LeShan, L. Psychotherapy and the dying patient. In L. Pearson (Ed.) *Death and dying: Current issues in the treatment of the dying person*. Cleveland: Case Western Reserve University Press, 1969, pp. 28–48.

Lewis, O. *The children of Sanchez*. New York: Random House, Inc., 1961.

Lieberman, M. Psychological correlates of impending death: Some preliminary observations. *Journal of Gerontology*, 1965, *20*, 181–190.

Lieberman, M. Vulnerability to stress and the processes of dying. *Proceedings of the Seventh International Congress on Gerontology*, 1966, Vol. 8, 513–519.

McNeil, E. B. *Human socialization*. Belmont, Calif.: Brooks/Cole Publishing Company, 1969.

Neugarten, B., Havighurst, R. J., & Tobin, S. S. Personality and patterns of aging. In B. Neugarten (Ed.) *Middle age and aging*. Chicago: The University of Chicago Press, 1968.

Pearson, L. (Ed.) *Death and dying: Current issues in the treatment of the dying person*. Cleveland: Case Western Reserve University Press, 1969.

Pikunas, J. *Human development: A science of growth*. New York: McGraw-Hill Book Company, Inc., 1969.

Plutarch. Life stories of men who shaped history, from *Plutarch's Lives*. E. Lindeman (Ed.) New York: Mentor Books, 1950.

Reichard, S., Livson, F., & Petersen, P. G. *Aging and personality*. New York: John Wiley & Sons, Inc., 1962.

Rosenfelt, R. H. The elderly mystique. *The Journal of Social Issues*, 1965, *21*, 37–43.

Sarnoff, I. *Personality dynamics and development*. New York: John Wiley & Sons, Inc., 1962.

Saunders, C. The moment of truth: Care of the dying person. In L. Pearson (Ed.) *Death and dying: Current issues in the treatment of the dying person*. Cleveland: Case Western Reserve University Press, 1969, pp. 49–78.

Shneidman, E. S. Orientations toward death. In R. W. White (Ed.) *The study of lives*. New York: Atherton Press, 1963, pp. 200–227.

Strauss, A. L. Awareness of dying. In L. Pearson (Ed.) *Death and dying: Current issues in the treatment of the dying person*. Cleveland: Case Western Reserve University Press, 1969, pp. 108–132.

Weisman, A. D., & Kastenbaum, R. *The psychological autopsy: A study of the terminal phase of life*. Community Mental Health Journal, Monograph #4, 1968.

Wolff, K. A new conceptualization of the geriatric patient. *Geriatrics*, August 1968, 157–162.

Index

441